Lecture Notes in Business Information Processing   **539**

Series Editors

Wil van der Aalst, *RWTH Aachen University, Aachen, Germany*

Sudha Ram, *University of Arizona, Tucson, USA*

Michael Rosemann, *Queensland University of Technology, Brisbane, Australia*

Clemens Szyperski, *Microsoft Research, Redmond, USA*

Giancarlo Guizzardi, *University of Twente, Enschede, The Netherlands*

AF173150

LNBIP reports state-of-the-art results in areas related to business information systems and industrial application software development – timely, at a high level, and in both printed and electronic form.

The type of material published includes

- Proceedings (published in time for the respective event)
- Postproceedings (consisting of thoroughly revised and/or extended final papers)
- Other edited monographs (such as, for example, project reports or invited volumes)
- Tutorials (coherently integrated collections of lectures given at advanced courses, seminars, schools, etc.)
- Award-winning or exceptional theses

LNBIP is abstracted/indexed in DBLP, EI and Scopus. LNBIP volumes are also submitted for the inclusion in ISI Proceedings.

Efi Papatheocharous · Siamak Farshidi ·
Slinger Jansen · Sonja Hyrynsalmi
Editors

Software Business

15th International Conference, ICSOB 2024
Utrecht, The Netherlands, November 18–20, 2024
Proceedings

 Springer

Editors
Efi Papatheocharous 🆔
RISE Research Institutes of Sweden
Gothenburg, Sweden

Siamak Farshidi 🆔
Wageningen University and Research
Wageningen, The Netherlands

Slinger Jansen 🆔
Universiteit Utrecht
Utrecht, The Netherlands

Sonja Hyrynsalmi 🆔
LUT University
Lahti, Finland

ISSN 1865-1348   ISSN 1865-1356 (electronic)
Lecture Notes in Business Information Processing
ISBN 978-3-031-85848-2   ISBN 978-3-031-85849-9 (eBook)
https://doi.org/10.1007/978-3-031-85849-9

This Springer imprint is published by the registered company Springer Nature Switzerland AG
The registered company address is: Gewerbestrasse 11, 6330 Cham, Switzerland

If disposing of this product, please recycle the paper.

Preface

It is our great pleasure to introduce the proceedings of the International Conference on Software Business (ICSOB) 2024. This volume compiles a rich collection of works that reflect both the breadth and depth of current research and practice in software business and related fields. The ICSOB community continues to thrive and grow, drawing diverse researchers, practitioners, and students who contribute to the ongoing exploration of how software drives economic and societal value.

This year's conference was hosted by Utrecht University, one of the oldest and most prestigious universities in the Netherlands. With a strong reputation in research excellence and an enduring commitment to fostering interdisciplinary collaboration, Utrecht provided an inspiring environment for thought leaders and innovators in the software business domain to come together and share their work. As one of the founding organizations of ICSOB, Utrecht University was long overdue to host the conference, and it was happy to comply.

The theme of ICSOB 2024 was "Ethics, Equity, and Sustainability in Software Business," which emphasized the importance of ethical practices, equitable opportunities, and sustainable engineering within the software business community. This theme encouraged participants to consider how software can contribute to a fairer and more sustainable world while balancing business goals and societal needs.

We received a total of 98 submissions for ICSOB 2024, from which 23 full papers and 13 short papers were accepted, after a rigorous double-blind review process, led by at least 3 experts for each submission who were engaged in the evaluation. Additionally, 8 PhD students were selected to participate in the PhD retreat, where they had the unique opportunity to receive mentorship from 5 experienced coaches. In addition, 1 journal-first paper was invited, and 7 posters were presented. The high quality of these submissions speaks to the vibrancy and rigor of our community, as well as its commitment to advancing the state of knowledge in software business.

In recognition of their outstanding quality and significance, authors of selected papers will be extended a journal invitation. They are going to be encouraged to submit an expanded version of their originally accepted ICSOB paper for inclusion in a Special Issue dedicated to Software Production within the Information and Software Technology journal (IST). We firmly believe that these extended papers will deliver substantial and influential contributions to the special issue, further advancing the discourse and knowledge in the field.

The research tracks at ICSOB 2024 encompassed a diverse array of topics, reflecting the conference's commitment to addressing contemporary challenges in the software business realm. Key areas of focus included ethical and governance challenges in software engineering, developer experience and ecosystem trust in software platforms, sustainable ICT and cloud adoption in software businesses, transparency and trustability in AI and software business, and diversity, equity, and inclusion in AI and software engineering. For example, one of the sessions addressed ethical decision-making in software engineering, focusing on how ethical frameworks can be integrated into software engineering practices to guide responsible innovation. These themes underscored the conference's dedication to exploring both foundational concepts and emerging issues, particularly those aligned with the overarching theme of ethics, equity, and sustainability in software business.

Artificial Intelligence (AI) also featured prominently in this year's program, highlighting its growing influence in software business. Contributions ranged from exploring AI-driven business models to examining the implications of AI on software engineering processes. The conference program included several sessions dedicated to AI, emphasizing its role as a transformative force across the industry. Notably, the Best Paper Award was presented to Ulrik Franke for his insightful work on the topic of explainable AI titled "How do ML students explain their models and what can we learn from this?"

ICSOB 2024 featured three distinguished keynote speakers who shared their expertise on critical topics in software business. Inge van de Weerd presented on "Workarounds are Everywhere! We'd Better Use Them." Her talk delved into how users adapt technology to meet their specific needs, often leading to workarounds that highlight mismatches between software, processes, and users. Van de Weerd introduced innovative approaches for the automatic detection of workarounds and discussed how process mining techniques could be utilized to study their emergence, evolution, and diffusion within organizations. This exploration aimed to enhance both processes and software by understanding the dynamics of workarounds.

Magne Jørgensen discussed "Successful Cost-Benefit Management of Agile Software Development Projects." His presentation focused on integrating cost-benefit management practices into agile software development. Drawing from empirical studies, Jørgensen provided insights into planning the realization of benefits, implementing continuous benefits management, and evaluating benefits realization. He also addressed the surprising finding that the front-end phase of agile software development often mirrored that of non-agile approaches, prompting a discussion on the potential benefits of increased agility in this phase.

Michiel Overeem presented on "The Role of Ethics in Software Business." His keynote explored the ethical considerations inherent in software engineering and business practices. Overeem discussed frameworks for integrating ethical decision-making into software engineering and business strategies, emphasizing the importance of aligning technological advancements with societal values and ethical standards.

ICSOB 2024 also featured the 2nd International Workshop on Advances in Software Intensive Startups (AiSIS). This workshop provided an active forum for researchers and practitioners to discuss the latest trends, challenges, and solutions in the dynamic landscape of software startups. Key topics included the impact of emerging technologies such as AI and requirements engineering advances on startups, the engineering of novel tools to support innovation, and sustainable practices in new product engineering. The workshop fostered interactive sessions, encouraging collaboration among participants to shape future research agendas and contribute to a planned book project on software startups.

The ICSOB 2024 conference featured a diverse set of awards designed to recognize excellence and foster growth within the software business research community. These included awards for early career researchers and the best research paper, aimed at encouraging innovative contributions and highlighting exemplary scholarship. Acknowledgment of outstanding reviewers emphasized the importance of constructive peer feedback in maintaining high academic standards, while the best poster award encouraged clear and engaging research communication. The diversity and inclusion award underscored the value of equitable practices and ethical considerations in technology development. Additionally, the most influential paper and lifetime achievement awards celebrated impactful contributions that have shaped the field over time, inspiring the community to build on these foundations. Together, these awards serve to motivate, inspire, and strengthen the collaborative spirit of the ICSOB community.

Overall, ICSOB 2024 once again demonstrated the continued interest and engagement of the community in exploring the evolving world of software business. The conference remains a vital forum for bringing together a wide array of topics, methodologies, and perspectives, fostering a deeper understanding of how software shapes our economies and societies. We recognize the value of focusing discussions to maximize impact, and we hope that next year's conference will aim to sharpen its thematic scope while preserving the diversity that makes ICSOB unique.

We hope that the theme of this year's conference will continue to inspire researchers and practitioners alike, serving as a beacon for the community. We look forward to an even greater ICSOB 2025, confident that the discussions initiated here will pave the way for future advancements and collaborations.

November 2024

Efi Papatheocharous
Siamak Farshidi
Slinger Jansen
Sonja Hyrynsalmi

Organization

General Chair

Slinger Jansen   Utrecht University, Netherlands

Program Committee Chairs

Siamak Farshidi   Wageningen University & Research, Netherlands
Efi Papatheocharous   RISE Research Institutes of Sweden, Sweden

Proceedings Chair

Sonja M. Hyrynsalmi   LUT University, Finland

PhD Retreat Chairs

Rodrigo Santos   UNIRIO, Brazil
Dron Khanna   Free University of Bozen-Bolzano, Italy

Poster Chair

Edona Elshan   Vrije Universiteit Amsterdam, Netherlands

Marketing Chair

Andrey Saltan   LUT University, Finland

Social Media Chair

Fernanda Madeiral   Vrije Universiteit Amsterdam, Netherlands

Special Issue Chair

Antti Knutas   LUT University, Finland

Sponsorship Chair

Slinger Jansen   Utrecht University, Netherlands

Student Volunteer Chair

Kate Labunets   Utrecht University, Netherlands

Awards Chair

Dominik Siemon   LUT University, Finland

Organization and Administration Registration Chair

Fang Hou   Utrecht University, Netherlands

Website Chair

Elena Baninemeh   Utrecht University, Netherlands

Companion Proceedings Chair

Deekshitha M.   Utrecht University, Netherlands

Program Committee

Bilal Al Ahmad   University of Jordan/Aqaba, Jordan
Matthew Ajimati   University of Galway, Ireland
Muhammad Azeem Akbar   LUT University, Finland
Jesper Andersson   Linnaeus University, Sweden

Antti Knutas	LUT University, Finland
Jacob Krüger	Eindhoven University of Technology, Netherlands
Alfons Laarman	Leiden University, Netherlands
Kate Labunets	Utrecht University, Netherlands
Patricia Lago	Vrije Universiteit Amsterdam, Netherlands
Casper Lassenius	Aalto University, Finland
Ulrike Lechner	Universität der Bundeswehr München, Germany
Hongxiu Li	Tampere University, Finland
Johan Linåker	RISE Research Institutes of Sweden, Sweden
Francesca Lonetti	CNR-ISTI, Italy
Fernanda Madeiral	Vrije Universiteit Amsterdam, Netherlands
Andrey Maglyas	LUT University, Finland
Tiziana Margaria	University of Limerick, Ireland
Gerardo Matturro	Universidad ORT Uruguay, Uruguay
Jorge Melegati	Free University of Bozen-Bolzano, Italy
Tommi Mikkonen	University of Jyväskylä, Finland
Rahul Mohanani	University of Jyväskylä, Finland
Jurgen Munch	Reutlingen University, Germany
Matti Muhos	University of Oulu, Finland
Tuomas Mäkilä	University of Turku, Finland
Niko Mäkitalo	University of Jyväskylä, Finland
Valdemar Vicente Graciano Neto	Universidade Federal de Goiás, Brazil
Emil Numminen	Blekinge Institute of Technology, Sweden
Helena Holmström Olsson	Malmö University, Sweden
Michiel Overeem	AFAS Software, Netherlands
Maria Paasivaara	LUT University, Finland
Efi Papatheocharous	RISE Research Institutes of Sweden, Sweden
Ella Peltonen	University of Oulu, Finland
Annabell Petri	Universiteit Twente, Netherlands
Wolfram Pietsch	Aachen University of Applied Sciences, Germany
Luís Ferreira Pires	University of Twente, Netherlands
Tero Päivärinta	Luleå University of Technology, Sweden
Usman Rafiq	Free University of Bozen-Bolzano, Italy
Guus Ramackers	Leiden Institute of Advanced Computer Science, Netherlands
Minna Rantanen	University of Turku, Finland
Andrey Saltan	LUT University, Finland
Luiz Olavo Bonino da Silva Santos	University of Twente, Netherlands
Rodrigo Santos	UNIRIO, Brazil
Dipti Sarmah	University of Twente, Netherlands
Marko Seppänen	Tampere University, Finland
Pertti Seppänen	University of Oulu, Finland

Contents

Software Startups and Digital Transformation

Ethical Challenges in Software Development

Five Darlings to Be Killed: Debunking Myths About Innovation in the Software-Intensive Embedded Systems Industry

Helena Holmström Olsson[1]([⊠])(ID) and Jan Bosch[2](ID)

[1] Malmö University, Malmö, Sweden
`helena.holmstrom.olsson@mau.se`
[2] Chalmers University of Technology, Gothenburg, Sweden
`jan.bosch@chalmers.se`

Abstract. Companies need to continuously innovate to stay competitive. For every innovation, there needs to be a customer, a way to monetize and a way to validate that what is developed adds value to the customer. With digitalization, however, the approach to innovation needs to change. Instead of technology-driven approaches, companies need to adopt more customer-driven approaches to innovation. In this context, we see that companies in the software-intensive embedded systems industry adopt practices that originate in the Software-as-a-Service (SaaS) domain. This has proven to be far from trivial, and these practices tend to be associated with several myths in the software-intensive embedded systems industry. In this paper, we present multi-case study research in which we identify five myths that permeate software-intensive embedded systems companies and that have become the typical representation of how these companies work, how they interact with customers and how they do business. We explore these myths referring to them as "five darlings to be killed", and we detail what the myth is about, why it is incorrect and what happens in companies instead.

Keywords: Software-intensive systems · Myths · Minimal Viable Product · Friendly customer · New business · Agile ways-of-working · New business model

1 Introduction

Software engineering is a discipline that keeps evolving. As a major shift, we see how digitalization is changing the ways in which companies innovate. Traditionally, companies in the software-intensive embedded systems domain took a technology-driven approach to innovation [24] in which focus was on minimizing the risks of introducing new technologies by making these available in the most cost-effective fashion. With digitalization, however, companies need customer-driven approaches to innovation since what adds value to customers is more

© The Author(s), under exclusive license to Springer Nature Switzerland AG 2025
E. Papatheocharous et al. (Eds.): ICSOB 2024, LNBIP 539, pp. 3–19, 2025.
https://doi.org/10.1007/978-3-031-85849-9_1

complex and often unclear. As recognized in Desouza et al. [8], companies need to change their innovation practices from "innovating for customers" to "innovating with customers" by finding ways to collect frequent and continuous feedback about what adds value.

If looking at the two most recent decades, the process of innovation and development of software-intensive systems has significantly changed. What used to be a sequential process with distinct phases such as requirements gathering, system design, development, testing, and deployment, is now a process in which developers use continuous development practices to integrate their code changes whenever changes are made and deploy new software to customers on a frequent basis [2,3,14]. What used to be a waterfall process with very limited opportunities for customer collaboration is now an agile process in which customer collaboration and short feedback loops are considered key [3,14,17]. As a major disruption, digitalization has forced companies to fundamentally rethink the ways in which they innovate, develop, and monetize their products [5,31,32]. For every innovation there needs to be a customer, a way to monetize and a way to validate that what is developed adds value to the customer. While this was always true, the ways in which to achieve this are changing.

In this context, we see that companies in the software-intensive embedded systems industry adopt practices that originate in the Software-as-a-Service (SaaS) domain and that reflect how these companies work. As an example, agile practices as well as experimentation practices, e.g., A/B testing, have been increasingly adopted by embedded systems companies as these have proven valuable in large online companies such as Google, Microsoft, and Amazon [10,23,25,26]. However, the adoption and use of these practices have proven to be far from trivial, and these practices tend to be associated with several myths in the software-intensive embedded systems industry.

In this paper, we identify five myths that permeate software-intensive embedded systems companies and that they suffer from holding on to. While these myths have become the typical representation for how these companies claim to work, interact with customers and do business, most often this is not the case in practice. In the paper, we refer to these myths as "five darlings to be killed", and we show that they are either incorrect or only partially correct. Our research builds on multi-case study research and long-term collaboration with companies in the software-intensive embedded systems industry.

The remainder of the paper is structured as follows. In Sect. 2, we review literature on how innovation and development practices are changing in software-intensive businesses. In Sect. 3, we outline the research method and the case companies involved in our study. In Sect. 4, we summarize the empirical findings. In Sect. 5, we identify five myths. In Sect. 6, we discuss threats to validity and in Sect. 7 we conclude the paper and we outline future research.

2   Background

Companies need to continuously innovate to stay competitive. This involves not only development of new products but also the adoption of novel ways-of-working and new business models. Below, we provide an overview of the changes we see in how companies engage with customers, how they monetize and how they validate customer value in relation to innovation of software-intensive products and systems.

2.1 Customer Engagement

During the 80's and 90's, the trend among companies was to adopt process-based and technology-driven approaches to innovation and development of products. During this period, many companies spent efforts on implementing e.g., the Capability Maturity Model Integration (CMMI). As recognized in [36] a main objective of the model is to reduce the cost of implementing process improvements by eliminating inconsistencies and establishing guidelines to assist organizations at various stages of a software project. During this period, following processes was considered the most effective approach to develop software, to ensure its quality and to provide value to customers.

Starting already in the 1990s, and formally coined as a term in the manifesto in 2001 [15], agile software development emerged as an alternative approach. Instead of rigorous processes, agile methods emphasized speed, incremental cycles and short iterations for engaging with customers. In [17], the authors outline the evolution of agile methods and how these have scaled. Today, agile methods are used also by companies in the software-intensive embedded systems domain as these seek ways to improve customer engagement [9,17]. More recently, however, agile development methods are being questioned as practitioners experience their limitations [18,19,40]. In [9], the authors identify 35 challenges that range from lack of cross-team coordination mechanisms and difficulties with adopting an autonomous team model to lack of support for creating user stories, difficulties with accommodating non-functional testing and uncertainty on how to adjust to an incremental delivery and launch model.

2.2 Monetization Models

Value is shifting from products to services with software being the main driver for this [5,31,32]. As recognized in [5], companies in the software-intensive embedded systems domain have, for decades, focused their value-creating activities on physical products involving mechanics and electronics components. In domains such as telecommunications, automotive, defense, security, and manufacturing, product sales is where the primary revenue is generated. Although companies in these domains have service offerings, the revenue generated from these services is still very limited. In traditional and product-oriented business models, the focus is on the short-term selling of the product rather than the long-term and continuously evolving customer needs [21].

However, with technologies such as software, data, and artificial intelligence (AI), new opportunities arise. In our previous work [5], we outline how companies in the embedded systems domain are in the midst of complementing their physical products with software-driven services that extend previous product offerings. With software, data and AI becoming increasingly important, also the monetization models shift towards more continuous and recurring revenue models [5, 32].

2.3 Validation with Customers

Traditionally, the customer relationship was transactional with the customer being at the receiving end of the product development life cycle. In [35], the authors report on a survey of 400 waterfall projects that shows that the software being developed is either not deployed or, if deployed, never used by customers. The main reason for this is the difficulty to respond to changing needs during the development process and the lack of opportunity to validate if the feature or functionality that is being develop adds value to customers.

With the introduction of agile development methods, customer collaboration was identified as key to development [15]. In emphasizing short sprints, incremental development and iterative cycles, agile practices involve customers in the development process and allow customer feedback throughout the development life cycle. As recognized in [16], agile methods expand the customer role by involving them in writing user stories, discussing product features, prioritizing the feature lists, and providing rapid feedback to the development team on a regular basis. Similarly, scaling agile frameworks such as SAFe consider user feedback and the usage of intrinsic customer knowledge as key [20, 39].

More recently, continuous integration, continuous delivery and continuous deployment [37] enable validation practices that go far beyond the agile definition of customer collaboration. Today, companies are increasingly adopting experimentation practices such as A/B testing to continuously evaluate hypotheses and collect data on what version of a software feature that customers appreciate the most and hence, that generates value as well as revenue [10, 12, 27].

3   Research Method

3.1   Case Study Research

Case study research is an appreciated method in software engineering research as it allows for in-depth empirical investigation of one, or a few, selected cases [41]. As recognized in [41], case studies are considered a rewarding method as they support research in which the aim is to observe, explain and explore phenomena in real-life settings. Since its introduction, case study research has only increased in popularity as a frequent aim of software engineering research is to investigate how activities associated with software development, operation, and maintenance are conducted, managed, and understood by software engineers and other stakeholders [41].

For more than a decade, we have used case study research as our primary method for exploring how companies in the embedded systems domain develop, deploy and continuously improve software-intensive products and systems. Throughout our research collaborations, we have had the privilege to interact with multiple case companies, multiple use cases and multiple roles/stakeholders within each of the companies. In what follows, we report on research conducted through workshops involving on-site and online sessions in six companies. In addition to these workshops, we build on the insights we got from our long-term research collaboration with companies in the embedded systems domain. Our research spans over more than a decade and during this time we have reported on e.g., the adoption and evolution of software development practices in the companies [3,4], experimentation and data-driven practices [11,13,29,30], digitalization and digital transformation [5,31], and new business opportunities and monetization models [7,32].

3.2 Case Companies

The case companies involved in this study are members of a larger research collaboration in which we aim to accelerate the digitalization capabilities in the member companies (for more information please visit www.software-center.se). For this paper, we selected six of the member companies as case companies. Below, we provide a short description of the selected companies.

- *Case company A* is a company manufacturing trucks, buses and construction equipment as well as a supplier of marine systems.
- *Case company B* is a food packaging and processing company.
- *Case company C* is a company manufacturing network cameras, access control, and network audio devices for the security and surveillance industries.
- *Case company D* is a company developing automation and digitalization solutions for process and manufacturing industries, intelligent infrastructure for buildings and distributed energy systems.
- *Case company E* is a company manufacturing pumps and electronic motors.
- *Case company F* is a company developing software and systems in the areas of connectivity, security, mobility solutions and AI.

The six companies that were selected as case companies were all interested in a close and active collaboration around the topic of this paper. In addition, we have rich experience from working with these companies for more than a decade. From that perspective, we know them well and they are eager to share their expertise.

3.3 Data Collection and Analysis

In this paper, we report on findings from workshops conducted between February 13th, 2024–August 27th, 2024. During this time, we organized four on-site workshops and five online workshops on topics closely related to innovation and development of software-intensive products and systems. As topics for discussion, we included agile ways-of-working, digitalization, innovation opportunities brought by software, data and AI, digital business models, and customer collaboration. The purpose of the workshops was to bring practitioners together to exchange expertise on topics that are critical for them and the organizations in which they work. From a research perspective, the workshops were organized and designed to collect empirical data on how companies approach innovation and how the practices they use are rapidly changing. Two *on-site workshops* were organized as cross-company workshops to which we invited all case companies (company A - F) as well as companies external to the member companies in the research collaboration. The workshops lasted for three hours and were documented in text, by collecting Post-it notes and by taking photos of the whiteboards that were used. At the first on-site workshop, we had 16 people attending of which half of the group were representatives from the case companies. At the second on-site workshop, we had 40 people attending of which 20 were representatives from the case companies. The other two on-site workshops were organized as company-specific workshops where we met with one case company at each workshop (company E and F). These workshops lasted for four hours and each company had invited key stakeholders relevant for the discussions. At company E, 20 people were invited and at company F, 5 people were invited. The workshops were documented by one of the researchers taking notes while the other researcher acted as facilitator for the discussions. For the on-site workshops, we followed a format in which we, the researchers and authors of this paper, opened the workshops with an introductory presentation to set the scene and provide the context. After this, we had different types of interactive elements depending on the type and size of the group and the time we had available. Typically, group discussions, break-out groups and/or PostIt note exercises were used. In our experience, the more we encouraged every participant to engage, the more rewarding the workshop discussions and results we got. The *online workshops* were organized as open workshops to which we invited all case companies as well as companies external to the member companies in the research collaboration. The online workshops lasted for one hour and were recorded and transcribed using Microsoft Teams. All workshops attracted roles ranging from developers, product owners and Scrum masters to software and system architects, product managers and project managers. For the on-line workshops, we followed the similar format as for the on-site workshops, i.e., an opening presentation followed by group discussion, but using shorter time for presentation and discussion. We focused the workshop discussions on topics related to digitalization, innovation and ways-of-working to capture the many challenges that companies face in their innovation of software-intensive systems and products.

In addition to the workshops, our findings build on the insights we got from studying the case companies for more than a decade. These insights provide the basis for understanding how the companies have evolved over time. During this collaboration, we have conducted case study research on a variety of topics using workshop sessions and semi-structured interview studies as our primary data collection techniques. For data collection and analysis, we use guidelines such as those presented in e.g., [34] and [28]. During analysis, the opportunity to use different data sources for triangulation, i.e., notes from on-site and online workshops, whiteboard pictures, PostIt notes and insights and experiences from our previous research, were valuable for enhancing validity and identify commonalities among the case companies. Also, as we were two researchers involved in this research, we had he opportunity to use investigator, or observer, triangulation to provide multiple observations and conclusions [34]. As part of the analysis, both researchers read through all the written documentation from the workshops, and we revisited the recordings of some of these, to identify themes and patterns in the discussions. For identifying themes and patterns in the empirical data, we followed thematic coding principles and especially the open coding practices as described in e.g., [43] and [6]. As recognized in [38], thematic coding allows for flexibility that is of particular value in analysis of qualitative data.

4   Empirical Findings

Below, we summarize our findings. In our summary, we present what we see are common patterns in the case companies, experiences they share, and beliefs on how they perceive themselves in relation to their innovation and development practices. We organize our summary according to customer engagement, monetization, and validation of customer value as these activities are key to stay competitive. Our findings build on the workshop sessions as detailed in Sect. 3.3 as well as on our insights and experiences from working closely with the case companies for more than a decade.

4.1   Every Innovation Needs a Customer

The workshop discussions revealed a common pattern in that the case companies seek to engage with customers more frequently and especially when developing new functionality. The typical approaches in the companies are customer interviews, customer surveys, on-site customer visits and larger customer conferences where the companies meet with multiple customers for several days. However, while these activities provide valuable input on a high level, e.g., general customer satisfaction, a common pattern is that the company representatives find it difficult to engage with customers in innovation of specific functionality and on a more continuous basis. In one of the workshops, the company representatives discussed the challenges in selecting the most appropriate customer for involvement in the innovation of new products. Based on this discussion, one approach could be to select the most valuable customers as developing functionality that serves their needs is critical from a revenue perspective.

However, as most innovations fail, or don't work as intended, the risks with involving the most valuable customers are high. The company representatives describe a situation in which the consequence could easily be a negative impact on their revenue, brand and future business. The last thing these companies want is to harm a relationship with a key customer, something that one of the workshop participants describe in the following way: *"You don't build your ecosystem, you earn it."* What we learnt is that the case companies are exceptionally careful with risking or harming their customer relationships in any shape or form. They rather keep to traditional approaches and even if they are aware of the experimentation practices that are applied in the B2C domains, they find these too risky to apply in effective ways in their own contexts. In addition, the case companies are B2B companies which means that typically, it is their customers that own the products the companies wish to experiment with to improve its performance. For the customer, the benefits of such experiments might not be obvious. Also, since the products are in operation, any risk of disruption or decrease in performance due to an unsuccessful experiment could cause damage and would not be well received by the customers. As one example on how to circumvent these challenges, several of the case companies involved in this study run experiments using internal resources, i.e., employees, as customers. In automotive companies we have seen experiments being run on e.g., test vehicles driven by employees. Another example is a company that used employees to experiment with configuration settings of their products before deployment to customers.

4.2   Every Innovation Needs a Business Model

All case companies are experiencing rapid changes due to the digitalization of their businesses. For the companies, software, data and artificial intelligence (AI), bring fundamentally new business and value creation opportunities. From developing products consisting primarily of hardware, the case companies are currently complementing their physical products with software-driven services and digital solutions that extend, and improve, their traditional product offerings. This is reflected in the following quote from one of the workshop participants: *"In the pipeline is the new technology where we make use of more intense data sets connected to the usage of AI-embedded applications, e.g., usage of vision, images, streaming of video to understand crashes, creation of digital twins."* For the majority of these services, data provides the foundation not only as the basis for development of the services but also as an asset that can be monetized using new business models. In the workshops, several participants reported on a situation in which digital technologies in general, and data in particular, are driving digital transformation initiatives. Representatives from company A shared that the company is looking to significantly increase the revenue from services and that the company is currently exploring services related to performance of the trucks, trailer services, resting services for the driver and the ability for a fleet owner to assess and compare the overall performance of the fleet.

However, even if there are endless opportunities and many promising business models for recurring revenue, the companies we studied find these difficult to realize in practice. While there are many reasons for this, the common ones that were referred to are unclear data ownership, lack of incentives for sharing data, and fear of upsetting the existing customers. Also, it should be noted that the companies we studied are incumbents in their business ecosystems and hence, keystone players for which it is very difficult to create and build emergent new businesses without risking the existing ones.

4.3   Every Innovation Needs to Be Validated with Customers

All case companies claim they use agile development methods and, over the years, they have adopted frameworks such as SAFe to help them scale these. Typically, agile practices were adopted by teams in the software organizations as a means to reduce cycle times and allow for more frequent release of software features. When asking what the company representatives perceive as the benefits of agile practices the typical answers are: fast feedback, iterations, cooperation, flexibility, fast development cycles, incremental, and cross-organizational. On the downside, the companies report on the too high focus on process, roles and organizational structure as this focus brings attention to the "how" to develop rather than the "what" to develop and "why". Also, people refer to bureaucracy, fragmentation, the paradigm being reactive. A recurring challenge is the difficulties in scaling agile practices. Although the case companies have worked in an agile fashion for more than a decade, these practices tend to remain within the software organization and the involvement of other functions has proven to be hard, if not impossible. As reflected on by one of the workshop participants: *"We say we adopted SAFe but we didn't change a thing".*

The concept of developing a Minimal Viable Product (MVP) is well-known in all case companies even if people are far from aligned on what this means, or how this can be achieved, in practice. In one of the workshops, the difficulty with thinking in terms of a MVP was described by one of the participants when saying: *"What would be the MVP of a truck? How do we even think about this...!?"* According to this person, running experiments typically requires a majority of the functionality in the system. With only a slice of the functionality in place, it is very hard, or even impossible, for customers to evaluate and provide relevant feedback on the new system. As a result of this, the case company participants reported on a situation in which the role of experimentation in the early phases of development is very limited.

More recently, several of the case companies have started using DevOps with the aim to continuously improve the product. This, however, shows to be challenging due to both internal and external reasons. Internally, DevOps practices require different teams and functions to work closely together in ways the organizational structures and boundaries were not designed for. Externally, customers are often hesitant to receive frequent software upgrades. As shared by one of the workshop participants: *"If deploying a new version of the software is perceived as effort-consuming, customers will instead reduce the release frequency as the cost of deploying them is perceived as higher than the intended benefits of the update."* Based on the workshops, we see that despite decades of agile transformation initiatives, and attempts to scale agile practices, most organizations did not fundamentally change. Although the case companies benefit from agile practices at the software team level, all levels above the team-level, as well as all other parts of the organizations, operate in a highly waterfall and project-based fashion.

5 Five Darlings to Be Killed

Below, we identify five myths that permeate software-intensive embedded systems companies and that they suffer from holding on to. These myths have become the typical representation for how the companies work, how they interact with customers and how they do business. In our experience, however, this is not the case in practice. Derived from our empirical data, we present these myths as "five darlings to be killed". Below, we detail each of these in terms of *what* the myth is about, *why* it is incorrect, and *what* happens instead.

5.1 There Is No Such Thing as "The Friendly Customer"

What is the Myth? In B2C SaaS companies, many innovation experts refer to the friendly customer when starting to test a new innovation. In this context, a friendly customer is a customer that is involved in testing of hypotheses and early-stage prototyping with the intent to provide feedback on the solution and the direction of development. The idea is that a friendly customer will not be upset about the limited maturity of the solution and provide valuable feedback that the company can use to iteratively improve the innovation. That allows the company to share the innovative solution with more customers beyond the initial, friendly ones. These latter customers will be more critical and less forgiving, but as the innovation has matured somewhat already, this is considered manageable.

Why is it Incorrect? Although companies in the B2B domain collaborate with customers, the ways in which this is achieved differs from the typical approach we see in B2C companies and as described above. The challenge with innovation experiments in a B2B context is twofold. First, different from B2C SaaS companies, it is often the customer that owns the product the company wants to experiment with. This is not just a server on your premises and that you own that will get some new software, but rather a product that you typically do not own. Second, this product is typically in operation at the customer and is used for commercial purposes. Disrupting or deteriorating the performance of the product is typically not received well by customers. Hence, involving a customer to experiment with solutions of limited maturity is a delicate request that needs careful consideration and customer approval.

In addition, and in relation to new products, a challenge is which customer to select for involvement in the innovation activities. The tendency is to select the most valuable customers as staying on their good side is the most relevant from a revenue perspective. However, many innovations fail and the consequence will easily be a negative impact on the revenue, brand and future business. Companies are exceptionally careful with risking or harming the customer relationship in any shape or form. The alternative is to target the edge customers (smaller and less critical customers), but then the challenge becomes that feedback from experiments with these customers will, by default, be less relevant (if relevant at all). Hence, the idea of a friendly customer is great in theory, but very difficult to realize in reality in B2B contexts.

What Happens Instead? Rather than going out with very early innovations, the companies that we studied spend significant resources on building mature innovations internally without, or with limited, customer feedback. In the cases where a customer is involved, the innovation is still mature to the extent that no harm can be done to the customer and to the system in operation. This significantly increases the investment per innovation before the companies know whether the innovation is viable or not, but the downside risk is generally considered to be too high.

5.2   There Is No Such Thing as "The New Business"

What is the Myth? In a digital world, all companies, including software intensive embedded systems companies, collect vast amounts of data from the products out in the field. This data is not just relevant for internal R&D purposes and other use cases inside the company, but is often also relevant for external parties that the company has not been in business with earlier. Hence, the available data could easily be commercialized with new customers that would open up an entirely new business, and generate new revenue streams, for the company. As an example of a new business, one could imagine a situation in which an automotive company would monetize e.g., road condition data with an external party who is not the typical and traditional customer in the automotive domain.

Why is it Incorrect? The empirical data shows that all the case companies have discussed the potential to commercialize data with new customers and we found proponents of pursuing this idea in most companies. However, in practice, it simply doesn't happen. The reasons for this are multiple, including unclear data ownership, lack of incentives for the teams closest to the data to share it, and fear of upsetting the existing customers. The primary reason, however, is that the companies we studied are incumbents in their ecosystems and virtually unable to create and build emergent new businesses. Typically it is a matter of priorities: the initial revenue from a new business is so small compared to the core business that it simply is not worth to pursue. This happens even if the potential revenue is quite significant in the long term as the key decision makers in the company are unable to imagine why others would pay any significant amounts for their data. The workshop discussions revealed that it is considered a too difficult and uphill battle to get the buy-in that is required from the organization as the potential use cases are hard to prove.

What Happens Instead? Rather than opening up entirely new avenues of business, the companies we studied look for ways to use the data they collect to serve their existing customers better. Most often, this takes the form of data-driven services that complement the core offering, such as performance and operations improvements to the system. Also, in several of the case companies data is increasingly used for comparative services in which a customer can assess and compare performance with other similar customers.

5.3   There Is No Such Thing as "The New Business Model"

What is the Myth? As companies enter the digital transformation, one of the typical assumptions is that the company will change the business model from a transactional business model where the customer pays upfront and acquires the product to one where there are continuous revenue models such as subscription or usage based monetization.

Why is it Incorrect? Although several of the companies in this study are exploring continuous business models, these are intended to complement rather than replace the upfront, transactional model. This is the case for two main reasons. First, changing from a transactional to a continuous business model has major cashflow implications. Rather than getting paid for the product at delivery, the company has to finance the product on behalf of the customer and instead collect revenue over time. Even if the total amount of revenue is significantly higher than the transactional revenue, the cashflow implications are hard to overcome. Second, adopting usage-based pricing models or seat-based subscription models is often counterproductive as the customer will then try to decrease its use of the solution provided. Companies typically look for business models that benefit the customer and where revenue is aligned and in continuous business models, this is typically not the case.

What Happens Instead? Rather than adopting business models that will cause the customer to limit their use and consumption, the companies we studied look for a business model where increased usage doesn't have negative cost implications on their customers. The result often is charging a license fee that is independent of usage or number of users. Even if the companies reference this as annual recurring revenue, in practice this brings us back to a traditional license model in anything but name.

5.4   There Is No Such Thing as "The MVP"

What is the Myth? Originating from the work of Steve Blank [1] and later Eric Ries [33], the principle advocated in the innovation community is that companies should build the absolute minimum of a product before releasing it to customers and collecting feedback. This is often referred to as the minimal viable product (MVP), see e.g., [22], or in some contexts as the minimal loveable product (MLP). In the context of innovation, a minimum viable product (MVP) is known as a version of a product with just enough features to be usable by customers who are involved early in the development process to provide feedback for future product development.

Why is it Incorrect? In the software-intensive embedded systems companies involved in this study, we learned that in most cases, being able to run realistic experiments requires the companies to build most of the functionality that is intended to be part of the product. Otherwise, the perceived or actual business benefits for the customer are not realized. The result is that the role of experimentation in the exploration phase is in practice "non-existing" (or very small). In the workshop discussions, the company representatives reported on how it is impossible to build an MVP for experimentation purposes since anything less than the full functionality doesn't work, i.e., to test with customers there is typically the need for about 80% of the new functionality.

What Happens Instead? Rather than building what could be considered to be MVPs, the companies spend significant amounts of time talking to and interviewing customers, i.e. listening to what customers say they do. Once there is a consensus in the company that the new product or feature has sufficient traction with customers, it gets built, with most functionality in place, and then released to selected customers for validation. Typically, the validation is concerned with quality issues, i.e. defects, and less with the market viability of the offering. Once the company establishes that the quality of the new offering is satisfactory, it is released to all customers.

5.5   There Is No Such Thing as "Agile Ways-of-Working"

What is the Myth? More than two decades after the introduction of the Agile Manifesto [15], few companies will claim to not have adopted agile practices. Also the companies studied in this research all claim to work using agile practices. Words like sprints, cross-functional teams, daily stand-ups, retrospectives, scaled agile framework and other terminology are used extensively, not only in the software parts of the companies, but also in other parts such as the electronics and mechanics departments. This reflects how these practices have moved far beyond the SaaS domain.

Why is it Incorrect? There are several beliefs on how companies should work in the engineering of products. However, these tend to be broadly held beliefs and illusions rather than methods and processes applied in practice. Our research shows that despite decades of agile transformations and attempts to scale agile practices in large-scale systems development, most organizations did not fundamentally change and the adoption of agile practices remains at the software side (if at all) but doesn't scale beyond this. The goal of agile is to achieve business agility, i.e. the ability to rapidly respond to customer requests or market developments. Although all case companies apply agile practices at the team level, above that the ways of working are still highly waterfall and project-based. Hence, the desire to achieve business agility by adopting agile methods remains but so far, none of the companies have seen any signs of this in practice.

What Happens Instead? Although most of the companies that we studied are discussing the broader adoption of agile, which would allow for business agility in relation to the functionality provided by software, the reality is that this is far from reality at this point. In most cases, the regulatory and certification practices are such that releases of mechanical and electronics parts, software, machine learning components as well as the systems as a whole require a heavy approval process that simply is too costly to conduct often.

6   Threats to Validity

As recognized in [34], there are different ways to classify aspects of validity and threats to validity. In our research, we use the four aspects as proposed in [44]. These are construct validity, internal validity, external validity and reliability. To address *construct validity* [28], we shared our understanding of digital transformation, and the ways in which innovation practices are changing, in the opening of each workshop. In this way, our workshop discussions were based on terminology that was familiar for all participants. To increase *internal validity*, we followed common and well-established guidelines for how to conduct case study research and hoe to plan workshops and interviews. Similarly, we applied such guidelines during data collection and analysis. With regards to *external validity*, we used our empirical insights and our experiences from working with the case companies to derive our findings with the intention to provide value for companies that have common characteristics as the case companies we studied. Hence, we view our contributions as related to the "drawing of specific implications" and as a contribution of "rich insights" [42]. We have no evidence that our findings would generalize beyond the case companies, However, with the opportunity to study companies from different domains we believe that the findings are relevant also in other embedded systems companies with similar characteristics as the companies we studied. Finally, to address *reliability*, we followed well-established guidelines for case study research and methods for data collection as presented in e.g., [34]. For example, the on-site workshops were carefully documented by one of the researchers, the online workshops were recorded, and we used coding techniques when analyzing the empirical data. Moreover, we used different data sources to collect information to ensure a holistic understanding of the topic. These data sources include the workshops arranged with, and referred to, in this paper as well as the research activities that provide the basis for the insights and experiences we collected during the years we have been working with the case companies.

7   Conclusions and Future Work

Companies need to continuously innovate to stay competitive. In this context, we see that companies in the software-intensive embedded systems industry adopt practices and principles that originate in the Software-as-a-Service (SaaS) domain and that reflect how these companies work. As an example, agile practices as well as experimentation practices have been adopted by embedded systems companies as these have proven valuable in companies such as Google, Microsoft, and Amazon [10,23,25,26]. However, translating these practices into the ways in which B2B embedded systems companies operate is far from trivial.

In this paper, we identify five myths that permeate software-intensive embedded systems companies and that they suffer from holding on to. The myths are related to "the friendly customer", "the new business", "the new business model", "the MVP" and "agile ways-of-working" and we show that despite these being the typical representations of how companies work, they don't happen in practice as the nature of embedded systems companies doesn't allow for effective adoption and use of these practices.

In future work, we aim to further explore the challenges associated with innovation of software-intensive embedded systems. This involves overcoming the myths we identified and finding viable approaches that apply in the B2B context. As part of this, we seek to explore solutions for how to overcome the challenges companies face and develop best practices that help companies to advance their innovation processes of software-intensive embedded systems. Also, we look to study each of the myths in more detail to reflect on situations in which they might hold value or be contextually appropriate.

References

1. Blank, S., Dorf, B.: The Startup Owner's Manual: The Step-by-Step Guide for Building a Great company. Wiley, New York (2020)
2. Booch, G.: The history of software engineering. IEEE Softw. **35**(5), 108–114 (2018)
3. Bosch, J.: Continuous software engineering: an introduction. In: Bosch, J. (eds.) Continuous Software Engineering, pp. 3–13. Springer, Cham (2014). https://doi.org/10.1007/978-3-319-11283-1_1
4. Bosch, J.: Speed, data, and ecosystems: the future of software engineering. IEEE Softw. **33**(1), 82–88 (2015)
5. Bosch, J., Olsson, H.H.: Digital for real: a multicase study on the digital transformation of companies in the embedded systems domain. J. Softw. Evol. Process **33**(5), e2333 (2021)
6. Castleberry, A., Nolen, A.: Thematic analysis of qualitative research data: is it as easy as it sounds? Curr. Pharm. Teach. Learn. **10**(6), 807–815 (2018)
7. Dakkak, A., Bosch, J., Olsson, H.H., Mattos, D.I.: Continuous deployment in software-intensive system-of-systems. Inf. Softw. Technol. **159**, 107200 (2023)
8. Desouza, K.C., et al.: Customer-driven innovation. Res. Technol. Manag. **51**(3), 35–44 (2008)
9. Dikert, K., Paasivaara, M., Lassenius, C.: Challenges and success factors for large-scale agile transformations: a systematic literature review. J. Syst. Softw. **119**, 87–108 (2016)
10. Fabijan, A., Dmitriev, P., McFarland, C., Vermeer, L., Holmström Olsson, H., Bosch, J.: Experimentation growth: evolving trustworthy A/B testing capabilities in online software companies. J. Softw. Evol. Process **30**(12), e2113 (2018)
11. Fabijan, A., Dmitriev, P., Olsson, H.H., Bosch, J.: The evolution of continuous experimentation in software product development: from data to a data-driven organization at scale. In: 2017 IEEE/ACM 39th International Conference on Software Engineering (ICSE), pp. 770–780. IEEE (2017)
12. Fabijan, A., Dmitriev, P., Olsson, H.H., Bosch, J.: Effective online controlled experiment analysis at large scale. In: 2018 44th Euromicro Conference on Software Engineering and Advanced Applications (SEAA), pp. 64–67. IEEE (2018)

13. Fabijan, A., Olsson, H.H., Bosch, J.: Data-Driven Decision-Making in Product R&D. Springer (2015)
14. Fitzgerald, B., Stol, K.J.: Continuous software engineering: a roadmap and agenda. J. Syst. Softw. **123**, 176–189 (2017)
15. Fowler, M., Highsmith, J., et al.: The agile manifesto. Softw. Dev. **9**(8), 28–35 (2001)
16. Hoda, R., Noble, J., Marshall, S.: The impact of inadequate customer collaboration on self-organizing agile teams. Inf. Softw. Technol. **53**(5), 521–534 (2011)
17. Hoda, R., Salleh, N., Grundy, J.: The rise and evolution of agile software development. IEEE Softw. **35**(5), 58–63 (2018)
18. Kasauli, R., Knauss, E., Horkoff, J., Liebel, G., de Oliveira Neto, F.G.: Requirements engineering challenges and practices in large-scale agile system development. J. Syst. Softw. **172**, 110851 (2021)
19. Kischelewski, B., Richter, J.: Implementing large-scale agile-an analysis of challenges and success factors. In: 28th European Conference on Information Systems (ECIS), p. 176 (2020)
20. Laanti, M.: Characteristics and principles of scaled agile. In: Dingsøyr, T., Moe, N.B., Tonelli, R., Counsell, S., Gencel, C., Petersen, K. (eds.) XP 2014. LNBIP, vol. 199, pp. 9–20. Springer, Cham (2014). https://doi.org/10.1007/978-3-319-14358-3_2
21. Lefaix-Durand, A., Kozak, R.: Integrating transactional and relational exchange into the study of exchange orientation in customer relationships. J. Mark. Manag. **25**(9–10), 1003–1025 (2009)
22. Lenarduzzi, V., Taibi, D.: MVP explained: a systematic mapping study on the definitions of minimal viable product. In: 2016 42th Euromicro Conference on Software Engineering and Advanced Applications (SEAA), pp. 112–119. IEEE (2016)
23. Liu, Y., Mattos, D.I., Bosch, J., Olsson, H.H., Lantz, J.: Size matters? Or not: A/B testing with limited sample in automotive embedded software. In: 2021 47th Euromicro Conference on Software Engineering and Advanced Applications (SEAA), pp. 300–307. IEEE (2021)
24. Maarse, J.H., Bogers, M.: An integrative model for technology-driven innovation and external technology commercialization. In: Open Innovation in Firms and Public Administrations: Technologies for Value Creation, pp. 59–78. IGI Global (2012)
25. Mattos, D.I., Bosch, J., Olsson, H.H.: Your system gets better every day you use it: towards automated continuous experimentation. In: 2017 43rd Euromicro Conference on Software Engineering and Advanced Applications (SEAA), pp. 256–265. IEEE (2017)
26. Mattos, D.I., Bosch, J., Olsson, H.H., Korshani, A.M., Lantz, J.: Automotive A/B testing: challenges and lessons learned from practice. In: 2020 46th Euromicro Conference on Software Engineering and Advanced Applications (SEAA), pp. 101–109. IEEE (2020)
27. Mattos, D.I., Dakkak, A., Bosch, J., Olsson, H.H.: Experimentation for business-to-business mission-critical systems: a case study. In: Proceedings of the International Conference on Software and System Processes, pp. 95–104 (2020)
28. Maxwell, J.A.: Qualitative Research Design: An Interactive Approach. Sage Publications, Thousand Oaks (2012)
29. Olsson, H.H., Alahyari, H., Bosch, J.: Climbing the "stairway to heaven"-a multiple-case study exploring barriers in the transition from agile development towards continuous deployment of software. In: 2012 38th Euromicro Conference on Software Engineering and Advanced Applications, pp. 392–399. IEEE (2012)

30. Olsson, H.H., Bosch, J.: The HYPEX Model: from opinions to data-driven software development. In: Bosch, J. (ed.) Continuous Software Engineering, pp. 155–164. Springer, Cham (2014). https://doi.org/10.1007/978-3-319-11283-1_13

31. Olsson, H.H., Bosch, J.: Going digital: disruption and transformation in software-intensive embedded systems ecosystems. J. Softw. Evol. Process **32**(6), e2249 (2020)

32. Olsson, H.H., Bosch, J.: Living in a pink cloud or fighting a whack-a-mole? On the creation of recurring revenue streams in the embedded systems domain. In: 2022 48th Euromicro Conference on Software Engineering and Advanced Applications (SEAA), pp. 161–168. IEEE (2022)

33. Ries, E.: The lean startup. New York: Crown Bus. **27**, 2016–2020 (2011)

34. Runeson, P., Höst, M.: Guidelines for conducting and reporting case study research in software engineering. Empir. Softw. Eng. **14**, 131–164 (2009)

35. Senapathi, M., Buchan, J., Osman, H.: Devops capabilities, practices, and challenges: insights from a case study. In: Proceedings of the 22nd International Conference on Evaluation and Assessment in Software Engineering, pp. 57–67 (2018)

36. Silva, F.S., et al.: Using CMMI together with agile software development: a systematic review. Inf. Softw. Technol. **58**, 20–43 (2015)

37. Stahl, D., Martensson, T., Bosch, J.: Continuous practices and DevOps: beyond the buzz, what does it all mean? In: 2017 43rd Euromicro Conference on Software Engineering and Advanced Applications (SEAA), pp. 440–448. IEEE (2017)

38. Terry, G., Hayfield, N., Clarke, V., Braun, V., et al.: Thematic analysis. SAGE Handb. Qual. Res. Psychol. **2**(17–37), 25 (2017)

39. Trienekens, J., Kusters, R., Himawan, H.B., van Moll, J.: Customer involvement in the scaled agile framework: results from a case study in an industrial company. In: 20th International Conference on Enterprise Information Systems, pp. 104–110. SCITEPRESS-Science and Technology Publications, Lda. (2018)

40. Uludag, Ö., Kleehaus, M., Caprano, C., Matthes, F.: Identifying and structuring challenges in large-scale agile development based on a structured literature review. In: 2018 IEEE 22nd International Enterprise Distributed Object Computing Conference (EDOC), pp. 191–197. IEEE (2018)

41. Verner, J.M., Sampson, J., Tosic, V., Bakar, N.A., Kitchenham, B.A.: Guidelines for industrially-based multiple case studies in software engineering. In: 2009 Third International Conference on Research Challenges in Information Science, pp. 313–324. IEEE (2009)

42. Walsham, G.: Interpretive case studies in is research: nature and method. Eur. J. Inf. Syst. **4**(2), 74–81 (1995)

43. Williams, M., Moser, T.: The art of coding and thematic exploration in qualitative research. Int. Manag. Rev. **15**(1), 45–55 (2019)

44. Yin, R.K.: Designing case studies. Qual. Res. Methods **5**(14), 359–386 (2003)

Digital Sovereignty: Affordances in Open Source Projects

Martha Klare[✉][iD] and Ulrike Lechner[iD]

Universität der Bundeswehr München, 85579 Neubiberg, Germany
{martha.klare,ulrike.lechner}@unibw.de

Abstract. Digital Sovereignty as a strategic concept encompasses equity and sustainability. We explore affordances in Open Source projects that have been initiated to achieve more Digital Sovereignty. Open Source has the potential to be central for Digital Sovereignty. Our primary data set include online interviews with project teams and literature in the context of Digital Sovereignty from 2013 to 2024. By evaluating the project outputs based on affordance theory, we identify digital and economical offerings. The analysis of the impact of these offerings on the projects forms the basis for formulating measures to improve sustainable actions through Digital Sovereignty. With this work we provide a better understanding of IT-enabled organizational change and the types of affordances that are required in Digital Sovereignty transformations.

Keywords: Digital Sovereignty · Open Source · Affordance Theory

1 Introduction

Digital Sovereignty (DS) is a strategic goal put in place by the European Union to be achieved until 2030 [29]. It encompasses sustainability through digital education [14], more self-determination in the digital space through politics [27] and reducing digital inequality through digital inclusion [1]. In the sustainability goals 2030 of the European Union, reduced inequalities, equity, high-quality education and, simultaneously, economical growth, innovation and partnerships to achieve these goals are also explicitly mentioned [24].

We note that practical approaches from the business sector, which describe the path to achieving DS goals, are scarce [12,17]. To gain deeper insight into organizational challenges and management of DS, we aim to analyze DS in daily development practices by utilizing the affordance theory. We analyze affordances to explore what open source (OS) projects are offering to achieve DS. The affordance theory enables us to analyze technical objects and economical services.

To gain new insights, two OS projects will be examined. These projects were initiated in a security-critical environment, with the aim of ensuring more security, availability and gaining control over content - in other words, being sovereign. OS technology and components play an important role when providing core functionalities for the projects. We specifically consider OS projects, as we found evidence that OS is an important element of DS [1,5,28].

E. Papatheocharous et al. (Eds.): ICSOB 2024, LNBIP 539, pp. 20–34, 2025.
https://doi.org/10.1007/978-3-031-85849-9_2

This paper addresses the following research questions:

1. What are the challenges in the usage of open source development teams in order to strengthen Digital Sovereignty?
2. How can affordances in open source projects be modified to gain more Digital Sovereignty?

Section 2 provides a theoretical framework, while Sect. 3 presents the methodology. The current and desired states are described in Sect. 4 and 5. Here, research question 1 with regards to the challenges in using OS to strengthen DS will be answered. An analysis between the current and desired states leads us to gaps. We use our data set as a basis for answering research question 2, namely how affordances can be modified to achieve DS (Sect. 6). The final section summarizes the results and provides an outlook for further research (Sect. 7).

2 Theoretical Background

Digital Sovereignty. The term 'sovereignty' has various definitions. Celeste [4] initially describes the core of the sovereignty concept, as originating from the idea of independence and control over a territorial area. Couture and Toupin [5] provide further specification. They explain that one might assume a necessity of a high degree of sovereignty in correlation with high authority; however, the opposite is true, in the past, sovereignty was often needed where authorities were weak and dependencies arose. The modern concept of 'Digital Sovereignty' now applies to the digital space. Celeste [4], Couture and Toupin [5], and Glasze et al. [13] understand DS as a strategical-political concept that can serve as a guide for acting more autonomously in the digital space. The authors all refer to Pohle [27], who describes the difference between achieving DS for an individual, a company, or a state. In this paper, we focus on DS as a strategic goal for companies. For us, DS aligns with political objectives. We use the goals of the European Union, which has placed achieving DS on the political agenda for 2030, as guidelines [29]. Specifically, in our understanding, DS aims to achieve greater autonomy in the digital space and more sustainable action.

Affordances and Affordance Theory. James Gibson first analyzed in 1986 how an object can be perceived and used differently by various living beings. His definition: *"The affordances of the environment are what it offers the animal, what it provides or furnishes, either for good or ill"* [11]. In psychology, where the term 'affordance' originates, it is increasingly understood as the possibility of perceiving actions through objects in the environment [16]. In Information Systems research, affordance analysis is increasingly used to analyze user behavior when utilizing technical objects [9]. It solidifies the understanding that information technology objects offer suggestions on how they should be used. Volkoff and Strong [34] suggest how to use the affordance theory in IS research. They define that affordances have an offering character that can produce a result between an object (we want to understand 'object' as technical objects or economical services) or through actors (we want to understand 'actors' as actors in companies). Affordance theory is therefore crucial for us to explain agency in the context of DS and IT-related organizational change. Affordances are not independent possibilities for action but an integral part of actions [20]. At the interface between humans, machines, and institutions, affordances arise and can be beneficial as well as inhibiting or limiting. Affordances are often confused with features, but they can also be constraints [34]. To apply affordance theory in the context of DS, we look at what is relevant for an IT strategy. We want to find IT affordances in OS projects in order to understand how these affordances need to be adapted to strengthen DS.

We provide one core definition of sustainability and open source.

Sustainability. Moore et al. [22] aim to understand the term 'sustainability' based on 209 definitions. They define sustainability as something that necessitates the introduction of new ways of working according to a norm and the adaptation of the systems used according to this norm. In recent years, the field of computer science has increasingly focused on sustainable technologies and sustainable human-machine interaction [35]. In contrast, business administration has increasingly addressed the question of how sustainable management [25] can be achieved. In our view of sustainability, we aim to unify these perspectives. In this work, we adopt a perspective where sustainable action in companies and a sustainable technology selection are harmonized through the lens of DS.

Open Source. OS can refer to software, development teams and projects in our work. One example, developers collaborate and, with the use of OS software, are allowed to copy the source code without paying for it [31]. Another example, there are ten criteria defined by the OS Initiative [26] that permit development teams to modify software and source code. Last example, within a project, OS software can be used [10]. DS encompasses efforts to develop and use IT systems in a self-determined and free way. OS can be an enabler to achieve this goal [2].

3   Research Design

The central method of this work is the gap analysis (see Fig. 1). It is based on a comparison between the current state and the target state [18]. In our research methodology, the current state is represented by online interviews with two project teams, while the target state has been determined by collecting goals and requirements for DS.

The data for the current state analysis were collected between October 2023 and March 2024, and the online interviews were conducted in Germany. For the online interviews, we followed the steps outlined by Lehmann [21]: determining the target group, preparing the questions, conducting two pre-tests, collecting and analyzing the data. The following questions were adapted from Przybyle

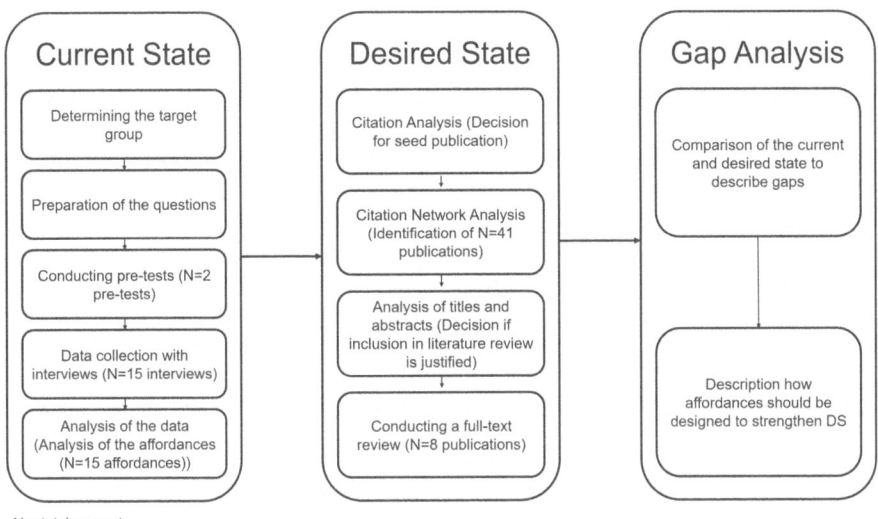

Fig. 1. Current State, Desired State, and Gap Analysis

and Kotecka [30] for the interviewees: 1) How does the IT architecture of the project look like? 2) What challenges did you encounter using open source to strengthen Digital Sovereignty? 2a) What would you do more of? 2b) What would you continue doing? 2c) What would you stop doing? 2d) What would you start doing now? 2e) What would you do less of? The interviewees were provided with a definition of DS.

For the first series of interviews (1st project), the following roles were obtained: the product owner, a scrum master, an IT architect, and five developers. The second series of interviews (2nd project) included a project manager, a product owner, a scrum master, a data engineer, a backend developer, a frontend developer, and a consultant. The interviewees listed were from the same company and they were familiar with the projects. These projects are seen as success stories for more DS. In our analysis with the affordance theory, we rely on Fromm et al. [9], who provide recommendations for applying affordance research in information systems. Under point 6 they recommend to identify contextual factors. To include an affordance in the overview, we determine three context-related factors: 1) Are they entrepreneurial, human, or technological action invitations? 2) Do they have a beneficial or inhibiting impact on the project team's ability to act? and 3) Is there a need to consider the affordance in the context of DS? We assign the affordances collected from the interviews to the following affordance clusters from the work of [33] and [32]: Standardizing, Basic, Controlling, Organizational Sensemaking, and Integrating Affordances.

For the target state analysis, we chose a representative literature review, using a snowball sampling by Lecy and Beatty [19]. We first conducted a citation analysis by searching the databases IEEE, Springer, and ScienceDirect, using the keywords 'Digital Sovereignty' and 'digitale Souveränität'. We find that Couture (2019) is suitable as a seed article. Next, we performed a network analysis using connectedpapers.com. Connectedpapers.com automatically matches which publications cite the seed article, the number of references, and the similarity to the original paper. This analysis results in 41 identified publications. Finally, we narrowed down the literature further by reviewing titles and abstracts to decide if an inclusion in the literature overview would be justified. Articles that address the project-specific challenges from the current state analysis are included. This lead to a selection of 11 publications.

In the final gap analysis, we compare the target state analysis with the current state analysis to identify gaps. Based on our data, we formulate measures that describe how affordances can be modified to close the identified gaps and strengthen DS.

4   Analysis of the Current State in the OS Projects

4.1   Results From the Online Interviews

The two OS projects (Messenger and Information Brief) were initiated due to geopolitical tensions and stricter security requirements. The aim of the first project is to develop a secure messenger for the public sector. The aim of the second project is to carry out forecasts on potential crisis areas.

How Does the IT Architecture of the OS Project Look Like? The project architecture for the Messenger development consists of four layers: data layer, chat app cloud infrastructure, geo-located server, and user layer (see Fig. 2). At the lowest layer, data from the metadata database are used to create user groups and chat rooms. The hot chat history allows the extraction of recent messages, while the cold chat history allows the restoration of archived chats. The chat app infrastructure is based on a public cloud, and a message queue is used to create message queues when the target system is unavailable. The OS community and external collaborations influence the project.

The project architecture for the development of the information brief is divided into data, backend, frontend, and user (see Fig. 3). At the data layer, external websites, documents, images, and audios are found. While information from external websites is scraped, documents, images, and audios are retrieved using a push method. There are also two databases at the data layer that store structured and unstructured data. The transition to the databases takes place via a transfer zone through an ETL pipeline. In the backend, data are analyzed and prepared for delivery. Specifically, this involves text extraction from HTML, JPG, PDF, MP4, information extraction with NLP (natural language processing), and geo-information extraction. The backend (Spring Boot) forms the bridge for running the application. It is coupled with 1) the cognitive service, which provides a collection of algorithms and APIs for AI applications, and 2) a semantic search that enables contextual search. The core of the frontend is the dashboard built with Grafana. Users can view the dashboard. The administrator can adjust configuration objects and assign roles and permissions.

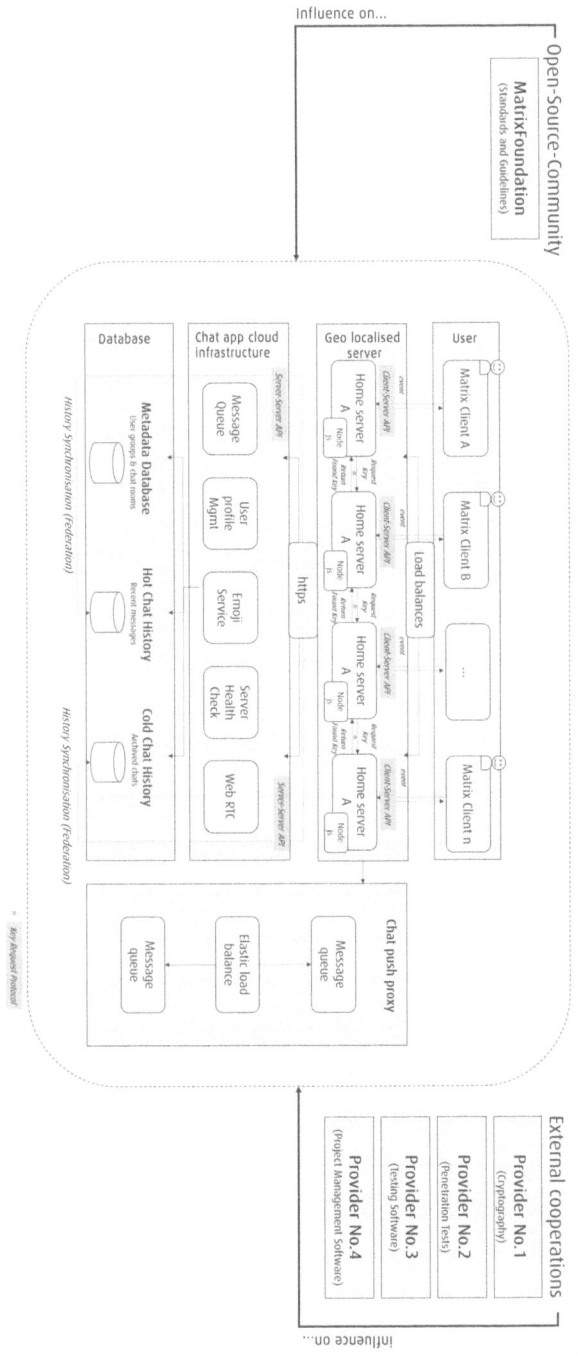

Fig. 2. Project Architecture Open Source Project No.1: Messenger

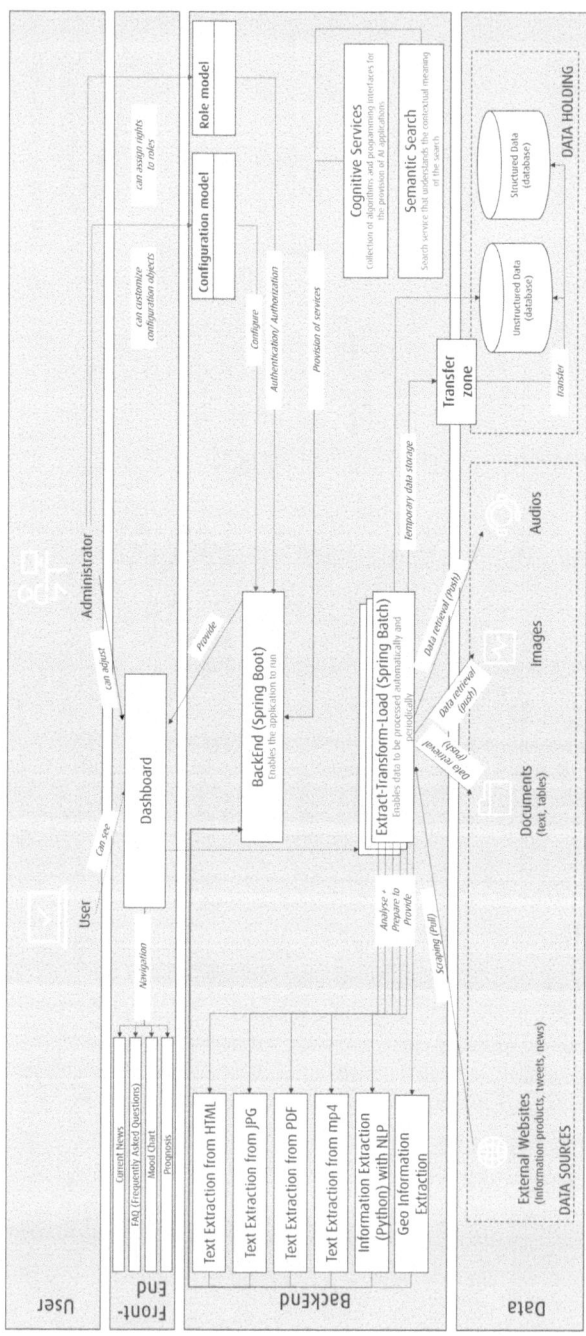

Fig. 3. Project Architecture Open Source Project No.2: Information Brief

What Challenges Did You Encounter Using Open Source to Strengthen Digital Sovereignty? Based on our interview results, it becomes clear that in the development of the messenger, standards and guidelines imposed by external entities such as the Matrix Foundation restrict the project's autonomy. One interviewee commented (I1): *"None of us are part of the Matrix Foundation. We have no influence on the Matrix ecosystem."* Additionally, expertise in cryptography and penetration testing lies within third parties. Another interviewee noted (I2): *"We lack expertise in core areas like cryptography. We don't have an expert on our team, so an external provider handles it."* Consequently, the selection of testing software and project management software also leads to dependencies. Another interviewee mentioned (I3): *"The use of specific proprietary tools is problematic."* Security weaknesses were identified in the front-end solution, the OS system, the database, and the database management solution for the information brief. One expert stated (I4): *"The use of open source should not come at the expense of security."* The cloud used in the project leads to dependencies and lock-in effects, which also limit the project team's autonomy. An interviewee explained (I5): *"We are dependent on market monopolists like Amazon or Microsoft for our development."* Another challenge is that automated extractions could lead to the misuse or disclosure of sensitive information. It is possible to infer personal data and the location of individuals. One interviewee noted (I6): *"It's challenging because we are expected to ensure 100% security. That's impossible."* The use of AI models particularly highlights the challenge of dependency on English-language NLP models. Finally, an interviewee commented (I7): *"There are hardly any good alternatives to the English NLP models."*

4.2 Results of the Affordance Analysis Based on the Online Interviews

We found standardizing, basic, controlling, organizational sensemaking and integrating affordances.

Based on the online interviews, we analyze the following affordances for the first OS project (see Table 1). 'Standards and guidelines' are provided by the Matrix Foundation in the project to guide the proper use of the Matrix protocol within the OS community. This affordance impacts the development within the project. 'Know-how' is the second affordance we identified. A third-party provider is responsible for the cryptography aspect of the project. This provider offers his know-how as a service. This affordance also impacts the development and the project work. Another affordance is 'penetration tests'. Here, another third party provider is responsible for testing security weaknesses. This affects the project's speed. The last provider offers testing software. Therefore, we include 'testing software' as an affordance since it is offered to the developers as a technical service, impacting the project's work. The testing software is used to verify that the messenger development performs as expected. The last two affordances are 'project management tools'. Jira by Atlassian offers a popular web application used for project tracking. Confluence, also by Atlassian,

Table 1. Affordance Analysis Open Source Project No. 1: Messenger

Cluster	Affordance	Exact solution	Explanation	Impact
		Open Source Project No. 1: Messenger		
Standardizing Affordances	Standards and guidelines	Standards and guidelines for matrix (Matrix.org Foundation)	Matrix.org Foundation is an open source community that sets standards for the use of the Matrix communication protocol and promotes the development of Matrix.	Project work (development)
Basic Affordances	Know how	Cryptography know how (Vector Informatik GmbH)	Vector Informatik GmbH offers cryptography know how. This means that they are working on how the messenger can be made resistant to manipulation and how critical information can be securely encrypted.	Project work (development)
Controlling Affordances	Penetration test	Penetration test know how (Secusmart GmbH)	Secusmart GmbH is the company responsible for penetration tests within the project. The six-monthly test is intended to ensure that security weaknesses in Messenger are detected quickly. They are also responsible for proposing mitigation measures, which the project team will then implement.	Project work (speed)
	Testing software	Eggplant (Keysight Technologies)	Keysight Technologies offers testing software that provides test cases identified by AI analysis and uses a twin approach to allow developers to navigate through the system under test as a user. As a testing software, Eggplant offers a fast way to check whether the messenger is doing what it is supposed to do.	Project work (development)
Organizational Sensemaking Affordances		Jira (Atlassian)	With Jira, Atlassian offers a web application that is used to track project processes. Jira has established itself as a monopolist for task management in software development projects for small and medium-sized development teams.	Project work (project management - quality, speed, budget)
	Project management tools	Confluence (Atlassian)	Atlassian offers Confluence as software to support knowledge sharing, document management and the creation of wikis in companies. It is used as a documentation platform in this project.	Project work (project management - quality, speed, budget)

provides software for document management and knowledge sharing. These two affordances impact the management of the project work.

Table 2 shows the results of the affordance analysis for the second OS project. Here, we identified 'front-end solution' as the first affordance. The front-end solution used in the project (Grafana) is based on OS. The front-end impacts the project work as it is delivered to the customer at the end. It also affects customer satisfaction, as it significantly influences the system's usability. The next affordance is 'open source system'. The OS solution used in the project is Kubernetes, a popular system among developers for managing containerized applications. The decision to use Kubernetes impacts the project work, particularly what is delivered to the customer. Additionally, from the project architecture, we identified MongoDB as the document management solution. The corresponding affordance is 'database management system'. The database management system impacts the development and thus the project work. Besides the database management system, another affordance is 'database'. The OS database used in this project is PostgreSQL, which also impacts the development. Cloud capacities are also used. The cloud computing platform used is AWS, influencing the development work. Therefore, we include 'cloud capacity' as an affordance. 'Automated extractions' are used in the project to extract texts, information, and location names. Automated extractions impact the speed and development of the project team. We also include 'AI models' as an affordance since they are used in the project to make predictions. AI models impact the customer outcome. The last affordances are 'open source product', 'collection of algorithms and APIs', and 'search technology'. All three affordances influence the development work.

Table 2. Affordance Analysis Open Source Project No. 2: Information Brief

Cluster	Affordance	Exact solution	Explanation	Impact
		Open Source Project No. 2: Information Brief		
Integrating Affordances	Front end solution	Grafana	Grafana is an open source application used in the project as a front-end solution for data analysis	Project work (customer provision), customer satisfaction (usability)
	Open source system	Kubernetes	Kubernetes is an open source system for developers. It was developed by Google to provide, manage and automate container-based applications.	Project work (customer provision), multi-provider management
Organizational Sensemaking Affordances	Database management solution	MongoDB	MangoDB is a modern database management solution from MangoDB, Inc. that enables developers to make their data queryable and quickly identifiable through a collection of JSON documents.	Project work (development)
Basic Affordances	Database	PostgreSQL	PostGreSQL is an open source database. It was developed in the 1980s by POSTGRES and is now being further developed by an open source community. It has been meticulously and continuously improved by a worldwide team of developers, making PostGreSQL one of the most convenient databases (for both relational and non-relational databases). Developers value the database for its flexibility (open standards) and reliability (largely compliant with the SQL standard SQL:2011).	Project work (development)
Integrating Affordances	Cloud Capacity	AWS (Amazon Cloud)	AWS is more than just the provision of cloud capacity. Compared to other market players, AWS scores points with developers thanks to its extensive density of functions (over 200 services). These services make it relatively easy to work with artificial intelligence (AI), machine learning, big data analytics and internet of things	Project work (development), multi-provider management,
		Text extraction	Text Extraction is a text tool for extracting JSON into a TXT file.	Project work (development, speed)
		Extraction of information	Information Extraction aims to automatically extract structured information from unstructured text using Spark NLP. Spark NLP offers several ways to extract, analyze and use entities from text data.	Project work (development, speed)
	Automated extractions	Extraction of geoinformation	Geo Information Extraction is a way to extract place names from text. With feedback to Open-Street-Map, the Python geoparsing library enables the analysis of large amounts of data. This approach is an alternative to the use of third-party APIs (e.g. Google Geocoding API).	Project work (development, speed)
	AI models	Natural language processing (NLP) model	The NLP model used in the project is called paraphrase-multilingual-MiniLM-L12-v2 and is an already pre-trained open source product that was used for this use case. While it achieves very good results in English, it should be noted that the developers are supposed to perform a prediction of the political situation in a country from the study environment. The output should be in German language.	Result at the customer (forecast results political situation in study environment)
	Open source product	Spring Boot	A Spring Boot is an open source product that developers use to develop microservices or web apps based on Java frameworks. Java Spring Boot allows to create stand-alone applications quickly and easily.	Project work (development)
	Collection of algorithms and APIs	Cognitive service	Cognitive Service is a collection of algorithms and programming interfaces for AI applications. The market monopolist in the field of cognitive services is Microsoft. Microsoft offers tools in cognitive services to design AI services and enable natural language understanding.	Project work (development), multi-provider management
	Search technology	Semantic search	Semantic Search enables contextual searches in the dashboard. To enable contextual searches, developers have to develop them on an open-source basis. Alternatively, they can use elasticsearch and Kibana to create a semantic search. In this project, the focus was on in-house development.	Project work (development)

5   Analysis of the Desired State in Terms of DS

5.1   Results from the Literature Review on DS

As depicted in quotes I1 and I2, the autonomy of the project teams is too restricted because of several dependencies. Our literature review indicates that autonomy in the digital space, in terms of DS, requires the acquisition of necessary capabilities and skills [8,12,27,28]. Pohle [27] points out that arrangements should be made that lead to more security and independence and that technological and economic skills are necessary for this. Another requirement for DS is to reduce dependencies [1,12,23,28]. We inferred this requirement from quotes I1 and I5, which highlighted dependencies on external foundations and companies. According to Moerel and Timmers [23], the dependency on a small number of suppliers and monopolists is particularly problematic. This is also reflected in quote I5, which showed the dependency on monopolists like Amazon and Microsoft in development activities. We take the achievement of technical sovereignty as an imperative. Glasze et al. [12] call for the examination of secure, European, sovereign cloud alternatives to get closer to the goal of technical sovereignty. Another requirement for strengthening DS is more product sovereignty [5,7]. The online interviews (see quote I3) showed that the use of a proprietary software in the projects led to lock-in effects. Couture and Toupin [5] criticize how companies deal with digital services from Google, Facebook, and other giants and call for the verification of digital services for more DS. In this context, it becomes clear that more DS is possible by reducing lock-in effects [8,23]. Fries et al. [8] suggest developing strategies to reduce lock-ins. Furthermore, quote I4 indicates that preventing security weaknesses which lead to misuse or disclosure of sensitive information is challenging. The related demand from Hummel et al. [15], Floridi [7], and Couture and Toupin [5] is: more data sovereignty. Data sovereignty is a significant sub-area of DS. Hummel et al. [15] analyze the term 'data sovereignty' based on 341 publications and conclude that data sovereignty aims at a self-determined handling of data. Glasze et al. [12], Pohle [27], and Moerel and Timmers [23] see a contribution to more data sovereignty in the reduction of security gaps. Moerel and Timmers [23] and Glasze et al. [12] call for trustworthy IT. Lastly, Broeders et al. [3] and Falkner et al. [6] see the opportunity to realize products considering economic competitiveness and enforceability as a way to strengthen DS. This requirement aligns with quote I7, which indicated that there are hardly any good alternatives to the common English NLP models.

6   Gap Analysis

6.1   Results from the Comparison of the Current and Desired State

Gap No. 1. Our results of the analysis showed that the affordances 'standards and guidelines' and 'know-how' influence the development work of the project teams, and 'penetration tests' affect the speed (see Sect. 4.2). The project team's autonomy is limited by external foundations and companies (see Sect. 4.1). The concept of DS demands the acquisition of necessary resources and skills to gain more autonomy in the digital space (see Sect. 5.1). Thus, we can identify a gap that calls for a balance between adhering to standards and guidelines and promoting skills for more autonomy in the digital space.

Gap No. 2. The affordances 'testing software,' 'project management tools,' and 'cloud capacity' also impact the work of developers and the management of OS projects (see Sect. 4.2). When comparing the current and desired state, we find that the project team is dependent on the know-how, software offerings, and infrastructure offerings of external partners (see Sect. 4.1). However, the concept of DS aims to reduce strong dependencies (see Sect. 5.1). Thus, we can identify a gap between offerings that lead to lock-in effects and the demand for independence. This balancing act must be considered if companies want to achieve more sustainable actions through the concept of DS.

Gap No. 3. We also analyzed the affordances 'front-end solution,' 'OS system,' 'database,' and 'database management solution' and found that they influence customer satisfaction, as well as project work in OS projects (see Sect. 4.2). Our current state analysis shows that the above-mentioned affordances have security weaknesses (see Sect. 4.1). Our desired state analysis indicates that the concept of DS requires trustworthy IT (see Sect. 5.1).

Gap No. 4. The affordance 'automated extractions' also impacts development and speed (see Sect. 4.2). Our current state analysis shows that misuse or disclosure of data is possible (see Sect. 4.1). The desired state analysis shows that the concept of DS demands data sovereignty and a more autonomous handling with data (see Sect. 5.1).

Gap No. 5. We also find that the affordance 'AI models' used in OS projects impacts customer outcomes. Our current state analysis reveals that there are hardly any good alternatives to the English AI models (see Sect. 4.1). However, the concept of DS aims to combine product and economic sovereignty and thus gain the ability to realize national products while considering economic competitiveness (see Sect. 5.1).

Finally, we analyzed the affordances 'collection of algorithms and APIs' and 'search technology' and their impact on development (see Sect. 4.2). We find that the project team has had good experiences with the OS products that can be used for the development of microservices and web apps and that relying on OS aligns with the concept of DS (see Sect. 5.1).

How Can Affordances in Open Source Projects Be Modified to Lead to More Digital Sovereignty? The affordance 'standards and guidelines' and 'know-how' should be balanced to strengthen DS (see Gap No. 1). This means that firstly, competence development through training and education, and secondly, adherence to standards and guidelines through clear political as well as corporate regulations are significant. These results are in line with Pohle [27], who also describes competence development and guidelines as significant for more DS in her work. The affordances 'testing software,' 'project management tools,' and 'cloud capacity' all exhibit dependencies on third-party providers (see Gap No. 2). We suggest that companies consider alternative partners in the digital space for their software, tools, and infrastructure (especially for the above-mentioned affordances) to become more independent. This contrasts with the view of Floridi [7] who aim to establish politically motivated alternatives. Our view differs from this view, as we prescribe the success of DS especially to companies considering politically motivated goals. The topic of cybersecurity and IT security cannot be overlooked when introducing the concept of DS with the affordances 'front-end solution,' 'open source system,' 'database,' and 'database management solution' (see Gap No. 3). We thus suggest that future projects specifically examine the mentioned affordances for risks and develop mitigation measures. The options for action should promote data and product sovereignty and should be geared towards trustworthy IT (see Sect. 5.1). The affordance 'automated extractions' can be aligned with the topic of data sovereignty. To address the challenges of Gap No. 4, developing a management strategy for data sovereignty is recommended. This aligns with the findings of Hummel et al. [15], who describe management strategies based on constitutive components, technical, epistemic, and legal facilitators to ensure data sovereignty. The affordance 'AI models' should thus be elevated to a strategic level. Gap No. 5 revealed that there are hardly any good alternatives to the common English AI models. Strategic alliances can help leverage synergy effects and save costs when implementing DS. Based on our data, we recommend to companies to build more know-how in the field of AI and NLPs, and minimize risks that were uncovered by the mentioned dependencies. However, the efforts involved in coordinating cooperation, different interests, and cultural differences should not be underestimated. Finally, we continue to recommend relying on OS and not changing the affordances 'collection of algorithms and APIs' and 'search technology' since the project teams have had good experiences with their configurations.

7   Summary and Outlook

In this paper, we analyzed affordances of open source projects to prove an embedding of DS in software development projects. Our results confirm that the concept of DS can be used to achieve more autonomous actions in the digital space. However, our results also show that there are still some challenges for project teams to align with DS and design affordances sovereignly. The challenges according to the project teams to achieve DS are dependencies on foundations, dependencies on specific proprietary software and dependencies on monopolists. A lack of expertise, high security requirements, and a lack of alternatives to English NLP models intensify the challenges. Our data shows that affordances should be adjusted as follows: First, align 'standards and guidelines' with 'know-how.' Second, consider alternative partners in the digital space for the affordances 'penetration tests,' 'testing software,' 'cloud capacity,' and 'project management tools' in future projects. Third, align the affordances 'front-end solution,' 'open source system,' 'database,' and 'database management solution' with trustworthiness and product sovereignty. Fourth, align 'automated extractions' with data sovereignty. Fifth, form strategic alliances to design the affordance 'AI models' more sovereignly, and consider economic and competitive challenges. We thus contribute new insights to two different areas of research: affordance research and DS research. On the one hand, we were able to demonstrate for Information Systems how affordances need to be adapted in order to strengthen DS. On the other hand, we are expanding DS research by offering specific examples from OS projects and highlighting measures that can make IT-supported transformation a success. The study is, however, subject to some limitations. The analysis presented here considered two projects. This limits the validity. Our next research step include more strategies for companies aiming to achieve DS through OS by analyzing more projects and consider organizational and cultural factors.

Acknowledgements. We thank our partners, research colleagues, and the LIONS project. LIONS is funded by dtec.bw of the Research Center for Digitization and Technology of the Bundeswehr, financed by the European Union, NextGenerationEU.

References

1. Avila Pinto, R.: Digital sovereignty or digital colonialism. SUR-Int'l J. Hum. Rights **15**, 15–27 (2018)
2. Bechara, J., Lechner, U.: Digital sovereignty and open-source software - a discussion paper. In: Phillipson, F., Eichler, G., Erfurth, C., Fahrnberger, G. (eds.) Innovations for Community Services, I4CS 2024. CCIS, vol. 2109, pp. 397–407. Springer, Cham (2024). https://doi.org/10.1007/978-3-031-60433-1_22
3. Broeders, D., Cristiano, F., Kaminska, M.: In search of digital sovereignty and strategic autonomy: normative power Europe to the test of its geopolitical ambitions. JCMS J. Common Mark. Stud. **61**(5), 1261–1280 (2023)
4. Celeste, E.: Digital sovereignty in the EU: challenges and future perspectives. In: Data Protection Beyond Borders: Transatlantic Perspectives on Extraterritoriality and Sovereignty, pp. 211–228 (2021)
5. Couture, S., Toupin, S.: What does the notion of "sovereignty" mean when referring to the digital? New Media Soc. **21**(10), 2305–2322 (2019)
6. Falkner, G., et al.: Digital sovereignty - rhetoric and reality. J. Eur. Public Policy 1–22 (2024)
7. Floridi, L.: The fight for digital sovereignty: what it is, and why it matters, especially for the EU. Philos. Technol. **33**, 369–378 (2020)
8. Fries, I, et al.: Towards a Layer Model for Digital Sovereignty: A Holistic Approach. In: Hämmerli, B., Helmbrecht, U., Hommel, W., Kunczik, L., Pickl, S. (eds.) Critical Information Infrastructures Security, CRITIS 2022. LNCS, vol. 13723, pp. 119–139. Springer, Cham (2022). https://doi.org/10.1007/978-3-031-35190-7_9
9. Fromm, J., et al.: A systematic review of empirical affordance studies: recommendations for affordance research in information systems. In: ECIS, pp. 1–11 (2020)
10. Gacek, C., Arief, B.: The many meanings of open source. IEEE Softw. **21**(1), 34–40 (2004)
11. Gibson, J.J.: The theory of affordances. Hilldale, USA **1**(2), 67–82 (1977)

12. Glasze, G., Odzuck, E., Staples, R.: Was heißt digitale Souveränität? Diskurse, Praktiken und Voraussetzungen individueller und staatlicher Souveränität im digitialen Zeitalter, vol. 3. transcript Verlag, 1–320 (2022)
13. Glasze, G., et al.: Contested spatialities of digital sovereignty. Geopolitics **28**(2), 919–958 (2023)
14. Herlo, B., Ullrich, A., Vladova, G.: Sustainable digital sovereignty: interdependencies between sustainable digitalization and digital sovereignty. Weizenbaum Series. 32. Weizenbaum Institute for the Networked Society - The German Internet Institute, Berlin. Working Paper, pp. 5–39 (2023)
15. Hummel, P., et al.: Data sovereignty: a review. Big Data Soc. **8**(1), 1–17 (2021)
16. Jones, K.S.: What is an affordance? How shall affordances be refined? Routledge, pp. 107–114 (2018)
17. Kagermann, H., et al.: Digitale Souveränitat: Status quo und Handlungsfelder. acatech IMPULS 1–29 (2021)
18. Kim, S., Yingru, J.: Gap analysis. Int. Encycl. Strateg. Commun. **8**, 1–6 (2018)
19. Lecy, J.D., Beatty, K.E.: Representative literature reviews using constrained snowball sampling and citation network analysis. SSRN Electron. J. 1–15 (2012)
20. Leonardi, P.: Affordances and agency: toward the clarification and integration of fractured concepts. MIS Q. **47**(4) (2023)
21. Lehmann, D.R., et al.: Marketing Research. Addison-Wesley, Reading (1998)
22. Moore, J.E., et al.: Developing a comprehensive definition of sustainability. Implement. Sci. **12**, 1–8 (2017)
23. Moerel, L., Timmers, P.: Reflections on digital sovereignty. EU cyber direct. Res. Focus Ser. 1–32 (2021)
24. United Nations: The Sustainable Development Goals Report. Department of Economic and Social Affairs, pp. 1–80 (2022). https://unstats.un.org/sdgs/report/2022/
25. Nosratabadi, S., et al.: Sustainable business models: a review. Sustainability **11**(6), 1–30 (2019)
26. Open Source Initiative. The Open Source Definition (2024). https://opensource.org/osd. Accessed 02 Oct 2024
27. Pohle, J.: Digital sovereignty. A new key concept of digital policy in Germany and Europe, pp. 1–26. Konrad-Adenauer-Stiftung, Berlin (2020)
28. Pohle, J., Thiel, T.: Digital sovereignty. Internet Policy Rev. **9**(4), 1–19 (2020)
29. European Parliament: Digital agenda for Europe (2024). https://www.europarl.europa.eu/factsheets/en/sheet/64/digital-agenda-for-europ
30. Przybylek, A., Kotecka, D.: Making agile retrospectives more awesome. Federated Conference on Computer Science and Information Systems (FedCSIS), vol. 11, pp. 1211–1216. IEEE (2017)
31. Perens, B.: The open source definition. Open Sources Voices Open Source Revol. **1**, 171–188 (1999)
32. Seidel, S., Recker, J., Vom Brocke, J.: Sensemaking and sustainable practicing: functional affordances of information systems in green transformations. MIS Q. **37**(4), 1275–1299 (2013)
33. Volkoff, O., Strong, D.M.: Critical realism and affordances: theorizing IT-associated organizational change processes. MIS Q. **37**(3), 819–834 (2013)
34. Volkoff, O., Strong, D.M.: Affordance theory and how to use it in IS research. In: Companion to Management Information Systems, pp. 232–245. Routledge (2017)
35. Weaver, P., et al.: Sustainable technology development, pp. 1–304. Routledge (2017)

The Ethical Landscape in Public Procurement of ICT Systems

Aapo Koski[1]([⊠]) [iD], Sinna Pirinen[2] [iD], and Tommi Mikkonen[2] [iD]

[1] Tampere University, Tampere, Finland
aapo.koski@tuni.fi
[2] University of Jyväskylä, Jyväskylä, Finland
sinna.e.pirinen@student.jyu.fi, tommi.j.mikkonen@jyu.fi

Abstract. In an era where Information and Communication Technology (ICT) systems are foundational to the delivery of public services, the ethical procurement of these technologies has never been more crucial. This paper embarks on a comprehensive exploration of the ethical dimensions inherent in the public procurement process of ICT systems in Finland, underscoring the significance of incorporating ethical considerations to safeguard public interest, promote equitable access, and ensure sustainable technological advancements. The discourse presented not only highlights the imperative for ethical vigilance in public procurement but also serves as a guiding framework for public entities striving to align their ICT procurement processes with broader societal values and priorities.

Keywords: Public procurement · ICT systems · information systems · organizational values · ethical integrity

1 Introduction

This is to inform you that corresponding authors have been identified as per the information available in the Copyright form. In the ever-evolving and complex landscape of public Information and Communication Technology (ICT) procurement, the intertwining of technology with the fabric of society has rendered the ethical dimensions of procurement practices not just relevant, but imperative. The procurement of ICT systems by public entities is more than a mere transaction. It is a critical decision-making process that shapes the very infrastructure upon which societies function and flourish. With each procurement decision, we are presented with an opportunity to uphold the values of fairness, transparency, and responsibility to the public we serve [6]. However, these decisions are fraught with ethical dilemmas; from ensuring fair competition among vendors to safeguarding the privacy and security of citizens' data. Moreover, there are numerous other concerns that have an impact to the competition, such as sustainability of the delivered solution [5].

© The Author(s), under exclusive license to Springer Nature Switzerland AG 2025
E. Papatheocharous et al. (Eds.): ICSOB 2024, LNBIP 539, pp. 35–43, 2025.
https://doi.org/10.1007/978-3-031-85849-9_3

Due to the above concerns, public ICT procurement requires paying constant attention to balance. Such balancing addresses technological advancement with ethical integrity, the drive for innovation with the imperative for equity and inclusivity, and the pursuit of efficiency with the unwavering commitment to the public good [3].

This article is a reflection of these balancing acts, an exploration of the ethical considerations that lie at the heart of public ICT procurement. Delving into the ethical fabric of ICT procurement requires exploring key issues, such as the importance of transparency and accountability in the procurement process, the need for fair competition to foster innovation and value, the critical nature of data privacy and security in an increasingly digital world, and the overarching responsibility to consider the social and environmental impacts of our technological choices. These considerations are not mere theoretical concepts but are practical challenges that demand human attention and action.

2   Imperative of Ethical Public Procurement

At the heart of public procurement lies responsibility that extends beyond the mere acquisition of goods and services [9]. It is a stewardship role that encompasses the guardianship of public trust, the equitable distribution of resources, and the advancement of societal well-being through judicious and transparent decision-making [8]. This stewardship is particularly pronounced in the ICT systems procurement, where the implications of procurement decisions ripple through the very fabric of society, influencing everything from individual privacy rights to the global competitive landscape. The imperative for ethical public procurement emerges not from a vacuum but from the complex interplay of societal expectations, technological advancements, and the inherent challenges posed by the public tendering process [2]. This process, designed to ensure fairness, efficiency, and value for public funds, is fraught with ethical dilemmas that demand rigorous scrutiny and adherence to ethical principles.

2.1   The Complex Nature of Ethical Tendering

The tendering process for public ICT procurement is a multifaceted endeavor characterized by its inherent complexity [11]. This complexity arises from several factors, including the following.

Multiplicity of Stakeholders: Public procurement involves a wide array of stakeholders, including government entities, vendors, citizens, and advocacy groups [1]. Each brings to the table divergent interests, expectations, and ethical considerations, making the balancing act between these interests a critical ethical challenge.

Rapid Technological Change: The fast-paced evolution of ICT poses unique challenges in ensuring that procurement decisions remain relevant, forward-looking, and aligned with ethical standards over time [10]. The dynamic nature of technology demands a procurement process that is both flexible and principled, able to adapt to new developments while upholding ethical standards.

Regulatory and Legal Frameworks: Navigating the intricate web of regulations and legal requirements that govern public procurement is an ethical imperative in itself. These frameworks are designed to ensure transparency, fairness, and accountability but can also introduce complex ethical considerations, especially when they intersect with emerging technologies and data protection laws [4].

Risk Management: ICT system procurement entails significant risks, from data breaches and privacy concerns to obsolescence and vendor lock-in. Ethical procurement practices must therefore encompass robust risk management strategies that consider not only the financial implications but also the broader societal and ethical impacts.

2.2   Upholding Ethical Standards in the Tendering Process

To navigate the complexities of the tendering process ethically, public entities must embrace a holistic approach that integrates ethical considerations into every phase of procurement, from planning, requirement specification and tender design to vendor selection and contract management [13]. This approach involves the following activities:

Developing and Enforcing Clear Ethical Guidelines: Establishing comprehensive ethical guidelines that define acceptable behaviors, decision-making criteria, and accountability mechanisms for all participants in the procurement process.

Ensuring Transparency and Openness: Fostering a culture of transparency by making procurement processes as open and accessible as possible: Ensuring that decisions are made in the public eye and that stakeholders have the opportunity to provide input and oversight.

Promoting Fair and Equitable Competition: Implementing procedures that guarantee a level playing field for all vendors, encouraging innovation and ensuring that the best technological solutions are selected based on merit and value. Equitable competition in public procurement also ensures that vendors can sustain healthy business operations by enabling fair pricing practices, which balance the value delivered with the costs of provisioning ICT systems.

Prioritizing Social Responsibility: Considering the broader societal implications of procurement decisions, including the environmental impact of ICT solutions and the social responsibilities of vendors, to ensure that procurement practices contribute positively to societal goals.

In conclusion, the imperative of ethical public procurement in the realm of ICT cannot be overstated. As stewards of public trust and resources, entities involved in the procurement process bear a profound responsibility to ensure that their actions reflect the highest ethical standards. By embracing the complexities of ethical tendering and committing to transparency, fairness, and social responsibility, public entities can navigate the ethical landscape of ICT procurement with integrity, building a digital infrastructure that serves the public good and stands as a testament to the values of society.

3   Key Ethical Considerations in Public ICT Procurement

As we venture deeper into the ethical intricacies of ICT procurement, it becomes evident that certain key considerations are foundational to fostering an ethical, transparent, and equitable process. These considerations are not merely guidelines but are integral to ensuring the procurement process upholds public trust and delivers on the promise of technology to enhance societal well-being. We propose the following key ethical considerations to form the cornerstone of a responsible procurement process.

Transparency and Accountability: At the forefront of ethical procurement is the commitment to transparency and accountability. This entails the clear, accessible, and timely dissemination of information regarding procurement opportunities, criteria for selection, and the decision-making process. Such openness ensures that the procurement process is not shrouded in secrecy but is open to scrutiny by stakeholders, fostering a culture of accountability. In the realm of ICT, where decisions have far-reaching implications on privacy, security, and public trust, transparency is not just ethical—it is essential.

Fair Competition: Equally critical is the principle of fair competition. Ethical procurement practices demand that all vendors have an equal opportunity to compete, ensuring that no single entity is unduly favored and that the selection process is merit-based, considering factors such as functionality, cost-effectiveness, and innovation. Fair competition not only underpins the integrity of the procurement process but also drives the market towards higher standards of quality and efficiency, ultimately benefiting the public sector and society at large. Fair competition also requires that vendors compete in a fair way, e.g. not trying to take advantage of some loopholes in the procurement materials or not offering services or products in prizes that do not allow running a healthy business.

Data Privacy and Security: In an era characterized by digitalization, concerns about data privacy and security are paramount. Ethical procurement of ICT systems necessitates prioritizing solutions that adhere to stringent data protection regulations, ensuring the confidentiality, integrity, and availability of data. This consideration goes beyond compliance, touching on the ethical responsibility to protect the privacy rights of individuals and safeguard against data breaches and cyber threats that could erode public trust in digital infrastructure.

Social and Environmental Impact: The procurement process must also account for the social and environmental impact of ICT solutions. This includes evaluating the sustainability of technologies, the ethical labor practices of vendors, and the potential societal implications of deploying certain technologies. By prioritizing vendors and solutions that demonstrate a commitment to sustainable and ethical practices, public entities can ensure that their procurement decisions contribute to the broader goals of social responsibility and environmental stewardship.

Vendor Responsibility: Finally, the ethical assessment of vendors' practices and policies is crucial. This involves scrutinizing potential vendors for their adherence to ethical business conduct, compliance with labor standards, and commitment to diversity and inclusion. Engaging with vendors who share a public entity's ethical values not only strengthens the procurement process but also builds long-term partnerships that can advance the public good. Vendors whose strategy is to set prices unsustainably low, potentially with the intention of undermining competition or establishing market dominance, do not ensure long-term business viability and therefore are not responsible vendors.

4 Implementing Ethical Considerations

Implementing the ethical considerations requires a proactive and committed approach [7]. Public entities must embed the ethical principles into their procurement policies, guidelines, and practices, ensuring that every step of the procurement process—from planning to contract management—is guided by ethical integrity. Moreover, fostering an organizational culture that values ethics, providing training on ethical procurement practices, and engaging in continuous dialogue with stakeholders are essential strategies to reinforce the ethical foundation of the procurement process.

Best Practices for Ethical Public Procurement. In the pursuit of ethical excellence in public procurement, especially within the ICT domain, it becomes imperative to establish and adhere to a set of best practices. These practices are designed to not only navigate the complexities and challenges inherent in the procurement process but also to ensure that every decision and action aligns with ethical principles and contributes positively to the public good.

The following best practices serve as a blueprint for public entities committed to ethical procurement (see Fig. 1).

Establish Clear Ethical Guidelines: The foundation of ethical procurement lies in the development and enforcement of clear, comprehensive ethical guidelines. These guidelines should articulate the values and principles that guide procurement activities, including transparency, fairness, accountability, and respect for privacy and security. By clearly defining what constitutes ethical behavior and decision-making, public entities set a standard for all participants in the procurement process to follow.

Ensure Stakeholder Engagement: Ethical procurement processes are inclusive, considering the perspectives and interests of a broad range of stakeholders, including government officials, suppliers, citizens, and advocacy groups. Engaging stakeholders in dialogue and consultation ensures that diverse viewpoints are considered, potential ethical concerns are identified early, and the procurement process is more transparent and accountable. This approach fosters trust and cooperation among all parties involved.

Conduct Regular Training and Capacity Building: To navigate the ethical complexities of ICT procurement, it is crucial for those involved in the procurement process to have a deep understanding of ethical issues and principles. Regular training and capacity-building initiatives can equip procurement professionals, decision-makers, and other relevant staff with the knowledge and skills needed to identify and address ethical challenges proactively. Training should cover topics such as ethical decision-making, risk management, data protection, and the evaluation of vendors' ethical standards.

Implement Rigorous Vendor Assessment: Assessing the ethical practices and policies of potential vendors is a critical step in ensuring that procurement decisions align with ethical and social responsibility goals. This assessment should go beyond mere compliance with legal requirements to evaluate vendors' commitment to ethical business practices, labor standards, environmental sustainability, and social impact. Transparent and objective criteria should be used to conduct these assessments, ensuring that only vendors who meet these high ethical standards are considered.

Monitor and Audit Procurement Activities: Ongoing monitoring and auditing of procurement activities are essential to ensure adherence to ethical guidelines and identify areas for improvement. Regular audits can help detect any deviations from established ethical practices, allowing for timely corrective action. Moreover, monitoring and auditing demonstrate a commitment to transparency and accountability, reinforcing public trust in the procurement process.

Foster a Culture of Ethical Integrity: Ultimately, the success of ethical procurement practices hinges on the cultivation of an organizational culture that values and prioritizes ethical integrity. This culture is characterized by open communication, ethical leadership, and a shared commitment to the public interest. Encouraging ethical behavior, recognizing and rewarding ethical decisions, and addressing unethical conduct promptly and decisively are all critical to fostering such a culture.

By implementing these best practices, public entities can navigate the intricate landscape of ICT procurement with a steadfast commitment to ethical principles. These practices not only ensure that procurement activities reflect the highest standards of integrity but also build a foundation for public trust and confidence in the digital infrastructure and services that shape our society. As the field of ICT continues to evolve, the commitment to ethical public procurement remains a constant beacon, guiding the way toward a more transparent, equitable, and responsible future.

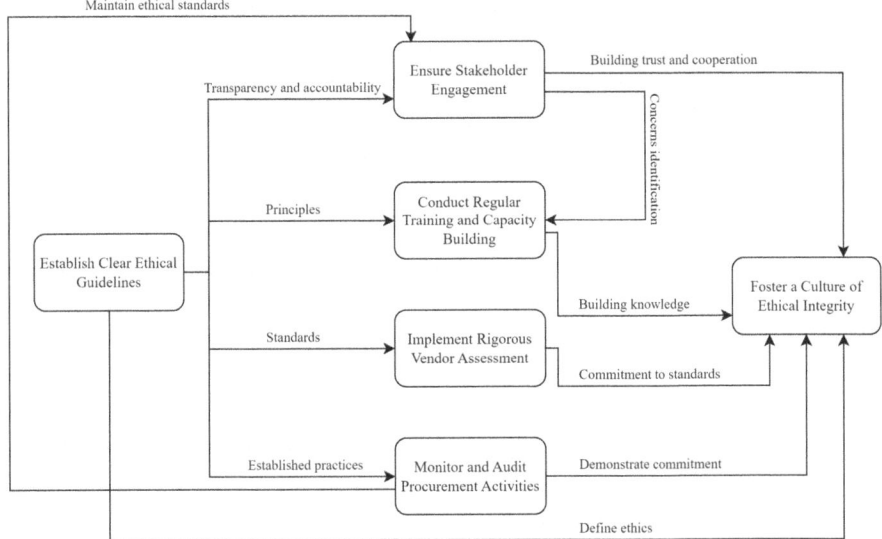

Fig. 1. Best Practices for Ethical Public Procurement.

5   Conclusions

In the rapidly advancing landscape of ICT, the public procurement of ICT systems stands at the crossroads of innovation and ethics. This article has navigated the multifaceted ethical considerations essential to fostering a procurement environment that not only advances technological capabilities but also upholds the core values of integrity, equity, and responsibility. Ethical considerations in public procurement are not peripheral concerns but integral to constructing a digital infrastructure that serves societal values and priorities.

By continuously prioritizing transparency, fair competition, data privacy, and responsible business practices, governments and public entities are positioned to ensure that the procurement process not only adheres to the highest standards of ethical conduct but also actively contributes to the well-being of citizens and the holistic advancement of society. These priorities are the pillars upon which trust in public institutions is built and maintained, ensuring that ICT systems deployment genuinely enhances public services and civic life.

As technology continues to evolve at an unprecedented pace, the principles of ethical public procurement serve as a crucial safeguard against the myriad potential risks and challenges associated with the ICT systems implementation. These principles guide us in navigating the complexities of digital transformation, ensuring that technological progress does not come at the cost of ethical compromise or societal harm. Instead, ethical procurement practices ensure that technological advancements are leveraged to promote inclusivity, sustainability, and the public good.

Looking ahead, the journey toward ethical excellence in public ICT procurement is both a challenge and an opportunity. It calls for a collective commitment from all stakeholders involved – from policymakers and procurement professionals to vendors and the broader community – to champion ethical practices that align with our shared values and aspirations [12]. Through this collective effort we can ensure the digital future we build is not only innovative and efficient but also equitable, secure, and reflective of the diverse needs and values of the society we aim to serve.

In conclusion, the ethical procurement of ICT systems is a critical endeavour that demands our attention, diligence, and commitment. As we forge ahead, let us remain guided by the principles of ethical integrity, ensuring that our digital infrastructure serves as a beacon of progress, inclusivity, and societal well-being. The path forward is clear: by embedding ethical considerations into every facet of the ICT procurement process, we can pave the way for a future where technology truly serves the common good, bolstering our collective journey towards a more ethical, equitable, and prosperous society.

References

1. Alanne, A., Hellsten, P., Pekkola, S., Saarenpää, I.: Three positives make one negative: public sector IS procurement. In: Tambouris, E., et al. (eds.) EGOV 2015. LNCS, vol. 9248, pp. 321–333. Springer, Cham (2015). https://doi.org/10.1007/978-3-319-22479-4_24
2. Badenhorst, J.A.: Unethical behaviour in procurement: a perspective on causes and solutions. J. Bus. Ethics **13**, 739–745 (1994)
3. Busch, T.: Capabilities in, capabilities out: overcoming digital divides by promoting corporate citizenship and fair ICT. Ethics Inf. Technol. **13**(4), 339–353 (2011)
4. Díaz, G.M., Hernández, J.J.G., Salvador, J.L.G.: Explainable artificial intelligence (XAI) and ethical decision-making in business. In: Smart Ethics in the Digital World: Proceedings of the ETHICOMP 2024. 21th International Conference on the Ethical and Social Impacts of ICT, pp. 19–22. Universidad de La Rioja (2024)
5. Ghezzi, R., Koski, A., Lautanala, J., Lehtisalo, M., Setälä, M., Mikkonen, T.: Towards sustainable software for public sector information systems. In: 2023 IEEE/ACM International Conference on Software and System Processes (ICSSP), pp. 86–91. IEEE (2023)
6. Ghezzi, R., Mikkonen, T.: On public procurement of ICT systems: Stakeholder views and emerging tensions. In: Hyrynsalmi, S., Münch, J., Smolander, K., Melegati, J. (eds.) ICSOB 2023. Lecture Notes in Business Information Processing, vol. 500, pp. 61–76. Springer, Cham (2023). https://doi.org/10.1007/978-3-031-53227-6_5
7. Johnson, B., Menzies, T.: Ethics: why software engineers can't afford to look away. IEEE Softw. **41**(1), 142–144 (2023)
8. Jones, D.S.: Public procurement ethics. Public Adm. Public Policy, 234 (2003)
9. Koski, A., Mikkonen, T.: What we say we want and what we really need: experiences on the barriers to communicate information system needs. Requirements Eng. Serv. Cloud Comput., 3–21 (2017)

10. Li, P.H., Balasubramaniam, D.: Highlighting ethical dilemmas in software development: Atool to support ethical training and deliberation. In: Smart Ethics in the Digital World: Proceedings of the ETHICOMP 2024. 21th International Conference on the Ethical and Social Impacts of ICT, pp. 117–121. Universidad de La Rioja (2024)
11. McMurray, R., Pullen, A., Rhodes, C.: Ethical subjectivity and politics in organizations: a case of health care tendering. Organization **18**(4), 541–561 (2011)
12. Menzies, T., Johnson, B., Roberts, D.L., Alvarez, L.: The engineering mindset is an ethical mindset (we just don't teach it that way... yet). IEEE Softw. **40**(2), 103–110 (2023)
13. Olsson, D., Öjehag-Pettersson, A.: Buying a sustainable society: the case of public procurement in Sweden. Local Environ. **25**(9), 681–696 (2020)

Exploring Classification Consistency of Natural Language Requirements Using GPT-4o

Fredrik Karlsson$^{(\boxtimes)}$ ⓘ, Panagiota Chatzipetrou ⓘ, Shang Gao ⓘ,
and Tanja Elina Havstorm ⓘ

Department of Informatics, Örebro University, 701 82 Örebro, Sweden
{fredrik.karlsson,panagiota.chatzipetrou,shang.gao,
tanja.havstorm}@oru.se

Abstract. Classifying natural language requirements (NLRs) is challenging, especially with large volumes. Research shows that Large Language Models can assist by categorizing NLRs into functional requirements (FR) and non-functional requirements (NFRs). However, Generative Pretrained Transformer (GPT) models are not typically favored for this task due to concerns about consistency. This paper investigates the consistency when a GPT model classifies NLRs into FRs and NFRs using a zero-shot learning approach. Results show that ChatGPT-4o performs better for FRs, a temperature parameter set to 1 yields the highest consistency, while NFR classification improves with higher temperatures.

Keywords: Requirements · Classification · Large Language Model · Zero-Shot Learning

1 Introduction

Requirements engineering (RE) is crucial in software engineering. Typically, requirements specifications are documented in natural language [1], serving as a bridge between the stakeholders' needs and the proposed solution. However, with many requirements, the risk of missing critical elements—whether related to system functionality or quality attributes—increases. To mitigate this, classifying natural language requirements (NLRs) helps organise and prioritise them [2], streamlining the focus on specific areas during design, development, and testing. By categorizing requirements into functional (FR) and non-functional (NFR), teams ensure that both what the system does and how well it performs are clearly defined and addressed in the development process.

In recent years, the RE discipline has evolved significantly. The advancements in natural language processing have been remarkable, introducing powerful new techniques. Research has demonstrated that Large Language Models (LLMs), a type of artificial intelligence (AI) capable of generating and understanding natural language text, can be used for classifying NLRs [3, 4]. This technology provides valuable support to requirements engineers, easing the tedious task of classifying large volumes of NLRs. Previous research has shown that supervised classification approaches can be applied for this purpose [5]. However, training LLMs is time-consuming, and the resulting model is

© The Author(s), under exclusive license to Springer Nature Switzerland AG 2025
E. Papatheocharous et al. (Eds.): ICSOB 2024, LNBIP 539, pp. 44–50, 2025.
https://doi.org/10.1007/978-3-031-85849-9_4

restricted to the classes it has been trained on [6]. Therefore, Alhoshan et al. [7] proposed the use of zero-shot learning (ZSL) approach to classify NLRs, which has shown
promising results. Their research focused on Bidirectional Encoder Representations
from Transformers (BERT) models, without exploring Generative Pretrained Transformer (GPT) models, such as OpenAI's GPT-series. GPT models seem less favoured
for this type of categorization task [7], partly due to concerns about their inconsistency
in producing reliable results. At the same time, the temperature parameter in GPT models controls the randomness of output [8], with zero making it more deterministic and
higher values increasing randomness, potentially impacting classification tasks. In addition, GPT models have significantly evolved, and recent models like GPT-4o, LLAMA3
70B, and Falcon 180B have demonstrated the ability to handle more complex tasks and
generate more accurate responses [9].

Against this backdrop, the aim of this paper is to investigate the consistency when
a GPT model classifies NLRs into functional and non-functional requirements using a
ZSL approach. We therefore pose the following research questions: 1) How consistent
does GPT-4o classify NLRs into FRs and NFRs using ZSL? 2) To what extent does
the temperature parameter affect GPT-4o's consistency when classifying NRLs into
functional and non-functional categories using ZSL?

2 Related research

ZSL [10] in LLMs refers to their ability to perform tasks without being explicitly trained
for them. When given a task, the model uses its pre-trained knowledge to deduce how
to complete the task based on the instructions, even if it has not seen specific examples
during training. Being task-agnostic means that the effectiveness of ZSLs relies heavily
on the quality of the prompt [11], making well-structured prompts crucial for success.
However, LLMs can struggle to maintain consistency over longer tasks or across multiple questions in a zero-shot setting. In LLMs like GPT, temperature is a parameter
that controls the randomness or creativity of the generated outputs. Lower temperature
settings in a zero-shot scenario should lead to more reliable and accurate outputs, while
higher temperature increases diversity but may sacrifice accuracy and coherence. The
ideal temperature for ZSLs depends on balancing creativity and reliability, with different
tasks benefiting from different temperature ranges.

According to a literature study on the application of AI techniques in requirements
classification [12], various AI techniques, such as machine learning techniques (e.g., Support Vector Machine), deep learning techniques (e.g., Convolutional Neural Networks),
and transfer learning-based techniques (e.g., BERT, GPT) have been employed for classifying requirements. For example, the findings by Kurtanović and Maalej [5] demonstrated that Support Vector Machines performed well in classifying FRs and NFRs.
Similarly, Winkler and Vogelsang [13] designed a classification approach based on Convolutional Neural Networks, achieving high precision in identifying requirements from
a real-world automotive specification. Furthermore, Bashir et al. [3] tested BERT for
requirements classification within the railway industry.

However, most existing studies tend to focus primarily on performance metrics such
as accuracy of different techniques for classifying requirements. To our knowledge, there

is a noticeable gap in the literature regarding the consistency of classifying NLRs with transfer learning-based techniques, which limits the advice that research can provide to practitioners in this area.

3 Research Method

Our research employs an experimental design. Below we discuss the selection of the dataset used as a starting point, the design of the experiment, and the data analysis. We use the PROMISE NFR dataset, introduced by Cleland-Huang et al. [14] that has been used in previous research on requirements classification [e.g., 4, 5, 7]. The dataset comprises 625 requirements, delineated into 255 FRs and 370 NFRs. Thus, the distribution is 41% FRs and 59% NFRs.

In our experiment, the classification task follows our research questions and is a binary classification of FRs versus NFRs. The objective of this task is to differentiate between FRs and NFRs, operating under the assumption that each requirement falls into one of these two distinct classes. To accomplish these tasks, we use ZSL when prompting GPT-4o to classify the requirements. The prompt we have used is the following: "Use temperature value of [insert temperature value] in our conversation. Classify the following requirements into functional and non-functional requirements. Only present the label associated with each requirement.

1. The data displayed in both the nodes within the graph and the rows in the table are MSEL Summary data
2. Aside from server failure the software product shall achieve 99.99% up time.
3. The system shall be available for use between the hours of 8am and 6pm.
4. …"

In order to assess consistency between the runs that classified the requirements, we used four different temperature settings: 0 (edge test with maximal determinism and minimal randomness), 0.7 (consistency testing with default setting in Chat-GPT4o), 1 (consistency testing with balancing determinism and randomness), and 2 (edge test with minimal determinism and maximal randomness). Each temperature setting was considered an independent experiment, ensuring that the impact of the temperature can be accurately assessed. The performance measures were calculated for each experiment. Each experiment included three runs where GPT-4o classified the requirements in the PROMISE NFR dataset. We have executed the classification in batches of 100 requirements. We tried to classify all 625 requirements in one run, but GPT-4o did not return a classification of all the requirements. Therefore, we settled on smaller batches.

For the data analysis we used two metrics: 1) *Machine learning evaluation metrics*: In order to measure the classification performance results, we used F1-score (F1), Precision (P) and Recall (R). F1-score is a metric for evaluating the accuracy of a binary classification model [15]. It balances precision and recall of an algorithm into one metric. A binary classification model classifies items as one of two values—i.e. in our case, Functional or Non-Functional. Precision quantifies the accuracy of positive predictions, while Recall measures the model's ability to identify all positive instances. This score is helpful in determining how well an algorithm classifies a dataset into two categories.

Moreover, it is useful when dealing with imbalanced datasets or when false positives and false negatives have different associated costs. An F1-score of 1 indicates a perfect algorithm, while an F1-score of 0 indicates an algorithm that has failed completely in either Recall, Precision, or both. *2) Fleiss' Kappa*: The robust statistical measure Fleiss' Kappa [16] was applied to access the reliability of the consistency between the different runs. We considered an agreement when the kappa value is above 0.5.

4 Results

4.1 Consistency of GTP-4o in Classification of NLRs

In this first stage of our analysis, we looked at the consistency of GPT-4o in classification of NLRs into FRs and NFRs. The results are shown in Table 1. We conducted four different trials depending on the temperature, with 3 runs each. Regarding the FRs, the results are similar for the different temperatures. In particular, in all the different combinations, F1 has achieved a high score of 0.83, with P = 0.73 and R = 0.97 (mean values). This indicates that GTP-4o performs extremely well in classifying the NLRs into FR. However, the performance of the GTP-4o model differs between the FR and NFR classification. Table 1 shows that for Default Temp = 0.7, Temp = 0 and Temp = 1, the model tends to have lower precision (P = 0.64) and recall (R = 0.75) (mean values) on NFR classification. This is an interesting result, since NFRs are more frequent in the dataset (59%). However, when we set the temperature to 2, the model substantially outperformed the other trials with different temperatures for classifying NFRs (F1 = 0.85, P = 0.97, R = 0.75) (mean values).

4.2 Temperature Parameter and Consistency of GTP-4o in Classification of NLRs

In the second step of our analysis, we examined how the temperature parameter affects GPT-4o's consistency in classifying NRLs into FR and NFR. In Table 1 and the right-most column, the Fleiss' kappa is used to measure the interrater agreement between the runs under the different trials. The results show that in all four different trials (Default Temp = 0.7, Temp = 0, Temp = 1 and Temp = 2), there is a strong agreement between the GTP-4o classification of NLRs into FRs and NFRs (p < 0.05, κ = 0.803, κ = 0.881, κ = 0,900, κ = 0.839 respectively). Moreover, Fleiss' kappa was run to determine if there is an agreement between the original (human) classification of NFRs and the GTP-4o. The results showed that for all the four different trials (Default Temp = 0.7, Temp = 0, Temp = 1 and Temp = 2), GTP-4o is very consistent in the classification of NFRs. There is a strong agreement between the original (human) classification and the GTP-4o classification of NFRs (p < 0.05, κ = 0.729, κ = 0.771, κ = 0,814, κ = 0.760 respectively).

Table 1. Evaluation metrics for classification between FR and NFR

Experiment	Run N	FR			NFR			Fleiss Kappa
		F1	P	R	F1	P	R	
Default Temperature = 0.7	Run 1	0.80	0.69	0.96	0.59	0.51	0.70	0.803*
	Run 2	0.80	0.68	0.97	0.58	0.50	0.68	
	Run 3	0.85	0.77	0.97	0.65	0.55	0.80	
Temperature = 0	Run 1	0.80	0.69	0.97	0.59	0.51	0.70	0.881*
	Run 2	0.83	0.71	0.99	0.60	0.52	0.72	
	Run 3	0.84	0.74	0.97	0.63	0.53	0.76	
Temperature = 1	Run 1	0.85	0.75	0.97	0.63	0.54	0.78	0.900*
	Run 2	0.85	0.77	0.96	0.65	0.55	0.81	
	Run 3	0.86	0.77	0.97	0.64	0.54	0.79	
Temperature = 2	Run 1	0.80	0.68	0.98	0.80	0.98	0.68	0.839*
	Run 2	0.84	0.74	0.97	0.86	0.97	0.77	
	Run 3	0.85	0.76	0.97	0.88	0.97	0.79	

* p-value < 0.05

5   Discussion and Conclusions

This study contributes to the literature on using LLMs for classifying NLRs. Specifically, we investigate the consistency of GPT-4o in classifying NLRs into FRs and NFRs using ZSL, as well as the impact of the temperature parameter on this consistency, complementing previous studies on BERT models [e.g., 7].

The results for RQ1 indicate that GPT-4o demonstrated strong consistency across multiple runs within each experiment, meaning its performance in classifying NLRs was stable. GPT-4o closely matched human classifications for FRs, showing its potential for real-world FR classification tasks. However, GPT-4o performed less effectively in classifying NFRs compared to FRs. While GPT-4o's performance in NFR classification was decent, there is still room for improvement to match the level of human classification. The results for RQ2 suggest a strong agreement in GPT-4o's classification of NLRs into FRs and NFRs, regardless of temperature settings. This implies that the temperature parameter has little effect on GPT-4o's consistency in NLR classification when using ZSL. Additionally, the classification of NFRs appeared to benefit from higher temperature values, potentially allowing GPT-4o to be more creative.

Regarding the validity threats of experiments [17], in our study all data were acquired from prompting thus we are not prone to researchers' personal biases (reliability), and no subjective measures were used (construct validity). Moreover, we repeated the prompting, but our subject (GPT 4o) was not aware that a test is conducted at any time (internal validity). However, regarding external validity, the study is clearly exploratory, and the findings cannot be generalized to an isolated company.

Future research could focus on several directions. First, we aim to further evaluate GPT-4o's performance in NFR classification using few-shot learning examples. Second, we plan to assess the consistency of other LLMs, such as LLAMA3 70B and Falcon 180B, in NLRs classification and compare these results with the findings from this study. Third, future studies should also include datasets other than PROMISE NFR dataset. Finally, using more intermediate temperatures may reveal additional insights.

References

1. Kassab, M.: State of practice in requirements engineering: contemporary data. Innov. Syst. Softw. Eng. **10**, 235–241 (2014)
2. Abad, Z.S.H., Karras, O., Ghazi, P., Glinz, M., Ruhe, G., Schneider, K.: What works better? A study of classifying requirements. In: 2017 IEEE 25th International Requirements Engineering Conference, pp. 496–501. IEEE (2017)
3. Bashir, S., Abbas, M., Ferrari, A., Saadatmand, M., Lindberg, P.: Requirements classification for smart allocation: a case study in the railway industry. In: 2023 IEEE 31st International Requirements Engineering Conference (RE), pp. 201–211. IEEE (2023)
4. Hey, T., Keim, J., Koziolek, A., Tichy, W.F.: NoRBERT: transfer learning for requirements classification. In: 2020 IEEE 28th International Requirements Engineering Conference (RE), pp. 169–179. IEEE (2020)
5. Kurtanović, Z., Maalej, W.: Automatically classifying functional and non-functional requirements using supervised machine learning. In: 2017 IEEE 25th International Requirements Engineering Conference (RE), pp. 490–495. IEEE (2017)
6. Wang, W., Zheng, V.W., Yu, H., Miao, C.: A survey of zero-shot learning: settings, methods, and applications. ACM Trans. Intell. Syst. Technol. **10**, 1–37 (2019)
7. Alhoshan, W., Ferrari, A., Zhao, L.: Zero-shot learning for requirements classification: an exploratory study. Inf. Softw. Technol. **159**, 107202 (2023)
8. Ouyang, S., Zhang, J.M., Harman, M., Wang, M.: LLM is like a box of chocolates: the non-determinism of ChatGPT in code generation (2023). arXiv:2308.02828
9. Chen, B., et al.: On the use of GPT-4 for creating goal models: an exploratory study. In: 31st International Requirements Engineering Conference Workshops (REW 2023), pp. 262–271. IEEE (2023)
10. Larochelle, H., Erham, D., Bengio, Y.: Zero-data learning of new tasks. In: Cohn, A. (ed.) AAAI'08: Proceedings of the 23rd National Conference on Artificial Intelligence, vol. Volume 2, pp. 646–651. ACM (2008)
11. Kojima, T., Gu, S.S., Reid, M., Matsuo, Y., Iwasawa, Y.: Large language models are zero-shot reasoners. In: Koyejo, S., Mohamed, S., Agarwal, A., Belgrave, D., Cho, K., Oh, A. (eds.) 36th Conference on Neural Information Processing Systems (NeurIPS 2022), pp. 22199–22213. ACM (2022)
12. Kaur, K., Kaur, P.: The application of AI techniques in requirements classification: a systematic mapping. Artif. Intell. Rev. **57**, 57 (2024)
13. Winkler, J., Vogelsang, A.: Automatic classification of requirements based on convolutional neural networks. In: 2016 IEEE 24th International Requirements Engineering Conference Workshops, pp. 39–45. IEEE, Beijing, China (2016)
14. Cleland-Huang, J., Settimi, R., Zou, X., Solc, P.: Automated classification of non-functional requirements. Requirements Eng. **12**, 103–120 (2007)
15. Goutte, C., Gaussier, E.: A probabilistic interpretation of precision, recall and F-score, with implication for evaluation. In: Losada, D.E., Fernández-Luna, J.M. (eds.) Advances in Information Retrieval, ECIR 2005. Lecture Notes in Computer Science, vol. 3408, pp. 345–359. Springer, Berlin, Heidelberg (2005). https://doi.org/10.1007/978-3-540-31865-1_25

16. Fleiss, J.L., Levin, B., Paik, M.C.: Statistical Methods for Rates and Proportions. Wiley, Hoboken (2013)
17. Wohlin, C., Runeson, P., Höst, M., Ohlsson, M.C., Egnell, B., Wesslen, A.: Experimentation in Software Engineering: An Introduction. Kluwer Academic Publishers, Boston (2000)

Developer Experience and Ecosystem Trust

Unveiling the Skills and Responsibilities of Serverless Practitioners: An Empirical Investigation

Muhammad Hamza[✉], Vy Kauppinen, Muhammad Azeem Akbar,
Wardah Naeem Awan, and Kari Smolander

Software Engineering Department, Lappeenranta-Lahti University of Technology,
15210 Lappeenranta, Finland
{muhammad.hamza,Vy.Kauppinen,azeem.akbar,
wardah.awan,kari.smolander}@lut.fi

Abstract. Enterprises are increasingly adopting serverless computing to enhance scalability, reduce costs, and improve efficiency. However, this shift introduces new responsibilities and necessitates a distinct set of skills for practitioners. This study aims to identify and organize the industry requirements for serverless practitioners by conducting a qualitative analysis of 141 job advertisements from seven countries. We developed comprehensive taxonomies of roles, responsibilities, and skills, categorizing 19 responsibilities into four themes: software development, infrastructure and operations, professional development and leadership, and software business. Additionally, we identified 28 hard skills mapped into seven themes and 32 soft skills mapped into eight themes, with the six most demanded soft skills being communication proficiency, continuous learning and adaptability, collaborative teamwork, problem-solving and analytical skills, leadership excellence, and project management. Our findings contribute to understanding the organizational structures and training requirements for effective serverless computing adoption.

Keywords: Serverless computing · Empirical Investigation · Job-ads · Roles and responsibilities

1 Introduction

Serverless computing is transforming software development by enabling developers to focus solely on writing code without managing infrastructure. This paradigm shift allows enhanced scalability, reduced operational costs, and improved efficiency [6]. Companies such as Amazon Prime Video, Netflix, and Coca-Cola have adopted serverless architectures to improve efficiency [9].

However, this shift presents new challenges, compelling practitioners to develop specialized skills. These skills are inadequately addressed in the existing literature, which predominantly focuses on technical aspects such as performance

© The Author(s), under exclusive license to Springer Nature Switzerland AG 2025
E. Papatheocharous et al. (Eds.): ICSOB 2024, LNBIP 539, pp. 53–67, 2025.
https://doi.org/10.1007/978-3-031-85849-9_5

optimization and cost efficiency. [9]. Nevertheless, there is limited empirical evidence on the specific requirements required from the practitioners to thrive in developing decoupled, event-driven, and stateless applications using serverless computing [9].

This study addresses this gap by analyzing 141 job ads from a dataset of 2,508 serverless-related job ads across seven English-speaking countries. Using thematic analysis, we seek to answer the following research questions:

RQ1: What are the roles and responsibilities of serverless practitioners as identified in job ads?

RQ2: What hard and soft skills are required from serverless practitioners as identified in job ads?

RQ3: What are the trends in programming languages, serverless technologies, and cloud platforms as indicated in job ads?

By addressing these questions, this study aims to align industry demands with practitioner capabilities, providing insights into the skills and structures necessary for successful serverless computing adoption.

2 Related Work

The unique nature of serverless architecture has prompted researchers and practitioners to explore various aspects, including architectural design, performance improvement, technological advancements, and challenges in testing and debugging [8].

For instance, [13] conducted an in-depth analysis of 619 discussions from Stack Overflow and identified the challenges developers face when developing serverless applications. Similarly, [7] analyzed 2,000 real-world opensource applications on GitHub, providing insights into the Function-as-a-Service (FaaS) ecosystem, including growth rates, architectural designs, and common use cases. Another study by [5] examined different aspects such as implementation strategies, traffic patterns, and usage scenarios.

Similarly, Research in other software engineering domains has also identified essential skills for practitioners in AI, requirements engineering, and testing. For instance, job advertisements highlight specific testing skills crucial for coders and testers, emphasizing their importance [4]. While existing literature thoroughly addresses the necessary profiles and competencies for AI engineers [11] and professionals in microservices architecture [1].

However, current research fails to adequately identify the specific skills and responsibilities required by serverless practitioners, particularly when developing greenfield projects or migrating from monolithic architectures to serverless environments. This transition demands an entirely new skill set, which is not yet thoroughly addressed in the existing literature.

3 Research Method

In this study, we use qualitative analysis methods, specifically thematic analysis techniques [3], to examine the roles, responsibilities, and skills required for serverless engineers. The analysis was conducted on a dataset of job ads sourced from Glassdoor[1], a global recruitment platform. The study is structured into four phases, as shown in Fig. 1.

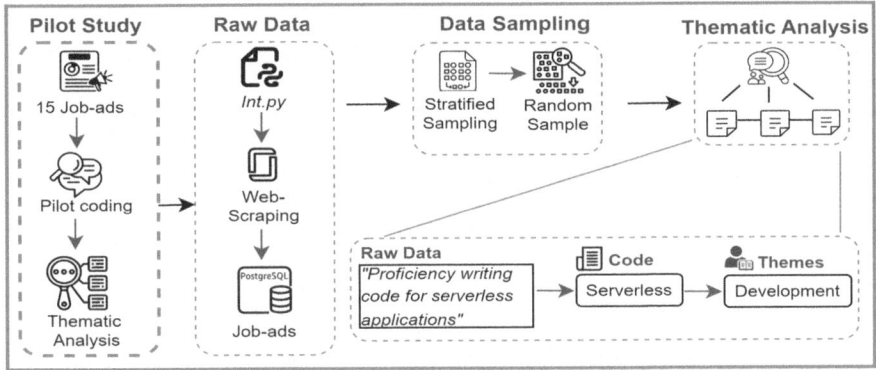

Fig. 1. Research Method

In the first phase, a pilot study was conducted where the first author gathered and analyzed fifteen job ads to identify key roles, responsibilities, and skills, and to refine the research questions. Based on the pilot findings, we conducted extensive data collection, resulting in 2,508 job ads. From these, we used stratified sampling to select 141 job posts for qualitative analysis.

3.1   Data Collection

The primary goal was to systematically collect job ads featuring serverless computing skills globally. We developed an automated Python script using Selenium, Selenium Stealth, and PostgreSQL to retrieve real-time job listings from Glassdoor. For example, the script extracted 800 U.S. job ads posted by April 5, 2024. The automation ensured data integrity by sorting listings chronologically and minimizing selection bias influenced by Glassdoor's algorithms. All the jobs ads were extracted on April 8,2024.

Job posts were gathered from seven countries across five continents: the United States, United Kingdom, Australia, United Arab Emirates, India, Singapore, and South Africa. These countries were selected because our daily search experiments consistently showed the highest number of job postings related to serverless computing in these regions. Further, the selection ensured English consistency and diverse representation, resulting in a dataset of 2,508 job ads. The script also collected metadata for each job ad, including recruiter details, enriching our analysis of regional and industry-specific demands for serverless skills shown in Fig. 2.

---

[1] https://www.glassdoor.com.

3.2   Data Sampling

After collecting job ads from Glassdoor, we employed stratified random sampling for thematic analysis, ensuring representative selection across regions [2]. This method, common in software engineering and social sciences, segments data by country, with each as a separate stratum. Our dataset included 2,508 job ads from seven countries. We sampled 5% from each stratum, calculating sample sizes using the formula $n_i = \lfloor 0.05 \times N_i \rfloor$, where N_i is the total jobs in country i. This yielded sample sizes: US (40), UK (17), AUS (5), India (57), UAE (1), South Africa (1), and Singapore (5). We then applied simple random sampling with Python's pandas library to ensure equal selection chances for each data point [10]. This approach preserves statistical integrity, and the replication package is available online [12].

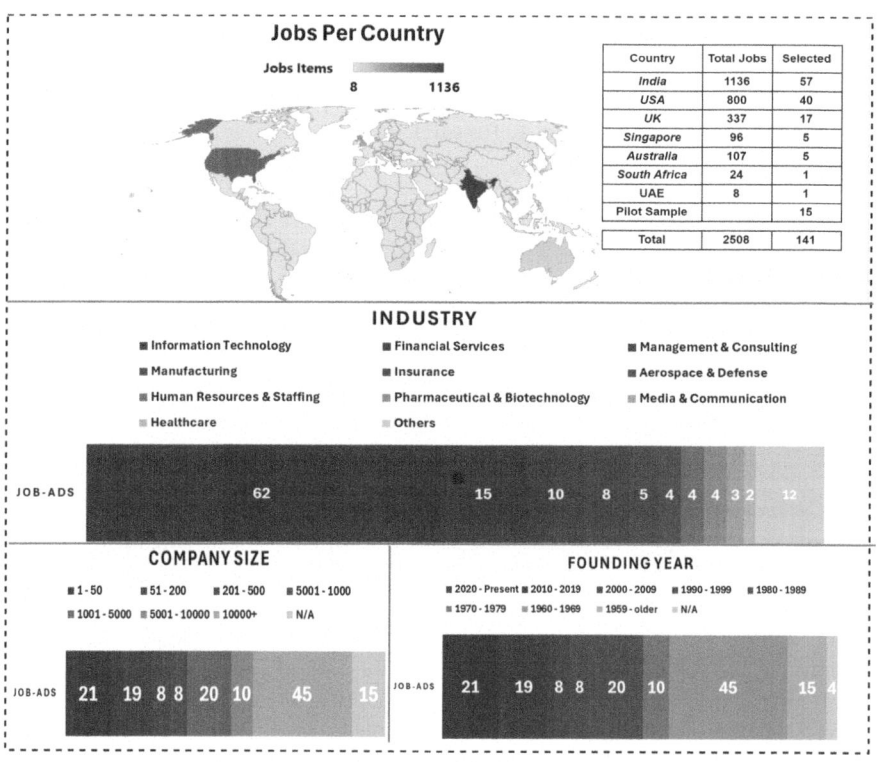

Fig. 2. Demographics

3.3   Data Analysis

This study utilizes a thematic analysis approach [3] to systematically code and categorize data from job ads, identifying significant themes. The process involved familiarization with the data, generating initial codes, and grouping these into sub-themes, which were then categorized into broader main themes by following the guidelines of Braun and Clarke [3]. The authors periodically analyzed the job ads throughout the study, regularly reviewing and discussing their findings to ensure consistency. After all 141 ads were analyzed, the authors collaboratively finalized the sub-themes and main themes.

4 Results

The analysis of 141 job posts provides insights into serverless practitioner roles, highlighting key responsibilities and required skills. We identified seven roles: software engineer (44 ads), data engineer (27 ads), architect (21 ads), web developer (18 ads), cloud engineer (14 ads), engineering leadership and management (14 ads), and product manager (3 ads). We further identified nineteen responsibilities and grouped them into four themes. Additionally, we mapped the hard and soft skills required for each role, offering a comprehensive overview of key competencies required from serverless practitioners.

RQ1: What are the roles and responsibilities of serverless practitioners as identified in job ads?

T1: Software Development: in the context of serverless computing involves the systematic process of designing, creating, testing, and maintaining software applications. This theme is critical for ensuring that applications are not only functional but also secure, scalable, and efficient. The sub-themes within software development highlight various aspects of this process. Architectural design focuses on structuring software systems to align with business goals and technical requirements. *"Knowledge of architectural design patterns, performance tuning, database, and functional designs."* – job-ad #26. Secure software development practices emphasize integrating security measures throughout the development lifecycle to safeguard applications from vulnerabilities. *"Partner with teams across the organization to perform architecture reviews, code security reviews, and promote secure development practices."* – Job-ad #28. Testing and quality assurance ensure that software meets specified requirements and is free of defects, thus guaranteeing reliability and performance. *"Write unit and integration tests which will pave the way for continuous deployment and aim for zero bugs."* – Job-ad #61. Integration and API management are vital for enabling seamless communication between different software components. *"Hands-on API and API Gateway implementations, managing integrations with external systems and internal modules/components."* – Job-ad #90.

The sub-themes include frontend and backend development, databases, APIs, software process improvement, development tools and technologies, data management and analytics, and AI/ML integration. These sub-themes collectively offer a comprehensive framework for understanding the diverse aspects of software development in serverless computing.

T2: Infrastructure and Operations: Despite serverless computing abstracting much of the infrastructure, our findings show that companies still expect practitioners to have knowledge in infrastructure management. This highlights the need for understanding foundational elements to ensure optimal performance, scalability, and reliability. Key sub-themes include configuration and management of infrastructure for scalable and efficient serverless applications. *"Experience with Infrastructure as Code tools, particularly Terraform and Packer."* – Job-ad #136. CI/CD *"Drive the implementation and maintenance of CICD pipelines to automate software delivery processes."* – Job-ad #58. Operations and support. *"Proactively identify and address performance bottlenecks, ensuring optimal system performance."* – Job-ad #141.

T3: Professional Development and Leadership emphasize the importance of continuous growth and strategic direction. First, Leadership and Strategic Planning highlight the necessity for serverless practitioners to possess strong leadership capabilities and strategic planning skills, enabling them to guide teams, make informed decisions, and set a clear vision to navigate the complexities of serverless environments effectively. *"Lead and contribute to complex technical projects and initiatives that span multiple engineering teams."* – Job-ad #2. Second, Professional Development Skills focus on the ongoing personal and professional growth of serverless practitioners, emphasizing the importance of staying current with industry trends, acquiring new skills, and fostering an environment of continuous improvement. *"Stay up-to-date with industry best practices and emerging .... and quality assurance initiatives within the organization."* – job-ad #11.

Together, these sub-themes underscore the critical role of leadership and professional development in ensuring that serverless practitioners can lead their teams effectively, plan strategically, and continuously enhance their skills to adapt to the evolving landscape of serverless computing.

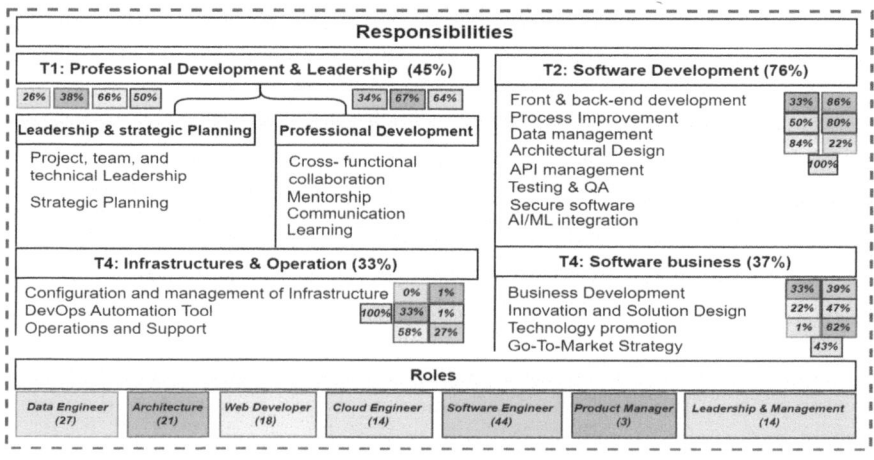

Fig. 3. Responsibilities

Responsibilities to roles: Our analysis revealed distinct distributions of responsibilities across roles, calculated by the percentage of specific tasks per role. For example, software engineers handle 80% of software development tasks, 39% of business activities, 34% of professional development, and 27% of infrastructure and operations. Data engineers contribute 22% to software development and 26% to professional development, with minimal involvement in other areas. Architects focus 86% on software development, 62% on business activities, and 38% on professional development. Web developers have 84% in software development, 58% in infrastructure, 22% in business activities, and 66% in professional development. Cloud engineers are fully involved in software development (100%) and contribute to infrastructure (58%), business activities (43%), and professional development (50%). Further details on the roles are depicted in Fig. 3.

Take Away: serverless practitioners are expected to excel in software development, infrastructure management, and professional development. They need to design and maintain secure, scalable applications, manage infrastructure effectively despite the abstraction, and continuously develop their skills while providing strategic leadership. Similarly, responsibilities vary by role, with each focusing on specific aspects like software development, infrastructure, and team leadership.

RQ2: What hard and soft skills are required from the serverless practitioner as identified in job ads?

Beyond roles and responsibilities, our analysis identified 28 essential hard skills required for practitioners working with serverless computing. These skills range from software development, including frontend, backend, and cloud architecture, to software process improvement methodologies like Agile. We categorized these hard skills into seven main themes: Software Development (Frontend, Backend, and Full Stack), Software Operations, Cloud Architecture, Security and Compliance, Software Process Improvement, AI/ML, and Software Business. Among them, three main themes for the hard skills are cloud architecture and infrastructure, software development, and software operations. These themes provide a comprehensive overview of the technical competencies needed to excel in serverless computing, highlighting the diverse and specialized skill sets required in this field as shown in Fig. 4.

The Cloud Architecture and Infrastructure theme covers the essential elements for building and maintaining cloud systems. Key sub-themes include Serverless Computing (e.g., AWS Lambda), focusing on application deployment without server management for scalability and efficiency. Big Data Management ensures optimized storage, processing, and analysis of large data sets. Scalable Systems and Distributed Computing address designing systems for efficient scaling across distributed environments. Application Migration involves moving existing applications to the cloud with minimal disruption. Architecture focuses on strategic cloud system design, and Software Design emphasizes creating robust, efficient, and maintainable software within cloud infrastructure. Together, these sub-themes outline the critical aspects of cloud architecture

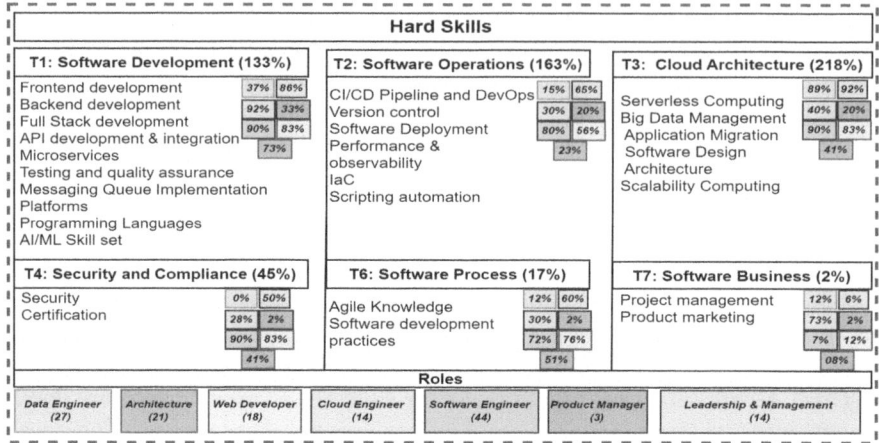

Fig. 4. Hard Skills

and infrastructure. *"Work with Solution Architecture to influence solutions and ensure High-Level Designs are implemented as intended."* – Job-ad #76.

The Software Development theme covers essential skills for serverless computing, including frontend and backend development, full-stack expertise, and API integration. Key sub-themes also involve proficiency in programming languages, frameworks, operating systems, microservices architecture, messaging queues, testing, and quality assurance. Together, these sub-themes emphasize the diverse skill set required for effective software development in serverless computing. *"Confidence to work in multiple programming languages could include C, Go, Rust, Python, Lua, and even PHP."* – Job-ad #69.

The DevOps and Software Operations theme is crucial for serverless computing, emphasizing CI/CD pipelines, DevOps practices, and version control. Key areas include software deployment, automation through scripting, and infrastructure as code (IaC). Performance and observability ensure efficient application operation. These sub-themes underscore the critical skills needed for maintaining robust and efficient serverless operations, ensuring seamless development, deployment, and monitoring of applications. *"Experience with IaC and Serverless tools like Terraform, Ansible, AWS Lambda."* – Job-ad #83.

Hard skills mapping to Roles: Our analysis identified distinct distributions of hard skills across various roles, calculated by the percentage of specific skills per role. For instance, we examined how many of the 27 data engineer job ads require skills in cloud architecture. Data engineers are responsible for 37% of software development tasks, while cloud engineers, web developers, and architects have higher involvement at 86%, 83%, and 73% respectively. Engineering leadership and management roles allocate 32% of their responsibilities to software development, while product managers have a lower engagement at 33%. Software engineers have the second highest involvement, with 90% of their responsibilities related to software development. In software operations, data engineers and architects are involved in 15% and 23% of tasks, whereas cloud engineers and web developers have higher involvement at 65% and 56%. Engineering leadership and management roles contribute 30% of their responsibilities to software operations, and product managers are engaged at 20%. Software engineers have the highest involvement at 80%. For cloud architecture, data engineers are significantly involved with 89% of their tasks related to this area. Cloud engineers and architects have even higher involvement at 92% and 86%. Engineering leadership and management roles dedicate 40% of their responsibilities to cloud architecture, while product managers are engaged at 20%. Software engineers and web developers also have substantial involvement, with 90% and 83% of their responsibilities related to cloud architecture. Regarding software process improvement, data engineers are involved in 12% of these tasks. Cloud engineers have more significant involvement at 60%. Engineering leadership and management roles dedicate 30% of their responsibilities to process improvement, while product managers have minimal involvement at 2%. Software engineers, architects, and web developers are highly engaged, with 72%, 51%, and 76% of their responsibilities respectively related to software process improvement. Figure 4 presents the complete taxonomy.

Soft Skills: Based on the analysis of 141 job posts, we identified 32 sub-themes that were categorized into 7 main themes representing the soft skills required for serverless practitioners. Among these, the six most demanded soft skills across all job ads are (i) communication proficiency, (ii) continuous learning and adaptability, (iii) collaborative teamwork, (iv) problem-solving and analytical skills, (v) leadership excellence, and (vi) project management. We further mapped the soft skills to the identified roles. The thematic findings of this research question are depicted in Fig. 5.

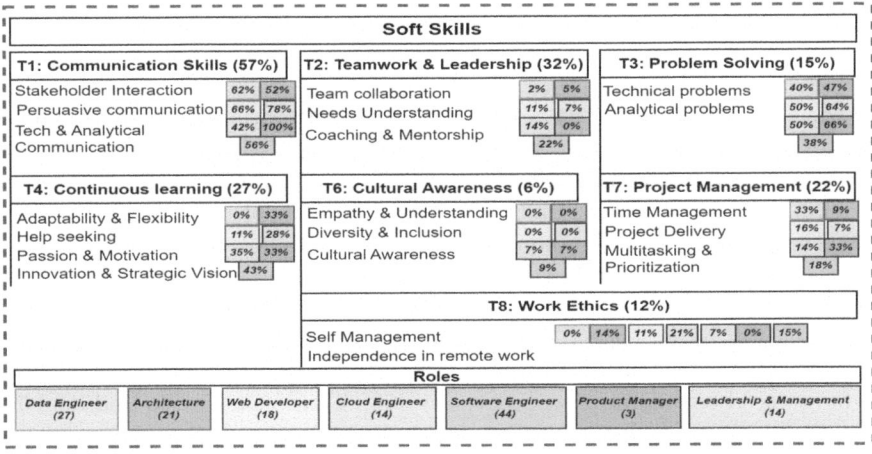

Fig. 5. Soft Skills

Communication proficiency is essential for clear and effective information exchange, enabling seamless collaboration and understanding among team members, stakeholders, and clients. This skill ensures that ideas, feedback, and instructions are conveyed accurately, reducing the risk of misunderstandings and errors. An example of the required soft skill in communication is: *"Strong ability to communicate ... variety of contexts and formats."* – Job-ad #15. Continuous learning and adaptability are crucial for staying ahead in the fast-evolving field of serverless architecture. These skills help practitioners remain current, integrate new tools and techniques into their workflows, and adjust to changing project requirements. An example of a soft skill in this area is adaptability in continuous learning. *"Stay up-to-date, ... internal teams on these developments."* – Job-ad #45. Collaborative teamwork is essential for successful project integration, fostering an environment where diverse skills and perspectives contribute to common goals. Effective teamwork enhances problem-solving, accelerates timelines, and improves overall project quality by leveraging the team's collective expertise. An example of collaborative teamwork is: *"Collaborate with cross-functional teams including product managers, ... alignment with business requirements."* – Job-ad #1. Problem-solving and analytical skills are necessary for identifying and addressing technical challenges, allowing practitioners to devise innovative and efficient solutions. *"Solves problems that have unique and/or broad implications for the technology architecture."* – Job-ad #43. Leadership excellence is crucial for guiding and inspiring teams, providing direction and motivation to achieve project goals and drive organizational success. Leaders in serverless architecture set the vision, allocate resources, and foster a positive team culture, enabling high performance and successful outcomes. An example of a leadership excellence soft skill is: *"Ensure high-quality deliverables by demonstrating leadership in code reviews and test practices."* – Job-ad #48. Finally, project management is key for ensuring project goals and timelines are met and coordinating resources and tasks to deliver successful outcomes within set parameters. An example of the project management soft skill is: *"Manage sole project priorities, deadlines, and deliverables."* – Job-ad #99.

The soft skills required for a data engineering role are unevenly distributed across the main themes. Key skills include communication proficiency (62%), problem-solving and analytical skills (41%), and project management skills (33%). Other soft skills are not commonly required for this role. For architects, the emphasis is on communication proficiency (52%), problem-solving and analytical skills (47%), and continuous learning and adaptability (34%), with empathy and cultural awareness not mentioned. Web developers primarily need communication proficiency (66%) and project management skills (16%), while other skills like sales orientation and independence are less mentioned. Cloud engineers need communication proficiency (78%), problem-solving and analytical skills (64%), and continuous learning and adaptability (28%). For engineering leadership and management roles, all identified soft skills are required, with communication skills (42%), continuous learning and adaptability (35%), and teamwork and leadership excellence (14%) being particularly important. Product managers need communication proficiency (100%), problem-solving and analytical skills (66%), continuous learning and adaptability (33%), and project management skills (33%). For software engineers, the essential skills include communication skills (56%), problem-solving and analytical skills (38%), and continuous learning and adaptability (43%).

Take Away: serverless practitioners need a diverse set of hard and soft skills. Key hard skills include software development, cloud architecture, and software operations. Essential soft skills are communication, continuous learning, teamwork, problem-solving, leadership, and project management. The required skills vary by role, with each position demanding a unique mix of technical and interpersonal abilities to succeed in serverless computing.

RQ3: What are the trends in programming languages, serverless technologies, and cloud platforms as indicated by serverless job ads?
We investigated evolving trends in serverless computing by analyzing job ads for programming languages, serverless technologies, and cloud platforms. This analysis identifies the most in-demand programming languages, popular serverless frameworks, and platforms, aiming to inform future educational and training programs.

Programming Languages: Programming language preferences in serverless job ads reveal an evolving software development landscape. Our analysis shows Python leading with 32 mentions (22.7%), highlighting its widespread adoption and versatility. Java and JavaScript follow with 27 (19.15%) and 23 (16.6%) mentions, respectively, reflecting their importance in enterprise applications and web services. Emerging languages like Node.js and TypeScript also show significant traction with 22 (15.6%) and 9 (6%) mentions, indicating a shift towards JavaScript-based technologies for better scalability and maintainability. Other languages such as C#, .Net, and Go are also noted in our replication package.

We further analyzed programming language trends in relation to specific roles and found Java and JavaScript are the most demanded for software engineering. Node.js is trending for engineering leadership and management roles. Python is highly sought after in data engineering and architect roles. For web developers, JavaScript and Node.js are the most demanded programming languages. Similarly, Node.js and Python are the preferred languages for cloud engineer roles. The results are depicted in Fig. 6.

Serverless Technologies: The analysis of serverless technologies in job advertisements reveals a significant dominance of AWS Lambda with 62 (45%) mentions, underscoring its preeminence in serverless computing. Azure Functions, while significantly trailing with 12 (9%) mentions, indicates Microsoft's growing influence in the market. The data also highlights a robust integration of AWS services, including API Gateway 11 (8%), SNS 7 (5%), SQS 7 (5%), DynamoDB 5 (4%), and other 34 (24%) reflects a preference for AWS's extensive suite of tools that cater to various aspects of serverless computing. This trend suggests that professionals in the serverless domain should focus on acquiring expertise in AWS technologies, while also considering the emerging relevance of Azure Functions to remain competitive in the job market.

Platforms: The analysis of cloud platform mentions in job advertisements shows AWS as the predominant platform with 83 mentions (58%), indicating its strong leadership in the serverless computing market. Azure follows with 36 mentions (25%), demonstrating its significant presence as a competitive alternative. Google Cloud Platform (GCP) has 22 mentions (17%), highlighting its niche but growing role in the serverless ecosystem. However, we did not find any open-source serverless frameworks such as OpenFaas, or Kubeless mentioned in any job posts, indicating a low trend in choosing open-source solutions for developing serverless applications.

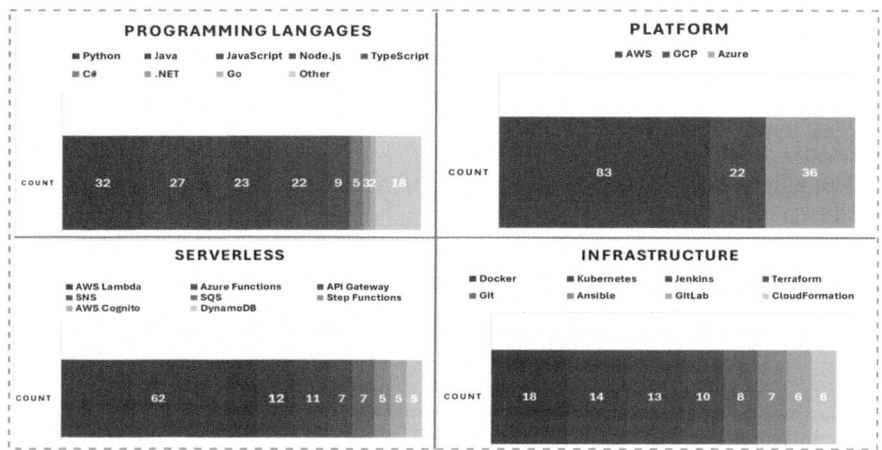

Fig. 6. Technology Implementation

Take Away: to excel in serverless computing, practitioners should focus on mastering Python, Java, JavaScript, Node.js, and TypeScript, along with key AWS services like Lambda, API Gateway, SNS, SQS, and DynamoDB. Additionally, proficiency in Azure Functions and Google Cloud Platform will provide a competitive edge.

5   Discussion

This study offers a comprehensive understanding of the roles, responsibilities, and skills essential for serverless practitioners, providing valuable insights for practitioners, educators, and organizations seeking to align with industry standards. To achieve this, we extracted 2,508 job ads from Glassdoor across seven English-speaking countries and selected 141 job ads through stratified sampling. These selected job ads were then analyzed using thematic analysis.

Organizational Structure: Our analysis conducted on the job ads revealed that organizations adopting serverless computing must address skill gaps by investing in continuous learning and professional development. Companies should prioritize hiring individuals with strong communication, problem-solving, and leadership skills to navigate the complexities of serverless projects successfully.

Implications for Education and Training: Educational and training programs should equip practitioners with a blend of both hard and soft skills necessary for success in serverless computing. These programs should emphasize cloud architecture, software development, and process improvement while integrating training in communication, continuous learning, problem-solving, leadership, and project management. By doing so, training programs can ensure that practitioners are well-prepared to handle the technical and collaborative demands of the industry.

Clarifying the Roles and Responsibilities: The analysis confirmed key roles in serverless computing, including software engineers, data engineers, architects, web developers, cloud engineers, engineering leadership, and product managers. Each role encompasses distinct responsibilities, with software engineers and cloud engineers heavily involved in both development and operations, highlighting the need for a comprehensive skill set.

Soft Skills as a Critical Component: Our analysis conducted on the job ads reveals that communication proficiency, continuous learning, and problem-solving are paramount across all roles. These skills are essential for effective collaboration, adaptation to new technologies, and innovative problem-solving. Leadership and project management skills are particularly vital for roles involving team guidance and strategic oversight, such as engineering leadership and management. This indicates the importance of balancing technical expertise with strong interpersonal and organizational skills to succeed in serverless environments.

6   Threats to Validity

This study acknowledges several threats to validity, categorized into external, internal, and construct.

External validity: concerns the generalizability of the findings beyond the sample. Our reliance on data from Glassdoor may limit the representativeness of serverless roles and skills, as not all employers use this platform. To mitigate this, we included data from a broad geographic range and all job posts mentioning *"serverless"* to enhance coverage.

Internal validity: relates to the accuracy of attributing study results to the investigated variables. Job ads may not fully reflect actual responsibilities, and their requirements may evolve. We addressed this by focusing on frequently mentioned responsibilities and skills, using stratified sampling, and cross-validating our sample with additional job sources.

Construct validity: pertains to how well our measurements reflect the studied concepts. Thematic analysis relies on consistent coding, and variations in interpretation could threaten validity. To mitigate this, all authors conducted rigorous analysis and collaboratively developed clear, well-defined themes.

7 Conclusion and Future Work

As serverless architecture gains traction, the underlying technologies are becoming increasingly diverse. This study develops a comprehensive taxonomy of the roles, responsibilities, and skills required for serverless practitioners by analyzing 141 job ads from Glassdoor. We identified 19 distinct responsibilities, categorized into four main themes: software development, infrastructure and operations, professional development and leadership, and software business. Additionally, we identified 28 hard skills across seven themes: Software Development (Frontend, Backend, Full Stack), Software Operations, Cloud Architecture, Security and Compliance, Software Process Improvement, AI/ML, and Software Business. Furthermore, we identified 32 soft skills, mapped into 10 themes, with the six most demanded being communication, continuous learning, collaboration, problem-solving, leadership, and project management.

Future research should broaden this study by incorporating additional data sources beyond Glassdoor to capture a more global view of the job market for serverless practitioners.

References

1. Ayas, H.M., Hebig, R., Leitner, P.: An empirical investigation on the competences and roles of practitioners in microservices based architectures. J. Syst. Softw. **213**, 112055 (2024)
2. Baltes, S., Ralph, P.: Sampling in software engineering research: a critical review and guidelines. Empir. Softw. Eng. **27**(4), 94 (2022)
3. Braun, V., Clarke, V.: Using thematic analysis in psychology. Qual. Res. Psychol. **3**(2), 77–101 (2006)
4. Cerioli, M., Leotta, M., Ricca, F.: What 5 million job advertisements tell us about testing: a preliminary empirical investigation. In: Proceedings of the 35th Annual ACM Symposium on Applied Computing, pp. 1586–1594 (2020)
5. Eismann, S., et al.: The state of serverless applications: collection, characterization, and community consensus. IEEE Trans. Softw. Eng. **48**(10), 4152–4166 (2021)
6. Eivy, A., Weinman, J.: Be wary of the economics of "serverless" cloud computing. IEEE Cloud Comput. **4**(2), 6–12 (2017)
7. Eskandani, N., Salvaneschi, G.: The uphill journey of FaaS in the open-source community. J. Syst. Softw. **198**, 111589 (2023)
8. Hamza, M.: Software architecture design of a serverless system. In: Proceedings of the 27th International Conference on Evaluation and Assessment in Software Engineering, pp. 304–306 (2023)
9. Hamza, M., Akbar, M.A., Smolander, K.: The journey to serverless migration: an empirical analysis of intentions, strategies, and challenges. In: Kadgien, R., Jedlitschka, A., Janes, A., Lenarduzzi, V., Li, X. (eds.) Product-Focused Software Process Improvement, PROFES 2023. LNCS, vol. 14483, pp. 100–115. Springer, Cham (2023). https://doi.org/10.1007/978-3-031-49266-2_7

10. Lohr, S.L.: Sampling: Design and Analysis. Chapman and Hall/CRC, London (2021)
11. Meesters, M., Heck, P., Serebrenik, A.: What is an AI engineer? An empirical analysis of job ads in the Netherlands. In: Proceedings of the 1st International Conference on AI Engineering: Software Engineering for AI, pp. 136–144 (2022)
12. Muhammad, H.: Unveiling the Skills and Responsibilities of Serverless Practitioners: An Empirical Investigation (2024). https://doi.org/10.5281/zenodo.11622664. https://zenodo.org/records/11622665
13. Wen, J., et al.: An empirical study on challenges of application development in serverless computing. In: Proceedings of the 29th ACM Joint Meeting on European Software Engineering Conference and Symposium on the Foundations of Software Engineering, pp. 416–428 (2021)

On the Way to the Best Information System of the Future – Reflections on Scenarios in Favor of Good Technology Development

Isabelle Fries$^{(\boxtimes)}$ ⓘ, Maximilian Greiner ⓘ, Manfred Hofmeier ⓘ,
Michael Hofmeier ⓘ, Razvan Hrestic ⓘ, and Ulrike Lechner ⓘ

University of the Bundeswehr Munich, Neubiberg, Germany
isabelle.fries@unibw.de

Abstract. Shaping the future is preceded by imaginations of a desired future. This applies in particular to imaginations in an ethical way. In technology development, future imaginations are traditionally represented through scenarios. Our paper builds on scenario development but supplements it with metaethics, a sub-discipline of ethics dealing with the moral connotations of language, alongside stakeholder theory. Our research design in favor of a good future accounted for various aspects of understanding the good (e.g., functional vs. moral) and different perspectives on the good (from various stakeholders). The interdisciplinary scientific foundations are supplemented in exemplary application with experts from computer science, information systems, ethics, psychology, education, and industry partners. We contribute a transdisciplinary perspective, viewing the future as a task to be shaped and making this tangible in technology development. We provide scientific and methodological guidance to developers, designers, and decision-makers to include ethical considerations in software development.

Keywords: Scenario Development · Future-oriented Technology Development · Value Sensitivity · Digital Ethics · Philosophy of Technology

1 Introduction

The future does not have to do with being but with becoming. We can imagine what is to come, but we cannot grasp or describe the future in the same way as it is possible for the present. The future remains elusive, imagining the future to a certain degree speculative. For those who do not advocate determinism and assume that actions are based on freedom of action and that freedom can shape the future, "speculative" is not the same as "arbitrary". For them, the future is partly a modelable mass (on the philosophical idea of shaping the future: [14], pp. 309–314; on ethical action theory: [10], p. 35). This applies to actions and their

E. Papatheocharous et al. (Eds.): ICSOB 2024, LNBIP 539, pp. 68–82, 2025.
https://doi.org/10.1007/978-3-031-85849-9_6

consequences in the future. It applies, in particular, to technology assessment and technology foresight (on future-oriented technology analysis: [6]). Research is required to show responsible paths in terms of ethics, equity and sustainability. However, a scientific challenge lies in envisioning a more responsible future rather than transferring the logic of the past onto the future [22]. According to societal expectations, research is supposed to shape the future in a (morally) good way. Information systems are intended to promote sustainability, social justice, or digital sovereignty. Public science and research, in particular, are subject to the demand for an ethically "good" future. The software industry also faces the challenge of addressing social and environmental needs. Even a company with established guidelines and strong IT governance encounters increasing ethical issues due to legal regulations - such as those ensuring human rights in the supply chain. As a result, proven strategies must be adapted to support the development of "good" technology. Integrating ethical considerations into software development and business strategies becomes crucial.

In this contribution, we present a methodology for "good" technology development, situating information systems within an ethical framework. We extend established methodologies with a broader vision, asking what the best possible future and information system might look like. Our approach is both transdisciplinary and innovative, combining philosophical and ethical expertise with computer science, information systems, and stakeholder theory, applied in scenario-based software development. Rather than designing the best information system, we focus on articulating the journey toward it. This flexible, partly abstract approach allows for a variety of applications. We modify traditional scenario development by placing it alongside stakeholder theory and metaethics (Sect. 2), where metaethics examines language for moral connotations [38]. Our distinctive approach considers pluralistic understandings of "good" among participants in system development. Our approach incorporates interdisciplinary scientific methods combined with empirical application. We developed an exemplary workshop for experts from various disciplines and practical software development (methodology: Sect. 3, results: Sect. 4). We contribute to the integration of ethical considerations in software development, both through the scientifically based method of the workshop itself and in the results and evaluation of the workshop we conducted as an example. In this way, our discussion (Sect. 5) provides orientation for developers, designers, and decision-makers. The formulated questions therein encourage time- and situation-sensitive reflection. In doing so, we are also opening the field for further research and scientific discourse.

2   Related Work

This section provides an overview of the current state of scenario development, as well as stakeholder theory. In addition, we present metaethical insights as key to our research approach. These elements underpin our workshop design.

2.1 Scenario Development

Thinking in Scenarios

Scenario development arose from the need to find ways to prepare for a future that is fundamentally not entirely tangible. Researchers had been used to looking retrospectively at chains of actions, identifying causal relationships, and learning from them. Looking to the future, they had been explorers. Like seafarers, they ventured into unknown waters. The history of technological development and its ethical evaluation gave a new impetus in the 20th century. Since then, research must be measured against the concept of responsibility [24]. Research could no longer experiment and hail every conceivable result as a scientific success. This sets a certain course for the current sailors of science. Responsible research requires an awareness of future consequences. The desire for sustainability, e.g., shows conceptually that it is about desirable future consequences. Public research should not simply stop to avoid misdevelopment but should be conducted in a socially beneficial manner. Thinking in causal relationships is transferred to the future. The aim is to achieve desired consequences and avoid undesired ones ([36], p. 27; [36]). This is the core of technology assessment as "a form of policy research that examines short- and long-term consequences [...]" of the application of technology" ([3], p. 7) and technology foresight as "process involved in systematically attempting to look into the longer-term future of science, technology, the economy, and society with the aim of identifying areas of strategic research and emerging technologies likely to yield the greatest economic and social benefits" ([33], p. 140). This raises two crucial questions for practice:

1. What is a desirable future state and what is an undesirable one?
2. How can we methodically prepare the best possible way to get to the former?

Before we outline scenario development, we analyze the term "scenario" ([35], p. 1404). It goes back to Latin "scena" or Greek "skené". Literally, it refers to the stage for a public event. This metaphor can be applied to today's practice of technology development:

1. What is developed has public significance, even if it is only for a subset of the public within a company or a smaller group. Others are expected to respond and interact positively (using an information system).
2. What is brought to the stage is a choice. Behind the scenes, there is a dramaturge or a group of decision-makers who select the specific piece, the particular protagonists, or the exact props. This could be a specific problem that is at the top of a company's or society's agenda. Often, the means are predetermined, such as when a problem is decided to be solved using a specific technology. The dramaturgy also decides whether and to what extent an audience (a group of users or stakeholders) is involved in the performance. Therefore, it is important to be aware of:

   – Who determines the dramaturgy?
   – Who is on stage?

- Who is in the audience and can interact and who is nearby, gains no benefit but hears the indistinct noise of the event?
- What is the chosen piece (what are alternatives)?
- What is the piece's purpose/what interests, or dependencies does it serve?

Whoever determines the dramaturgy determines the answer to the question of what is "good." This affects others who might have answered differently if they had the opportunity to do so. Subsequently, we also include stakeholder theory in our research method. We show that the above-mentioned questions find empirical support and are reflected in our considerations for practice (Sect. 6).

Working with Scenarios

In the literature, a scenario is defined as a coherent and plausible model of a potential future reality, encompassing information about the paths of development leading to that future, which can contribute to informed decision-making and action [28,42]. Scenario development offers a strategic planning method to explore complex and uncertain futures and gain in-depth insight into possible developments and their implications [29,41]. The objective is not to accurately predict the future but rather to devise different possible visions of the future to make policymakers, business leaders or researchers more aware of new potential trends, key factors and players that may produce major shifts in the existing conditions, as well as unknown eventualities or threats [42,47]. Over time, scenario development has evolved to include a range of methodologies, from sophisticated techniques to simple approaches [8]. This enhances the flexibility of scenario development as a strategic tool that enables customized environments to meet the specific requirements and challenges of various situations [32]. Henrichs et al. [21] distinguish between three scenario development types: explorative ("what can or might happen?"), normative ("how can a specific target be reached?") and reference scenarios ("what is expected to happen?"). The work of van Notten et al. [45,46] distinguish four types of scenario development approaches. On the one hand, approaches can be categorized by considering their content and thematic coverage (1) in complex and simple [45]. Second, approaches that address the design of the process (2) from formalized to intuitive methods [32]. Third, concepts that are classified according to the typology of the data (3), be it quantitative input or qualitative input [28]. Lastly, scenario development techniques can also be differentiated according to their input into the scenario process (4), such as analyst-led and participatory approaches. Scenario development is used in multiple disciplines, including information systems [4], business model development [9], environmental impact assessment [19], and public policy making [49], serving as a critical tool to anticipate future scenarios and facilitate informed decision-making. The development of scenarios for information systems design is used to explore future technological landscapes [26], assess potential risks [23], and inform strategic decision-making [31], thus improving the adaptability and effectiveness of system architectures in dynamic environments [7,48]. Recent studies explore the impact of disruptive technologies, such as Artificial Intelligence [1,25] and Blockchain [18,43]. Use cases, requirements, and architectures have a role in design and management of information systems, and they focus on interactions of users with systems to achieve a goal. Goal-oriented requirements engineering provides a means to elicit requirements from various stakeholders to document how systems meet these requirements [30].

2.2 Stakeholder Theory

Important for the development of information systems - and thus for scenario development - is the need to define and consider stakeholders. Various interests and needs are also ethically significant. In the research field, there are different conceptualizations of information system stakeholders. Freeman [13] defines seven stakeholder groups focusing on form stakeholders: government, competitors, customers, shareholders, employees, suppliers, and civil society. An interesting aspect is the inclusion of civil society, which is crucial. Ruohonen [39] examines information system stakeholders focusing on managerial groups: top management group, user management group and information management group. This limits the stakeholder perspectives to views from within the organization, in which an information system is used. A more open conceptualization can be found in the work of Ballejos et al. [2]. They define the following stakeholder roles for information systems: beneficiary, negative (adversely impacted by the system), responsible, decision-maker, regulators, operators, experts, consultants, and developers.

As existing conceptualizations were not fully applicable for our purpose, we defined our own stakeholder groups based on aspects of existing concepts considering the three levels of state, organization, and individual. The result is an abstract framework that could inform further research as necessary and be adapted for subsequent concrete applications. The most distinctive feature is that, due to our ethical research interest, we have also included "animate and inanimate nature" as relevant stakeholder: *Animate and inanimate nature, legislative (state, supranational institution), developers (organizations), providers (organizations), advertisers and sellers (organizations), users (organizations), affected (organizations), creators (individuals)* (such as designers and developers of information systems), *users (individuals), affected (individuals)*, and *society/citizens.*

These stakeholder groups, listed in Table 1 (Sect. 6), are not isolated and a single organization or individual can be part of multiple stakeholder groups.

2.3 Metaethics

When inquiring about the best information system of the future, one must presuppose an awareness of what "good" actually means. Without an understanding of what "good" entails, it would be impossible to determine what constitutes "the best". However, there are various interpretations of the word "good". An important distinction is between objective good and subjective good ([40], p. 50): Individual reasons can lead to the perception of something as good, even if objective reasons might suggest otherwise.

Furthermore, "good" can be understood in different contexts. For instance, the statement "Your behavior yesterday was not good" employs the term "good" in a different manner than "The new knife is good". Good behavior represents a moral understanding of "good". In contrast, it is its functionality that makes the knife "good" in a non-moral sense. This is a relational use: good in relation to functionality [27]. Also a person can be considered "good" in relation to their role (function), such as being a good scientist, as the ancient thinker Homer has already explained ([11], p. 21). Being a good scientist does not necessarily imply being a good person. The mentioned examples illustrate a difference between a moral and a functional understanding of "good", beyond objective or subjective.

Scholars such as George Edward Moore, Richard Hare, and Philippa Foot have extensively examined the word "good". We cannot represent the sophisticated discussion here (e.g. whether the goodness of a knife stands and falls with the motives of the person using it). To outline the most important ideas: Moore was a co-founder of metaethics. His notable work, "Principia Ethica" [34], introduces the "open question argument", which remains influential in academic discourse. Moore argues that "good" is an independent value that cannot be reduced to other descriptions, such as "promoting well-being" ([44], pp. 147–150). Although he does not give the example of the (functionally) good knife, he already distinguishes talk of a "good book" or a "good horse" from talk of good human behavior. Hare's metaethical ideas became influential in the second half of the 20th century. His work "The Language of Morals" [20] contains an approach of Universal Prescriptivism. "Universal" and "prescriptive" are qualities that Hare saw in the word "good". The idea of prescriptiveness is then linked in the further discussion to the understanding that certain terms entail inherent normativities (if a person says that behavior X is good, then they also know that they are entitled to do X; [17]). In "Virtues and Vices" [12], Foot actually brought the much-noticed example of the good knife into the discussion. Against Hare's idea of prescriptivism, however, she advocated a virtue ethics approach. Crucial for our purpose is to recognize that "good" can be used across various dimensions and that it is worth exploring these dimensions. They can shed light on different ways of understanding and thus encourage communicative exchange. They help to cognitively grasp the "good" in multiple perspectives as a prerequisite for being able to aim for a multi-perspective good in practice.

The well-known example of a functionally good knife can be replaced, for our purpose, with a functionally good information system. Societal or organizational expectations regarding information systems are not met solely by good functionality. Information systems should not only be technically well-made or pleasing in design but they should also contribute to a morally understood good [15]. They should ensure data protection, help reduce CO_2 emissions, or aid in ensuring adherence to human rights. These examples also apply to the business sector, even if it is only legal requirements that drive them. Various understandings of the good come together, often without transparency among the involved stakeholders regarding the diversity of associations and demands. In our research approach (see Fig. 1), we have integrated these insights to create transparency

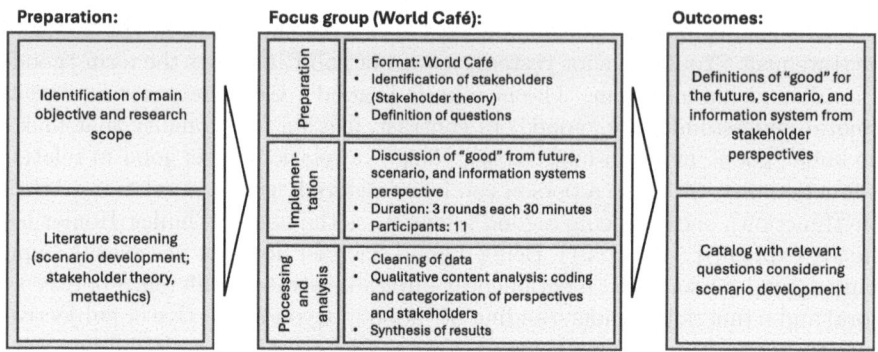

Fig. 1. Procedure

and thereby address different stakeholder perspectives and legitimate interests in the development of good information systems in favor of a good future.

3   Research Design

The research design utilizes a structured approach that merges qualitative methodologies, stakeholder theory, and metaethics (see Fig. 1). The preparation phase addresses the identification of our main objective and the research scope. Literature in the fields of scenario development, stakeholder theory, and metaethics was screened. To gather data to define a "good" future, a "good" scenario, and "good" information system, we conducted a focus group in a world café format. This participatory discussion method facilitates an open and collaborative dialogue through a series of small group conversations, often structured around specific topics of interest, to gather collective insight [5]. Participants have a new composition in each round of discussions. We incorporated abstract stakeholder types into the discussion method, each of which should address future, scenario, and information system perspectives. This approach not only involved various disciplines but also prompted experts to consider multiple shifts in perspective in favor of different interest groups.

The workshop was carried out within the interdisciplinary research environment of the LIONS project. The project's topics range from the design of (blockchain) technology to psychology, ethics, and media pedagogy with the goal of increasing resilience and sovereignty. Discussions, e.g., on whether technical designs of blockchains actually meet society's interests, are frequent, and certain designs are necessary to meet security requirements but pose risk of excluding marginalized communities and stakeholders. Before the discussion rounds, the participants were introduced to the topic. They were given an overview of the methodological foundations (scenario development, stakeholder theory, metaethics) and informed about the research goal, which aims to contribute to the development of "good" information systems. During three 30-minute rounds, a total of 11 participants, including ethics experts, system developers, psychology and education experts, and industry partners, engage in discussions that are documented and analyzed. This group of participants ensures a thorough exploration of the topic while capturing a wide range of insights from various professional perspectives. The participants were presented with three questions for discussion: "What is a 'good' information system?"; "What is a 'good' scenario?"; "What is a 'good' future?" The conception of the questions was preceded by the knowledge of context-related possibilities of understanding the good. These possibilities of understanding were to be called up. In answering, participants should adopt the perspectives of the proposed stakeholder groups. This was aimed at the perspectivity of the possibilities of understanding the good. Following the data collection phase, the research design incorporates a data cleaning process.

The analytical phase employs qualitative content analysis techniques. This step is pivotal, as it synthesizes the diverse perspectives of stakeholders into categories that reflect the understanding of "good" across the three dimensions: future, scenario and information system. This analysis leads to relevant basic questions that researchers and practitioners can consider engaging with the development of information systems (Sect. 5).

4   Results

Table 1 shows the stakeholder groups' perceptions of "good" for the future, scenario, and information system. In addition, we emphasize a few comments.

For example, a good future is seen as sustainable in terms of resources. It should simultaneously enable growth and profits, and provide both individuals and animate and inanimate nature with a good and undisturbed life. A good scenario should also consider everyone, be legally compliant and user-friendly, and demonstrate long-term consequences, including considerations of fairness, at low cost. The participants associated a good information system with a catalog of relatively specific requirements: sustainability, resource efficiency, legality, usability, controllability, security, compatibility, and so on.

It is evident that ideas of a "good" future manifest themselves in respective perceptions of scenarios and information systems. Regarding animate and inanimate nature, for example, a "good" future is one with an environment that allows existence and serves the required resources. This manifests itself in sustainability aspects in scenarios and information systems, such as low energy consumption. It is also noteworthy that the collected perceptions of a good future reflect, among others, general human needs and rights, such as existence, peace, freedom, justice, and solidarity. It is also evident that "good" scenarios and information systems reflect impacts on society and the environment, such as privacy, transparency, or sustainability aspects.

It should be emphasized that the perceptions collected in Table 1 include both moral and functional understandings of "good", as described in the metaethics section (Sect. 2.3). The connections also become clear. For example, usability is both a moral concern and a functional requirement.

Table 1. Definitions of "good" from stakeholder perspectives.

Stakeholder	What is a "good" future?	What is a "good" scenario?	What is a "good" information system?
Animate and inanimate nature	an environment that allows existence, resources such as food or water, and therefore a sustainable economic system	highlighting the importance, significance and relevance (e.g. sustainability)	Low consumption of resources (energy, materials), environmentally friendly system output
Legislative (state, supranational institution)	lively political participation; political and economic stability; functional systems	compliance with the law; adaptation of the scenario to the law (development process - scenarios are often adapted retrospectively); adequate representation of the superior authority	Controllable, traceable, clear responsibilities, compliance with laws (e.g. data protection), verifiability of transactions (e.g. through blockchain)
Developers (organizations)	economic viability; availability of resources such as raw materials or people (with according competencies)	knowledge and information generation; consideration of the relevant perspectives of the scenario; description of the prototype or demonstrator; Few waste products	Short development time, familiar technologies, agile/non-agile process, sovereignty, expertise, sustainable business model, open source libraries
Providers (organizations)	economic viability; availability of resources such as raw materials or people (with according competencies)	consideration of the cost factor (economic); low effort; scalability	Cost efficiency, low effort, good administrability, quality assurance, scalability, availability, sustainable business model, open source (costs)
Advertisers and sellers (organizations)	profit; high purchasing power of customers	addressing current relevance; optimal readability for target groups	Proprietary nature, system dependency, marketable trends (technology), scalability, sustainable business model
Users (organizations)	achievement of the organizational goals; growth of the own potential	uncovering potentials, problems, added value, impacts; high user-friendliness; reduced complexity; comprehensibility; problem solving (actual-future situation)	Security of internal data, compatibility with other systems/processes, quality assurance, scalability, updates, verifiability of transactions

(*continued*)

Table 1. (*continued*)

Stakeholder	What is a "good" future?	What is a "good" scenario?	What is a "good" information system?
Affected (organizations)	no unwanted impact by information systems	demonstration of effects (subjective construction); representation of individual interests; description of empiricism in the creation and development process; description of roles within the scenario and the implications	Compatibility with other systems/processes, transparency of interests and processes, security of internal data
Creators (individuals)	creative self-realization, good working conditions	clarity, easy handling, practical relevance, orientation with regard to future strategy	Low effort, high acceptance, great popularity, understandable scenario(s)
Users (individuals)	availability of useful information systems; having knowledge about their interaction with information systems and understanding the systems' decisions (e.g. in AI systems)	uncovering potentials, problems, added value, impacts; high user-friendliness; reduced complexity; comprehensibility; problem solving (actual-future situation); Realistic depiction of living conditions	Security of own personal data, good usability/user experience, reasonable behavior/results, regular updates, open source (consumer systems)
Affected (individuals)	no unwanted side-effects of information systems; no disturbance by information systems	demonstration of effects (subjective construction); representation of individual interests; description of empiricism in the creation and development process; description of roles within the scenario and the implications	Security of own personal data, transparency with regard to the purpose of processing, clarification of necessity
Society/ Citizens	optimistic atmosphere; peaceful discussion culture; being able to achieve one's goals; quality of life; general human needs and rights such as existence, peace, freedom, justice, and solidarity	fairness/equal opportunities; demonstrating public relevance; describing what role they play	Cross-linking, dedication, education about benefits/dangers, no monopolies, social benefits, common good

Contradictions caused by the perspectivity rarely came to light. One example of a possible conflict is that the advertisers and sellers group perceives information systems as "good," that are primarily marketable, while the society/citizens want information systems to be for the common good and reject monopolies.

5   Discussion

We offer a framework for ethical considerations in the development of information systems. Identifying stakeholders, their interests, and imaginations enables the integration of different needs into the development of technology. Changing perspectives will also change the development process. Blind spots can be reduced. This is particularly evident when looking at animate and inanimate nature, which is, thus, given a voice. The participants occasionally found it difficult to think from other perspectives. However, this exercise can broaden the horizon. As an ethical reference, John Rawls' thought experiment of the original position is noteworthy: A group agrees on just principles for a future society without knowing which social role they will later occupy [16,37]. By incorporating theories of justice like those of Rawls or discourse ethics according to Jrgen Habermas when negotiating divergent visions of the future, metaethical descriptions find a substantial complement. Our approach can complement traditional scientific methods in favor of a responsible future in terms of ethics, equity, and sustainability. The results may suggest that the best information system of the future aims to be a kind of "Jack-of-all-trades." Outcomes, which risk being labeled "utopian," are intended. Participants were encouraged to speculate and not restrict their thinking with present-day logics. It is human nature not to let go of old logics completely, as some participants did with regard to growth logic. However, by framing the broad question of a good future, courageous steps have been taken toward future responsibility. With this overall perspective, strategies such as internal IT governance can also be adjusted in an agile way.

Table 2. Questions for "good" scenarios.

1.	Which stakeholders are relevant and should be included in the scenario? This potentially includes adversely affected organizations or individuals and society as a whole
2.	What quality of data is required for scenario development and which methods are useful (e.g. literature review, interviews with stakeholder representatives)? Our workshop is an option
3.	Which design criteria, such as security and protection of individual stakeholders' data, play an important role in scenario development?
4.	What characteristics does a new/disruptive technology offer and how can synergies be created with stakeholders and the environment?
5.	What risks are associated with disruptive technologies and how can they be accounted for?
6.	How can ethical values and system requirements such as sustainability, resilience, or scalability be represented and ensured?

This is relevant for scenario development in a research context, but also in practice. If a specific information system is to be developed, the questions and the list of possible stakeholders can be used (Table 1). Our framework even takes into account those who typically lack a voice in the development process: the structurally disadvantaged, as well as animate and inanimate nature. The three questions we have chosen on the basis of metaethical considerations show that imaginations of the good depend on stakeholders, but also on contexts. Whether it concerns a moral or functional good, there is initially no judgment regarding legitimate interests. Recognizing the different levels, however, promotes communicative exchange among participants, fostering a process towards achieving the best possible outcome: a future that accounts for the good in a multidimensional sense. Our basic questions for practice (Table 2) build on this. They refer to the points set out in Sect. 2.1 on the "dramaturgy" of a scenario and motivate time- and situation-sensitive reflection on potential outcomes and ethical considerations inherent in the design and implementation of new systems and technologies. The questions (Table 2) are intentionally kept brief and intuitively understandable. They can serve as a compact checklist when one cannot integrate a workshop into software development following Table 1 or wishes to independently review all mentioned fields. When consciously integrated as a reflection step in the scenario development process, they can also highlight pathways toward good technology development. Thus, the focus is less on the originality of the questions and more on integrating them as a conscious component of the development process. However, the reflection process and the results outlined in Table 1 can offer even more impact, where the abstract stakeholders can also be specified according to one's specific application.

There are some limitations. As the participants predominantly originate from the same research environment and a similar socio-cultural background, there may be biases. It is possible that the personal background influences the perceptions of the good. To examine this point, the workshop could be repeated in different cultural settings, which could be part of future research. However, it is important to consider that culturally conditioned notions of good are reflected in the corresponding cultural law. For example, a commitment to sustainability is supported by relevant EU legislation. A group with different cultural values would still need to comply with this legislation for projects within the EU. When asked to describe a "good" future, the participants independently named values that correspond to a consensus at the EU level such as freedom or justice.

During the workshop, some participants commented that they found it difficult to draw a clear distinction between scenario and the future in general. This is probably due to the fact that the idea of the future is linked to the idea of superordinate abstract scenarios and that no concrete scenario was mentioned in the discussion of the scenario question in favor of the advantages of an abstract framework. The blurring of boundaries between scenario and future also demonstrates that the horizon-expanding question of a good future has successfully integrated into scenario thinking. In future research, it could be examined through a control group to what extent the overarching question of a good future also frames the responses towards a good scenario, especially in ethical terms.

6   Conclusion and Outlook

Our paper contributes a methodology of fostering "good" technology development combining scenario development, stakeholder theory, and metaethics. A transdisciplinary workshop illustrated what constitutes a "good" future, scenario, and information system. This method can be concretized for any application in scenario-based software development. For this purpose, it was kept general and open for situational modifications. Participant involvement has allowed us to gather diverse perspectives, fostering a multidimensional understanding of "good". In addition, we have formulated reflection questions. Both serve as foundational tools for practitioners aiming to integrate various stakeholders' needs directly and embed ethical considerations into future-oriented research. The presented future imaginations can guide developers and researchers in assessing ethical dimensions of technology and scenario development in terms of diverse interests, long-term impacts, and societal consequences. Furthermore, the proposed questions (which can be expanded) can serve as an overall checklist to ensure that technological development is aligned with ethical and social goals. As the discourse on technology development continues, more research should expand on the foundations laid by our study. Future work could explore how the reflection questions are applied or extended in different contexts and industries. This ongoing exploration, the journey to the best information system of the future, will not only refine the current results, but also adapt them to the shifting technological landscape, ensuring relevance and practical utility in promoting "good" technology development.

Acknowledgments. This work originates in the LIONS research project. LIONS is funded by dtec.bw - Digitalization and Technology Research Center of the Bundeswehr which we gratefully acknowledge. dtec.bw is funded by the European Union - NextGenerationEU. We also thank all the experts who participated in the world café.

References

1. Alahi, M.E.E., Sukkuea, A., et al.: Integration of IoT-enabled technologies and artificial intelligence (AI) for smart city scenario: recent advancements and future trends. Sensors **23**(11), 5206 (2023)
2. Ballejos, L.C., Gonnet, S.M., et al.: A stakeholder model for interorganizational information systems. In: Paech, B., Rolland, C. (eds.) Requirements Engineering: Foundation for Software Quality, pp. 73–87. Springer, Cham (2008)
3. Banta, D.: What is technology assessment? Int. J. Technol. Assess. Health Care **25**(1), 7–9 (2009)
4. Bonilla, S.H., Silva, H.R., et al.: Industry 4.0 and sustainability implications: a scenario-based analysis of the impacts and challenges. Sustainability **10**(10), 3740 (2018)
5. Brown, J.: The World Café: Shaping Our Futures Through Conversations That Matter. Berret-Koehler, San Francisco (2010)

6. Cagnin, C., Keenan, M.: Positioning future-oriented technology analysis. In: Cagnin, C., Keenan, M., et al. (eds.) Future-Oriented Technology Analysis. Strategic Intelligence for an Innovative Economy, pp. 1–13. Springer, Cham (2008)
7. Carrol, J.M.: Five reasons for scenario-based design. In: Proceedings of the 32nd Annual Hawaii International Conference on Systems Sciences. HICSS-32. Abstracts and CD-ROM of Full Papers, pp. 11–pp. IEEE (1999)
8. Dean, M.: Scenario planning: a literature review. A report of project (769276-2) (2019)
9. Di Vaio, A., Boccia, F., et al.: Artificial intelligence in the agri-food system: rethinking sustainable business models in the COVID-19 scenario. Sustainability **12**(12), 4851 (2020)
10. Fenner, D.: Ethik: Wie soll ich handeln? Attempto, Tübingen (2020)
11. Fischer, J., Gruden, S., et al.: Grundkurs Ethik: Grundbegriffe philosophischer und theologischer Ethik. Kohlhammer, Stuttgart, 2nd edn. (2007)
12. Foot, P.: Virtues and Vices and Other Essays in Moral Philosophy. Blackwell, Oxford (1978)
13. Freeman, R.E.: Strategic Management: A Stakeholder Approach. Pitman, Boston (1984)
14. Fries, I.: Ich und Wir: Der Begriff der Gemeinschaft bei Martin Buber. Gütersloher Verlagshaus, Gütersloh (2023)
15. Fries, I.: Ethical guidelines for DLT-based information systems. In: Fries, I., Grabatin, M., et al. (eds.) Sovereign by Design: The LIONS Approach to Digital Sovereignty, pp. 57–90. Logos, Berlin (2024)
16. Fries, I., Greiner, M.: Technology-enabled fairness? Reflections on fairness within blockchain-based supply chain consortia. In: European Academy of Management 2023, Conference Proceedings (2023). ISSN 2466-7498
17. Garza Vázquez, O.: The capability approach: ethics and socio-economic development. In: Routledge Handbook of Development Ethics, pp. 68–83. Routledge, London (2019)
18. Greiner, M., Seidenfad, K., et al.: The digital product passport: enabling interoperable information flows through blockchain consortia for sustainability. In: Innovations for Community Services: 24th International Conference, I4CS 2024, Maastricht, The Netherlands, 12–14 June 2024, p. 377. Springer, Cham (2024). https://doi.org/10.1007/978-3-031-60433-1_21
19. Hallström, E., Carlsson-Kanyama, et al.: Environmental impact of dietary change: a systematic review. J. Clean. Prod. **91**, 1–11 (2015)
20. Hare, R.M.: The Language of Morals. Clarendon Press, Oxford (1952)
21. Henrichs, T., Zurek, M., et al.: Scenario development and analysis for forward-looking ecosystem assessments. Ecosyst. Hum. Well-Being: Manual Assess. Practitioners **10** (2010)
22. Horkova, D., Peter, S.: Research perspectives: from other worlds: speculative engagement through digital geographies. J. Assoc. Inf. Syst. **22**(6), 1736–1752 (2021)
23. Jacobsson, A., Boldt, M., et al.: A risk analysis of a smart home automation system. Futur. Gener. Comput. Syst. **56**, 719–733 (2016)
24. Jonas, H.: Das Prinzip der Verantwortung: Versuch einer Ethik für die technologische Zivilisation. Insel, Frankfurt (1979)
25. Kieslich, K., Diakopoulos, N., et al.: Anticipating impacts: using large-scale scenario writing to explore diverse implications of generative AI in the news environment. AI Ethics 1–23 (2024)

26. Kirchner, M., Schmidt, J., et al.: Ecosystem services and economic development in Austrian agricultural landscapes - the impact of policy and climate change scenarios on trade-offs and synergies. Ecol. Econ. **109**, 161–174 (2015)
27. Korsgaard, C.M.: The relational nature of the good. In: Shafer-Landau, R. (ed.) Oxford Studies in Metaethics, pp. 1–26. Oxford University Press, Oxford (2023)
28. Kosow, H., Gaßner, R.: Methods of Future and Scenario Analysis: Overview, Assessment, and Selection Criteria, vol. 39. DEU, Bonn (2008)
29. Lindgren, M., Bandhold, H.: Scenario Planning. The Link Between Future and Strategy. Revised and Updated Edition. Palgrave Macmillan London (2009)
30. Lucke, C.: Stakeholder-orientierte Unternehmensarchitekturmodellierung: Konzeption, Entwurf und Anwendung des ASTEAM-Ansatzes. WiKu-Wiss.-Verlag, Duisburg / Köln (2014)
31. Mahmoud, M., Liu, Y., et al.: A formal framework for scenario development in support of environmental decision-making. EMS **24**(7), 798–808 (2009)
32. Martelli, A.: Models of Scenario Building and Planning: Facing Uncertainty and Complexity. Springer, Cham (2014)
33. Martin, B.R.: Foresight in science and technology. Technol. Anal. Strateg. Manag. **7**(2), 139–168 (1995)
34. Moore, G.E.: Principia Ethica. Cambridge University Press, Cambridge (1903)
35. Pfeifer, W.: Etymologisches Wörterbuch des Deutschen. Kramer, Berlin (2012)
36. Rader, M., Porter, A.L.: Fitting future-oriented technology analysis methods to study types. In: Cagnin, C., Keenan, M., et al. (eds.) Future-Oriented Technology Analysis, pp. 25–40. Springer, Cham (2008)
37. Rawls, J.: A Theory of Justice. Harvard University Press, Cambridge (1971)
38. Ricken, F.: Metaethik. In: Philosophisches Wörterbuch, pp. 296–297. Karl Alber, Freiburg (2010)
39. Ruohonen, M.: Stakeholders of strategic information systems planning: theoretical concepts and empirical examples. J. Strateg. Inf. Syst. **1**(1), 15–28 (1991)
40. Rüther, M.: Ein bemerkenswertes Projekt? Die objektive Theorie des guten Lebens in der Metaethik. In: Glück – Werte – Sinn, pp. 49–72. De Gruyter, Berlin /Boston (2013)
41. Schoemaker, P.J.: Scenario planning: a tool for strategic thinking. MIT Sloan Manag. Rev. (1995)
42. Schwartz, P.: The art of the long view: planning for the future in an uncertain world. Crown Currency, New York (1996)
43. Seidenfad, K., Wagner, et al.: Demonstrating feasibility of blockchain-driven carbon accounting – a design study and demonstrator. In: International Conference on Innovations for Community Services, pp. 28–46. Springer, Cham (2022)
44. Soames, J.: Philosophical Analysis in the Twentieth Century. Princeton University Press, Princeton / Woodstock (2003)
45. Van Notten, P.: Scenario development: a typology of approaches (2006)
46. Van Notten, P., Rotmans, J., et al.: An updated scenario typology. Futures **35**(5), 423–443 (2003)
47. Wack, P.: Scenarios: uncharted waters ahead. Harv. Bus. Rev. **63**(5), 72–89 (1985)
48. Weidenhaupt, K., Pohl, K., et al.: Scenarios in system development: current practice. IEEE Softw. **15**(2), 34–45 (1998)
49. Wright, D., Stahl, B., et al.: Policy scenarios as an instrument for policymakers. Technol. Forecast. Soc. Chang. **154**, 119972 (2020)

What Affects Developer Experience in Software Platforms?

Rodrigo Oliveira Zacarias[1]([⊠]) [iD], Léo Carvalho Ramos Antunes[1] [iD],
Marcos César da Rocha Seruffo[2] [iD], Rodrigo Pereira dos Santos[1] [iD],
and Patricia Lago[3] [iD]

[1] Federal University of the State of Rio de Janeiro, Rio de Janeiro, Brazil
{rodrigo.zacarias,leo.antunes}@edu.unirio.br, rps@uniriotec.br
[2] Federal University of Pará, Belém, Brazil
seruffo@ufpa.br
[3] Vrije Universiteit Amsterdam, Amsterdam, The Netherlands
p.lago@vu.nl

Abstract. Developer experience (DX) is a decisive coefficient both for the performance of developers and for keeping developers actively contributing to software platforms. When it comes to understanding what affects DX in software platforms, researchers and practitioners recognize several factors. This topic still lacks a roadmap regarding the main DX factors, primarily when considering platforms in software ecosystems. Thus, this study aims to investigate and characterize the factors that affect DX in software platforms. After investigating the literature, we selected 35 studies to analyze the state-of-the-art of DX in development on software platforms. As the main contribution, we provided a set of factors organized into six categories that affect DX in software platforms. This set of DX factors can be used as a reference guide to support researchers and practitioners in improving the development processes of the products and services on software platforms.

Keywords: Developer experience · Software platform · Software development · Software ecosystem

1 Introduction

Some companies have invested in opening their architectures to allow third-party developers to collaborate in the production of their components on a common technological platform, which contributes to the emergence of software ecosystems (SECO) [5]. Developer experience (DX) is a decisive coefficient both for the performance of developers and for keeping developers actively contributing to software platforms [2,6].

Fagerholm and Münch [1] define DX as a broader concept that captures how developers feel about, think about, and value their work. An unsatisfactory

E. Papatheocharous et al. (Eds.): ICSOB 2024, LNBIP 539, pp. 83–88, 2025.
https://doi.org/10.1007/978-3-031-85849-9_7

DX in the SECO environment can lead to a lack of interest and engagement among third-party developers to the software platform. In more severe cases, it can culminate in the SECO "death" [2,3,8]. Despite the importance of the DX concept for software development, its characterization is still incipient. When it comes to understanding what affects DX in software platforms, researchers and practitioners recognize several factors. This topic still lacks a roadmap regarding the main factors that affect DX. When we consider software platforms in SECO, this gap is even greater.

In this context, this study aims to investigate and characterize the factors that affect DX in software platforms. To do so, we reviewed the existing literature on scientific databases and digital libraries to map and analyze the state-of-the-art of DX in development on software platforms. As the main contribution, we provide a set of DX factors as a reference guide to support researchers and practitioners in improving the development processes of the products and services on software platforms.

The remainder of this paper is organized as follows: Sect. 2 depicts the protocol followed for the systematic mapping study (SMS). Section 3 shows the results of the study. Furthermore, a discussion of the main aspects identified and the mapping contributions are presented in Sect. 4. Finally, Sect. 5 presents the conclusion and future work.

2   Research Method

To review the state-of-the-art of DX in software development and SECO, we conducted an SMS following the guidelines proposed by Petersen et al. [7]. To address the purpose of the study, we define the following main research question (RQ): **"How DX factors have been investigated in software platforms?"** To answer the RQ, the following sub-questions (SQ) were elaborated: (SQ1) "What are the factors that influence DX in development on software platforms?"; (SQ2) "What are the research methods used for obtaining these factors?"; and (SQ3) "What factors are specific to software platforms in SECO?".

After some refinements, the following search string was used and Fig. 1 illustrates an overview of the process: *"software" AND ("developer experience" OR "programmer experience" OR "developer satisfaction" OR "developer relation" OR "newcomer experience")*. We performed the search string on the databases of IEEE, ACM, Scopus, and Web of Science. In our searches, we have covered studies until 2022 with the support of Parsifal[1], an online tool designed to help researchers perform systematic literature reviews within the context of SE.

We used the following inclusion (IC) and exclusion (EC) criteria for the studies returned by the search string: **IC1** - The study approaches DX in development on software platforms; **IC2** - The study presents at least one factor that influences the DX in development on software platforms; **EC1** - The study brings the concept of DX as the time of experience or seniority; **EC2** - The study is

---

[1] https://parsif.al/about.

not related to software development; **EC3** - The study is not primary; **EC4** - The study is not accessible; and **EC5** - The study is duplicated.

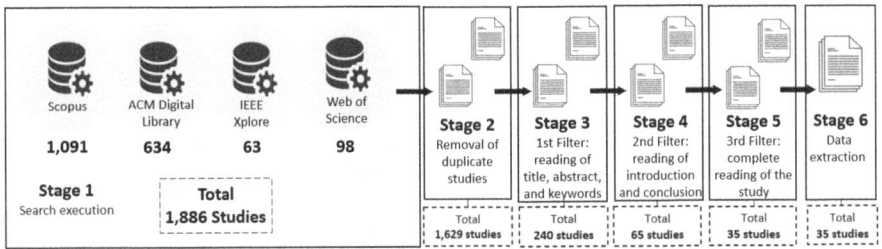

Fig. 1. Number of remaining studies in each step.

3 Results

After executing the SMS process described in Sect. 2, information was extracted from 35 selected studies, which were numbered from S01 to S35. Further details about the selected studies are available via Zenodo[2]. To respond to the main RQ, SQs were answered, as described next.

SQ1: "What are the factors that influence DX in development on software platforms?" To answer this SQ, we searched in the selected studies factors that impact DX. So, we identified the most relevant factors in software platforms, grouped them into categories, and elaborated the scheme seen in Fig. 2. The number in the parentheses means the frequency of them in the studies. These factors affect DX in development on software platforms, which is one of the main activities inserted in the SECO context.

To design the scheme and organize the factors, we used the categories proposed by the framework of Greiler et al. [4]. It lists DX factors in four categories in order: **Development and Release (A)**, **Product Management (B)**, **Collaboration and Culture (C)**, and **Developer Flow and Fulfilment (D)**. To adequate the classification of factors found in this study, we created two more categories: **Mood/Emotions (E)** and **Software Ecosystems (F)**.

SQ2: "What are the research methods used for obtaining these factors?" The most used method is survey/questionnaires (S2, S3, S4, S5, S6, S7, S8, S9, S13, S15, S19, S20, S22, S23, S24, S25, S26, S28, S31, S33), followed by interviews (S1, S2, S6, S11, S14, S15, S16, S19, S28, S29, S30, S34, S35). We believe that this happens because the evaluation of the experience is subjective and influenced by several variables and each one can have their perceptions. Thus, these two methods help researchers deeply understand these nuances.

Moreover, we can highlight that interviews allow understanding each factor more deeply, going into the details of each aspect of it. Although it is more

---

[2] https://doi.org/10.5281/zenodo.13738490.

Developer Experience (DX) Factors					
A. Development and Release	**B.** Product Management	**C.** Collaboration and culture	**D.** Developer flow and fulfilment	**E.** Mood / Emotions	**F.** Software Ecosystems
1. appropriate tools and resources (14)	1. defined process and roles (7)	1. team collaboration and communication (18)	1. challenging and stimulating work (11)	1. enjoyment and fun (7)	1. entry barriers (4)
2. development environment (14)	2. changes and time issues (5)	2. getting recognition and feedback (12)	2. engagement and ideology achievement (11)	2. self-confidence (6)	2. platform openness (3)
3. technical knowledge (11)	3. clear goals scope and planning (5)	3. work culture (7)	3. compensation and personal benefit (8)	3. bad feelings (5)	3. platform market potential and innovativeness (3)
4. codebase health (10)	4. domain expertise (4)	4. code review process (3)	4. focus and productivity (7)	4. stress or break of expectation (2)	4. platform technical dependencies (3)
5. documentation problems (8)	5. transparency and privacy (4)	5. knowledge sharing (3)	5. making progress without obstacles (6)	5. satisfaction (2)	5. social influence (2)
	6. organization governance (3)	6. language proficiency and geolocation (1)	6. learning (6)	6. peace of mind (1)	6. partnership model (2)
	7. bad decision making (2)		7. new opportunities (5)		7. contributing-to-OSS experience (1)
	8. providing value to the business (1)		8. sense of control (5)		8. value of the content (1)
			9. being an important contributor (3)		9. efficient information channels (1)
			10. stability of job and team (2)		

Fig. 2. General and specific factors that influence the developer experience in the context of software platforms in SECO.

difficult to go over these details for surveys, it can reach more developers also due to the characteristics of geolocation. The other methods appeared more isolated in some studies but also brought valid and relevant results, most of them also related to qualitative analysis.

SQ3: "What factors are specific to software platforms in SECO?" As we can observe in Fig. 2, some factors are more intrinsically related to software platforms in SECO. If the platform imposes **entry barriers (F1)** (such as registration fees for developers or submission fees for apps - S15, S24, S27, S33), this impacts negatively the DX. This may discourage newcomers, causing them even to give up using the technology platform. **Platform openness (F2)** has also been noted as one important factor in improving DX (S2, S13, S19). Additionally, it includes the availability of free content (S2) on the platform. The **platform market potential and inovativeness (F3)** (S2, S19, S33) is another relevant factor. The individual who is contributing to the platform needs the guarantee it is up to date with the most recent trends and it is worth contributing to it. Not far behind, we can highlight **platform technical dependencies (F4)** (S15, S18, S27) as something that affects developers. Some characteristics as performance or developer authentication time (S15), limited API use cases (S27), and other dependencies (S18) can hold developers back.

Another factor that affects DX is **social influence (F5)** (S19, S31). Since ecosystems involve different actors around a common technological platform, a good relationship can make developers' lives easier when collaborating. Furthermore, having a **partnership model (F6)** (S24, S27) can improve developers' experience since they are part of an organized process that aims to benefit both sides (developers' and keystone's). Additionally, when dealing with open source software (OSS), the **contributing-to-OSS experience (F7)** (S8) is something that can motivate the developer to contribute. A study also mentioned that the **value of the content (F8)** (S9) is relevant for the developer. Finally, **efficient information channels (F9)** (S19, S35) are also a key factor in SECO, because they support processes of technology learning for newcomers, promoting interaction between the community and bringing them closer to the keystone.

4 Discussion

During the selection of studies for this SMS, we observed that many of them define DX based on seniority level. This work chose to consider the definition of DX by Fagerholm and Münch [1] in the selection process, excluding studies that did not fit in this view. When analyzing the selected studies, we realized that DX is a recent term for academia and industry, and research and investments focus on the types of strategies for good DX and the benefits that can be generated for the business. Corroborating with Nylund [6], the analysis, interpretation, and compilation of DX factors is somewhat complex, as many studies implicitly address the term. Something similar happens in the context of software platforms in SECO, mainly in older works. Therefore, our research strategy sought to bring the maximum number of studies that could be filtered.

Regarding the research methods used by the selected studies to identify the DX factors, we observed that the majority opted for conducting surveys (questionnaires) and interviews. Surveys allow for reaching a large number of participants, on the other hand, interviews allow for greater depth in the analyses. Given the intrinsic subjectivity of research involving DX, these methods are successful because they enable collecting the perception of those who experience it daily. The results obtained through the SMS described factors that impact DX in software platforms. We organized them into 6 categories, as presented in Fig. 2. The two last categories - **Mood/Emotions (E)** and **Software Ecosystems (F)** - expand the framework of DX from Greiler et al. [4]. Besides the Software Ecosystems category, we can highlight the Mood/Emotions category, which did not receive much prominence in the framework from Greiler et al. [4].

As mentioned in Fontão et al. [3], affective reactions influence work-related behaviors, i.e., the emotional state of a person, plays a crucial role in many domains where it can make or break a team's ability to produce successful products. Therefore, it is important to understand these emotional factors, identified in Fig. 2, such as enjoyment, fun, satisfaction, anxiety, or stress, and think of ways to consider them during the DX assessment process. Furthermore, although Fontão et al. [3] mentioned feelings and emotions as factors, our research complements these results by listing the types of feelings and emotions. Regarding the category of specific factors for Software Ecosystems, we identified 9 factors that are linked to business characteristics, mainly influencing the retention of developers actively contributing to SECO's common technological platform. This allows us to infer that the SECO's business characteristics can influence the experience and how the keystones manage the business of their platforms are crucial to provide a good DX.

5   Conclusion

We conducted an SMS to investigate and characterize the factors that affect DX in software platforms. As the main contribution, we provided a set of DX factors that can be used as a reference guide to support researchers and practitioners in improving the development processes of the products and services on software platforms. Regarding threats to validity, to minimize the researchers' bias, when there was doubt when executing the selection process, this was discussed between two researchers extensively and the differences were analyzed together by a third researcher until there was a consensus. We also recognize that if the snowballing technique had been used, other studies could have been selected.

The main takeaway message of this paper is to present a set of DX factors as a reference guide to support researchers and practitioners in improving the development processes of the products and services on software platforms. For future work, we suggest conducting a field study to understand how specific DX factors in software platforms of SECO can positively or negatively affect the business perspective of keystones and what strategies should be adopted.

Acknowledgments. This work was financed in part by the Coordenação de Aperfeiçoamento de Pessoal de Nível Superior - Brazil (CAPES) - Finance Code 001 and Grant 88887.928989/2023-00, CNPq (Grant 316510/2023-8), FAPERJ (Grant E-26/204.404/2024), and UNIRIO.

References

1. Fagerholm, F., Münch, J.: Developer experience: concept and definition. In: 2012 International Conference on Software and System Process (ICSSP), pp. 73–77 (2012)
2. Fontão, A., Cleger-Tamayo, S., Wiese, I., Pereira dos Santos, R., Claudio Dias-Neto, A.: A developer relations (DevRel) model to govern developers in software ecosystems. J. Softw. Evol. Process e2389 (2021)
3. Fontão, A., Dias-Neto, A., Viana, D.: Investigating factors that influence developers' experience in mobile software ecosystems. In: 2017 IEEE/ACM Joint 5th International Workshop on Software Engineering for Systems-of-Systems and 11th Workshop on Distributed Software Development, Software Ecosystems and Systems-of-Systems (JSOS), pp. 55–58 (2017)
4. Greiler, M., Storey, M.A., Noda, A.: An actionable framework for understanding and improving developer experience. IEEE Trans. Softw. Eng. 1 (2022)
5. Jansen, S.: A focus area maturity model for software ecosystem governance. Inf. Softw. Technol. **118**, 106219 (2020)
6. Nylund, A.: A multivocal literature review on developer experience. Master's thesis, Aalto University. School of Science (2020)
7. Petersen, K., Vakkalanka, S., Kuzniarz, L.: Guidelines for conducting systematic mapping studies in software engineering: an update. Inf. Softw. Technol. **64**, 1–18 (2015)
8. Steglich, C., et al.: Factors that affect developers' decision to participate in a mobile software ecosystem. J. Syst. Softw. **205**, 111808 (2023)

Enabling Inter-organizational Data Sharing: Towards a Method for Assessing Data Assets

Maximilian Werling[1]($\boxtimes$), Kim Stuber[2], Dimitri Petrik[2], Jens Lachenmaier[1], and Georg Herzwurm[2]

[1] Ferdinand Steinbeis Institute, Filderhauptstr. 142, 70599 Stuttgart, Germany
`{maximilian.werling,`
`jens.lachenmaier}@ferdinand-steinbeis-institut.de`
[2] Graduate School of Excellence Advanced Manufacturing Engineering (GSaME), Nobelstraße 12, 70569 Stuttgart, Germany
`{kim.stuber,dimitri.petrik,`
`georg.herzwurm}@gsame.uni-stuttgart.de`

Abstract. As companies increasingly develop data products and follow data-driven strategies for competitive advantage, the decisions about sharing data become important. In practice, however, organizations are hesitant to participate in data sharing. To address this problem, this paper presents a taxonomy to characterize data assets and improve structured assessment of data assets for decisions on inter-organizational data sharing. The aim of the taxonomy is to aid organizations engaged in data spaces or data ecosystems in making informed decisions whether to share data assets and under what terms, based on their value, possible risks and the resulting criticality associated with sharing. To develop the taxonomy, we conducted a multivocal literature review, synthesizing scientific literature related to data sharing, descriptions of data assets used in real-world use cases, and shared in data space initiatives. The taxonomy structures data key dimensions and characteristics important for understanding business value and risks associated with data sharing. The taxonomy is an initial result of a method for data assessment, and lays groundwork for future theorizing on inter-organizational sharing of sensitive data assets.

Keywords: Data Sharing · Data Assessment · Taxonomy · Data Assets · Data Spaces

1 Introduction

The increasing operation of smart products, which can generate vast amounts of data, impacts the way companies create value [1]. This development allows companies to analyze data to improve, accelerate, or automate decisions, creating opportunities for internal efficiency gains, new services, or business models [2]. However, data-driven value cannot be fully embraced when organizations do not sufficiently participate in the data economy, which requires them to engage in sharing data with other parties

E. Papatheocharous et al. (Eds.): ICSOB 2024, LNBIP 539, pp. 89–96, 2025.
https://doi.org/10.1007/978-3-031-85849-9_8

[3]. This is referred to as inter-organizational data sharing, which is defined as the domain-independent process of organizations giving third-parties access to their data assets [4]. While the concept of data sharing is not new, recent research acknowledges the emergence of new institutionalized approaches, such as data marketplaces [5], data platforms [6] and data spaces [7]. In practice, however, there is considerable reluctance to share data. Companies keep their data assets closed to third parties, even though they recognize the potential of sharing data assets. Despite the progress made, and the emergence of a new sharing-oriented narrative in academia, the increase of inter-organizational data sharing has been slow in practice [8], as organizations, for instance, consider data as a strategic asset and these are worth protecting [9]. Reflecting on this paradox, we argue that a sufficient foundation for decision-making whether to provide third parties access to data assets or not is still lacking. This claim is supported by the existing literature, which indicates a certain complexity in determining the suitability of data assets for sharing and the associated risks [8, 10, 11]. To address this problem, our ongoing research intends to develop a method for characterizing data assets to support informed decision-making about the potentials and risks associated with the sharing of data assets. With the present paper, we perform a morphological analysis of data assets. from the perspective of data-sharing companies and data trustees to answer the question: *What dimensions and characteristics are suitable to assess criticality of data assets and their suitability for data sharing?*

2 Background and Related Work

When organizations have data that has certain value and can be capitalized by sharing it with other organizations, it fits the notion of data assets. Data assets are defined as *"data resources that are owned or controlled by an enterprise and have real or potential value, comply with data laws and are recorded electronically."* [12]. However, data assets may incorporate sensitive data and sharing them can lead to risks, resulting in uncertainty about whether to share at all [11]. Considering this problem, the concept of data sovereignty was established. It is considered an important prerequisite for sharing data across organizations [13], and *"refers to the self-determination of individuals and organizations with regard to the use of their data"* [7]. Data sovereignty means retaining control and autonomy over digital infrastructure, technologies, data, and digital content, which could positively influence data sharing considering the existing reservations in practice [13, 14]. By implementing techniques and providing means to enable sovereign data sharing, data spaces are a concept that enables data sharing in practice. Data spaces (e.g., Catena-X for the automotive supply chain or the Mobility Data Space for the mobility domain) aim to create a trustworthy environment to facilitate data sharing between data consumers and data providers. Data spaces provide means for actors to share data assets in a sovereign way, as well as engage in matchmaking between data providers and data consumers [7].

However, companies engaged in data spaces still shy away from the risk of making wrong decisions related to sharing data assets [8]. This phenomenon stems from the fact that the realization of data-driven added value often requires the sharing of data perceived as sensitive. For example, the precise calculation of a CO_2 footprint for a product, which is produced throughout a supply chain, requires data on machine utilization, material data, supplier data, and others. Such data is often considered critical to competitive advantage as it may contain intellectual property or sensitive contract terms. This data is worth protecting and may bear competitive risks when shared with other companies. Therefore, sharing of data assets requires careful decision-making to anticipate the added value in order to correctly estimate the price of the data asset on the one hand and to weigh up the risks of sharing. To make informed decisions on sharing data assets, further instruments are needed to help data consumers and providers better understand and characterize data assets.

3 Taxonomy Development

To develop and evaluate our taxonomy, we use the iterative method described by [15] and [16]. This approach is appropriate to our research goals, as it allows the integration of scientific literature and empirical sources. The taxonomy aims to support the systematic assessments of data assets to enable informed decisions of roles involved in data sharing and is developed iteratively. We defined five subjective and eight objective ending conditions and checked whether the taxonomy met these conditions after each iteration. As a start, we conducted a multivocal literature review (MLR) to collect and synthesize scientific papers as well as examples from practice relevant to data sharing, existing data space initiatives and data-driven use cases [17]. An MLR enabled us to follow a conceptual-to-empirical (C2E) approach by analyzing scientific papers and an empirical-to-conceptual (E2C) approach by analyzing practical initiatives relevant to deriving (meta-) dimensions and the characteristics for assessing data assets. Detailed information on the ending conditions, the literature and use case review as well as the resulting samples can be found in an online appendix: https://bit.ly/49ZEmTt.

In total, we performed four iterations to come up with the proposed taxonomy. In the first iteration, we followed the C2E approach by analyzing existing taxonomies and classifications found scientific literature. The literature sample led to the inductive definition of the meta-dimensions *data, pricing, access, value creation,* and *service domain* to structure our dimensions and characteristics that were derived from the scientific literature and the data space websites. In the second iteration, we followed the C2E approach again to improve the taxonomy through existing literature. In the third iteration, we followed the E2C approach by focusing on existing real-world data-sharing use cases and data initiatives. In the final iteration, we followed the E2C approach, evaluating the taxonomy with additional use case documentations from our sample an additional 20 use cases from our sample. In this iteration, no changes were made, indicating the robustness and completeness of the taxonomy. All the objective ending criteria have been satisfied, and the authors have discussed the subjective ending criteria.

4 Results

The proposed taxonomy, illustrated in Fig. 1, consists of 5 meta-dimensions, 19 dimensions, and the corresponding characteristics relevant for data assessment by data-sharing actors (i.e., data providers and data consumers). The column "E/N" indicates whether the characteristics of a dimension are mutually exclusive ("E") or not ("N"). The column "role" signifies whether a dimension is relevant to data providers, data consumers or both roles.

Meta-dimension data asset: The first meta-dimension, *data asset*, is concerned with describing the different qualities of a data asset. Its dimensions are used to characterize basic properties of a data asset. The meta-dimension comprises the dimensions of *type, timeframe, privacy level, focal point, structure, compliance, and creation.* Data consumers can use the dimensions to specify data requirements for their service or data product. Data providers, on the other hand, can use the dimensions to characterize their data assets and assess their suitability for data sharing. If deemed suitable, the characterization also serves as a description of the data supply. Having descriptions of data demands and supplies using the same characteristics, may enable data trustees to provide a better matching functionality to better facilitate data exchange between data consumers and providers.

Meta-dimension	Role	Dimension	Characteristics				E/N
Data Asset	Data consumer Data provider	Type	Measured	Aggregated		Transactional	N
		Timeframe	Past	Current		Future	N
		Privacy level	Raw	Pseudonymized		Anonymized	N
		Focal point	Object	Process		Person	N
		Structure	Structured	Semi-structured		Unstructured	N
		Compliance	Generic	Specific		No	E
		Creation	Event-driven	Frequent		Occasionally	N
(Preferred) Pricing	Data consumer Data provider	Payment model	Free	One-time payment		Subscription	E
		Price Discovery	Fixed price	Auction		Negotiation	N
		Compensation	Money	Digital assets		Data assets	N
(Preferred) Data Exchange	Data consumer Data provider	Format	Open			Proprietary	E
		Interface	File-based	Standardized API		Proprietary Interface	E
		Delivery	Batch			Stream	E
Value creation	Data consumer	Service delivery	Downloadable application	Web-based Application		Specialized service API	N
		Main value	Monitoring	Quality Control	Predictive Operations	Other	N
		Main outcome	Efficiency gains	Improved quality	New offerings	Other	N
Data product	Data consumer	Spatial	Local	Regional		Global	E
		Temporal	Static			Dynamic	E
		Domain	Domain-specific			Cross-domain	E

Fig. 1. Taxonomy for data assessment by data sharing participants

Data assets can provide a whole range of different types of data. *Measured* data refers to data from smart assets, sensors or other types of data often produced by smart objects. *Aggregated* data refers to data that has already been processed (e.g., consisting of calculated or aggregated values). Transactional data refers to data typically found in traditional information systems, such as customer or product data. The three characteristics are non-exclusive, since the line between the type of data cannot always be drawn precisely. Data may cover different *timeframes*. The three non-exclusive characteristics distinguish between data that is describing the *past* (e.g., time-series data of past events), the *present* (e.g., current status-related data of a smart object), or the *future* (e.g., simulations or predictions of events). The privacy level refers to the identifying properties that me be contained within a data asset. They can either be *raw* (identifying properties are part of the data asset), *pseudonymized* (identifying properties would be obfuscated using methods of pseudonymization) or *anonymized*, eliminating identifying properties. The *focal point* refers to the main context from which this data originates. The focal point of a data asset may be an *object* (e.g., a smart object producing status-related data), a *process* (e.g., a manufacturing process) or a *person*. Data can exhibit varying degrees of *structure*, ranging from *structured data* (e.g., data from relational database), semi-structured data (e.g., documents, NoSQL databases), to *unstructured* data (e.g., video feeds). Data may be *compliant* to various standards, frameworks, or reference architectures. The three mutually exclusive characteristics are *generic* (for compliance with generic frameworks such as Gaia-X), *specific* (compliance with domain-specific frameworks or standards), or *none*, meaning no compliance with standards. The interval at which new data is created is referred to as *creation*. Data can be created *frequently*, *infrequently* (or occasionally), or based on things happening (*event-driven*).

Meta-dimension (preferred) pricing: The sharing of data may involve compensation. Data providers and consumers often hold different views on the optimal price for a data asset. To facilitate an agreement, the meta-dimension encompasses the three dimensions of *payment model*, *price discovery*, and *compensation*, which are pertinent to both data consumers and data providers. Data providers can use these characteristics to describe their conditions or preferences when it comes to the compensation for providing the data access. Data consumers may use these characteristics as a marker for their preferred way of compensation for data assets they want to consume. By affording both roles the opportunity to assess their preferred pricing mechanisms, the matching between provider and consumer can be enhanced.

There are various payment methods that may be employed when sharing data. Data may be shared for *free*, with no compensation, in exchange for a *one-time payment*, or a *subscription* (e.g., a fixed subscription or volume-based pricing). A price may be set as a *fixed price* (e.g., set by the seller, the buyer, or a third party), or discovered through an *auction* or *negotiation*. *Compensation* for data assets may not be limited to *monetary* assets; digital assets (e.g., like crypto currency) or data itself can also serve as payment.

Meta-dimension (preferred) data exchange: Data can be exchanged in different ways. The meta-dimension comprises several dimensions that are used to describe the circumstances under which the data asset is exchanged. As with the pricing meta-dimension, data providers may use characteristics of the dimension to describe the general conditions under which the data exchange can take place. Data consumers can describe their preferred way of consuming data. In contrast to the conditions of payment, technical requirements often exert a significant influence on the framework conditions for the exchange of data. These requirements may relate to the systems or objects used, or the interfaces chosen.

All data is subject to a *format*. These formats may be *open* (e.g., based on open standards, such as JSON or XML), or *proprietary* (e.g., some computer-aided design [CAD] file formats). Furthermore, there are numerous methods for interfacing with data assets. They may be accessed in the form of a downloadable file, through a *standardized* application programming interface (API) (e.g., a REST API), or a *proprietary interface* (e.g., CAD data exchange). Data may be delivered either as a *batch* (e.g., one or more discrete transactions of data) or as a *stream* of data (e.g., a continuous stream of data).

Meta-dimension value creation: The meta-dimension value creation encompasses three non-mutually exclusive dimensions: *service delivery, main value,* and *main outcome.* The meta-dimension is concerned with the description of the intended value-creation processes, on shared data assets. Data consumers may use the characteristics of the dimension to describe their intended way of using the data. These intentions should be made known to potential data providers, as this will allow them to better understand the value of their data assets regarding the intended use. *Service delivery* provides several characteristics to describe the method of delivery, including as a *downloadable application, web-based applications,* and *special interfaces,* such as dedicated service APIs or embedded services. The *main value* of a data-driven service can be *monitoring, quality control, prescriptive operations,* or some combination of these (*other*). The *main outcome* of the service may be *efficiency gains, improved product or process quality,* or entirely *new data-based offerings.*

Meta-dimension data product: This meta-dimension is aimed at data consumers to provide even more context for their intended service or data product and consists of three mutually exclusive dimensions: *spatial, temporal,* and *domain.* Providing context about the intended scope of the data product gives potential data providers a better foundation for their decision to share a data asset or not (e.g., if it threatens their competitive position). Despite the digital nature of the data products, the geographical scope or access to the service can be either *local, regional,* or *global.* The temporal dimension describes the timeliness of the data product, which can be either *static* (e.g., providing a report) or *dynamic* (e.g., providing an interactive application). Finally, the data product may be *domain-specific* (e.g., health-related) or *cross-domain* (e.g., a service that combines mobility and energy-related data, crossing traditional domain boundaries).

5 Conclusion and Outlook

This paper presents the first results of an ongoing research project to develop a method, to assist organizations in assessing the criticality of data asset and to reduce the resulting complexity on whether a data asset can be shared (i.e., for profit), requires certain treatment for sharing, or should not be shared at all. The proposed taxonomy is suitable for decomposing the complex construct of data assessment, by helping to assign individual characteristics for data assets, before they are shared. Therefore, as part of the intended method, and an intermediary artifact, the taxonomy supports informed decisions about data sharing from both perspectives of a transaction - the supply and the demand perspectives on data assets; since they evaluate data assets for different purposes (i.e., sale or search for your own data product). Since data assets should be carefully assessed before sharing, we consider the proposed taxonomy as a relevant addition to existing taxonomies [18–20] and current data sharing practices [10].

This study is subject to some noteworthy limitations that necessitate additional research. Foremost, the proposed taxonomy requires empirical evaluation. Accordingly, the next steps planned by the researchers comprise evaluative interviews and focus groups with data-sharing experts. Nevertheless, to increase the generalizability of our results, we encourage other researchers to validate the taxonomy in other domains with emerging data spaces, such as mobility or health [21]. Furthermore, each data assessment is an essential part of a unique decision regarding data sharing, raising some uncertainty about the final role of the proposed taxonomy. Therefore, during future development, we plan to develop and validate a holistic assessment method that follows the principles of method engineering [22]. In our future research, the taxonomy represents the first step towards a method to help data providers and data consumers in determining the value and the criticality of the data assets prior to sharing.

Acknowledgements. The project on which this report is based was funded by the Federal Ministry of Education and Research of the Federal Republic of Germany under grant number 16DTM238A. The responsibility for the content of this publication lies with the authors.

References

1. Lee, J.Y.H., Hsu, C., Silva, L.: What lies beneath: unraveling the generative mechanisms of smart technology and service design. JAIS **21**, 1621–1643 (2020)
2. Hunke, F., Thomsen, H., Satzger, G.: Investigating modular reuse as an underlying mechanism of conceptualization during service design: the case of key activity orchestration. In: Association for Information Systems (AIS) (ed.) Proceedings of the 54th Hawaii International Conference on System Sciences (2021)
3. Sestino, A., Kahlawi, A., Mauro, A. de: Decoding the data economy. a literature review of its impact on business, society and digital transformation. Eur. J. Innov. Manag. (2023)
4. Jussen, I., Schweihoff, J., Dahms, V., Möller, F., Otto, B.: Data sharing fundamentals: characteristics and definition. In: Bui, T. (ed.) Proceedings of the 56th Hawaii International Conference on System Sciences (2023)
5. Spiekermann, M.: Data marketplaces: trends and monetisation of data goods. Intereconomics **54**, 208–216 (2019)
6. de Reuver, M., Ofe, H., Agahari, W., Abbas, A.E., Zuiderwijk, A.: The openness of data platforms. a research agenda. In: Laoutaris, N. (ed.) Proceedings of the 1st International Workshop on Data Economy. ACM Digital Library, pp. 34–41. Association for Computing Machinery, New York, NY ,United States (2022)
7. Jarke, M., Otto, B., Ram, S.: Data sovereignty and data space ecosystems. Bus. Inf. Syst. Eng. **61**, 549–550 (2019)
8. Brechtel, M., Petrik, D., Hölzle, K.: From challenges to solution pathways for industrial data ecosystems: a socio-technical perspective. In: Association for Information Systems (AIS) (ed.) Wirtschaftsinformatik 2023 Proceedings (2023)
9. Fassnacht, M., Benz, C., Heinz, D., Leimstoll, J., Satzger, G.: Barriers to data sharing among private sector organizations. In: Bui, T. (ed.) Proceedings of the 56th Hawaii International Conference on System Sciences (2023)
10. Fassnacht, M., Benz, C., Bode, J., Heinz, D., Satzger, G.: Systematizing data sharing practices: a taxonomy. In: Association for Information Systems (AIS) (ed.) Proceedings of the 32nd European Conference on Information Systems (ECIS) (2024)
11. Cutolo, D., Kenney, M.: Platform-dependent entrepreneurs: power asymmetries, risks, and strategies in the platform economy. AMP **35**, 584–605 (2021)
12. Xu, T., Shi, H., Shi, Y., You, J.: From data to data asset. conceptual evolution and strategic imperatives in the digital economy era. APJIE **18**, 2–20 (2024)

13. Abbas, A.E., van Velzen, T., Ofe, H., van de Kaa, G., Zuiderwijk, A., de Reuver, M.: Beyond control over data. Conceptualizing data sovereignty from a social contract perspective. Electron. Markets **34**, 1–21 (2024)
14. von Scherenberg, F., Hellmeier, M., Otto, B.: Data sovereignty in information systems. Electron. Markets **34**, 1–11 (2024)
15. Nickerson, R.C., Varshney, U., Muntermann, J.: A method for taxonomy development and its application in information systems. Eur. J. Inf. Syst. **22**, 336–359 (2013)
16. Kundisch, D., et al.: An Update for taxonomy designers: methodological guidance from information systems research. Bus. Inf. Syst. Eng., 421–439 (2021)
17. Garousi, V., Felderer, M., Mäntylä, M.V.: Guidelines for including grey literature and conducting multivocal literature reviews in software engineering. Inf. Softw. Technol. **106**, 101–121 (2019)
18. Gelhaar, J., Groß, T., Otto, B.: A taxonomy for data ecosystems. In: Association for Information Systems (AIS) (ed.) Proceedings of the 54th Hawaii International Conference on System Sciences (2021)
19. Gelhaar, J., Groß, T., Otto, B.: Towards a taxonomy of incentive mechanisms for data sharing in data ecosystems. In: Association for Information Systems (AIS) (ed.) Proceedings of the 54th Hawaii International Conference on System Sciences (2021)
20. Gieß, A., Möller, F., Schoormann, T., Otto, B.: Design options for data spaces. In: Association for Information Systems (AIS) (ed.) Proceedings of the 31st European Conference on Information Systems (ECIS) (2023)
21. Nienstedt, J., Schulze, L., Trenz, M.: Interorganizational data sharing in health ecosystems. A case study. In: Association for Information Systems (AIS) (ed.) Proceedings of the 31st European Conference on Information Systems (ECIS) (2023)
22. Brinkkemper, S.: Method engineering. engineering of information systems development methods and tools. Inf. Softw. Technol. **38**, 275–280 (1996)

Transparency and Trust in AI

Fairness in AI Systems Development: Beyond EU AI Act Compliance

Salla Westerstrand$^{(\boxtimes)}$ (iD)

University of Turku, Turku, Finland
`salla.k.westerstrand@utu.fi`

Abstract. Rapid popularisation of Artificial Intelligence (AI) has accelerated initiatives for ethical AI development. In the European Union (EU), the Artificial Intelligence Act (AIA) entered into force on the 1st of August 2024, which has steered the focus in many organisations towards compliance. As the AIA is not an ethics guideline, it is reasonable to assume that measures beyond compliance are required for ethical AI systems development. To help unravel what is already covered by the AIA and what not, this paper studies the premise the AIA lays out for ethical AI systems development. Drawing from critical theory and using John Rawls's theory of justice, the paper shows how the Act provides limited support for basic liberties, equality of opportunity and the least advantaged members of society, which calls for attention concerning ethical reflection in the AI system lifecycle to ensure ethically sustainable AI development. Recommendations are given on what kinds of ethical considerations organisations should include in Agile AI development process to steer the development towards justice as fairness.

Keywords: Ethical AI development · John Rawls · Fair software business

1 Introduction

The rapid popularisation of Artificial Intelligence (AI) systems has provoked AI companies to explore new governance mechanisms for AI system lifecycle. In the European Union (EU), European Commission gave a proposal for a regulation of the European Parliament and of the Council Laying Down Harmonised Rules on Artificial Intelligence (Artificial Intelligence Act, hereinafter, AIA) In April 2021. After political debate and several rounds of negotiations, it entered into force on the 1st of August 2024.

For businesses developing AI systems, law is often the first normative framework with which they seek compliance. Perhaps unsurprisingly, compliance has been identified as one of the key dimensions of organisational AI governance [1]. What we do not yet understand is *how far* compliance takes us with *ethical* AI development. We could ask: is it justified to develop a software product for active surveillance in public spaces and hence limit human freedom to protect citizens' physical safety against a terrorist attack [2, 3]? Can it be acceptable to develop AI for recruitment and thus find better fitting workplaces for most people more efficiently, even if that means a higher risk for systematic discrimination of minorities [4]? Both are scenarios regulated by the AIA, as it

E. Papatheocharous et al. (Eds.): ICSOB 2024, LNBIP 539, pp. 99–113, 2025.
https://doi.org/10.1007/978-3-031-85849-9_9

includes prohibitions of AI-powered mass surveillance and deems AI used in recruitment high-risk, hence subject to detailed requirements. However, as legal compliance is not a guarantee of being ethical, software businesses need to figure out the extent to which AIA compliance fosters societally and ethically sustainable AI development practices.

This paper seeks understanding of the extent to which the AIA covers questions in ethics, which offers businesses developing AI systems a better understanding of what can be achieved by AIA compliance and what needs to be addressed with other governance measures during the AI development lifecycle. It thus contributes to the research traditions of ethical systems development [5–7], AI ethics [8] and organisational AI governance [1]. It helps researchers and practitioners to start exploring practical methods and solutions for integrating ethics into software development practices.

The paper seeks response to the following research question: *What kind of premise does the EU AI Act lay out for ethical AI development?* The question is approached from the perspective of critical theory and an analysis of the AIA using a combination of critical discourse studies and political discourse analysis, which allows for a rigorous qualitative analysis of the AIA and enables academically justified critique and recommendations on how to steer AI development to a more ethical direction. To ensure the analysis is philosophically robust, the AIA is studied using John Rawls's theory of justice as fairness. The findings indeed demonstrate a lack of alignment with Rawls's principles, which is why considerations are then proposed to be included in Agile software development practices.

In what follows, I start by exploring the background of ethical AI governance and the potential for ethics to inform AI systems development. Next, the methodological approach for analysing the AIA is explained. I then walk through the empirical analysis of the AIA in light of Rawls's theory of justice and end up with conclusions and discussion about the next steps towards ethical AI development.

2 Background: Ethics in Governing AI Systems Development

2.1 Ethics in AI Systems Development

In recent years, several frameworks have been suggested to govern AI systems development towards ethical direction [1, 9]. Simultaneously, the discussion around the ethics of AI has intensified, leading to several guidelines, recommendations and ethics principles [10–12] and models for operationalising the principles in AI development processes [13–15]. Both AI ethics and governance have a similar goal: to steer the AI systems development to a more ethical direction. Yet, there seems to be a divide between the two fields, which risks slowing down the development of measures and their implementation into software development processes.

One of the issues this gap brings forth is a risk of losing sight of ethics in AI development practise. This originates from two main sources. First, there is a tendency of AI ethics to focus overmuch on principles [16, 17], which risks losing its potential to actively direct AI towards ethical outcomes [18–20]. Considering that ethics is mainly an active process of reasoning, principles should not be the end of ethics but one tool in the process. Second, despite the long tradition of researchers in addressing ethical questions in information systems and software development [5–7, 21, 22], AI governance has primarily adopted the principled approach of ethics into their frameworks (see, e.g., [1, 9]). Whereas principles can be one useful tool for ethical AI development [23], if these principles lack ethical justifications and definitions, we oversimplify ethics [10]. This is further emphasised by the narrative around operationalisation (e.g., [13]), in which implementing ethics focuses on putting principle into action. Considering that these principles often lack ethical justifications [10], using them as a basis for practical governance can hardly be seen as operationalising *ethics* [18].

Meanwhile, practitioners developing AI systems for the European market are seeking solutions from AI governance to get prepared for the obligations of the recently adopted AIA. Unlike ethics guidelines or governance frameworks, the AIA is legally binding, giving an incentive for businesses to focus their efforts on compliance. This focus risks drifting the attention in AI development ever further from moral justifications: Why and by whom were these requirements decided and how were they justified? Which interests guided the drafting of the AIA? Lastly, what remains for the software businesses to do after compliance if they want to develop AI systems ethically?

As the above discussion indicates that the current AI governance frameworks only offer partial answers to such questions, relying on moral philosophy seems to be a welcome addition. Let us now explore one such perspective to ethical AI development beyond compliance: John Rawls's theory of justice as fairness.

2.2 Justice as Fairness as a Perspective to Ethical AI

In the realm of moral philosophy, we are positioned in the layer of applied ethics, which applies normative ethics theories to solve ethical dilemmas in real-life situations (see, e.g., [24] for a categorisation of ethics in information systems research). As the vast number of ethical frameworks forces makes it impossible to cover all theories in one paper, I limit the scope of this analysis to a perspective that has been shown relevant in the context of technology development [25–28], as well as organisational and business studies [29–31]: John Rawls's theory of justice as fairness.

Rawls established his theory mainly in *Theory of Justice* [32] (revised in 1999 [33]) and *Political Liberalism* [34]. He aimed to develop a theory for fair distribution of inequalities in a way that would form the "most appropriate moral basis" for democratic societies [32, p. viii]. He directed his principles of justice to the basic structure of society, which can be seen to encompass all organisations with profound impacts on people's lives and their abilities to act as free and equal beings [35–37] (vs. [38]). In the context of AI, software businesses that are involved in the lifecycle of impactful AI systems can be considered subject to the following principles of justice:

a) *"Each person has an equal right to a fully adequate scheme of equal basic liberties which is compatible with a similar scheme of liberties for all. b) Social and economic inequalities are to satisfy two conditions. First, they must be attached to offices and positions open to all under conditions of fair equality of opportunity; and second, they must be to the greatest benefit of the least advantaged members of society." (Rawls 2005, p. 291).*

In the context of AI systems development, Rawls's theory has been used as a basis for developing morally acceptable algorithms [25, 26, 39]. Yet, attempts in aligning broader business ecosystems with the principles of justice has been little discussed (with one notable exception [37]). In analysing the AIA in the light of Rawls's theory of justice, I thus critically evaluate the extent to which the AIA is aligned with the principles of justice, which would lead to the benefits of AI development being distributed fairly. Doing so, we can gain better understanding of what remains for software businesses to do after AIA compliance, if they wish to develop ethical AI systems.

It must be noted that one ethics perspective never gives a complete picture of ethical questions. It could be justified, for example, to explore the Act using virtue ethics [40], consequentialism [41], or other deontological approaches [42]. However, as fitting all perspectives into one paper is impossible, I have decided to start from the Rawlsian analysis for its emphasis on the role of the basic structure of society, which for Rawls is the subject of justice – the very societal structure that should safeguard a fair distribution of social primary goods (such as rights, liberties, opportunities, income and wealth) [33, p. 54]. When businesses that develop AI systems with profound impact on people's lives take a role in the basic structure, we enter an underdiscussed area of how such AI development is governed. Rather than looking at theories that guide individual moral decisions, we can thus focus on the organisational responsibilities that enable moving towards more ethical software business ecosystems.

3 Methodology

As the choice of methodological approach is less typical for software business research, it is worth a detailed description. The choice of epistemological approach and methods was informed by 1) the need to understand the complex premise of the AIA for ethical AI development, and 2) doing it in a way that enables pronouncing scientifically justified critique and recommendations for action that AI businesses can take in practice. Therefore, this study's methodology draws from critical epistemology, which highlights the pragmatic nature of science and knowledge by aiming at changing the society through challenging existing paradigms and suggesting alternatives [43–46]. Critical theory also takes freedom, autonomy and human emancipation as central concepts [47], which makes it a fitting companion for the theory of justice as fairness that is based on an idea of people as free citizens.

In this paper, the critical stance is built on the principles for critical information systems research of Myers and Klein [48]. The AIA is approached as a discourse, relying on Jürgen Habermas's critical discourse theory e.g., [49]. According to Habermas, discourse that fulfils the validity claims of truth, truthfulness and rightness (normative validity) contributes to communicative action [49, pp. 306–307], which is a prerequisite for ethical action [50]. As the AIA is communicated using language, adopting a critical discourse perspective is justified for studying the premise it gives for ethical AI.

To ensure the analysis is coherently structured and takes into consideration the political nature of the discourse in question, Political Discourse Analysis (PDA) introduced by Fairclough and Fairclough [51] is used as a method for structuring the analysis as a practical argument. Their approach centres around "the reproduction and contestation of political *power* through political discourse" [51, p. 17]. Accordingly, arguments are shaped by value-driven goals and circumstances of the speaker, which leads to a claim for action. The research process is summarised in Fig. 1.

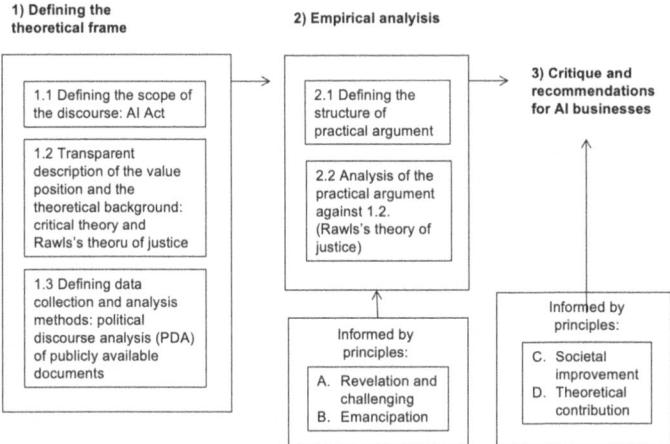

1) Defining the theoretical frame

2) Empirical analyisis

1.1 Defining the scope of the discourse: AI Act

1.2 Transparent description of the value position and the theoretical background: critical theory and Rawls's theoru of justice

1.3 Defining data collection and analysis methods: political discourse analysis (PDA) of publicly available documents

2.1 Defining the structure of practical argument

2.2 Analysis of the practical argument against 1.2. (Rawls's theory of justice)

Informed by principles:

A. Revelation and challenging
B. Emancipation

3) Critique and recommendations for AI businesses

Informed by principles:

C. Societal improvement
D. Theoretical contribution

Fig. 1. The research process described.

The theoretical frame has been defined in the previous Sections. The empirical study (phase 2) was conducted in three rounds of analysis. The first round focused on defining the structure of practical argument (step 2.1 in Fig. 1), and during the second round, the AIA was coded based on the theoretical frame (step 2.2). The third round was used to make connections between the structure of practical argument and the theoretical frame, ensuring rigour of analysis and inclusion of observations potentially missed during the first two rounds. These rounds were informed by principles of challenging the existing paradigm and revealing prevailing power structures and related imbalances. This is followed by phase 3, which revolves around formulating critique and recommendations for software businesses on developing ethical AI systems. This phase was informed by principles of societal improvement and contribution to theory development.

4 EU AI Act in the Light of Justice as Fairness

The analysis comprises the final AIA [52], as well as the four preceding benchmark versions of the proposal [53–56]. Earlier versions were included as I assume that changes between versions provide information about the value basis and the goal setting of the regulatory bodies and other stakeholders. Therefore, relevant changes between versions are included in the discussion below.

4.1 Practical Argument of the EU AI Act

Using the structure of practical argument [51], I have identified the structure leading to the main claim for action. The result of this analysis round is illustrated in Fig. 2.

The value basis and the goals of the AIA are mainly laid out in the explanatory memorandum of the original proposal [53], as well as in the recitals. Accordingly, the AIA is rooted in EU values laid out in the Treaty on the European Union (TEU), Article 2, as well as in the Charter for Fundamental Rights of the European Union (Charter), the

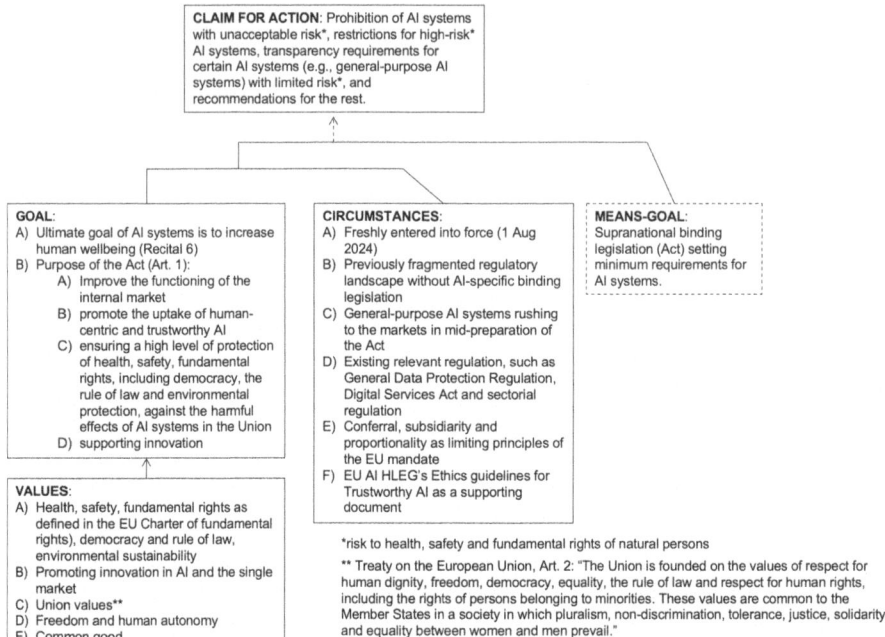

Fig. 2. Practical argument in the EU AI Act: values, goals, circumstances and the means-goal leading to the claim for action.

values being *human dignity, freedom, democracy, equality, rule of law* and *human rights* [57]. In addition, three values are central for evaluating the risk level of an AI system: *health, safety* and *fundamental rights* of natural persons. The European Parliament added emphasis on democracy and environmental sustainability in its amendments, which was partially carried through to the final AIA. The regulation aims to support and protect the European single market, which can be seen as values driving the goal setting of the regulation. From this background, the ultimate goal for the use of AI is to *increase human wellbeing* [52, recital 6]. Therefore, the AIA highlights values found in human rights conventions and puts human wellbeing in the centre of proper use of AI. On the other hand, fostering the single market and innovation and preventing market fragmentation are goals towards stronger economy and accumulation of wealth.

This choice of goals is likely to be influenced by the *circumstances*. Firstly, due to the principles of conferral, subsidiarity and proportionality, the EU can only impose regulations on the Member States according to its legal mandate (conferral), if the proposed goals cannot be achieved via national regulation (subsidiarity), and to an extent necessary considering its goals (proportionality). Secondly, the regulatory process was influenced by AI companies [58]. In addition, the AIA was influenced by the introduction of general-purpose AI systems (GPAIs) to the markets during the regulatory work in the late 2022–early 2023 onwards. The AIA went through several modifications to target the risks posed by GPAIs, such as applications mimicking human language and producing real-like images and video footage. It can also be assumed that some relevant aspects are regulated in other existing regulations indicated in Fig. 2 and non-binding guidance given in the High-Level Expert Group's Ethics Guidelines for Trustworthy AI, and thus not addressed in the AIA.

As a *means-goal*, the EC settled on a binding legislation. Accordingly – unlike in the case of, e.g., directives – it is directly applicable in all EU Member States when it enters into force. As a *claim for action*, the AIA lays out prohibitions for AI systems the risk of which is deemed unacceptable, specific requirements for developers and deployers of AI systems that are high-risk, transparency requirements for certain AI systems, and recommendations for systems with minimal risks. The risks are reflected against health, safety and fundamental rights of natural persons. I will next look at how the AIA and its claim for action relate to Rawls's theory of justice as fairness.

4.2 EU AI Act and Justice as Fairness

Principle 1: Basic Liberties. Let us begin with Rawls's first principle of justice. To be aligned, the AIA should ensure that "[e]ach person has an equal right to a fully adequate scheme of equal basic liberties which is compatible with a similar scheme of liberties for all" [34, p. 291]. Rawls gives a non-exhaustive list of basic liberties that he considers should be protected [34, p. 291]: freedom of thought and liberty of conscience; political liberties and freedom of association (the right to vote and to hold public office); liberty and integrity of the person (incl. Freedom from psychological oppression, physical assault and dismemberment); liberties covered by the rule of law.

Looking at the values and goals, the AIA seems aligned with the first principle, as the liberties are widely covered in the Charter [57]. This is also highlighted by the risk categorisation that is based on the impacts on health, safety and fundamental rights. However, looking at the Articles of the AIA, the measures appear more ambiguous.

Regarding political liberties and freedom of association, all citizens should be equally able to gather political information, assess how decisions influence their lives, and participate in agenda setting and political discussion [33, p. 198], leading to a "fair rivalry for political office and authority" [33, p. 199]. In the AIA, transparency requirements set to systems interacting with natural persons and producing human-like contents [52, Article 50] can be seen as measures to support deliberation based on high-quality, accurate information.

However, whereas the amendments of the European Parliament in 2023 emphasised risks to democracy to accompany those to the health, safety and fundamental rights, this was toned down in the final Act (e.g., Article 9.2(a) [52] vs. 9.2(a) [55]). Moreover, the requirements set for GPAIs are particularly relevant when it comes to ensuring political liberties and freedom of association, as they can have a significant influence on the functioning of democracy when used to influence opinion formation and elections (see, e.g.,[59, 60]). As Rawls notes, political liberties lose value when public debate is controlled by business interest, as it will lead to over-emphasis on property owners' interests in legislative process [33, p. 198]. Critiques have been voiced regarding the heavy lobbying of AI companies in the regulation process [58], which can be seen to have influenced the extent of measures to support political liberties and freedom of association. From the perspective of Rawls's political liberties, such influence is in contradiction with basic political liberties, as it leads to an uneven ground for people to influence decisions concerning their lives.

People's ability to retain agency over decisions that concern them is linked to another dimension of Rawls's basic liberties: freedom and human autonomy. The AIA prohibits AI systems that deploy manipulative or deceptive techniques that cause or "is reasonably likely to cause" significant harm [52, Art. 5.1(a)]. Therefore, although addressing human autonomy in the level of prohibitions can be seen positive in the light of basic liberties, the prohibition is conditional: a system is only prohibited if the (potential) harm *significant*. Hence, the AIA does not prohibit these systems based on their impacts on autonomy itself but based on harms resulting from impaired autonomy, treating autonomy as an instrumental value instead of an intrinsic one – in the AIA, some loss of autonomy is acceptable, even if harm occurs, as long as the harm is not significant.

Principle 2a: Equality of Opportunity. As for Rawls's second principle, ambiguities persist. According to Rawls, necessary inequalities "must be attached to offices and positions open to all under conditions of fair equality of opportunity" [34, p. 291]. In this context, the use of AI should not be used in determining access to offices or positions of privilege and power in a discriminatory manner, nor should it lead to weaker opportunity to seek influence in AI business. The AIA attributes support for Small and Medium-Sized Enterprises (SMEs) and startups (e.g., [52], Art. 62), which supports equality of opportunity in the market. Still, it is not clear whether the measures of the AIA are sufficient to guarantee a level playing field in a way intended by Rawls. As the field of AI development is already mainly dominated by few big tech companies (see, e.g.,[3]), it seems that more than minimum requirements would be necessary to ensure fair equality of opportunity.

In addition, AI systems used in recruitment, promotions and performance evaluation at work, as well as access to and performance evaluation in education and vocational training are categorised as high-risk systems [52, Annex III, 3 and 4], which supports equality of opportunity by mitigating the risk of discrimination in these instances that are essential for people's opportunities to seek advantageous positions. Yet, despite these systems being subject to additional requirements, it remains unclear whether the measures would be sufficient to mitigate systematic biases in algorithms already impacting for example recruitment, as they are rooted in convoluted social structures reflected in redundant encodings [61]. It is worth noting that many of the organisations deploying such systems are private organisations, thus exempt from conducting a fundamental rights impact assessment that could bring to light some of these impacts more efficiently, and thus enable them to be effectively mitigated.

Principle 2b: Difference Principle. Lastly, when it comes to the difference principle, all necessary inequalities should be to the greatest benefit of the least advantaged members of society. The AIA sets requirements that aim to protect the rights of people belonging to vulnerable groups (e.g., Article 6.1(b)), which does aim to assure the condition of the vulnerable groups is not further worsened. Yet, there is no indication that the AIA would direct the *greatest benefits* of AI development to the least advantaged members of society. Instead, the AIA lists measures to support innovation in a way that seeks maximum profits for the providers of the AI systems (e.g., Chapter VI), which includes, for instance, testing high-risk AI systems under development in real-life conditions under regulated circumstances (Art. 60). Following the logic of the (much debated) maximin principle, taking the risk of serious incidents arising from such testing would make the worst-case scenario far worse than it would be if testing in real-life conditions were prohibited. Therefore, there is no indication that AI development would bring most benefit to the least advantaged when compliant with the AIA.

As discussed above, the EU's mandate to legislate is dictated by principles of conferral, proportionality, and subsidiarity. Therefore, the EU only proposed minimum requirements in the scope of its mandate, leaving several areas untouched. Despite some unclarities in the areas of EU's mandate [62, pp. 22–25], EU has generally weaker mandate in areas such as social policy, taxation, employment, environment, freedom, security and justice, and protection and improvement of human health (see TFEU, Articles 3 to 6). It is thus possible that the type of social justice called by the difference principle could be addressed in policy areas outside the EU's exclusive mandate. In addition, several media have reported how the regulators faced particularly heavy lobbying during the negotiations on the AIA from companies developing AI systems [58, 63, 64], which seems to have diverted the emphasis of benefits towards providers of AI systems, rather than people subjected to them. Therefore, additional governance measures would be needed to fulfill the difference principle.

The results of the analysis are summarised in Table 1.

Table 1. Results of the analysis.

Principle of justice	Alignment with the principle
Basic liberties	**Partial alignment**: The goals of the Act are aligned through requirements to follow the EU Charter of fundamental rights and further enforcement for public sector high-risk systems through a requirement for fundamental rights impact assessment (Article 27). However, the enforcement mechanisms notably concerning private sector providers, as well as protection of human autonomy and democratic liberties, are limited
Equality of opportunity	**Partial alignment** through support for SMEs and start-ups and assigning high-risk category to AI systems used in recruitment, promotions, and performance evaluation at work
Difference principle	**Weak alignment**, as only minimal protection of rights is offered to the least advantaged members of society, and considering the minimal requirements to GPAI providers. The main beneficiaries of AI development are indicated to be the businesses and their owners

5 Conclusions and Discussion

The AIA has become a key element for businesses in their efforts to establish governance measures for AI development. Still, we are yet to understand what kind of premise the recently adopted regulation gives for ethical AI development. This study has sought an answer to the following question: *What kind of premise does the EU AI Act lay out for ethical AI development?*

In this paper, I have approached this question using Rawls's theory of justice as fairness as a normative stance. Placing AI businesses with profound impact on people's lives into the basic structure of society attributes them moral responsibility over fair AI development, which in Rawlsian ideal is best achieved by follow his principles of justice. Using critical discourse analysis, I have studied the AIA and the extent to which it is aligned with these principles, which revealed significant gaps that would need to be tackled during AI system lifecycle to end up with fair AI (see Table 1). The results of the analysis indicate an urgent need to integrate ethics into the governance mechanisms of AI businesses throughout the lifecycle of the AI system. It seems that for the society to be aligned with Rawlsian idea of justice as fairness, mere compliance with the AIA is only an initial step towards the right direction.

From the perspective of AI businesses, the enforcement of the protection of basic liberties is especially weak, as they are not required to conduct fundamental rights impact assessment prior to deploying their high-risk AI systems, unless they provide public services. These systems can, however, equally impact basic liberties (e.g., AI systems used in political campaigns or private health care). Addressing the lack in equality of opportunity and the difference principle can also seem particularly challenging for an AI business, as that would require making trade-offs that might occasionally go against profit maximisation. However, can we talk about a well-functioning and a robust system if it is ethically dubious? As institutions belonging to the basic structure of society, it is high time to harness innovation with a broader societal and social impacts in mind. Approaching the process from the perspective of traditional Agile software development approach commonly used in AI projects, I propose including Rawlsian considerations into the development process to steer it towards ethically more sustainable direction. This is illustrated in Fig. 3.

From this background, the next step would be to bring the considerations into daily software development tasks. Whereas some illustrated in Fig. 3 are directly related to software development tasks (e.g., choosing AI models), some of them are broader considerations that go beyond technical problem-solving. Laying out task lists and allocating them to different roles in the developer team would be a useful next step to better facilitate the adoption of the considerations in software development practice. Considering the scope of the present paper, this remains a challenge for future research.

Also, asking questions does not yet count for a governance framework. This framework is not meant to illustrate all layers of governance identified in previous literature [1]. Rather, it is a contribution towards bringing clarity into the type of considerations that should be included in AI development if we wish to steer it to a more ethical direction. It adds to the existing governance models in one essential aspect: it distributes ethical consideration throughout the lifecycle of the AI system, which has shown to be a viable approach in software development contexts [15]. It suggests embedding ethics

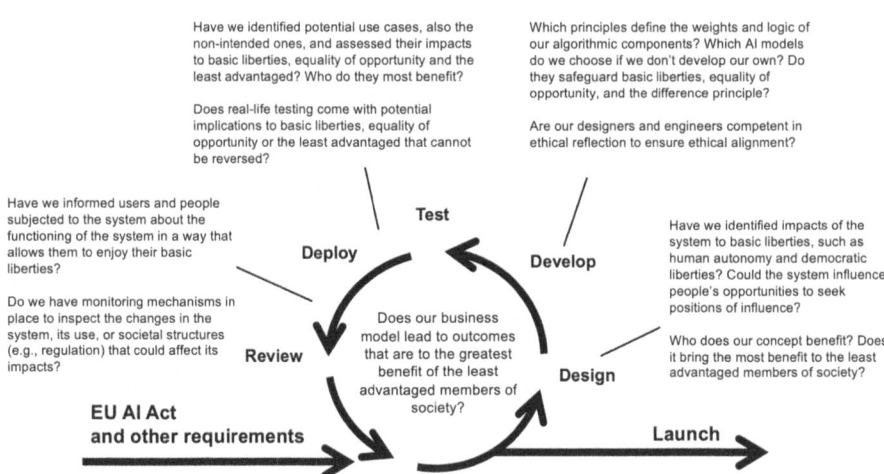

Have we identified potential use cases, also the non-intended ones, and assessed their impacts to basic liberties, equality of opportunity and the least advantaged? Who do they most benefit?

Does real-life testing come with potential implications to basic liberties, equality of opportunity or the least advantaged that cannot be reversed?

Which principles define the weights and logic of our algorithmic components? Which AI models do we choose if we don't develop our own? Do they safeguard basic liberties, equality of opportunity, and the difference principle?

Are our designers and engineers competent in ethical reflection to ensure ethical alignment?

Have we informed users and people subjected to the system about the functioning of the system in a way that allows them to enjoy their basic liberties?

Do we have monitoring mechanisms in place to inspect the changes in the system, its use, or societal structures (e.g., regulation) that could affect its impacts?

Have we identified impacts of the system to basic liberties, such as human autonomy and democratic liberties? Could the system influence people's opportunities to seek positions of influence?

Who does our concept benefit? Does it bring the most benefit to the least advantaged members of society?

Test

Deploy

Develop

Review

Does our business model lead to outcomes that are to the greatest benefit of the least advantaged members of society?

Design

EU AI Act and other requirements

Launch

Fig. 3. Rawlsian considerations in an Agile AI systems development process.

into the mundane processes and practices of AI development in conversation with established normative frameworks, such as regulation. Whereas regulation can be seen as is a top-down normative guidance, ethics is a bottom-up consideration that originates from the organization itself rather than an external source of authority. It plays into harnessing the demonstrated potential ethics can have in AI innovation [65] when it is seen as an active process of reflection followed by action [18–20].

This study is a contribution towards more ethically robust AI development, which I argue is the only possible way towards sustainable value creation with AI development. It demonstrates how principles can serve as a basis for interpreting key ethical concepts into contextual applications, all while calling for bringing them into action. By choosing to root the analysis into ethics principles instead of principles based on political agreement (e.g., human rights, regulation, standards) or a mere opinion, I have resulted in a framework that opens a path towards taking ethically justified actions in AI development process. After all, as Bleher and Braun [18] note, if we do not ground our justifications regarding our choice of principles and how they are applied into rigorous ethical reasoning, the principles and the tools for their operationalisation easily become "either inappropriate, meaningless, or merely an end in themselves" (p. 10).

It is worth noting that in this framework, the accountability to follow the principles of justice is essentially attributed to the organisation developing AI systems due to its role in the basic structure of society. It is therefore not a tool that an organisation can give to its developers and conclude ethical alignment. Instead, enabling ethical reflections and action based on observation still requires establishing governance processes, which is a topic for further research. Similarly, Rawls's theory only offers one (also criticised [66, 67]) perspective to ethical AI development. Hence further analyses from perspectives of other ethics theories could add to the understanding of how we can steer AI development to a more ethical direction. It is also possible that another researcher could have made differing interpretations of the AIA during analysis, which is a factor that needs to be taken into consideration when evaluating the validity of this study. Moreover, focusing on the AIA neglects other technology related regulatory initiatives, as well as those in other regions, such as Northern America and China, which also play a role in global AI software business. We hope that this study encourages others, too, to take on this challenge and contribute to the work on understanding the normative landscape in AI business and designing actions towards ethical AI development.

References

1. Birkstedt, T., Minkkinen, M., Tandon, A., Mäntymäki, M.: AI governance: themes, knowledge gaps and future agendas. Internet Res. **33**(7), 133–167 (2023). https://doi.org/10.1108/INTR-01-2022-0042
2. Almeida, D., Shmarko, K., Lomas, E.: The ethics of facial recognition technologies, surveillance, and accountability in an age of artificial intelligence: a comparative analysis of US, EU, and UK regulatory frameworks. AI Ethics **2**(3), 377–387 (2022). https://doi.org/10.1007/s43681-021-00077-w
3. Zuboff, S.: The Age of Surveillance Capitalism (2019)
4. Hunkenschroer, A.L., Luetge, C.: Ethics of AI-enabled recruiting and selection: a review and research agenda. J. Bus. Ethics **178**(4), 977–1007 (2022). https://doi.org/10.1007/s10551-022-05049-6
5. Mumford, E.: Problems, Knowledge, Solutions: Solving Complex Problems, ICIS Research Papers (1998). https://dl.acm.org/doi/pdf/10.5555/353053.353134
6. Mumford, E.: Redesigning Human Systems. Idea Group Inc (IGI) (2003)
7. Mingers, J., Walsham, G.: Toward ethical information systems: the contribution of discourse ethics. MIS Q. **34**(4), 833–854 (2010). https://doi.org/10.2307/25750707
8. Stahl, B.C.: From computer ethics and the ethics of AI towards an ethics of digital ecosystems. AI Ethics **2**(1), 65–77 (2022). https://doi.org/10.1007/s43681-021-00080-1
9. Mäntymäki, M., Minkkinen, M., Zimmer, M., Birkstedt, T., Viljanen, M.: Designing an AI governance framework: from research-based premises to meta-requirements. ECIS 2023 Research Papers (2023). https://aisel.aisnet.org/ecis2023_rp/295
10. Franzke, A.S.: An exploratory qualitative analysis of AI ethics guidelines. J. Inf. Commun. Ethics Soc. **20**(4), 401–423 (2022). https://doi.org/10.1108/JICES-12-2020-0125
11. Hagendorff, T.: The ethics of AI ethics: an evaluation of guidelines. Mind. Mach. **30**(1), 99–120 (2020). https://doi.org/10.1007/s11023-020-09517-8
12. Jobin, A., Ienca, M., Vayena, E.: The global landscape of AI ethics guidelines. Nat. Mach. Intell. **1**(9) (2019), https://doi.org/10.1038/s42256-019-0088-2
13. Ibáñez, J.C., Olmeda, M.V.: Operationalising AI ethics: how are companies bridging the gap between practice and principles? Exploratory Study. AI & Soc **37**(4), 1663–1687 (2022). https://doi.org/10.1007/s00146-021-01267-0
14. Morley, J., Kinsey, L., Elhalal, A., Garcia, F., Ziosi, M., Floridi, L.: Operationalising AI ethics: barriers, enablers and next steps. AI & Soc. **38**(1), 411–423 (2023). https://doi.org/10.1007/s00146-021-01308-8
15. Vakkuri, V., Kemell, K.-K., Jantunen, M., Halme, E., Abrahamsson, P.: ECCOLA — A method for implementing ethically aligned AI systems. J. Syst. Softw. **182**, 111067 (2021). https://doi.org/10.1016/j.jss.2021.111067
16. Mittelstadt, B.: Principles alone cannot guarantee ethical AI. Nat. Mach. Intell. **1**(11) (2019). https://doi.org/10.1038/s42256-019-0114-4
17. Ryan, M., Stahl, B.C.: Artificial intelligence ethics guidelines for developers and users: clarifying their content and normative implications. J. Inf. Commun. Ethics Soc. **19**(1), 61–86 (2020). https://doi.org/10.1108/JICES-12-2019-0138

18. Bleher, H., Braun, M.: Reflections on putting AI ethics into practice: how three AI ethics approaches conceptualize theory and practice. Sci. Eng. Ethics **29**(3), 21 (2023). https://doi.org/10.1007/s11948-023-00443-3

19. Rességuier, A., Rodrigues, R.: AI ethics should not remain toothless! A call to bring back the teeth of ethics. Big Data Soc. **7**(2), 205395172094254 (2020). https://doi.org/10.1177/2053951720942541

20. Heilinger, J.-C.: The ethics of AI ethics. Constr. Critique. Philos. Technol. **35**(3), 61 (2022). https://doi.org/10.1007/s13347-022-00557-9

21. Hirschheim, R., Klein, H.K., Lyytinen, K.: Information Systems Development and Data Modeling: Conceptual and Philosophical Foundations. Cambridge University Press, Cambridge (1995)

22. Lurie, Y., Mark, S.: Professional ethics of software engineers: an ethical framework. Sci. Eng. Ethics **22**(2), 417–434 (2016). https://doi.org/10.1007/s11948-015-9665-x

23. Seger, E.: In defence of principlism in AI ethics and governance. Philos. Technol. **35**(2), 45 (2022). https://doi.org/10.1007/s13347-022-00538-y

24. Stahl, B.: Morality, ethics, and reflection: a categorization of normative IS research. J. Assoc. Inf. Syst. **13**(8) (2012). https://doi.org/10.17705/1jais.00304

25. Leben, D.: Ethics for Robots: How to Design a Moral Algorithm. Routledge, London (2018). https://doi.org/10.4324/9781315197128

26. Leben, D.: A Rawlsian algorithm for autonomous vehicles. Ethics Inf. Technol. **19**(2), 107–115 (2017). https://doi.org/10.1007/s10676-017-9419-3

27. Keeling, G.: Against Leben's Rawlsian collision algorithm for autonomous vehicles. In: V. C. Müller, (ed.) Philosophy and Theory of Artificial Intelligence, pp. 259–272. Springer, Cham (2018). https://doi.org/10.1007/978-3-319-96448-5_29

28. Douglas, D.M.: Towards a just and fair Internet: applying Rawls' principles of justice to internet regulation. Ethics Inf. Technol. **17**(1), 57–64 (2015). https://doi.org/10.1007/s10676-015-9361-1

29. Wood, D.: Business justice: transactions, resources, and organisations. J. Bus. Ethics **13**(6), 481–4861(994)

30. Cohen, M.A.: The narrow application of rawls in business ethics: a political conception of both stakeholder theory and the morality of markets. J. Bus. Ethics **97**(4), 563–579 (2010). https://doi.org/10.1007/s10551-010-0525-y

31. Fia, M., Sacconi, L.: Justice and corporate governance: new insights from rawlsian social contract and sen's capabilities approach. J. Bus. Ethics **160**(4), 937–960 (2019). https://doi.org/10.1007/s10551-018-3939-6

32. Rawls, J.: A Theory of Justice, Original Harvard University Press, Cambrudge (1971)

33. Rawls, J.: A Theory of Justice, Revised Harvard University Press, Cambridge (1999)

34. Rawls, J.: Political liberalism. Columbia University Press, New York City (2005)

35. Blanc, S., Al-Amoudi, I.: Corporate institutions in a weakened welfare state: a Rawlsian perspective. Bus. Ethics Q. **23**(4), 497–525 (2013). https://doi.org/10.5840/beq201323438

36. Berkey, B.: Rawlsian institutionalism and business ethics: does it matter whether corporations are part of the basic structure of society? Bus. Ethics Q. **31**(2), 179–209 (2021). https://doi.org/10.1017/beq.2020.14

37. Gabriel, I.: Toward a theory of justice for artificial intelligence. Daedalus **151**(2), 218–231 (2022)

38. Singer, A.: There is no Rawlsian theory of corporate governance. Bus. Ethics Q. **25**(1), 65–92 (2015). https://doi.org/10.1017/beq.2015.1

39. Heidari, H., Loi, M., Gummadi, K.P., Krause, A.: A moral framework for understanding fair ml through economic models of equality of opportunity. In Proceedings of the Conference on Fairness, Accountability, and Transparency, in FAT* 2019, pp. 181–190. Association for Computing Machinery, New York (2019). https://doi.org/10.1145/3287560.3287584

40. Bynum, T.W.: Flourishing ethics. Ethics Inf. Technol. **8**(4), 157–173 (2006).https://doi.org/10.1007/s10676-006-9107-1
41. Card, D., Smith, N.A.: On Consequentialism and fairness. Front. Artif. Intell. **3** (2020). https://doi.org/10.3389/frai.2020.00034
42. Aylsworth, T., Castro, C.: Kantian ethics and the attention economy (2024). https://doi.org/10.1007/978-3-031-45638-1
43. Delanty, G., Harris, N.: Critical theory and the question of technology: the Frankfurt school revisited. Thesis Eleven **166**(1), 88–108 (2021). https://doi.org/10.1177/07255136211002055
44. Orlikowski, W.J., Baroudi, J.J.: Studying information technology in organizations: research approaches and assumptions. Inf. Syst. Res. **2**(1), 1–28 (1991). https://doi.org/10.1287/isre.2.1.1
45. Stahl, B.C.: The ethical nature of critical research in information systems. Inf. Syst. J. **18**(2), 137–163 (2008). https://doi.org/10.1111/j.1365-2575.2007.00283.x
46. Waelen, R.: Why AI ethics is a critical theory. Philos. Technol. **35**(1) (2022). https://doi.org/10.1007/s13347-022-00507-5
47. Adorno, T. W., Horkheimer, M.: Dialectic of enlightenment. Verso (1979)
48. Myers, M.D., Klein, H.K.: A set of principles for conducting critical research in information systems. MIS Q. **35**(1), 17–36 (2011). https://doi.org/10.2307/23043487
49. Habermas, J.: The Theory of Communicative Action, Volume 1. Polity Press (1984)
50. Habermas, J.: Between facts and norms. Transl. William Rehg. Oxford: Polity (1996)
51. Fairclough, I., Fairclough, N.: Political Discourse Analysis: A Method for Advanced Students. Routledge, Milton Park (2013)
52. European Union, 'Regulation (EU) 2024/1689 of the European Parliament and of the Council of 13 June 2024 laying down harmonised rules on artificial intelligence and amending Regulations (Artificial Intelligence Act)' (2024)
53. European Commission: 'Proposal for a Regulation of the European Parliament and of the Council laying down harmonised rules on artificial intelligence (Artificial Intelligence Act) and amending certain Union legislative acts (COM/2021/206 final)'. European Commission (2021)
54. Council of the European Union: 'Proposal for a Regulation of the European Parliament and of the Council laying down harmonised rules on artificial intelligence (Artificial Intelligence Act) and amending certain Union legislative acts - General approach (ST 15698 2022 INIT)'. Council of the European Union (2022)
55. European Parliament: 'Amendments adopted by the European Parliament on 14 June 2023 on the proposal for a regulation of the European Parliament and of the Council on laying down harmonised rules on artificial intelligence (Artificial Intelligence Act) and amending certain Union legislative acts (COM(2021)0206 – C9–0146/2021 – 2021/0106(COD))' (2023)
56. European Parliament: 'European Parliament legislative resolution of 13 March 2024 on the proposal for a regulation of the European Parliament and of the Council on laying down harmonised rules on Artificial Intelligence (Artificial Intelligence Act) and amending certain Union Legislative Acts (COM(2021)0206 – C9–0146/2021 – 2021/0106(COD))' (2024)
57. European Union, 'Charter of Fundamental Rights of the European Union'. Official Journal of the European Union C83, 53 (2012)
58. Corporate Europe Observatory: Byte by Byte: How Big Tech undermined the AI Act (20230. https://corporateeurope.org/en/2023/11/byte-byte. Accessed 24 Aug 2024
59. Feezell, J.T., Wagner, J.K., Conroy, M.: Exploring the effects of algorithm-driven news sources on political behavior and polarization. Comput. Hum. Behav. **116**, 106626 (2021). https://doi.org/10.1016/j.chb.2020.106626
60. König, P.D., Wenzelburger, G.: Opportunity for renewal or disruptive force? How artificial intelligence alters democratic politics. Gov. Inf. Q. **37**(3), 101489 (2020). https://doi.org/10.1016/j.giq.2020.101489

61. Hardt, M., Price, E., Price, E., Srebro, N.: Equality of opportunity in supervised learning. In: Advances in Neural Information Processing Systems, Curran Associates, Inc. (2016). https://proceedings.neurips.cc/paper/2016/hash/9d2682367c3935defcb1f9e247a 97c0d-Abstract.html. Accessed 01 May 2023

62. Rosas, A., Armati, L.: EU Constitutional Law: An Introduction. Bloomsbury Publishing, London (2012)

63. Axiotes, C.: Lobbying for loopholes: the battle over foundation models in the EU AI act. https://www.euractiv.com/section/digital/opinion/lobbying-for-loopholes-the-battle-over-foundation-models-in-the-eu-ai-act/. Accessed 24 Aug 2024

64. Perrigo, B.: Exclusive: OpenAI Lobbied E.U. to Water Down AI Regulation. TIME. https://time.com/6288245/openai-eu-lobbying-ai-act/. Accessed 24 Aug 2024

65. Bednar, K., Spiekermann, S.: The power of ethics: uncovering technology risks and positive value potentials in IT innovation planning. Bus. Inf. Syst. Eng. **66**(2), 181–201 (2024). https://doi.org/10.1007/s12599-023-00837-4

66. Sen, A.: The Idea of Justice. Penguin books, London (2009)

67. Anderson, B. C.: The antipolitical philosophy of John Rawls. Public Interest (151), 39–51. https://www.proquest.com/magazines/antipolitical-philosophy-john-rawls/docview/222108464/se-2

The EU AI Act is a Good Start But Falls Short

Chalisa Veesommai Sillberg[1]([✉])([iD]), José Siqueira De Cerqueira[2]([iD]),
Pekka Sillberg[1]([iD]), Kai-Kristian Kemell[1]([iD]), and Pekka Abrahamsson[1]([iD])

[1] Faculty of Information Technology and Communication Sciences,
Tampere University, Pori, Finland
chalisa.sillberg@tuni.fi
[2] Faculty of Information Technology and Communication Sciences,
Tampere University, Tampere, Finland

Abstract. The EU AI Act (EU AIA) was created to ensure ethical and safe Artificial Intelligence development and deployment across the EU. Enterprises will face stringent requirements when complying with the EU AIA, which many organizations currently find confusing. This study aims to identify key challenges and strategy development that organizations face regarding the EU AIA and to help them comply with it. To achieve this aim, we conducted a Multivocal Literature Review (MLR) to explore the sentiments of both the industry and the academia. From 130 articles, 56 met our criteria. We found 199 primary keywords in the literature. The three following concepts were the key ones: liability, discrimination, and a adequacy of tool. Additionally, both industry and academia expressed negative sentiments around regulatory interpretations, specific requirements, and transparency issues. Based on our findings, we highlight three themes for enterprises. First, a risk-based regulatory compliance system, emphasizing the importance of developing systems that ensure adherence to regulatory requirements by focusing on risk management. Second, the need for ethical frameworks and principles in technology development. Third, the importance of policies and systems regulatory risk management. These results highlight key challenges and strategies, while also highlighting less commonly discussed themes, thus enabling enterprises to align their systems with the requirements and better position themselves in relation to the EU market.

Keywords: EU AIA · MLR · Ethical AI for Enterprises · Ethics

1 Introduction

The European Commission launchs the first European Union's (EU) regulatory framework for Artificial Intelligence (AI), namely the EU AI Act (EU AIA), in April 2021 [WL6: *WL/GL* see section Data availability]. The EU AIA aims to regulate AI while preserving innovation and upholding fundamental rights, a challenging balance to achieve. It sets out four specific objectives: 1) to ensure

E. Papatheocharous et al. (Eds.): ICSOB 2024, LNBIP 539, pp. 114–130, 2025.
https://doi.org/10.1007/978-3-031-85849-9_10

that AI systems in the EU market comply with safety laws and respect fundamental rights and Union values; 2) to promote a legal framework that encourages investment and innovation in AI; 3) to improve the effective enforcement of laws related to fundamental rights and safety in AI systems; and 4) to facilitate the development of a single market for safe, legal and trustworthy AI systems, preventing market fragmentation [WL14].

To achieve this goal, the EU AIA proposes a proportionate regulatory approach with the minimum requirements necessary in terms of the risks and potential problems associated with AI. The EU AIA outlines prohibited AI systems, explains the requirements for high-risk AI systems, and provides guidelines to increase transparency while fostering development. Performing a risk classification is the first step toward knowing the risk category and complying with regulatory requirements. The EU AIA categorizes AI systems into four risk levels: 1) unacceptable risk, which includes AI functionalities such as subliminal manipulation, exploitative techniques, biometric categorization, social scoring, real-time remote biometric identification, emotional state assessment, predictive policing, and facial image scraping, all of which are banned in the EU; 2) high risk, which includes AI systems such as those used to assess consumer creditworthiness; and 3) limited risk, which is risk of impersonation or deception such as chatbots, emotion recognition, deep fake; and 4) minimal risk, which includes AI-powered spam filters, video games [3]. In the context of the EU AIA, enterprises, i.e., providers, deployers, importers, distributors, and product manufacturers, are faced with detailed documentation, strategies, and processes related to compliance. These may include various practical, operational, and strategic issues. Therefore, the process and framework should be in the form of practical terms. According to current law, the Secretary of Government Operations is required to create a coordinated plan that looks into the viability and challenges of creating standards and technology that state agencies can use to identify the provenance of digital content by analyzing the effects of the rise in deepfakes, among other things [13].

Since the emergence of the EU AIA, several academic articles have been published to share good practics, such as the challenges posed by AI-driven trading in the EU's financial markets [WL17], the effect on mobility within the EU [GL34], a framework for collaborative governance [WL11], the articulation of ethical charters, legal tools, and technical documentation in Machine Learning (ML) [WL24]. Furthermore, valuable insights may be available not in traditional academic databases but in the media, such as the EU AIA's recommendations for business [GL39], a proposed framework with current developments meant for businesses, a comprehensive regulatory framework for businesses [GL31, GL39], and implications and strategies for UK businesses [GL36], to name but a few. Thus, this work recognises that valuable knowledge and insights can be found in various types of publications and media, not just academic articles [5]. Accordingly, we aim to aid companies in better understanding EU AIA by conducting a secondary research study using a Multivocal Literature Review (MLR) and Natural Language Processing (NLP) to investigate the EU AIA practices.

In this study, we aim to gather a more comprehensive and multifaceted understanding of the EU AIA by considering multiple perspectives, including those from practitioners, industry experts, and other stakeholders. For this reason two research questions (RQs) were formulated for conducting this study: RQ1) *What are the key challenges perceived by both industry and academia in complying with the EU AIA*, and RQ2) *What strategies and processes are enterprises developing to implement the EU AIA*, through MLR and NLP approaches. MLR is a comprehensive literature review approach and systematic process that incorporates various sources of information, namely "Grey Literature" (GL). MLR has become notable in various fields because it is an approach able to 1) integrate both academic and GL, 2) provide a comprehensive overview of a topic with diverse perspectives, and 3) raise the strictness and applicability in the literature review of that field for proving the significance of practical and knowledge [5,7].

This study is structured similarly to the MLR guidelines [5], in terms of 1) planning and surveying the MLR guidelines, 2) conducting the review and data analysis, and 3) presenting the findings or results. The rest of the paper is organized as follows. The content in Sect. 2 describes 1) how to search, select, and stop data sources with criteria, 2) how to control the quality of the data used, and 3) how to analyze the key challenges and identify/underline the strategies. The content in Sect. 3 deals with the key challenges and the strategy themes that will benefit companies in complying with the EU AIA. Section 4 describes and provides a practical framework and its limitations. Finally Sect. 5 concludes the study and suggests future research work.

2   Methodology

This study employs MLR method to examine the EU AIA for businesses, integrating perspectives from both academic literature and GL, which we collectively refer to as MLR. MLR, as a form of systematic literature review (SLR), includes GL sources to capture insights relevant to both researchers and practitioners. This approach allows us to integrate diverse viewpoints, making it particularly suitable for analyzing the compliance and impact landscape within the EU AIA. Our approach to conducting the MLR follows the structured framework outlined by Garousi [5], adapted to ensure the method aligns with our study's objectives.

In this study, a systematic MLR and NLP approach to EU AIA in business was applied in three parts. In the first part, a process for conducting the review and gathering the significant data was established. It also looked outside of academic forums, according to the search process criteria, and made data preparation and formation for determining the relevant data without overlaps and duplicate data, in accordance with the selection criteria and performance of the data selection. In the second part, quality was assessed for determining the satisfactory and free of bias nature of the data source. Lastly, data was analyzed to find the key challenges, and underline the themes of the strategies and processes being developed to implement the EU AIA.

2.1 Search Strategy and Literature Review Protocol

There are several specific data sources related to the EU AIA available in scientific databases. In practice, the vast array of data sources with valuable insights also exists outside the realm of scientific publications, often obtained by practitioners and not discussed or published in the scientific literature. Therefore, an MLR approach to systematic review is beneficial as it incorporates GL.

Search Data Source. Four digital academic research databases-Science-Direct, ACM Digital Library, Google Scholar, and IEEE Xplore-were used to search white literature (WL). ScienceDirect proved useful for accessing both policy and technical perspectives on AI applications across sectors, offering broad coverage of scientific disciplines including AI, ethics, technology policy, and applied research. The ACM Digital Library, specializing in computer science and information technology, particularly covers emerging technologies, data science, and ethical implications. It also emphasizes EU AIA research, especially in areas such as ethics and privacy studies, research on AI in high-risk sectors, and frameworks for compliance. Google Scholar aggregates a wide range of academic articles, reports, conference papers, theses, and more across various disciplines. This platform's diverse sources, including law, ethics, and computer science, are pertinent to the EU AI Act's regulatory aspects. Additionally, Google Scholar offers access to gray literature, making it valuable for both WL and GL searches. In contrast, IEEE Xplore yielded limited results relevant to the EU AIA. Google search engine was utilized for the GL search.

Search Strings. Keyword search is crucial for efficiently locating relevant information by targeting specific terms. Effective keyword searches help filter out irrelevant data, allowing researchers to focus on pertinent literature. To establish relevant keywords, a systematic approach was used: *Basic Keywords:* Initially, direct keywords related to the research topic were identified, including "EU," "AI," "Act," and "business". *Phrase Search:* These basic keywords were then combined into a phrase to derive relevant keyword searches, resulting in the phrase `"EU AI Act" AND "business"`. *Web Search Engine:* The phrase search was employed in a general search engine, specifically Google, which is a conventional tool for web search and GL review studies across many fields.

Pre-selection. To narrow down the vast amount of available data sources, a pre-selection process was applied to enhance the likelihood of finding relevant, high-quality sources. This process aimed to cover all aspects of the research topic comprehensively. Inclusion data (ID) and exclusion data (ED) criteria were defined for selecting data sources and are depicted in Fig. 1.

Stop Search. To ensure a thorough and efficient search, stopping criteria for the GL search were applied in this study, referred to as control stopping criteria. Two criteria were used: effort bounded and bound limitation with a condition. The effort-bounded criterion limited the search to the first 100 search engine hits, with the option to extend if exclusion data (ED) were found among these hits. Additionally, the ratio of relevant results to total search results was monitored. If this ratio fell below 0.5, indicating the bound limitation condition, the search process was terminated [2].

2.2 Quality Assessment for the Literature Review Approach

The quality assessment criteria were reviewed and set to ensure the selected data sources were relevant, unbiased, and of high quality. Some GL quality assessment processes overlap with inclusion/exclusion criteria, add exclusions, and are integrated with study assessments. Garousi's model was selected for its comprehensive approach to evaluating both academic and GL, ensuring a robust assessment of source relevance and quality. Therefore, we used the advanced criteria from Garousi [5] for this purpose, as outlined in Table 1. Then, the dataset of GL data sources was transformed into a CSV format for database creation and quality assessment analysis.

Table 1. Quality assessment criteria of GL for EU AI Act in Business [5]

Criteria	Exclusion Questions (EQ)	Satisfy
1. Authority	1. Is the publishing organization reputable?	3/4
	2. Is the individual author associated with a reputable organization?	
	3. Has the author published other work in the field?	
	4. Does the author have expertise in the area?	
2. Methodology	1. Does the source have a clearly stated aim?	4/6
	2. Does the source have a stated methodology?	
	3. Is the source supported by authoritative, contemporary references?	
	4. Are any limits clearly stated?	
	5. Does the work cover a specific question?	
	6. Does the work refer to a particular population or case?	
3. Objectivity	1. Does the work seem to be balanced in presentation?	4/4
	2. Is the statement in the sources as objective as possible, or is the statement a subjective opinion?	
	3. Is there vested interest, or are the conclusions free of bias?	
	4. Are the conclusions supported by the data?	
4. Date	1. Does the item have a clearly stated date?	1/1
5. Position w.r.t. related source	1. Have key related GL or formal sources been linked to / discussed?	1/1
6. Novelty	1. Does it enrich or add something unique to the research?	2/2
	2. Does it strengthen or refute a current position?	
7. Impact	1. Normalize following impact metrics into a single aggregated value: citations, backlinks, social media shares, comments, view counts	1/1
8. Outlet type	1st tier GL (m = 1) is high outlet control and high credibility	0-1
	2nd tier GL (m = 0.5) is moderate outlet control and credibility	
	3rd tier GL (m = 0) is low outlet control and low credibility	

2.3   Data Analysis Approach

The aim of this approach was to gain a comprehensive understanding of the key challenges and strategies perceived by both industry and academia in complying with the EU AIA. We utilized an approach similar to the one utilized by Bourdin [1]. This approach was conducted using Altair AI Studio software (version 2024.0.1), which combines both qualitative and quantitative, providing an analysis of the research question.

Data Extraction. A summary and key takeaway context of each data source were extracted to provide a broad overview of all essential points. This extraction process was conducted primarily through careful, manual analysis, allowing for a thorough interpretation of each source's content. Following this, Natural Language Processing (NLP) techniques were employed in the data analysis stage to systematically categorize and synthesize the extracted information.

Data Analysis. The NLP algorithm is part of AI and has been created for numerous purposes. It aims to achieve human language understanding, focusing on enabling computers to analyze and interpret text data [9,10]. There are two analysis approaches in this part: the first process analyzes the key challenges by implementing text processing, Term Frequency-Inverse Document Frequency (TF-IDF), and sentiment analysis in the summary context, and the second process identifies and underlines the theme of strategies and processes by applying text processing, TF-IDF, and the Latent Dirichlet Allocation (LDA) model in the key takeaway context. The data analysis process of this study is shown in Fig. 1, and is described as follows:

Text processing implements several operations, such as: 1) token splitting to split text into individual words or tokens; 2) filtering stop-words to remove common words that do not carry significant meaning; 3) stemming to reduce words to their base root form; and 4) transforming cases to convert all text to lowercase. *Text vectorization processing* implements term frequency and the reciprocal document frequency (TF-IDF) operation to convert text into a numerical representation based on TF-IDF. It processes with 2 criteria: 1) how frequently it is used in the text provided (TF) and (2) how rarely it appears across the other documents in the corpus (IDF) [8]. *Sentiment Analysis* is applied to determine the sentiment of the text, which can provide additional insights into the nature of the challenges. *Latent Dirichlet Allocation (LDA)* performs topic modeling and identifies underlying themes or topics in text data by applying an LDA model. The model produces two outputs: the distribution of terms within each topic and the distribution of topics across each document [8]. *Visualization* utilizes 1) word clouds to visualize the most frequent terms or topics, and 2) graphs to represent results for better understanding.

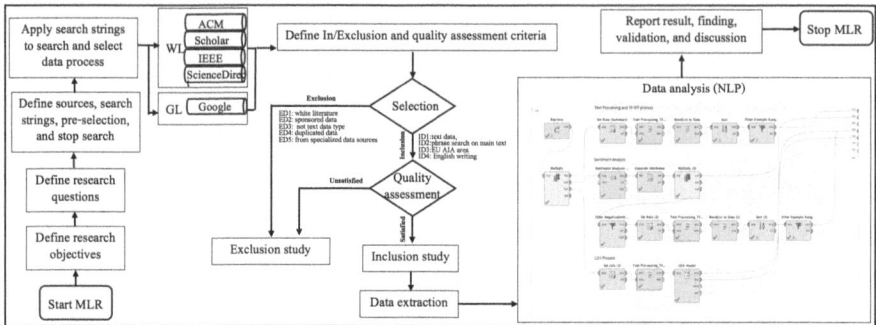

Fig. 1. The system architecture of this study.

3   Results

We report our results in this section, seeking to answer the RQs outlined in Sect. 1. The addition outlet types in this study are updated to the literature type of shades of GL with the same criteria. The results of the selected and satisfied data sources are presented in Subsect. 3.1. Lastly, the results of the analyzed data and validated outcome are presented in Subsect. 3.2.

3.1   MLR Execution, Protocol and Quality Assessment

Data was collected through a phrase search ("EU AI Act" AND "business"), pre-selection, and stopping criteria. A Google search conducted on June 17, 2024, returned approximately 214 million results, with relevant findings extending across 30 pages. After pre-selection and applying stopping criteria, 100 results were found on the first 12 pages. Of these, 26 data sources were excluded based on various criteria of ED (ED1: white literature, ED2: sponsored data, ED3: not text data type, ED4: duplicated data, and ED5: from specialized data sources) and shown as Fig. 2(a).

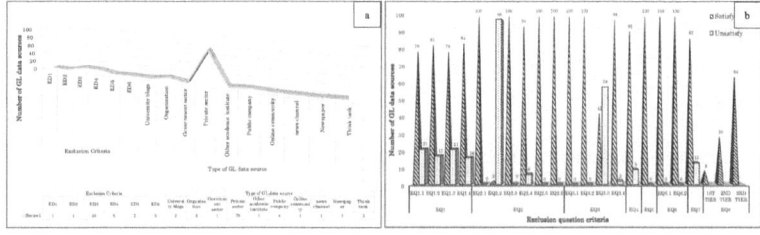

Fig. 2. The results of a) the selected data sources from pre-selection and b) the results of data source quality assessment.

The quality assessment criteria were applied to 100 data sources from the selected results. Based on these criteria, 26 sources were deemed suitable for inclusion as GL in this study. The excluded sources were primarily rejected due to vested interests or bias, lack of reputable authors or relevant expertise, failure to address specific questions, insufficient impact metrics, and outdated information. An example of the quality assessment is shown in Table 2 and Fig. 2(b).

Regarding the quality assessment of authority, all Exclusion Questions (EQs) related to authority were satisfied. In the methodology quality assessment, twenty EQs were examined. All data sources qualified as GL based on five of these questions. However, question 2.2, regarding stated methodologies, was omitted since formal methodologies are not typically used in these articles. Regarding objectivity, 40 sources passed the quality assessment. Specifically: most of the texts provided a balanced view, discussing both challenges, benefits, statements were generally objective, focusing on facts and expert opinions, and conclusions free of bias/vested interest in terms of the EU AIA (EQs 3.1–3.4). Concerning date quality assessment, 91 articles have clearly stated publication dates, ranging from August 2021 to May 2024, as per EQ 4.1. With respect to related sources quality assessment, all articles discuss and are linked to key regulatory frameworks, including the EU AIA, as assessed by EQ 5.1. In the novelty quality assessment, each article offers unique insights or practical advice on EU AIA compliance, enhancing current understanding with detailed explanations and updates, as assessed by EQs 6.1 and 6.2. In the impact quality assessment, EQ 7.1, each article's impact was normalized into a single aggregated metric. Professional networks were assessed via LinkedIn, Wikipedia, and Trustpilot. Backlink counts were determined using Ahrefs, and social media shares were measured using SharedCount.

Some finding outcome types in this study are not listed in the "shades of GL". These were classified by shades of GL criteria by using expertise and outcome control, equivalent to the criteria used. The additional classification outcome types are shown in Table 3.

3.2   Interpreted Insights from the Data Analysis Approach

RQ1: What are the key challenges perceived by both industry and academia in complying with the EU AIA? In this approach, NLP, a text processing TF-IDF method, was implemented. The analysis was conducted on the text dataset, analyzing 199 words. This method was used to identify the most significant terms in the documents by considering both their frequency within individual documents (Term Frequency) and their rarity across all documents (Inverse Document Frequency). Through this approach, three key challenges were identified, i.e., liability, discrimination, and the adequacy of the tool. "Liability" with the highest TF-IDF scores was considered the most challenging and relevant to specific documents (total occurrences: document frequency: 10:2). The insight finding revealed that enterprises need to adapt their compliance and liability management. The second and third challenges are discrimination and tools, i.e., enterprises must manage discrimination risk both for legal compliance

Table 2. Example of the quality assessment for GL data sources for EU AIA in Business

EQ*	GL Source					Note
	A	B	C	D	E	
1.1	1	1	1	1	1	All GL data sources are reputable publishing organizations
1.2	1	1	1	1	1	All GL data sources are published by an individual author
1.3	1	1	1	1	1	All GL data sources have other work published in the field
1.4	1	1	1	1	1	All GL data sources have expertise in the area
2.1	1	1	1	1	1	All GL data sources have a clearly stated aim
2.2	0	0	0	0	0	No GL data source has a stated methodology
2.3	1	1	1	1	1	All GL data sources are supported by authoritative, contemporary references
2.4	1	0	1	1	0	All GL data sources, except B and E, have clearly statedlimits
2.5	1	1	1	1	1	All GL data sources cover a specific question on EU AIA and business
2.6	1	1	1	1	1	All GL data sources refer to a particular population or case in context
3.1	1	1	1	1	1	All GL data sources seem to be balanced in presentation
3.2	1	1	1	1	1	The statements in all five GL data sources are objective and adhere strictly to factual information, avoiding subjective opinions
3.3	1	1	1	1	0	All GL data sources, except E, provide unbiased conclusions with no indication of vested interests. E promotes its compliance services, indicating a vested interest.
3.4	1	1	1	1	1	The conclusions in all GL data sources are supported by the data
4.1	1	1	1	0	0	All GL data sources, expect D and E, have a clearly stated date
5.1	1	1	1	1	1	All GL data sources discuss the EU AI Act thoroughly, referencing specific provisions, expert opinions, and impacts on the tech industry. They include related sources and formal documents, examining implications for businesses, compliance requirements, and regulatory alignment.
6.1	1	1	1	1	1	All GL data sources provide detailed guidance for businesses on EU AIA compliance, with sector-specific insights, particularly for financial services and UK businesses. They offer practical steps for implementing human oversight and improving business competitiveness
6.2	1	1	1	1	1	All GL data sources emphasize the need for comprehensive AI regulations for ethical deployment and proactive compliance strategies for the EU AIA. They highlight balanced regulation to avoid excessive burdens, international alignment, and human oversight to ensure safety and compliance.
7.1	1	1	1	0	1	All GL data sources, except D, provide impact metrics. Two impact metrics are used for analysis, namely number of backlinks and social media shares.
8.1	.5	0	1	0	0	GL data source A is an *Informational Article*, B is an *Informational Blog Post*, C is a *Position Paper*, D is an *Advisory Article*, and E is a *Blog Post*
Nor.	.9	.8	.9	.7	.8	Normalized mean value of the sum of scores, rounded up

* see criteria and EQ explanations from Table 1

and to maintain customer trust and the adequacy of the tool. The 199 extracted primary keywords are visualized in Fig. 3 along with their frequency for both industry and academia when complying with the EU AIA.

Table 3. The additional classification type of GL data sources based on Shades of GL

GL Tier	Shades of GL [5]	Additional classification types in this research study
1st tier	Book, full paper, position paper, abstract, poster, conference paper	Expert commentary, position paper, analysis article, insights legal analysis and guidance article
2nd tier	Annual reports, news articles, video, Q/A site (e.g. StackOverflow), Wiki article	Client alert publication, insight article published, information report, legal advisory publication, advisory publication
3rd tier	Blog posts, emails, tweets, presentations	Information article, information blog post, legal advisory blog post, consulting report, opinion blog post, business insights article

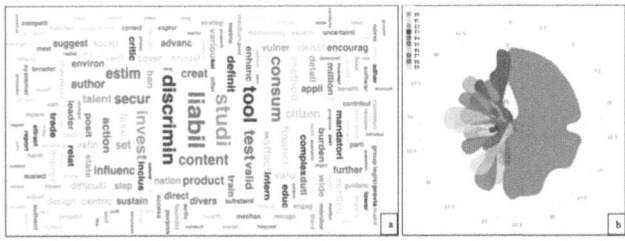

Fig. 3. The extracted results of a) the challenges and b) the strategies and processes required in complying with the EU AIA.

Furthermore, the results from sentiment analysis identified a few negative points of concern when enterprises, both in industry and academia, comply with the EU AIA regulation, in terms of requirements and transparency in the AI system, mainly in the high risk level category. Concerning regulation, the findings suggest implementing a risk-based classification with stringent requirements, with the aim of conducting thorough assessments and compliance checks as laid down in the Act's regulatory framework. The findings identified requirements such as: 1) balancing innovation with safety and ethical standards through specific compliance measures, and 2) updating AI strategies and categorizing AI solutions to ensure compliance with the new regulations. In addition, concerns were raised about transparency. The insights suggest that a human rights-based approach should be emphasized in risk management and human oversight [GL10, GL17, GL21].

RQ2: What strategies and processes are enterprises developing to implement the EU AIA? To address this question, NLP, i.e., the text processing TF-IDF method and LDA, was implemented for analyzing the underlying themes of strategies and processes being developed to implement the EU AIA. Through this approach, the model analyzes ten themes regarding strategies and processes, with each theme represented by a set of words most strongly associated with it. The analyzed results also revealed that our contexts cover more topics evenly and have more commonality between topics, which are indexed by the alphaSum (0.9008) and beta (0.1582) indicators.

Figure 3 represents the 10 themes of strategies and processes being developed to implement the EU AIA, where the wider areas of the themes are addressed by the tokens index. Then, the coherence index was applied to underline three crucial themes: 1) *T8: risk-based regulatory compliance systems*, 2) *T3: ethical frameworks and principles in technology development*, and 3) *T4: policies and systems for regulatory risk management*. Each theme is described below:

T0: Proposed legislation and financial liabilities seems to focus on themes related to liability, financial implications, directives, and legislation. The presence of words like "liability," "financial," and "legislation" with high exclusivity scores suggests that these are central to the theme of this topic.

T1: Regulatory standards and testing processes for consumer protection appears to revolve around themes of standards, testing processes, and regulatory concerns. Despite the strong coherence score, the high exclusivity for words like "test" and "vulner" suggests that these are key aspects of the topic.

T2: Studying discrimination and trust in regulatory demand focuses on themes related to discrimination, demand, and trust. The high exclusivity of "discrimin" and "rbi" suggests a specific focus on issues surrounding discrimination and a regulatory body or measure.

T3: Ethical frameworks and principles in technology development centers on ethics, practices, and frameworks, particularly in the context of development. The high exclusivity of terms like "ethic" and "practic" indicates a strong focus on ethical principles and best practices within this topic.

T4: Policies and systems for regulatory risk management revolves around regulatory frameworks, policies, and risks. The terms "regulatori" and "act" are central to the theme, while the lower exclusivity of "system" and "risk" indicates that these concepts are prevalent across multiple topics.

T5: User information and labeling systems impact focuses on information systems, impacts, and labeling. The high exclusivity of "inform" and "label" suggests these are central concepts to the topic, while "system" appears to be a common term across multiple topics.

T6: Cost estimation and compliance in system development related to costs, compliance, and estimates. The high exclusivity of "cost" and "estim" indicates a strong focus on financial or resource-related aspects within this topic.

T7: Global market dynamics and investment in European talent focuses on themes around markets, investments, and talent. The terms "invest" and "talent" have high exclusivity, suggesting a strong emphasis on investment strategies and human resources, particularly in a global or European context.

T8: Risk-based regulatory compliance systems is centered on risk, compliance, and regulatory requirements. The term "risk" has high exclusivity, indicating that risk management and assessment are primary concerns in this topic.

T9: Justice and bias in sustainable development goals is highly concentrated on Sustainable Development Goals (SDG), justice, and related terms. The high exclusivity of "sdg" and "justic" indicates that this topic is very specialized, likely addressing a niche but important area within the broader context.

To validate these outcomes, we crosschecked our results with other existing academic publications. A similar trend of key challenges was found in Arcila, B.B., Gerke S. et al., and Van K.H. [WL18] [6,12] as there is an effect on liability when an AI system is harmful, which then affects and harms fundamental rights and safety. Then discrimination, privacy, and decision-making are impacted after fundamental rights. The publication by Foffano et al. highlights: 1) ethical principles and policies as a part of the main AI strategy for the social good based on the perspective of the EU; 2) compliance management, risk-based compliance systems, and regulation for enterprises to lead their organizations [4,11].

4   Discussion

This section comprises a detailed discussion of the extracted insights on: 1) the three key challenges—liability, discrimination, and tools, and 2) the three crucial themes for developing strategies to implement the EU AIA—risk-based regulatory compliance systems, ethical frameworks in technology, and regulatory risk management systems. We then outline the framework of key challenges and strategies for complying with the EU AIA, as shown in Fig. 4. Lastly, we discuss the limitations of this study. We begin by discussing the three key challenges:

4.1   Key Challenges

Liability. Insight extraction revealed that enterprises need to adapt their compliance and liability management. Based on this finding we divided how to deal with it into the following four key areas: 1) Penalties for non-compliance issues. This issue creates significant financial liability for businesses that fail to comply with regulations. To address this, enterprises must: i) proactively establish governance and compliance frameworks to mitigate risks, and ii) ensure adherence to the new regulations; 2) Risk assessments. Thorough risk assessments for identifying and addressing potential compliance issues should be conducted [GL2]; 3) Maintain documentation. By documenting AI systems, risk assessments, and compliance efforts, the records serve as evidence of compliance and help mitigate liability during regulatory scrutiny; and 4) Human oversight. To mitigate liability risk, human oversight mechanisms for AI systems need to be implemented

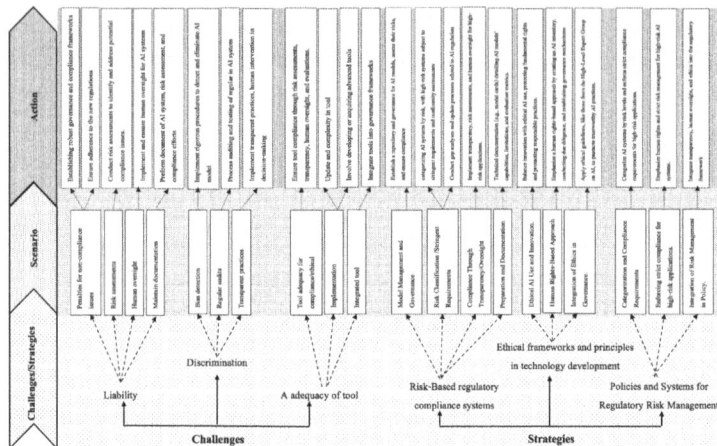

Fig. 4. The framework outline of key challenges and strategies when complying with the EU AIA.

and ensured, particularly in critical decision-making areas like healthcare, where errors can have severe consequences [GL8].

Discrimination. Managing discrimination risk is important for both legal compliance and maintaining customer trust. If an enterprise fails regarding discrimination, it could result in penalties under the EU AIA and also damage the company's reputation and trust from customers. Therefore addressing discrimination proactively is crucial for compliance and maintaining public trust. Insight extraction revealed three key parts for managing discrimination risk, as follows: 1) Bias detection. Perceptions of discrimination strongly influence the demand for regulation. Implementing rigorous procedures to detect and eliminate biases in the AI model will minimize discrimination. This includes using diverse and representative datasets during the training phase to prevent discriminatory outcomes [WL22]; 2) Regular audits. The process of regular auditing and testing in AI systems is important and recommended as it leads to identification of any unintended discriminatory patterns that may emerge over time [GL34]; and 3) Transparent practices. Such practices are crucial to represent where the accountability for any discriminatory outcomes lies. To implement transparent practices, it could be a benefit to include human intervention in the decision-making process to ensure fairness [GL31]. Furthermore, one extracted insight was the integration of non-discrimination and fairness into AI development practices, as these are beneficial to fill the gaps between AI ethical guidelines and industry practices [WL29].

Adequacy of tool insight indicates that effective, adaptable, and compliant tools are required to address the challenges faced when complying with the EU AIA, as well as ensuring that enterprises can meet the regulatory demands and maintain ethical AI practices. The insight extraction of three key parts concerning tool adequacy is as follows: 1) Tool adequacy for compliance and supporting ethical AI practices. To ensure that they have the appropriate tools to support ethical AI practices, this insight proposes enterprises use risk assessments, transparency, human oversight, other assessments, and compliance checks [GL21, GL54]; 2) Implementation, updating and complexity of the tool. This insight highlights the need for adaptation, updates, and tool complexity to meet evolving compliance requirements, especially as the EU AIA introduces new regulatory frameworks, and to manage the complexities of AI systems. Enterprises should ensure their tools undergo risk assessments, transparency evaluations, human oversight, and other compliance checks [GL10, GL18]; and 3) An integrated tool for governance and risk management. This insight underlines the benefits of effective AI system management and helps enterprises meet EU AIA compliance standards. Enterprises should integrate tools into governance by establishing frameworks to mitigate risks and ensure adherence to the new regulations [GL2].

4.2   Themes for Strategy Development

Next, we discuss the three crucial themes for developing strategies and processes to implement the EU AIA:

First theme: *Risk-based regulatory compliance systems.* This theme highlights the central focus on risk followed by compliance, system, and regulatory requirements. It suggests that this theme is concerned with systems that are designed to ensure compliance with regulatory requirements through a risk-based approach. The analysis results pointed to five ways to help enterprises ensure compliance with regulatory requirements through a risk-based approach such as 1) Model Management and Governance. The key point is that enterprises must establish a repository and governance for AI models, assessing their risk levels and ensuring compliance [GL2]; 2) Risk Classification and Stringent Requirements; 3) Focus in AI systems is categorized by risk, with high-risk systems subject to stringent requirements and conformity assessments. This suggests that enterprises must conduct gap analyses and update processes related to AI regulation [GL34, GL38, GL49]; 4) Compliance through Transparency and Oversight. This refers to implementing compliance requirements in terms of transparency, risk assessments, and human oversight for high-risk applications [GL29, GL32]. In the case of SMEs, they may face significant costs and legal uncertainty (compliance burden) [GL41]; and 5) Preparation and Documentation. This recommends that enterprises integrate ethical charters, legal tools, and technical documentation to establish a comprehensive governance framework for AI. Technical documentation, such as model cards, is vital for auditing AI systems, ensuring transparency and educating users on proper usage. It details AI models' capabilities, limitations, and evaluation metrics. For example, the Big Science Workshop illustrated how collaborative AI development can effectively incorporate ethical, legal, and technical compliance [WL24].

Second theme: *Ethical frameworks and principles in technology development.* This theme underscores the importance of ethical frameworks and principles in technology development, highlighting how ethical considerations guide the practical creation of technological solutions. The analysis identified three approaches to assist enterprises in addressing ethical frameworks and principles in technology development, as follows: 1) Ethical AI Use and Innovation. This proposes that enterprises implement ethical AI use while balancing innovation which i) protects fundamental rights, ii) promotes responsible AI practices, iii) focuses on ethics, safety, transparency, and human oversight to protect democratic processes [GL34, GL37, GL38]; 2) Human Rights-Based Approach. This emphasizes that a human rights-based approach by enterprises should be prepared by creating an AI inventory, conducting human rights due diligence, and establishing governance mechanisms [GL17]; and 3) Integration of Ethics in Governance. In this theme, enterprises are advised to apply ethical guidelines from a high-level expert group on AI integrated into the regulation, promoting trustworthy AI practices [WL9].

Third theme: *Policies and systems for regulatory risk management*. This theme highlights the central topic of regulatory acts and systems, and the policy put in place for managing risks. It suggests a focus on how regulations guide the development and implementation of risk management systems within various policy frameworks such as 1) Categorization and Compliance Requirements. This outlines how to categorize AI systems by risk levels and imposes strict compliance requirements, especially for high-risk applications [GL23], 2) Enforcing strict compliance for high-risk applications, 3) Emphasis on Human Rights and Risk Management by implementing strict requirements for high-risk AI systems, with the emphasis on compliance in term of transparency, risk management, and human oversight [GL39, GL49]; and 4) Integration of Risk Management in Policy. This encourages enterprises to integrate the transparency, human oversight, and ethical considerations in the regulatory framework [WL21].

Limitations. The empirical results reported herein should be considered in the light of some limitations. We divided these limitations into two types, i.e., internal and external threats. The internal threat of this study is related to 1) how we classified and interpreted the type of GL and 2) how we set the normalization impact metrics of GL in quality assessment for the literature review approach. For example, some GL types were not indicated in the GL classification, and some of the information was not always easy to retrieve. To mitigate this threat, we applied "shades of gray" criteria to classify the type of GL [5], we manually counted the number of citations, backlinks, social media shares, and the number of comments posted, and we manually checked the author's reputation and/or expertise in the area. This problem was also found in GL [7]. A minor internal threat, reducing words to their root forms in text processing can obscure differences between word forms. Mitigate this by manually rechecking the original words or sentences. One external threat of this study is related to the methodology, objectives, and impact criteria in quality assessment for the literature review approach. For example, not all of the GL data was stated in formal methodology, which is typically used in this literature, and although some of the GL data was not presented objectively, it had an impact index (n = 74). Therefore, one criterion in RQ 2.2 was omitted and GL without an objective and impact index was not used in the data analysis approach. Concerning the omitted methodology criteria, it was necessary to use those samples as the GL in question contained the most relevant data. However, comparing the sample, including threats from the objective and impact index, we checked the context manually and showed quite a similar trend for the interpreted results.

5   Conclusion and Future Work

We conducted an MLR and utilized NLP to help analyze the academic articles and gray literature on the EU AI Act in business contexts to aid enterprises in complying with and benefiting from the EU AIA. We examined 56 of 130 articles for comprehensive understanding, identifying 199 keywords, including liability, discrimination, and tool adequacy, as major obstacles for enterprises. We also noted negative aspects in the articles, such as regulatory interpretations, specific requirements, and transparency issues of the Act. Additionally, we identified ten strategic themes, with three key areas: risk-based regulatory compliance, ethical frameworks in technology development, and policies for regulatory risk management. We checked our findings against existing academic literature and discussed the results while establishing a practical framework for EU AIA compliance. These findings will benefit enterprises and research in the EU AIA domain. In future work, the focus is more likely to be on sectors with specific challenges and strategies such as "Deep Dive into High-Risk Sectors," with the implementation of AI in healthcare, finance, or transportation. This could involve exploring how these sectors are preparing for compliance and the unique challenges they face.

Acknowledgments. This work was co-funded by the European Union and the Regional Council of Satakunta (Generative artificial intelligence as a business enabler Project, GENT), with additional support from the Jane and Aatos Erkko Foundation through the CONVERGENCE of Humans and Machines Project (grant No. 220025).

Data Availibility Statement. A list containing all the *WL/GL* labeled references of this study is available at https://doi.org/10.6084/m9.figshare.26968498.v2

Declaration of competing interest. The authors have no competing interests to declare that are relevant to the content of this article.

References

1. Bourdin, M., Paviot, T., Pellerin, R., Lamouri, S.: NLP in SMEs for industry 4.0 opportunities and challenges. Proc. Comput. Sci. **239**, 396–403 (2024)
2. Butijn, B.-J., Tamburri, D.A., van den Heuvel, W.-J.: Block-chains: a systematic multivocal literature review. ACM Comput. Surv. (CSUR) **53**(3), 1–37 (2020)
3. European Commission, Brussels, Belgium. Proposal for a Regulation laying down harmonised rules on artificial intelligence (2021). COM/2021/206 final

4. Foffano, F., Scantamburlo, T., Cortés, A.: Investing in AI for social good: an analysis of European national strategies. AI & Soci. **38**(2) (2023)
5. Garousi, V., Felderer, M., Mäntylä, M.V.: Guidelines for including grey literature and conducting multivocal literature reviews in software engineering. Inf. Softw. Technol. **106**, 101–121 (2019)
6. Gerke, S., Minssen, T., Cohen, G.: Ethical and legal challenges of artificial intelligence-driven healthcare. In: Artificial Intelligence in Healthcare, pp. 295–336 (2020)
7. Kamei, F., et al.: Grey literature in software engineering: a critical review. Inf. Softw. Technol. **138** (2021)
8. Kim, D., Seo, D., Cho, S., Kang, P.: Multi-co-training for document classification using various document representations: TF-IDF, LDA, and Doc2Vec. Inf. Sci. **477**, 15–29 (2019)
9. Loor-Torres, R., et al.: A systematic review of natural language processing methods and applications in thyroidology. Mayo Clin. Proc. Digit. Health **2**(2), 270–279 (2024)
10. Pilowsky, J.K., et al.: Natural language processing in the intensive care unit: a scoping review. Crit. Care Resuscitation (2024)
11. Savin, A., Bagley, C.E.: On a strategic management approach to the new EU risk-based compliance regulations. Int. In-house Counsel J. **16**(64), 1–13 (2023)
12. Van Kolfschooten, H.: EU regulation of artificial intelligence: challenges for patients' rights. Common Market Law Rev. **59**(1) (2022)
13. Wiener, S., Roth, R., Rubio, S., Stern, H.: SB 1047: safe and secure innovation for frontier artificial intelligence models act (2024)

Professionals' Opinions on the Use of AI Software for HRM

Nasreen Azad$^{(\boxtimes)}$, Maryam Hina , and Najmul Islam

LUT University, Lappeenranta, Finland
{nasreen.azad,maryam.hina,najmul.islam}@lut.fi

Abstract. This study explores how Artificial Intelligence (AI) is changing recruitment practices and the skills recruiters need to succeed in AI-driven environment. We conducted a survey using open-ended questions and received responses from 32 professionals. The goal was to understand how AI is influencing the roles and responsibilities of recruiters. The findings highlight the importance of efficiency, bias reduction, learning and improvement, speed and consistency, and data-driven insights in promoting effective collaboration between humans and AI in recruitment. This insight has valuable implications for understanding the impact of AI on recruitment and the essential skills recruiters need to understand and adapt to AI-driven processes.

Keywords: Artificial Intelligence · Recruitment · Human Resource Management

1 Introduction

The Human Resource Management (HRM) processes have been significantly shaped by digitalization. Digital technologies have been progressively incorporated into HRM practices to enhance process efficiency [33]. This has also led to the rapid development of the Human Resource Information System, which has captured the attention of organizations and HR leaders due to its confirmed contributions to cost-saving and gaining a competitive advantage. Researchers have also focused on assessing its actual impact and understanding adoption factors across diverse business segments.

HRM is crucial for a company's success. Due to the digital technologies such as automation, big data, and artificial intelligence, HRM operations have significantly transformed. These changes involve various areas such as talent management, job design, recruitment, training and development, performance management, and employee engagement. As a result, scholars have taken a keen interest in studying this paradigm shift. Various research contributions [16,19,22] are evidence of this attention. In particular, AI-based HR solutions, including smart HR systems, have received increased attention, promising to automate administrative processes, particularly in areas like recruitment and selection. Recruitment processes, which are time-consuming and costly, have witnessed early integration of AI [31]. Smart systems, such as chatbots and search engines, are now utilized in sourcing, shortlisting, and interacting with job applicants, aiming to improve the efficiency of the selection process. Despite the potential advantages in terms of time, cost, and mitigating human bias, there remains skepticism among HR professionals, warranting further investigation into the trustworthiness of these technologies [15].

Building and retaining a skilled, dedicated, and highly motivated workforce requires significant resources and careful consideration [1]. AI can be integrated into the recruitment process, including resume scanning, interview analysis, and selection decision-making. AI-powered tools help speed up the hiring process and improve the selection of suitable candidates by analyzing resumes, skills, and job requirements. This leads to better hiring decisions and reduced employee turnover rates [1]. Although significant progress has been made, fully automating HR decision-making is still challenging, and various obstacles persist [6]. The gap between human comprehension and AI neural networks poses a challenge for HR professionals unfamiliar with programming [25], leading to reduced trust and reluctance to adopt AI-based processes. Additionally, AI developers often simplify information to improve efficiency, resulting in a lack of transparency for external stakeholders, making it difficult for them to comprehend AI-based processes and outputs [20]. Furthermore, the interpretation of individual emotions by AI systems poses a significant challenge for integrating them into HRM [32]. Despite these crucial aspects, scholarly attention on these topics has been limited. In particular, there exists a gap in our understanding of how AI impacts the recruitment process. In this paper, we address the following two research questions.

RQ:1 What are professionals' perspectives regarding utilizing AI tools for recruitment?

RQ:2 What advice do professionals have for addressing challenges when using AI recruitment tools?

We employed a qualitative approach to gain insight into our research questions. We used open-ended questions in our survey, following the critical incident approach (CIT) [8], and collected data from participants who previously had experience with AI technologies in HRM. We gathered data from 32 participants to understand their experiences and perceptions regarding using AI in HR recruitment. After analyzing the data, we identified factors such as efficiency, productivity, bias, continuous learning, speed, and data-driven insights may influence the use of AI in recruitment. We also highlight strategies to overcome challenges while using AI for recruitment. Our study contributes to literature in three main ways. Firstly, we highlight the critical issues and opportunities of using AI at work. Secondly, we emphasize the importance of trust issues in AI, which recent studies have shown to be crucial for AI and humans to work together effectively. Finally, we explained the role of training and HR practices in integrating AI into organizations while protecting employees' data.

2 Background

2.1 AI in Hiring

AI is increasingly being integrated into the different phases of the recruitment process, including initial outreach, candidate screening, in-depth assessment, and final selection, as highlighted by Leicht (2022) [21]. Notably, most human resource professionals acknowledge AI as a powerful tool for streamlining processes and saving time in the recruitment domain [11].

Use of AI may start right at the outreach stage, where it can craft compelling job advertisements, target specific audiences, and efficiently identify potential candidates. Moving into the screening phase, AI can review and analyze resumes, effectively ranking candidates based on predefined criteria. Progressing further, AI assists through facial and voice recognition technology, alongside sophisticated linguistic analysis, during the assessment and selection stages, to scrutinize video interviews and writing samples. Moreover, AI can help to rigorously evaluate candidates, looking into their skill sets, capabilities, and even psychological profiles [17].

AI tools can analyze extensive volumes of unstructured data, ranging from numerical, textual, to video content, and produce precise results [23]. Moreover, AI serves to streamline the hiring process by engaging with applicants, addressing inquiries, arranging interviews [27], and even dispatching job offers [29]. Therefore, many organizations have adopted AI for their algorithmic pre-screening assessments [11]. Notably, large tech companies such as IBM and Xerox Services promote AI-enabled hiring tools, highlighting heightened efficiency and accuracy in identifying person-job fit [11,26], positioning AI as superior to traditional methods, in terms of biased human intuition and error [13]. Overall, AI-enabled tools are viewed as democratizing processes and liberating humans from labor-intensive tasks in hiring [10]. However, empirical evidence indicates that individuals may also be over optimistic regarding the potential of AI-enabled tools [11]. In particular, a growing concern is about the ethical considerations surrounding deploying AI-enabled tools in hiring [34]. In a recent analysis conducted by IBM, it was discovered that artificial intelligence systems exhibited inherent discriminatory biases within their algorithms. These biases could potentially alienate users based on their characteristics and even result in the disqualification of competent candidates from employment [11]. Additionally, further evidence highlights ethical concerns regarding the fairness of outcomes that deviate from established HR decision paths [34].

2.2 AI Ethics for Hiring

As discussed previously, there exists significant ethical challenges when using AI for hiring [11,14,18]. One of the crucial question to consider: who bears accountability for the decision-making outcomes of AI? This prompts an examination of the ethical responsibility of the algorithm developer versus the organization implementing the technology [14].

The ethical challenge associated with incorporating AI into the hiring process partly stems from the limited access to the proprietary code behind AI-enabled tools, which is owned and controlled by firms [11]. This lack of transparency makes it challenging to identify HR ethical risks before these tools are used in real-world scenarios [21]. Additionally, the algorithms powering these proprietary codes are designed based on past employment trends, perpetuating biases related to race, gender, and other forms of discrimination [24]. The limited control that HR managers have over the underlying design of AI-enabled tools used in the hiring process emphasizes the need to investigate how individuals perceive the organizations using AI tools and whether they trust them.

3   Research Method

3.1   Data Collection

We based our research on the Critical Incident Technique (CIT) principles, which helped ensure that a rigorous and structured approach guided our study [12]. We administered the survey through the Prolific Academic Platform to reach a broad audience. We wanted to ensure we received relevant responses, therefore we included a screening question that prompted only those who had utilized AI-powered tools for hiring.

The survey questionnaire was designed to gather demographic information and insights into the benefits and risks of utilizing AI in HRM context. We also asked participants to share positive and negative experiences they encountered while using AI for recruitment purposes. We received responses from 32 participants with diverse backgrounds in various industries, such as IT, manufacturing, healthcare, education, and finance. All respondents had prior experience using AI for recruitment purposes. Through our research study, we aimed to provide a deeper understanding of the role of AI in HRM and its potential benefits and risks.

3.2   Data Analysis

We utilized qualitative methods to analyze our data, specifically the thematic analysis approach described by Castleberry [9]. This method involves assigning codes to text segments and translating those codes into higher-order themes. Two researchers performed the coding and theme-generation process to ensure accuracy [9]. This process allowed us to identify similar and dissimilar codes from different data segments collected from our open-ended survey transcripts. The coding process allowed us to create themes that helped us understand human-AI collaboration in the context of HRM. Our analysis discovered five categories of codes that describe AI collaboration in HRM. We explain these themes in the result sections.

4   Results

Several key themes emerged regarding how humans and AI can collaborate in recruiting and the benefits and drawbacks of using AI-based tools in the recruitment process. We found that the collaboration between humans and AI is crucial, with each complementing the other's strengths. AI excels at tasks like resume screening and data analysis, while humans excel in assessing soft skills, cultural fit, and making final decisions. This collaborative approach ensures that the recruitment process remains fair, unbiased, and efficient. Next, we discuss the themes from our analysis. Table 1 comprehensively summarizes each aspect of Human AI collaboration with HRM and describes the advantages and disadvantages of using AI tools.

4.1   Efficiency and Productivity

Our findings show that AI simplifies recruitment by providing recruiters with tools that help process vast amounts of data quickly. With AI-powered tools, recruiters can focus on tasks such as analyzing candidate profiles and interviewing potential hires [4]. This collaboration between recruiters and AI has proven highly beneficial, allowing for optimized time management and improved productivity. The ability to process large volumes of data in a shorter time frame means that recruiters can make better-informed decisions and find the right candidates more efficiently [7]. A professional stated that,

> *"AI simplifies the recruitment process by quickly scanning resumes and evaluating candidates based on predefined criteria, promoting fairness and diversity in hiring practices. It also provides valuable data and insights about the recruitment process, allowing organizations to make data-driven decisions about their hiring criteria and strategies".*

4.2   Bias Reduction

Our findings further show that AI significantly reduces human biases in the hiring process [28]. The AI-powered system promotes fairness and diversity in hiring practices by objectively screening candidates based on predefined criteria [30]. Unlike humans, AI is unbiased and does not discriminate based on race, gender, or ethnicity if the system is trained with unbiased data. By utilizing AI-based tools during the initial stages of the recruitment process, recruiters can minimize biases and ensure fair hiring decisions. AI-powered systems can help identify the most qualified candidates based on their skills and experience rather than subjective factors such as race, gender, or ethnicity [35]. Thus, incorporating AI into the recruitment process can lead to more diverse and inclusive workplaces, which can help businesses thrive. A professional stated that,

> *"AI is unbiased and should be able to adhere to legislation so that there is no discrimination, as well as quickly review resumes to filter out unsuitable candidates."*

Another professional stated that

"Benefits of using AI tools include faster and more efficient resume screening, reduced bias in initial candidate selection, improved data analysis for decision-making, and a potential increase in overall hiring quality. As it is done by AI no biases are included in the selection process".

4.3   Learning and Improvement

AI constantly improves performance by learning from human interactions and feedback. By processing and analyzing vast amounts of data, AI can present it in a way that is easy for humans to comprehend and use. A professional stated that,

"It's not very sensitive, and probably AI has to learn from humans and properly interact with the candidates. Talking with an AI tool during a recruitment process without empathy would feel very cold".

Our research question pertains to the advice given by professionals on AI recruitment tools. Our findings show that AI recruitment tools have some notable benefits that address RQ2.

4.4   Speed and Consistency

With AI-powered screening, evaluating candidates becomes faster and more consistent, allowing companies to reduce their time-to-hire without sacrificing quality [3]. AI HRM tools improve recruitment by evaluating candidates based on specific criteria, reducing time-to-hire, and allowing recruiters to focus on strategic aspects. While beneficial, relying solely on AI may overlook candidates with non-traditional qualifications. Therefore, it's crucial to use AI as a supportive tool alongside human judgment, and including human review to ensure a balanced approach. A participant reported the following,

"AI brings some new tools that can have advantages in the recruitment process such as speeding up the process, especially regarding sifting, ensuring a consistent approach to applications and introducing new technology that can improve functions such as advert writing and attracting candidates".

4.5   Data-Driven Insights

Our results also highlight that organizations can gain invaluable insights into their hiring processes from data. These insights enable them to make informed decisions and optimize recruitment strategies to attract and retain top talent [5]. By analyzing large volumes of data, AI can uncover trends and patterns, enabling organizations to make informed decisions about their recruitment strategies. With these insights, HR teams can identify effective candidate channels, relevant

Table 1. Summary of the findings

Themes	Advantages for using AI	Disadvantages of using AI
Efficiency and Productivity	Increases speed and efficiency of data processing, Optimizes time management and Enhances decision-making.	May require a significant initial investment, which can lead to over-reliance on automated processes.
Bias reduction	Reduces human biases in hiring, Promotes diversity and fairness, Ensures objective screening.	Risk of biased outcomes if AI relies on flawed data, Lack of transparency in decision-making.
Learning and Improvement	Continuously learns and enhances performance, Provides insights for various applications, and Can enhance accuracy and efficiency.	Can lack sensitivity and empathy in interactions, May need to understand nuanced contexts fully.
Data-driven Insights	Enables data-driven decision-making, Helps optimize recruitment strategies, and Provides actionable insights.	Potential misuse of sensitive data may require advanced data management and analysis skills.
Speed and Consistency	Streamlines many repetitive tasks, Enhances consistency and Improves the overall recruitment process.	May fail to capture human nuances in hiring, Can lead to over-dependence on technology, Potential resistance from staff due to lack of trust.

qualifications for specific roles, and predict future hiring needs. However, using AI for data analysis requires careful management of sensitive information and an understanding of potential biases. Establishing clear data privacy protocols and providing training on responsible data interpretation allows organizations to fully benefit from AI-driven insights while maintaining ethical standards and protecting candidate privacy [2]. A professional stated that,

> "Humans and AI can collaborate in recruiting by using AI for tasks like resume screening, initial candidate assessments, and data analysis. Human recruiters can then focus on more nuanced tasks, such as conducting interviews, assessing cultural fit, and making final hiring decisions, where human judgment and empathy are crucial."

Professionals also stated some disadvantages to using AI tools for the recruitment process. AI may need help to grasp nuanced contexts and unconventional qualifications, potentially overlooking suitable candidates. There could be bias in the Data. AI algorithms may inherit biases from historical data, leading to unfair outcomes if not carefully monitored and adjusted. Excessive reliance on AI may diminish the role of human judgment and intuition, particularly in assessing soft skills and cultural fit. Finally, trust and understanding issues are another concern in the recruitment process. Some individuals may have reservations or need more understanding about AI tools, affecting their acceptance and usage in recruitment processes. A professional stated that,

> "Always having to depend on artificial intelligence for hiring personnel is a bit too dependent on them; you cannot leave everything to them and trust

everything one hundred percent in the future, maybe something, but I would never trust the election 100 percent. They learn from any candidate, and we do not know exactly what will happen in the future."

Another Professional stated that,

"I feel that sometimes the human element may be taken away as the AI can see things as very black or white - ie someone may not have completed a degree that is required for the role but their experience may be adequate for them to proceed to interview. This may be overlooked by AI but could be considered by human sifting".

While AI-based tools offer significant benefits in efficiency, bias reduction, and data-driven insights, organizations must be mindful of potential limitations related to contextual understanding, bias in data, and the need for human oversight and judgment in recruitment processes. Collaborative efforts that leverage the strengths of both humans and AI can optimize the recruitment process and lead to more effective hiring outcomes.

5 Discussion

The use of AI in recruitment processes has led to discussions about how AI and humans can work together effectively. This study examines the opinions of 32 individuals regarding the collaboration between AI and HRM in recruitment processes.

5.1 Key Findings

The participants noted that AI helps in tasks such as resume screening and data analysis, which can speed up the recruitment process, analyze large amounts of data and improve recruitment efficiency. However, concerns about AI's limited contextual understanding and potential biases in data highlight the importance of human oversight and judgment. The benefits of using AI-based tools include faster processing, consistent and unbiased candidate selection, and data-driven insights for informed decision-making. However, there are also drawbacks, such as challenges related to contextual understanding, bias in AI algorithms, and over-reliance on technology. Therefore, a collaborative approach that combines AI's strengths with human judgment and intuition is recommended to optimize recruitment outcomes.

5.2 Implications

It is crucial for organizations to recognize that the quality of the input data has a direct impact on the quality of the output. Should erroneous data be incorporated into the AI tools, they will learn from it and consequently generate inaccurate decisions. Therefore, it is important for organizations to ensure that the data utilized in the recruitment and selection processes remains unbiased and fair. Moreover, transparency in the utilization of algorithms and AI tools is important to ensure.

In the future, these tools may assume the duties of HR professionals in specific aspects of the recruitment and selection process, possibly even making final decisions. However, in areas as sensitive as job selection, the human factor is imperative due to its direct involvement with individuals. Consequently, we suggest organizations to be transparent and outline the workings of their algorithms to establish trust with clients and candidates.

Finally, successful implementation of these systems requires employees to fully embrace them. This necessitates involving employees in the process and illustrating the tools' advantages. Additionally, organizations must invest in new competencies for HR professionals to encourage growth.

5.3 Limitations and Future Work

Our research offers valuable insights into the evolving role of HR professionals in recruitment due to AI implementation. However, it's crucial to acknowledge the limitations of our study. Our research is exploratory, and our findings are based solely on respondents' perceptions.

Another limitation is the small sample size of 32 respondents, and a larger sample size would provide a more representative picture of different organizations that have integrated AI into their recruitment and selection processes. Additionally, our focus was mainly on the organization's perspective. Future research could explore how clients and candidates perceive the introduction of AI in recruitment and selection processes.

Further research is necessary to validate our findings and examine the impact of AI on recruitment processes. Confirmatory studies could assess the effectiveness of AI in streamlining the recruitment process. Furthermore, it would be intriguing to investigate whether the introduction of AI enables HR professionals to assume a more strategic role and bring more significant value to the organization.

6 Conclusion

Our study explores how the implementation of AI affects HR professionals at different stages of the recruitment and selection process. Our study involves an open-ended questionnaire that was answered by 32 professionals and analyzed using thematic analysis. The aim is to uncover the experiences, perceptions, expectations, and challenges of recruiters who use AI-supported recruitment processes. The findings suggest that efficiency and productivity, bias reduction, learning and improvement, speed and consistency, and data-driven insights are essential for Human AI collaboration in recruitment. The goal of this research is to add to the current body of knowledge by providing a thorough understanding of how AI will shape the role of recruiters in the future. The study's discoveries will give practical insights for HR professionals, recruiters, and organizations looking to maximize AI in recruitment. Furthermore, this research will guide future research directions and stimulate conversations regarding the ethical, social, and organizational consequences of AI-supported recruitment processes.

References

1. Ahammad, T.: Personnel management to human resource management (HRM): how HRM functions. J. Mod. Account. Auditing **13**(9), 412–420 (2017)
2. Avellan, T., Sharma, S., Turunen, M.: AI for all: defining the what, why, and how of inclusive AI. In: Proceedings of the 23rd International Conference on Academic Mindtrek, pp. 142–144 (2020)
3. Basu, S., Majumdar, B., Mukherjee, K., Munjal, S., Palaksha, C.: Artificial intelligence-HRM interactions and outcomes: a systematic review and causal configurational explanation. Hum. Resour. Manag. Rev. **33**(1), 100893 (2023)
4. Bhagyalakshmi, R., Maria, E.F.: Artificial intelligence and HRM: an empirical study on decision-making skills of HR through AI in HRM practices. Ann. Rom. Soc. Cell Biol. **25**(6), 11568–11578 (2021)
5. Böhmer, N., Schinnenburg, H.: Critical exploration of AI-driven HRM to build up organizational capabilities. Empl. Relat. Int. J. **45**(5), 1057–1082 (2023)
6. Brynjolfsson, E., Mitchell, T., Rock, D.: What can machines learn and what does it mean for occupations and the economy? In: AEA Papers and Proceedings, vol. 108, pp. 43–47. American Economic Association 2014 Broadway, Suite 305, Nashville, TN 37203 (2018)
7. Budhwar, P., Malik, A., De Silva, M.T., Thevisuthan, P.: Artificial intelligence-challenges and opportunities for international HRM: a review and research agenda. Int. J. Hum. Resource Manage. **33**(6), 1065–1097 (2022)
8. Butterfield, L.D., Borgen, W.A., Amundson, N.E., Maglio, A.-S.T.: Fifty years of the critical incident technique: 1954–2004 and beyond. Qual. Res. **5**(4), 475–497 (2005)
9. Castleberry, A., Nolen, A.: Thematic analysis of qualitative research data: is it as easy as it sounds? Curr. Pharm. Teach. Learn. **10**(6), 807–815 (2018)
10. Du, J.: Unlocking the potential: literature review on the evolving role of AI in HRM. Front. Manage. Sci. **3**(1), 28–33 (2024)
11. Figueroa-Armijos, M., Clark, B.B., da Motta Veiga, S.P.: Ethical perceptions of AI in hiring and organizational trust: the role of performance expectancy and social influence. J. Bus. Ethics **186**(1), 179–197 (2023)
12. Flanagan, J.C.: The critical incident technique. Psychol. Bull. **51**(4), 327 (1954)
13. Giermindl, L.M., Strich, F., Christ, O., Leicht-Deobald, U., Redzepi, A.: The dark sides of people analytics: reviewing the perils for organisations and employees. Eur. J. Inf. Syst. **31**(3), 410–435 (2022)
14. Gunz, S., Thorne, L.: Thematic symposium: the impact of technology on ethics, professionalism and judgement in accounting (2020)
15. Hmoud, B.I., Várallyai, L.: Artificial intelligence in human resources information systems: investigating its trust and adoption determinants. Int. J. Eng. Manage. Sci. **5**(1), 749–765 (2020)
16. Huang, M.-H., Rust, R.T.: Engaged to a robot? The role of AI in service. J. Serv. Res. **24**(1), 30–41 (2021)

17. Hunkenschroer, A.L., Luetge, C.: Ethics of AI-enabled recruiting and selection: a review and research agenda. J. Bus. Ethics **178**(4), 977–1007 (2022)
18. Johnson, B.A., Coggburn, J.D., Llorens, J.J.: Artificial intelligence and public human resource management: questions for research and practice. Pub. Pers. Manage. **51**(4), 538–562 (2022)
19. Kim, G., Shin, B., Lee, H.G.: Understanding dynamics between initial trust and usage intentions of mobile banking. Inf. Syst. J. **19**(3), 283–311 (2009)
20. Langer, M., König, C.: Explainability of artificial intelligence in human resources. In: Handbook of Research on Artificial Intelligence in Human Resource Management, pp. 285–302. Edward Elgar Publishing (2022)
21. Leicht-Deobald, U., et al.: The challenges of algorithm-based HR decision-making for personal integrity. In: Business and the Ethical Implications of Technology, pp. 71–86. Springer (2022)
22. Mikalef, P., Islam, N., Parida, V., Singh, H., Altwaijry, N.: Artificial intelligence (AI) competencies for organizational performance: a B2B marketing capabilities perspective. J. Bus. Res. **164**, 113998 (2023)
23. Munoko, I., Brown-Liburd, H.L., Vasarhelyi, M.: The ethical implications of using artificial intelligence in auditing. J. Bus. Ethics **167**(2), 209–234 (2020)
24. Noble, S.U.: Algorithms of oppression: how search engines reinforce racism. In: Algorithms of oppression, New York University Press (2018)
25. Pan, Y., Froese, F., Liu, N., Hu, Y., Ye, M.: The adoption of artificial intelligence in employee recruitment: the influence of contextual factors. Int. J. Hum. Resour. Manage. **33**(6), 1125–1147 (2022)
26. Peck, D.: They're watching you at work. Atlantic **312**(5), 72–84 (2013)
27. Rąb-Kettler, K., Lehnervp, B.: Recruitment in the times of machine learning. Manage. Syst. Prod. Eng. **27**(2), 105–109 (2019)
28. Roselli, D., Matthews, J., Talagala, N.: Managing bias in AI. In: Companion Proceedings of the 2019 World Wide Web Conference, pp. 539–544 (2019)
29. Sánchez-Gordón, M., Colomo-Palacios, R.: A multivocal literature review on the use of devops for e-learning systems. In: Proceedings of the Sixth International Conference on Technological Ecosystems for Enhancing Multiculturality, pp. 883–888 (2018)
30. Silberg, J., Manyika, J.: Notes from the AI frontier: tackling bias in AI (and in humans). McKinsey Global Inst. **1**(6), 1–31 (2019)
31. Sivathanu, B., Pillai, R.: Smart HR 4.0-how industry 4.0 is disrupting HR. Hum. Resour. Manage. Int. Digest **26**(4), 7–11 (2018)
32. Stark, L., Hoey, J.: The ethics of emotion in artificial intelligence systems. In: Proceedings of the 2021 ACM Conference on Fairness, Accountability, and Transparency, pp. 782–793 (2021)
33. Strohmeier, S.: Research in e-HRM: review and implications. Hum. Resour. Manag. Rev. **17**(1), 19–37 (2007)
34. Tambe, P., Cappelli, P., Yakubovich, V.: Artificial intelligence in human resources management: challenges and a path forward. Calif. Manage. Rev. **61**(4), 15–42 (2019)
35. Vasconcelos, M., Cardonha, C., Gonçalves, B.: Modeling epistemological principles for bias mitigation in AI systems: an illustration in hiring decisions. In: Proceedings of the 2018 AAAI/ACM Conference on AI, Ethics, and Society, pp. 323–329 (2018)

Emotion AI in Workplace Environments: A Case Study

Joni-Roy Piispanen$^{(\boxtimes)}$ ⓘ and Rebekah Rousi ⓘ

University of Vaasa, 65200 Vaasa, Finland
{joni.piispanen,rebekah.rousi}@uwasa.fi

Abstract. Emotion AI is an emerging field of artificial intelligence, intended to be utilized by organizations to manage and monitor employees' emotional states, supporting employee wellbeing and organizational goals. The current paper presents a case study that took place in a Finnish research institute, in which research participants (N = 11) were interviewed about their experiences of working in an Emotion AI environment. Our findings indicate that employees have a positive predisposition towards wellbeing monitoring in the workplace when benefits are perceived firsthand. Concerns however, manifest even in settings where there is existing familiarity with the technology, how it operates, and who is conducting the data collection, these are discussed in the findings. We additionally note that employee concerns can be mitigated via robust organizational policies, transparency and open communication.

Keywords: Emotion AI · Employee · Wellbeing · Organization · Privacy

1 Introduction

The emerging field of Emotion Artificial Intelligence (Emotion AI), or data-driven technology that collects, analyzes and interprets emotional data is currently being researched and developed to support future employee wellbeing. Recently, Emotion AI comprising sensor-based technologies, passively and continuously measuring employee wellbeing in real-time, have been utilized to unobtrusively measure engagement, productivity, job satisfaction, mood, stress, organizational relationships and outcomes [1–3]. Yet, this type of technology designed to identify and respond to emotional states does not come without its dark sides [4]. Employees can be vulnerable to technological interventions in workplace contexts, when considering heightened surveillance, privacy, coercive control, marginalization and biases, power asymmetries and lack of explicit consent [5–10]. In fact, recent regulations by the European Union specifically restrict the use of emotion recognition in critical public sectors [11]. This illustrates the necessity to elucidate employee experiences, perspectives, attitudes and concerns regarding Emotion AI in workplace environments.

Currently, there are substantial gaps in empirical investigations of human-centered experiences in Emotion AI and its associated data collection in the workplace. Previous research consists mostly of theoretical and conceptual level studies, utilizing speculative

E. Papatheocharous et al. (Eds.): ICSOB 2024, LNBIP 539, pp. 142–148, 2025.
https://doi.org/10.1007/978-3-031-85849-9_12

methods. Empirical studies of privacy experience are still in their infancy, particularly in terms of experimental studies that probe how privacy experience manifests in context. Thus, we chose to focus on employee perspectives and experiences, as examining the phenomenological aspects of Emotion AI is imperative to understanding how the technology impacts employee wellbeing. Our aim is to contribute to a growing body of interdisciplinary research surrounding Emotion AI's ethical and social implications in workplace environments [9, 10, 12]. We argue that employee concerns over Emotion AI and data collection in workplace environments can be reconciled through establishing pathways for communication and building trust.

2 Methods

We conducted a case study on the practicalities of utilizing Emotion AI in workplace environments, based on a previous research project at a Finnish research institute. The project collected data from environmental sensors (air quality, sound levels, motion detectors), work equipment (virtual sensors, pressure-sensitive chairs, video cameras, keyboard and mouse trackers), and wearable devices (smartphone trackers, sports watches, HRV monitors). This data was combined with employees' self-reported emotional states via surveys in a longitudinal study to track workplace wellbeing. The aggregated data was used to monitor employee wellbeing and functioning. The data was subsequently made available to employees for self-reflection.

We leveraged two qualitative research methods: secondary observation and semi-structured interviews. The former consisted of reviewing accounts, reports, and representations created by the researchers in the previous research project. The latter consisted of interviewing research participants about their experiences of working in an Emotion AI workplace environment, and interviewing researchers to validate their observations and experiences. Two research questions (RQs) guided our research:

- RQ1: How do employees experience and perceive an Emotion AI workplace environment designed to support their wellbeing?
- RQ2: What are employees' experiences of privacy and trust in Emotion AI workplace environments?

We recruited participants from the previous project who were willing to express their perspectives and experiences regarding working in an experimental Emotion AI workplace environment. In total, 11 participants consented to participate in our study. Nine participants (P1-P9) were employees who had participated in the previous research project, while two participants (P10-P11) were researchers conducting the research project in question. All participants were employees in research institutes and worked in Finland. Four of the participants were female and seven were male. Ages ranged between 25 and 64, with the largest age bracket being 45 to 54.

We adopted a semi-structured interview approach to collect participant experiences [13]. The interviews lasted between 30 and 120 min. The interviews were conducted in Finnish to facilitate disclosure by participants and to provide a more comfortable experience. The interviews were subsequently transcribed verbatim by the interviewer and translated from Finnish into English by hand for analysis. The translations were verified with translation software for accuracy and revised when necessary. We designed the interview protocol to begin with general topics and questions to establish rapport with participants, delving into more specific and sensitive topics further on in the interviews to avoid influencing the participant's answers. We felt it was necessary to mitigate potential researcher bias, recall bias, response bias and social desirability bias, given the sensitive and emotionally charged subject matter. The interview transcripts were analyzed utilizing reflexive thematic analysis [14]. Firstly, the interview transcripts were open-coded by paying close attention to the language and meaning used by the participants. Secondly, the codes were further refined to resolve any ambiguity or disagreements regarding granularity. Thirdly, following an iterative process the codes were developed into successively higher-level themes. Through this process patterns and commonalities in participant experiences could be identified.

3 Results

Our results indicate that: 1) employees have a generally positive attitude towards improving wellbeing in workplace environments even through embedded data-intensive technologies; 2) employees have an appreciation and a positive predisposition towards wellbeing monitoring at the workplace, given that they also benefit from this process; 3) even employees who have previous familiarity with the technology, its operation and data collectors are concerned about their privacy; 4) existing trust in employers, researchers, data infrastructures and operational procedures are not sufficient by themselves to alleviate privacy concerns; 5) the objectives of data collection, anonymity and the nature of organizations involved in data collection are the primary factors affecting employee experiences; and 6) transparency and open communication build trust, positively impacting experiences of Emotion AI in workplace environments. A summary of the results is depicted in Table 1 with thematic codes and evidence from interviews.

Table 1. Summary of results indicated by thematic codes and evidence from interviews.

Thematic Codes	Interview Questions	Interview Quotes
Perceived Benefits of Data Collection	If we are only thinking about the risks and benefits, what perspective would you arrive at?	Well, in terms of benefits, (…) understanding what is stressful and how it can be reduced, that is valuable, and why not only from the employee's point of view, but also from the employer's point of view. (P2) The enormous benefit of it was that you started to learn, you could see your activity in those applications (…) In it, perhaps, one became more aware of one's own ability to work and function. (P5) However, since it was for a good cause, I wouldn't have minded no matter what kind of sensors there were. (P9)

(continued)

Table 1. (*continued*)

Thematic Codes	Interview Questions	Interview Quotes
Concerns over Privacy and Data Use	Did you have any particular concerns in terms of data privacy or ethics, and if you did, what kinds?	I'm of course interested in the fact that my data doesn't go to the wrong parties, those who could possibly misuse it. (P3) Hmm, well there are risks. They are much easier to come up with. There is always a question about whether exactly what is said in the notices is being done. (P4) (…), but I think it is a big risk if it is used for some kind of control. (P5) I was wary of how the information would be utilized. What kind of data is collected (…) These were my initial concerns. (P7)
Trust in Data Handling	What is your overview, if we are talking about data protection and the ethical aspects?	Well as far as I can see, at least it had been well considered and it was brought up several times. Particularly, in what way the data is collected, for what purpose and what kind of people have access to what information and how well that data can or cannot be connected to individuals. (P1) Of course, since this is a research project and I myself am an employee there, I knew at what level of ethics and other things this would be treated. So, there was nothing to worry about. (P6) Additionally, knowing the researchers or at least at an organizational level knowing how these issues are approached, you can have a trusting attitude. (P8)

(*continued*)

Table 1. (*continued*)

Thematic Codes	Interview Questions	Interview Quotes
Transparency and Communication of Procedures	What was your general idea of how well it was communi-cated to you, for example, what the purposes are and what is done with the data afterwards? What kind of notion did you have?	I think communication and informing are really important in that regard. Being open about challenges and that some things don't work. (P5) We did everything we came up with. To make it transparent and intelligible. (P10) During the project, we tried to take into account and invested into data protection and privacy-related issues. (...) In the early stages, the extra headache that this caused was sizable, however, through the value of the data and the trust of the participants, it paid back in the end. (P11) Users expressed that it motivates them when you get answers. Considering the level of understanding the end user has when answering questions was important. (...) You can't just give a robotic answer, like, look at the documentation on page so and so. (P11)

Participants in our study expressed a general appreciation for wellbeing monitoring at the workplace and experienced it as beneficial on both an individual level as well as organizational level. Employees expressed an appreciation for continually receiving data about their wellbeing, mood and efficiency. Participants even expressed preparedness for more extensive data collection, given that they have some access to the data that is collected and, in turn, benefit from the process. If the end goal is promoting wellbeing at work and sufficient anonymity is preserved, employees feel more comfortable with data collection at the workplace. Anonymity, awareness of data collection and its purposes appear to be the primary factors affecting employee experiences, attitudes and perceptions.

Concerns by employees were varied, even if the perceptions related to the acceptability of monitoring technologies at the workplace were positive. Participants in our study considered themselves privacy conscious, yet in their view do not actively preserve their privacy or keep up to date with technological advancements and best practices. In relation to data privacy, the acceptance of data collection, and its processing in a workplace environment, participants were mainly worried about the purposes of data collection and whether the employer was monitoring their activity with the aim of scrutinizing their work. However, with sufficient anonymity, transparency and explainability of data collection processes these concerns were mitigated.

The shared sentiment among both researchers and research participants was that effective communication is needed. The results show indications that transparency and open communication build trust, resulting in a positive impact on employee experience. Especially on the researcher's side, the relationship between communication and trust was emphasized. However, organizational cultures and relationships to data collectors also affect trust in a significant manner.

4 Discussion

Our findings indicate that employees appear highly interested in receiving data about their wellbeing at work, while also showing an appreciation for organizations monitoring and managing how employees fare in workplace environments. In this respect, recent literature has emphasized employee opportunities to opt-out of workplace monitoring, adequate opportunities for exercising employee's rights, and the actual distribution of benefits from Emotion AI as contentious aspects [9, 10, 12, 15, 16]. Organizations planning to utilize Emotion AI need to consider transparency, communication and the purposes of data collection, when attempting to convince employees of the benefits. Additionally, geographical and cultural differences should be considered [17, 18].

There were some limitations to this study that should be considered when evaluating the results. Participants in our study were employed by research institutes involved in the previous research project and indicated existing trust towards institutions and the research institutes conducting the research project. Additionally, participants in the previous research project volunteered to work in the experimental Emotion AI workplace environment, which could indicate a positive predisposition towards wellbeing monitoring and data collection. Furthermore, the research institutes in question are located in Finland and have an excellent reputation within the country both for their research quality as well as ethics and security standards. Moreover, all participants expressed knowledge of the European General Data Protection Regulation and at least a passing familiarity with organizational policies at the organization conducting the previous research project. As such, attitudes towards researchers, participation and data collection might be biased.

Further research is required to establish and validate commonalities in employee experiences of Emotion AI in workplace environments. Additionally, the relationship between age, gender and privacy-related behavior requires more comprehensive analysis.

References

1. Constantinides, M., Šćepanović, S., Quercia, D., Li, H., Sassi, U., Eggleston, M.: ComFeel: productivity is a matter of the senses too. Proc. ACM Interact. Mob. Wearable Ubiquitous Technol. **4**(4), 1–21 (2020)
2. Mirjafari, S., et al.: Differentiating higher and lower job performers in the workplace using mobile sensing. Proc. ACM Interact. Mob. Wearable Ubiquitous Technol. **3**(2), 1–24 (2019)
3. Morshed, M.B., et al.: Prediction of mood instability with passive sensing. Proc. ACM Interact. Mob. Wearable Ubiquitous Technol. **3**(3), 1–21 (2019)

4. Marsh, E., Vallejos, E.P., Spence, A.: The digital workplace and its dark side: An integrative review. Comput. Hum. Behav. **128** (2022)
5. Bernhardt, A., Kresge, L., Suleiman, R.: The data-driven workplace and the case for worker technology rights. ILR Rev. **76**(1), 3–29 (2023)
6. Manokha, I.: The implications of digital employee monitoring and people analytics for power relations in the workplace. Surveill. Soc. **18**(4) (2020)
7. Das Swain, V., Gao, L., Wood, W.A., Matli, S.C., Abowd, G.D., De Choudhury, M.: Algorithmic power or punishment: information worker perspectives on passive sensing enabled AI phenotyping of performance and wellbeing. In: Proceedings of the 2023 CHI Conference on Human Factors in Computing Systems, pp. 1–17 (2023)
8. Glavin, P., Bierman, A., Schieman, S.: Private eyes, they see your every move: workplace surveillance and worker well-being. Soc. Currents **11**(4), 327–345 (2024)
9. Roemmich, K., Schaub, F., Andalibi, N.: Emotion AI at work: implications for workplace surveillance, emotional labor, and emotional privacy. In: Proceedings of the 2023 CHI Conference on Human Factors in Computing Systems, pp. 1–20 (2023)
10. Corvite, S., Roemmich, K., Rosenberg, T.I., Andalibi, N.: Data subjects' perspectives on emotion artificial intelligence use in the workplace: a relational ethics lens. Proc. ACM Hum. Comput. Interact. **7**(CSCW1), 1–38 (2023)
11. European Union Artificial Intelligence Act. O.J. (L 207) 1 (2024)
12. Mantello, P., Ho, M.T.: Emotional AI and the future of wellbeing in the post-pandemic workplace. AI & Soc. **39**(4), 1883–1889 (2024)
13. Kallio, H., Pietilä, A.-M., Johnson, M., Kangasniemi, M.: Systematic methodological review: developing a framework for a qualitative semi-structured interview guide. J. Adv. Nurs. **72**(12), 2954–2965 (2016)
14. Braun, V., Clarke, V., Hayfield, N., Davey, L., Jenkinson, E.: Doing reflexive thematic analysis. In: Supporting Research in Counselling and Psychotherapy: Qualitative, Quantitative, and Mixed Methods Research, pp. 19–38 (2023)
15. Chowdhary, S., Kawakami, A., Gray, M.L., Suh, J., Olteanu, A., Saha, K.: Can workers meaningfully consent to workplace wellbeing technologies? In: Proceedings of the 2023 ACM Conference on Fairness, Accountability, and Transparency, pp. 569–582 (2023)
16. Kawakami, A., et al.: Sensing wellbeing in the workplace, why and for whom? Envisioning impacts with organizational stakeholders. Proc. ACM Hum. Comput. Interact. **7**(CSCW2), 1–33 (2023)
17. Mantello, P., Ho, M.T., Nguyen, M.H., Vuong, Q.H.: Bosses without a heart: socio-demographic and cross-cultural determinants of attitude toward emotional AI in the workplace. AI & Soc. **38**(1), 97–119 (2023)
18. Rousi, R., Piispanen, J.R., and Boutellier, J.: I trust you dr. researcher, but not the company that handles my data–trust in the data economy. In: Proceedings of the 57th Hawaii International Conference on System Sciences, pp. 4632–4641 (2024)

Exploring the Factors that Impact the Half-Life of Software

Krzysztof Wnuk[1]($\boxtimes$), Theresia Harrer[3], Piotr Tomaszewski[2],
and Ehsan Zabardast[1]

[1] Blekinge Institute of Technology, Karlskrona, Sweden
{krw,ehsan.zabardast}@bth.se
[2] RISE Research Institutes of Sweden, Lund, Sweden
piotr.tomaszewski@ri.se
[3] Hanken School of Economics, Helsinki, Finland
theresia.harrer@hanken.fi

Abstract. This vision paper explores the factors that impact the aging and depreciation of software. Based on the exploration of related work in software aging, software anti-aging, the financial aspect of technical debt and accounting of intangible assets, we postulate that a more holistic approach towards obsolescence should be taken as most research focuses solely on the technical aspects of software aging, leaving the business and accounting aspects greatly unexplored.

Keywords: software aging · software half-life · software technical debt

1 Introduction

Software business is fiercely competitive with rapidly changing market trends, customer needs and technologies [7]. The intangible and flexible nature of software makes it a suitable mechanism to respond to these changes, however at the risk and cost of rapid obsolescence and aging of produced software artifacts. Software aging is not a new concept, it was discussed in 1994 by Parnas, who claimed that programs like people get old despite software programs being mathematical products and therefore immortal [14]. Parnas lists two types of aging: 1) failure to meet changing needs, 2) the results of changes made to the software. Software users get dissatisfied unless software is frequently updated, and often look for an alternative that will satisfy their needs. Software that is unchanged is considered as "old" or "outdated" despite providing the requested functionalities with sufficient quality and reliability. This pressure for change confuses even the most skilled software architects. The "design for change" offers limited support in coping with software aging, especially if the entire product or the fundamental principles of this product are changed [14].

Aging of software is one of the factors that impact software obsolescence, explored by several authors. Rajagopal et al. highlighted the lack of data related

E. Papatheocharous et al. (Eds.): ICSOB 2024, LNBIP 539, pp. 149–155, 2025.
https://doi.org/10.1007/978-3-031-85849-9_13

to software obsolescence and management strategies to handle software obsolescence [16]. Bowlds et al. developed a software obsolescence risk assessment approach using multi-criteria decision-making, listing internally controlled criteria (defect corrections, enhancements added, customer code complexity) and externally controlled elements (COST application, operating system and hardware) [3]. What remains greatly unexplored is a holistic view on aging and obsolescence that takes into consideration both business and technological trends as well as software internal aging aspects, e.g., technical debt.

This vision paper makes an attempt to occupy this research gap by discussing the factors that impact software aging and suggesting an introduction of the concept of the half-life of software, which we define as a point in time where the alternative cost to keeping your product alive is lower than an increasing investment to prevent it from aging. We also look at the amortization of software as an intangible asset and relate our definition of half-life to the finite useful life concept from accounting [9]. This work extends our previous efforts on understanding what is asset degradation in software engineering [21].

2   Software Aging, Anti-Aging, Financial Aspects of Technical Debt (TD)

A recent literature review on software aging shows two focus areas [15]: 1) mitigation strategies for software aging, often called software anti-aging [13] and 2) strategies for identifying software aging. Castelli et al. looked into management of software aging by proactive fault management and software rejuvenation (occasionally terminating an application and restarting it) [4]. Rahman et al. [15] list the following factors that contribute to software aging: 1) complex and unmaintainable code, 2) data corruption, 3) exhaustion of system resources, 4) memory bloating, 5) memory leaking, 6) numerical error accumulation, 7) storage space fragmentation, 8) unplanned system changes, 9) unreleased file locks, and 10) unterminated threads. Interestingly, none of these factors is related to revenue or business. Still, the majority of the research is focusing on the technical aspects of software aging, e.g., predicting the aging-related bugs using software complexity metrics [6] while the business aspect remains greatly ignored.

Software anti-aging has been studied by several researchers. Yahaya et al. [20] developed the anti-aging model based on the following software aging factors: functional, human, environment and product profile. They also encourage the following external software aging factors: dynamic environment, technology challenge (hardware and software), competition, business stability and consistency. At the same time business demand and technology demand are among the top software change factors listed by Yahaya et al. [20]. Shao et al. explored the anti-aging rules of software reliability design, including triple modular redundancy (TMR) and logical partitioning [18].

Another area of software aging is dead code analysis. Romano et al. postulate that dead code is harmful not only in the maintenance and evolution phases, but also in the design and implementation phases [17]. Knoop developed an algorithm that eliminates the partially dead code (only dead on some program paths) [10].

Technical Debt (TD) is another aspect associated with software aging and obsolescence. Ampatzoglou et al. surveyed the literature on the financial aspects of managing technical debt, concluding that principal and interest are the terms used most, with Return on Investment used only in about 10% of the publications [2]. Real options, portfolio management, cost/benefit analysis and value-based analysis are the most commonly used financial approaches for managing technical debt. Chatzigeorgiou et al. proposed an approach to estimate the breaking point in technical debt, an estimate of the time point at which accumulated interest from TD will exceed the initial savings obtained by not repaying the principal [5].

This paper builds on that line of thinking by considering not only technical debt and internal factors that a company can partially control but also external factors, such as business and market influences, that affect the lifespan of a product. Ampatzoglou et al. proposed a technical debt interest theory, where they map money supply to principal (the amount of money that a software development company has, after incurring TD), and they map money demand to the accumulated amount of interest, the extra amount of money that is demanded by the company when performing future maintenance activities, caused by the TD [1]. The authors define the equilibrium point as a time stamp in which the company has spent the complete amount of money from the internal loan (i.e., initial principal - P0) in extra maintenance activities because of the incurred TD. However, the authors do not consider high revenue regardless of spending the complete amount of money from the internal loan, or external forces that may render the software obsolete.

3   Accounting of Intangible Assets

Measuring intangible capital has became a more and more significant element of company valuation and accounting [8]. Intangibles, i.e., software assets [21], have less explicit physical boundaries than regular assets, the unit of account usually is more fluffy for the prior. It is however important to a) determine whether the item is a software asset and if so b) calculate the value of the software asset.

The International Accounting Standard 38 on Intangible Assets defines intangible assets as "identifiable non-monetary asset without physical substance" [9]. What is important to understand in our discussion is that an asset is a resource controlled by the entity as a result of past events and from which future economic benefits are expected (IAS 38.8). Past events refer to prior software development and maintenance activities when a product has been developed in-house, or to integration and modification efforts when substantial components have been sourced externally. However, the degree of control can differ depending if the software is shared with other companies within a software ecosystem or an open source ecosystem. The asset is "controlled by the entity" which means that the entity needs to have the power to obtain the future economic benefits. For software producing companies this means checking if the licenses of software allows the company to generate future economic benefits.

The word identifiable in the definition of an asset is important because it implies that to be an asset an item must be either separable from the entity (i.e., sold, licensed or exchanged individually or together with a contract) regardless if the entity wants to do that, or arising from contractual and other legal rights regardless of whether those rights are separable from the entity. Future cash flows, control and separation are all hard to estimate for software-intensive products. For software products the separation can be done via servitization or extraction of software components or platforms that can be monetized. The intangibles that qualify as assets according to the accounting definition, can be written off using amortization. Accounting differentiates between internally generated and externally acquired intangible assets. This is important because for internally generated assets only the development expenses (i.e., those expenses that relate to the use of new research findings for the production of new or substantially improved materials, products, devices, services, etc.) are recognized as assets in the balance sheet and subject to potential write-offs. Research expenses are recognized as normal expenses (in the P/L statement, not in the balance sheet) and hence not subject to amortization (IAS 38.54) [9].

Once the asset is recognized it is normally measured at cost less accumulated amortization and annual impairment (IAS 38.74) [9]. The assumption here is that the asset has a so-called "finite useful life" and the ability of the asset to deliver on what it is supposed to do (generate future economic benefits) needs to be reflected in its value accordingly. Amortization usually begins when the asset is available for use. It ends when the asset is de-recognized or when it is "held for sale". Note that those assets that have an indefinite (not infinite) useful life aren't amortized but only subject to annual impairment testing.

Finite useful life usually arises from contractual and other legal rights and must not exceed this, but it can be shorter if a company expects shorter usage of the asset. If a life can be renewed then this extension can only be included in the useful life of an asset, if the renewal doesn't incur significant cost for the company (e.g., significant rework of architecture). Software lives are usually assumed to be short (but not too short) and they shall be chosen based on a prudence principle. Software, in theory, can have an indefinite useful life: there is no foreseeable limit to the period over which the asset generates benefits, however as pointed out by Parnas the changing needs make software obsolete and therefore contribute to shortening its finite useful life [14].

Amortization has to reflect the pattern of the economic benefits that the asset is expected to generate, i.e., it needs to take place over the useful life of the asset and reflect the future economic benefits. It is then calculated as the Net (purchase) value of the asset – residual value (i.e., what it is worth at the end), divided by the useful life (years). The residual value is usually zero unless: there is a commitment of a third party to purchase the asset at the end of its useful life (which can be challenging for software assets due to their high sunkeness cost), or there is an active market for this software product (which is also challenging given the unique nature of software solutions). The residual value can be calculated by reference to that market. However, there rarely is an active market for internally generated intangibles [12].

4   Towards the Holistic Approach Towards Software Aging, Obsolescence and the Half-Life of Software

We believe that a more holistic approach towards software aging and obsolescence should be taken as most research focuses solely on the technical aspects of software aging, leaving the business and accounting aspects greatly unexplored. Therefore, we suggest to represent the causes or factors impacting software aging and obsolescence as a three dimensional space as the first step towards understanding its half-life. The dimensions are: 1) People, Processes and Technology, 2) Market and Customer Needs and 3) Business. Each of the three dimensions contains internal and external aspects. We postulate that the external forces became dominant aspect in all three dimensions and thus should be taken more into consideration.

We postulate that software products undergo an exponential decay where the half-life is a point in time where it loses half of its initial value, as inspired by the work of Rutherford [11][1]. The half-life of the software can be considered as an equilibrium point that takes into consideration both internal and external aspects that impact the deprecation of software as an intangible asset. Software arrives at its half-life not only as a result of internally controlled forces, e.g., accumulated technical debt, but also in response to external forces. We describe and exemplify these dimensions below:

- **People, Processes and Technology** - this dimension includes internal aspects that impact product development, e.g., technical debt accumulated by an organization [2, 15], aging of software engineering processes and routines (e.g., low productivity), or external forces that impact the software technology and process, e.g., introduction of new programming language or ways of deploying software (e.g., DevOps) to the customers offered by competitors to the market. This dimension relates to the first type of aging suggested by Parnas [14]. Another internal factor in this dimension is the competence required to continue developing software in your current technology, e.g., developers experienced in a programming language that the software is developed.
- **Market and Customer Needs** - this dimension describes the internal and external factors that impact the ability to cope with changing customer needs and requirements as pointed by Parnas [14], an example of the internal factor is the inability to accommodate the changing needs of existing customers in the product and thus the depreciation of its value in their eyes. An example of an external factor is other products or actors that managed to better respond to changing customer needs and requirements.

---

[1] https://en.wikipedia.org/wiki/Half-life.

– **Business** - internal business (e.g., business models, monetization) or external business (e.g., product becoming obsolete due to change in legal regulations or disappearance of a market segment). Examples of internal business factors include obsolescence of the business model and monetization strategies, e.g., failure to migrate to the subscription model[2]. Examples of external business factors include rapid shrinking of point-and-shot camera market in favor of mobile phones, introduction of ecosystem based mobile phone platforms like Android that rendered feature phones obsolete, or introduction of new regulations and law that impact the business. External business aspects are related to Yahaya's competition and business stability aspects [20].

5   Discussion and Conclusions

This paper explores software obsolescence by looking at the external forces that impact people, process, technology, needs and business. We surveyed software aging, software anti-aging, the financial aspect of technical debt and accounting of intangible asset and structured the potential causes of software obsolescence into three highly interconnected dimensions.

The current literature is favoring technical aspects and often abstracting away business perspective. We believe this leads to situations when software companies continue investments despite the fact that their products are becoming obsolete. Examples of such cases are plentiful, e.g., continued investment in Symbian platform despite the appearance of Android [19]. The work presented in this paper is the first step towards exploring the impact and interplay between the business, market, people and technology on software obsolescence and aging. We believe that the introduced half-life concept is a step towards finding an equilibrium point in asset investment that can help decision makers.

In future work we plan to explore the interactions and potential trade-offs between the proposed dimensions (e.g., balancing technical debt with rapidly evolving market needs) to provide guidance for decision-makers. Lastly, defining specific metrics to measure each factor within the three dimensions would help to measure the half-life of software.

References

1. Ampatzoglou, A., Ampatzoglou, A., Avgeriou, P., Chatzigeorgiou, A.: Establishing a framework for managing interest in technical debt. In: 5th International Symposium on Business Modeling and Software Design, BMSD (2015)
2. Ampatzoglou, A., Ampatzoglou, A., Chatzigeorgiou, A., Avgeriou, P.: The financial aspect of managing technical debt: a systematic literature review. Inf. Softw. Technol. **64**, 52–73 (2015)

---

[2] https://www.forbes.com/councils/forbestechcouncil/2021/09/21/lift-shift-and-drift-when-cloud-migrations-fail-miserably/.

3. Bowlds, T.F., Fossaceca, J.M., Iammartino, R.: Software obsolescence risk assessment approach using multicriteria decision-making. Syst. Eng. **21**(5), 455–465 (2018)
4. Castelli, V., et al.: Proactive management of software aging. IBM J. Res. Dev. **45**(2), 311–332 (2001)
5. Chatzigeorgiou, A., Ampatzoglou, A., Ampatzoglou, A., Amanatidis, T.: Estimating the breaking point for technical debt. In: 2015 IEEE 7th International Workshop on Managing Technical Debt (MTD), pp. 53–56. IEEE (2015)
6. Cotroneo, D., Natella, R., Pietrantuono, R.: Predicting aging-related bugs using software complexity metrics. Perform. Eval. **70**(3), 163–178 (2013). Special Issue on Software Aging and Rejuvenation
7. Cusumano, M.A.: The Business of Software: What Every Manager, Programmer, and Entrepreneur Must Know to Thrive and Survive in Good Times and Bad. Simon and Schuster, New York (2004)
8. Eckstein, C.: The measurement and recognition of intangible assets: then and now. Account. Forum **28**(2), 139–158 (2004)
9. Ias 38 intangible assets. Standard, IFRS Foundation, Geneva, CH (2000)
10. Knoop, J., Rüthing, O., Steffen, B.: Partial dead code elimination. In: Proceedings of the ACM SIGPLAN 1994 Conference on Programming Language Design and Implementation, PLDI 1994, pp. 147–158. Association for Computing Machinery, New York (1994)
11. Kragh, H.: Rutherford, radioactivity, and the atomic nucleus. *arXiv preprint*arXiv:1202.0954 (2012)
12. Lim, S.C., Macias, A.J., Moeller, T.: Intangible assets and capital structure. J. Bank. Financ. **118**, 105873 (2020)
13. Morshidi, M.K., Nor, R.N.H., Mahdin, H.: Initial review on icts governance for software anti-aging. JOIV: Int. J. Inform. Vis. **1**(4–2), 232–235 (2017)
14. Parnas, D.: Software aging. In: Proceedings of 16th International Conference on Software Engineering, pp. 279–287 (1994)
15. Rahman, T., Nwokeji, J., Manjunath, T.V.: Analysis of current trends in software aging: a literature survey. Comput. Inf. Sci. **15**(4), 19 (2022)
16. Rajagopal, S., Erkoyuncu, J., Roy, R.: Software obsolescence in defence. In: Procedia CIRP, vol. 22, pp. 76–80 (2014). 3rd International Conference in Through-life Engineering Services
17. Romano, S., Vendome, C., Scanniello, G., Poshyvanyk, D.: A multi-study investigation into dead code. IEEE Trans. Softw. Eng. **46**(1), 71–99 (2020)
18. Shao, Q., Gou, X., Huang, T., Yang, S.: Anti-aging analysis for software reliability design modes in the context of single-event effect. Softw. Qual. J. **28**(1), 221–243 (2020)
19. West, J., Wood, D.: Evolving an open ecosystem: The rise and fall of the symbian platform. In: Collaboration and Competition in Business Ecosystems, vol. 30, pp. 27–67. Emerald Group Publishing Limited (2014)
20. Yahaya, J.H., Deraman, A., Abdullah, Z.H.: Evergreen software preservation: the anti-ageing model. In: Proceedings of the International Conference on Internet of things and Cloud Computing, pp. 1–6 (2016)
21. Zabardast, E., Frattini, J., Gonzalez-Huerta, J., Mendez, D., Gorschek, T., Wnuk, K.: Assets in software engineering: what are they after all? J. Syst. Softw. **193**, 111485 (2022)

Diversity and Inclusion in Software Business

Exploring Diversity-Driven Power Dynamics in Software Engineering Environments: Insights from a Qualitative Study

Konstantinos Tsilionis[1](✉)(iD), Jesse Stoels[2], and Yves Wautelet[2](iD)

[1] Eindhoven University of Technology, Eindhoven, The Netherlands
k.tsilionis@tue.nl
[2] KU Leuven, Leuven, Belgium
{jesse.stoels,yves.wautelet}@kuleuven.be

Abstract. The presence of gender inequality in working environments is linked to broader societal issues, such as impediments to democratization and economic growth, affecting both developing and developed countries. In the Software Engineering (SE) field, gender imbalances seem to persist. While extensive research exists on the causes of these gender-based disparities, there is a notable gap in studies exploring how gender intersects with other diversity factors, particularly race, which may intensify discriminatory behaviors in the workplace. This paper investigates whether gender and racial diversity in certain educational and work environments drives the manifestation of power-mediated behaviors (i.e., influencing actions and goals or reshaping personal beliefs) within SE roles. We conducted semi-structured interviews with students in SE-related programs and professionals working in SE roles in Belgium to explore their perceptions of gender and racial diversity within their academic and professional environments. Utilizing an abductive research approach, we applied open, axial, and selective coding to structure the interview data. Our analysis aimed to identify key thematic maps (termed 'code-trees') and integrate them with a specific power-exertion framework. This exercise led us to derive specific interpretations (inferences) that illustrate how diversity influences and is influenced by power dynamics in SE environments. These interpretations can inform policy recommendations to foster equity, inclusivity, and representation in such environments. Our results demonstrate that power-exerting behaviors are primarily triggered by the presence of gender minorities, who experience discrimination in both study and work environments. In contrast, racial diversity does not appear to be consistently linked to coercive behaviors.

Keywords: Diversity Dynamics · Gender Inequality · Racial Discrimination · Power Dynamics · Software Engineering

1 Introduction

The impact of gender inequality can be more accurately assessed by examining specific social contexts where gender discrimination is actively present. For example, Inglehart

E. Papatheocharous et al. (Eds.): ICSOB 2024, LNBIP 539, pp. 159–173, 2025.
https://doi.org/10.1007/978-3-031-85849-9_14

et al. [14] and Bellamy et al. [2] link the pervasive presence of gender inequality within society to a broader decline in the democratization of modern institutions. Additionally, Busse & Spielmann [4] find that gender disparities in labor force participation in both developed and developing countries undermine the comparative advantages in labor-intensive industries, which can, in turn, hinder economic growth.

Despite the negative externalities of gender imbalances, the Software Engineering (SE) field remains notably male-dominated [6,7]. Several studies aim to uncover the origins of such imbalances and analyze their effects on the field. For instance, Riegle-Crumb et al. [23] suggest that the misrepresentation of Science, Technology, Engineering, and Mathematics (STEM) course subjects at a high-school level as solely career-oriented fields contributes to gender imbalances in SE-related occupations. They argue that framing STEM subjects primarily in terms of their career benefits may discourage female students, who might be more interested in the intrinsic value and broader applications of these subjects, from pursuing them further. Gisler et al. [11] highlight the need to differentiate between various STEM fields when examining gender disparities, noting that stagnation in women's participation is particularly evident in computer science-related programs and roles. However, despite existing research on gender gaps within SE, there seems to be a dearth of studies exploring how gender-based disparities intersect with other diversity factors, such as race. In fact, race is often recognized as a latent diversity factor that, in conjunction with gender, frequently incurs behaviors attributed to bias in the field of SE [15]. Furthermore, research on how the combination of these diversity factors contributes to the creation and perpetuation of power inequalities within SE roles and environments remains scarce. Following the paradigm of Thomas et al. [30], racial discrimination in this study is defined as biased behaviors based on ethnic characteristics. These characteristics include skin color, facial features, other physical traits associated with specific racial groups, accents, and specific attire.

The present study seeks to examine whether gender and racial diversity within specific organizational environments is linked to the emergence of certain power-influenced behavioral traits in those settings. These traits may sometimes be misconstrued as positively connoted social characteristics associated with the exertion of power, such as dominance or assertiveness. Our study will primarily draw on the works of Lukes [16] and Milne & Maiden [18] which conceptualize the exhibition of *power* across three distinct dimensions: (i) *Influencing*, defined as the ability to affect someone's behavior, (ii) *Autonomous Goal Setting*, which refers to the capacity to set goals that individuals pursue independently, without needing further assistance, and (iii) *Exerting Normative Control*, which involves the ability to define values, norms, and ideologies. The choice of the particular framework was justified based on a preliminary review of relevant literature (for example, see [15,22]) which suggest that power dynamics are a critical aspect of diversity-related perceptions in professional and academic settings.

To achieve the objectives of this study, we conduct a comparative qualitative analysis of educational and professional (workplace) environments in Belgium, concentrating on areas where SE curricula and roles are most prevalent and active. This targeted approach allows for an in-depth examination of these settings within a specific socio-cultural and organizational context. Indeed, studies such as Sandell & Tupy [25] and Ryan et al. [24] highlight that cultural awareness and behavioral idiosyncrasies among professionals begin to develop in earlier educational settings. As a result, the following Research Question (RQ) has been formulated: *How do perceived minority diversity factors, such as gender and race, influence power-exertion behavioral traits within SE roles in specific educational and professional (workplace) environments?*. To address this question, we begin by conducting semi-structured interviews with students engaged in SE-related curricula and professionals practicing SE-related roles. These interviews aim to gather data on their perceptions of gender and racial diversity within their educational and professional environments. We then apply open, axial, and selective coding to analyze the data and extract insights (specific inferences) into the motivations behind certain behaviors exhibited towards specific minority groups. In that sense, our paper aims to assess the extent of gender and racial impartiality within the SE field and provide recommendations for educational institutions and organizations on how to gain a deeper understanding of the social dynamics affecting students wishing to enter the labor market with an SE-related degree and current employees already fulfilling SE-related roles.

The paper is organized as follows: Sect. 2 details the research methodology. Section 3 presents and discusses key inferences drawn from our data analysis, showing how diversity factors like gender and race impact power dynamics and behaviors in SE environments. Section 4 notes some limitations during the conduct of the study. Section 5 draws conclusions and suggests future directions for extending the study.

2 Research Methodology

2.1 Research Approach

To the best of our knowledge, few studies explore the interplay between diversity factors (primarily gender and race) and power perceptions in SE environments and roles. To address this gap, we chose to conduct an exploratory study [3] by collecting empirical data to identify and document behavioral characteristics that permeate educational and professional SE settings in Belgium. Our research focused on capturing the perceptions and experiences of students and professionals to uncover themes and patterns that explain the evolution of behavioral traits in individuals practicing various SE roles before and after tertiary education. We began by identifying key informants within the student body and technology-oriented organizations in Belgium. We collected qualitative data with the intention to explore mostly **informal** communication and influence mechanisms–often more challenging to evaluate and change– through which organizations shape behavior, particularly in relation to the treatment of specific minorities.

To capture substantive content from our respondents regarding their opinions and experiences, we adopted a qualitative research methodology [17] by conducting semi-structured interviews. Following the rationale described in the study of Yin [31], each respondent agreeing to participate in these interviews was treated as a source of valuable information. This approach allowed us to gather rich in-content qualitative data, which was then analyzed using open, axial, and selective coding. The analysis aimed to uncover latent behavioral trends taking place within the respondents' social environments and to identify the factors influencing these trends. The insights gained from this phase were then empirically associated to a power-exertion framework as presented in the works of Lukes [16] and Milne & Maiden [18].

Overall, an abductive research approach (i.e., a combination of induction and deduction [26]) was adopted due to its iterative exploration of inferences that best explain empirical data [27]. The abductive process involves identifying themes through qualitative data analysis (induction), applying the power-exertion framework to interpret these themes (deduction), and iteratively refining inferences to develop the most plausible explanations for how power dynamics shape perceptions of gender and racial diversity in specific SE environments. The approach is structured into three major tasks, each designed to build upon the previous one while maintaining a clear distinction between inductive pattern identification and deductive framework application:

1. **Data Collection:** The first task focuses on the collection of qualitative data through targeted sampling and semi-structured interviews. The aim is to gather rich, descriptive data without preconceived notions, consistent with inductive reasoning. We employed a purposive sampling strategy (see Sect. 2.2) to select participants from diverse academic and professional backgrounds within the SE field. An interview protocol (see Sect. 2.3) was developed to guide the semi-structured interviews, ensuring that while specific themes were explored (e.g., gender and racial diversity), participants had the freedom to introduce additional topics relevant to their experiences. Overall, this phase yielded raw, qualitative data in the form of interview transcripts, which served as the foundation for subsequent analysis.

2. **Pattern Identification:** The second task involves the inductive analysis of interview data to identify patterns and themes. This phase is purely exploratory, aimed at developing an understanding of the participants' experiences and perceptions without imposing a predefined theoretical framework. We utilized open, axial, and selective coding methods, consistent with grounded theory [21], to analyze the data (see Sect. 2.4). During the *open coding* step we deconstructed the interview transcripts into discrete concepts directly emerging from the data. During the *axial coding* step we linked these concepts to form broader themes and identified relationships between them. During the *selective coding* step we refined the themes further, identifying core thematic categories and structuring them into hierarchical code-trees. Six code-trees were developed (i.e., *Gender diversity at university, Racial Diversity at university, Power according to students, Gender diversity at work place, Racial Diversity at work place, Power according to professionals*), each representing a different aspect of the perceptions related to gender and racial diversity in both academic and professional settings (see Appendix[1] for an explicit description of these code trees). Overall, this phase resulted in a set of emergent themes and categories that provide insight into diversity-related issues in SE.

3. **Framework Integration:** The third task integrates the inductively derived themes with a power-exertion framework to draw structured inferences. We employed the aforementioned power-exertion framework as a lens to interpret the emergent themes. In this third task, to facilitate the integration of inductive themes with the power-exertion framework, a research team member utilized the *OpenCode* tool [20]

---

[1] The Appendix can be accessed in: https://bit.ly/4eg9GQi.

to run coding queries. These queries explored the frequency and contextual occurrence of specific themes within the code trees alongside keywords and concepts from the power-exertion framework. This step enabled the creation of thematic maps that represent the relationships between various themes within the code-trees and terms associated with power dynamics (Sect. 2.4 offers an example for how specific themes within a code-tree align with terms from the power-exertion framework). Next, each member of the research team revisited the code-trees, identifying overlapping codes and themes, and organizing them into four major dimensions: *Perceptions on Gender Diversity*, *Perceptions on Racial Diversity*, *Perceptions on Power*, and *Potential Implications for the SE Field*. Following this, the team convened for an extensive discussion to refine the findings, culminating in a final list of inferences (see Table 3) that best explained our empirical data and provided answers to our research question.

The following sections provide details on our data collection approach, interview protocol, and data analysis technique for retrieving code trees.

2.2 Sampling Technique and Data Collection

Given our focus on comparing behavioral traits between SE students and professionals in educational and work settings, we chose a non-probability sampling technique. This decision arises from the absence of a comprehensive sampling frame, which makes selecting a representative sample challenging [26].

To achieve a balanced representation of SE students and SE professionals in our study, we employed a combined approach of quota and purposive sampling techniques [10, 19]. Specifically, we implemented quotas where 50% of our sample comprised SE students and the other 50% were professionals. This method ensured equitable and robust participation from both groups, thereby enhancing the comprehensiveness and validity of our findings across educational and professional environments. The purposive sampling technique enabled us to select respondents possessing specific traits relevant to our study. Specifically, we targeted individuals who were either currently in academic training or already academically trained and who demonstrated professional competence in various roles within the SE field. We targeted final-year bachelor's students and those pursuing master's degrees, as we considered that students in the earlier years of their bachelor's studies might lack sufficient experience to recognize subtle behavioral traits indicative of potential infringing conduct. We did not prioritize any specific SE role or subject for either students or professionals. In essence, we perceived SE as an 'umbrella' term encompassing all roles involved in developing, delivering, or consistently utilizing software that adds value to a business context. This inclusive approach allowed us to capture diverse perspectives and behaviors within the SE field. While we encouraged the participation of individuals who identify as members of gender or ethnic minorities, to mitigate potential participation bias that could influence our results, we also welcomed participation from individuals who do not identify as members of these minorities. Moreover, we did not restrict the industries of professionals, aiming to capture diverse perspectives from various sectors. Last, given the topic and purpose of the study, we did not limit ourselves to a single gender dimension (i.e., male-female) when investigating gender equality in specific SE roles. On the contrary, our work acknowledges the multitude of dimensions open for exploration, including interactions involving male, female, and non-binary genders.

Regarding our data collection process, an initial number of candidates (students and professionals) was selected primarily from the professional network of a research team member, using *LinkedIn*[2], with consent from the other team members. A snowball sampling technique [1] was then followed from those initial cases in order to retrieve additional survey candidates whose profiles could adhere to the selection criteria as set by the research team. At the end, one student-candidate had to be eliminated from the interviewing process as the study profile was not directly related to the SE field; this brought the final number of participants to 4 students and 5 professionals. Due to privacy reasons, the names of these respondents will not be revealed; however, Tables 1 and 2 provide an overview of their characteristics. We acknowledge that the respondent numbers do not align with what Hennink & Kaiser [13] describe as the point of data saturation[3]. However, due to the sensitive nature of the questions included in our research, we encountered challenges in attracting a larger number of participants. We chose not to offer incentives to prospective candidates for participating in our survey, as several studies (e.g., [9] and [28]) have critiqued various incentive methods to increase the participation numbers. These studies advocate for broader improvements in survey design, such as clear communication of the survey objectives, which we prioritized in our approach.

Table 1. Characteristics of Respondents (Professionals)

Respondent	Gender	Ethnicity	Role	Years of Experience in SE
Respondent 1	Trans-woman	European	Software developer	3
Respondent 2	Non-binary	Middle Eastern	Data scientist	1
Respondent 3	Cis woman	East Asian	Software engineer	4
Respondent 4	Cis woman	European	Software engineer	4
Respondent 5	Cis woman	European	Software developer	7

*The term 'Cisgender' refers to individuals whose gender identity matches the sex they were assigned at birth.

At a later stage, these nine potential interview participants received a formal email invitation with detailed information about the interview process. The interviews were to be conducted as 45-min, individual conversations at a designated location. For the purposes of our study, we utilized a semi-structured interview format. This approach enabled us to engage directly with the interviewees and conduct in-depth dialogues guided by a set of questions. The questions were slightly modified to account for the differing focus on students and professionals. Nonetheless, the core focus of the interview questions remained consistent in both cases. They were designed to investigate how

---

[2] More information can be found at: https://about.linkedin.com/.

[3] Saturation in qualitative studies is typically reached between 9 and 17 cases [13].

Table 2. Characteristics of Respondents (Students)

Respondent	Gender	Ethnicity	Study Program	Year of Study
Respodent 6	Cis male	Mixed heritage	MSc in Computer Science	2nd
Respodent 7	Cis woman	East Asian	MSc Applied Computer Science	1st
Respodent 8	Cis woman	East Asian	MSc in Applied Computer Science	1st
Respodent 9	Cis woman	African descent	MSc in Computer Science	1st

*The term 'Cisgender' refers to individuals whose gender identity matches the sex they were assigned at birth.

gender and race, as diversity factors, impact professional experiences, team dynamics, and career opportunities within the SE field. Given the sensitivity of the study, we adhered to the guidelines outlined by Smyth [29], paying special attention to the design of question wording and order in our interview questionnaire. This approach aimed to avoid leading questions and to enhance the clarity and objectivity of respondents' answers. The interview questionnaire was piloted with one participant from each group. This testing was conducted to evaluate the design of the questions and to ensure they effectively measured the intended constructs. After the pilot testing, no changes were deemed necessary for the questions. The interview protocol is outlined below.

2.3   Interview Protocol

Overall, the interview protocol was organized into four major thematic areas. The first thematic area contained different sets of questions for each group. For the SE professionals, this initial cluster of questions aimed to gather background information, including their academic qualifications, years of experience in various SE-related roles, current job responsibilities, and an overview of their duties in their present positions within their companies. For the SE students, the first cluster focused on their current field of study and their motivations for pursuing a study curriculum in SE. Both groups were asked to define how they would perceive the exertion of power within their respective environments. This introductory section concluded with an explanation of how the concept of power would be applied in the context of this study, based on the definitions provided by Lukes [16] and Milne & Maiden [18] (see Sect. 1).

The second thematic area aimed to explore the respondents' gender self-identification and ethnic background. For the SE professionals, the questions of this theme also focused on their current roles, including job descriptions, responsibilities, and any perceived discrepancies between what was described during the hiring process and the actual duties performed on the job (e.g., *Do you notice any discrepancy between the described responsibilities and the actual responsibilities of your role? If yes, where do you attribute such a discrepancy? To what extent would you attribute such a discrepancy to any perceived diversity factors?*). These questions also investigated the perceived gender and racial diversity within the respondents' teams, their interactions with colleagues based on gender and race, and the organizational policies on diversity. For the SE students, various questions were asked about their university experiences to understand how the existence of gender and racial attributes (the latter mainly through ethnicity) impacted some aspect of their academic lives (e.g., *On a scale of 1 to 5, with 1 being 'nonexistent' and 5 being 'significant', how would you rank gender and racial diversity at your university, and why?, To what extent does this gender diversity status affects your university experience? To what extent does this racial diversity status affects your university experience? Are there any initiatives or programs aimed at attracting and retaining racially (ethnically) and gender-diverse individuals in SE studies at your university?*). Other questions explored how frequently the student respondents reflected on their colleagues' perceptions about gender and racial diversity, how these perceptions impacted their own behavior within the student body, and the identification of any positive or negative effects these perceptions inflicted on their academic experience.

The third thematic area included questions to investigate how gender and race affect career advancement prospects. SE professionals were asked whether they perceive any direct or indirect link between belonging to a specific gender and/or race category and an individual's career trajectory in their workplace. (e.g., *Have you observed any differences in career development opportunities between different genders or races within your work environment?, If yes, can you provide an example? To what extent has your organization implemented policies to address concerns from perceived gender minorities that affect career progression?, To what extent has your organization implemented policies to address concerns from racial minorities that affect career progression?, Can you name a few policies that your organization has implemented to promote gender and racial diversity in career progression?*). Questions were also posed to examine the level of inclusiveness in the work environment, as well as to explore experiences of stereotypes or biases related to gender and racial attributes in the working environment. These questions aimed to investigate how likely respondents were to adapt their behavior to conform to pre-established gender norms in order to fit in with their colleagues. For this thematic area, similar questions were posed to SE students, but were tailored to assess how gender and race were perceived by students in their classroom and group-work experiences. The aim was to understand how these perceptions influenced their study experiences and career aspirations.

The last thematic was meant to ask respondent some suggestions and recommendations about improvements that can happen in the academic/professional environment that can increase diversity and inclusiveness in the SE field (e.g., *What specific strategies or practices would you recommend for improving gender and racial diversity and inclusivity your SE organization/academic environment? Please provide examples based on your experiences*).

2.4   Data Analysis and Creation of Code-Trees

To reiterate, we conducted a structured analysis of the semi-structured interviews. The discussions that took place during the interview sessions were recorded in audio format after obtaining the consent of the interviewees. Upon completion of the interviews, the subjects' recordings/answers were subsequently transcribed into text and analyzed.

We approached the analysis of the interview data using open, axial, and selective coding methodologies, employing the *OpenCode* tool [20]. To enhance the reader's understanding, we will describe the coding process used to create the code-tree titled *"Power according to students"* as an illustrative example. During the **Open Coding** part of the analysis, we managed to retrieve some first-level categorization of the data based on the transcribed answers. For example, when questioned about their own definition of power in the organizational context of their the education program, the 9th respondent mentioned ... *"I really want to expand my power in order to encourage the other girls to do what they want and to be more in this field of computer science.".* This allowed us to create a first code labeled as *"Power as form of female encouragement".* The same process was followed iteratively for all the transcribed answers for the respondents. For example, the open code *Gender-Based Exclusion in Leadership Positions* was assigned to the statement made by the 7th respondent, who mentioned ... *"feeling uncertain about achieving a leadership position due to never seeing an Asian IT role model in pop culture while growing up".* The respondent also expressed that her gender further contributed to this lack of confidence. During the **Axial Coding** part of the analysis, we searched for connections amongst the retrieved open codes and grouped them into more abstract thematic categories. The aforementioned examples, combined with some other open codes retrieved from the student transcriptions, such as *Gender-based Stereotypes in SE Curricula* and *Feeling of Isolation Due to Lack of Female Role Models*, provided us with our first axial code category labeled as *Low Amount of Females in Leadership Positions*. Additional axial categories identified within the data include:

- *"Wanting to Express Power"* which encompasses the open codes *"Goal of Career Advancement"* and *"Driving Change."*
- *"Perceived as Bossy by Friends,"* including the open codes *"Power as a Pathway to Being Heard"*, *"Gender Bias in Behavior Perception"* and *"Reactions to Female Figures of Authority.".*

Lastly, during the **Selective Coding** phase of the analysis, we integrated the axial categories identified in the previous step into core thematic categories that offer a comprehensive explanation of the main findings. For example, one core thematic category that was used to provide context to all of the aforementioned axial categories is *Motivation in pursuit of power*. This category captures one of the various dimensions of power as described by the student respondents, highlighting their underlying reasons and motivations for seeking power and leadership roles. The clustering of similar in-context core thematic categories led to the creation of Fig. 1, which visualizes a conceptual map summarizing the code-tree titled *"Power According to Students".* This code-tree illustrates the various facets and manifestations of power as perceived by the students.

Overall, students conceptualize power in various ways, including the ability to control others and the courage to remain steadfast despite expressing opinions that may be disapproved by others. In many cases, the attainment of formal or informal managerial roles (e.g., leadership positions in student associations or as team leaders in group works) influences "blind followership," which underscores a dynamic where compliance with the position holder is perceived as *influence* (1st power dimension). According to the students, the exertion of power is reflected in a series of actions that demonstrate the *capacity to prevent others from interfering with one's goals and agendas* (2nd power dimension), such as choosing willingly to leave a company in response to racism, confronting team members about discrimination, notifying higher authorities, and seeking punitive measures against offenders. Additionally, most students perceive

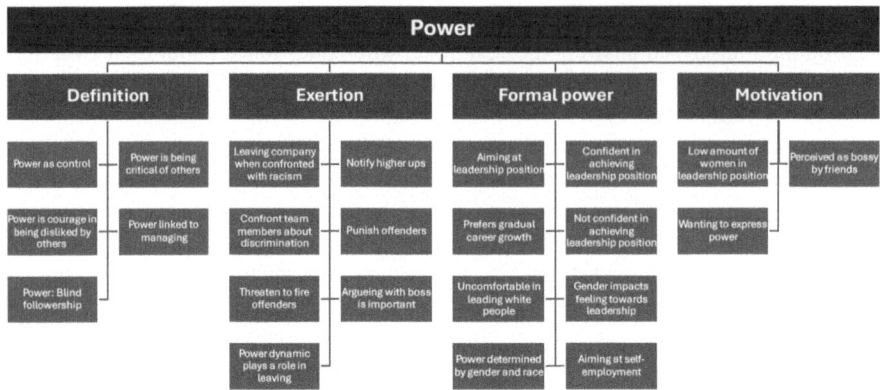

Fig. 1. Example of a Code-Tree: Power According to Students

that the display of formal power in an academic setting is influenced by factors such as race and gender. Specifically, adherence to established gender and racial stereotypes appears to exert a form of *normative control* (3rd power dimension) that can undermine students' confidence and comfort in pursuing leadership roles, due to these influences. The motivation to exert power is often driven by a recognition of the low representation of women in leadership, the desire to avoid being perceived as bossy, and the aspiration to express power in environments traditionally dominated by others. Due to space constraints, we will not detail the development of the remaining code-trees and their association to the power-exertion framework. However, it is important to note that the process followed for these trees adhered to the same logic previously described.

3   Results and Discussion

This section presents the compiled and empirically-grounded inferences in Table 3, which constitute one of the key contributions of this study. Due to space constraints, we present below a summarized overview of these inferences and highlight key implications that can be drawn from them. Overall, these inferences suggest significant gender imbalances in SE-related study programs, particularly those focused on computer science. Due to low rates of participation, female students often experience isolation, critiques of their competence, and, in some cases, intimidation by the dominating behavior of their male peers. This is a strong indication of the existence of a link between gender disparity and power-exertion where female students' behaviors are often *influenced* by the prevailing behavior of a predominant gender group in SE study programs. To counteract these challenges and enhance their social dynamics, female students tend to form and actively engage in various support networks during their studies. This gradual development of the notion of support, the need for female empowerment, and the creation of camaraderie amongst female students seems to be once again caused, even unintentionally, by the assertiveness exhibited by their male peers in their daily activities and group works. So, we see here the act of *normative control* to be in play according to the power classification of Lukes [16] and Milne & Maiden [18]. An important

Table 3. Student and Professional Insights on Diversity and Power Dynamics in SE

Dimension	Students (S)	Professionals (P)
Perceptions on Gender Diversity	**Inference S.1.1:** Under-representation of female students in SE curricula leading to isolation. **Inference S.1.2:** Female students actively seek out each other for support. **Inference S.1.3:** Need for initiatives and role models to attract females to SE curricula.	**Inference P.1.1:** Work environments are often dominated by masculine-led leadership. **Inference P.1.2:** Pressure to adapt to masculine behaviors to fit in. **Inference P.1.3:** Stereotypes and gender discrimination are often prevalent in the work environment.
Perceptions on Racial Diversity	**Inference S.2.1:** Racially diverse students often form groups based on shared ethnic backgrounds. **Inference S.2.2:** The existence of racial diversity is not a great cause of concern for racially diverse students.	**Inference P.2.1:** Opinions on existence of racial diversity in work environment vary significantly among professionals. **Inference P.2.2:** Racial minorities feel limited in career prospects. **Inference P.2.3:** Racial diversity often considered less critical than gender diversity, although some professionals highlight its importance.
Perceptions on Power	**Inference S.3.1:** Power mostly perceived as control over others, managing others, and courage in being disliked by some. **Inference S.3.2:** Females seek leadership roles to serve as role models, although their confidence levels vary. **Inference S.3.3:** Power perceived as a means to challenge gender norms.	**Inference P.3.1:** Power perceived as the ability to influence others and set boundaries. **Inference P.3.2:** Gender and racial minorities use power to advocate for inclusivity (e.g., awareness). **Inference P.3.3:** Professionals feel sometimes powerless due to systemic barriers (e.g., glass ceiling). **Inference P.3.4:** Preference to enhance technical skills over managerial roles among some female professionals.
Implications for the SE Field	**Inference S.4.1:** Gender diversity as a prerequisite to create a more inclusive environment in SE. **Inference S.4.2:** Lack of gender and racial diversity may deter some students from further pursuing a career in SE. **Inference S.4.3:** Organizations that are perceived as diverse are more appealing to students.	**Inference P.4.1:** Need for more gender and racial diversity in SE to avoid a homogeneous work culture. **Inference P.4.2:** Gender diversity requires industry-wide efforts, including female role models and diverse leadership. **Inference P.4.3:** Racial diversity is viewed as less urgent yet important for making the SE field more globally inclusive.

implication of our analysis is that, even in highly democratized socio-cultural environments for SE studies, there is a noticeable lack of (i) strong female role models who exemplify success within the SE community, and (ii) what Bystydzienski & Brown [5] characterize as 'early sensitization programs' intended to introduce young females to STEM-oriented subjects and their diverse applications. In contrast, racial diversity does not seem to play a decisive role in shaping SE students' experiences. While many racially diverse students prefer to form groups with peers of similar racial backgrounds, this preference is largely due to the ease of communication in their native languages rather than evidence of prejudice from peers in predominant racial groups. However, students did express a preference for diverse workplaces to avoid feelings of isolation.

Comparatively, SE professionals who identify as gender minorities often find themselves in a precarious situation, having to essentially adapt their behavior to align with what they report as 'predominantly masculine environment' within their workplaces. Similar to the SE study environment, this suggests that gender mismatches in SE roles in a workplace environment are heavily influenced to adapt their behavior in the effort to adopt more masculine traits (e.g., raise their tone of voice or adopt a more masculine way of speaking) to fit preconceived stereotypes. They proceed with these behavior-modification patterns, even if it means suppressing their personal beliefs regarding gender multiplicities, and engage in what they consider to be behavior that inadvertently perpetuates gender biases (e.g., accepting maternity leave as a justification to avoid promoting females to higher-level management positions). This realization underscores the link between gender asymmetries in the work environment and two of the power dimensions as prescribed by Lukes [16] and Milne & Maiden [18]. To be specific, the respondents (i) are *influenced* by predominant gender stereotypes to modify their behavior, and (ii) feel compelled to suppress (i.e., consciously inhibit) their own values and/or beliefs to better fit into their work environment. The latter case describes a situation where the respondents are being subjected to some form of *normative control*, which pressures them to redefine their values and beliefs. In contrast to SE students, SE professionals exhibit a distinct reluctance to seek positions of formal authority within their work environments. Despite recognizing the need for more gender non-conformist role models in positions of power, these professionals, upon entering the SE workforce, preferred to focus on enhancing their technical skills to justify their competence while maintaining a healthy work-life balance. A future extension of this study could further examine the reasons behind this desire to augment their technical competence upon entering the workforce—whether it stems from a true knowledge gap or some form of impostor syndrome. Nonetheless, this observation indicates that respondents might be the subjects of an extrinsic power-related instrument (e.g., prevailing culture within work environment), which causes them to significantly alter their long-term goals and ambitions (inability to exhibit *Autonomous Goal Setting* according to Lukes [16] and Milne & Maiden [18]). Similar to the experiences of SE students, race alone was not considered a major cause of power abuse in an SE work environment. However, respondents who exhibited both gender and racial diversity characteristics noted that internal procedures for career advancement within their current companies are indirectly (though inherently) structured to favor specific groups. This observation highlights another significant implication of our study which is the need to revise hiring processes and training procedures for SE-related roles.

4   Limitations

At this stage, it is essential to critically evaluate the limitations that may have influenced our results. **First**, we acknowledge that our sample size and sample diversity may not have been ideal in providing a comprehensive representation of the internal dynamics of the two complex socio-cultural environments studied. Additionally, a significant portion of the interviewees in our study belonged to minority groups, which may have led to an imbalanced representation of perspectives from gender and racial majorities. For instance, inference S.2.2 suggests that racial diversity is not a significant concern in student environments; however, this perspective may be influenced by the predominance of non-male participants in our sample. Including male participants from racial minority groups could have offered a more nuanced and accurate representation of the diverse realities within student environments. Despite the limited sample size posing a threat to the generalizability of our results, we align with Saunders et al. [26], who argue that purposive sampling techniques can effectively capture highly informative cases. In addition to using a neutral tone in formulating the interview questions, we chose our sampling technique to ensure that the participants selected for our study would occupy relevant roles and possess experiences directly applicable to mapping the current state of their educational and organizational contexts. **Second**, a more comprehensive view of the SE field would include a cross-country comparison of educational and professional environments. Currently, our study is limited to Belgium, which may restrict the generalizability of our findings to other countries or sectors within the software industry. Future research that includes diverse geographical and professional contexts could offer a deeper understanding of gender and racial diversity issues in SE. **Third**, the study conflates *racial* attributes with *ethnic* characteristics. However, ethnicity[4] is a broader concept that includes various cultural, social, and ancestral factors [8]. This conflation oversimplifies identity and diversity, potentially affecting the accuracy and depth of our analysis. Future research should clearly distinguish between race and ethnicity for a more nuanced understanding of these dimensions in the SE field. **Fourth**, the deductive linking of core thematic areas within the code trees to key terms in the power-exertion framework could be enhanced by adopting a more rigorous analytical approach. For instance, using a text mining technique could have quantitatively evaluated how well the terms within the themes align with the dimensions of the framework, potentially providing a more objective measure of congruence. However, several factors influenced our decision to use an empirical, iterative refinement approach. Primarily, we aimed to keep the analysis closely connected to participants' perspectives, preserving the authenticity of the qualitative data. This approach allowed for a detailed and nuanced understanding of emerging themes, ensuring findings were deeply grounded in evidence. Practical constraints, such as the dataset size, also influenced our methodological choice.

5 Conclusion

At this stage, we can get back to the stated RQ: *How do perceived minority diversity factors, such as gender and race, influence power-exertion behavioral traits within SE roles in specific educational and professional (workplace) environments?*. To address this question, we have outlined the development of a specific methodological approach. This approach involves the gathering of qualitative data from individuals actively

---

[4] Cornell & Hartmann [8] describe *ethnicity* as a fluid and socially constructed concept that involves group identification based on shared cultural traits (e.g., language, religion), and shaped by historical context and social interactions.

engaged in specific SE-related subjects and roles and directly experiencing the effects of specific behavioral attributions in their respective environments. This data, organized through systematic coding, formed the basis for connecting themes with a power-exertion framework. This approach highlighted how gender and racial diversity factors manifest in SE study and work environments and explored how power dynamics shape perceptions on diversity. Overall, the data suggest that gender minorities are indirectly pressured to adjust their behaviors to align with the prevailing masculine profile in SE study and workplace environments. This dominant masculine culture subtly intimidates gender minorities while fostering a sense of collegiality and solidarity among female SE students. Although racial diversity is considered less important than gender diversity in both study and work environments, possessing both gender and racial diversity traits complicates securing a job or advancing in a SE-related career. Future research should include all relevant groups within these environments. For instance, interviews with academic professors and policy coordinators, in addition to SE students, would provide a more comprehensive view. Similarly, incorporating perspectives from senior managers and HR professionals would offer valuable insights into gender and racial advocacy programs. Following the example of Heng et al. [12], these insights could be used to identify, visually represent, and analyze key actors in educational and professional environments. This approach would enable us to chart the SE field as a sociocultural network of actors to improve hiring and employee retention processes.

References

1. Baltes, S., Ralph, P.: Sampling in software engineering research: a critical review and guidelines. Empir. Softw. Eng. **27**(4), 94 (2022)
2. Bellamy, R.P., et al.: Challenges of Inequality to Democracy. Cambridge University Press, Cambridge (2018)
3. Benbasat, I., Goldstein, D.K., Mead, M.: The case research strategy in studies of information systems. MIS Q. 369–386 (1987)
4. Busse, M., Spielmann, C.: Gender inequality and trade. Rev. Int. Econ. **14**(3), 362–379 (2006)
5. Bystydzienski, J.M., Brown, A.: "I just want to help people": young women's gendered engagement with engineering. Feminist Formations **24**(3), 1–21 (2012)
6. Campero, S.: Hiring and intra-occupational gender segregation in software engineering. Am. Sociol. Rev. **86**(1), 60–92 (2021)
7. Canedo, E.D., Mendes, F., Cerqueira, A., Okimoto, M., Pinto, G., Bonifacio, R.: Breaking one barrier at a time: how women developers cope in a men-dominated industry. In: Proceedings of the XXXV Brazilian Symposium on Software Engineering, pp. 378–387 (2021)
8. Cornell, S., Hartmann, D.: Ethnicity and Race: Making Identities in a Changing World. Sage Publications (2006)
9. Curtin, R., Presser, S., Singer, E.: Changes in telephone survey nonresponse over the past quarter century. Public Opin. Q. **69**(1), 87–98 (2005)
10. Etikan, I., Musa, S.A., Alkassim, R.S., et al.: Comparison of convenience sampling and purposive sampling. Am. J. Theor. Appl. Stat. **5**(1), 1–4 (2016)
11. Gisler, S., Kato, A.E., Lee, S., Leung, D.W.: One size does not fit all: gender inequity in stem varies between subfields. Ind. Organ. Psychol. **11**(2), 314–318 (2018)
12. Heng, S., Tsilionis, K., Scharff, C., Wautelet, Y.: Understanding AI ecosystems in the global south: the cases of Senegal and Cambodia. Int. J. Inf. Manag. **64**, 102454 (2022)

13. Hennink, M., Kaiser, B.N.: Sample sizes for saturation in qualitative research: a systematic review of empirical tests. Soc. Sci. Med. **292**, 114523 (2022)
14. Inglehart, R., Norris, P., Welzel, C.: Gender equality and democracy. In: Human Values and Social Change, pp. 91–115. Brill (2003)
15. Kohl, K., Prikladnicki, R.: Benefits and difficulties of gender diversity on software development teams: a qualitative study. In: Proceedings of the XXXVI Brazilian Symposium on Software Engineering, pp. 21–30 (2022)
16. Lukes, S.: Power: A Radical View. Bloomsbury Publishing (2021)
17. Mack, N.: Qualitative research methods: a data collector's field guide (2005)
18. Milne, A., Maiden, N.: Power and politics in requirements engineering: embracing the dark side? Requirements Eng. **17**, 83–98 (2012)
19. Moser, C.A.: Quota sampling. J. R. Stat. Soc. Ser. A (General) **115**(3), 411–423 (1952)
20. OpenCode4: ICT services and system development and department of epidemiology and global healthopencode 4 (2015). https://bit.ly/3XauIJu
21. Pidgeon, N., Henwood, K.: Grounded theory. In: Handbook of Data Analysis, pp. 625–648 (2004)
22. Powell, A., Bagilhole, B., Dainty, A.: How women engineers do and undo gender: consequences for gender equality. Gender Work Organ. **16**(4), 411–428 (2009)
23. Riegle-Crumb, C., King, B., Grodsky, E., Muller, C.: The more things change, the more they stay the same? Prior achievement fails to explain gender inequality in entry into stem college majors over time. Am. Educ. Res. J. **49**(6), 1048–1073 (2012)
24. Ryan, S.D., Magro, M.J., Sharp, J.H.: Exploring educational and cultural adaptation through social networking sites. J. Inf. Technol. Educ.: Res. **10** (2011)
25. Sandell, E.J., Tupy, S.J.: Where cultural competency begins: changes in undergraduate students' intercultural competency. Int. J. Teach. Learn. High. Educ. **27**(3), 364–381 (2015)
26. Saunders, M., Lewis, P., Thornhill, A.: Research Methods for Business Students. Pearson Education Limited (2016)
27. Schurz, G.: Patterns of abduction. Synthese **164**, 201–234 (2008)
28. Singer, E., Ye, C.: The use and effects of incentives in surveys. Ann. Am. Acad. Pol. Soc. Sci. **645**(1), 112–141 (2013)
29. Smyth, J.D.: Designing questions and questionnaires. In: The SAGE Handbook of Survey Methodology, p. 218 (2016)
30. Thomas, J.O., Joseph, N., Williams, A., Burge, J., et al.: Speaking truth to power: exploring the intersectional experiences of black women in computing. In: Research on Equity and Sustained Participation in Engineering, Computing, and Technology, pp. 1–8. IEEE (2018)
31. Yin, R.K.: Validity and generalization in future case study evaluations. Evaluation **19**(3), 321–332 (2013)

Towards Sustainable ICT Solutions: Analyzing Call for Tender Documents

Markus Takamaa[(✉)] [iD] and Samuli Pekkola [iD]

University of Jyväskylä, 40014 Jyväskylä, Finland
{Markus.k.t.takamaa,Samuli.j.Pekkola}@jyu.fi

Abstract. Currently, all public development initiatives are expected to consider environmental sustainability, economic sustainability, social sustainability, and, more broadly, the UN's sustainable development goals. This requirement also applies to periodically renewable or replaceable IT systems and services. However, little is known about how the development goals are actually addressed in IT. As public sector organizations are obliged to acquire new systems through public procurement procedures, we collected all Finnish ICT-related calls for tenders from a public repository in May 2024. By qualitatively analyzing 106 calls for tenders, we aimed to understand how the sustainability goals appear and are addressed in public ICT acquisitions. Surprisingly, only 7,55% of the calls mentioned the goals indirectly in their descriptions. Even more surprising was the absence of generic reasons and motives for the renewal initiative. Only 9,43% of the calls clearly stated the objective of the system renewal or provision. These low numbers have several consequences. First, they illustrate that sustainability goals are not considered in the IT field in practice; They are dead letters there. Second, the absence of explicit motives for the system renewal makes it challenging to design, develop and implement the system and reach and assess whether the initiative has reached its goals. This could be one of the main reasons why so many IT projects are said to fail – not knowing why they were developed makes it impossible to assess whether they have reached their targets.

Keywords: Sustainability · Information Technology · Provision · Acquisition · Green IT

1 Introduction

1.1 A Subsection Sample

During the last few years, ICT research on sustainability has rapidly increased. United Nations Sustainability Development Goals, Green IT, and other buzzwords have also gained much attention in the ICT field [1, 2]. This trend is emphasized by the governmental and political initiatives that request various actors to consider, assess, and publish their sustainability goals, progress, and scores [1, 3]. For example, public sector ICT procurement initiatives are asked to assess their support for different sustainability goals, explicitly state how they contribute to solving major societal challenges and describe their support towards sustainable societies [3]. Environmental, economic, and social sustainability are especially expected to be supported by development initiatives.

E. Papatheocharous et al. (Eds.): ICSOB 2024, LNBIP 539, pp. 174–185, 2025.
https://doi.org/10.1007/978-3-031-85849-9_15

In the public sector, ICT systems and solutions are usually renewed through a public tendering process where the system needs and its goals, requirements, and constraints, and the procurement practices are published so that anyone interested can make a bid [4]. In this situation, public sector organizations are currently obliged to state how their renewal initiative addresses various sustainability goals. Previous studies have shown that when public procurement initiatives mandate environmental selection criteria, the likelihood of the introduction of more environmentally friendly products increases by 20% on average [5]. Therefore, public organizations have a significant stand in guiding the market toward more sustainable solutions.

However, very little is known about how different development goals are considered in the procurement of new ICT systems and solutions. This paper aims to fill this research gap. We aim to provide an understanding of how public organizations present their sustainable development goals in their system renewal initiatives, namely in the call for tenders. We thus aim to answer the following research question: *How environmental, economic and social sustainability goals are considered in public ICT call for tender documents?*

We provide a cross-sectional, qualitative case study on the call for tender documents published in May 2024 in a public, official repository. In the repository, all public organizations must publish their call for tenders, and anyone interested in bidding them may gain the documents and necessary information. The documents thus represent a cross-sectional sample of public tenders and further illustrate the consideration of sustainable development goals.

Our paper is organized as follows: We first provide the background of the study. We then explain the research methods and provide our findings. We end the paper by discussing our findings and their implications.

2   Literature Review

Public procurement is defined as a government's or public organization's act of acquiring goods or services [6]. As public organizations operate on public money, public procurement processes are defined as open and transparent – by the law. This means any party interested in offering products, goods, or services to public organizations must be able to do so. Legislation has thus defined principles for public procurement: publishing call for tenders openly in an open portal, financial thresholds defining the scope of the audience, strict practices for the procurement process and communicating and collaborating with interested actors, and a procedure for the complaints to be handled [4, 7].

Also, sustainable development issues, often through the UN sustainable development goals or sustainability pillars, that is, economic, social, and environmental [8–10], have been lately included in the public procurements. Sustainable procurements incorporate these goals or pillars into their requirements, attempting to maximize the benefits both for the procurer and the society. This is ensured by explicit statements in the tendering documents, which state how they are considered and assessed in the procurement processes [9]. The goals related to environmental protection and sustainability have been seen as a contributing factor in solving climate change, the loss of biodiversity and the reduction of inequality [3]. As the EU states spend 2 trillion euros annually on their procurements [11], public spending can contribute significantly to solving environmental and social issues.

Previous ICT-related studies on sustainability issues and UN sustainable development goals have traditionally focused on environmental sustainability, often using terms such as "Green IT" [9, 12, 13]. In the context of green public procurements, the focus has mainly been on national-level topics, and national or industry-specific themes. These include, for example, whether and how green values are seen as a critical factor in the service provider selection since green products have helped achieve environmental objectives, reduce energy and water consumption, and support innovation. However, how sustainability policies are extensively adopted in public procurement remains unknown [14].

Research on green values has overshadowed other sustainability issues [9]. For example, social sustainability, such as sustaining the humans' basic needs, making behavioral changes to support biophysical environmental objectives, and maintaining sociocultural characteristics during change, are mostly ignored – at least technology-related research [15]. However, Montalban-Domingo et al. [16] showed that social sustainability objective assessment has been absent in nations' public procurements and that the number of social categories is related to the contract size.

The third pillar of sustainability, economical sustainability, comprises economic expenses and benefits, and it's often evaluated based on operational efficiency, effectiveness, and productivity. Economic sustainability reflects long-term financial sustainability [17] and is often linked directly to the level of digitalization [18]. Even though a link has been found between ICT usage and the nations' GPD, it is still contested whether this is directly the result of ICT technology [19]. However, ICT usage can increase financial integration and economic activities, therefore improving the economic system [20].

All three sustainability factors can be seen manifested in the UN's sustainable development goals. The UN sustainable development goals include 17 specific areas that call for, for example, conserving life on land and water, building sustainable cities and communities, and providing decent work and economic growth. They also support goals for sustaining basic needs, such as hunger reduction, as well as good health and wellbeing [10].

3   Research Methods

Our study is a qualitative case study [21] in which we used document analysis [22] to examine the sustainability factors in public tenders in Finland. Finland is one of the most advanced nations in creating strategic sustainability objectives for public procurements in the public sector. For example, the Finnish government alone spent over 1 billion Euros on ICT procurements in 2020, making it one of the biggest ICT procurers in Finland [23]. As the EU legislation obligates an explicit statement of how the sustainability goals are reached, the procurement documents provide a cross-sectional sample of their contemporary expression.

We collected our research data from the Hilma service, which is used to publish public procurements in Finland. Public organizations must publish their call for tenders there if the initiative exceeds 60000 Euros. These calls are public so they can be accessed any time upon request. For our study, we gathered all ICT related calls for tenders published during May 2024 and included only the ICT-focused procurements. In other words, we excluded procurements that were closely related to the IT field but did not directly focus on it. Also, market research or sales management related to ICT were excluded.

We examined the call for tenders in detail. We first summarized their general descriptions and contents and explicit statements about reaching the sustainability goals. We then analyzed the procurement documents and their texts in detail to understand the consideration of goals beyond the legislation-driven statements. We especially aimed to identify any signs of social, economic or environmental sustainability-related goals and whether any significant trends emerged.

Most call for tenders contained additional documents with eight obligatory questions related to sustainability. These questions were answered bipolarly, either "Yes" or "No". The first five questions focused on environmental sustainability, while the last three focused on social sustainability. The questions were:

- Does the procurement foster energy efficiency?
- Does the procurement foster low carbon emissions?
- Does the procurement foster circular economy?
- Does the procurement foster biodiversity?
- Does the procurement foster sustainable food system?
- Does the procurement foster fair working conditions?
- Is the procurement have a minimum code of conduct?
- Does the procurement include a requirement for employment clause?

We also collected data from these additional documents and analyzed how the questions are answered within the documents. If the additional documents contained extra information on the procurement descriptions, we also evaluated this information in our study analysis.

The data was gathered on an Excel spreadsheet. First, we entered all "facts", i.e. explicit statements about procurement size, content, organization, and goals. This also includes answers to required sustainability questions and whether the descriptions contain any sustainability-related information. We also qualitatively assessed whether the objectives and goals were unambiguous and labelled them as "Yes", "Partially", "No", or "Assessed". If the documents explicitly stated the procurement objective, the objective was seen as unambiguous. The "Assessed" category refers to cases where the objectives seem clear in the description but are not directly articulated. Some examples of our interpretations of the call for tenders are illustrated in Table 1.

Table 1. Examples of quotes and our interpretation of them.

Organization	Quote	Interpretation
DigiFinland Oy	"The objective is to create working processes for selecting, buying and monitoring software licenses in a way in which the procurer has clear procedures for controlling and inventory managing/auditing software assets"	The objectives are unambiguous
Port of Turku Ltd. Oy	"The aim of this procurement is to integrate and automate vehicle check-in and boarding processes in the upcoming Ferry Terminal Turku port with up to two roro ferries turning around together in less than one hour. Concurrent departures will be handled from a single waiting area and check-in processes with as little personnel as possible"	The objectives are partially clear but where the processes are integrated remains unspecified
Kouvola Vocational Institute Ltd	"The procurement concerns about a finance - and payroll administration system for Kouvola Vocational Institute Ltd.'s finance management and payroll calculations as a SaaS service, including the system implementation, maintenance and support."	The objectives are unclear
Aalto University Foundation sr	"The procurement concerns about the transference of Aalto Space mobile application maintenance to a provider (including) the expert work needed for maintenance and development."	Based on our assessment, the objective is to outsource the application maintenance work

4 Findings

In total, 106 calls for tenders were published in May 2024 and included in our study. Out of the 106 calls for tender, 70 contained additional documents on sustainability-related questions. The answers to mandatory sustainability questions are shown in Table 2.

Table 2. Distribution of answers to obligatory sustainability questions in 70 calls for tenders.

Question	Yes	No	Percentage of "Yes"-Answers
Energy efficiency	11	59	15,71%
Low carbon emissions	3	67	4,29%
Circular economy	6	64	8,57%
Biodiversity	1	69	1,43%
Sustainable food systems	0	70	0,00%
Fair working conditions	23	47	32,86%
Uses a minimum code of conduct	26	44	37,14%
Includes an employment requirement clause	1	69	1,43%

From the 70 calls for tender documents with additional information about sustainability goals, approximately one-third explicitly described the fair working conditions to be supported. At the same time, the minimum code of conduct was said to be implemented in 37,14% of the cases. On the other hand, almost all documents abstained from supporting biodiversity and sustainable food systems or providing employment positions. Few calls for tenders claimed to support energy efficiency and circular economy.

Next, we present our findings on whether the descriptions of the call for tenders contain any sustainability-related requirements and information in Table 3.

Table 3. How many procurements contain sustainability-related requirements or goals in their detailed description? (n = 106)

Sustainability type	Number of call for tenders	Percentage
Social Sustainability	3	2,83%
Environmental Sustainability	3	2,83%
Economical Sustainability	2	1,89%

The results are astonishing. Despite 70% of the calls for tenders fulfil the letter of the law and explicitly claim how they are sustainable, only very few address the issue in their actual tendering documentation. One of the few examples is a welfare district organization that provides healthcare in a region. The organization aimed to procure a feedback system as a software service and increase social sustainability with it. The intention was to collect feedback on the inhabitants' wellbeing, public family and social services, and support related service processes. These goals were explicitly stated as its aims. The objectives were thus classified as unambiguous Since wellbeing can also be considered as one of the human beings' basic needs, the procurement was deemed to support social sustainability. This also supports the UN's sustainability goal concerning good health and wellbeing.

On the other hand, the Ministry of the Environment's call for tenders clearly considered environmental sustainability. The call aimed to acquire expert services for logical data modelling for a system to collect data from various environmental protection actors and authorities. The aim was to streamline the processes and practices and make the operations more efficient. Since improving the operations in environmental protection can be seen as supporting environmental sustainability, we considered the call for tender to support these tasks.

Next, we will look at the clarity of the objectives discovered. This is summarized in Table 4.

Table 4. Are the objectives and goals of the procurement clear? (n = 106)

Question	Yes	Percentage
Yes	10	9,43%
Partially	5	4,72%
No	83	78,3%
Assessments	8	7,55%

Table 4 shows the documents mostly lack detailed information on the objectives of the procurements. Instead, we found that they mainly focused on other requirements, such as technical or service-wise, instead of explicitly stating *why* the procurement was intended to be made.

Only about 10% of the call for tenders explicitly mentioned their generic goals and objectives, not just sustainability-related goals. For example, the Finnish Innovation Fund was searching for a service design partner to plan an update to the Lifestyletest app. The app evaluates a person's carbon footprint and encourages a more environmentally sustainable lifestyle. The update was targeted to add new features and expand the app so that it can assess the one's impact on biodiversity and provide respective tips to reduce these impacts. Even though the call for tender documents did not explicitly articulate these objectives, we interpreted that the goal was to prepare for introducing an app update. Therefore, the procurement was deemed in the "assessed"-category. The call for tenders also seemed to support environmental sustainability goals due to its fundamental purpose and its update.

Another example is the procurement of a check-in and boarding-system for a ferry terminal at Port of Turku. Its objective was to automate and integrate the check-in and boarding processes with as little human service intervention as possible. The requirements description ignored all sustainability-related information. An additional appendix, however, provided answers to mandatory sustainability questions. A "Yes" was answered to energy efficiency, fair working conditions, and the code of conduct-related questions. The procurement documents, however, left a more detailed description of how this energy efficiency would be implemented absent. Interestingly, it also remains unclear how the procurement can promote fair working conditions if it aims to minimize the number of staff in the check-in process.

Another unclear example is the procurement of Software as a Service for critical communication in an in-house company[1]. The procurement includes the service and its installation, update, and support services. The procurement focuses on explaining the system's functional requirements, such as being able to send communication through an app, email, or SMS, being available 24/7, and being reliable, coherent and ready for use. Regarding sustainability-related questions, fair working conditions and a minimum code of conduct are said to be used. However, again, they are left undetailed, leaving it ambiguous whether the service provider should support fair working conditions for its employees or for the personnel using the service.

This kind of sloppiness is apparent in almost every call for tenders answering "yes" to any sustainability questions; They do not provide any more information. As the procurement's general objectives and goals are vague simultaneously, addressing the sustainability goals will be very difficult and random. The vendors may succeed, and the target might be good and meet all objectives, assuming one can make the right guesses and decisions.

This vagueness is apparent despite the type of organization or of the procurement. Tables 5 and 6 summarize our sample and the organizations and their type of procurements, respectively. Note that a single procurement may contain various goods and services, explaining the number of goods and services exceeding the number of call for tenders.

Table 5. Types of organizations and number of appearances within call for tender documents (n = 106).

Organization	Number	Percentage
In-House Company	29	27,36
City	17	16,04%
Specialized organization	16	15,09%
Welfare District	11	10,38%
Tertiary Education	8	7,55%
Municipality	7	6,60%
Agencies	6	5,66%
Municipal Union in Education	5	4,72%
Others	7	6,60%

---

[1] In-house companies operate as any firm but are owned by a public organization. This increases their flexibility in their operations but hides public spending and reduces the transparency of the public sector.

Table 6. Types of procurements within the call for tenders (n = 106). There are 151 procurement occurrences.

Question	Yes	Percentage
Expert Services	46	30,46%
Information Systems	23	11,26%
SaaS-service	17	11,26%
Hardware/It-Equipment	14	9,27%
Software-service	13	8,61%
Software/System-licenses	5	3,31%
Undefined Digital solution	3	1,99%
Other Software	3	1,99%
Others	26	17,22%

5 Discussion

Most of our procurements leave sustainability requirements absent and unanswered. This implies that environmental, social, and ecological sustainability are unconsidered when public organizations acquire new ICT systems and solutions. The reasons for this phenomenon remain largely unclear and necessitate more research. For example, one could speculate that the absence is a result of the lack of knowledge and understanding about the sustainable development goals, their broad definitions, the lack of usable and applicable metrics and means, the actors' ignorance and opposite values, inappropriate pressure and sanctions from the legislation, unclear generic goals, or something else. Our analysis of the call for tenders does not reveal these issues.

However, our data shows one potential explanation: the call for tenders very seldom defines their generic goals, like the example of Kouvola Vocational Institute Ltd's procurement, as seen in Table 1. Considering, for example, an ERP system, it can be used to optimize the processes (faster lead time [24]), increase risk management (more control points), connect different parts of the company (system integration [25, 26]), or provide better information sharing and understanding about the situation (information flows [26]). These goals can be (at least partly) contradictory. Under the circumstances, just providing both technical and functional requirement specifications will not help the developers and vendors to deliver the systems and services, the procurers to compare different offerings, or the managers to assess whether some offering is appropriate or the acquisition project successful. Leaving a simple question: "Why is this system needed, and what are its goals" unanswered creates many unclarities later.

We argue this unclarity is one of the reasons, but not necessarily the only one, why the sustainability development goals appear so rarely in the call for tender documents. If the procurers themselves do not define the generic system and service objectives, it is very difficult to address some particular sustainability goal. An easily tick-able "yes"-box on some portal provides very little value for the system providers who do not understand the rationale behind the choice or how the choice should be implemented, for the governmental officials analyzing whether the sustainability development goals are reachable and reached, or for the procurer organization itself if there is no information why the "yes"-box was marked, and what were the reasons for such a decision. We thus argue that to advance sustainable development goals, the goals of the public sector ICT systems and services should first be explicitly defined.

These results imply that the public organizations in general do not consider adding sustainability related goals in their ICT-procurements. Instead, the focus is on the technical and practical fulfillment of the organizations' daily needs. At this moment sustainability related issues are mostly dead letters. Even though the focus in Europe is on finding sustainable solutions, they seem to be ignored and absent.

These results are surprising considering the current governmental and political initiatives in Europe and the impacts the public procurements are known to have. This knowledge is unused in Finland to encourage introducing more sustainable products to the market. Instead, the focus is on more technical requirements of the call for tender documents, which causes unclear objectives for the provisions.

6   Summary and Conclusions

Sustainability factors seem to be out of focus in the procurement of ICT systems and solutions in the public sector. When the call of tenders asks for explicit claims and support for sustainability goals, the answers are ungrounded, without the rationale for reasons or instructions on how they should be considered. Instead, the focus seems to be on the technical and functional requirements, not on the objectives and reasons for making the procurement at all. The absence of explicit reasons for the system goals implies that the responses to sustainability-related goals are also unjustified.

Our study contributes to the research by scoping the current procurement practices. Our findings on the absence of sustainable development goals in the practitioners' lives open up several questions: Why do they ignore them? Is there a lack of knowledge, understanding, or tools and methods? or are there any conflicts between the values and practices? or is there some other explanation? These issues urge for more research. Similarly, the rareness of explicitly articulated motives for the system and service renewal or acquisition encourages more research: Is this a reason why so many ICT projects are said to fail? If one does not know why a project was started in the first place, how can it be evaluated and assessed later?

We also contribute to the practice by providing immediately actionable instructions: please define the reasons why an ICT systems and services acquisition was initiated and what are its explicit goals? This will help the vendors in their work and all the actors participating in or observing the initiative. This will then help them articulate the sustainability goals in the calls for tenders.

There are some limitations. First, our sample consisted of call for tenders posted during May 2024. The procurements published at other times of the year may differ – although we doubt it. Second, our data originates from a single country, Finland, and its public sector. This means that in other countries or firms, the situation might be different. This urges more research in other countries, perhaps even cross-country comparisons, and private companies. Third, the reasons for the lack of sustainability goals may be due to the context of our study. We deliberately focused on ICT-related procurements. As they do not directly provide food and water security without other supporting processes and infrastructure, their safety is not a concern in Finland, which is a stable, high-income country that does not have such issues.

References

1. Nash, K., Wakefield, R.L.: The role of identity in green IT attitude and intension. J. Comput. Inf. Syst. **62**(5), 998–1008 (2022)
2. Nchofoung, T., Asongu, S.: ICT for sustainable development: global comparative evidence of globalisation thresholds. Telecommun. Policy **46**(5) (2022)
3. Merisalo, M., Hyytinen, K., Oksanen, J., Pihlajamaa, M., Uyarra, E.: Navigating the multiple views of value in assessing public procurement. Sci. Public Policy **51**, 463–476 (2024)
4. Ghezzi, R., Mikkonen, T.: Public procurement of ICT systems: stakeholder views and emerging tensions. In: Hyrynsalmi, S., Münch, J., Smolander, K., Melegati, J. (eds.) Software Business: 14th International Conference, ICSOB 2023, vol. 91, pp. 61–76. Springer, Lahti (2024)
5. Krieger, B., Zipperer, V.: Does green public procurement trigger environmental innovations?. Res. Policy **51**(61) (2022)
6. Bleda, M., Chicot, J.: The role of public procurement in the formation of markets and innovation. J. Bus. Res. **107**, 186–196 (2020)
7. Nurmi, J., Piipponen, J., Pekkola, S., Seppänen, V.: Towards successful information system procurement: lessons from the Finnish public sector. Submitted to a Journal (2024)
8. Purvis, B., Mao, Y., Robinson, D.: Three pillars of sustainability: in search of conceptual origins. Sustain. Sci. **14**, 681–695 (2019)
9. Manta, O., Panait, M., Hysa, E., Rusu, E., Cojocaru, M.: Public Procurement, a tool for achieving the goals of sustainable development. Amfiteatru Econ. **24**(61), 861–876 (2022)
10. United Nations, Department of Economic and social affairs, The 17 Goals. https://sdgs.un.org/goals. Accessed 15 Aug 2024
11. European Commission: Internal Market, Industry, Entreoreneurship and SMEs. Public Procurement. https://single-market-economy.ec.europa.eu/single-market/public-procurement_en. Accessed 13 Aug 2024
12. Dwivedi, Y.K., et al.: Climate change and COP26: are digital technologies and information management part of the problem or the solution? An editorial reflection and call to action. Int. J. Inf. Manag. **63** (2022)
13. Gholami, R., Watson, R.T., Hasan, H., Molla, A., Bjorn-Andersen, N.: Information systems solutions for environmental sustainability: how can we do more?. J. Assoc. Inf. Syst. **17**(8), 521–536 (2016)
14. Chersan, I.C., Dumitru, V.F., Gorcan, C., Corgan, V.: Green public procurement in the academic literature. Amfiteatru Econ. **22**(53), 82–101 (2020)
15. Vallance, S., Perkins, V., Dixon, J.: What is social sustainability? A clarification of concepts. Geoforum **42**(3), 342–348 (2011)
16. Montálban-Domingo, L., García-Segura, T., Sanch, M.A., Pellicer, E.: Social sustainability criteria in public-work procurement: an international perspective. J. Clean. Prod. **198**, 1355–1371 (2018)
17. Alsayegh, M., Rahman, R., Homayoun, S.: Corporate economic, environmental and social sustainability performance transformation through ESG disclosure. Sustainability **12**(9) (2020)

18. Evangelista, P., Hallikas, J.: Exloring the influence of ICT on sustainability in supply management: evidence and directions for research. **44** (2022)
19. Fernández-Portillo, A., Almodóvar-González, M., Coca-Pérez, J.L., Jiménez-Naranjo, H.V: Is sustainable economic development possible thanks to the deployment of ICT?. Sustainability **11**(12) (2019)
20. Avom, D., Nkengfack, H., Fotio, H.K., Totouom, A.: ICT and environmental quality in sub-Saharan Africa: effects and transmission channels. Technol. Forecast. Soc. Change **155** (2020)
21. Walsham, G.: Doing interpretive research. Eur. J. Inf. Syst. **15**(3), 320–330 (2006)
22. Wach, E., Ward, R.: Learning about qualitative document analysis (2013)
23. Ghezzi, R., Korhonen, M., Vilpponen, H., Mikkonen, T.: The role of in-house procurement according to Finnish municipalities' purchase invoice data. In: Dang, C.T., Cifuentes-Faura. J. (eds.) Proceedings of the 2nd International Conference on Business and Policy Studies, vol. 17, pp. 1040–1072. EWA Publishing (2023)
24. Quereshi, H., Asim, M., Manzoor, S.: To determine the impact of ERP implementation in improving the SCM operation in manufacturing. CenRaPS J. Soc. Sci. **2**(1), 103–121 (2020)
25. Katuu, S.: Enterprise resource planning: past, present, and future. New Rev. Inf. Netw. **25**(1), 37–46 (2020)
26. Munthe, R.: Benefits of company management systems with combination of ERP (enterprise resource planning). JRSSEM **01**(06), 610–620 (2021)

Exploring Perceptions of Blockchain in Cross-Border Workforce Mobility

Anastasiia Gurzhii$^{(\boxtimes)}$ ⓘ, A. K. M. Bahalul Haque ⓘ, Bilal Naqvi ⓘ,
Jaakko Vuolasto ⓘ, Janne Parkkila ⓘ, and A. K. M. Najmul Islam ⓘ

LUT University, 53850 Lappeenranta, Finland
anastasiia.gurzhii@lut.fi

Abstract. While most research focuses on the technical side of blockchain-based solutions, empirical studies with HR professionals and the workforce on verification processes remain limited. This paper aims to resolve these gaps, exploring the issues and processes that need to be considered before utilizing blockchain solutions in recruiting. We collected data using 13 semi-structured interviews among experts who are involved in the applicants' credentials verification process and 1 workshop among applicants. We analyzed the data from interviews using the content analysis approach, focusing on 3 themes, namely key motivators, challenges faced and proposed solutions. These were then validated and expanded during a workshop. Based on the collected data we provide essential design requirements for future systems and align them to all stakeholders involved in the process (individuals, certificate issuers and HR department). Our study extends prior research on blockchain-based verification systems, enhancing collaboration between recruiters and applicants.

Keywords: blockchain · credential verification · recruitment · design requirements

1 Introduction

Digitalization is becoming increasingly important across various domains due to many reasons such as focus on sustainability in organizations [1], disruption of the competitive landscape [2], changes in consumer behavior and expectations [3], structural changes in the business environment [4], etc. Even though the potential of information technologies in this process is vivid, certificates have stubbornly resisted integration into digital platforms. One of the reasons is they exist in different formats in disparate databases and often require labor-intensive manual verification [5]. Additionally, those certificates are still predominantly distributed in physical formats [6] rather than electronically. This situation creates several challenges when verifying the certificates such as reliance on multiple accrediting bodies, time-consuming procedures and administrative processes supplemented with the potential loss or document damage [7].

Fake credentials are seen as a widespread phenomenon. Ezell and Bear [8] discussed that such problems are growing exponentially since producing academic diplomas and certificates from deceptive websites is not a daunting task these days. A recent Forbes [9] research survey revealed that more than 70% of applicants provide false information in their resumes, such as education credentials falsification, previous work experience exaggeration, employment dates and workplaces. However, the fraud is not limited only to educational credentials, but also trust in the whole traditional certification system experiences a significant decline in value and reputation [10]. In addition to compromising ethical position, holders of fake diplomas do not possess the necessary knowledge, which may pose a serious threat in the professional environment. Recent research highlights the degree of fraud that has permeated in critical sectors such as healthcare [11], aviation [12] and even governmental positions [13].

In credentials management, blockchain technology has the potential to accelerate document processing, improve talent acquisition and increase productivity during the verification process [14, 16]. Despite the potential and existing efforts [15, 16, 18], in the IS literature, there is a lack of empirical evidence for understanding what challenges organizations face while recruiting and verifying educational or work-related certificates and design requirements for such verification systems. Therefore, our objective is to explore the sentiment in credential verification, provide a detailed overview on how the data for a prototype system that demonstrates a practical realization of the design principles were gathered [17] and in this study, we aim to (i) validate and expand the existing challenges that job seekers and employers face during recruitment regarding credential verification through an empirical investigation and (ii) identify essential design requirements for the blockchain-based credential verification platform development based on the comments and recommendations from potential users.

This research makes four valuable contributions. First, it identifies the main motivators influencing the adoption and usage of blockchain-based credential verification. Second, it identifies the main challenges associated with existing verification processes across various domains and our research provides a set of design requirements that support future development. Third, our findings may attract more attention from the business organization perspective and encourage individuals to initiate the verification and support of emerging technologies from relevant institutions. Fourth, the goal is to navigate the creation of an effective, fair and adaptable hiring process that can meet the organisation's immediate needs and ensure the workforce's long-term sustainability by utilizing emerging technologies.

The remaining part of the paper is structured as follows. In Sect. 2 we provide a literature review regarding blockchain in the recruiting and verification domain. Section 3 contains data about the method used in this research. Section 4 highlights the results of the data collection and blockchain-based systems design requirement. Section 5 summarizes the whole research alongside limitations and future research direction.

2 Literature Background

In recent years, the interest in blockchain has become incredibly high due to its inherent characteristics such as integrity, non-repudiation, transparency, and privacy [21]. In simple words, blockchain is a cryptographically secure protocol that facilitates the creation of an immutable digital data structure where asset transactions are securely shared between parties in public or private peer-to-peer networks. The main attributes of the technology include trust, transparency, and elimination of all potential third parties that are common to traditional systems [22]. Blockchain has become a transformative innovation, marking a significant milestone using distributed data storage, peer-to-peer transmission, cryptographic algorithms and consensus mechanisms, the technology provides a range of benefits including fraud prevention, data transparency, decentralization, traceability, immutability and trust establishment [14, 15]. While the predominant application of blockchain is associated with financial and supply chain domains, the deployment of the technology in certificate verification and recruitment gained more attention both among businesses and in academia [18, 23].

While existing research reveals attempts and solutions on how to prevent the misuse of official documents, they continue to occur in higher education institutions [20], various cases of document forgery continue to be reported, especially of diplomas, the most important identity document for jobseekers in both the public and private sectors. Even though blockchain offers opportunities for document verification in higher education, it has not been adopted widely yet due to obstacles (e.g. operational issues, cost of new technology, human resource challenges, regulative environment, etc.) [24]. Research is focused on the platforms that generate, verify, and revoke diplomas [25, 26], receive degree verification [27], models on how to design the system and frameworks [28–30], blockchain-based projects overview in this domain [10, 31] and development of private solutions [32]. The adoption of blockchain technology in higher education institutions provides transparent and online access to public data. The legitimacy of records remains uncompromised and concerns about data integrity are lowered due to the immutability inherent in blockchain. Any ambiguities associated with degree records can be easily resolved and verified on the blockchain system [24].

In today's competitive environment, companies must align their operations with innovative technologies and reshape their existing business models to survive in an ever-changing world [33]. Despite advances in research on hiring, performance management and training, Blockchain's adoption in these areas remains limited [19]. The lack of understanding of Blockchain's impact on human resource management (HRM) has encouraged scholars to further explore how the technology could support hiring practices, performance management systems, and training protocols. Hence, in the literature researchers pay attention to fraud prevention through the interviews and identification of qualified employees [34–37], certifications, training and verification [38–40] and overall innovation in the employment relationships [40, 41]. Overall, blockchain technology offers new prospects for improving security, efficiency, cost-effectiveness, and overall quality of HR (Human resources) procedures. Scholars state that the adoption of blockchain-based verification systems is expected to be gradual [33]. In addition, the role expectations of recruiters may also change, with an increasing focus on understanding technology mechanisms, assessing the cultural fit of candidates, rather than just performing routine tasks. Overall, the literature shows that many educational institutions are already using blockchain technology and how it can improve the efficiency, reliability, and decentralization of certificate verification processes.

3 Method

The data was collected in two stages. The first one consisted of semi-structured inter-views and the second was a jobseeker workshop. In the first stage, we carried out 13 interviews representing university admission services, corporate HR managers, and SME representatives. The interviews focused on discussing the challenges and provided us with a detailed overview of the validation process of received documents. In the second stage, we arranged one workshop with jobseekers to complement the findings from the interviews. The workshop data shed light on the drivers, challenges, and requirements for certificate verification from the jobseeker's perspective.

3.1 Interviews Protocol

We conducted 13 semi-structured interviews in 2023. The participants of the interview were employees of companies from various sectors and sizes, with different positions and roles in the applicant certificates authenticity validation process. The interviews duration was from 20 min to 1 h. Each interview process was divided into 4 themes: (i) background and problem description in the domain of employment credentials verifi-cation, (ii) verification procedure in more detail, (iii) requirements for the new system, and (iv) financial aspects of the platform and potential costs. Overall, the interviews focused on understanding the possible adoption and use of verification services from third-party providers and the common challenges related to the certificate's validation in their domains. The experts' experience was more than 2 years on their current position.

3.2 Co-creation Workshop Protocol

To identify the challenges faced with current verification schemes, and the design require-ments for a prospective system, a co-creation workshop was conducted [36]. The work-shop was attended by job seekers from 10 countries and lasted 90 min. During the workshop, the participants were divided into 3 groups. It was intended that each group contained members from different countries for a more detailed discussion of their own certificate verification experiences. The workshop had the following objectives: 1. To identify challenges faced by you in the verification of documents issued from abroad. 2. To develop a concept of an ICT-based solution that helps overcome the challenges.

In line with these objectives, each group was tasked to first identify the challenges they have faced in their respective countries and while considering these challenges develop a concept of how an ICT-based solution could help overcome those challenges. For execution purposes, the following 5-step protocol was followed [42]:

Step 1 – Introducing the workshop goals and objectives: At the beginning of the workshop session, participants were introduced to the key objectives and goals. The workshop facilitators communicated these objectives framed in a "What? How? Why?" outline, using short and simplified statements.

Step 2 – The challenges: This step is intended to explore the challenges that job seekers face in general. This step involved the following activities:

- Identifying the role of document verification in employment.
- Discussing current verification schemes that are used.
- Identify the challenges with the current schemes.

Step 3 – The solutions: During this step, the participants were asked to discuss a prospective solution that will help overcome the challenges identified earlier. The participants were asked to consider the output of Step 2 to devise their version of the solution. While proposing the solution the participants were asked to think about the role of blockchain there. Additionally, the participants were also tasked to document at least one merit and one limitation of their solution.

Step 4 – Voting the best one: Each group presented the solutions formulated in Step 3 and after discussion, the participants were tasked to vote for the one, while considering the challenges identified in Step 2.

Step 5 – Additional requirements and design principles: For the best-voted solutions, the requirements were documented primarily by involving the group that proposed, and discussion among all groups helped generate additional requirements.

3.3 Data Analysis and Validation

The collected data from both interviews and the workshop was analyzed using content analysis using theorization and annotations of concepts [43] and pattern-matching logic [44]. The data through interviews among experts that are involved in credentials verification was collected, transcribed, and broken down into smaller text units and coded according to identified themes namely key motivators, challenges faced and proposed solutions. The line-by-line coding of the interviews aimed to identify recurring patterns and key concepts common among experts in relation to credentials verification. In some cases, dual coding occurred, which was resolved through discussion and regular meetings between the authors of the current research to reach an agreement and ensure inter-coder reliability. Validation of the interviews data involved the workshop organization to collect additional thoughts from applicants utilizing the same themes. Additionally, we used pattern matching to compare findings from the literature review, interviews, and the workshop. This approach expanded the findings of the study by identifying common patterns and themes. As a result, it contributed to comprehensive answers to the research questions.

4 Findings

In this section, we analyzed the combined empirical evidence from interviews with experts and workshop discussions to answer research queries and fill research gaps. We explore the key challenges associated with the current certificate verification procedure, the contextual elements influencing the motivators that may lead to the new system consideration and propose design requirements out of the collected data to support the blockchain-based verification system development.

4.1 Analysis of Interviews Data

To analyze the interviews data, we divided the 3 Groups as well namely Group A – recruiting specialists, Group B – representatives from small and medium enterprises that are involved in the hiring process to some extent and Group C – representatives from the admission services from universities. The diversity of viewpoints expressed in the interviews highlights the lack of guidance from the business community that companies developing blockchain-based verification solutions should aspire and conduct rigorous research that examines this critical issue in various domains. Table 1 presents the outcomes of the experts' opinions. Hence, experts from Group A provided a detailed overview of the existing hiring process in the EU. The findings highlight the need to reconsider the importance of certificates in various companies and focus more on the practical experience and personality of the candidate. At the same time, an emphasis on the existence of fraud and data fragmentation in the certificate industry highlights the potential of blockchain-based solutions.

However, there are still some misconceptions regarding blockchain as a technology among experts. To address this issue, there is a need to clearly position the solution as a tool for the verification, not for the selection of applicants.

This is critical for managing the expectations of potential users. Additional integration with existing popular platforms (e.g., LinkedIn) and the introduction of additional services (e.g. video or AI-based recommendations) can improve the efficiency of the verification process and increase the number of users. Overall, the experts' opinions highlight the importance of balancing technological solutions with practical considerations.

Group B highlighted that certificates are not the most important part of the recruitment process which leads to the urgent need for the improvement of skills accessibility, especially in the context of expanding the global labor pool access for companies. The high emphasis on practical skills and the challenges associated with lengthy government verification procedures for foreign workforce supplement the need for the new way of credentials validation. However, companies are still reluctant to adopt new verification systems and the trust in such methods is low. Among possible solutions experts mentioned possible incentives as a reward for companies to join the system and letting individuals initiate the verification process themselves.

Finally, Group C experts are representatives from universities and the main issues that were discussed relate to the applicant for a degree from all over the world and their documents for admission. The requirement to validate all certificates, especially for applicants from abroad, is the complete responsibility of the certificate owner. To improve verification efficiency and eliminate fraud universities suggest providers that students may choose and follow the guidelines of the particular country. Overall, the findings highlight the critical importance of ensuring accuracy and authenticity in the document verification process, as well as transparency as to the origin of documents. Data integrity and efficiency of the admission process improvements are crucial, especially in the case of manual data processing. We found that universities are open to collaborations with blockchain-based solutions providers and are positive about blockchain technology.

Table 1. Analysis of interviews data

Theme	Group A	Group B	Group C
Key motivators	1. Adapting certificates importance for various domains 2. Faster and simplified search of qualified specialists 3. Effective verification system 4. Streamlining personal data management	1. Increased time of skills verification and hiring process 2. Need to expand the global talent pool and quick verification of qualifications 3. Applicant-driven verification process and emphasis on practical skills	1. Need for authenticity and accuracy in the document verification process 2. Importance of documents' origin transparency and need for data integrity maintenance and improved efficiency
Challenges faced	1. Personal data fragmentation and difficulty in engaging companies 2. Varying the importance of certificates and focus on personal experience and skills 3. Misconceptions regarding blockchain-based solutions 4. Potential data granularity and complexity in the candidate evaluation just based on the certificates	1. Time-consuming government procedures for applicants from abroad 2. Low relevance of educational certificates 3. Difficulty of companies' motivation to join new systems 4. Focus on specific domains with sensitive data 5. Lack of global temper-proof pool of qualified specialists	1. Time-consuming process of manual document handling 2. Difficulty in verifying double-degree applicants 3. Inability to meet increasing application demand and lack of external funding for third parties in the verification process 4. Complexity in the detection of fraudulent activities

(*continued*)

Table 1. (*continued*)

Theme	Group A	Group B	Group C
Proposed solutions	1. Focus more on companies' requirements regarding certificates validation 2. Offer options for individuals to exclude certain data elements of their experience	1. Advocate for simplifying visa grant procedures 2. Assess practical skills and relevant work experience rather than relying solely on diplomas and certificates	1. Introduce digital tools for document analysis and validation to enhance accuracy and minimize human error 2. Implement advanced fraud detection tools to identify and prevent fraudulent document submissions
	3. Clearly define the tool's purpose as verification rather than selection to manage expectations effectively 4. Provide a connection with existing HR tools 5. Add additional services: video ref. or AI-based recommendations to filter the data 6. Clarify who validates entities and bears the cost, considering various business models	3. Simplify the verification process; create a solution that requires one-time verification 4. Offer incentives for companies that participate in the verification process (e.g., access to the database of verified specialists) 5. Empower individuals to initiate the verification process from relevant institutions	3. Consider various partnerships with verification tool providers to replace costly funding models 4. Establish clear protocols for verifying documents applicants and consider leveraging partner university verifications

4.2 Analysis of the Workshop Data

The workshop participants were divided into 3 groups and Table 2 shows the results from the analysis of the workshop evidence and the responses provided by each of the 3 groups during the discussion. Determining the key challenges during the certificates verification process and finding an optimal solution based on the empirical evidence is a dominant concern of this research. The groups presented different perspectives regarding the future system, while the challenges associated with certificates authenticity are common in different parts of the world.

Table 2. Analysis of workshop data

Theme	Group A	Group B	Group C
Key motivators	1. Simplified verification process using blockchain and encryption technology	1. Digital transformation for document verification 2. Transparent and simple process 3. Use of blockchain and encryption technology	1. Online verification by means of blockchain and other digital technologies 2. Global acceptance and unified standards for verification
Challenges faced	1. Finding an authorized agency and sending original documents 2. Apostille sticker processing 3. Document transferring challenges and risk of losing documents	1. Attestation from the university, educational ministry, and foreign ministry 2. Verification for birth and marriage certificates for the local embassies	1. Time-consuming verification process 2. Excessive costs for document processing 3. Need to visit various places for certification 4. Restricted schedule (Monday to Friday)
Proposed solutions	1. Develop a system that will enable a criteria-based verification 2. Use digital copies only, no printed documents 3. Implement API access for verification and authentication 4. Integrate payment mechanisms through apps and local currencies systems 5. Conduct a pilot program to test the effectiveness of the proposed solutions	1. Establish a common website for document uploads 2. Include government entities in the system 3. Collaborate with various service providers like embassies and universities 4. Ensure online services and availability of digital documents 24/7 5. Implement API access for verification 6. Focus on user training to ensure a smooth transition to system	1. Develop an online application system available worldwide 2. Implement the use of QR-codes 3. Streamline the certification process to reduce time and costs by the system integration into the governmental systems 4. Enable online verification without the physical presence 5. Suggest conducting a feasibility study to assess the practicality

Group 1 focused on the foundational principles of blockchain-based solutions with a strong emphasis on the encryption, transparency, and decentralized nature of the technology. Comments from participants revealed that the described problems of traditional document verification processes, including the need to find authorized agencies, undergo complex apostille procedures and difficulties in transferring documents, highlight the urgent need for innovative solutions and improved verification mechanisms.

The proposal of a pilot test run to validate the effectiveness of the blockchain-based solution represents a proactive desire of individuals to participate in the implementation process. This way, we can make sure that any improvements in verification technologies are thoroughly tested and improved before widespread adoption.

At the same time, Group 2 emphasized the importance of collaboration with various certificates providers and authorities to ensure continuous access to the document verification process. Among the solutions they provided were the establishment of a common website and the incorporation of API access. The results of the group discussion revealed the need for the documents verification process and data storage modernization utilizing digital technologies. A huge emphasis should be placed on the participation of multiple stakeholders, including universities and other certificate issuers, ministries of education and foreign affairs to support the solution's collaborative nature. Moreover, potential users and more emphasis on the blockchain as a solution training is key to ensuring smooth use of the new online system alongside a unified website and engaging government agencies.

Finally, participants from Group 3 supported the findings from the previous 2 groups and highlighted common issues. Nevertheless, they extended the challenges part underscoring time-consuming procedures, high costs, and the inconvenience of multiple certification locations and working hours limitations. Moreover, integrating the verification system into governmental frameworks alongside QR codes for quick access can significantly reduce both the time and costs associated with the process for all parties involved. Overall, all participants showed a profound awareness regarding the challenges related to the traditional and commonly recognized verification process.

The proposal to conduct an in-depth case study demonstrates a willingness to thoroughly evaluate the practicality and effectiveness of blockchain-based solutions before implementation.

4.3 Proposed Design Requirements for a Blockchain-Based System

The diversity of viewpoints heard at the workshop emphasised the lack of guidance on the level of quality and convenience of the traditional certificate verification process. The workshop data also revealed the need for rigorous research examining this critical issue in different contexts in the recruitment process. We have identified that the challenges of certificate verification are related to lack of centralized storage and verification, transparency in the whole process, lack of flexible and user-friendly mechanism for verification, time consuming nature, lack of coordination among the verification entities and lack of proper data protection mechanism. Upon investigation we have identified several design requirements that can contribute to the design of a blockchain-based system. These requirements can act as guidelines for the system development, even though new requirements will likely arise during the development of such a system. Therefore, there is need for further testing and validation in the future from practitioner's perspective. The requirements that we propose are as follows:

DR1: **Inclusive solution**. The proposed solution should include all relevant parties involved in the verification process, so that, the user can use this service as one stop solution for any of verification from all required and relevant entities.

DR2: **Fast verification**. The proposed solution for a Blockchain-based credential verification system should provide a quick and flexible verification mechanism so that the users will be able to reduce the time needed for verification in the current process.

DR3: **Unified interface**. The proposed system should provide the users with a single system/interface that can be used for uploading, verifying and downloading relevant documents so that, users will not have to rely on/go through multiple parties again.

DR4: **Flexible data sharing**. The proposed system needs to have a flexible data sharing mechanism such as QR code, so that, users can share this QR code with relevant parties for necessary verification.

DR5: **Payments' flexibility**. The system needs to incorporate flexible payment mechanisms such as integration with the local currency and credit card for international payment so that users can use this system from any place they require with any flexible payment method to choose from.

DR6: **Data protection and privacy**. The proposed system should include proper data protection, privacy mechanisms to comply with existing laws on data privacy (e.g. EU's GDPR) so that, users' valuable data is not hampered in case of system failure.

DR7: **Interoperability**. The proposed system should include interoperability among the credential providers, so that, the users can easily upload and download their document from any platforms.

DR8: **Scalability**. The proposed systems need to be scalable so that, it can efficiently store and analyse increased number of users, especially if more companies are willing to participate in the system.

DR9: **Transparency and integrity**. The proposed system needs to facilitate the companies about the transparency and integrity of the credential provider and their authenticity.

DR10: **Bonus/reward model**. The system can introduce incentives for participating and using this service, therefore more users (both companies and individuals) are willing to participate in the ecosystem.

DR11: **Individuals' empowerment**. The system developers should empower individuals to initiate verification themselves and provide options to connect with certificate issuers in a quick and simple manner.

4.4 Synthesized Framework of Requirements

Based on the insights obtained from the empirical data analysis, we identified 3 main parties involved in the verification process in the recruiting context: individuals (certificate holders), certificate issuers, and HR departments/admission services office (Fig. 1). We provide a simplified framework that addresses important requirements for every stakeholder involved in the process. In this case, individual entities that initiate the verification from relevant institutions, certificate issuers confirm the authenticity of the document, and HR specialists validate the outcomes of the verification process. The challenges section explains the main constraints that every party involved faces; design requirements are meant to resolve those issues and make the system more attractive to potential users. Our findings complement the existing progress in this domain [7, 12] by focusing on the empirical data and the importance of such system in the verification domain.

Overall, we found that individuals focus on convenience, price and efficiency, emphasizing the need for a comprehensive, fast and secure verification process of their documents. Certificate issuers emphasize functionality and scalability, with a huge focus on interoperability, simplified processes and efficient data management. HR departments and admission service representatives prioritize efficiency and reliability, looking for rational processes, fast validation and transparent, reliable validation results that will be accepted by other parties without an additional timely verification request. Understanding these priorities is critical to developing a solution that meets the needs of all stakeholders and maximizes the benefits of blockchain technology for certificate verification.

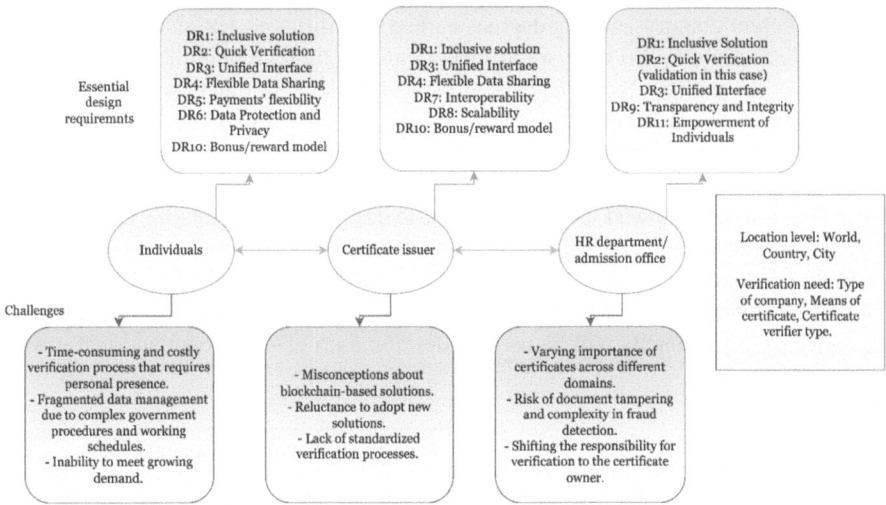

Fig. 1. A framework for scoping blockchain-based verification solutions

Additionally, we found that the general adoption of blockchain-based verification systems depends on several factors. First, individuals who initiate the verification from relevant institutions and encourage other parties to consider alternative options. Second, certificate issuers may collaborate with certificates verification providers to eliminate time-consuming procedures for their students in the future. Finally, HR or admission departments could allow individuals to be more flexible in case of choosing verification methods. Fourth, verification systems providers should unite all parties involved by providing bonus systems, a pool of talented and verified specialists and the creation of viable business models without a stick focus on one stakeholder only.

5   Implications and Discussion

The paper has several contributions. First, even though numerous papers discuss the role of blockchain in certificate verification and recruiting in particular [5, 12, 20, 24], the overall knowledge regarding the blockchain-based system in the certificate verification process is still limited. Our findings emphasize that even though blockchain can revolutionize and completely transform credential verification in recruiting, our findings show that both companies and individuals are wary about the technology. Nevertheless, while scholars [28–30, 32] focus on the technical perspective and the development process, we provide a discussion with experts from various domains and job applicants to reveal challenges and design requirements that are essential to consider blockchain in credential verification based on their feedback. Second, the findings complement the existing research with empirical data that can be expanded in the future and encourage scholars to focus more on blockchain-based solutions not only in the verification domain but also in the technology adoption in educational institutions. Third, the investigation revealed several challenges for credential verification, especially when a job seeker is applying from a different country and has degrees earned in a different region than that of the employer's country. In this case, a job seeker must go through multiple steps and visit multiple verifier entities. Issues have been noticed while recruiting people from around the world in terms of fake credentials, identifying the verifier entities, and establishing the integrity and trustworthiness of the credential provider. Fourth, we have outlined and identified the novel research challenges from both job seekers' and employers' perspectives. The data also allowed us to propose basic design requirements for developing a trustworthy, transparent, and efficient credential verification system.

Future research will focus on a broader empirical validation of blockchain-based solutions' potential for credential verification, particularly in recruiting. Additionally, the collected requirements will be used to develop a proof-of-concept and test it with field experts.

6   Conclusion

In this study we identified the existing challenges that job seekers and employers face during recruitment regarding credential verification and identified design requirements for the blockchain-based credential verification platform development based on the comments and recommendations from potential users. The current research derived the following conclusions. First, we empirically validated the importance of a blockchain-based verification system among certificates' owners and career experts. Second, based on the data collected through interviews and the workshop we identified essential design requirements that will support future systems development. Third, the deeper insights into HR managers' and business owners' perspective in the case of verification revealed a huge load on applicants. This leads to the significance of focusing not solely on business owners and HR departments but also towards involving individuals and certificate issuers in the adoption of blockchain-based verification system.

Acknowledgments. This project is supported by the Business Finland project, SafeRecords. Project number 7441/31/2022.

References

1. Duerr, S., Holotiuk, F., Beimborn, D., Wagner, H.-T., Weitzel, T.: What is digital organizational culture? Insights from exploratory case studies. In: Hawaii International Conference on System Sciences, Waikoloa Beach, HI, pp. 5126–5135 (2018)
2. Delmond, M.-Hh., Coelho, F., Keravel, A., Mahl, R.: How information systems enable digital transformation: a focus on business models and value coproduction. SSRN Electron. J. **14**(3), 7–40 (2016)
3. Bassano, C., Gaeta, M., Piciocchi, P., Spohrer, J.C.: Learning the models of customer behavior: from television advertising to online marketing. Int. J. Electron. Commer. **21**(4), 572–604 (2017)
4. Hansen, R., Sia, S.K.: Hummel's digital transformation toward omnichannel retailing: key lessons learned. MIS Q. Executive **14**(2), 51–66 (2015)
5. Turkanovic, M., Holbl, M., Kosic, K., Hericko, M., Kamisalic, A.: EduCTX: a blockchain-based higher education credit platform. IEEE Access **6**, 5112–5127 (2018)
6. Vidal, F.R., Gouveia, F., Soares, C.: Revocation mechanisms for academic certificates stored on a blockchain. In: 15th Iberian Conference on Information Systems and Technologies (CISTI) (2020)
7. Chen, Z.: Revolutionising HRM practice with blockchain technology: unleashing disruptive paradigms of work and overcoming management challenges. Technol. Anal. Strateg. Manag. 1–14 (2023)
8. Ezell, A., Bear, J.: Degree Mills: The Billion-Dollar Industry That Has Sold Over a Million Fake Diplomas. Prometheus Books, Amherst (2012)
9. Forbes Careers. https://www.forbes.com/sites/bryanrobinson/2023/11/05/70-of-workers-lie-on-resumes-new-study-shows/. Accessed 10 May 2024
10. Tariq, A., Binte Haq, H., Ali, S.T.: Cerberus: a blockchain-based accreditation and degree verification system. IEEE Trans. Comput. Soc. Syst. **10**(4), 1503–1514 (2023)
11. Telegraph Media Group. https://www.telegraph.co.uk/education/2018/01/16/nhs-consultants-nurses-accused-buying-fake-degrees-online/. Accessed 14 Feb 2024
12. The Express Tribune. https://tribune.com.pk/story/1706726/24-active-pia-pilots-fake-degrees-caa-informs-sc. Accessed 14 Feb 2024
13. The news: FIA probing fake degrees attestation by HEC officials. https://www.thenews.com.pk/print/392649-fia-probing-fake-degrees-attestation-by-hec-officials. Accessed 14 Feb 2024
14. Chillakuri, B., Attili, V.S.: Role of blockchain in HR's response to new-normal. Int. J. Organ. Anal. **30**(6), 1359–1378 (2021)
15. Zhu, P., Hu, J., Li, X., Zhu, Q.: Using blockchain technology to enhance the traceability of original achievements. IEEE Trans. Eng. Manag. **70**(5), 1693–1707 (2023)
16. Hegadekatti, K.: Blockchain and human resources management. SSRN Electron. J. **10**(2) (2018)
17. Parkkila, J., et al.: Designing GDPR compliant credential verification using blockchain: a design science research approach. In: ECIS 2024 Proceedings, vol. 5 (2024)
18. Keck, I.R., Vidal, M.E., Heller, L.: Digital transformation of education credential processes and life cycles - a framework of research questions based on the main challenges. Int. J. Adv. Intell. Syst. **13**(3), 204–211 (2020)
19. Salah, D., Ahmed, M.H., ElDahshan, K.: Blockchain applications in human resources management. Proc. Eval. Assess. Softw. Eng. 383–389 (2020)
20. Rustemi, A., Dalipi, F., Atanasovski, V., Risteski, A.: A systematic literature review on blockchain-based systems for academic certificate verification. IEEE Access **11**, 64679–64696 (2023)

21. Rajasekaran, A.S., Azees, M., Al-Turjman, F.: A comprehensive survey on Blockchain technology. Sustain. Energy Technol. Assess. (52), 102039 (2022)
22. Chowdhury, N.: Inside Blockchain, Bitcoin, and Cryptocurrencies. Auerbach Publications, Boca Raton (2019)
23. Hughes, L., Dwivedi, Y.K., Misra, S.K., Rana, N.P., Raghavan, V., Akella, V.: Blockchain Research, practice and policy: applications, benefits, limitations, emerging research themes and research agenda. Int. J. Inf. Manag. **49**, 114–129 (2019)
24. Dwivedi, S., Vig, S.: Blockchain adoption in higher-education institutions in India: identifying the main challenges. Cogent Educ. **11**(1) (2023)
25. Kwok, A.O., Treiblmaier, H.: No one left behind in education: blockchain-based transformation and its potential for Social Inclusion. Asia Pac. Educ. Rev. **23**(3), 445–455 (2022)
26. Salau, O., Adeshina, S.A.: Secure document verification system using blockchain. In: 1st International Conference on Multidisciplinary Engineering and Applied Science (ICMEAS), Abuja, Nigeria, pp. 1–7 (2021)
27. Nguyen, D.-H., Nguyen-Duc, D.-N., Huynh-Tuong, N., Pham, H.A.: CVSS: a blockchainized certificate verifying support system. In: Proceedings of the Ninth International Symposium on Information and Communication Technology - SoICT 2018, pp. 436–442 (2018)
28. Cernian, A., Vlasceanu, E., Tiganoaia, B., Iftemi, A.: Deploying blockchain technology for storing digital diplomas. In: 2021 23rd International Conference on Control Systems and Computer Science (CSCS), Bucharest, Romania, pp. 322–327 (2021)
29. Kontzinos, C., Markaki, O., Kokkinakos, P., Karakolis, V., Skalidakis, S., Psarras, J.: Leveraging blockchain, analytics and decision support to facilitate qualifications' verification, recruitment and competency management: the QualiChain project and initial results. Int. J. Adv. Intell. Syst. **13**, 177–191 (2020)
30. Reza, A.W., Islam, K., Muntaha, S., Abdur Rahman, O.B., Islam, R., Arefin, M.S.: Education certification and verified documents sharing system by Blockchain. Int. J. Intell. Eng. Syst. **15**(6), 682–691 (2022)
31. Enescu, F.M., Bizon, N., Ionescu, V.M.: Blockchain technology protects diplomas against fraud. In: 2021 13th International Conference on Electronics, Computers and Artificial Intelligence (ECAI), (Pitesti, Romania), pp. 1–6 (2021)
32. Wicaksana, A., Wira, J.: Security analysis of private blockchain implementation for digital diploma. Int. J. Innov. Comput. Inf. Control **18**(5), 1–15 (2022)
33. Kişi, N.: Exploratory research on the use of blockchain technology in recruitment. Sustainability **14**(16), 10098 (2022)
34. Signet Screening: How to discover resume falsifications. https://www.signetscreening.com/false-resume/. Accessed 6 Feb 2024
35. Bamberger, K.A., Canetti, R., Goldwasser, S., Wexler, R., Zimmerman, E.: Verification dilemmas, law, and the promise of zero-knowledge proofs. SSRN Electron. J. **37**(1) (2021)
36. Jones, P.: Contexts of co-creation: designing with system stakeholders. In: Jones, Kijima, K. (eds.) Systemic Design, pp. 3–52. Springer, Tokyo (2018)
37. Yi, C.S., Yung, E., Fong, C., Tripathi, S.: Benefits and use of blockchain technology to human resources management: a critical review. Int. J. Hum. Resour. Stud. **10**(2) (2020)
38. Jain, G., Sharma, N., Shrivastava, A.: Enhancing training effectiveness for organizations through blockchain-enabled training effectiveness measurement (Betem). J. Organ. Chang. Manag. **34**(2), 439–461 (2021)
39. Fachrunnisa, O., Hussain, F.K.: Blockchain-based human resource management practices for mitigating skills and competencies gap in workforce. Int. J. Eng. Bus. Manag. **12**, 1–11 (2020)
40. Adel, H., ElBakary, M., ElDahshan, K., Salah, D.: BC-HRM: a blockchain-based human resource management system utilizing smart contracts. Lecture Notes in Networks and Systems, vol. 309, pp. 91–105. Springer, Cham (2021)

41. Marella, V., Vijayan, A.: Document verification using blockchain for trusted CV information. In: Proceedings of the Americas Conference on Information Systems (AMCIS 2020), Virtual Conference, pp. 15–17 (2020)
42. Bakhaev, S., Naqvi, B., Wolff, A., Smolander, K.: Co-creating requirements for the emerging electronic identity management platform. In: Scandinavian Conference on Information Systems, vol. 1 (2023)
43. Hsieh, H.-F., Shannon, S.E.: Three approaches to qualitative content analysis. Qual. Health Res. **15**(9), 1277–1288 (2005)
44. Trochim, W.M.K.: Outcome pattern matching and program theory. Eval. Program Plann. **12**(4), 355–366 (1989)

Experience of Gender Among Professionals in Finnish IT Companies

Aila Kronqvist[1]([✉]) [iD] and Rebekah Rousi[2] [iD]

[1] Faculty of Information Technology, University of Jyväskylä, Jyväskylä, Finland
`aila.j.kronqvist@student.jyu.fi`
[2] School of Marketing and Communication, University of Vaasa, Vaasa, Finland

Abstract. Issues of equality and fair treatment in the workforce have held a position in professional discourse across fields for decades. Gender equality is particularly relevant in fields such as information technology (IT), where developed products and systems affect all segments of society. The current paper presents a study that probed professional experiences in the field of IT, in Finland, from the perspective of gender. The study was implemented as a questionnaire where $N = 93$ individuals participated. Our results show that women paid close attention to how their gender influenced multiple aspects of their professional lives, reporting both negative and positive impacts on several categories. Men generally perceived their gender as irrelevant in most of the categories except salary. Women also highlighted experiences of sexual harassment and biased behavior. These statistically significant results contribute to advancing knowledge on gendered conditions of professionals and how they influence the IT industry.

Keywords: Gender · Professionals · Information Technology · Equality · Industry

1 Introduction

Like all professional fields, including healthcare, education and politics, IT is riddled with gender challenges. Some of the traditional issues arising when considering gender have been [1, 2]: 1) participation; 2) pay levels; 3) workload; 4) task allocations and expectations; 5) sexually-oriented treatment; 6) credibility issues; and 7) psychological obstacles attached to all of the above, including self-doubt [2, 3]. These are crucial aspects from a professional perspective, none-the-least that of individuals working in the IT field. Greater equality and diversity in professional IT development roles mean more likelihood of the development of systems that are relevant and valuable for diverse user groups [4]. The present study aimed to examine differences of professional experience in the field of IT based on gender. The research furthered this insight by probing the factor of age, and how age has influenced this experience of gender as a professional in IT. In doing so, the authors have additionally been able to gauge minor potential generational changes in the professional climate of IT. The research question was: *How does gender affect the professional experiences of individuals working in IT?*

E. Papatheocharous et al. (Eds.): ICSOB 2024, LNBIP 539, pp. 202–208, 2025.
https://doi.org/10.1007/978-3-031-85849-9_17

The study was implemented in questionnaire form, and focused on individuals working in Finland, and/or Finnish companies abroad. The reason for focusing on Finland was two-fold: 1) Finland is known internationally as being a country that values equality and equal opportunities among the genders; and 2) the authors of this paper both identify as cis-female (born as female and identify as female) and have been working in the IT sector for over two decades. The aim was to capture both the state of professional experience in relation to gender in the Finnish IT field – i.e., opportunities, perceived value and contribution, obstacles and challenges etc. – and probe the less discussed nuances in the industry that inevitably affect the ways in which IT products and services are designed, developed and delivered. The study advances a growing body of work on diversity in the field of IT and related business. The results are a part of a larger research project that examines the relationship between treatment of female IT professionals, cognitive-affective effects resulting from this treatment, and the challenges resulting from biased and distorted representation in design and development processes. The paper begins by describing the method of the empirical study, describing the questionnaire utilized, ethics and data privacy compliance, recruitment and analysis. Due to the concise nature of a short paper, we simply acknowledge that substantial effort (see e.g., [5]) has been undertaken towards understanding gender distributions, roles and conditions in IT. Most of the research has focused on university students. Here, we examine the experiences of actual professionals with varied levels of experience in the field. We then present the results, followed by the conclusion that includes limitations and future research directions.

2   Method

Data were collected through an online mixed-methods questionnaire, incorporating both quantitative and qualitative open-ended questions that was distributed via Webropol from March to June 2024. All data was collected anonymously, and in accordance with both the General Data Protection Regulation (GDPR) and the research ethics guidelines outlined by the Finnish National Board on Research Integrity, participants were provided with information about the research and use of data; information on data handling practices; and an informed consent form. This information was already available via links during the recruitment stage of the research. Professional participants were recruited via public social media postings (LinkedIn, Author 1 and 2's combined LinkedIn analytics reports 2279 views) and Author 1's internal business communication channels including 1320 members. Participation was asked from people who work at IT companies in Finland, and/or in Finnish IT companies abroad. Of the 181 respondents who opened the questionnaire, 129 started it, and 93 completed it. It took approximately 20 min to complete and was formulated according to the results derived from a written narrative inquiry study undertaken earlier (see e.g., [6]) in 2023 where female IT professionals wrote narratives about their gender-related experiences in work life (positive, neutral, negative).

Questionnaire themes were career – how gender has affected career choice; types of work and/or tasks applied for; types of work or tasks obtained; the level of pay offered to the respondents or the level paid; experiences of sexual harassment; belittlement or bias when interacting with co-workers and/or clients; the ability to participate in the decision-making processes of technical design; and the ability to express ideas. The data was analyzed in SPSS (quantitative data) for statistics. Qualitative data was collected with open-ended questions, but the current paper focuses only on the statistical reporting of quantitative data. Qualitative results are not reported in this paper. In total, $N = 93$ professionals responded to the questionnaire, of which, $N = 54$ were female, $N = 37$ male, and $N = 2$ identified as 'other'. Because only two participants identified as 'other', their responses were excluded from the analysis as they could not be adequately compared to the other two groups. The respondents were divided into the following groups according to age: 1) 21–30 years old (16); 2) 31–40 years old (32); 3) 41–50 years old (33); 5) 51–60 years old (8); and 6) over 61 years old (4). Thus, the largest respondent groups were group 2 and 3.

3   Results

In the first part of the questionnaire the respondents were asked to state why they had chosen to enter the professional field of information technology. Participants were given the selection of career prospects, interest in IT, ending up there, and other. Out of these, $N = 27$ stated that their selection was based on career prospects, $N = 64$ stated that they had an interest in IT; $N = 33$ stated that they had just ended up there, and $N = 6$ selected 'other'. Most participants ($N = 27$) had between six and ten years of experience, followed by those with less than five years of experience ($N = 20$). The other distributions of years worked in the field were 11–15 years, 16–20 years, 21–25 years and over 26 years. Eleven to thirteen participants identified with each of these categories. Data did not follow normal distribution (p-values for both Shapiro-Wilk and Kolmogorov-Smirnov tests are all <0.001 for each variable), thus non-parametric tests were used. Yes/no questions were also featured regarding participant experience of sexual harassment, belittlement or bias, and if they felt that they had the ability to participate in decision-making of technical designs and could contribute ideas. Significant gender differences were recognized: reasons for entering IT; perceived career advancement impacts; job application impacts; job attainment impacts; pay and salary impact; experiences of sexual harassment; experiences of condescending behavior; and participation in technical decision-making. Females reported higher positive and negative impacts of gender, yet males only in relation to salary.

The results of the gender affected career can be seen in Table 1. 'Reasons for entering the field' proved to hold significant difference between men and women regarding 'interest in IT'. Males were more likely than females to report interest in IT. There were significant differences observed in the impact of gender on professional experiences. Women felt that their gender had a more positive impact on career progression, while men reported fewer positive impacts.

Women perceived that their gender had a negative impact on career advancement, a trend also reflected in the types of jobs they applied for. While women reported a more positive gender-based influence on job applications, they were also more negative about how gender affected their opportunities. Similarly, in the types of jobs secured, women felt their gender had both a more positive and negative influence compared to men. They also reported a stronger positive influence of gender on participation in

Table 1. Results of the quantitative questions

Question	Mann-Whitney U	Wilcoxon W	Z	Asymp. Sig. (2-tailed)
Career: Positive	567.000	1270.000	−3.758	**<.001**
Career: Negative	381.000	1084.000	−5.299	**<.001**
Types of work/ tasks applied for: Positive	742.000	1445.000	−2.621	.009
Types of work/ tasks applied for: Negative	648.000	1351.000	−3.370	**<.001**
Types of jobs/tasks obtained: Positive	573.500	1276.500	−3.915	**<.001**
Types of jobs/tasks obtained: Negative	585.000	1288.000	−3.760	**<.001**
Pay level offered or paid: Positive	821.500	1524.500	−1.761	.078
Pay level offered or paid: Negative	391.000	1094.000	−5.304	**<.001**
Participation in technical decision-making: Positive	671.500	2156.500	−3.250	**.001**
Participation in technical decision-making: Negative	527.500	2012.500	−4.498	**<.001**
Ability to express own ideas	671.500	2156.500	−3.250	**.001**

technical decision-making, yet they simultaneously felt their gender negative affected their involvement in such processes. Regarding salary, women experienced significantly more negative impacts related to gender than men, although no significant differences were observed in the positive influence of gender on salary.

Table 2 shows a significant difference emerged in how men and women perceived the impact of gender on sexual harassment, with 46.3% of women and 13.5% of men reporting such experiences. Women also experienced more instances of sexist or dismissive behavior, reporting these at a much higher rate than men. In terms of biased or dismissive behavior, participants could select different types of belittlements and discrimination, including: 1) being referred to as "girl" or "boy"; 2) disregard for skills and capabilities; and 3) being assigned specific roles based on gender (e.g., women as organizers or managers, men as technical professionals). A significant difference in the experience of sexist or dismissive behavior was found between age groups, with younger

Table 2. Results of the experiencing harassment or prejudiced behavior

Variable	Chi-Square Value	Degrees of Freedom (df)	p-value	Women Reporting (%)	Men Reporting (%)
Experienced sexual harassment	10.874	2	0.004	46.3%	13.5%
Experienced sexist or dismissive behavior	20.505	2	<0.001	79.6%	32.4%

participants (21–30 and 31–40) reporting more frequent occurrences compared to older groups (51–60 and 61+). However, for other variables, such as belittling terms, skill dismissal, role assignment, and other gender-based issues, no statistically significant differences were observed between age groups (Table 3).

Table 3. Results of age group differences

Variable	Chi-Square Value	Degrees of Freedom (df)	p-value
Experienced sexist or dismissive behavior	10.523	4	0.032
Experienced belittling terms (e.g., 'boy' or 'girl')	6.312	4	0.177
Experienced belittling of skills	2.376	4	0.667
Assigned specific roles based on gender stereotypes	3.887	4	0.422

4 Conclusion

This paper presents a study examining the experience of gender on professional conditions and opportunities in the IT industry. A questionnaire was designed and implemented to test the validity of findings from a previous qualitative study. The study reveals a series of significant differences indicating not only that gender was perceived as negative influencing crucial aspects of careers in IT, but that women in gender experienced *gender* consciously. We argue this based on the results that show women also experienced gender positive in many respects. Male participants only demonstrated a significant experience of the positive impact of their gender on salary levels. Moreover, in comparison to women, men were significantly different to women in the reason why they entered the IT field – i.e., out of interest. Moreover, the results are striking in terms of their statistical significance between men and women in the domain of sexual harassment.

Women were significantly more likely to report that they had been sexually harassed than men. Women also reported more biased or dismissive behavior. When comparing women across age groups, no statistically significant differences are found except for the experience of "sexist or dismissive behavior", where the age groups (21–30 and 31–40) reported experiencing this behavior more frequently, while older age groups (51–60 and 61+) reported fewer instances.

There are several limitations to the current study. First, less than 100 people responded to the survey. While it is often difficult to recruit professionals from specific sectors, and $N = 93$ participants is an adequate sample size for conducting statistical analyses (see e.g., [7, 8]) given the number of people employed in the IT field, a larger sample would have been more representative. Moreover, there was abnormal distribution among the age groups. It would also be apt to recruit participants from more companies and organizations to ensure that the results are valid and reliable for the IT industry in Finland, in general. However, the results of the survey should be seen as a reflection of real problems and challenges not only experienced by women, but by IT business in general. This is a question of both employee wellbeing, as well as increasing positive impact through employee-driven value propositions that are not strongly biased. Further, a more thorough analysis of the types of comments, names and changes over the years would be enlightening in terms of understanding how the gendered conditions of workers have evolved. This study is part of a larger project examining how cognitive-emotional effects of gender-based inequities in the IT field influence design processes. We assume that inequality on the basis of gender stifles creative thinking due to environmental stressors (i.e., discrimination, negation and exclusion, see e.g., [9, 10]). Further, there is much talk about cultural differences regarding the experiences of gender, and equal treatment. Future research should engage in examining these differences, while questioning why countries known for equality still house bias in the workforce.

Acknowledgements. Thanks to Solita Oy, University of Jyväskylä, Research Council of Finland (funding 348391), and University of Vaasa.

References

1. Tokbaeva, D., Achtenhagen, L.: Career resilience of female professionals in the male-dominated IT industry in Sweden: toward a process perspective. Gend. Work Organ. **30**(1), 223–262 (2023)
2. Trinkenreich, B., Britto, R., Gerosa, M.A., Steinmacher, I.: An empirical investigation on the challenges faced by women in the software industry: a case study. In: Proceedings of the 2022 ACM/IEEE 44th International Conference on Software Engineering: Software Engineering in Society, pp. 24–35 (2022)
3. Wolff, A., Knutas, A., Savolainen, P.: What prevents Finnish women from applying to software engineering roles? A preliminary analysis of survey data. In: Proceedings of the ACM/IEEE 42nd International Conference on Software Engineering: Software Engineering Education and Training, pp. 93–102 (2020)
4. Dyaram, L., Kamalanabhan, T.J.: Diversity in software development teams: the moderating effects of interdependence, team tenure and project type. Int. J. Bus. Innov. Res. **5**(2), 159–178 (2011)

5. Armstrong, D.J., Riemenschneider, C.K., Giddens, L.G.: The advancement and persistence of women in the information technology profession: an extension of Ahuja's gendered theory of IT career stages. Inf. Syst. J. **28**(6), 1082–1124 (2018)
6. Kronqvist, A., Rousi, R.A.: A quick review of ethics, design thinking, gender, and AI development. Int. J. Des. Creativity Innov. **11**(1), 62–79 (2024)
7. Kish, L.: Survey Sampling. Wiley, New York (1965)
8. Louangrath, P.: Minimum sample size method based on survey scales. Int. J. Res. Methodol. Soc. Sci. **3**(3), 44–52 (2017)
9. Isen, A.M.: On the relationship between affect and creative problem solving. In: Affect, Creative Experience, and Psychological Adjustment, pp. 3–17. Routledge, London (2015)
10. Vartanian, O., Saint, S.A., Herz, N., Suedfeld, P.: The creative brain under stress: considerations for performance in extreme environments. Front. Psychol. **11**, 585969 (2020)

Secondary Use of Health Data: Centralized Structure and Information Security Frameworks in Finland

Hannu Vilpponen[1,2], Antti Piirainen[2], Miikka Kallberg[3(✉)], and Tommi Mikkonen[1]

[1] University of Jyväskylä, Jyväskylä, Finland
{hannu.v.vilpponen,tommi.j.mikkonen}@jyu.fi
[2] Finnish Social and Health Data Permit Authority Findata, Helsinki, Finland
antti.piirainen@findata.fi
[3] CSC – IT Center for Science Ltd., Espoo, Finland
miikka.kallberg@csc.fi

Abstract. The utilization of health data for secondary purposes, such as research, statistics, and development, has become increasingly significant in advancing healthcare systems. To foster the above, Finland has established a framework for the secondary use of health data through legislative measures and the creation of specialized institutions, which are the first of their kind in the world. In this paper, we give an overview of our implementation for using secondary health data in a centralized fashion. As a technical contribution, we also address key implementation aspects related to implementing the framework.

Keywords: Health data · information security · regulation

1 Introduction

The utilization of health data for secondary purposes, such as research, statistics, and development, has become increasingly significant in advancing healthcare systems. In April 2024 the European Parliament adopted an agreement for European Health Data Space (EHDS) regulation [6]. The aim of the EHDS is to make it easier to access and exchange health data across borders (primary use of data) and inform health research and policy-making (secondary use of data) [5]. The benefits of EHDS include empowering individuals to manage their health data, supporting the use of health data to improve healthcare services, research, innovation, and decision-making, and providing the EU with the means to safely harness the potential for the seamless exchange, use and re-use of health data. Finland, known for its robust healthcare infrastructure and innovative data practices, has established a framework for the secondary use of health data through legislative measures and the creation of specialized institutions.

The Nordic countries have a long tradition of population-based health registers. Record-keeping in the Nordic countries started in the 1950s [7]. While the Nordic registries were established at various times, they generally follow a similar overall structure.

E. Papatheocharous et al. (Eds.): ICSOB 2024, LNBIP 539, pp. 209–217, 2025.
https://doi.org/10.1007/978-3-031-85849-9_18

Each country has a significant number of registries and databases, with Denmark having over 200 alone [7] and Finland having several hundred as well. In Finland, the recognition of the need for more streamlined, secured and standardized secondary use of health data led to the establishment of the necessary authority, Findata, in 2019. Findata is the data permit authority in the social welfare and healthcare sector, and its assigned role is to organize and maintain a centralized contact point for health data for researchers [2].

In this paper, we outline the framework for the secondary use of health data in Finland. In doing so, we address the role of Findata in defining and implementing data usage environments. As a technical contribution, we also consider key implementation aspects. The rest of this paper is structured as follows. In Sect. 2, we present the background and motivation for the work. In Sect. 3, we outline the framework used for information security in Finland. In Sect. 4, we discuss the technical implementation. Finally, in Sect. 5, we draw some final conclusions.

2 Background and Motivation

The secondary use of health data has been studied in several reports [8–11, 32]. For example, "Operationalizing Research Access in Platform Governance" by Algorithm Watch [8] identifies best practices for research access in platform governance by learning from legal frameworks in environmental law and medical research. It highlights the need for better data access to ensure accountability, using two case studies to address transparency challenges and data protection concerns, from which the other showcases an in-depth examination of Findata's operations.

Center for Data Innovation's report "How the EU Can Unlock the Private Sector's Human-Mobility Data for Social Good" by Hodan Omaar [9] has a different goal, as it discusses how businesses collect mobility data, and how this data can be valuable for addressing societal challenges such as disease spread, urban planning, and disaster response. While researchers and governments benefit from such data, access is often limited due to privacy concerns, high costs, and legal uncertainties. As an example of national legislation which takes on to tackle these issues, the report examines Findata and the Finnish Act on Secondary Use of Health and Social Data.

Nuffield Trust's "Fit for the future: What can the NHS learn about digital health care from other European countries?" [10] examines how digital health care is crucial for sustainable healthcare systems and improving public health. By studying five European countries—Denmark, Finland, Sweden, Estonia, and Portugal—the report highlights that countries with strong digital policies and public trust in digital services have made significant progress. Key factors include effective governance, public confidence, and collaborative design of digital tools.

The Sanitas Health Insurance Foundation's study, "Are smartwatches eroding solidarity?" [11] explores future healthcare scenarios, reflecting on the impact of data-driven health systems on societal cohesion and solidarity. It uses Finland as an example of government-driven action regarding data utilization.

VTT Technical Research Centre of Finland has studied the subject from a more technical point of view and concentrates on secure processing environments. The report [32], commissioned by the Finnish Ministry of Social Affairs and Health, examines the

Act's impact on AI research through interviews with stakeholders, exploring challenges in developing secure processing environments. It identifies technological solutions and provides recommendations for efficient data use in research.

Despite the comprehensive studies, such as the aforementioned and others in the field, the structure and information security frameworks and key implementation aspects have not yet been thoroughly addressed.

Furthermore, the European Health Data Space (EHDS) initiative is expected to enhance cross-border data sharing and collaboration, amplifying the potential for secondary use of health data at a European level. This will pave the way for more comprehensive research opportunities and healthcare improvements across Europe, fostering a unified approach to health data utilization and innovation. Presently, there are several recent projects that aim to define security and design principles for research environments for health data, listed in Table 1.

Table 1. Projects to define research environments for health data in Europe.

EOSC ENTRUST [24]	EOSC-ENTRUST aims to create a European network of Trusted Research Environments (TREs) for sensitive data and drive European interoperability by joint development of a common blueprint for federated data access and analysis
TEHDAS & TEHDAS2 [25]	The TEHDAS Joint Action provided background information for the preparation of the EHDS regulation proposal. TEHDAS2 Joint Action is doing the same for the implementing acts of the EHDS and prepares the ground for the harmonized implementation of the secondary use of health data
TRE (UK) [26]	TRE (UK) aims to prepare a blueprint for Trusted Research Environment in the UK for researching Health data
Healthdata@EU Pilot [28]	The HealthData@EU Pilot project brought together 17 partners including health data access bodies, health data sharing infrastructures and European agencies. It will build a pilot version of the EHDS infrastructure for the secondary use of health data which will serve research, innovation, policy making and regulatory purposes
EHDS2 Communities of Practice [27]	The HDABs-CoP mission is to foster collaboration and knowledge sharing among Competent Authorities and Affiliated Entities involved in establishing the HDABs and responsible for the secondary use of health data within the EHDS

3 Framework for Secondary Use of Health Data in Finland

The Act on the Secondary Use of Health and Social Data provides the legal foundation for the secondary use of health data in Finland [1]. The legislation aims to facilitate the use of social welfare and healthcare data while ensuring data protection and privacy. It defines the conditions under which health data can be used for purposes beyond direct patient care, such as scientific research, statistics, and policy development. Findata has established a regulation on Secure Processing Environments (SPE), which is used as one of the audit criteria in the audit processes of SPE's [3]. The primary objectives of the framework for Secondary Use of Health Data include:

• Enhancing the quality and effectiveness of health and social services.
• Promoting research and innovation.
• Ensuring the security and privacy of health data.
• Facilitating the efficient and ethical use of health data for secondary purposes.

Findata, the Finnish Social and Health Data Permit Authority [2], was established in 2019 under the Act on the Secondary Use of Health and Social Data and is the national permit authority. Findata's responsibilities include:

• Granting permits for the secondary use of health and social data.
• Compiling and pre-processing the data stated in permits and data requests.
• Ensuring compliance with data protection regulations.
• Providing secure data environments for data transfer, processing and analysis.

Data Usage Environments. Findata grants data permits, collect, links and pseudonymises the data and produces aggregated data on request. It plays a crucial role in defining the environments where health data can be accessed and analyzed. These SPEs are designed to provide secure and controlled access to data, ensuring that data privacy and integrity are maintained. On the other hand, the service providers of SPEs are under constant pressure to meet the demand for up-to-date software and performance. Research data can include numerous variables from several registers, even covering the entire population along with comparison data. The size of a single SPE can reach several terabytes.

According to the legislation, Findata is tasked with issuing specific requirements for SPEs, against which security audits are conducted to ensure compliance. Findata must provide a SPE of its own, but other organizations, both public and private, can build audited SPEs as well. In this way, they can manage SPE system configuration and costs independently [12–21]. In Finland, there are currently ten audited SPEs, whose compliance with the law is overseen by Valvira, the National Supervisory Authority for Welfare and Health [4]. SPEs established today are listed in Table 2.

Table 2. Secure Processing Environments and their approximate volumes in Finland.

Name of the SPE	Provider	Ownership	Active environments	Active users
HUS Academic	HUS Helsinki University Hospital	Wellbeing services county	406	1 300
T3 Researchers workspace	Istekki Oy	Publicly-owned private company	112	354
SPESiOR	ESiOR Oy	Private company	n/a	n/a
FIMM Sandbox	University of Helsinki	University (public)	1	2
FinnGen SandBox	University of Helsinki	University (public)	30	816
Kapseli	Findata	Public authority/Government	145	1 000
FIONA remote access system	Statistics Finland	Public authority/Government	301	1 204
SD Desktop	CSC - IT Center for Science Ltd	Publicly-owned special interest company	21	65
SECDATA	Aalto University	University (public)	4	10
Auria's Atolli	Auria Biobank	Wellbeing services county	55	260
Total			1 075	5016

4 Technical Implementation

Secure Data Processing Environments. The technical implementation of secure data environments involves the development of platforms and tools that allow researchers and other authorized users to access and analyze data without compromising security. Key features of these environments include:

- **Data Anonymization and Pseudonymization:** Before transferring health data to SPEs, permit authorities use safeguard measures to protect personal identities while allowing data analysis.
- **Isolation**: The SPE is isolated from other parts of the system, such as the operating system or applications running on the main processor. This isolation helps prevent unauthorized access or tampering with the sensitive data processing environment.
- **Access Control and Monitoring:** Systems log control and monitor who accesses the data and how it is used.
- **Encryption:** Ensures that data is encrypted both in transit and at rest to prevent unauthorized access.

Findata Kapseli. CSC – IT Center for Science Ltd., plays a pivotal role in the technical implementation by providing a secure data environment called Kapseli. Kapseli is designed to meet stringent data protection requirements and supports the secure processing of sensitive health data.

Kapseli Security. Kapseli is audited by an external auditor to match Findata's requirements for a secure data environment [3]. In Finland, there are two companies that are authorized by the National Cyber Security Center to audit the regulation on the requirements set for SPEs. The regulation is based on the existing National Security Auditing Criteria (KATAKRI) framework and legislation of secondary use of health data. Kapseli has been built using existing security recommendations including Microsoft Admin Tier model [22], MFA and other well-known security frameworks, such as CIS Benchmarks [23]. The CIS Benchmarks™ are prescriptive configuration recommendations for more than 25+ vendor product families. They stand for the consensus-based effort of cybersecurity experts globally to help you protect your systems against threats more confidently.

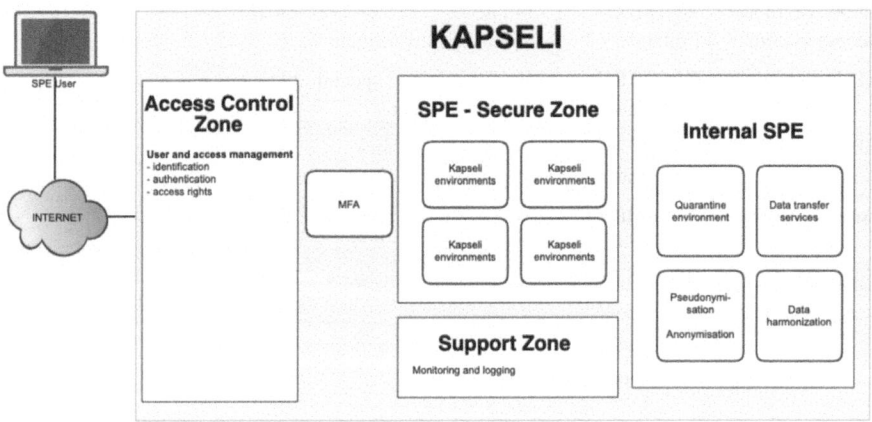

Fig. 1. Kapseli high-level architecture.

Kapseli Architecture. The architecture of Kapseli (Fig. 1) ensures robust security and efficient data management. In terms of the underlying implementation, Findata's Kapseli environment is built on top of CSC ePouta - private cloud. ePouta is designed for processing sensitive data and is located in Finland. Key Kapseli components include the following:

- **Data Isolation:** Each research project operates in a separate, isolated environment to prevent data leakage and unauthorized access.
- **High-Performance Computing Resources:** Kapseli leverages CSC's high-performance computing infrastructure to support large-scale data analysis.
- **Scalable Storage Solutions:** The environment is equipped with scalable storage options to accommodate varying data sizes and types.

Kapseli is partitioned to a number of different zones, called Access Control Zone, SPE-Secure Zone, Support Zone and Internal SPE. The Access Control Zone contains services for user authentication and identification. Access to this zone is limited to requested IP addresses. Users are identified by using existing identification federations, for example Suomi.fi [30], which utilizes banks' electronic identification for user identification in an eIDAS [29] compliant way. Other supported federations are Haka, the identity federation of the Finnish universities, polytechnics and research institutions [31], and Virtu, the Finnish Government's joint single sign-on solution, provided by the Government ICT Centre Valtori [32]. After successful identification, users are redirected to Multifactor authentication before accessing the Kapseli environment in the SPE-Secure zone.

The SPE-Secure Zone contains all Kapseli environments. Currently there are approximately 145 permit specific user environments in the SPE-Secure Zone of Kapseli. Each Kapseli environment is isolated from other Kapseli environments and from the internet. Kapseli environments can be either Windows or Ubuntu Linux virtual machines. Findata maintains a list of pre-approved software that can be installed on Kapseli environments, some are installed by default and others as requested. Users don't have administrative permissions to Kapseli environments. All data and software must pass through Findata's inspection before it can be brought to Kapseli environments. The research data is provided to specific Kapseli environments by Findata.

The Support Zone contains necessary support functions to ensure data security and privacy, such as monitoring services on other zones and logging. Internal SPE zone is dedicated to the use of Findata officials for processing the health data before it can be provided to the Kapseli environment, like pseudonymisation, anonymisation and data harmonization. It also contains necessary services for transferring the data and tools to check data anonymization before it is released outside the Kapseli environment.

5 Discussion and Conclusions

The secondary use of health data in Finland is supported by a robust legislative framework and the dedicated efforts of Findata and CSC. Through secure data environments such as Kapseli and comprehensive support systems, Finland ensures that health data can be used effectively for research and development while maintaining the highest standards of data protection and privacy. The successful implementation of these systems highlights Finland's commitment to leveraging health data for the betterment of healthcare services and public health.

References

1. The Act on the Secondary Use of Health and Social Data. https://www.finlex.fi/fi/laki/aja ntasa/2019/20190552. Accessed 30 Oct 2024
2. Findata - Finnish Social and Health Data Permit Authority. https://findata.fi/en/. Accessed 30 Oct 2024
3. Regulations for SPE Regulations. https://findata.fi/en/services-and-instructions/regulations/. Accessed 30 Oct 2024

4. Database of secondary-use environments Database of secondary-use environments. https://valvira.fi/en/healthcare-and-social-welfare/astori-register. Accessed 30 Oct 2024

5. European Health Data Space (EHDS). https://www.european-health-data-space.com/. Accessed 30 Oct 2024

6. EU Parliament. https://ec.europa.eu/commission/presscorner/detail/en/IP_24_2250. Accessed 30 Oct 2024

7. Laugesen, K., et al.: Nordic health registry-based research: a review of health care systems and key registries. Clin. Epidemiol. 533–554 (2021). https://doi.org/10.2147/CLEP.S31495

8. Operationalizing Research Access in Platform Governance What to learn from other industries?. https://algorithmwatch.org/en/wp-content/uploads/2020/06/GoverningPlatforms_IViR_study_June2020-AlgorithmWatch-2020-06-24.pdf. Accessed 30 Oct 2024

9. How the EU Can Unlock the Private Sector's Human-Mobility Data for Social Good. https://datainnovation.org/2022/03/how-the-eu-can-unlock-the-private-sectors-human-mobility-data-for-social-good/. Accessed 30 Oct 2024

10. Hutchings, R., Scobie, S., Edwards, N.: Fit for the future: International learning on digital health care Research report, Nuffield Trust Fit for the future: What can the NHS learn about digital health care from other European countries? (2021). https://www.nuffieldtrust.org.uk/research/fit-for-the-future-what-can-the-nhs-learn-about-digital-health-care-from-other-european-countries. Accessed 30 Oct 2024

11. Scenarios for a data-driven healthcare system. https://www.sanitas.com/content/dam/sanitas-internet/Dokumente/2021_EN_Studie_Entsolidarisiert_die_Smartwatch.pdf. Accessed 30 Oct 2024

12. HUS Acamedic HUS Acamedic - secure operating environment. https://www.hus.fi/en/research-and-education/hus-acamedic-secure-operating-environment. Accessed 30 Oct 2024

13. T3 researchers workspace. https://www.pirha.fi/ammattilaiselle/tutkimus/tutkimus-ja-opinnaytetyoluvat/rekisteritutkimukset/rekisteritutkimukseen-liittyvat-hinnat. Accessed 30 Oct 2024

14. SPECIOR SPESiOR - Secure Processing Environment. https://esior.fi/spesior/. Accessed 30 Oct 2024

15. Fimm SandBox. https://www.helsinki.fi/en/infrastructures/fimm-technology-centre/fimm-it. Accessed 30 Oct 2024

16. FinnGen SandBox. https://sandbox.finngen.fi/. Accessed 30 Oct 2024

17. Findata Kapseli. https://findata.fi/en/kapseli/. Accessed 30 Oct 2024

18. Fiona FIONA remote access system. https://stat.fi/tup/tutkijapalvelut/fiona-etakayttojarjestelma_en.html. Accessed 30 Oct 2024

19. SD Sesktop SD Desktop. https://sd-desktop.csc.fi/guacamole/#/. Accessed 30 Oct 2024

20. SECDATA Secure operating environment for sensitive data. https://www.aalto.fi/en/services/secure-operating-environment-for-sensitive-data. Accessed 30 Oct 2024

21. Auria's Atolli Auria Tietopalvelu. https://www.auria.fi/tietopalvelu/atolli/index.html. Accessed 30 Oct 2024

22. Microsoft Admin Tier model. https://learn.microsoft.com/en-us/microsoft-identity-manager/pam/tier-model-for-partitioning-administrative-privileges. Accessed 30 Oct 2024

23. CIS Security. https://www.cisecurity.org/. Accessed 30 Oct 2024

24. EOSC ENTRUST. https://eosc-entrust.eu/. Accessed 30 Oct 2024

25. Tehdas 2. https://tehdas.eu/. Accessed 30 Oct 2024

26. TRE UK. https://www.uktre.org/en/latest/. Accessed 30 Oct 2024

27. EHDS Community of practice. https://health.ec.europa.eu/ehealth-digital-health-and-care/eu-cooperation/health-data-access-bodies-community-practice_en?prefLang=et. Accessed 30 Oct 2024

28. HealthData@EU Pilot. https://ehds2pilot.eu/. Accessed 30 Oct 2024

29. eIDAS. https://digital-strategy.ec.europa.eu/en/policies/eidas-regulation. Accessed 30 Oct 2024
30. Suomi.fi identification. https://www.suomi.fi/e-authorizations. Accessed 30 Oct 2024
31. Haka identification. https://wiki.eduuni.fi/x/NYigAQ. Accessed 30 Oct 2024
32. Virtu identification. https://wiki.eduuni.fi/x/6ISwAQ. Accessed 30 Oct 2024

Sustainable ICT

Sustainable ICT Procurement: Data-Driven Decision-Making in B2B Green ICT Adoption

Md Ariful Islam[1]($\boxtimes$)(iD), Shola Oyedeji[2](iD), and Jari Porras[2](iD)

[1] Faculty of Information Technology, University of Jyväskylä, Jyväskylä, Finland
ariful.m.islam@jyu.fi
[2] Department of Software Engineering, LUT University, Lappeenranta, Finland
{shola.oyedeji,jari.porras}@lut.fi

Abstract. The rapid growth of the Information and Communication Technology (ICT) sector has led to escalating environmental and social impacts. This study develops and validates the Sustainable ICT Device Acquisition (SIDA) framework and tool, incorporating a Supplier Selection Questionnaire (SSQ) and Sustainability Guidelines to address these challenges. Employing a mixed-methods approach, we identify key barriers and enablers to sustainable ICT procurement. The proposed SIDA tool operationalizes the framework, empowering decision-makers with data-driven insights and comprehensive sustainability information. Workshops with industry practitioners and academic experts validate the tool's potential to raise awareness, streamline supplier evaluation, and enhance decision-making in alignment with sustainability goals. This research contributes a theoretically grounded and empirically validated framework and tool, promoting responsible ICT procurement decisions.

Keywords: green ICT · sustainable decision making · data-based decision making · sustainable ICT procurement · circular economy · B2B

1 Introduction

The modern era is heavily influenced by ICT devices and services, which have significantly altered organizational operations and individual lives through enhanced efficiency and global connectivity. However, this technological growth, partly fueled by advancements in artificial intelligence (AI), is accompanied by substantial environmental and social impacts, such as significant energy usage and waste production. For instance, the global embodied CO2 emissions of the key ICT user devices (laptops, desktops, monitors, smartphones, tablets) were estimated to total 180 Megatonnes, which is very likely to increase as the sector expands [1]. For the scope of this study, these key user ICT devices will be referred to as "ICT products" or "ICT devices".

© The Author(s), under exclusive license to Springer Nature Switzerland AG 2025
E. Papatheocharous et al. (Eds.): ICSOB 2024, LNBIP 539, pp. 221–235, 2025.
https://doi.org/10.1007/978-3-031-85849-9_19

Life cycle assessment (LCA) research shows that the majority of emissions are attributed to both the embodied phase ranging from 12% to 97% and use-phase emissions varying from 3% to 88%. The increasing production and rapid innovation cycles within the ICT sector have indeed enhanced ICT device capabilities but have also reduced product lifetimes, resulting in the generation of substantial amounts of e-waste as well as increasing energy consumption annually. In 2019 alone, the global production of electronic waste (e-waste) reached approximately 50 million tons, with a projected annual growth rate of 3–5% [6], and predictions suggesting the ICT sector could account for 14% of the global carbon footprint by 2040 [2], there is an urgent need to address sustainability in ICT procurement.

The importance of procurement in this context cannot be emphasized enough. Scope 3 emissions, primarily arising from purchased goods and services, often constitute over 75% of an industry sector's carbon footprint [4]. The CDP's[1] 2020 report further emphasizes the critical role of procurement in addressing these indirect emissions. This emphasis on supply chain emissions is further supported by recent findings from the same report showing that supply chain emissions are on average 11.4 times higher than operational emissions, more than double previous estimates. Corporate buyers face potential costs of up to US$120 billion from environmental risks in their supply chains within the next five years. Despite these challenges, only 37% of suppliers are engaging their own suppliers to reduce emissions, indicating a significant gap in cascading sustainable practices through the supply chain.

These findings underscore the need for effective procurement frameworks, yet while research has explored various aspects of sustainable ICT, the literature reveals a notable gap in comprehensive frameworks and models for ICT procurement decision-making. This gap is evident in practice, where 75% of Finnish ICT sector organizations report no attempts at green ICT procurement [7], and challenges are further exacerbated by the absence of consistent carbon footprint data for 78% of device models [5]. Both public and private organizations struggle to integrate sustainability due to unreliable data, fragmented practices, and a lack of standardized criteria [9].

However, the possibility for substantial positive transformation is significant [3]. Organizations, regardless of their public or private status, could mitigate the negative impacts of ICT through strategic decision-making processes that prioritize sustainability [11]. As [12] emphasize, the very nature of ICT's impact is shaped by the decision-making process itself.

To address these theoretical and practical gaps we introduce the Sustainable ICT Device Acquisition (SIDA) Framework. The framework advances sustainable ICT procurement theory through an integrated decision support model that systematically connects stakeholder engagement, sustainability criteria, and assessment metrics. Its contribution lies in bridging the research-practice gap through structured supplier evaluation methods and evidence-based decision

---

[1] https://www.cdp.net/en/research/global-reports/transparency-to-transformation.

support mechanisms, providing organizations with a systematic approach to incorporating sustainability in ICT procurement processes.

The remainder of this study is organized as follows: Sect. 2 reviews existing literature on sustainability in ICT procurement. Section 3 delineates the research methodology employed. Section 4 reports the findings of this study. Section 5 discusses the implications of the findings, linking them to the research questions and broader sustainability goals. Lastly, Sect. 6 summarizes the key conclusions drawn from this research.

2   Related Works

This section briefly overviews the current state of knowledge regarding sustainable procurement of ICT products. It investigates the environmental impacts of ICT, delves into the idea of sustainable procurement, assesses established frameworks and models, and analyzes pertinent standards, regulations, and policies.

2.1   Environmental Impacts of ICT Products

The aspects of environmental impacts vary depending on the ICT products or services in consideration. The ICT sector's environmental impact extends beyond its carbon footprint, encompassing significant raw material consumption. This impact is exacerbated by continuous technological advancements, potentially leading to global scarcity of essential raw materials including metals, crystals, water and energy. Recent LCA studies reveal that both the embodied and use phases contribute substantially to overall emissions, with the embodied phase accounting for anywhere between 12% to 97% and the use phase for 3% to 88% of the total emissions, depending on factors such as the materials and electrical efficiency [5]. In addition to environmental impacts, the ICT sector also has significant social impacts, including labor practices in manufacturing, digital divide, and the potential for ICT to perpetuate or mitigate social inequalities. These social considerations are also integral to a holistic understanding of sustainability in ICT procurement.

Table 1 shows the significant carbon footprint of ICT devices across their lifecycle stages particularly in the production phase. Extending device lifespans can substantially reduce annual carbon footprints. For instance, increasing a tablet's lifespan from 3 to 8 years can halve its yearly footprint. However, the rapid turnover of ICT devices contributes to the growing e-waste problem, as only 17.4% of the 53.6 million tonnes of e-waste generated was properly recycled in 2019 [13]. These findings highlight the need for sustainable procurement strategies prioritizing energy efficiency, longevity, and responsible end-of-life management in the ICT sector. While these studies provide valuable insights into ICT's environmental impact, they rarely translate into actionable procurement frameworks, creating a gap between impact assessment and practical decision-making.

Table 1. Estimated Total Carbon Footprint (kg CO2e) of ICT Devices across Lifecycle Stages (Source: [2])

	Useful Life (years)		Production Energy (kg CO_2-e)		Use Phase Energy (kg CO_2-e/yr)		Lifecycle Annual Footprint (kg CO_2-e/yr)	
	Min	Max	Min	Max	Min	Max	Min	Max
Desktop	5	7	218	628	69	75	100	200
Notebooks	5	7	281	468	20	23	60	117
CRT Displays	5	7	200	200	51	95	79	135
LCD Displays	5	7	95	95	23	43	37	62
Tablets	3	8	80	116	4.5	5.25	14.5	43.9
Smart Phones	2	2	40	80	4.5	5.25	24.5	45.3

2.2 Sustainability in ICT Procurement and Existing Frameworks

Sustainable procurement in ICT is crucial for reducing the sector's environmental impact [15]. It integrates economic, environmental, and social considerations into procurement processes, aiming to create value while minimizing negative environmental effects [16]. This approach differs from traditional procurement by focusing on whole-life value rather than just lowest price. The procurement process typically includes needs identification, market analysis, specification development, supplier evaluation and selection, contract management, and performance review [17,18]. Each stage offers opportunities to incorporate sustainability criteria [19]. Ecolabels, such as EU Ecolabel, Energy Star, and EPEAT, provide information on products' environmental performance [20]. LCA evaluates environmental impacts throughout a product's lifecycle. Life Cycle Costing (LCC) considers total costs over a product's lifespan. The Triple Bottom Line framework assesses environmental, social, and economic impacts. Sustainable Supply Chain Management (SSCM) extends these principles across the entire supply chain. Although recent frameworks offer theoretical foundations and incorporate resource optimization and circular economy principles [22], they lack specific guidance for ICT procurement decisions. Current approaches tend to treat sustainability criteria in isolation, without providing integrated decision support mechanisms that procurement professionals require.

2.3 Regulations, Policies and Standards

The regulatory landscape for sustainable ICT procurement is rapidly evolving, driven by global climate commitments and the increasing demand for responsible resource management. Key regulations and standards shaping this field include the EU's Green Public Procurement[2] (GPP) criteria [24] and the Ecodesign for Sustainable Products Regulation (ESPR) [26], which introduces the Digital

---

[2] https://circabc.europa.eu/ui/group/44278090-3fae-4515-bcc2-44fd57c1d0d1/
   library/bf592737-c5a8-43ce-99e1-dea61648d3f9/details.

Product Passport (DPP) to enhance product traceability and promote circular economy principles. Additionally, Germany's Supply Chain Due Diligence Act [27] and the EU's Corporate Sustainability Reporting Directive (CSRD) [25] emphasize increased corporate accountability and transparency. In the standardization domain, ISO 20400 and ISO 14001 [23] provide frameworks for sustainable procurement and environmental management, while sector-specific guidelines from the International Telecommunication Union (ITU) align with Paris Agreement targets [10].

While these regulations and standards establish comprehensive requirements, organizations face significant challenges in their practical implementation. The complexity of integrating multiple standards, coupled with the rapid evolution of ICT technologies, creates a substantial gap between regulatory compliance and effective procurement practices. This implementation gap is notable in three areas: the translation of standards into actionable procurement criteria, the integration of sustainability requirements with existing procurement processes, and the evaluation of supplier compliance with these standards.

This evolving landscape presents both challenges and opportunities for organizations. Compliance efforts can drive innovation and create competitive advantages, while also influencing organizational behavior and decision-making. However, the lack of structured frameworks for putting these standards into practice often results in fragmented approaches to sustainable procurement, emphasizing the need for integrated decision support systems that can close the gap between regulatory requirements and practical implementation.

Future research should focus on the practical implementation and impact of these regulations, particularly on developing systematic approaches that can help organizations translate complex regulatory requirements into effective procurement decisions, as well as explore the potential of emerging technologies to enhance transparency and traceability in the ICT supply chain.

3   Methodology

This study employs a mixed-methods approach to investigate sustainability integration in ICT procurement processes and develop evidence-based frameworks and tools. The methodology integrates a Systematic Literature Review (SLR), semi-structured interviews, and quantitative survey analysis, enhancing the validity and reliability of the findings [8]. The research process, illustrated in Fig. 1, unfolds across three primary phases:

- **Phase 1 - Problem Identification:** Initial discussions with the industry practitioners shaped the problem formulation, followed by a Systematic Literature Review (SLR)[3] to establish the state of the field and identify knowledge gaps. The SLR addressed specific questions about existing sustainability integration approaches in ICT procurement, barriers encountered, and successful implementation strategies. Findings from the SLR informed the formulation

---

[3] https://tinyurl.com/SLR-Protocol.

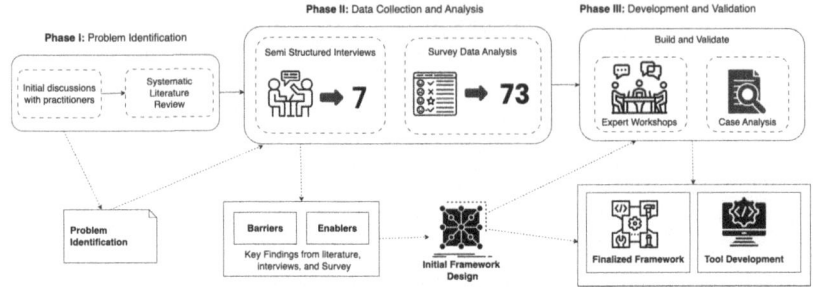

Fig. 1. The research process and design

of this study's research questions RQ1 and RQ2 (see Sect. 3.1) and guided subsequent data collection.

– **Phase 2 - Data Collection and Analysis:** Semi-structured interviews[4] with 7 industry experts were conducted to gather qualitative insights on existing practices, challenges, and opportunities in sustainable ICT procurement. Additionally, a quantitative survey analysis was performed on data collected from 73 respondents in a separate study by the Green ICT ecosystem [14] offering a broader perspective on barriers and enablers. The respondents represented organizations of varying sizes (48% large, 52% SMEs) across both private (62%) and public (38%) sectors.

– **Phase 3 - Development and Validation:** The analysis findings informed the iterative development of the Sustainable ICT Decision and Acquisition (SIDA) framework and its supporting components: a decision support tool, Supplier Selection Questionnaire (SSQ), and practical sustainability guidelines. This involved 5 expert workshops and stakeholder feedback sessions, and case analysis to ensure alignment with real-world challenges and opportunities, with a particular emphasis on facilitating decision-making and behavior change within procurement teams.

Data analysis involved thematic analysis of interview transcripts using NVivo software,[5] and statistical analysis of survey data using Python and specialized libraries. The iterative evaluation process, incorporating stakeholder engagement and collaboration, ensured that the final framework and tools were both theoretically grounded and practically relevant. This methodology enabled a comprehensive approach to addressing the research questions, integrating insights from literature, industry experts, and quantitative data to develop practical tools for sustainable ICT procurement.

---

[4] https://tinyurl.com/Semi-Interview-protocol.
[5] https://lumivero.com/products/nvivo/.

3.1 Research Questions

This research aims to investigate sustainability integration in organizational ICT procurement processes through the following research questions:

- **RQ1:** What are the key barriers and enablers for integrating sustainability criteria into ICT procurement processes in organizations?
- **RQ2:** How can organizations effectively integrate sustainability into the decision-making process of ICT procurement processes?

4 Results

The section is structured to provide a comprehensive understanding of the results, encompassing the problem identification phase, qualitative analysis of the interview data, quantitative analysis of the survey data, and the iterative design, refinement and validation of the SIDA framework and tools.

4.1 Problem Space and Literature Analysis

Several initial meetings were conducted with practitioners to understand the problem space and potentially identify key challenges in integrating sustainability into ICT procurement. Barriers identified include the absence of **clear sustainability criteria, difficulty in assessing supplier performance, resistance to change, fear of increased costs, and a lack of supportive tools**. Addressing these requires understanding decision-makers' tendencies to overlook sustainability, lowering or removing these barriers, and developing effective support mechanisms to encourage sustainable ICT procurement.

The SLR identified six primary categories of barriers and enablers influencing the integration of sustainability into ICT procurement: Environmental, Economic, Technical, Awareness and Training, Policy and Regulations, and Organizational Dynamics. Environmental barriers include the complexity of eco-labels and the lack of standardized CO_2 emission data, creating confusion in product evaluation [5, 28]. Economic challenges are rooted in the uncertainty of return on investment and the higher upfront costs associated with sustainable options [29]. Technical barriers arise from the absence of standardized frameworks and inadequate information management systems [5, 21]. Awareness and Training obstacles stem from insufficient knowledge and training programs, while unclear policies and fragmented regulations create a challenging landscape for organizations [29, 31]. Organizational dynamics, including a lack of senior management commitment and stakeholder resistance, further complicate the adoption of sustainable practices.

Conversely, the SLR identified enablers such as environmental consciousness and the use of eco-labels, long-term financial benefits [32], technical advancements like sustainability assessment frameworks and decision support tools [33], increased awareness and training foster behavioral change within organizations, supportive policies and regulations [34], and organizational dynamics such as pressure from ESG-focused investors [29].

4.2   Interview and Survey Data Collection and Analysis

Table 2. Interview Participants

Job Title	Experience (years)	Country	Company Size
Senior IT Procurement Manager	15	Finland	Large
Head of Sustainability	12	Finland	Medium
IT Procurement Specialist	10	Finland	Medium
Sustainability Manager	8	Finland	Very Large
IT Operations Manager	14	Finland	Large
Chief Technology Officer	13	Germany	Medium
Procurement Analyst	9	Germany	Small

Interviews with industry experts and analysis of survey data further validated and expanded upon the identified barriers and enablers. Seven industry experts from Finland and Germany were interviewed (see Table 2). Their insights validated and expanded upon the literature findings, particularly emphasizing practical implementation challenges. The study identified several key barriers to sustainable ICT procurement. Technical barriers emerged as a significant challenge, particularly regarding data management and accessibility. As one sustainability manager explained:

"We have so much data on different products and suppliers, but it's scattered across multiple spreadsheets. It's difficult to find the information we need, and it's even harder to make sense of it all in a meaningful way."

This highlights the pressing need for improved data management and decision support tools. Organizational resistance was another critical barrier. As one practitioner noted:

"How can we make ICT sustainable? Like how does it work? They don't really believe in it. They just say it's a buzzword or something".

This highlighted the challenge of establishing organizational commitment to sustainable practices.

Factor analysis of the survey data revealed the average impact of identified barriers and enablers on a scale from 0 to 10, as illustrated in Fig. 2. The bar charts presents a comparative view of the most significant barriers and enablers in sustainable ICT products procurement, as perceived by survey respondents.

Figure 3 illustrates that the survey responses further validated and expanded upon the barriers identified in the literature review and interviews. The barriers highlighted in yellow indicate convergence across all three data sources - literature review, interviews, and survey data - underscoring their significance and prevalence in the context of sustainable ICT procurement.

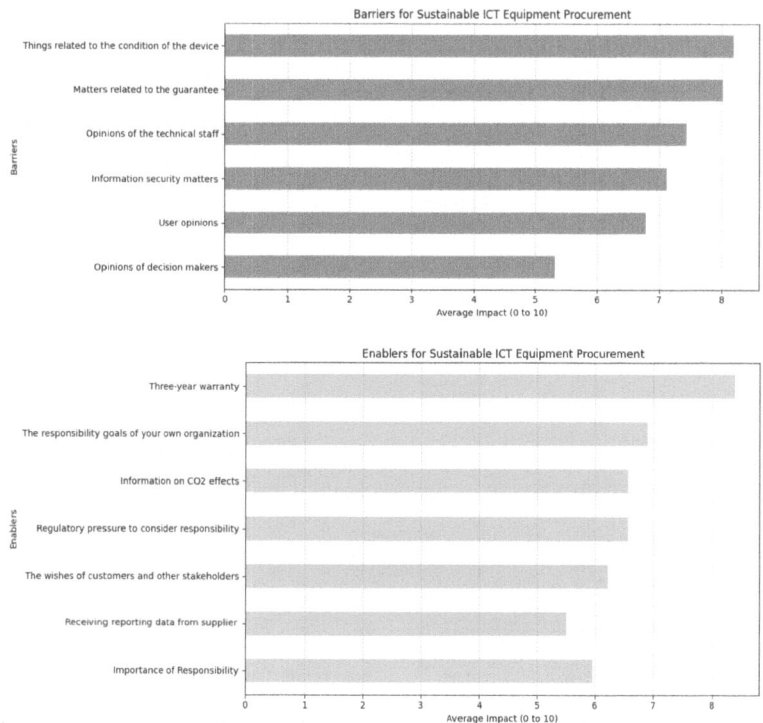

Fig. 2. Average Impact of Barriers and Enablers

In Fig. 4, the enablers highlighted in yellow signify convergence of the survey data with the findings from both the literature review and the interviews, underscoring their consistent importance across different data sources. These converged enablers, such as **regulatory pressures, organizational sustainability goals, and the availability of clear sustainability information**, represent key factors that organizations perceive as crucial in facilitating the adoption of sustainable ICT procurement practices. While 'Transparency & Data Availability' and 'Carbon Footprint data availability' appear as separate technical enablers, this distinction is intentional. The former encompasses broad product lifecycle and supply chain information, whereas the latter specifically focuses on greenhouse gas emissions metrics—a critical factor in sustainable ICT procurement decisions. This separation ensures dedicated attention to carbon footprint while maintaining comprehensive transparency requirements.

4.3 SIDA Framework Development and Supporting Tools

To address the lack of a comprehensive framework for sustainable ICT procurement, we developed the Sustainable ICT Device Acquisition (SIDA) framework combining theoretical insights from literature with practical knowledge

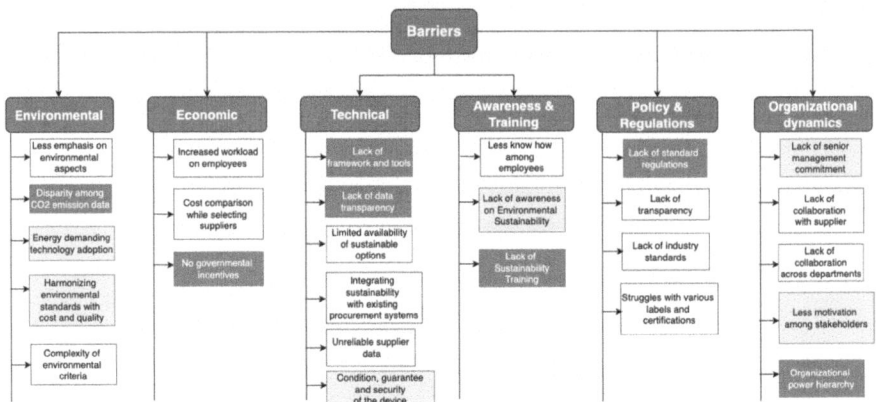

Fig. 3. Merged Barriers supported by Survey data. Highlighted Yellow Barriers indicate convergence across literature review, interviews, and survey data. (Color figure online)

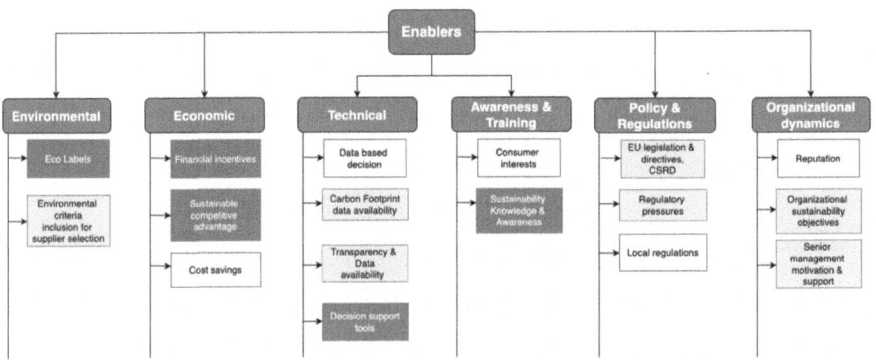

Fig. 4. Merged Enablers supported by Survey data. Highlighted Yellow Enablers indicate convergence across literature review, interviews, and survey data. (Color figure online)

gained through empirical research. The SIDA framework comprises the following components: Policy and regulations compliance, Sustainability criteria, Carbon footprint information, Supplier selection and performance evaluation, Assessment metrics, scoring, and weighting, Measurable KPIs, Stakeholder engagement mechanisms, Decision support, and Awareness and training. The framework was iteratively improved to better reflect practical needs and implementation considerations. Workshops with academic peers and industry experts provided valuable feedback on the initial SIDA framework, leading to its refinement.

Key suggestions included consolidating certain components (e.g., merging "Carbon Footprint Information" with "Sustainability Criteria"), emphasizing active stakeholder engagement in defining metrics and KPIs, and improving the visual representation of the framework's interactions. Additionally, the need for supporting tools, such as a Supplier Selection Questionnaire and Sustainability Guidelines, was identified to facilitate practical implementation.

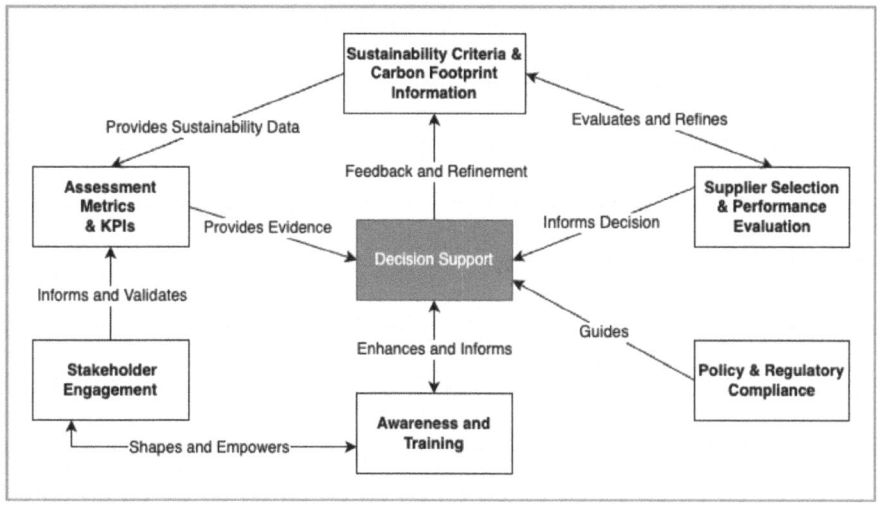

Fig. 5. Sustainable ICT Decision and Acquisition (SIDA) Framework

Incorporating feedback from workshops, the SIDA framework was refined to enhance its usability and effectiveness (see Fig. 5). The revised framework emphasizes decision support, stakeholder engagement, and the crucial role of defining clear sustainability criteria, assessment metrics, and KPIs. Each framework component serves a specific purpose: Carbon Information guides emissions-related decisions, Policy & Regulatory Compliance ensures adherence to sustainability standards, and Stakeholder Engagement facilitates collaborative decision-making. Detailed specifications of framework elements and their relationships are available in the supplementary documentation.[6] To support the framework, we developed a Supplier Selection Questionnaire (SSQ)[7] and Sustainability Guidelines[8]. The SSQ evaluates potential suppliers based on environmental, social, and economic criteria, while the guidelines provide step-by-step recommendations for integrating sustainability into ICT procurement. However, the workshop also highlighted the need for a dedicated SIDA Tool to translate the theoretical concepts of the framework into actionable steps, further supporting its practical application.

Due to time constraints, we were unable to fully develop the SIDA Tool. However, we outlined its proposed design, features, and functionalities, focusing

---

[6] https://tinyurl.com/SIDA-Framework.

[7] https://bit.ly/Supplier_Selection_Questionnaire.

[8] https://bit.ly/SustainabilityGuidelines.

on sustainable software development practices. The SIDA Tool[9] aims to bridge the gap between theory and practice by providing a platform that operationalizes the SIDA framework. It will offer features such as:

- **Sustainability Data Repository:** Centralized access to sustainability data for ICT products.
- **Supplier Evaluation:** Interactive module for assessing supplier sustainability performance.
- **Assessment Metrics and KPIs:** Platform for defining, tracking, and visualizing KPIs.
- **Stakeholder Engagement:** Features for fostering collaboration and communication.
- **Decision Support:** Tools for analysis, comparison, and visualization of sustainability data.
- **Awareness and Training:** Gamified modules for enhancing understanding and promoting sustainable procurement.
- **Policy and Regulatory Compliance:** Repository of relevant information and a compliance checker.

The SIDA Tool's development is guided by sustainable software principles, including **energy efficiency, resource optimization, modularity, data minimization, and ethical considerations**. These principles ensure the tool itself aligns with the sustainability goals it promotes.

While full implementation was not feasible within the project timeframe, validation workshops with practitioners and academic peers confirmed the framework's effectiveness in improving decision-making and raising sustainability awareness. Participants particularly valued the structured approach to supplier evaluation and the practical guidance provided by the supporting tools. The final validation phase demonstrated the framework's significant potential in multiple areas. It provides a systematic approach to sustainable ICT procurement while enhancing stakeholder awareness and engagement throughout the process. The framework effectively supports evidence-based decision-making and facilitates comprehensive supplier evaluation and selection. Additionally, it promotes continuous improvement through measurable KPIs. Moving forward, future work will focus on full implementation of the SIDA Tool and continued refinement based on practical application feedback.

5 Discussion

This study addresses the pressing need for sustainable ICT procurement in the B2B sector by developing and validating the SIDA framework and conceptualizing the SIDA tool. The identified challenges, such as the lack of carbon footprint data transparency [5] and the perceived higher costs of sustainable options [29], echo concerns raised in previous research. The SIDA framework, developed through rigorous mixed-methods research, offers a structured approach

---

[9] https://tinyurl.com/SIDA-dashboard.

to overcome these barriers and facilitate the integration of sustainability into ICT procurement decisions. The SIDA framework goes beyond existing models by explicitly incorporating behavioral and organizational factors crucial for successful implementation. This aligns with calls in the literature for a more holistic approach to sustainable procurement that considers not only technical aspects but also the human and organizational dimensions [19]. By integrating stakeholder engagement, decision support tools, and awareness-building mechanisms, SIDA empowers decision-makers to navigate the complexities of sustainable ICT procurement, addressing a key gap identified in previous research [5, 21, 30].

An important consideration in sustainable ICT procurement is the potential for rebound effects, where efficiency improvements may lead to increased consumption that partially offsets the intended environmental benefits. This is particularly relevant in the context of energy-efficient ICT devices, where cost savings might drive increased device acquisition or usage. The SIDA framework's comprehensive approach, particularly through its Assessment Metrics and Decision Support components, helps organizations recognize and account for these potential rebound effects in their procurement strategies, though this remains an area for further investigation and refinement.

Furthermore, the conceptualization of the SIDA tool demonstrates the potential to bridge the gap between theory and practice. While not fully implemented in this study, workshops with industry practitioners and academic experts validated its potential to enhance decision-making, raise awareness, and facilitate sustainable procurement. This resonates with the literature's emphasis on the need for practical tools and decision support systems to enable sustainable procurement [33].

The alignment of the SIDA framework with specific SDG targets, such as 12.5 (waste reduction), 12.8 (awareness raising), 9.1 (resilient infrastructure), 8.4 (decoupling growth from environmental degradation), and 8.5 (decent work and economic growth), highlights its potential for broader societal impact.

The SIDA framework and tool hold significant implications for both research and practice. For practitioners, they offer a practical and effective solution for integrating sustainability into ICT procurement, potentially leading to improved environmental and economic outcomes. For researchers, this study opens avenues for further investigation into the framework's effectiveness across various industries, its long-term impact on organizational behavior and sustainability performance, the quantification and mitigation of rebound effects, and the exploration of diverse methods for organizing sustainability criteria.

6   Conclusion

This study addressed the pressing need for sustainable ICT procurement in the B2B sector by developing the SIDA framework and conceptualizing the SIDA tool. The SIDA framework provides a structured approach for integrating sustainability into procurement decisions, while the SIDA tool offers a practical platform for implementation. By adopting the SIDA framework and tool, organizations can expect significant benefits, including reduced environmental impact, enhanced social responsibility, and cost savings. While the SIDA tool shows promise, further research is needed to assess its long-term efficacy and explore scalability challenges. This research contributes a valuable solution for organizations striving to align ICT procurement with sustainability goals. By addressing current limitations and pursuing future research directions, we can continue advancing sustainable ICT procurement practices.

References

1. Lövehagen, N., et al.: Assessing embodied carbon emissions of communication user devices by combining approaches. Renew. Sustain. Energy Rev. **183**, 113422 (2023)
2. Belkhir, L., Elmeligi, A.: Assessing ICT global emissions footprint: trends to 2040 & recommendations. J. Clean. Prod. **177**, 448–463 (2018)
3. Zimmer, M.P., Järveläinen, J.: Digital-sustainable co-transformation: introducing the triple bottom line of sustainability to digital transformation research. In: IFIP International Conference on Human Choice and Computers, pp. 100–111. Springer (2022)
4. Hoyer, C.: Accelerating climate action beyond company gates. In: Handbook of Climate Change Management: Research, Leadership, Transformation, pp. 1365–1386. Springer (2021)
5. Sutton-Parker, J.: Is sufficient carbon footprint information available to make sustainability focused computer procurement strategies meaningful? Procedia Comput. Sci. **203**, 280–289 (2022)
6. Chen, Z., et al.: Recycling waste circuit board efficiently and environmentally friendly through small-molecule assisted dissolution. Sci. Rep. **9**(1), 17902 (2019)
7. Abdullai, L., Sipilä, A., Porras, J.: Green ICT adoption and challenges: evidence from the Finnish ICT sector. In: International Conference on Software Business, pp. 337–343. Springer (2022)
8. Johnson, R.B., Onwuegbuzie, A.J., Turner, L.A.: Toward a definition of mixed methods research. J. Mixed Methods Res. **1**(2), 112–133 (2007)
9. McMahon, K., Mugge, R., Hultink, E.J.: Overcoming barriers to circularity for internal ICT management in organizations: a change management approach. Resour. Conserv. Recycl. **205**, 107568 (2024)
10. Data Bridge Market Research: Future of Carbon Footprint of Information and Communication. https://tinyurl.com/databridgemarket. Accessed 12 July 2024
11. Ramautar, V., et al.: Sustainable development goals in the ICT sector. In: 2023 International Conference on ICT for Sustainability (ICT4S), pp. 108–119. IEEE (2023)
12. Rugeviciute, A., Courboulay, V., Hilty, L.M.: The research landscape of ICT for sustainability: harnessing digital technology for sustainable development. In: 2023 International Conference on ICT for Sustainability (ICT4S), pp. 97–107. IEEE (2023)
13. Forti, V., et al.: The global e-waste monitor 2020. United Nations University (UNU), International Telecommunication Union (ITU) & International Solid Waste Association (ISWA), Bonn/Geneva/Rotterdam, p. 120 (2020)
14. TIEKE: Green ICT Ecosystem. https://greenict.fi/en/etusivu-english/
15. Reynolds, S.: Exploring sustainable procurement practices: a qualitative study of supplier selection criteria (2024)

16. Asquer, A., Marcialis, I.: Exploring the discourse on sustainability in public procurement: AQ methodology study in development cooperation programmes. Yearb. Swiss Adm. Sci. **5**(1) (2014)
17. Walker, H., Brammer, S.: Sustainable procurement in the United Kingdom public sector. Supply Chain Manage.: Int. J. **14**(2), 128–137 (2009)
18. Chartered Institute of Procurement and Supply: The Procurement and Supply Cycle (2024). https://tinyurl.com/cipsProcure
19. Brammer, S., Walker, H.: Sustainable procurement in the public sector: an international comparative study. Int. J. Oper. Prod. Manage. **31**(4), 452–476 (2011)
20. Harris, K., Divakarla, S.: Supply chain risk to reward: responsible procurement and the role of ecolabels. Procedia Eng. **180**, 1603–1611 (2017)
21. Sonnichsen, S.D., Clement, J.: Review of green and sustainable public procurement: towards circular public procurement. J. Clean. Prod. **245**, 118888 (2020)
22. Yang, C.-H., Wang, T.-S., Tsai, H.-T., Hsu, C.-L., Huang, J.-S.: Incorporating resource optimization for sustainable airline service innovation business decision model: toward circular economy policy achievement. Ann. Oper. Res. 1–27 (2024)
23. Salim, H.K., et al.: Global trends in environmental management system and ISO14001 research. J. Clean. Prod. **170**, 645–653 (2018)
24. GPP Criteria and Requirements. https://green-business.ec.europa.eu/green-public-procurement/gpp-criteria-and-requirements_en. Accessed 23 May 2024
25. Directive (EU) 2022/2464 of the European Parliament on Corporate Sustainability Reporting. https://eur-lex.europa.eu/eli/dir/2022/2464. Accessed 12 July 2024
26. European Commission. Ecodesign for Sustainable Products Regulation. https://tinyurl.com/EUcommissionClimate. Accessed 22 Aug 2024
27. Koos, S.: The German supply chain due diligence act 2021 and its impact on globally operating German companies. In: 2nd Riau Annual Meeting on Law and Social Sciences (RAMLAS 2021), pp. 111–115. Atlantis Press (2022)
28. Yokessa, M.M., Marette, S., et al.: A review of eco-labels and their economic impact. Int. Rev. Environ. Resour. Econ. **13**(1–2), 119–163 (2019)
29. Bomfim, C., et al.: Modelling sustainability in a procurement system: an experience report. In: 2014 IEEE 22nd International Requirements Engineering Conference (RE), pp. 402–411. IEEE (2014)
30. Kozuch, A.C., von Deimling, C., Eßig, M.: Implementing green public procurement: a replication study. J. Clean. Prod. **377**, 134424 (2022). https://doi.org/10.1016/j.jclepro.2022.134424
31. Igarashi, M., de Boer, L., Fet, A.M.: What is required for greener supplier selection? A literature review and conceptual model development. J. Purchas. Supply Manag. **19**(4), 247–263 (2013)
32. Dey, P.K., Malesios, C., De, D., Budhwar, P., Chowdhury, S., Cheffi, W.: Adoption of circular economy practices in small and medium-sized enterprises: evidence from Europe. Int. J. Prod. Econ. **248**, 108496 (2022)
33. Ramkumar, M., Jenamani, M.: Sustainability in supply chain through e-procurement–an assessment framework based on DANP and liberatore score. IEEE Syst. J. **9**(4), 1554–1564 (2014)
34. Pouikli, K.: Towards mandatory green public procurement (GPP) requirements under the EU green deal: reconsidering the role of public procurement as an environmental policy tool. Era Forum **21**(4), 699–721 (2021)

Integrating Sustainability into Scrum Agile Software Development: An Action Research Approach

Shola Oyedeji[1]([✉]) [iD], Hatef Shamshiri[1] [iD], Mikhail Ola Adisa[1] [iD],
Rafael Capilla[2] [iD], and Ruzanna Chitchyan[3] [iD]

[1] LUT University, Lappeenranta, Finland
shola.oyedeji@lut.fi
[2] Rey Juan Carlos University, Móstoles, Spain
[3] University of Bristol, Bristol, UK

Abstract. Software plays a crucial role in promoting sustainability, yet there is no standardized approach for embedding sustainability into Scrum agile software development process. With many systems now built using agile methods, integrating sustainability into these practices is essential. This paper presents an action research conducted with an industry partner to demonstrate how sustainability concerns can be incorporated into the Scrum agile framework using previously published sustainability elicitation techniques (e.g., we used the Sustainability Awareness Framework for this action research). The goal of this study is to guide software development practitioners in making sustainability-conscious design and development decisions. Our findings show that even practitioners with limited prior sustainability knowledge, were able to successfully adapt their agile processes to integrate systematic treatment of sustainability concerns.

Keywords: Agile · Scrum · Sustainability · Software Development

1 Introduction

Software systems play a pivotal role in all human activities [12] and are essential for driving economic transformation and advancing digitization across various sectors, presenting opportunities to mitigate environmental impacts, enhance social equity, and improve individual well-being [3,12]. In today's digital age, one of the key drivers to achieve the digital transformation is to promote sustainability in the systems we produce or use. Because software systems can undermine sustainability via, for example, resource depletion for hardware and software production needs, related carbon emissions, or biodiversity degradation [15,18].

To illustrate the magnitude of this prospective dual impact in terms of global CO_2 equivalent emissions, it is reported that at present the (rapidly growing)

impact from ICT itself amounts to roughly 3% [14] of worldwide emissions and is estimated to exceed 14% of the 2016-levels by 2040 [7]. At the same time, ICT with software systems at the core is claimed to be able to reduce the global footprint of other sectors by up to 15% [13]. It is not a surprise, then, that the software industry needs to concertedly address the sustainability issues of their products and integrate sustainability into software design and development processes.

Given that agile software development process is the current most widely used process [1,3] in software development companies, integration of sustainability consideration into this process is paramount. To demonstrate the feasibility of this proposal, this paper presents an action-research of a commercial software product development, undertaken by a collaborative team of software practitioners and academic researchers. This action research explores: *how to integrate sustainability concerns into the Scrum framework to help software practitioners make decisions that consider sustainability?* The goal is to provide valuable insights into how sustainability can become integral to decision-making in scrum agile software development.

The remainder of this paper is structured as follows. We start outlining the background and related works regarding sustainability in software development processes in Sect. 2. Section 3 details the study design and research approach taken, while 4 outlines the steps in conducting the action research. Section 5 provides the findings of our work and Sect. 6 highlights the limitations of this research. Finally, we provide our conclusions and future work in Sect. 7.

2   Background and Related Work

Sustainable software development involves continuously evaluating and addressing the software system's sustainability impacts throughout its life cycle to optimize performance [26]. In software engineering, sustainability can be examined from five dimensions: technical, environmental, economic, social, and individual [6]. The impact of software systems across these dimensions spans time: immediately, in the mid-term, and further away future [24] by causing various effects or systemic impacts on software systems.

Sustainability in software engineering [16] can be approached from two directions: *software for sustainability* and *sustainable software*. "Software for sustainability" involves using software to achieve sustainability goals in other sectors, such as managing energy consumption in buildings to reduce CO_2 emissions [11]. On the other hand, "sustainable software" aims to minimize the negative impacts of production, use and decommissioning of the software systems themselves [19] which is the main focus of this study. Overall, software or technical sustainability is perceived as a property to achieve system endurance [25].

In addition, there is the need to identify the sustainability impacts of software systems and provide well-defined standardized practices for sustainability impact identification and mitigation in each of the sustainability dimensions (technical, environmental, economic, social, and individual). One framework applied in this study is the **Sustainability Awareness Framework -SuSaF**. A question-based framework to help identify the potential sustainability impacts of software system impacts. The SusAF[1] [8] requires both engaged conversations with stakeholders (software development practitioners and end users) for the identification of sustainability impacts of the developed software systems (across social, individual, environmental, economic, and technical dimensions as well as for direct, indirect, and systemic effects) and provides a set of questions that facilitate the sustainability-related impact elicitation.

However, the awareness of software professionals about the software sustainability impacts remains limited because developers lack a common perspective on integrating sustainability into design and development processes [6]. While researchers argue that software designs created with sustainability in mind can lead to more sustainable socio-technical systems [8–10,12], and recent studies have explored how sustainability can be considered during agile software development [3,5], the actual integration of sustainability concerns into the software development process remains fragmented. For instance, research on Agile practices for green and sustainable software [22] identified different agile practices to support green software development, but the tool support to integrate the practices in agile software development is missing. Another study [4] proposed a Sustainability-Aware Scrum Framework to support the integration of sustainability impacts into Scrum, but it was presented without an applied case example. This study addresses critical gaps in agile practices by embedding sustainability considerations within the scrum product backlog and sprint retrospective, providing agile teams with a practical way to operationalize sustainability within Scrum processes.

3   Methodology

In order to evaluate how sustainability concerns can be applied in software development processes, we aim to analyze its role in the context of agile methods, being one of the most used software development processes by companies today [1]. To address this challenge, we conducted an action research [23][2] between an industrial partner and the paper authors. In action research, we establish an active collaboration between the researchers and the partners in order to generate new knowledge. The action research was conducted to help software practitioners integrate sustainability concerns into Scrum. The process started with forming a research partnership and undertaking collaborative action research in iterative cycles of planning, action, observation, and reflection [23].

3.1   Forming Partnership

The partnership formation began with three researchers and a product manager from a software development company who reached out to the researchers

---

[1] https://www.suso.academy/en/sustainability-awareness-framework-susaf/.
[2] https://www2.sigsoft.org/EmpiricalStandards/docs/standards.

(authors) to explore how sustainability could be embedded into the company's agile processes. The product manager recruited the software development team to collaborate with the researchers. Table 1 outlines the roles of the agile development team members who participated in the study.

Table 1. Software development practitioners (Agile Team) from the company

No	Job Title	Years of Experience
1	Scrum Master	9
2	Product Owner	6
3	Programmer	6
4	Software Developer/Architect	6
5	UX Specialist	5
6	IT Manager	4
7	Software Developer	2
8	Software Developer	2
9	Junior Software Developer	1

3.2 Conducting Action Research

Planning: The action research study began with identifying the need to integrate sustainability into the development process of a company's software product, "Labour Hire", a platform for connecting service seekers with providers. To address this, the company organized an initial *Business Requirements Workshop*, involving three researchers and the agile team. During this workshop, the product manager introduced the Labour Hire software and outlined its goals, while the product owner presented user stories. A primary challenge was raised: *how to embed sustainability concerns into their Scrum process and encourage sustainability considerations during design and development.* After reflecting on this challenge, the researchers identified the Sustainability Awareness Framework (SusAF) as a suitable approach. This framework was chosen based on its effectiveness in raising sustainability awareness among developers by focusing on five sustainability dimensions and three orders of effects [12,21]. Additionally, the researchers and agile team used insights from the SusAF workshop to plan enhancements to the Scrum product backlog, incorporating sustainability concerns, and to improve sprint retrospectives to address sustainability.

Action: With SusAF as a foundation, two researchers organized a second workshop to train the agile team to use SusAF framework for the Labour Hire project. This interactive session utilized online sticky notes for real-time collaboration, allowing team members to actively participate in understanding and applying SusAF. Following the training, the agile team collaborated with the researchers to develop a set of artefacts, including a list of potential sustainability impacts specific to Labour Hire and the Sustainability Awareness Diagram (SusAD), which visualized the software's sustainability effects. Additionally, the researchers and agile team used the data from the SusAF workshop to create two templates that will support concrete steps for integrating sustainability concerns into the scrum process:

- The Sustainability Agile Requirements Toolbox (SART) integrates sustainability impacts into the product backlog template within the Scrum framework, serving as a key reference for development tasks during sprint planning.
- The Sustainability Sprint Retrospective template includes sustainability related questions designed to encourage agile team members to consider sustainability in their discussions. This helps ensure that sustainability is integrated into the next sprint's planning and informs their design decisions.

The Agile team applied SART during the development phase by adding product backlog items (PBIs) that included user stories, story points, owners, and the sustainability impacts associated with each PBI. They also used the Sustainability Sprint Retrospective template during retrospective meetings.

Observation: During the five two-week sprints following the workshops, the agile team applied these new templates (SART and Sustainability Sprint Retrospective template) to support their sustainability thinking and track the sustainability impacts identified from SusAF workshop during the development process. The agile team documented items from the Labour Hire project in SART, ensuring that sustainability concerns were actively considered as items moved from the product backlog to the sprint backlog.

Reflection: Throughout the project and sprints, the researchers and agile team members analyzed the outcomes and collaboratively reflected on the effectiveness of the interventions. The team evaluated the integration of sustainability into the product backlog and sprint retrospectives, noting successes and identifying areas for improvement. This reflective process not only validated the use of SusAF, SART and Sustainability Sprint Retrospective template but also highlighted potential adjustments for enhancing sustainability practices in future agile projects.

4 Action Research: Integrating Sustainability with Scrum

The action research is applied to a software development project referred to as the "Labour Hire" solution for anonymity - is an online marketplace connecting labour service providers with service seekers, including companies and households. The processes and activities to support integrating sustainability concerns into agile process as depicted in Fig. 1. The findings from each part of the action research are further discussed below:

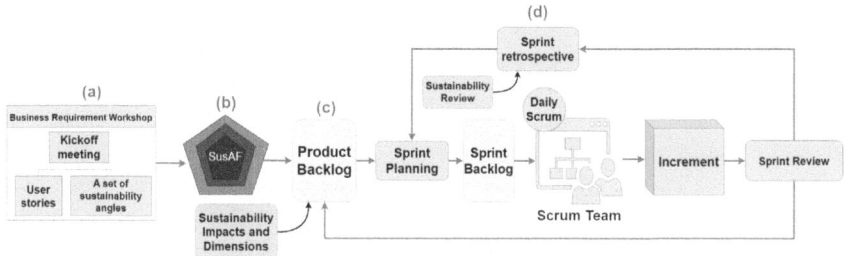

Fig. 1. Integrating Sustainability into Agile Process (Scrum)

4.1 Business Requirements Workshop

The study commenced with the product owner presenting the Labour high software with all the user stories and explained the goals for developing such a software product. This was followed by a review of the company's software development processes and practices at a **business requirements workshop** (see Fig. 1(a)). The Labour Hire product owner and agile team provided details of their then current agile software development process as summarized below:

- Requirements were gathered through user stories involving customers/users of the software products and the agile team (product owner, developers, UX expert).
- User and customer interviews were carried out, involving direct communication between the design and development teams to better clarify user needs and ensure alignment during requirement elicitation.
- Using a template, each team member took notes during customer or user interviews to cross-reference and delve deeper into customer problems and needs for the software products and services.
- Software product and service development was carried out using the Scrum agile framework through several sprints.

Next, the product manager and the Labour Hire product owner expressed the company's wish to integrate sustainability concerns into their agile software development process and increase sustainability awareness among their agile software development teams but lacked knowledge of methods and experience on how to do it within their company. Considering the outlined user-centered requirements elicitation process and the lack of understanding of sustainability concerns, the researchers proposed the Sustainability Awareness Framework (SusAF) [12,21] as a tool well-suited to the given context for sustainability considerations.

4.2 Sustainability Awareness Framework

The suggested use of SusAF was deemed relevant by the agile team, and a **SusAF application workshop** was arranged (see Fig. 1(b)) to elicit the potential sustainability impacts of Labour Hire. The workshop participants identified

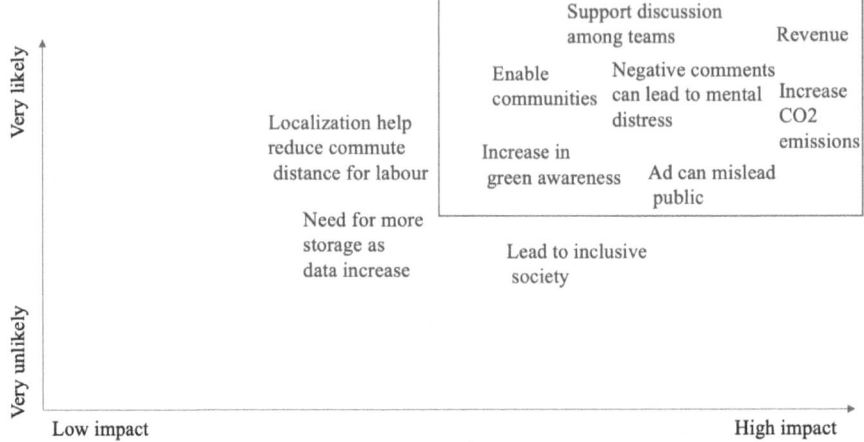

Fig. 2. Prioritize – Likelihood and Level of Impacts for the Labour Hire software (Color figure online)

and prioritized the sustainability impacts of the Labour Hire software, as illustrated in Fig. 2. Impacts were categorized by likelihood and significance: high impact and very likely to occur, high impact but very unlikely to occur, low impact and very likely to occur, or low impact and very unlikely to occur. Positive impacts are highlighted in blue, while negative impacts are shown in red. High-impact, likely-to-occur impacts are displayed within the square box in Fig. 2, while impacts with lower likelihood or significance are positioned outside the box.

The SusAF tool also suggests utilizing the sustainability awareness diagram (SusAD) - an adapted radar chart used to facilitate discussions on *chains of effects* (i.e., how impact on one aspect could evolve over time and cause other impacts). The development team was invited to consider what issues or concerns of the Labour Hire system would have positive or negative impact on the environment, society, economic, technical or personal well being of its users as well as makers in the near, medium and long term. Starting with an empty template, the team populated the SusAD for the sustainability effects for the Labour Hire software as shown in Fig. 3.

For example, the SusAD diagram (Fig. 3) highlights key sustainability impacts across various dimensions. **Technical Dimension:** In the immediate effects, data gathering can enhance system accessibility (positive effect). However, the same data may be exploited for ad manipulation of end users (negative effect). **Environmental Dimension:** The increased energy demand of the Labour Hire software is expected to lead to higher CO_2 emissions. **Economic Dimension:** In the short term, ad campaigns can generate revenue for service providers within the Labour Hire software. Over time, the company is projected to grow, reflecting the long-term structural effects. Thus, Fig. 3 facilitated the examination of the Labour Hire system's chains of effects and prompted the agile team to seek ways of integrating the impacts and effects identified through SusAF into their Scrum process.

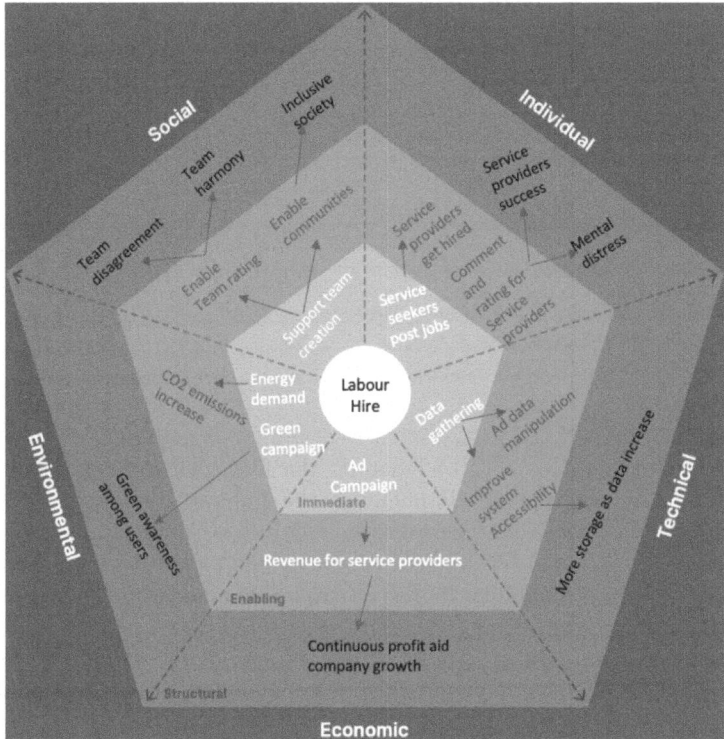

Fig. 3. Chain of Sustainability effects for the Labour Hire software

4.3   Inclusion of Sustainability Dimensions

Figure 4 details a snapshot of the populated SART product backlog. The product owner and agile team used the data from the identified sustainability impacts in the SusAD diagram (Fig. 3) to discuss and populate the SART product backlog (see Fig. 1(c)). Linking each Product Backlog Item (PBI) to a sustainability impact and dimensions. This approach enabled the team to address sustainability concerns consistently throughout each sprint as they designed and developed the Labour Hire software.

4.4   Sustainability Sprint Retrospective

Every sprint concluded with a sustainability review as part of the sprint retrospective process using a template created by the agile team and researchers

User Story	Priority	Story Points	Social Impact	Individual Impact	Economic Impact	Environmental Impact	Technical Impact
1							
As a user, I want to create an account to	High	3	Enhances inclusivity by	Provides access to flexible work	Increases platform user	Minimal impact at this stage	Requires secure user data handling
2							
As a user, I want to verify my email after	High	2	Builds trust within the	Enhances individual	Reduces potential costs	Low environmental	Improves platform security
3							
As a service seeker, I want to post a task with details like title,	High	5	Supports community-building and	Empowers service providers with job	Drives local economic activity	Reduces emissions if local matches are	Scalable infrastructure required
4							
As a service seeker, I want to categorize my task for easier	Medium	2	Improves accessibility for users by making	Reduces user search time, improving	Increases task visibility, boosting	Less search time means reduce energy used for	Enhances platform usability
5							
As a service provider, I want to browse available tasks by	High	5	Increases opportunities for service	Reduces time spent on job search,	Facilitates efficient task matching	Potential reduction in CO2 with local task	Needs efficient search performance
6							
As a service provider, I want to filter tasks	Medium	3	Enhances user experience with	Saves time, reducing stress	Supports productivity,	Lower emissions if commuting is	Needs efficient querying to
7							
As a service seeker, I want to book a service provider for	High	3	Encourages trust in the community	Gives control to users, enhancing experience	Supports economic transactions	Limited impact if local tasks are prioritized	Requires reliable booking system
8							

Fig. 4. SART product backlog for the Labour Hire software system

(see Table 2 and Fig. 1(d)). Table 2 details the five sprint retrospectives from the agile team during the development of the Labour Hire software system. The results highlight the *significance of having a dedicated sustainability representative* within the agile development team. Green coding techniques and the appointment of a sustainability representative were among the early initiatives that the team employed to stay focused on sustainability objectives. Through the work of the sustainability representative as part of the agile team, sustainability became a crucial component of the development process throughout every sprint.

Modular architecture and *constant reworking* were cited as tactics that supported the upkeep of a sustainable and adaptable codebase. The team also understood the significance of *reducing resource consumption in their software product as well as the CI/CD pipeline*. The agile team admitted that throughout the sprints, they ran into problems as a result of their *lack of experience with sustainability*, which they were able to resolve by using the SusAF results and backlog as well as the retrospective templates. Furthermore, there were challenges while *using Jira and Excel templates for product backlog at the same time*, which underscores the need for more efficient procedures to support the agile team. The team also faced issues with the *high energy usage* of the Labour Hire software during testing, and the pressure to deliver features quickly which can result to technical debt.

The retrospective meetings show a strong desire for process improvement, with particular recommendations to evaluate sustainability results through metrics, refine sprint planning to prioritize code quality, and integrate sustainability impacts into the sprint backlog. During the sprints, the team also targeted a 15% reduction in the energy consumption of the software as well as improved resource utilization. These initiatives demonstrate the agile team's dedication to actively promoting sustainability as well as improving their overall practice.

Table 2. Sprint Retrospective: Observations, Reflections, Plans

Sprint	OBSERVING: What worked best and helped sustainability design decisions	OBSERVING: What were the obstacles and challenges	REFLECTING: What can we do differently to improve the overall sprint process?	PLANNING: What should be incorporated in the next sprint?
Sprint 1	One developer played the role of sustainability rep to keep the team on track as they made design decisions during this sprint	It was challenging to use Jira and Excel templates at the same time. Team lacked sustainability knowledge and relied on SusAF, templates, and the researchers	Incorporate the sustainability impacts into the sprint backlog. Establish some metrics to measure the sustainability of each sprint outcome	Add sustainability impacts the sprint backlog. The researcher should join our sprint planning as a sustainability stakeholder
Sprint 2	The continuous refactoring sessions helped reduce technical debt and keep the codebase clean. The cost-benefit analysis was useful to prioritize features that deliver maximum value	Despite efforts to optimize, the software product energy consumption is still higher than the desired consumption, especially during testing phases	Identify and use better optimization strategies to improve the overall software product energy consumption	Target reduction of energy consumption by 15% in the next sprint. Increase efforts to ensure diverse team participation in decision-making
Sprint 3	The optimization of CI/CD pipelines reduced the energy consumption for the build and deployment processes	Rapid iterations forced fast development and release, risking inefficient code results. This could cause technical debt and affect future maintainability	Create a better plan for each sprint iteration with a focus on supporting the team to create quality codes and test cases	Work on efficient resource allocation to reduce delays in certain tasks that affect cost-effectiveness
Sprint 4	The implementation of a modular architecture is good, which will aid in better long-term maintainability and adaptability in subsequent development iterations	For individual sustainability, there is still a lack of personalization features, which might affect the ability of the software to meet the diverse needs of all users	Prioritize the implementation of personalization features for the software	Add at least two new personalization features for the next sprint. Add a green awareness campaign feature to educate users about sustainability. Add accessibility features for disabled users
Sprint 5	Developers researched and adopted green coding practices, producing more efficient code. The sustainability representative pushed to improve environmental impact	Some team members felt overworked because of the tight deadlines	Introduce a system that will monitor the workload of the developers in each sprint to prevent burnout	Monitor team workload. Add content filtering to detect and block hate comment

Additionally, the agile team recognized that implementing *personalization* features was essential to satisfying the diverse needs of different users which prompted the agile team to include features to improve accessibility for disabled users and educate users about sustainability. *These design decisions demonstrate an understanding that sustainability is not only about the environment but also about developing inclusive and adaptable software systems for end users.*

The tight deadlines and team workload led to concerns of potential team burnout which prompted recommendations to implement workload monitoring tools to manage the team workload in each sprint to avoid exhaustion. This shows attention to the agile team well-being which is important to maintain a sustainable pace of work for the team to meet its goals without sacrificing their morale and health. The retrospectives also indicate awareness of ethical considerations by the agile team with the recommendation to include content filtering for detecting and blocking hate comments in the Labour Hire software. This is an important step towards making the software socially responsible.

5 Findings

Drawing on our action research, we present a set of key findings, which are likely to be relevant to the wider software practitioner audiences:

5.1 On Key Components for Integrating Sustainability with Scrum

At present, to our knowledge, there are limited practical references that exemplify how agile software development takes into account the social, economic, and environmental sustainability concerns in software development within software companies [2, 22]. Fortunately, as illustrated by the action research (see Sect. 4), *all key components necessary for such change towards integrating sustainability into agile software development process are already present*. More specifically:

- The SuSAF framework supports the familiarization of software practitioners with the notions of sustainability (i.e., its 5 dimensions, orders of effects, chains of effects and impact magnitude), as well as
- The framework provides a set of questions that foster the initial identification of sustainability requirements and effects.
- The adapted product backlog and sprint retrospective templates support the agile team in considering sustainability impacts during software development and design decisions.

5.2 On Scrum Process for Integrating Sustainability

It is even more encouraging to note that *the agile development process (the most commonly used process of the present day) does not require any foundational changes to support accountability for sustainability-related practices*. The Labor Hire team was able to start practicing a sustainability-supportive software engineering process after only 2 workshops (i.e. after spending about 3 h) with the researchers. This demonstrates that an agile development team starting with no previous knowledge or expertise of sustainability in software engineering can integrate sustainability considerations and expand their own software engineering practices quite immediately. Additionally, these results address the question raised by [4] regarding the impact of adding sustainability concerns on Scrum's lightweight nature and confirm that integrating sustainability into Scrum Framework can preserve Scrum's lightweight nature. Integrating sustainability complements rather than disrupts agile practices, allowing teams to incorporate sustainability seamlessly while maintaining Scrum's flexibility.

5.3   On Change of Mindset of the Agile Team

We also note that the few simple *changes we co-designed into the team's Scrum process resulted in an astonishing impact on the mindset of the agile development team* of the Labor Hire system. The team is now adjusting their own development practice so as to improve the sustainability impact of their software product, as well as focusing on the individual well-being of the team members themselves and the societal impacts of their software, and, finally, the team is working towards spreading sustainability considerations across the wider company.

Additionally, organizational culture plays a crucial role in embedding sustainability into agile processes. In this action research study, the shift in the agile team's mindset toward sustainability was facilitated by a collaborative, open culture where sustainability concerns were actively discussed and supported. Integrating sustainability into agile frameworks requires cultural adjustments that promote continuous learning and openness to new practices of the software development team. The above observations are confirmed by the comments that the team provided when requested to comment on what (if anything) has changed in their practice so far due to using the adapted SusAF framework:

- Throughout the sprints, the team now holds conversations about their mental and physical well-being
- The sustainability footprint of the software product is now evaluated at the end of each sprint using the sustainability impacts and effects using SusAF
- To make comparisons with other providers easier, the team proactively asked their cloud service providers for information on their CO_2 emissions during deployment
- The team has committed to ongoing sustainability dialogues within their company, enabling them to make more informed decisions. For instance, while transitioning to more sustainable cloud service providers might incur additional costs, they are exploring options to influence their existing partners and suppliers to reduce environmental impact
- Emphasizing inclusivity and community engagement, the team has prioritized accessibility in their product development endeavors
- The company has now started initiatives to investigate green coding techniques and create teaching plans for their junior developers

In summary, our collaborative exploration of integrating sustainability into the agile software engineering process of the Labor Hire team has led to transformative changes within the agile scrum process used by the team, the team's mental model on sustainability, and the development company's activities. As we co-developed ways to integrate sustainability considerations and effects into the team's Scrum process, it also progressively advanced the team's understanding of sustainability in software development. Our research focuses on the integration of sustainability concerns into scrum agile software development. How such integration impacts maintenance and evolution is equally important. Future research could identify best practices, such as regular assessments and adaptable frameworks, to sustain these efforts as the software system evolves.

Furthermore, the frequently pointed out software practitioners' lack of understanding of sustainability in software development [8,17,20] was effectively
addressed through consistently applying the SART and the sustainability sprint
retrospective templates. The team's understanding of what sustainability means
for their software product and process keeps developing, growing and evolving.
The commitment of the Labor Hire team to continuously seek ways of improving their agile software development process with sustainability considerations
(despite their initially limited sustainability knowledge) shows how a holistic
approach can grow. This, in turn would lead to software solutions that balance
sustainability concerns in any service delivery.

6   Limitations

The industry partner's interest drove the choice of the partner for this action
research. The researchers did not set out any objective selection criteria. Thus,
we make no claims about the representatives of this company or their context.
Given that the team members' knowledge, motivation, and buy-in impact the
ease and speed of the process change, teams with other contexts will likely have
different barriers to adopting the suggested process changes.

The co-design of the Sustainability Agile Requirement Toolbox (SART) to
integrate sustainability into the scrum process was tailored specifically to the
needs of the collaborating company. SART may be more effective within software
development companies that are already motivated and interested in integrating
sustainability into their agile development processes. The data collected is limited to one company project. However, the data collected and analyzed in this
action research provide valuable insights, guidance and inform the development
of specific sustainability practices for other companies interested in sustainability
in agile software development.

7   Conclusions

The action research undertaken with our industry partner demonstrated how
Agile development teams can effectively identify and prioritize sustainability
effects within Agile software development using SusAF. The use of SusAF to
identify potential sustainability impacts of the Labour Hire software system
before development enabled the Agile development team to link sustainability
effects to each item in the product backlog and conduct a sprint retrospective
with sustainability concerns covered at the end of each sprint.

Furthermore, the transformative shifts seen in the agile team's practices,
mindset, and organizational activities demonstrate how sustainability integration can spark significant change in software development processes. A promising
move towards more sustainable software engineering practices was shown by the
agile team developing the Labor Hire system with a commitment to addressing
sustainability concerns, fostering inclusiveness, and engaging with stakeholders.
Future work based on the ongoing action research will involve exploring with the

agile development team the other components of the Scrum Framework (sprint planning and backlog, daily sprints, sprint review) that can facilitate better sustainability integration in agile software development and also report on the evolving software development practices within the company. Looking ahead, we envision a future where sustainability is inherently integrated into agile software development approaches.

References

1. 17th state of agile report: 71% use agile in their SDLC. Business Wire (2024). https://www.proquest.com/docview/2914167913/citation/7FA46A48642845A8PQ/1
2. Bambazek, P., Groher, I., Seyff, N.: Sustainability in agile software development: a survey study among practitioners. In: 2022 International Conference on ICT for Sustainability (ICT4S), pp. 13–23 (2022). https://doi.org/10.1109/ICT4S55073.2022.00013
3. Bambazek, P., Groher, I., Seyff, N.: Application of the sustainability awareness framework in agile software development. In: 2023 IEEE 31st International Requirements Engineering Conference (RE), pp. 264–274 (2023). https://doi.org/10.1109/RE57278.2023.00034
4. Bambazek, P., Groher, I., Seyff, N.: Requirements engineering knowledge as a foundation for a sustainability-aware scrum framework. In: 2023 IEEE 31st International Requirements Engineering Conference (RE), pp. 311–316 (2023). https://doi.org/10.1109/RE57278.2023.00041
5. Barroca, L., Gregory, P., Kuusinen, K., Sharp, H., AlQaisi, R.: Sustaining agile beyond adoption. In: 2018 44th Euromicro Conference on Software Engineering and Advanced Applications (SEAA), pp. 22–25. IEEE (2018)
6. Becker, C., et al.: Sustainability design and software: the Karlskrona manifesto. In: 2015 IEEE/ACM 37th IEEE International Conference on Software Engineering, vol. 2, pp. 467–476. IEEE (2015)
7. Belkhir, L., Elmeligi, A.: Assessing ICT global emissions footprint: trends to 2040 & recommendations. J. Clean. Prod. **177**, 448–463 (2018). https://doi.org/10.1016/j.jclepro.2017.12.239, https://www.sciencedirect.com/science/article/pii/S095965261733233X
8. Betz, S., et al.: Lessons learned from developing a sustainability awareness framework for software engineering using design science. ACM Trans. Softw. Eng. Methodol. (2024)
9. Chitchyan, R.: What can requirements engineering do for emerging system of systems? Case of smart local energy. In: International Conference on Software Engineering: Software Engineering in Society Track (2024)
10. Chitchyan, R., Bird, C.: Theory as a source of software and system requirements. Requirements Eng. **27**(3), 375–398 (2022)
11. Condori-Fernandez, N., Lago, P.: Towards a software sustainability-quality model: insights from a multi-case study. In: 2019 13th International Conference on Research Challenges in Information Science (RCIS), pp. 1–11. IEEE (2019)
12. Duboc, L., et al.: Do we really know what we are building? Raising awareness of potential sustainability effects of software systems in requirements engineering. In: 2019 IEEE 27th International Requirements Engineering Conference (RE), pp. 6–16 (2019). https://doi.org/10.1109/RE.2019.00013

13. Ericsson: Ericsson report: Technology for good (2015). https://www.ericsson. com/assets/local/about-ericsson/sustainability-and-corporate-responsibility/ documents/2015-corporate-responsibility-and-sustainability-report.pdf
14. Freitag, C., Berners-Lee, M., Widdicks, K., Knowles, B., Blair, G.S., Friday, A.: The real climate and transformative impact of ICT: a critique of estimates, trends, and regulations. Patterns **2**(9) (2021)
15. Gil, D., Fernández-Alemán, J.L., Trujillo, J., García-Mateos, G., Luján-Mora, S., Toval, A.: The effect of green software: a study of impact factors on the correctness of software. Sustainability **10**(10) (2018). https://www.mdpi.com/2071-1050/10/ 10/3471
16. Heldal, R., et al.: Sustainability competencies and skills in software engineering: an industry perspective. J. Syst. Softw. **211**, 111978 (2024)
17. Karita, L., Mourão, B.C., Machado, I.: Software industry awareness on green and sustainable software engineering: a state-of-the-practice survey. In: Proceedings of the XXXIII Brazilian Symposium on Software Engineering, pp. 501–510 (2019)
18. Konda, S.R.: Ethical considerations in the development and deployment of AI driven software systems. Int. J. Comput. Sci. Technol. (IJCST) **6**(3) (2022). http:// www.ijcst.com.pk/index.php/IJCST/article/view/376/336
19. Naumann, S., Dick, M., Kern, E., Johann, T.: The greensoft model: a reference model for green and sustainable software and its engineering. Sustain. Comput.: Inform. Syst. **1**(4), 294–304 (2011)
20. Oyedeji, S., Adisa, M., Seffah, A., Coello, F.L., Naqvi, B.: Galapagos: a design pattern for sustainability of ICT interactive software and services. In: International Working Conference on Human-Centered Software Engineering, pp. 78–98. Springer (2024)
21. Penzenstadler, B., et al.: Sustainabilty awareness frameowrk (2023). https://www. suso.academy/en/sustainability-awareness-framework-susaf/
22. Rashid, N., Khan, S.U.: Agile practices for global software development vendors in the development of green and sustainable software. J. Softw.: Evol. Process **30**(8), e1927 (2018)
23. Somekh, B.: Action Research: A Methodology for Change and Development. McGraw-Hill Education, Maidenhead (2005)
24. Venters, C.C., et al.: Software sustainability: research and practice from a software architecture viewpoint. J. Syst. Softw. **138**, 174–188 (2018)
25. Venters, C.C., et al.: Sustainable software engineering: reflections on advances in research and practice. Inf. Softw. Technol. **164**, 107316 (2023)
26. Venters, C.C., et al.: Software sustainability: the modern tower of babel. In: CEUR Workshop Proceedings, vol. 1216, pp. 7–12. CEUR (2014)

Optimizing for Sustainability: Product Ops and Software Waste Reduction

Bogdan Moroz[ID], Andrey Saltan[(✉)][ID], and Sami Hyrynsalmi[ID]

LUT University, Lahti, Finland
bogdan.moroz@student.lut.fi, {andrey.saltan,sami.hyrynsalmi}@lut.fi

Abstract. In today's competitive software-intensive industries, the pursuit of sustainability is increasingly recognized as one of the important drivers of long-term performance. While lean methodologies focusing on waste reduction are widely adopted across various domains, the software-intensive industries face unique challenges when applying these principles. The emergence of Product Operations (Product Ops) in product-led companies presents new opportunities for improving operational efficiency and reducing waste within software development processes. This paper investigates the role of Product Ops in addressing different types of software development waste by mapping the responsibilities and impacts of Product Ops to these types of waste. The results indicate that Product Ops may help reduce multiple forms of waste, contributing to the sustainability of software businesses. This exploratory study lays the foundation for further research examining the impact of Product Ops on the sustainability of software companies.

Keywords: Product Operations · Product Ops · Product Management · Sustainability · Software Engineering · Software Business · Lean · Waste Management

1 Introduction

Over recent decades, sustainability has gained significant importance across various sectors, including software-intensive industries [3]. Similarly, lean principles that emphasize waste minimization have gained traction, with software companies adopting these methodologies. Historically, sustainability is conceptualized along three dimensions: environmental, economic, and social [29]. While the environmental aspect has received considerable attention, the economic dimension—particularly within business operations—is gaining recognition as a significant factor in long-term success. In the software-intensive businesses, where rapid product cycles and constant innovation are the norm, achieving sustainable practices requires a focus on operational efficiency and waste reduction.

Lean methodologies prioritize the identification and elimination of waste in processes, offering clear metrics and methods to enhance efficiency [8]. In software development, various types of waste have been identified, including delays,

E. Papatheocharous et al. (Eds.): ICSOB 2024, LNBIP 539, pp. 251–267, 2025.
https://doi.org/10.1007/978-3-031-85849-9_21

defects, and miscommunication between teams [2]. However, despite acknowledging the need for sustainability, many software companies struggle to integrate these considerations into their development processes effectively [21].

Product managers, while aware of the importance of sustainability, often lack practical tools or support to drive meaningful change [13]. The emergence of Product Operations (Product Ops) in product-led organizations may provide product managers with the means to do just that. Product Ops has been defined as a function that makes product companies more efficient, and allows them to scale without friction [19]. It serves to optimize processes, improve communication between product teams, and streamline product management workflows [19], all of which may contribute to reducing inefficiencies and waste. In previous studies, Product Ops has been explored from the perspective and context of product management, but its specific role in sustainability—particularly in reducing waste—has not yet been thoroughly investigated.

This paper aims to bridge this gap by exploring how Product Ops contributes to both operational efficiency and economic sustainability. Formally, the study addresses the following research question: *How does Product Operations affect different kinds of* **waste** *of the software product development process, and contribute to the sustainability of software companies?* The findings provide a better understanding of how Product Ops can contribute to the sustainability of the software development process.

Due to the scarcity of academic literature on the subject, this study relies on grey literature sources for its analysis. Through systematic coding of grey literature, we identified the responsibilities and impacts of Product Ops, constructing a multifaceted view of the role based on recurring themes across sources. The result of this exploratory study is a mapping between the responsibilities, outputs, and impacts of Product Ops and the various types of waste in software development processes.

2   Background

2.1   The Concept of Sustainability

The concept of sustainability has its roots in discussions from the Industrial Revolution, when thinkers like Adam Smith and John Stuart Mill explored the trade-offs between social justice and wealth generation [29]. However, the modern understanding of sustainability is most often traced back to the 1987 UN Brundtland Report, which emphasized the need for "a new era of economic growth [...] forceful and at the same time socially and environmentally sustainable" and introduced the widely-accepted definition of sustainable development as the "development that meets the needs of the present without compromising the ability of future generations to meet their own needs" [29]. Since then, a range of further interpretations of sustainability has been articulated. Sustainability has gained considerable attention across academia, business, and the public sphere, marked by a rise in publications and global initiatives [3,29]. One of the most widely adopted frameworks is the "three pillars" model, encompassing environmental, economic, and social dimensions [29].

In the early 2000s, sustainability began to attract attention from a broader range of industries, including the rapidly growing software-intensive ones [23]. These industries faced both challenges and opportunities in this shift. On the one hand, they exacerbated environmental issues such as energy consumption and electronic waste [15]. On the other hand, advancements in software have been instrumental in promoting sustainability by improving efficiency, optimizing resource use, and providing tools to monitor and mitigate environmental impacts [6]. This dual role underscores the importance of integrating sustainability into all aspects of operations within software-intensive companies as the industry continues to expand.

2.2 Lean

The concept of lean originated with the Toyota Production System (TPS), renowned for its ability to reduce waste and enhance production efficiency [17]. Lean principles emphasize minimizing waste—defined as any activity that does not add value to the customer—while increasing productivity, quality, and speed of the value creation process [2,17,28]. Over time, lean methodologies spread beyond manufacturing, influencing a wide range of industries, including software development [9,17].

In software-intensive industries, lean practices gained traction with the rise of cloud technology and continuous delivery, enabling rapid, automated updates to software products [5,8,32]. The principles of continuous discovery and experimentation, as outlined by Eric Ries in his book "Lean Startup", and adapted for software engineering by Tom and Mary Poppendieck in their "Lean Software Development" book series, have become central to modern software product management [8,9]. These practices, such as frequently releasing minimum viable products (MVPs) and using A/B testing, allow software teams to minimize risk, reduce inefficiencies, make data-driven decisions, and rapidly improve their products and services [8,12]. It is within this industry landscape that Product Ops emerged on the scene.

2.3 Impacts of Lean on Sustainability

Martínez and Calvo-Amodio identified both positive and negative impacts of lean practices on sustainability [17]. In the economic dimension, lean practices like waste elimination, Just-In-Time (JIT) production, and continuous improvement help reduce operational costs, improve resource utilization, and increase profits, giving companies a competitive edge through lower costs and higher quality [17]. However, implementing lean practices may require significant upfront investments in training, process redesign, and new technologies. Moreover, overly emphasizing cost-cutting and efficiency may lead to a lack of flexibility, reducing the ability to respond to market changes, and might also lead to higher energy consumption, carbon emissions, and waste generation [17].

In the environmental dimension, the lean goal of waste reduction aligns directly with the goal of preserving resources [17]. The mindset of continuous improvement and waste reduction can facilitate broader adoption of green practices[1] in organizations. It is possible however to overlook some of the negative environmental impacts when solely focusing on reducing costs. In the manufacturing context, for example, the environmental benefits of consuming less resources while producing products in smaller batches may be offset by the increased frequency of transporting these smaller batches [17].

Finally, in the social dimension, lean practices can enhance employee well-being by fostering continuous learning, engagement, and manageable workloads [17]. These can be offset by the pressure to constantly maintain and increase personal efficiency, causing stress [17].

2.4   Sustainability, Lean, and Waste Reduction in Software Engineering

Sustainability in Software Engineering (SE) is understood from two perspectives: sustainable software and sustainability through software [21]. Sustainable software refers to software whose creation, deployment, and use do not negatively impact the economy, society, or the environment. Sustainability through software emphasizes using software to achieve sustainability-oriented objectives. An industry survey by Oyedeji et al. revealed "a lack of progress in practically integrating sustainability considerations into software development activities" [21].

Waste reduction is a cornerstone of the lean philosophy, and lean manufacturing identified seven types of waste: defects, overproduction, waiting, non-utilized talent, transportation, inventory excess, motion, and extra processing [2]. When adapting the lean principles for software development, this typology of waste has been redefined to better address the unique aspects of software development processes and practices. Over time, researchers and practitioners have expanded upon and refined these categories to better fit the context of software development [2].

3   Methodology

This study originates from a broader research project aimed at understanding the role and impact of Product Operations (Product Ops) within product-led, software-intensive businesses. Recognizing that much of the relevant knowledge about Product Ops is disseminated through non-academic channels due to its emergent nature and the rapid evolution of industry practices, we conducted a systematic exploratory analysis of practitioner publications.

---

[1] Any action performed across the supply chain to eliminate or reduce any kind of negative environmental impact [4].

Grey literature encompasses publications produced outside traditional academic channels, such as books, industry reports, white papers, blog posts, webinars, and other non-peer-reviewed materials [1]. Incorporating grey literature into research has become particularly widespread in fields like software engineering and product management, where industry practices often outpace academic research, and valuable insights are frequently shared informally among practitioners [10,14]. By integrating these practical perspectives, multiple studies seek to bridge the gap between theory and practice, capturing real-world applications, challenges, and emerging trends not yet represented in academic discourse [11,18,30].

The primary data collection method involved usage of Google Search with the keywords "Product Ops" and "Product Operations", which generated a wide range of resources, including blog posts, web pages, white papers, and books. Out of the initial 187 search results for "product ops" and 167 for "product operations", we identified 133 unique and relevant sources for further analysis. Selection criteria included the level of detail, practical applicability, and specific focus on Product Ops. Additionally, we identified 9 sources through the snowballing technique, a method in which relevant references from initial sources led to the discovery of further pertinent materials. Another 6 sources were manually added due to their industry prominence or specialized insights, even if they did not emerge from the search results.

The selected publications were manually reviewed one by one, and key concepts were labeled. The labeling process was flexible, allowing labels to be applied to a phrase, sentence, paragraph, or multiple paragraphs, depending on the context. The label size was not restricted, and the labels were assigned in a case-by-case manner to capture the nuances of the text or audio transcript. Throughout this process, recurring labels emerged, that highlighted common themes and areas of focus within Product Ops, such as its responsibilities, strategic impact, and operational roles in product-led companies.

After reviewing 34 sources, we reached a point of theoretical saturation, where additional sources did not introduce new codes or categories. This saturation suggested that the sample provided a comprehensive representation of the Product Ops literature. Consequently, we concluded the source analysis after reviewing these 34 sources.

Proprietary software was utilized to review each label and the text snippets with that label. The software allowed to group related labels in a hierarchical structure by specifying parent-child relationships between them. During this iterative analysis, labels were reassigned, restructured, or regrouped as necessary to reflect emerging patterns. Each decision regarding the movement or reclassification of labels was documented when not self-evident. This process ultimately resulted in a structured typology of responsibilities typically assigned to Product Ops roles, and the reported effects of Product Ops on organizations.

In the subsequent phase, we mapped the identified responsibilities and impacts of Product Ops to the types of software development waste outlined by Alahyari et al. [2]. Each type of waste was examined to determine how Product Ops could address or mitigate it. This mapping aimed to illustrate the potential of Product Ops to reduce inefficiencies and contribute to operational sustainability within software development processes.

The final step involved synthesizing the insights gained from the mapping exercise and validating the findings against industry practices. The synthesis provided a framework for understanding how Product Ops can contribute to greater sustainability by addressing waste in software product development. It also outlined future research directions on the operational impact of Product Ops.

4 Results

Having conducted the analysis, we found that the adoption and practice of Product Ops may reduce the waste in the software product development process. In this section, we go over each of the waste types established in the Software Engineering Body of Knowledge (SWEBOK) (as collected by Alahyari et al. [2]), and describe how Product Ops may be able to reduce them. Each subsection begins by providing the name of the type of waste, the source where that waste was first introduced, and the definition of the waste. The impact of Product Ops on this type of waste is then described, based on the results of the literature study. At the end of each subsection, the labels identified in literature associated with the reduction of the waste are listed. Figure 1 presents a mapping between the waste types and these labels, which are the responsibilities, outputs, and impacts of Product Ops professionals that may help reduce or eliminate the linked types of waste. In several cases, two types of waste are addressed in a single subsection— this was done either when the definitions of the wastes largely overlapped, or the impact of Product Ops on both types of waste was similar, to avoid belaboring the point. Table 1 links the labels to the grey literature sources in which they were encountered.[2]

Partially Done Work [27]. This is software work that is started and developed for a while, but never integrated with the rest of the environment, nor delivered to production to provide value to the user and the business [27]. The resources invested into this development are sometimes capitalized, and sometimes need to be written off as expenses [27]. Certainly, it is the responsibility of software product managers to direct the development effort to be of value— product management is defined by Ebert and Brinkkemper [7] as "the discipline and business process which governs a product from its inception to the market or customer delivery and service in order to **generate biggest possible value to the business**".

---

[2] For full details on each source, including links to their full contents, refer to the supplementary package online at: https://tinyurl.com/4uzufawa.

Table 1. Responsibilities, outputs, and impacts of Product Ops linked to reviewed grey literature sources

Label	Encountered in sources
Increasing visibility	G2, G23, G24, G30, G32, G69, G77, G78, G85, G99, G100, G118, G134, G142, G145
Supporting SPM	G1, G2, G49, G78, G86, G134
Creating standard templates	G2, G24, G78
Process management	G2, G48, G67, G77, G82, G142
Process improvement	G1, G31, G55, G71, G77, G100
Automation	G2, G77, G78, G146
Accelerating feedback loops	G1, G23, G31, G32, G77
Increasing feature adoption	G1
Reducing administrative burden	G5, G31, G32, G78, G85
Letting SPM focus on core SPM	G1, G2, G48, G49, G66, G69, G77, G78, G82, G85, G134
Centralized knowledge	G2, G24, G30, G32, G55, G66, G78
Decision support	G1, G2, G5, G6, G30, G48, G66, G67, G69, G71, G77, G78, G82, G86, G99, G103, G134, G145, G146
Everyone aligned around strategy	G24, G71, G77, G78, G99, G118, G145
Experiment sequencing	G1, G24, G134, G142
Release management	G32, G78, G134
Facilitating communication & collaboration	G1, G2, G5, G23, G24, G31, G48, G49, G55, G69, G71, G77, G78, G82, G85, G87, G86, G100, G118, G142, G145
QA role	G2, G24, G48, G55
Preventing silos	G30, G48, G78, G82
Data enablement	G1, G49, G71, G77, G78, G82, G134, G145, G146
Raising the bar	G2, G24, G48, G82, G86
Best practice sharing	G1, G2, G6, G32, G48, G66, G77, G78, G85, G103, G142
Facilitating staff professional development	G6, G22, G30, G85
Helping scale	G2, G31, G32, G67, G69, G77, G78, G85, G87
Preventing SPM burnout	G78
Inspiring others	G24

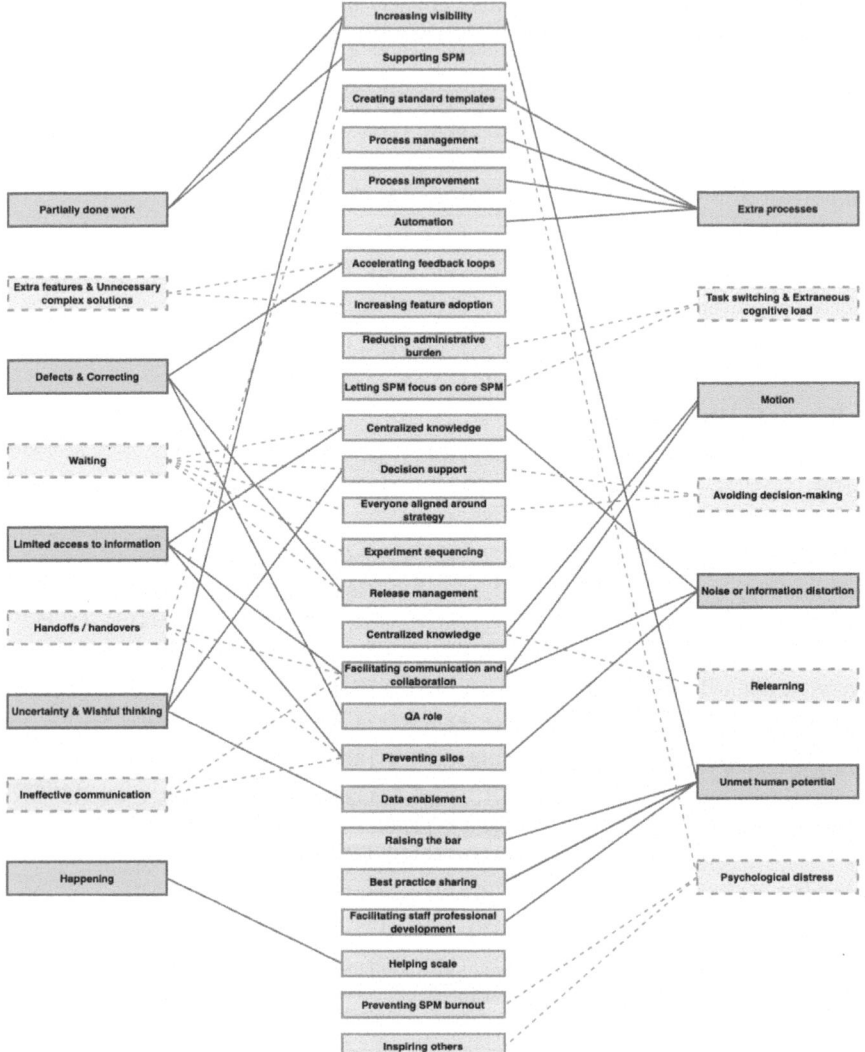

Fig. 1. A mapping between SE process waste types (orange and red, left and right) and the responsibilities, outputs, and impacts of Product Ops that may help reduce them (green, center). Shapes and colors used for visual clarity, no additional meaning. (Color figure online)

Product Ops, being a supporting and enabling role, help Software Product Managers (SPMs) achieve this more efficiently. However, compared to other types of wastes presented below, there is less direct impact here. Product Ops do increase visibility of the work done across the organization, and in some cases serve to quantify the costs of development efforts, which may help spot instances of partially done work earlier.

Labels: *increasing visibility, supporting SPM*

Extra Processes [27]. This is the sometimes necessary paperwork required in addition to the development of the software, such as requirements matrices traceable to code, and various customer sign-offs [27]. While unavoidable in some domains, such as safety-critical systems, these activities take time and may become excessive [27]. Poppendieck & Poppendieck [27] suggest template-driven approaches and constant evaluation of processes for efficiency—both these aspects are commonly mentioned as core activities of Product Ops.

When it comes to templates, the literature focuses on templates for documentation and communication within the organization. For example, the Product Ops team at Reddit has created a template for announcing feature launches, which reportedly accelerated the flow of informative emails across the company. Templates are also used at Reddit to share experiment results in a standard way. This both accelerates informative communication, and helps remain consistent and maintain this efficiency as the company grows.

Process management is a major area of Product Operations' work. In includes standardization and documentation of existing processes, establishment of new ones, and continuous process improvement—with the ultimate goal to streamline product development. A Product Ops team at Calendly reported conducting regular productivity meetings, where the efficiency of each meeting in the product development process is reevaluated, and low productivity meetings are cut or restructured. A team at a health tech company Oscar Health has designed a lightweight process for annual planning, where each development team surfaced initiatives they are considering to pursue in the coming year. Each initiative was summarized in a one-pager, which decision makers at the company voted on.

Automation is another aspect of this process management work. Product Ops automates repetitive time-consuming tasks, either by finding off-the-shelf tools for the job, or developing custom tooling for the unique needs of their organization.

Labels: *creating standard templates, process management, process improvement, automation*

Extra Features [27] **& Unnecessary Complex Solutions** [31]. Poppendieck & Poppendieck [27] write that any feature that is not needed by the customer right away only increases the complexity of the system, and development teams should resist the temptation to add these until absolutely necessary. Unnecessary complex solutions may manifest, for example, in a product requiring the user to fill form fields unrelated to the task they are trying to accomplish with the software [31]. A report from *Pendo* claims that up to 80% of the features released by software product vendors remain unused, and positions Product Ops as the solution [22].

Product Operations is reported to increase process efficiency and ability to deliver features to the customers faster. This allows product teams to learn about the usage of the product and improve quicker, and ensure the features released are useful and used. In Product Ops literature this is commonly referred to as "accelerating feedback loops", or making those feedback loops tighter, in order to understand the users better and respond to their needs faster.

Labels: *accelerating feedback loops, increasing feature adoption*

Task Switching [27] & Extraneous Cognitive Load [31]. The "task switching" waste is the time wasted getting into the flow of a particular project or task, after switching from something else [27]. While Poppendieck & Poppendieck [27] talk specifically about software developers switching between projects and teams, multitasking is a major challenge for many knowledge workers [20], including product managers [24]. Extraneous cognitive load is defined by Sedano et al. as "the cognitive load unnecessarily added by the task environment, or the way the task is presented", and reducing the burden on working memory by reducing this load is assosiated with better decision making and overall outcomes [31].

Product Operations is positioned as a solution to product managers "having too much on their plates", and is supposed to take away some of the administrative burden product managers face, especially as companies scale. Publications motivating the companies to adopt Product Ops often begin by painting a picture of an overwhelmed product manager lacking the time to do high-value, core product management work—such as conducting product discovery activities, developing strategy, and updating roadmaps. Product Operations takes over some of the work that is typically lower on the prioritized task list for SPM—this work needs to be done, but it takes an additional effort to do it really well, and product managers' time is better spent focusing on achieving product market fit and aligning business and customer needs. Product Ops is described as giving product managers their time back, allowing them to focus on 'what' they work on, instead of the 'how'.

Labels: *reducing administrative burden, letting SPM focus on core SPM*

Waiting [27]. This is waiting for things to happen, such as for a project to start, the right specialist to be hired, or a decision or a piece of documentation to be ready or approved [27].

Product Ops increase transparency across the organization via proactive communication and setting up centralized repositories and communication channels for the information about the company's products. This enables product teams to make independent decisions faster, while still remaining in alignment with the strategy, and grounded in the latest user insights. The role of Product Ops in product experimentation and release management was also associated with reduced waiting in our analysis. When it comes to experimentation, Product Ops is commonly in charge of experiment scheduling and sequencing, allowing the companies to plan and roll out experiments faster, and run as many experiments as possible concurrently, as long as those experiments do not risk interfering with each other's results. Product Ops also creates efficient processes for planning and coordinating launches of new features and updates. For example, a Product Ops team at Stripe instrumented tooling for improved coordination of various teams and departments involved in each release. The product team preparing the release fills out a form specifying the scope and impact of the release, and the relevant stakeholders and departments are immediately notified.

Labels: *centralized knowledge, decision support, everyone aligned around strategy, experiment sequencing, release management*

Motion [27]. This refers to the amount of effort it takes a developer to get a question about the project they are working on answered [27]. How many stakeholders do they need to talk to get their answers? Handing over artifacts such as documentation between teams and departments also leads to a partial tacit knowlege loss [27].

The impacts of Product Ops on waiting are also suitable to tackle motion. The centralized knowledge base makes it easier for product teams to look up relevant information about the product to get their questions answered. Product Ops may also establish clear communication channels that can be followed when some input is needed from different teams or departments.

Labels: *centralized knowledge, facilitating communication and collaboration*

Defects [27] **& Correcting** [25]. Defects are quantified by the size of the defect multiplied by the time it takes to detect it [27]. Correcting is defined as "redoing or scrapping, due to feedback" [25]. Product Ops accelerate the flow of the feedback to the product teams, potentially reducing the scope of correcting by catching issues earlier. Several of the sources reviewed indicate Product Ops is involved in the quality assurance of the products, in particular leading up to and after the launch of a feature or an update. When preparing for a launch, Product Ops in some organizations make sure the product is up to a certain level of quality, and analyse the impact of a new feature or update on existing features, to make sure there are no regressions to existing functionality. In some cases Product Ops are tasked with monitoring the features after launch and working together with the customer support team to collect and summarize issues with the release. These are then communicated back to the product teams for improvements.

Labels: *release management, QA role, accelerating feedback loops*

Relearning [26]. This is defined as rediscovering information that had been previously known, but forgotten [27]. The centralized knowledge bases established by Product Ops have the potential to reduce the amount of information forgotten.

Labels: *centralized knowledge*

Handoffs [26] **& Handovers** [28]. Handoffs are defined by the Poppendiecks as the "loss of tacit knowledge when work is handed over to others" [26], and the definition of handovers by Power and Conboy is quite similar—waste is generated when incomplete work is handed over from one team to another, leading to delays, more people required, and tacit knowledge loss [28].

Product Ops can be argued to reduce this waste by facilitating better communication and collaboration between the parties involved in the handover. They can do that by arranging shared meetings and setting up communication channels between the teams or departments. Templates can also be used for ensuring the work handed over is sufficiently documented. Product Ops is commonly described as "breaking down silos" between departments in an organization, making it easier to communicate cross-functionally.

Labels: *creating standard templates, facilitating communication and collaboration, preventing silos*

Avoiding Decision-Making [16]. This can be caused both by organizational factors, such as teams or individuals lacking the power to make decisions, or the individual personalities of the employees [16]. Product Ops empowers product teams to make independent decisions by equipping them with the necessary data, tools, and insights to make informed choices. By organizing and presenting qualitative and quantitative data in a clear, actionable format, Product Ops reduces ambiguity and provides a structured approach to decision-making. They reportedly foster a data-driven culture that encourages teams to base their decisions on evidence rather than assumptions, which may reduce indecision. Product Ops may be seen as trusted advisors, ready to consult teams to ensure their work is aligned with the strategy, and help them prioritize. This support system may help teams feel more confident and prepared to make decisions, diminishing the tendency to avoid them.

Labels: *decision support, everyone aligned around strategy*

Limited Access to Information [16]. Product decisions need to be made with all the relevant context taken into account, and may otherwise be harmful [16]. Information sharing and "preventing silos" is one of the core tasks of Product Ops professionals, as already elaborated above. Various initiatives, such as establishing and running product newsletters across the organization, are commonly mentioned, both as a means for Product Ops to quickly make an impact on the organization, and as a tool for stakeholders across the organization to remain engaged with the product development milestones with little effort.

Labels: *centralized knowledge, preventing silos, facilitating communication and collaboration*

Noise or Information Distortion [16]. Mandić et al. [16] distinguish temporal and spacial distortion. Time distortion may occur when the information is forgotten or not updated on time. Space distortion refers to passing the information across levels and departments in an organization, where context may be lost, or things interpreted differently based on a different context [16]. Clear parallels to 'relearning [26]' and 'handoffs [26]/handovers [28]' can be observed here, and the reported impact of Product Ops on this kind of waste is similar.

Labels: *centralized knowledge, preventing silos, facilitating communication and collaboration*

Uncertainty [16] **& Wishful Thinking** [25]. Mandić et al. [16] distinguish the uncertainty of predictions, decision assumptions, and quality of the information on which the decisions are based on [16]. Pessôa et al. [25] define wishful thinking as making decisions based on incomplete data (which is incorrectly perceived to be complete), or operating according to incorrect controls.

Product Ops equip product teams with the data to base their decisions on, providing more confidence in making decisions. Product Ops is commonly described as the enabler of data-driven decision making, contrasted with the often emotional opinion-based decision making of early-stage startups. Product Ops make the insights from user research and product analytics more visible and actionable by creating easily available dashboards.

Labels: *data enablement, decision support, increasing visibility*

Unmet Human Potential [28]. Power and Kieran [28] define this as "not using or fostering people's skills and abilities to their full potential". This is an opportunity cost for an organization—the potential of individuals, teams, and the entire organization is underutilized [28]. Motivation research indicates this waste can be mitigated by fostering a sense of purpose and providing opportunities to develop employees' skills and abilities [28].

Product Operations is described as unlocking hidden potential and raising the bar for the organization. The literature is rife with metaphors for Product Ops as the "connective tissue", "the oil in the gears" that is "fueling the momentum" and "raising the data IQ" of the oranisation. By sharing best practices, tools and approaches with product teams, Product Ops may help elevate their skills, and help ensure that all product teams operate at the same level. Some organizations involve Product Ops in creating learning paths for product managers, onboarding and training new product managers and designers, and coaching them on various product discovery techniques.

Labels: *raising the bar, best practice sharing, facilitating staff professional development, increasing visibility*

Happening [25]. Happening is described as all the reactions to unexpected changes, which can be external (market shifts, incorrect forecasts) or internal (restructurings, policy changes) [25]. Little was found in the reviewed literature to address this type of waste directly, except for the role of Product Ops in helping organizations scale. Introducing Product Ops at a company that found a product-market fit and is growing is commonly described as the perfect time to establish the position. This ensures that the company maintains its ability to deliver and innovate despite the increasing customer base and headcount.

Labels: *helping scale*

Psychological Distress [31]. Related to the "task switching" and "extraneous cognitive load", this type of waste hinders productivity when employees are overwhelmed by the pressure to meet deadlines or perform an expanding workload [31]. Product Ops is described as "giving product managers their time back", and alleviating some of their administrative burden as proactive assistants. Product Ops makes it easier for SPMs to access product-related data and analytics, which makes their job of making decisions on the strategy and roadmap easier. When a dedicated Product Operations unit takes care of the various intricate yet routine tasks—such as creating dashboards that aggregate data across departments and products—SPMs can spend more time on experimentation and big-picture planning. By communicating and visualizing the impact of product teams' and individual members' work, Product Ops also has the potential to inspire and motivate them to contribute more, and experience more satisfaction.

Labels: *preventing SPM burnout, supporting SPM, inspiring others*

Ineffective Communication [31]. "Incomplete, incorrect, misleading, inefficient, or absent communication", leading to reduced productivity [31]. Efficient communication and collaboration is a major focus in most of the Product Ops literature reviewed, as already described at length above. The 2020 global pandemic is mentioned as one of the catalysts for the broad adoption of Product Ops around that time—the transition to remote work exacerbated the challenges of asynchronous and distributed communication, which Product Ops can effectively tackle.

Labels: *facilitating collaboration and communication, preventing silos*

5   Discussion

The study analyzed the claims about Product Operations found in the grey literature written by a variety of industry stakeholders, including product managers, consultants, and reporters. Many potential positive impacts of Product Ops on waste reduction were identified and illustrated. The overall picture of the impact of Product Ops on waste reduction is a positive one, with examples of potential reduction identified for each type of waste established in software engineering literature. This positive 'skew' of the literature may be partly attributed to some of the sources aiming to present Product Ops in a positive light, to motivate further adoption of this discipline across the industry.

It is therefore worthwhile to consider the possible negative impacts of Product Ops on waste reduction as well. The process management responsibility of Product Ops in particular may be a double-edged sword in terms of reducing the "extra processes" waste. On the one hand, Product Ops has the potential to ensure highly efficient processes. On the other, they may introduce additional processes, or additional steps to existing processes, for more consistency across the organization. The trade-offs between the potential reduction in the performance of individual teams and the productivity gains of the company as a whole need to be studied closer. Less competent implementations of Product Ops could even see process creation as their primary responsibility, and the skepticism by some of the product managers in the literature reviewed is driven by the apprehension of Product Ops as "process people", coming into the company to drown it in bureaucracy and build procedural barriers between product teams and users.

Looking broadly on the relationship between Product Ops and company sustainability, we can see that a significant portion of the waste reductions described are within the **economic** domain—they drive the costs of the company down by reducing unnecessary waiting and relearning already known information, for example. Some of the waste reductions, however, veer into the **social** domain. The role of Product Ops in preventing SPM burnout, reducing extraneous cognitive load, and providing support and motivation to product team members, has the potential to make the workplace less draining, and the work more satisfying. **Environmental** waste reduction is indirect, and is primarily the result of using company resources more efficiently. Here also the possible negative impacts should be considered—for example, the experiment sequencing role of Product Ops may allow the launch and execution of more experiments in parallel, but the relationship between that and the overall energy consumption of the organization may warrant attention.

Finally, while we have shown that Product Ops is capable of reducing costs for businesses in many ways, the role itself is not directly generating revenue. It may therefore be tempting for companies to eliminate Product Ops in times of economic downturn, and in fact there is some indication that hiring for Product Ops positions has slowed, in line with the overall labour market in the technology industry. A better understanding and quantifying of the positive impacts of Product Ops on sustainability may prove to be another argument to motivate the industry to invest in this discipline going forward.

6   Conclusion

In today's competitive and rapidly evolving software-intensive industries, sustainability is becoming increasingly relevant. As businesses prioritize operational efficiency and sustainable practices, Product Operations (Product Ops) emerges as an enabler of waste reduction and long-term success. This paper highlights the role of Product Ops in driving sustainability by addressing inefficiencies in the software development process, ultimately contributing the most to economic and social sustainability of software businesses.

Through a systematic mapping of Product Ops responsibilities to various types of software development waste, the study demonstrates how Product Ops contributes to reducing waste, improving operational efficiency, and enhancing economic sustainability. Product Ops helps mitigate delays, task switching, and unnecessary features, while fostering data-driven decision making and streamlining processes. Moreover, by alleviating the administrative burden on product managers, Product Ops allows them to focus on strategic, high-value tasks, ultimately leading to better product outcomes.

While the overall impact of Product Ops on waste reduction is largely positive, potential challenges, such as the risk of introducing additional processes or creating bureaucratic inefficiencies, should be considered. The majority of waste reduction is linked to the economic dimension of sustainability, but there is also potential to foster social benefits, such as lessening the likelihood of employee burnout and enhancing job satisfaction. Environmental benefits, while indirect, may result from more efficient usage of different types of resources.

This study underscores the growing importance of Product Ops in achieving sustainable software development and lays the groundwork for future research. As companies face continuous pressures to improve efficiency and uphold social, economic, and environmental responsibilities, Product Ops may play a vital role in fostering operational efficiencies and synergies that support waste reduction and sustainable advancements in software-intensive industries.

References

1. Adams, R.J., Smart, P., Huff, A.S.: Shades of grey: guidelines for working with the grey literature in systematic reviews for management and organizational studies: shades of grey. Int. J. Manage. Rev. **19**(4), 432–454 (2017). https://doi.org/10.1111/ijmr.12102

2. Alahyari, H., Gorschek, T., Svensson, R.B.: An exploratory study of waste in software development organizations using agile or lean approaches: a multiple case study at 14 organizations. Inf. Softw. Technol. **105**, 78–94 (2019). https://doi.org/10.1016/j.infsof.2018.08.006

3. Andersson, S., et al.: Sustainable development–direct and indirect effects between economic, social, and environmental dimensions in business practices. Corp. Soc. Responsibil. Environ. Manage. **29**(5), 1158–1172 (2022). https://doi.org/10.1002/csr.2261

4. Azevedo, S.G., Carvalho, H., Machado, V.C.: The influence of green practices on supply chain performance: a case study approach. Transp. Res. Part E: Logist. Transp. Rev. **47**(6), 850–871 (2011). https://doi.org/10.1016/j.tre.2011.05.017

5. Cagan, M.: Inspired: How to Create Tech Products Customers Love, 2nd edn. Wiley, Hoboken (2018). ISBN 978-1-119-38750-3

6. Charfeddine, L., Umlai, M.: ICT sector, digitization and environmental sustainability: a systematic review of the literature from 2000 to 2022. Renew. Sustain. Energy Rev. **184**, 113482 (2023). https://doi.org/10.1016/j.rser.2023.113482

7. Ebert, C., Brinkkemper, S.: Software product management - an industry evaluation. J. Syst. Softw. **95**, 10–18 (2014). https://doi.org/10.1016/j.jss.2013.12.042

8. Forsgren, N., Humble, J., Kim, G.: Accelerate: The Science Behind DevOps: Building and Scaling High Performing Technology Organizations, 1st edn. IT Revolution, Portland (2018). ISBN 978-1-942788-35-5

9. Frederiksen, D.L., Brem, A.: How do entrepreneurs think they create value? A scientific reflection of Eric Ries' Lean Startup approach. Int. Entrep. Manage. J. **13**(1), 169–189 (2016). https://doi.org/10.1007/s11365-016-0411-x

10. Garousi, V., Felderer, M., Mäntylä, M.V.: Guidelines for including grey literature and conducting multivocal literature reviews in software engineering. Inf. Softw. Technol. **106**, 101–121 (2019). https://doi.org/10.1016/j.infsof.2018.09.006

11. Giamattei, L., et al.: Monitoring tools for DevOps and microservices: a systematic grey literature review. J. Syst. Softw. **208**, 111906 (2024). https://doi.org/10.1016/j.jss.2023.111906

12. Gilad, I.: Evidence Guided: Creating High-impact Products in the Face of Uncertainty (2023). ISBN 978-84-09-53639-9

13. Gnanasambandam, C., Harrysson, M., Singh, R.: Responsible product management: the critical tech challenge (2022). https://www.mckinsey.com/industries/technology-media-and-telecommunications/our-insights/responsible-product-management-the-critical-tech-challenge (visited on 04/09/2024)

14. Kamei, F., et al.: Grey literature in software engineering: a critical review. Inf. Softw. Technol. **138**, 106609 (2021). https://doi.org/10.1016/j.infsof.2021.106609

15. Kern, E., et al.: Sustainable software products - towards assessment criteria for resource and energy efficiency. Futur. Gener. Comput. Syst. **86**, 199–210 (2018). https://doi.org/10.1016/j.future.2018.02.044

16. Mandić, V., Oivo, M., Rodríguez, P., Kuvaja, P., Kaikkonen, H., Turhan, B.: What is flowing in lean software development? In: Abrahamsson, P., Oza, N. (eds.) LESS 2010. LNBIP, vol. 65, pp. 72–84. Springer, Heidelberg (2010). https://doi.org/10.1007/978-3-642-16416-3_12

17. Martínez León, H.C., Calvo-Amodio, J.: Towards lean for sustainability: understanding the interrelationships between lean and sustainability from a systems thinking perspective. J. Clean. Prod. **142**, 4384–4402 (2017). https://doi.org/10.1016/j.jclepro.2016.11.132
18. Melegati, J., Guerra, E., Wang, X.: Understanding hypotheses engineering in software startups through a gray literature review. Inf. Softw. Technol. **133**, 106465 (2021). https://doi.org/10.1016/j.infsof.2020.106465
19. Moroz, B., Saltan, A., Hyrynsalmi, S.: Product ops: understanding and defining an emerging discipline. In: Proceedings of the first International Conference on Software Product Management, Frankfurt am Main, GI (2023)
20. Newport, C.: Slow Productivity: The Lost Art of Accomplishment Without Burnout. Portfolio/Penguin, New York (2024). ISBN 978-0-593-54485-3
21. Oyedeji, S., et al.: Integrating Sustainability Concerns into Agile Software Development Process (2024). http://arxiv.org/abs/2407.17426
22. Pendo.io. The rise of product ops. Technical report, Pendo.io (2019)
23. Penzenstadler, B., et al.: Sustainability in software engineering: a systematic literature review. In: 16th International Conference on Evaluation & Assessment in Software Engineering (EASE 2012), Ciudad Real, Spain, pp. 32–41 (2012). https://doi.org/10.1049/ic.2012.0004
24. Perri, M., Tilles, D.: Product Operations: How Successful Companies Build Better Products at Scale, 1st edn. Product Institute Inc. (2023)
25. Pessôa, M.V.P., et al.: Understanding the waste net: a method for waste elimination prioritization in product development. In: Chou, S.Y., Trappey, A., Pokojski, J., Smith, S. (eds.) Global Perspective for Competitive Enterprise, Economy and Ecology. Advanced Concurrent Engineering, pp. 233–242. Springer, London (2009). https://doi.org/10.1007/978-1-84882-762-2_22
26. Poppendieck, M., Poppendieck, T.: Implementing Lean Software Development: From Concept to Cash. The Addison-Wesley Signature Series. Addison-Wesley, London/Munich (2007). ISBN 978-0-321-43738-9
27. Poppendieck, M., Poppendieck, T.: Lean Software Development: An Agile Toolkit. Nachdr. The Agile Software Development Series. Addison-Wesley, Boston (2003). ISBN 978-0-321-15078-3
28. Power, K., Conboy, K.: Impediments to flow: rethinking the lean concept of 'waste' in modern software development. In: Cantone, G., Marchesi, M. (eds.) XP 2014. LNBIP, vol. 179, pp. 203–217. Springer, Cham (2014). https://doi.org/10.1007/978-3-319-06862-6_14
29. Purvis, B., Mao, Y., Robinson, D.: Three pillars of sustainability: in search of conceptual origins. Sustain. Sci. **14**(3), 681–695 (2018). https://doi.org/10.1007/s11625-018-0627-5
30. Saltan, A., Smolander, K.: Bridging the state-of-the-art and the state-of-the-practice of SaaS pricing: a multivocal literature review. Inf. Softw. Technol. **133**, 106510 (2021)
31. Sedano, T., Ralph, P., Peraire, C.: Software development waste. In: 2017 IEEE/ACM 39th International Conference on Software Engineering (ICSE), Buenos Aires, pp. 130–140 (2017). https://doi.org/10.1109/ICSE.2017.20
32. Torres, T.: Continuous Discovery Habits: Discover Products That Create Customer Value and Business Value, 1st edn. Talc (2021). ISBN 978-1-73663-330-4

Designing for Sustainability When Architecture Standards are Involved: An Industrial Case Study

Markus Funke[✉], Priyeta Saha, and Patricia Lago

Vrije Universiteit Amsterdam, Amsterdam, The Netherlands
{m.t.funke,p.lago}@vu.nl, priyetasaha@gmail.com

Abstract. Many software businesses face increasing regulatory pressure and requirements changes that target more sustainable software systems. Therefore, integrating sustainability into software architecture is crucial for the long-term viability of organizations. In this study, we explore how new sustainability concerns can be effectively tackled within software architecture, especially when established architecture standards are followed. We present two main contributions derived from an industrial case study. First, we present the extension of existing architecture views, called decision maps, to trace the involvement of architecture standards. Such extension supports architects through informed decision making by integrating sustainability aspects while adhering to architecture standards. Second, we propose a set of key performance indicators to monitor the ongoing application of these standards and assess their impact on the software architecture and its sustainability *over time*. Our findings provide valuable insights and instruments for experts to first assess sustainability within the constraints of architecture standards, and then monitor their sustainability impact. This will help to meet regulatory requirements and align software design with strategic sustainability goals. We provide tangible guiding steps to improve sustainability awareness and decision-making.

Keywords: Software Architecture · Sustainability Practices · Key Performance Indicator (KPI) · Design Decision-making

1 Introduction

Through the increasing concern for sustainability across various sectors, sustainability has become a critical topic in the realm of software engineering [1,2]. This concern extends beyond the environmental aspects, encompassing also economic, technical, social, and individual concerns [3,4] which collectively aim for

This paper is based on thesis results from the M.Sc. student Priyeta Saha of the Erasmus Mundus SE4GD program. We thank all architects and experts participating in this study and the company for providing the case.

long-term viability and the reduction of (negative) impacts of software systems. Many industries are pushing towards sustainable practices due to new regulations, such as the Energy Efficiency Directive for Data Centers [5] in the EU. Therefore, the development of methodologies and tools to assess and enhance the sustainability of software systems *by design* has gained momentum.

Organizations maintain a set of enterprise and software architecture standards, ranging from principles or guidelines to standard tools or platforms, to be applied in their solutions. Boh et al. [6] presents a detailed overview of enterprise standards and how organizations use them to manage software solutions uniformly. However, there is only little research (e.g., [7,8]) on how to effectively integrate such standards into sustainability frameworks and assess their trade-offs across all the sustainability dimensions involved.

Despite integrating sustainability into software architecture, a current gap remains in keeping track of the expected impact. Sustainability is a dynamic and multifaceted concept, necessitating continuous refinement and adaptation of existing frameworks and standards to keep pace with evolving business needs and standards. Key Performance Indicators (KPIs) could help monitoring such continuous assessment. KPIs have established as essential for measuring the success and performance of organizations [9], offering quantitative data that can guide decision-making and improvement efforts. However, the current practice lack a cohesive structure that integrates sustainability-focused KPIs into the software architecture process [1], posing a challenge for professionals aiming to design and maintain sustainable software architectures.

The motivation behind this research stems from the need to address both **research gaps**, (i) addressing sustainability at software design time by using architecture standards, and (ii) facilitating informed decision-making by providing long-term monitoring on the sustainability impact of architecture standards. We partnered with a leading financial institution in the Netherlands to conduct this research. Our **study goal** is to explore how the new evolved sustainability concerns[1] can be effectively tackled and integrated withing software architecture by building on established architecture standards and using KPIs as monitoring method.

The **main contributions** of this research are as follows:

- We present an extension of existing architecture views to trace the involvement of architecture standards;
- We propose a set of KPIs to allow monitoring the sustainability concerns of the standards and assess their impact over time;
- We provide an example in the form of an industrial case study;
- Based on the case study, we derive tangible guiding steps for experts in the field to enable sustainability awareness and informed decision-making.

Our contributions are based on existing work in the area of sustainable software engineering and software architecture. To trace the involvement of archi-

---

[1] Sustainability concerns may pertain both design concerns or quality concerns. Our focus is on the latter as we want to frame sustainability impacts.

tecture standards, we facilitate an existing architecture view, i.e., design Decision Maps (DMs) [10] which are part of the larger Sustainability Assessment Framework (SAF) Toolkit [11]. The SAF Toolkit addresses multiple sustainability dimensions and provides a comprehensive methodology that experts can follow to design and assess software systems with respect to sustainability concerns. DMs act as thinking framework and architecture view at software design time to frame and uncover architecture design concerns with respect to sustainability to facilitate sustainability-driven decision making [10, 11]. We reuse and extend this view, assessing the sustainability of architecture standards. Leveraging standards promotes broader industry adoption through the reuse of established concepts.

Fatima et al. [12] propose a KPI framework aid at guiding experts in framing sound KPIs especially in a software context. The model consists of a KPI model which is based on fundamental literature, a KPI creation, and a checklist to validate their soundness. We reuse this framework in our study to define robust KPIs for the chosen architecture standards and monitoring their impact on sustainability. The designed KPIs are defined and proposed in the context of our collaboration partner, i.e., the bank, but can be translated to other contexts and showcase a way on how KPIs for architecture standards can be streamlined. The outcomes of this research are expected to aid software architects and decision-makers in designing and maintaining software systems that are not only technically sound but also sustainable in the long term.

2   Related Work

Architecture Sustainability Assessment Methods. In recent years, researchers have explored different techniques to evaluate the sustainability of software architectures. However, many of the works demonstrate a prominent focus on technical sustainability over the other dimensions.

Shaikh et al. [13] explore the sustainability of software architectures through modularization. They examine the correlation between package-level modularization and other software quality metrics using empirical data from open-source Java software systems. The authors demonstrate that well-executed package modularization significantly influences architectural sustainability and the overall software quality. Their focus on modularization metrics narrows the scope of their research to technical sustainability compared to our work, although we find similarities in the use of existing metrics.

Volpato et al. [14] investigates the concept of sustainability in the context of reference architectures. The authors argue that reference architecture elements, such as non-functional requirements and architectural descriptions can be used to create sustainable software architectures. While this work does not introduce a new method or framework for assessing the sustainability of software architecture, it draws attention to reference architectures—a concept similar to architecture standards, which is a pivotal component of our approach.

To evaluate how well an architecture meets sustainability requirements, Ojameruaye et al. [15] defined architectural sustainability as an architecture's ability to deliver value while considering individual, environmental, social, economic, and technical aspects throughout its lifecycle. The authors suggest an "economics-driven" method that combines a Cost Benefit Analysis Method (CBAM) with principles from modern portfolio theory. This method helps assess the costs and risks associated with linking sustainability requirements to design decisions. While the paper shares the same motivation with our work, it defines the concept of "sustainability debt", which reflects the potential future cost of not addressing sustainability requirements effectively today. One considerable difference with our approach is that we aim to develop KPIs impacted on application level and monitor sustainability beyond their potential economic costs and risks.

KPIs in Sustainable Architecture. Using KPIs in the context of software architecture sustainability is a fairly new concept. Therefore, the research in this area is also quite limited so far.

Venters et al. [1] reflect on the state of the art in sustainable software engineering by reviewing 102 relevant studies based on their previous work [16]. In both of their papers, they point to KPIs as an essential tool for assessing and monitoring sustainability over time. However, five years after the first publication, they found that "there is still a lack of [software] metrics and good KPIs that can explain how sustainable a software system or an architecture is". Moreover, while technical sustainability was the priority in the original paper, KPIs are now needed across all sustainability dimensions and cross-cutting domains. With our research we want to contribute to this gap by identifying concrete KPIs and proposing a way to develop new KPIs for software architecture and its impact on sustainability.

Funke et al. [7] investigate a process for monitoring how well software architecture principles influence a system's sustainability. Their focus is on creating a reusable approach that can be applied to real-world software solutions for monitoring and evaluating the sustainability impact of architecture principles. They used existing measurement tools and visualizations to track the sustainability impact. The authors specified KPIs and measurement tools for the identified sustainability quality concerns. As such, they expanded the PRSM model introduced by Gupta et al. [8] to the PRSM+T model, where the T stands for Tool. They used the SMART [17] (Specific, Measurable, Attainable, Relevant, and Time-bound) assessment method to evaluate their KPIs. This is possibly the closest to our work in terms of goals and approach. However, we have a stronger focus on exploring whether it is more sustainable to apply or deviate from architecture standards. We also specified the KPIs from our case study using a more systematic model (i.e., the proposed KPI framework by Fatima et al. [12]).

Research Gap. Most of the aforementioned works did not consider software sustainability holistically and covered only one or two dimensions of sustainability [13,18,19]. Only three of the cited papers focused on concepts similar to architecture standards (reference architecture [14], architecture principles [7,8]) in the context of software sustainability assessment. In some cases, the research outcomes were solely qualitative [14, 19]. While these results are still valuable, quantitative data from KPI measurements can make sustainability assessments significantly more credible. Finally, our research meaningfully combines the concepts of multi-dimensional software sustainability and measurable KPIs in the context of architecture standards, providing a more comprehensive approach to the sustainability assessment of software architecture.

3   Study Design

Research Questions. The primary objective of this research is to investigate how DMs can be used to model sustainability concerns of architecture standards and their application in different software solutions. After the expected concerns of a certain standard has been modeled, we want to monitor the standards' concerns over time to eventually assess the expected impact on sustainability. Only having both (i) the qualitative modelling via an architecture view, i.e., the DM, and (ii) the quantitative assessment via KPIs allow us to provide informed decision making for software architects about their choices of architecture standards and their business concerns. We formulated the following RQs:

RQ1 *How can design **Decision Maps** be extended to trace the sustainability impact of using architecture standards?*
RQ2 *How can **Key Performance Indicators** facilitate monitoring the sustainability impact of using architecture standards?*

To achieve our goals and answer our RQs, we utilize instruments from two existing frameworks, i.e., Decision Maps [10] and the KPI framework [12].

Research Phases. Figure 1 presents an overview of the study design.

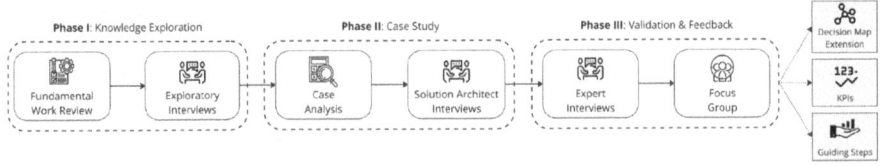

Fig. 1. Overview of the study design

Phase I: Knowledge Exploration. Since this research started with the intention of utilizing two existing instrument, reviewing material on these instruments was an indispensable first step. At the same time, it was also essential to understand current practices in the partnering institution, especially in the domains of software architecture and KPIs. We interviewed experts who work on architecture governance, KPI monitoring, and dashboarding within the organization. These interviews were exploratory nature to get a grasp on what is already being done and what the organization's needs for sustainable software. In fact, the motivation to facilitate architecture standards appeared after this first set of interviews. The outputs of this phase are (i) knowledge about the used instruments, and (ii) initial guiding steps to model and monitor sustainability concerns.

Phase II: Case Study. We conducted a case study to apply our initial guiding steps to a real software solution. We reached out to people within the organization in search of an appropriate case fulfilling the following criteria:

- The solution should have well-defined concerns and attributes.
- The solution should preferably be implemented and operational.
- The solution should have data available on common metrics or KPIs.

The solution "Belgium Securities Tax" satisfied all our criteria and was therefore selected for our case study. Section 4 provides more information on this solution. We collected documentation on the architecture of the solution, analyzed it, and came up with preliminary results in the form of two DMs and first KPI definitions. Then, we organized two rounds of semi-structured interviews [20] with the leading architect of this solution. First, we gained further insights in the cases' solution architecture and the rational behind the taken decisions. Then, we presented our intermediate results and collected feedback accordingly. All the insights derived from the case study are detailed in Sect. 4. After the case study, we honed in on the problems we faced in this phase and revised our preliminary results accordingly. The outputs of this part are an initial (i) version of the extended DM to trace the architecture standard(s) related to the chosen case, and (ii) set of KPIs to monitor the impact of such standard(s) over time.

Phase III: Validation and Feedback. The goal of the last phase was to validate our findings from the case study and gather more feedback from experts knowledgeable in the software architecture domain who were not directly involved with the solution. We organized two additional semi-structured interviews with experts working in different levels of architecture within the organization. Finally, we conducted a focus group [20] to facilitate some open discussions among architects regarding the application of our proposed approach in practice. The observations and ideas acquired in Phase III helped us to revise our results. The findings from this phase have been elaborated in Sect. 5.

4   Results

First, we outline the selected case to provide a better understanding of the context; then, we show the (final) extended DM for the architecture standard related to our case; last, a subset of the KPIs derived for this case are presented.

In this paper, we focus only on the final results derived from our research. The full set of concerns and KPIs is available in our online supplementary material[2].

4.1   Case Study Description

We use a case study to conceptualize our DM extensions, frame the KPIs, and derive our guiding steps along the way. Based on the selection criteria mentioned in Sect. 3, we chose the solution "Effectentaks 2021" (in Dutch) or "Belgium Securities Tax" (in English) for our case study, to be referred to as "Securities Tax" hereafter. The solution manages the annual wealth tax on securities accounts mandated in Belgium.

Figure 2 shows the main features of the Securities Tax solution and visualizes (i) design decisions, (ii) design alternatives, and (iii) the related architecture standards. We base this architecture view on the notation from DMs [10]. This view allows us to visualize design decisions regarding architecture standards, which were actually textually described in the provided architecture documentation. After conducting the interviews with the solution architect in Phase II, we did also derive tacit knowledge [21]. Our visualization, i.e., architecture view helps us in representing multiple design decisions, their alternatives, and potential architecture standards in one view capturing both textual and tacit architectural knowledge.

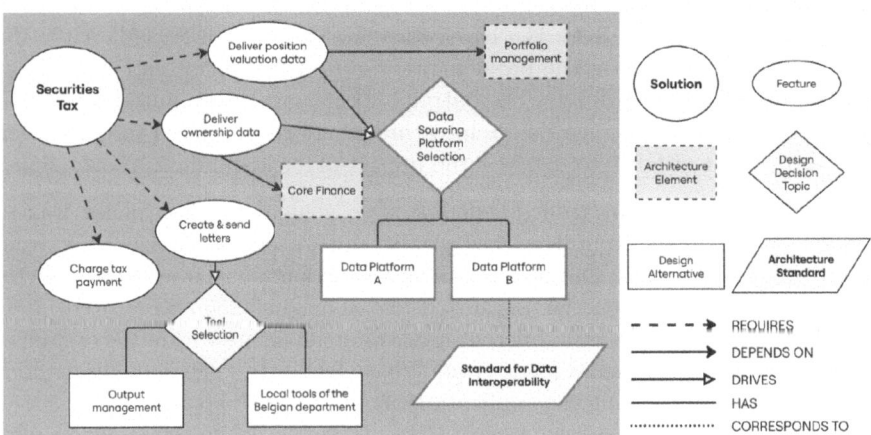

Fig. 2. Overview of solution architecture of our chosen case. Elements with red border are relevant for our work (Color figure online)

Four key features are required in this application and they raise two design decision topics. Between the two topics, *Data Sourcing Platform Selection* was

---

[2] Online supplementary material—https://github.com/S2-group/ICSOB24_DESIGN 4SUS/.

more critical according to the architecture documentation and the interviews. Therefore, we concentrated our attention on that design decision and its two alternatives. The interviews reviled that in its current implementation, the company wide architecture standard was not followed due to time constraints. With our research, we want to explore the impact on sustainability of this *deviation*, i.e., not following an architecture standard.

The two design alternatives are using either *Data Platform A (DP-A)*[3] or *Data Platform B (DP-B)* as the data sourcing platform. Both platforms aim to enforce efficient and secure data access, processing, and distribution between two involved (international) parties, i.e., banks. While both platforms offer a similar range of capabilities, DP-A is the more recent approach and is designed to be the new *standard*, whereas DP-B is slightly outdated and more niche. At the time the solution was designed, a trade-off had to be made between using the newer DP-A platform, which was not yet widely established among all architects, or DP-B, which had been in use for several years. In the next section, we use a DM to explore the consequences and trade-offs of choosing DP-B instead of the architectural standard that suggests the default use of DP-A. This analysis serves as an example of how architectural standards can be analyzed using a DM together with our extension to evaluate their impact on sustainability concerns.

4.2   Decision Map for Architecture Standards

After a thorough analysis of the input material (i.e., documentations), we prepared two separate DMs for the two design alternatives under consideration. Then we conducted the two interviews with the solution architect to discuss the identified sustainability concerns. The DMs along with the architect's rationale determining the types of effects. Due to space restrictions, we present and discuss only DP-B, i.e., the deviation from the newer standard DP-A, as this is the platform which was actually implemented[4].

Figure 3 depicts the DM and the sustainability concerns impacted by the decision to deviate from the (newer) standard by using DP-B in the Securities Tax solution. We extended this DM by illustrating the weights of the different sustainability concerns in two ways: (i) adding the weight values on the arrows; (ii) sizing the concerns according to their assigned weights (higher weight resulting in bigger font size and vice versa).

To determine the weights we asked the architect which concerns are possibly the most crucial factors in making the decision. Together, we assigned weights to the concerns in a way that reflects their significance in the decision making process. The weights sum up to 100. The majority of the concerns adhere to the definition in the ISO/IEC 25010:2012 Standard [22]. If not available (e.g., Time to Market), we created our definition and aligned it during the interviews.

---

[3] Names of specific components have been omitted or generalized due to confidentiality agreements and security policies imposed by the collaborating company.

[4] The DM for DP-A, i.e., the alternative, is available online in the supplementary material.

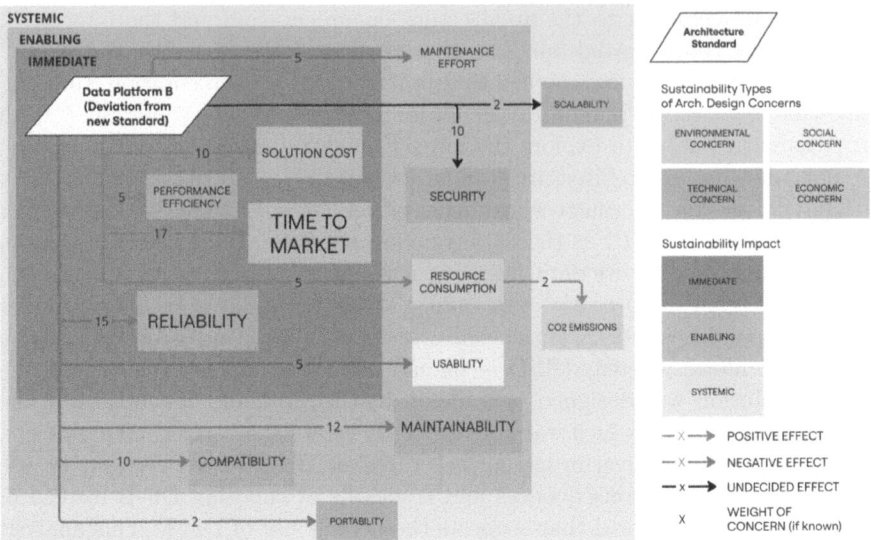

Fig. 3. (Extended) Decision map for DP-B. We extended the notion of DMs from Lago [10] via the architecture standard and the weighted concerns (X)

The full list with our derived concerns and defintions can be found in the online supplementary material. From the architect's perspective and considering the assigned weights, we highlight the three most relevant concerns that contributed to the decision to choose DP-B over DP-A at the decisive moment.

Time to Markt (TTM). The choice of DP-B over DP-A for the Securities Tax application was driven by the need for a quick solution. Since the architects and developers were already familiar with the data structures and the requirements of DP-B, allowed the architects and developers to meet their time-to-market goals. This was highlighted by the architect as: *"Also the timeline [...] we have to be ready on time because this is tax regulation and at a certain date, the tax has to be paid. And if you use [DP-A], it would take longer to develop"*. However, this decision came at the cost of increased complexity and maintenance effort, as the dedicated DP-B interface was more tightly coupled with the application.

Reliability. The smaller scale of DP-B offered some performance benefits crucial for the reliability of the Securities Tax application. An increased performance efficiency, in turn, leads also to less resource consumption and therefore to reduced CO_2 emissions in the long term. The development team also had the flexibility to tailor DP-B specifically to the needs of the solution, ensuring compatibility and reducing concerns about reliability within the limited scope of the project. However, the reliability of the solution could be at high risk in the long term due to the lack of active development and support, which could lead to potential challenges and risk in the future. The architect mentioned: *"The point is if you say [DP-B] is end of life-cycle and there will be less and less support for it, then, of course, you have an influence on the reliability"*.

Maintainability. As mentioned for reliability, while the DP-B solution was initially easier and faster to implement, it introduced long-term maintainability concerns. The small size of the DP-B team and the lack of ongoing development pose significant risks. As team members leave, the remaining or future personnel may lack the necessary knowledge to maintain or update the system, leading to potential issues in maintainability, usability, and portability. In contrast, DP-A, with its standardized interface and broader support, would likely have offered a more maintainable solution over time. This is emphasized by the architect as: *"If you want to compare now, you have to add the conversion cost or migration cost. If you consider going to [DP-A], then you have the replacement cost"*.

4.3 Key Performance Indicators

We associated each of the identified sustainability concerns from the DM with a corresponding KPI. The template proposed by Fatima et al. [12] supported us in streamlining KPIs in a coherent and systematic way, allowing us to identify components that were either (i) already existing in the company, (ii) or missing. Some of the KPIs were already established and monitored within the organization, enabling us to fill in certain fields directly. However, we had to align the "Goal" and "CSF" fields with the organization's IT strategy, as their KPI documentation mostly lacks a connection to organizational goals.

For some sustainability concerns, we did not find a relevant KPI or metric and hence suggested potential ones, drawing inspiration from the company's existing KPIs and metrics. The company has thresholds for most KPIs, with level "A" being the most desired. Below, we provide the filled KPI templates and a brief discussion for each of the three highlighted sustainability concerns. The complete set of KPIs is available in the online materials. In the templates (Table 1, 2 and 3), color coding indicates which fields were existing and reused (gray), or missing and added (white).

Time to Markt. TTM typically refers to the duration between the initial product request and its availability for sale or use. This KPI illustrates how the current or estimated *future lead time* fares against the *target time*. If the lead time deviates more than expected, then it can put the company on the back foot in the market for that specific product or service. On the other hand, a successful launch within the due date can bring about financial gains for the company.

Reliability. SonarQube[5] is used to provide a reliability grade for the application which can be directly mapped to the reliability concern. This KPI represents reliability from a code quality perspective, i.e., code bugs. Good code is expected to

---

[5] https://docs.sonarsource.com/sonarqube/latest/.

Table 1. KPI for Time to Market

Sustainability Concern: Time to Market					
Goal	**CSF**	**KPI**		**Metric**	**Measure**
Gain competitive market advantage	Launch product within target time	Time Deviation (%)		$TimeDeviation =$ $(|LeadT -$ $TargetT|/TargetT) \times$ 100	Lead time, Target time
		Target	**Action**		
		A: $\leq$ 5% B: 6 to 10% C: 11 to 20% D: 21 to 50% E: $\geq$ 50%	Streamline development and production processes		

contain fewer bugs, making the application more reliable. For any organization, catering to the needs of end users by providing reliable products and services is paramount—especially in the financial domain.

Table 2. KPI for Reliability (gray fields taken from SonarQube)

Sustainability Concern: Reliability					
Goal	**CSF**	**KPI**		**Metric**	**Measure**
Offer reliable service to users	Pass quality check	Reliability		Severity level of the worst open bug	Severity level of bugs, Number of bugs
		Target	**Action**		
		A: 0 Bugs B: at least 1 Minor Bug C: at least 1 Major Bug D: at least 1 Critical Bug E: at least 1 Blocker Bug	Resolve open bugs, prioritizing the most severe ones		

Maintainability. Similar to reliability, the maintainability KPI also comes from SonarQube. It is based on the ratio of the size of the project to the estimated time to fix all outstanding code smells. A code smell is a maintainability-related issue in the code. These smells make it harder to introduce changes to the code and may confuse maintainers, increasing the likelihood of bugs in the future. This KPI contributes towards lowering technical debt [23]. If code smells remain unidentified or get ignored, then they might result in considerable refactoring costs in the future.

4.4   Guiding Steps

Based on the experience gained throughout the case study and the expert feedback in research Phase II, we synthesize this learning into four concrete guiding steps. These steps provide architects with the necessary guidance to effectively evaluate their architecture standards and design decisions in terms of impact on sustainability. The steps do also enable continuous monitoring through KPIs. Long-term monitoring is essential for informed decision making. By using such insights, architects can reflect on (i) past decisions, (ii) architecture standards in place, (iii) their own deviations from such standards, and (iv) apply these lessons to future projects.

Table 3. KPI for Maintainability (gray fields taken from SonarQube and IT Strategy)

Sustainability Concern: Maintainability					
Goal	CSF	KPI		Metric	Measure
Reduce technical debt	Pass quality check	Maintainability		Maintainability = LOC / Estimated code smell fix time	Lines of Code (LOC), Estimated time to fix code smells
		Target	Action		
		A: ≤ 5% B: 6 to 10% C: 11 to 20% D: 21 to 50% E: ≥ 50%	Static code analysis, code review, and refactoring		

① **Identify** relevant architecture standards from the solution architecture.

② **Create** an individual DM for the standard.

③ **Assign** weight, type, and impact level to each of the sustainability concerns.

④ **Translate** the sustainability concerns into measurable KPIs.

5   Discussion and Threats to Validity

We discuss the results obtained by evaluating them through the expert interviews and the focus group[6] as described in our study design in Phase III (cf. Sect. 3). Along evaluating the results, we try to answer our RQs.

Expert Interviews to Evaluate the RQs. Unlike the interviews with the solution architect in Phase II, we interviewed two different experts within the organization to gain a more diverse feedback and reduce bias: a principal enterprise architect (E1) and an architecture governance lead (E2). Both are familiar with the architecture standards (e.g., DP-A, DP-B) but were not directly involved in the Securities Tax application. The goal of these interviews was to derive feedback on the DM with its weights and the KPIs.

RQ1: Design Decision Maps to Trace the Sustainability of Standards.
To answer RQ1, we have extended a DM with the notion of *architecture standards* and assigned weights to the impacts. Such extension adds a *quantitative layer* (i.e., the weights in numbers) on top of the *qualitative layer* (i.e., positive, negative, undecided impact) and hence allows a quantitative ranking of the sustainability concerns. We used interviews to evaluate our extension.

The experts raised some concerns about how such a DM would be applied in practice and, especially, what the advantage would be if the decision was already taken. We clarified that the sustainability concerns and their weights should be kept flexible. New concerns might arise in the future. Old concerns might become more or less important than they were first deemed to be. In such scenarios, the architects should be able to modify the weights. The updated concerns and weights might drive future architecture design decisions. E2 agreed

---

[6] The complete interview and focus group guide are available in the online material.

to our explanation with: *"And the benefit is [that] you are comparing. [...] And maybe that will then also trigger you in the future to make different choices irrespective of this solution that you navigate back to a certain target direction, maybe for a future purpose"*.

The interviewees found the self-assessment via the added weights somewhat problematic. Architects often prefer quicker, deviating solutions reflecting their own biases against an established standard. For a more objective assessment, other stakeholders, such as the solution owner should be involved. E2 added: *"I think the architect [..] will not see it or be biased"*.

While we were presenting the DM to the experts, E1 recognized our approach's intended benefit: *"What you actually 'officialized' is the architectural trade-off for a specific decision line"*. This statement captures our overarching idea and answers RQ1: by creating a DM for design alternatives and architecture standards, enriched with quantitative values, we can visualize architecture trade-offs. In the future, however, it should be investigated how the (cognitive) bias from the architect in charge can be mitigated while assigning the weights.

RQ2: Use KPIs for Monitoring Sustainability. To answer RQ2, we created KPIs for each identified sustainability concern. This allows architects to keep track of the concerns over time and quantitatively assess the impact and re-assess taken choices—if necessary. This information is vital for businesses to be more agile and adapt to future sustainability regulations and reporting requirements.

In the interviews, "assumptions" and "estimations" were a common point of discussion. While designing the solution architecture, the architects usually take assumptions based on their experience (i.e., usage of tacit knowledge). The exerts concluded, having actual measurement data in the future can give architects the opportunity to come back and reassess their original assumptions.

One major benefit the interviewees recognized is comparing the architect's initial thoughts to the reality with the help of KPIs. This might also trigger the architects to make different choices in the future. E2 also remarked that this assessment could be presented in the form of a sustainability rating for architecture if all the relevant KPIs are properly measured and monitored: *"We have now specific ratings for confidentiality, integrity, availability, but there could definitely be categorization on sustainability as well"*.

Focus Group to Evaluate the Guiding Steps. In our final Phase III, we conducted a focus group with one solution architect (P1), one domain architect (P2), and one enterprise architect (P3). Similar to the previous interviews, participants were familiar with the organization's architecture process and standards but were not directly involved in designing the application. The goal was to gather feedback on our research approach, which we summarize and put forward as our *Guiding Steps* in Sect. 4.4.

While discussing the DM and sustainability concerns, P2 expressed the need for an exhaustive list of sustainability concerns and definitions tailored to the organization's goals and processes: *"who can define the entire list of concerns which need to be tackled for every solution?"* Although this is valid, current research (e.g., [11]) tries to address this need by examining relevant sustainability concerns in practice. Ultimately, each solution targets their own subset of concerns. We can only provide the tools to identify the subset and assist the selection process (e.g., via thinking frameworks such as DMs).

P2 felt that even before an architect starts designing a solution architecture, weights need to be set from the business side. This way, the considerations for money, regulations, implementation time, etc. would be specified from the beginning. We agree with this point as meaningful weights can only be established by having sound strategic business goals (cf. [7]).

Participants mentioned, the KPIs should be first evaluated on the standard itself. This would give a high-level understanding of its sustainability. This knowledge could be applied to the solution context with comparisons against alternatives. Experts highlighted, there should be revisiting timelines checking whether the architect's assumptions about positive or negative impacts were correct.

As concluding benefit, participants mentioned that our approach might make the architects indeed aware of different sustainability concerns. It could also add more transparency to the decision-making process of architects. Most importantly, however, they emphasised the fact that without concrete measurements the approach would only provide *soft* benefits. With the measurements coming from the KPIs, the whole process would become much more beneficial. P3 concluded: *"if you really want [to change] something [...] we need to have more measurements".*

Threats to Validity. Potential threats to validity have been categorized according to the classification framework proposed by Wohlin et al. [20]. The major threat for **internal validity** is the intertwined nature of software architecture elements. It is difficult to decipher concretely whether a certain sustainability impact is caused by one specific architecture standard or not. Multiple architecture standards may contribute to a certain effect. Proper attribution and distribution of the impacts can prove to be extremely challenging in this case.

External factors that might threaten **external validity** include a lack of objectivity from software architects, and a lack of time and established processes to perform both qualitative and quantitative sustainability assessments. Also, if organizations do not have well-defined architecture standards in place, that might pose a barrier to the application and generalizability of our results; however, as KPIs are widely adopted, our approach can be readily integrated across various domains.

A potential threat to **construct validity** might have occurred as our approach is heavily influenced by existing research, i.e., the DM and KPI framework. However, the multiple rounds of interviews and the focus group were intended to mitigate this threat by continuously revising our results. To avoid a potential misinterpretation of our results obtained and posing a threat to **conclusion validity**, we used different groups of interviewees and focus group partners for cross-validation.

6 Conclusion

We have used a case study to address sustainability concerns in software architecture when architecture standards are involved. Based on expert feedback, we conclude that adding a quantitative layer (i.e., weights) to an architecture view (i.e., DMs) could indeed improve informed decision making and increase accountability for sustainability among architects. As interesting feedback, building on the results of our study, architects expressed the need for tools to assist them make the right decisions regarding sustainability. Beyond that, future research should validate the proposed KPIs in diverse software environments. We also observe that having tangible measurements coming from KPIs is perceived as beneficial to justify or reconsider decisions made. However, an important takeaway remains that although experts recognize the importance of sustainability KPIs, their adoption in industrial contexts is still lagging behind.

References

1. Venters, C.C., et al.: Sustainable software engineering: reflections on advances in research and practice. Inf. Softw. Technol. (2023)
2. Heldal, R., et al.: Sustainability competencies and skills in software engineering: an industry perspective. J. Syst. Softw. **211** (2024)
3. Lago, P., Koçak, S.A., Crnkovic, I., Penzenstadler, B.: Framing sustainability as a property of software quality. Commun. ACM **58**(10) (2015)
4. Duboc, L., et al.: Requirements engineering for sustainability: an awareness framework for designing software systems for a better tomorrow. Requirements Eng. **25**(4) (2020)
5. European Commission: Reporting requirements on the energy performance and sustainability of data centres for the Energy Efficiency Directive. https://data.europa.eu/doi/10.2833/304891 (2023) Accessed 31 July 2024
6. Boh, W.F., Yellin, D.: Using enterprise architecture standards in managing information technology. J. Manage. Inf. Syst. **23**(3) (2006)
7. Funke, M., Lago, P., Verdecchia, R., Donker, R.: A process for monitoring the impact of architecture principles on sustainability: an industrial case study. Software **3**(1) (2024)
8. Gupta, S., Lago, P., Donker, R.: A framework of software architecture principles for sustainability-driven design and measurement. In: IEEE 18th International Conference on Software Architecture Companion (ICSA-C) (2021)
9. Parmenter, D.: Key Performance Indicators: Developing, Implementing, and Using Winning KPIs, 3rd edn. Wiley, Hoboken (2015)
10. Lago, P.: Architecture design decision maps for software sustainability. In: IEEE/ACM 41st International Conference on Software Engineering: Software Engineering in Society (ICSE-SEIS) (2019)
11. Lago, P., Condori Fernandez, N., Fatima, I., Funke, M., Malavolta, I.: The sustainability assessment framework toolkit: a decade of modeling experience. Softw. Syst. Model. (2024). https://doi.org/10.1007/s10270-024-01230-9
12. Fatima, I., Funke, M., Lago, P.: Providing guidance to software practitioners: a framework for creating KPIs. IEEE Softw. (2024). https://doi.org/10.1109/ms.2024.3456446

13. Shaikh, M., Ibarhimov, D., Zardari, B.: Assessing architectural sustainability during software evolution using package-modularization metrics. Int. J. Adv. Comput. Sci. Appl. **10**(12) (2019)
14. Volpato, T., Oliveira, B.R.N., Garcés, L., Capilla, R., Nakagawa, E.Y.: Two perspectives on reference architecture sustainability. In: Companion Proceedings of the 11th European Conference on Software Architecture (ECSA-C). Association for Computing Machinery (2017)
15. Ojameruaye, B., Bahsoon, R., Duboc, L.: Sustainability debt: a portfolio-based approach for evaluating sustainability requirements in architectures. In: Proceedings of the 38th International Conference on Software Engineering Companion (ICSE). Association for Computing Machinery (2016)
16. Venters, C.C., et al.: Software sustainability: research and practice from a software architecture viewpoint. J. Syst. Softw. **138** (2018)
17. Ishak, Z., Fong, S.L., Shin, S.C.: SMART KPI management system framework. In: IEEE 9th International Conference on System Engineering and Technology (2019)
18. Koziolek, H., Domis, D., Goldschmidt, T., Vorst, P., Weiss, R.J.: Morphosis: a lightweight method facilitating sustainable software architectures. In: Joint Working IEEE/IFIP Conference on Software Architecture and European Conference on Software Architecture (2012)
19. Unphon, H.: Architecture-level evolvability assessment: assessing sustainability of software product evolution. IT University of Copenhagen (2010)
20. Wohlin, C., Runeson, P., Höst, M., Ohlsson, M.C., Regnell, B., Wesslén, A.: Experimentation in Software Engineering. Springer, Heidelberg (2012)
21. Ali Babar, M., Dingsøyr, T., Lago, P., van Vliet, H.: Software Architecture Knowledge Management. Springer, Heidelberg (2009)
22. International Organization for Standardization [ISO]: Systems and software engineering - Systems and software Quality Requirements and Evaluation (SQuaRE) - System and software quality models. Technical report ISO/IEC 25010:2011 (2011)
23. Cunningham, W.: The WyCash portfolio management system. In: Addendum to the Proceedings on Object-Oriented Programming Systems, Languages, and Applications (Addendum). OOPSLA. Association for Computing Machinery (1992)

Challenges in Incorporating Sustainability Practices in the Software Lifecycle

Mercy Bamiduro[1], Iffat Fatima[1(✉)], Patricia Lago[1], and Sophie Vos[2]

[1] Vrije Universiteit Amsterdam, Amsterdam, The Netherlands
m.d.bamiduro@student.vu.nl, {i.fatima,p.lago}@vu.nl
[2] Accenture, Amsterdam, The Netherlands
sophie.vos@accenture.com

Abstract. As software becomes more integral to daily life and business operations, its sustainability impact is increasing, and increasingly recognized. This study investigates the key challenges hindering stakeholders from adopting and implementing sustainability practices within organizations. To this aim, we interview 15 practitioners in two organizations to identify the challenges in sustainability adoption and implementation of sustainability practices in the daily workflow of software professionals. Our results highlight the practical challenges, recommendations, and benefits of implementing sustainability practices in real-world organizational settings. Lack of sustainability prioritization, knowledge awareness, measurement tools, scarce resources, and organizational culture are the key challenge areas. By balancing priorities, the investment in sustainability education and tool support coupled with cultural change and resource-rich incentivization programs can motivate practitioners to use sustainability practices. If so, organizations could save money and energy, improve overall productivity, and foster personal satisfaction.

Keywords: Sustainability · Software Development Life Cycle (SDLC) · Stakeholder Perspectives · Challenges

1 Introduction

As technology advances, software drives innovation but also presents sustainability challenges making sustainable software engineering a crucial concern in the software industry [1]. Organizations are recognizing the competitive edge of sustainable solutions with major tech companies integrating sustainability into

This publication is part of the project SustainableCloud (OCENW.M20.243) of the research programme Open Competition which is (partly) financed by the Dutch Research Council (NWO). We extend our gratitude to Accenture for their generous support and resources, which significantly contributed to the successful execution of this research. We thank our interview participants for their contribution to this project. We utilized OpenAI's ChatGPT for language refinement, ensuring all generated text was reviewed and adjusted to fit our requirements.

E. Papatheocharous et al. (Eds.): ICSOB 2024, LNBIP 539, pp. 284–290, 2025.
https://doi.org/10.1007/978-3-031-85849-9_23

their business models [11], which has been accelerated further with sustainability compliance attributed to the CSRD reporting regulation in Europe [3].

In the context of digital solutions, Lago [7] defines sustainability as 'the preservation of the beneficial use of digital solutions, in a context that continuously changes'. Lago et al. [9] also define four dimensions of sustainability, namely economic, environmental, social, and technical.

To develop sustainable software, practitioners need a solid understanding of sustainability strategies and access to the necessary tools [6], according to their specific needs. Research shows that many practitioners lack the knowledge and experience to address sustainability effectively [12]. A poor understanding of stakeholder perspectives on sustainability hinders the adoption of sustainability practices in organizations and presents various challenges.

This research was carried out in collaboration with Accenture over a period of 6 months. The company's sustainable technology mission is twofold: to leverage the power of technology to drive sustainability transformations and to continuously innovate to improve the sustainability of technology itself. With this study, we aim to understand the key challenges that hinder practitioners from embracing and implementing sustainability practices within organizations. To this aim, we conduct semi-structured interviews with 15 different participants from two organizations. We gather insights into the practical challenges they face, regarding sustainability integration. We then provide recommendations that practitioners can use to adopt sustainability practices while overcoming the challenges.

2 Methodology

This study aims to analyze the sustainability challenges hindering the acceptance and implementation of sustainability practices within organizations. We pose the following research question (RQ). **What are the key challenges hindering stakeholders from accepting and implementing sustainability practices within organizations?** To answer this RQ, we conducted semi-structured interviews. The details of the protocol are as follows.

Interview Design. We used the interview guide approach by Kallio et al. [5] for conducting the semi-structured interviews. We chose this approach to ensure the contextual extraction of information by having the flexibility to ask follow-up questions. We used a list of open-ended questions to give room for the respondents to offer more detailed qualitative data. We provide these questions as an appendix in our Online Material[1]

Interview Participants. The interview participants were chosen from two organizations, Accenture, and one of their clients, a Bank (Anonymized due to non-disclosure agreement). Appendix (see footnote 1) (Table 1) provides an overview of the 15 participants of both organizations, highlighting their roles and contributions to SDLC. Our goal was to include a diverse range of stakeholders as interview participants who are involved in the SDLC stage, as each

---

[1] Online Material: https://zenodo.org/records/14012044.

contributes uniquely to the development process of a software solution. The participant selection process was facilitated by the Technology and Sustainability Consultant at the first organization. For the second, their Technology Lead facilitated the process of outreach and selection. For both companies, at least one practitioner was requested from each stage of SDLC. Furthermore, the participants were expected to meet the following criteria to be eligible for participation. Participants can (i) discuss their work without confidentiality issues, (ii) respond to additional questions, if necessary, and (iii) Participants speak in English.

Execution of Interview. To ensure a shared understanding of sustainability, we gave each interviewee a brief One-Pager introducing the topic. We also provided role-specific sustainability practices from related work to assist discussion. Interview questions sought to uncover: (i) Participants' roles and phases of involvement, (ii) Views on sustainability's relevance and feasibility in the organization, (iii) Challenges to stakeholder acceptance and implementation, (iv) Suggestions for overcoming these challenges, (v) The relevance to their roles, and (vi) Benefits of adopting sustainability practices.

Pilot Test. We conducted one interview as a pilot test as per the recommendation by Kallio et al. [5], with a product manager within Accenture. This helped identify and address flaws in the interview guide. This process led to the exclusion of some questions and the refinement of others. We obtained consent for audio recording, which was transcribed using Otter.ai.

Data Analysis. We performed a thematic data analysis [15] to analyze interview data. We performed coding of the transcripts by identifying and labeling key phrases and concepts within the transcripts. The coded data were reviewed and examined to determine how different codes may be combined according to shared meanings and grouped into potential themes. Together with the second author, these potential themes were further reviewed and refined by revisiting the coded data segments, the themes were modified, merged, or discarded based on their relevance. Finally, themes were clearly defined and named. Based on the interview insights and related literature, we present recommendations that can help organizations include sustainability practices in their SDLC.

We provide the possible threats to validity and their mitigation in Online Material (see footnote 1).

3   Results and Discussion

3.1   Challenges

We discovered the following themes of sustainability challenges from the interview data.

Lack of Organizational Priority and Support. Sustainability still often takes a back seat in comparison to other organizational needs, such as performance and security. Sustainability is often seen as a *"nice to have"* (P4, P5)[2]

---

[2] P#s are the IDs of the interview participants. See Appendix (see footnote 1) Table 1.

but not prioritized. This lack of prioritization from the organization is also evident through the insufficient allocation of resources like time and cost that are essential to incorporate sustainability practices in the software lifecycle. Organizations are reluctant to invest in sustainability because they do not recognize its added value (P12). Also, sustainability practices might be difficult to implement without strong support and clear guidelines from top management (P1, P11).

Knowledge and Awareness Gaps. A general lack of knowledge and awareness regarding sustainability hinders its integration into the software life cycle (cf. *"[...] But the knowledge, it's not really there."* (P12)). Stakeholders have different awareness levels of sustainability, its potential effect, and the specific actions required to incorporate sustainability practices. The lack of clear guidance leads to uncertainty and misunderstanding, e.g., among cross-functional teams.

There is a lack of knowledge of the importance and benefits of sustainability; some stakeholders view it as irrelevant to their roles (P4, P12). IT professionals often associate sustainability only with CO_2 emissions, which can make it seem less relevant. However, sustainability is also closely linked to other software qualities, like resource usage and performance (P12).

Measurement and Evaluation. Lack of adequate measurement tools, clear metrics, and key performance indicators (KPIs) limit the ability to track progress and show the value of sustainability initiatives. Without these measurement tools, it becomes challenging to maintain and sustain the continued implementation of sustainability practices. One participant, (P2), said, *"But if it's not being measured, then it will die a very early death"*. They suggested that monitoring with KPIs might make sustainability seem more abstract than actionable.

Competing Priorities and Resource Constraints. Sustainability often competes with other non-functional requirements, such as performance, security, availability, and compliance, which are usually prioritized (P12). Such competition complicates the integration of sustainability practices within the SDLC (P4). The difficulties are further complicated by resource limitations, such as time, money, or human resources. Stakeholders must find a way to balance available resources (P6). However, strong time pressure leaves stakeholders with little or no room to consider sustainability (P2).

Team Collaboration and Commitment. Incorporating sustainability practices requires the effort and willingness of cross-functional teams. The misalignment between team priorities and sustainability goals can hinder progress, making collective commitment essential (P6).

3.2   Benefits of Sustainability Practices

Interviews revealed several benefits of implementing sustainability practices. Communication of such benefits can help motivate teams to integrate sustainability into the software lifecycle.

Cost Savings. Sustainability practices can lead to significant cost savings and freeing up the budget (P2). By cutting energy use, optimizing resources, and minimizing waste, organizations lower operational costs and increase financial flexibility.

Performance Improvement. Sustainability practices lead to an efficient and leaner architecture. Improving processes and adopting best practices boosts functionality, productivity, and overall effectiveness (P12).

Energy Efficiency. Sustainability practices improve energy efficiency and reduce long-term expenses by lowering the environmental footprint.

Personal Satisfaction. Sustainability boosts personal satisfaction by increasing motivation and fulfillment (P2, P6), highlighting the social and non-financial benefits of sustainability.

3.3 Recommendations

To incorporate sustainability in the software lifecycle, based on our study results we present the following recommendations.

Balance Competing Priorities. Integrate sustainability into project planning from the start. Set clear goals and allocate resources. Create a framework to balance sustainability with other non-functional requirements.

Build Sustainability Knowledge. Address the knowledge gap with role-specific guidelines and training. Offer webinars, workshops, and certifications. Use internal platforms to share best practices and success stories.

Develop Measurement Tools and KPIs. Invest in tools to measure energy consumption and sustainability performance. Implement solutions that show sustainability scores. Define and track sustainability KPIs.

Promote Cultural and Behavioral Change. Organize events and workshops focused on sustainability. Use rewards and gamification to motivate employees. Embed sustainability into the company's core values.

Allocate Resources for Sustainability. Appoint sustainability experts to lead initiatives. Set realistic targets and involve top management to ensure commitment to sustainability goals and provision of resources. Provide practitioners with incentives for practicing sustainability.

4   Related Work

Mohankumar et al. [10] highlight challenges in each SDLC phase affecting environmental sustainability and propose treating sustainability as a primary quality objective. Raisian et al. [13] recognize that the traditional SDLC method lacks sufficient focus on sustainability and green practices. The study also includes a survey that seeks to understand from the perspective of the software practitioners, how they perceive the importance of each phase in the Green SDLC, which is also confirmed by our results. Shenoy and Earatta [14] propose a Green Software Development Life Cycle Model that introduces some practices throughout the software development process. They also provide recommendations for positive/improved impacts on the environment, however ignore social aspects covered by our study. The interview study by Groher et al. [4] highlights that practitioners consider sustainability only as a technical concern and ignore its environmental aspect. Similar results, but specific to practitioners in digital architecture, are by and large confirmed by the mixed-method study of Lago et al. [8] and extended with recommendations for researchers and practitioners. Chitchyan et al. [2], in turn, identify barriers in the application of sustainability from a requirements engineering perspective and provide mitigation strategies. The results of their interview study show that lack of sustainability education, resistance to change, risks and economic trade-offs, lack of standards, and long-term change impacts.

The current literature is quite rich in providing sustainability practices, however, the representation of stakeholder perspectives in terms of their challenges is limited. With our study, we shed light on these challenges along with benefits and recommendations.

5 Conclusion

In this study, we conducted semi-structured interviews to identify the challenges faced by practitioners and organizations in adopting sustainability practices. The challenges include a lack of knowledge dissemination, training, and sustainability prioritization. We recommend that organizations improve sustainability awareness, prioritize and incentivize sustainability, and foster cultural changes. Our results suggest adopting sustainability practices that can lead to cost savings, improved performance, and energy efficiency.

References

1. Calero, C., Piattini, M.: Puzzling out software sustainability. Sustain. Comput.: Inform. Syst. **16** (2017)
2. Chitchyan, R., et al.: Sustainability design in requirements engineering: state of practice. In: Proceedings of the 38th International Conference on Software Engineering Companion (2016)
3. European Commission: CSRD directive. https://x.gd/hecGA
4. Groher, I., Weinreich, R.: An interview study on sustainability concerns in software development projects. In: 2017 43rd Euromicro Conference on Software Engineering and Advanced Applications (SEAA) (2017). https://doi.org/10.1109/SEAA. 2017.70
5. Kallio, H., et al.: Systematic methodological review: developing a framework for a qualitative semi-structured interview guide. J. Adv. Nurs. **72**(12) (2016)
6. Kern, E., Naumann, S., Dick, M.: Processes for green and sustainable software engineering. Green Softw. Eng. (2015)

7. Lago, P.: The digital society is already here – pity it is 'unsustainable'. In: Connected World - Insights from 100 Academics on How to Build Better Connections. VU University Press (2023)
8. Lago, P., Greefhorst, D., Woods, E.: Architecting for sustainability. In: International Conference on Informatics for Environmental Protection: Environmental Information and Communication Technologies (EnviroInfo), pp. 199–209 (2022)
9. Lago, P., Koçak, S.A., Crnkovic, I., Penzenstadler, B.: Framing sustainability as a property of software quality. Commun. ACM **58**(10) (2015)
10. Mohankumar, M., Kumar, D.: Empirical study on green and sustainable software engineering. Adv. Softw. Eng. Syst. (2015)
11. Oyedeji, S., Seffah, A., Penzenstadler, B.: A catalogue supporting software sustainability design. Sustainability **10**(7) (2018)
12. Oyedeji eet al.: Software sustainability: academic understanding and industry perceptions. In: Software Business. Springer (2021)
13. Raisian, K., Yahaya, J., Deraman, A.: Sustainable software development life cycle process model based on capability maturity model integration: a study in Malaysia. J. Theor. Appl. Inf. Technol. **95** (2017)
14. Shenoy, S.S., Eeratta, R.: Green software development model: an approach towards sustainable software development. In: Annual IEEE India Conference (2011)
15. Vaismoradi, M., Snelgrove, S.: Theme in qualitative content analysis and thematic analysis. Forum Qual. Sozialforschung **20** (2019)

Experimentation and Innovations

Pre-release Experimentation in Indie Game Development: An Interview Survey

Johan Linåker[1]([✉]), Elizabeth Bjarnason[1], and Fabian Fagerholm[2]

[1] Department of Computer Science, Lund University, Lund, Sweden
{johan.linaker,elizabeth.bjarnason}@cs.lth.se
[2] Aalto University, Helsinki, Finland
fabian.fagerholm@aalto.fi

Abstract. [Background] The game industry faces fierce competition and games are developed on short deadlines and tight budgets. Continuously testing and experimenting with new ideas and features is essential in validating and guiding development toward market viability and success. Such continuous experimentation (CE) requires user data, which is often limited in early development stages. This challenge is further exacerbated for independent (indie) game companies with limited resources. [Aim] We wanted to gain insights into CE practices in pre-release indie game development. [Method] We performed an exploratory interview survey with 10 indie game developers from different companies and synthesised findings through an iterative coding process. [Results] We present a CE framework for game development that highlights key parts to consider when planning and implementing an experiment and note that pre-release experimentation is centred on qualitative data. Time and resource constraints impose limits on the type and extent of experimentation and playtesting that indie companies can perform, e.g. due to limited access to participants, biases and representativeness of the target audience. [Conclusions] Our results outline challenges and practices for conducting experiments with limited user data in early stages of indie game development, and may be of value also for larger game companies, and for software intensive organisations in other industries.

Keywords: Game development · Continuous Experimentation · User Research · User data · Indie Game Company

1 Introduction

The game industry is ever growing with increasing yearly turnarounds and number of employees. For example, the Swedish game industry represents 4.1% of the country's national gross service export with a yearly turnaround of 86.5 billion SEK (including international subsidiaries) and a workforce of around 25,000 people globally, including 8,500 employees in 939 companies located in Sweden [12]. The industry is fiercely competitive, and game development companies are

E. Papatheocharous et al. (Eds.): ICSOB 2024, LNBIP 539, pp. 293–308, 2025.
https://doi.org/10.1007/978-3-031-85849-9_24

pressured by short deadlines and need to stay cost-efficient [21]. Therefore, betting on a wrong idea or a feature that is not technically or commercially viable poses a significant business risk.

In the broader industry, software-intensive organisations have started to adopt Continuous Experimentation (CE) practices [18] to mitigate the risk of releasing products with weak market viability. An experiment-driven development approach is then used to continuously evaluate new features and qualities based on user feedback [8], and hypotheses are defined upfront based on the expected outcome in terms of technical and/or commercial viability [3].

Experimentation would ideally be performed throughout game development from ideation and pre-release to post-launch, and thereby guide development and product planning in producing an engaging game experience that maximises the value creation [24]. The stages prior to releasing a game are extra critical as this is where the majority of the development occurs. As development progresses, the cost and impact of pivoting increase.

CE requires access to user data to test hypotheses [8], which is especially challenging prior to release of a game. Since the number of users is naturally limited at this point, so is the amount of available user data and feedback [24]. This challenge is especially taxing for smaller game development companies with limited resources and without the backing of larger game publishers. These companies, also referred to as independent (*indie*) game companies are commonly small and new companies with limited resources, experience and practice comparable to established game companies and studios [9].

There is limited research of CE practices in the game industry, and specifically for indie game studies [7], with some notable exceptions [6,24]. In this study, we aim to address this gap by investigating *how CE may be applied in the context of pre-release indie game development*. We conducted an exploratory semi-structured interview survey with 10 game developers from different indie game companies. Findings are synthesised into an emerging framework of continuous experimentation in game development that highlights five key parts to consider when planning and implementing experimentation in game development. In the future, we aim to further validate and refine our initial framework through case studies and expand our research to include larger game companies.

2   Related Work

Continuous Experimentation (CE) is a software development approach where product design decisions are based on results from field experiments with real users [3,8]. Several methods and frameworks have been proposed for CE, involving similar activities: identifying and articulating product assumptions, turning these into testable hypotheses, running experiments to validate the hypotheses, and interpreting the experiment results to determine whether the assumption held or not [8,10]. This allows the product organisation to iteratively find designs that promote desired user behaviours, such as increased purchases.

Many CE-like activities can be observed in game development. Game analytics is a common practice that has been used for, e.g., in-game balancing, identifying bottlenecks in game levels, detecting bugs, reducing costs and risks, and negotiating with investors and publishers [23]. Its use of field data to drive decision-making is common with CE. Some specific aspects of CE have received direct attention in game development [7], e.g., the exploratory use of prototyping in the requirements engineering process [4], and monetary feature-optimisation in post-deployment. The area of User research also provides some input into how user feedback can guide game development [16]. User research shares with CE the overall idea of basing development on an empirical approach.

Research describes a need to match experimentation practices to the different stages of game development [1]. Qualitative methods are primarily used in early development stages when the amount of quantitative user data is limited [24]. Play-testing is highlighted as the main overarching method, while A/B testing is common in the later post-production stages [11]. Identifying and isolating features for evaluation is a challenge [14], especially in the early development stages [13]. The feature set needs to be holistic enough to not loose important aspects required to enable game-play, while still enabling the experiment to evaluate defined Key Performance Indicators (KPIs) [11].

A distinction can also be noted in relation to the game genre and context. For example, in the mobile game context and freemium-type games [14], there is a strong belief in quantitative methods. Andersen et al., demonstrate the potential of quantitative experimentation in guiding feature development in gaming [2]. However, many game companies also rely on unstructured approaches.

Depending on the purpose and aspects being experimented on, different metrics are required, such as game mechanics (the rules of the game), game dynamics (what happens when the game is played), and aesthetics (the feeling of fun experienced by the player) [13]. When designing an experiment, each aspect requires specific consideration regarding the technical implementation and commercial viability [19]. Validation of aesthetics, or fun factor (regardless of technical or commercial viability) is specifically highlighted as a key challenge, due to the need to connect with a relevant target audience [21], while limiting the risk of leaking differentiating ideas and details to the public and potential competitors [1]. Therefore, play-testing is usually performed with internal developers or trusted associates, despite the risk of cognitive and confirmation biases [24]. Chueca et al. points to the need for new methods, tools, and processes to identify and validate requirements relating to the user experience of games [5].

Regardless of the many investigated aspects, the full CE cycle in game development has to date received limited attention with only recent work starting to emerge [6,24]. Scientific studies on holistic experimentation frameworks and processes are still missing despite the competitive and high-paced nature of the gaming industry, which points to a need for more research in this context on continuous and iterative experimentation. Specifically, the early stages of game development are highlighted as critical since many game ideas never enter the production stage [21]. Thus, this is an area for future research [1,5].

3   Research Design

An interview survey [17] of how CE may be applied within indie game development prior to releasing a game has been performed. We sampled interviewees with the goal of gaining a wide understanding of practice across different indie game companies. One representative per indie company was deemed sufficient to gain an understanding of the practice and experience at these very small companies. Representatives from ten indie company were identified at an indie game conference based on informal conversations from which initial observations were collected in field notes. These company representatives were then interviewed online, see Table 1 for an overview of interviewees I1–I10.

Table 1. Overview of interviewees (years of experience, current role) and their indie company (number of employees, game genre and platform, geographic location.

ID	Exp. (Yrs)	Role(s)	Nbr Empl.	Game genre(s)	Platform(s)	Main loc.
I1	7	Producer, Co-Founder	4	First-person-shooter	Desktop	CH
I2	18	Lead developer, Founder	1	Open world, Strategy	Desktop	SE, US
I3	13	CEO, Lead developer and Designer, Founder	3	AI-based Role play	Desktop	SE
I4	2	Director, Lead developer, Co-Founder	8	3D vehicle combat action roguelite	Desktop	SE
I5	6	Lead designer, Co-Founder	2,5	3D rougelite	Desktop	NL
I6	5	Game director, Co-Founder	9	3D Role Play	Desktop, console	SE
I7	14	CEO, Co-Founder	50+	Puzzle, Brawler, Action	Mobile	UA
I8	4	Development and design lead, Co-Founder	2	Cozy wholesome games	Desktop	SE
I9	5	Lead Developer, Founder	1.5	Platform, action	Desktop	NL
I10	5	CEO, Co-Founder	2.5	Sustainability-focused cozy games	Mobile	SE

Each interview lasted for about 30 min. I1–I6 were interviewed by the first and second author together, while I7–I10 were interviewed by the first author only. The interviews were semi-structured using an interview questionnaire [15] focused on open questions regarding the use and experience of CE and related practices such as game user research, testing, and requirements engineering.

Review of literature provided authors with an initial understanding of the problem domain, enabling probing questions during interviews.

The interviews were recorded, transcribed with an offline instance of WhisperX, and analysed using open and axial coding techniques [20]. The 1st and 2nd author coded I1 and I2 separately, and their two code books were merged and disagreements settled. For the remaining interviews the two authors took turns in coding and peer-reviewing each interview, and settled disagreements.

The coding rendered ten high level themes, in addition to demographics. These themes were informed inductively from the interview data and from our knowledge of related work. The final code book can be found in the supplementary material [15]. When coding I6, we noted some saturation among the findings and first-level codes introduced. By I10, the data was mainly of a confirming nature, adding only nuances to existing first-level codes.

Steps were taken to address **threats to validity** of the study. An audit trail was maintained to retain traceability throughout data collection, analysis, and reporting using references to I1-I10. Inclusion of quotes has been prioritised to provide richness and context in the reporting, and to enable anecdotal generalisation based on the data. Each interviewee was provided with an early version of this article to enable member-checking and validation of our synthesised findings. Collaborative and peer-review coding together with peer-debriefing was used to enhance construct validity and reduce the risk of researcher bias.

4 Results: Continuous Experimentation Framework

Our results are synthesised into a framework for CE in game development, see Fig. 1. The framework consists of five main parts involved in experimentation, namely *goal definition, design strategy, experiment object, sampling strategy*, and *execution strategy*. Each part is described based on our empirical data and with quotes derived from our interviewees (I1–I10, see Table 1).

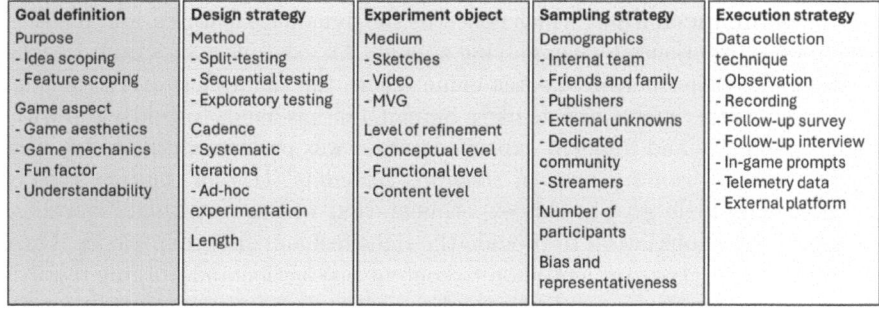

Goal definition	Design strategy	Experiment object	Sampling strategy	Execution strategy
Purpose - Idea scoping - Feature scoping	Method - Split-testing - Sequential testing - Exploratory testing	Medium - Sketches - Video - MVG	Demographics - Internal team - Friends and family - Publishers - External unknowns - Dedicated community - Streamers	Data collection technique - Observation - Recording - Follow-up survey - Follow-up interview - In-game prompts - Telemetry data - External platform
Game aspect - Game aesthetics - Game mechanics - Fun factor - Understandability	Cadence - Systematic iterations - Ad-hoc experimentation Length	Level of refinement - Conceptual level - Functional level - Content level	Number of participants Bias and representativeness	

Fig. 1. Overview of our framework for CE in game development including key parts of experimentation in the early stages of game development.

4.1 Goal Definition

We find that the goal of experimentation consists of a combination of the *purpose* of an experiment and the *game aspect* being evaluated. In the very early stages of development, the **purpose** primarily concerns the scoping of the overarching *game idea*, while it later shifts to *feature scoping*. Selecting and **scoping the game idea** is critical since it determines the future direction of the development and, ultimately, the success of the game. This scoping affects the development team, the target audience, and potential stakeholders, including publishers. For example, I6 described experimenting with three game ideas by presenting conceptual sketches of these to a potential publisher and using this feedback to select which idea to pursue and to invest further development effort into. When experimenting for the purpose of **feature scoping** *"the decision on what to include in the game"* (I2) is based on experimentation results, both regarding which features to include and the detailed scoping of these.

Experiments often focus on validating one or more **game aspects**, and four such aspects emerged through our interview survey, namely *game aesthetics, game mechanics, fun factor*, and *understandability*. Experimentation is performed for these aspects, both with the purpose of idea scoping and feature scoping. An experiment that focuses on **game aesthetics** considers the graphical style and artwork of the game. While the final artwork is conceived and evaluated in the later stages of pre-release (Alpha and Beta), we found some instances where the aesthetics are considered already in the idea-generation stage. For example, I10 described experimentation using early sketches that were shown to the target audience before any playable demo was created. Our interviewees described that the goal when experimenting with game aesthetics is to evaluate the conceptual look and feel of the game rather than the exact artwork to be implemented in the final product. For example, I9 described using placeholder-level art created by an AI-based image generator (Midjourney AI) to experiment and get the right *feel* early on, and that this cost-effective means of experimentation enabled creating a playable demo after only one month.

In the early stages of development, there is a strong focus on experimentation with the **game mechanics**, which concerns the dynamics, features, and physical mechanics as experienced when playing a game. An example comes from I1, who is developing a first-person-shooter game where the main character is a non-human who neither moves or acts like a human, nor has hands to hold a gun with. In this case, early and frequent experimentation was performed to develop *"the core mechanics... running around, shooting, reloading"* (I1) for this new type of character. The main goal of this experimentation was to figure out how these new mechanics should work to provide the right feel and game experience. Once this was in place, the team moved on to content production and working towards a beta release. Similarly, another interviewee described focusing on *"mechanics like weapons and items... to see what kinds of choices players were making and if they felt that those were satisfying"* (I4).

The mechanics and aesthetics of a game tie into the softer aspect of the **fun factor**, which regards the user experience, feel, and fun experienced by the user, i.e., the *game user experience* [22]. I1 highlights how this aspect can, and should, be evaluated early on in development, even before the game has nice-looking aesthetics. *"Players would have fun in a level that is pretty much a grey box. There is actually not much in there, but you still have your features... That is basically the best position. If you can test it so far that players enjoy it and actually have fun, even though the level is still ugly as hell"* (I1). This experimentation with game mechanics to evaluate fun factor should ideally continue throughout the development. I4 describes first focusing on evaluating players' game user experience and how they react to the core loop and mechanics of a game, and later shifting to experiment with *"different areas of the mechanics, [e.g.,] its weapons and items. We really wanted to see what kind of choices players were making and if they felt that those were satisfying"* (I4).

The **understandability** of a game is an aspect that is closely related to *fun factor*, and concerns how easily players comprehend and understand the logic of a game. The complexity of this aspect varies depending on the type of game. For example, for a strategy game, the player needs to *"learn... and understand the basic game mechanisms"* (I2) to play and enjoy the game and thus has a steeper learning curve compared to a first-shooter game. In this case, I2 performed experimentation with a tutorial to validate the learning aspects and to see how well players understood and learnt to use the game mechanisms.

4.2   Design Strategy

Our interviewees describe a range of strategies used when designing and setting up experiments that vary regarding the kind of *method* used, and the *cadence* and *length* of experiments. The described design strategies vary regarding formality and scope, and depend on the experimentation goals, type of game, current development stage, and available resources.

We observe three main **experimentation methods** in our material, namely *split*, *sequential*, and *exploratory testing* that represent strategies for exploring different options. Either, two versions are compared (split), options are exploring one by one (sequential), or the design space is freely explored (exploratory). **Split testing** is generally considered to be expensive in terms of resources, which is why this was mostly described for the early ideation and prototyping parts of pre-release. Split testing is usually limited to two versions (i.e., A/B testing). Several interviewees (I3, I5, I6) described experimenting by implementing two and three early alternative versions of their games, ranging from playable demos to conceptual art, and presenting these to potential publishers. The obtained feedback was often used to guide the indie game companies decisions on which alternative to pursue. However, I3 described that the experiment was inconclusive due to conflicting feedback from different publishers, and in the end the company decided to go with the game that had the lowest development cost.

In later stages of the pre-release, split-testing often becomes more focused on specific features. In this stage, the cost of implementation is still perceived as low, or reasonable in relation to the perceived benefit. I3 describes developing two versions of their main game, one of which contained more advanced AI functionality. The participants of the experiment selected which version they preferred to play and feedback was collected through a survey. Based on 60–70 survey responses the decision was to adopt the new, more advanced functionality. I1 also described using multiple prototype variants to experiment with in the early parts of pre-release. I7 stands out in our survey by describing comparatively mature experimentation practices using A/B-tests. The interviewee's experience of this is from development assignments for larger mobile game development companies. This includes the case where *"you have [game] mechanics that you are not sure will work for your game... so we develop two different versions in which those mechanics could be done in two different ways. Our team generates a hypothesis that [the new functionality] will improve for the specific KPI, for example, the play time"* (I7).

Sequential testing is an experimentation method where the option considered to have the best potential is evaluated first, and if the feedback is negative, the alternative solution is implemented and evaluated. Our interviewees generally prefer this method when development matures beyond the early ideation and prototyping stages. One interviewee described focusing their experimentation on functionality that is *"not working, and then we try to iterate on it, and then see if it has improved. But, it is not really A/B testing. We just test the new version and see if the reactions have improved... Most of the time, it is an improvement"* (I5). I6 exemplifies a more comprehensive form of sequential testing where they experimented with alternative artwork and game mechanics compared to the main game. Based on the obtained feedback, the ideas considered successful were then re-implemented in the main game. Another example of sequential testing was described by I9, where they had experimented by replacing a gun with an alternative mechanisms to evaluate the hypothesis that the gun was being used too repetitively, impacting negatively on the user experience. In this case, the experiment revealed that the users enjoyed, and preferred, the gun, which led to re-implementing it.

Exploratory testing is a less formal experimentation method where there is no predefined hypothesis but rather a set of questions or an open mind when entering an experiment, e.g. when playtesting. The goal of the experiment can be general, or aimed at considering specific aspects such as game mechanics or fun factor. I5 explains it as: *"Sometimes, we go in with a questionnaire, sometimes we just have some questions at the back of our minds while observing, and sometimes we are going in [with a] fully open [mind]... If we have something that we know we want to know more about, then it is really focused... if it is more ...how does the game play experience feel ... then it is more open."* Also, I4 describes typically having a set of predefined questions when entering a playtest. Lessons and takeaways help inform the backlog and prioritise feature development and bug fixing. I10 describes maintaining an open mind in playtests focusing on game mechanics and fun factor, and then observing how players move around and interact with the game environment. As stated by I6, *"fun is so subjective"* and the evaluation of fun factor requires more than pure quantitative data.

The **cadence** with which experiments are perofmred varies through *structured systematic experimentation* to *ad-hoc experimentation*. I1 describes using systematic experimentation in early prototyping stages through small and quick iterations. For this, a small set of easily available participants from within their co-working space are used as playtesters. In later stages, more development and refinement are conducted between tests, adding longer periods in between experiments. I2 describes a similar approach, but notes that he sometimes mixes the cadence, e.g. *"if I do one month of rapid play testing, I might afterwards pause for a bit to take more long-term decisions, and introduce larger feature implementations, followed again by more intense testing"*. Several interviewees (I1, I4, I6, I9) note how the time and resources required to plan, execute, and analyse the playtests are costly and limited in comparison to what larger AAA game development companies can perform. Others, such as I5 and I8, describe a more *ad-hoc experimentation*, e.g., dependent on the availability of local and externally hosted playtesting sessions.

The **length** of the experiments is described to range between a weekend to a week by the majority of our interviewees. I4 describes how experiments may be longer, spanning up to several weeks, during which the game is continuously updated, e.g. with corrections. The consequences of experimenting with a constantly changing version of the game is that the *"feedback that you get at the beginning of the playtest and the feedback that you get at the ending of the playtest is actually feedback on two different builds"* (I4).

4.3   Experiment Object

The experiment object refers to the artefact that is evaluated in an experiment. The *medium* (sketches, video, or MVG) and *level of refinement* (conceptual, functional, or content level) of the experiment object need to be aligned to the goals and the design strategy of the experiment. Game developers also need to consider the time and resources required to produce the experiment object, which also relates to the current stage of the game development. For the **medium** in the initial stages, interviewees describe using *sketches* and conceptual designs of the art and imagined gameplay to evaluate the overall game idea. *Videos* demonstrating gameplay may be an option to communicate an idea quickly, while playable *Minimum Viable Games (MVGs)* offer a direct experience for the participants of the experiment. Even if these *"early versions of the game … aren't very refined, they work"* (I5) and allow game developers to get early feedback on their ideas which *"informs our backlog"* (I4) and is thus fed directly back into the game design and development. For this reason, experimenting with an MVG is often preferred even if the MVG is *"very unpolished"* (I2) and requires more time and effort to produce than prototyping a new idea in isolation. One interviewee motivated this preference with a desire to *"get it [the change] into the game as quickly as possible … to see if it works with the rest"* (I2).

We have identified three main **levels of refinement** of the experiment object with increasing complexity and maturity, namely *conceptual*, *functional*, and *content level*. On the **conceptual level**, high-level ideas and visions are evaluated using, e.g., sketches, videos of gameplay, and rough prototypes of the art work and envisioned gameplay. For example, I6 described using three conceptual designs to present their game ideas to publishers early one, while I10 described presenting various art designs to the intended target audience. I4 described using non-executable (abstract) experimentation objects, such as design and conceptual art and descriptions, to evaluate ideas and design options internally within the company. When experimenting at the **functional level**, the core mechanics and loop of the game are demonstrated. I1 describes how they *"focused on getting the core mechanics of the game, the core loop right, which basically meant … running around, shooting needles, reloading, tapping at the right time… that's basically the core loop… [We] would look deeply into things like how much head bobbing, … [should there be] when [moving side-ways] left or right?"*. I4 described how the length of an experiment initially was limited to a two-week iteration to present a functional prototype, followed by a longer 2–3 month iteration where an early playable demo was created and evaluated by friends and family. On the **content level**, art work and level design is added and finalised, but not necessarily at a very polished level as hinted by I4. One interviewee differentiates between the functional and content levels as *"…you need the feature side, which is all the logic, which is design dictating what code to build, and whether it works, whether it's a proof of fun … And, the content side is stretching out that fun, putting these features in varied situations, [i.e.,] level design"* (I1).

4.4   Sampling Strategy

The people that participate in an experiment are selected, or sampled, to represent a certain population. The sampling strategy involves selecting the **demographics** and **number of participants** of an experiment, and considering risks related to **biases and representativeness** of those selected.

Indie game companies use participants from a diverse set of **demographics**, typically depending on the current stage of game development and the availability of participants. Our interviewees specifically distinguish between experimenting with their *internal team, friends and family, publishers, external unknowns, dedicated communities*, and *streamers* (i.e., individuals recording and sending live while they play and comment the game simultaneously). Several interviewees (I2, I5, I6, I10) describe how the first testing usually involves the company's **internal team** to ensure that the game *"feels good"* (I2). Several interviewees (e.g. I5, I6) describe performing internal experimentation on a weekly basis, e.g. through *show-and-tell sessions*. In a second step, indie game companies generally move towards including **friends and family**, e.g., through online observations or physical playtesting sessions. For example, I1 and I2 describe often recruiting users from a combination of friends and colleagues within the industry and their connections. The physical playtests are commonly hosted by local incubators or co-working spaces, where co-workers, students, and developers from the local gaming community can be found. Another important source of participants are **publishers** who are kept in the loop throughout the development.

Several interviewees stress the importance of including publishers in the testing when deciding on which idea to focus on, commonly at the beginning of the pre-release stage (I2, I3, I6). As development progresses, interviewees commonly turn to **external unknowns**, i.e. to external participants in general. These are commonly recruited from indie game platforms such as Itch.io and Steam. Indie game companies publish early game versions, or demos, on these platforms to attract attention and invite players into their Discord channels (a chat platform). The Discord channels serve as an infrastructure for growing and facilitating **dedicated communities** of fans and potential playtesters that can be used in experiments on a reoccurring basis. External playtesters can also be acquired monetarily from third party platforms where the company can define the desired characteristics of the participants, to better ensure that the correct audience is reached. Another means of gaining inputs from an external audience is through the use of **streamers**. Reactions from the streamers and their audience provide valuable insights as described by I3 and I5.

The **number of participants** in an experiment varies and depends on several factors, including the type of experiment (goals, design strategy, and experiment object), type of participants, and the current stage of the game development. For physical playtests, interviewees generally converge and agree that 8–10 individuals is satisfactory. For the online and external playtests with players from the community or unknown externals, the number of participants can range from a few up to 60–70. For example, I3 indicated that around 60–70 people could be involved in an A/B test within their dedicated community. Another interviewee said that *"10 players [will] often get you... [a] visible micro trend"* (I1). In contrast, I7 stated that they require a minimum of 100 testers for the input to be significant and trustworthy. However, the other interviewees explained that it is difficult to recruit that many testers. In particular, I10 highlighted the difficulty in attracting playtesters as a major challenge for their company. Generally, our interviewees described that as development progresses towards release of a game, the type and extent of experimentation shifts towards evaluation using more quantitative data from a larger number of participants.

Several interviewees described challenges in attaining **un-biased** participants (I2, I3, I4, I6) with a good **representativeness** of the target audience (I6, I7, I9). For example, friends and family often have a positive bias and are predisposed to approve of the company's work. Several interviewees (I1, I8, I9) mentioned that game developers provide *"feedback [that is] even more useful ... [since] they have some development knowledge"* (I1). Also, game developers tend to *"see things that regular gamers do not think about"* (I2).

4.5 Execution Strategy

Feedback from those participating in an experiment is collected through a multitude of **data collection techniques**, as exemplified by the interviewees. All interviewees describe using **observations** of participants performing external game play testing. While one interviewee described the value of observing people's facial expressions (I3), most of the interviewees expressed a preference for observing *"not their faces, but [to] record the screen and [to see] how they play the game"* (I2). Such recordings are *"worth gold"* (I2) since they can give insights into how the game is played, and if participants get stuck or do not understand certain aspects of the game. Watching people play is described as being especially useful in mitigating biases, for example, in friends and family, or when game players know that they are talking to the developer and are, thus, less likely to criticise. Also, several interviewees described the importance of not interfering with the participants when doing live observations by asking leading questions or helping them, since this may influence their responses (I1, I3, I4).

Several interviewees (I1-I4) described using **follow-up surveys** to complement observations. The surveys mainly consist of specific questions that the game developers want answers to, e.g. on game mechanics (if this is the focus of the experimentation), but also open questions. I2 often asks specific questions such as *"did you do this? Dig there, press that button?"*, since this indicates that the gamer has understood the game logic.

Sometimes open **follow-up interviews** are used where participants are asked to described their experience after playing the game. However, this *"takes up too much time for ... sole developers"* (I2) and is an aspect for which the cost-benefit balance is a constant challenge. I6 described how experimenting with external participants takes time from development, but reduces the risk of *"running into problem that are very hard or costly to correct"* (I6).

One interviewee suggested that **in-game prompts** and (existing) plugins for enabling in-game feedback could be used to gather feedback from players. For example, by inserting pops-up in the game when users *"encounter issues or want to suggest something"* (I1). Such popups can be used to take screenshots and record the gamer's description of a situation. Such a feature may potentially provide valuable feedback to game developers.

The potential and challenges of collecting and analysing large amounts of in-game **telemetry data** was raised by several interviewees (I1, I6, I7, I10). I6 uses analytics during play testing to measure, e.g. duration and progress of game play. Such information can inform about game play, e.g. difficulties, engagement, bugs etc. However, it is also *"very difficult to know in advance what data you want"* (I6), which is a requirement in GDPR in order to save data. In the mobile context, I7 states that many events in these games are tightly connected to analytics, e.g. to record time from one game action to another to tell how quickly a player progresses compared to an average user. I10 reports using Google Analytics to get certain metrics, e.g., the number of active users, new players, monthly active users, day-one retention, and day-seven retention. While these general KPIs are considered helpful, I10 would prefer more detailed in-game metrics, but this would *"require us to implement more analytics tooling"*. In addition to requiring technical implementation of data pipelines and processing infrastructure of the back-end, time and resources are required of the developers to collect, manage, and analyse the large amounts of data produced (I1).

External platforms and tools can also be used for experimentation, by disseminating games, gathering playtesters, and simultaneously collecting feedback.

This data collection technique was described by I5. In this case, a prototype, or a small demo of a game was created and published as a preview on Steam to poll interest. Releasing an early access version on an external platform can provide valuable *"feedback from people who explore the game'... [but also yield] very divided feedback from enthusiastic to very disappointed [gamers]"* (I5). Analysing and deciding how to address such divided feedback can be very challenging. Another common publication platform referred to is Itch.io. I9 mentioned an issues related to the limited amount of metrics this platform provides, beyond number of downloads, is used to assess the experienced fun and popularity of a game.

5   Discussion and Conclusions

We find that indie game development involves a continuous experimentation approach to explore, design, and develop new game ideas and features. Our interviews confirm previous research, and provide new insights into the experimentation practices used in early stages of indie game development, prior to release. In this paper, we describe these practices for five key parts of experimentation, namely goal definition, design strategy, experiment object, sampling strategy, and execution strategy, see Fig. 1.

Experimentation is commonly used in the pre-release stages for the purpose, and with the **goal** of *scoping the game idea and features* for different aspects of the game. In particular, the *fun factor* is characterised as a complex and difficult aspect to evaluate. Our findings align well with extant work that describes the aspects of *game mechanics, aesthetics,* and *fun factor* [13]. In addition, we identify the cognitive and pedagogic aspect of *understandability* of the game logic as an important aspect to evaluate for more complex games.

We note that the **design strategy**, and the formality and structure of experimentation practices, vary depending on the targeted platform (desktop vs. mobile), the level of experience and resources available to the indie company. *Experimentation methods* range on a spectrum from more or less structured *split (A/B) testing* (where two alternatives are evaluated in parallel) to *sequential testing* (where the solution with the highest potential is evaluated) and *exploratory testing* (without any pre-defined hypotheses). In contrast to earlier work [11], our findings suggest that split testing is often performed in the initial idea stage and in early prototyping stages. In these early development stages, **experiment objects** at the *conceptual level* are used predominantly. The higher cost and complexity of developing and evaluating different versions are the main reasons for limiting the split-testing to early development stages.

The **sampling strategy** used by indie companies is greatly affected by their limited access to participants for experimentation, which presents a major challenge. However, our interview survey also reveals that in the early stages of development, indie game developers gain useful feedback from smaller sets of participants through qualitative data collection methods, such as observations and recordings of game play. In addition to obtain sufficient numbers of participant, indie companies need to consider the representatives of the target audience and the risk of obtaining biased answers, e.g., from friends and family, or monetarily awarded participants. In alignment with extant work, we also find that internal testing is commonly performed in combination with playtesting with friends and family. This risks steering the development in a direction deviating from the actual target audience [24].

Indie game developers commonly experiment in the early development stages using an **execution strategy** that involves *data collection techniques* based on qualitative data such as *observations* of uninterrupted players' reactions and facial expressions. Our interviewees indicate that this is due to the limited number of users available, and is in line with other research by Yaman et al. [24]. The use of quantitative data collection methods were described primarily by interviewees with experience of mobile games, which aligns with Koskenvoima and Mäntymäki [14]. However, we observed a general interest in leveraging *telemetry data* to assess player engagement and understandability, e.g. by measuring the time spent on certain tasks or between two points in a game. Currently, the cost and complexity of acquiring and integrating the tools necessary to collect, manage, and analyse such data, is a barrier for small indie companies in extending their use of telemetry data in experimentation. Enabling and collecting quality feedback from the players is also reported as time consuming.

Our results may be of interest to many software-intensive organisations, irrespective of industry, and can provide insights into how experimentation can be conducted also in the early development stages when data is limited. Despite many challenges, the surveyed indie companies show high promise and resourcefulness, in particular considering the overarching high pace and competitiveness of the game industry [21]. Our qualitative investigation is limited to a small set of interviews of indie game developers from different studios, of which many are geographically located in Sweden. Any generalisation should be anecdotal considering the characteristics of the indie game companies surveyed and the contexts provided in this article.

In future work, the key parts of the experimentation practices and factors influencing these will be explored and formalised further. Specific attention needs to be paid to the resource and efficiency requirements of the indie game companies, concerning tools and processes that need to be developed. Another avenue regards the exploration of perspectives and practices among more established and resourceful game companies, and how these contrast against findings of this study. An additional avenue regards the cost and benefit of introducing different practices highlighted in the proposed framework, which could guide practitioners with resource constrains as is common for indie-game developers. Further, while the focus of this study has been on the pre-release process of game development, future work should investigate how CE can be applied post-release as well.

References

1. Aleem, S., Capretz, L.F., Ahmed, F.: Game development software engineering process life cycle: a systematic review. J. Softw. Eng. Res. Dev. **4**(1), 1–30 (2016). https://doi.org/10.1186/s40411-016-0032-7
2. Andersen, E., Liu, Y.E., Snider, R., Szeto, R., Cooper, S., Popović, Z.: On the harmfulness of secondary game objectives. In: Proceedings of the 6th International Conference on Foundations of Digital Games, FDG 2011, pp. 30–37. ACM (2011)
3. Auer, F., Ros, R., Kaltenbrunner, L., Runeson, P., Felderer, M.: Controlled experimentation in continuous experimentation: knowledge and challenges. Inf. Softw. Technol. **134**, 106551 (2021)
4. Bjarnason, E., Lang, F., Mjöberg, A.: An empirically based model of software prototyping: a mapping study and a multi-case study. Empir. Softw. Eng. **28**(5) (2023)
5. Chueca, J., Verón, J., Font, J., Pérez, F., Cetina, C.: The consolidation of game software engineering: a systematic literature review of software engineering for industry-scale computer games. Inf. and Softw. Technology 107330 (2023)
6. Edison, H., Melegati, J., Bjarnason, E.: Experimentation in early-stage video game startups: Practices and challenges. In: International Conference on Software Business, pp. 360–366. Springer (2023)
7. Engström, H.: Game development research (2020)
8. Fagerholm, F., Guinea, A.S., Mäenpää, H., Münch, J.: The right model for continuous experimentation. J. Syst. Softw. **123**, 292–305 (2017)
9. Grabarczyk, P.: Is every indie game independent? Towards the concept of independent game. Game Stud. **16**(1) (2016)
10. Olsson, H.H., Bosch, J.: The HYPEX model: from opinions to data-driven software development. In: Bosch, J. (ed.) Continuous Software Engineering, pp. 155–164. Springer, Cham (2014). https://doi.org/10.1007/978-3-319-11283-1_13
11. Hyrynsalmi, S., et al.: What is a minimum viable (video) game? Towards a research agenda. In: 17th IFIP WG 6.11 Conference on e-Business, e-Services, and e-Society, pp. 217–231. Springer (2018)
12. Swedish Games Industry: Swedish Games Industry 2023 Game Developer Index. Swedish Games Industry (2023)
13. Järvi, A., Taajamaa, V., Hyrynsalmi, S.: Lean software startup–an experience report from an entrepreneurial software business course. In: Software Business: 6th International Conference, pp. 230–244. Springer (2015)
14. Koskenvoima, A., Mäntymäki, M.: Why do small and medium-size freemium game developers use game analytics? In: 14th IFIP WG 6.11 Conference on e-Business, e-Services, and e-Society, pp. 326–337. Springer (2015)
15. Linåker, J., Bjarnason, E., Fagerholm, F.: Online supplementary material (2024). https://doi.org/10.6084/m9.figshare.26934910
16. Pagulayan, R.J., et al.: Applied user research in games. Wiley Handb. Hum. Comput. Interact. **1**, 299–346 (2018)
17. Ralph, P.: ACM sigsoft empirical standards for software engineering research. Qualitative surveys. arxiv:2010.03525 [cs.se] (2021). https://www2.sigsoft.org/EmpiricalStandards/docs/standards?standard=QualitativeSurveys#
18. Ros, R., Runeson, P.: Continuous experimentation and A/B testing: a mapping study. In: Proceedings of the 4th RCoSE, pp. 35–41 (2018)
19. Rosenfield Boeira, J.N., Rosenfield Boeira, J.N.: MVPs: do we really need them? In: Lean Game Development: Apply Lean Frameworks to the Process of Game Development, pp. 33–48 (2017)

20. Saldaña, J.: The Coding Manual for Qualitative Researchers. Sage (2021)
21. Schmalz, M., Finn, A., Taylor, H.: Risk management in video game development projects. In: 47th HICSS, pp. 4325–4334. IEEE (2014)
22. Stahlke, S.N., Mirza-Babaei, P.: Usertesting without the user: opportunities and challenges of an AI-driven approach in games user research. Comput. Entertain. **16**(2) (2018)
23. Su, Y., Backlund, P., Engström, H.: Comprehensive review and classification of game analytics. Serv. Orient. Comput. Appl. **15**(2), 141–156 (2021)
24. Yaman, S., Mikkonen, T., Suomela, R.: Continuous experimentation in mobile game development. In: Proceedings of 44th SEAA, pp. 345–352 (2018)

Marketplace for Multi-party Development of Artificial Intelligence Systems: Perceptions on Value Creation

Yuliyan V. Maksimov[1]([⊠]) [iD] and Samuel A. Fricker[2]

[1] Blekinge Institute of Technology (BTH), Karlskrona, Sweden
yuliyan.maksimov@bth.se
[2] University of Applied Sciences Northwestern Switzerland (FHNW), Windisch, Switzerland
samuel.fricker@fhnw.ch

Abstract. The field of artificial intelligence (AI) has yet to fully capitalise on the potential to develop AI systems through collaboration between system developers and data scientists, especially when they belong to different organisations. We studied how using a marketplace creates value in such value chains by allowing organisations to advertise and share AI assets like data and models and enable multi-party development of AI systems while protecting these assets. The paper describes an embedded multi-case study of a marketplace under development, the Bonseyes marketplace. The cases were a collaboration between universities, a large company outsourcing data science, and a small business offering AI models as products. Value creation was linked to reduced development time, streamlined product communication, and protection of shared assets. However, participants required data protection concerns to be addressed, as well as marketplace maturity. The marketplace created value with clear goals for developing an AI system and supporting tools, templates, and examples. Our study benefits researchers wanting to advance AI systems development by offering rich examples of how a marketplace can enable multi-party collaborations.

Keywords: marketplace · AI systems engineering · case study-based evaluation

1 Introduction

Artificial intelligence (AI) can transform industry and society [1]. Combining AI with environment-sensing devices enables machines to learn independently, interact with humans, make decisions, and respond effectively. This significantly expands AI's applications, enabling industrial and social innovations [2]. Over the last decade, developing AI systems with machine learning (ML), especially in vision and language modelling, has received much attention. ML system development involves data collection, cleaning, labelling, feature engineering, model training, evaluation, and deployment [3], each handled by separate tools integrated into a pipeline [4]. This process creates a value chain of services and assets, transforming data into an inference-ready model. Effective training requires large, clean datasets [5]. While model training is brief, data preparation and feature engineering are the most time-consuming phases in ML projects [5].

© The Author(s), under exclusive license to Springer Nature Switzerland AG 2025
E. Papatheocharous et al. (Eds.): ICSOB 2024, LNBIP 539, pp. 309–323, 2025.
https://doi.org/10.1007/978-3-031-85849-9_25

For small players like research teams at universities or small and medium-sized enterprises (SMEs), it is difficult to participate in the AI business and compete with large organisations that manage the entire AI value chain [6]. Vendors like IBM Watson, Microsoft Azure, and Google Cloud have opened their doors for collaboration but require data to be uploaded to their cloud and processed with their tools. However, giving up control over data is risky and limits collaboration. Also, the usefulness of open data may be limited in commercial AI systems projects [7].

To address this challenge, collaboration between legally distinct organisations is increasingly studied [8, 9]. Marketplaces have been proposed to facilitate collaboration by enabling the trading of data and AI models and supporting value chains built around these exchanged assets [10, 11]. Marketplaces further offer licencing of assets being traded [12], promise automation of data processing with tools chained into AI development pipelines [3, 4], and protect data by decentralising machine learning, e.g., with federated learning [13] or secure premises [12].

As of today, we still lack a clear understanding of how to design an AI marketplace that will be widely adopted for multi-party AI development. Specifically, we need to identify the incentives that would encourage AI developers and data scientists to use the marketplace and the barriers that must be addressed. Beyond proposing marketplace technologies and architecture, empirical research is essential to determine the value propositions the marketplace should offer.

This paper empirically examines AI developers' and data scientists' views on a marketplace supporting multi-party AI development across organisations. Using an embedded multiple case study [14], we explored the marketplace's value creation and barriers to collaboration. The cases involved university collaboration, a large company outsourcing data science, and a small company offering AI models to the market. Data was gathered in three workshops and eight interviews and analysed using conventional content analysis [15].

The document is structured as follows: Sect. 2 covers the background. Section 3 describes the research method. Section 4 presents cases and practitioners' views on value creation and barriers. Section 5 discusses the results. Section 6 concludes.

2   Background

2.1   Multi-party Collaboration for AI Systems Development

Underlying our work is the following definition of collaboration: "*the agreement among specialists to focus their abilities on a specific process to achieve the project's broader objectives*" [16]. It can form virtual organisations when companies share and integrate their infrastructure, expertise, and resources [17]. Key elements include the collaboration agreement, shared goals, involved parties, structured processes, and exchanging expertise, resources, and assets.

In AI system development, common assets include data for machine learning, trained models, AI components or services with APIs, runtime environments for executing models on target hardware, and complete AI systems. Collaborators include data scientists, who curate data and train models, and AI systems engineers, who integrate models into services, deploy them on hardware platforms, and develop products or solutions for market or customer needs.

Multi-party collaboration can create value for AI systems development. Approaches like federated learning may reduce AI model development time and enhance quality [18–21]. These benefits arise from shared data processing pipelines that automate data preparation and training workflows for machine learning [3].

Despite promises of value creation, diverse barriers can hinder collaboration. Organisational barriers to multi-party AI collaboration include cultural incompatibility and communication challenges [3]. Solutions include adaptive processes that account for cultural differences, standardised communication models, culture-sensitive icons for non-experts, user environments that address interface variances, and organisational practices that foster cross-cultural collaboration, such as mergers and acquisitions [22]. Privacy and data confidentiality concerns also limit data-sharing trust. Solutions like federated learning [18, 20, 21], centralised intermediate data representations [19], and secure premises restricting AI asset access [12]—as in our studied marketplace—offer some mitigation, though each has trade-offs; for example, federated learning may reduce model quality [21]. Technical concerns include dataset compatibility [23, 24], data provenance affecting model quality [23, 25], and AI model explainability [23]. Standardisation initiatives aim to address some of these issues [26, 27].

2.2 Bonseyes Marketplace

Kumar et al. [28] describe an AI marketplace as *"an online marketplace facilitating the buying and selling of AI models among various actors, such as AI developers [...] [and] AI customers."* Marketplaces like Kaggle (https://www.kaggle.com/) and Hugging Face (https://huggingface.co/) support publishing AI assets and collaboration. Others, like Gravity AI (https://www.gravity-ai.com/) and AI Marketplace (https://aimarketplac e.co/), focus on model monetisation for AI developers. Our study focused on the Bonseyes marketplace (https://www.bonseyes.eu/), which supports multi-party collaborative AI development for embedded devices, emphasising data and model protection while enabling collaboration.

The Bonseyes marketplace enables AI system developers to post specifications ("challenges") for AI models they want to procure, while data scientists can offer models as solutions that meet these specifications. The marketplace supports collaboration by providing a secure environment where data can be uploaded for machine learning without human access, targeted at developers and data scientists across academia, large companies, and SMEs. Bonseyes offers user management, authentication, asset search and management, asset creation and validation tools, documentation, and secure, license-based asset access [12].

Figure 1 shows the value chain for which Bonseyes was designed, utilising the e^3 value notation [29]. An AI systems developer posts a challenge for data science work to be outsourced to a third-party data scientist, who can accept the task. Upon agreement, AI systems developer-provided data (D1) and data scientist-provided data (D2) are uploaded to a secure premise. The data scientist then trains an AI model, and the marketplace assists the developer in wrapping it with an API for benchmarking and deployment on target hardware. The resulting AI component ("AI App") is a building block for the whole AI system.

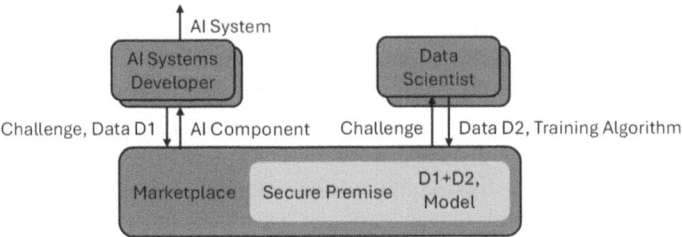

Fig. 1. Key asset exchanges between the AI systems developer, data scientist, and marketplace actors (notation based on e^3 value [29]).

The Bonseyes marketplace includes a web-based interface (Fig. 2), a repository for assets (challenges, data, models, platform environments, and AI components), and a secure environment for machine learning. Users register, manage identities, and post challenges or AI components through the interface. The secure environment enforces license-based access to AI assets, allowing regulated asset usage while restricting full access to asset owners only.

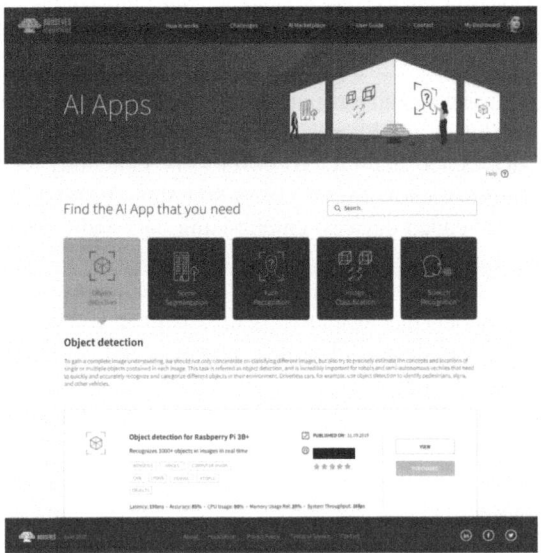

Fig. 2. User interface of the Bonseyes marketplace.

Our work contributed to demonstrating the use of the Bonseyes marketplace in relevant environments (technology readiness level TRL6). This implied that Bonseyes was not complete and qualified yet. For example, the monetisation of AI models and other assets was not fully implemented during the study. AI challenges could, however, be advertised, and in the third studied use case, a commercial organisation offered AI models to the market.

3 Method

3.1 Interview- and Observation-Based Multi-Case Study

We used an embedded multi-case study [14, 30] to research practitioners' perspectives on value creation and barriers that all used the same marketplace in three different real-world contexts and scenarios of AI systems development.

The study answered two research questions (RQ). *RQ1: how do AI systems practitioners perceive the value creation of the Bonseyes marketplace in support of multi-party collaborative AI systems development?* This research question allowed us to adopt the perspective of the end-users of the marketplace and understand how they perceive its value creation. Given that the Bonseyes marketplace was in the development stage, we kept the question open. We allowed the practitioners to share their opinions regarding value creation experienced in their marketplace trials and potential value creation with an eventually completed and mature marketplace. The answers to this question will be candidates for value propositions of the Bonseyes marketplace.

RQ2: what barriers do AI systems practitioners perceive blocking the adoption or value creation of the Bonseyes marketplace? This research question allowed us to understand experienced or potential reasons why they would not use the marketplace, even if its proposed values could be realised. The answer to this question will be a basis for designing barrier-mitigating features in the Bonseyes marketplace, adapting the supported AI systems development processes, and defining terms and conditions for using the marketplace.

We selected the cases based on a maximum variation sampling. The chosen collaborations differ in their aims and the involvement of academic vs. industrial as well as in large-scale and small organisations. Also, we explored the different scenarios of how to engage in multi-party collaborations, including challenges advertised as a competition for data scientists, procurement of data science services, and advertisement of AI models as a product. For reasons of the marketplace still being under development, the participants had to be sufficiently motivated to explore multi-party collaboration, be open to experimentation, and be interested in developing AI with deep neural networks.

We collected data in 3 workshops and 8 interviews between December 2019 and February 2020: observations, interview data, and assets created by the participants. For the observation, we decided to use Focus Group workshops [31]. We had one round of 3 workshops, one for each case. During the workshops, we first explained the scope of our research and asserted the anonymity of the personal data. Then, the marketplace development team presented the marketplace and the procedure for its use. In the end, the collaboration parties had the opportunity to experience the marketplace by trying it out, and we also discussed how the particular cases would be executed. The participants then worked on the cases independently from the researchers but received support from the Bonseyes marketplace developers whenever they needed it through e-mails and chats. Additionally, we had two rounds of additional talks with the first two cases since these were the more complex collaboration cases, where we checked the execution status, discussed mostly technical issues with the participants and the marketplace developers, and did some planning for further steps in the cases.

After utilising the Bonseyes marketplace by the parties and their work on the cases, we conducted 3 rounds of semi-structured interviews [32], 8 in total. Three interviews were conducted for cases CA and CB, and two were conducted for case CC since the case was shorter and did not have an opposite collaboration party. The interview questions matured, and their number increased between the rounds. They were given to the participants before the interviews. The second interview with case CC was during the third round of questions for cases CA and CB, so case CC got the same mature questions as the other two cases. Additionally, we had some shorter sessions between the first author and some of the case participants, as well as e-mail exchanges and chats to clarify some answers to the questions.

For conventional content analysis of the collected empirical data [15], we utilised the in-vivo, concept and pattern coding techniques described in the coding manual of Saldaña [33]. We spreadsheeted the codes and, where possible, linked them to the research questions, e.g., the code being related to an incentive or a barrier for using the Bonseyes marketplace. Then, in discussions between the authors, we further aggregated the codes building categories and subcategories of factors for value creation and barriers. The higher categories are the factors we report on in the Results and Analyses section.

3.2 Threats to Validity

Key threats to case study validity include construct, internal, and external validity and reliability [14, 30]. We outline how these apply to our study, mitigating measures, and the remaining threats.

Construct validity concerns the quality of measures used to collect data—specifically, whether we observed subjects truly collaborating in AI development through the Bonseyes marketplace and whether interview responses reflected this perspective. To mitigate these concerns, participants used the marketplace over time, with interviews spaced throughout. This enabled us to connect discussions to the assets they exchanged (see Fig. 1). The remaining threats were the marketplace's limited maturity, affecting participants' collaboration ease.

Internal validity concerns factors that may have skewed participants' opinions, such as their learning curve for collaborative AI development or challenges with marketplace usability. To mitigate these concerns, participants first practised using the MNIST challenge, then used the marketplace in their actual AI projects with ongoing assistance. While this reduced internal validity threats, marketplace usability limitations still influenced participants' opinions somewhat.

External validity concerns whether the study's findings can be generalised. We enhanced generalisability by selecting diverse contexts and marketplace usage scenarios, covering academia, industry, large and small organisations, and project-based and product-focused collaborations. Future research should replicate the study with other marketplaces and involve people and organisations in other industries and geographical regions.

Reliability concerns the rigour of study execution and analysis of results. To address reliability threats, both researchers collaborated throughout the study and documented the chain of evidence linking data to conclusions.

4 Results and Analysis

4.1 Overview of Cases

The three cases covered different approaches to using a marketplace for multi-party collaboration and were embedded in different contexts. Case CA concerned a researcher working with another remote researcher in a Kaggle-like collaboration for the science-driven development of an innovative AI system. Case CB concerned a large-case industrial developer of AI-based products working together with a small specialist enterprise acting as a science service provider in data science. Case CC concerned a small business offering AI components as a product to a wider market of AI systems developers. The marketplace was not a party in the collaboration but offered the infrastructure for enabling collaboration.

Case CA: University Collaboration Two research institutions wanted to collaborate on the development of an AI system able to recognise surgical instruments in laparoscopic images. The AI system was intended to be integrated into a Raspberry Pi-based system for real-time recognition of how far surgery has progressed. One collaborating party, a medical researcher working in a university hospital in Germany, was in the customer role and was willing to share surgery video sequences to obtain the AI system. The other party, an AI researcher working in an AI university institute in Spain, was in the developer role and wanted to use the video sequences to train an AI model able to detect surgical instruments in the video frames and embed that model in the AI solution to be shared with the medical researcher.

Case CB: Outsourcing of Data Science. Two commercial organisations wanted to collaborate on developing two AI systems: one for detecting pedestrians in street scenes and one for assessing a car driver's drowsiness. The AI systems were intended to be deployed into an AMV ALPHA Board-based integrated system for car safety. One collaborating party, a tier-1 automotive systems developer working for an automotive supplier in Germany, was in the customer role and willing to share relevant video sequences to obtain the AI components. A more senior automotive engineer working as an algorithm developer in computer vision supported the systems developer. Still, both used the same Ubuntu 18 workstation and user account for the Bonseyes marketplace-related work. The other party, a team of two AI software engineers working for a service provider for AI systems development located in Switzerland, was in the developer role and wanted to use the video sequences to train AI models able to solve the two AI challenges.

Case CC: AI Models as Products. A small business wanted to offer AI components to the market. The party was the product unit of a service provider for AI systems development located in Switzerland. It wanted to explore using the Bonseyes marketplace for advertising, selling, and lifecycle management of AI components as a software product for body posture recognition targeting primarily automotive contexts. The product unit was represented in the use case by an AI software engineer working as a release manager for the unit's software products.

4.2   RQ1: Value Creation with the Marketplace

When asked about the marketplace's benefits, the participants elaborated on their experiences during the use cases and the broader perspective of using the marketplace in the future. In the following, we summarise the value creation factors generated using the Bonseyes marketplace: increased work efficiency, trust for multi-party collaboration, universal reuse of assets, customer self-service and maintained work flexibility.

Work Efficiency. The participants would use the marketplace to develop proof of concepts and integrate them across platforms efficiently: *"[...] for instance, a new student project you can try out, see if it works. [...] it is about easy and efficient working"* (CA). They would share and source assets, making them available for peers in other organisations, which is useful specifically for such organisations lacking development resources: *"[...] you can search for existing AI assets, deploy them directly on a target device. This is useful for smaller companies lacking resources to develop their own AI assets"* (CB). Also, centralised sharing would increase visibility and referencing possibilities and reduce communication efforts: *"offer AI products more efficiently – reduced communication effort, multiple operations done by the tools"* (CC).

Trust. Participants emphasised the importance of collaborating and building trust with peers. They found it useful to operate AI components without disclosing data, ensuring privacy and protection of intellectual property (IP): *"My data is never leaving the premises, so it would be a kind of like inhouse development"* (CA). For medical research, privacy and IP protection are crucial, especially when working with private companies, costing a lot of effort until reaching an agreement on how data is protected and utilised: *"Our legal department negotiates a lot with companies on data exchange"* (CA). In CB, distributing challenges only to selected suppliers was valued to protect internal information: *"For sensitive challenges, a distribution to selected suppliers under an NDA would be desired"* (CB). Trust is also built by allowing AI customers to benchmark components on their data, with control over visibility and access: *"I can prove optimisation with a large or small data set"* (CA).

Reuse. CB and CC highlighted the ability to access, use, and reuse assets across organisations: *"One asset might be used by different customers"* (CB). The participants specifically appreciated that the marketplace tools enable efficient integration of AI components on various platforms: *"Easy to upload the AI app to different platforms"* (CC). The marketplace's procedures, such as challenge definitions and reusable assets like datasets, support AI training and benchmarking: *"I can offer a challenge to my students by giving them the data so that they can train their models"* (CA).

Self-service. Participants appreciated acquiring assets from the marketplace without interacting with suppliers, increasing flexibility and efficiency: *"It enables self-service for our customers, and it does not cost us anything"* (CB). Publishing challenges would allow to recruit multiple parties and to compare results: *"[We can be] selling data,* *exchanging data, not only private data but also new datasets [...], maybe selling AI apps and the AI models to other schools to compare the results"* (CA). Browsing through challenges and AI components was also appreciated since it simplified finding needed assets. The release manager noted the benefits of a centralised marketplace for sharing AI apps and improving visibility (CC).

Flexibility. The benefits include performing tasks incrementally with flexibility for involving different partners at each step. *"It depends on how easy it is to define your data tools and evaluation tools. But then, of course, if you post your challenge and get some assets back. That's probably quite easy."* (CA). Another advantage is the quick and easy use of platform tools, which allows for deployment across different platforms like Raspberry Pi4 or NVIDIA Jetson Xavier: *"It is easier to share, you can collaborate, you can deploy really easily on different platforms"* (CA). *"The platform tools make it easy to upload the AI app to different platforms"* (CC).

4.3 RQ2: Barriers to the Use of the Marketplace

Several barriers could block the adoption of the Bonseyes marketplace or the creation of value with it. They relate to the marketplace's maturity, its alignment with the users' contexts, and the significance of the user community.

Maturity. The marketplace's still limited technical maturity implied technical issues, making it hard to use. For instance, the front-end was criticised for being unreliable, especially in the early interviews: *"most front-end functionalities do not work"* (CB). The repository also faced criticism: *"problem: after uploading to GitHub, error when publishing"* (CA). *"It could be simpler by removing the need to use GitLab"* (CC). Also, the integration of the secure premise into the marketplace was insufficient: *"The secure premise should be [fully] implemented"* (CB). Participants needed support from the marketplace developers. For example, when learning how to specify or adapt a challenge: *"To do the first challenge from scratch, you will definitely need some kind of support."* (CB). Early documentation lacked clarity, particularly around local deployment, troubleshooting, and FAQs. *"The documentation is not very straightforward"* (CA). *"No troubleshooting of common errors"* (CB). *"FAQs section [missing]"* (CC). Though improved later, more work remained. Examples provided were incomplete and not directly usable, leaving participants wanting more relevant, out-of-the-box solutions: *"if you have like one or two examples per problem, where you can basically look up and then adapt to your problem"* (CA).

Intuitiveness and Learning. User interaction with the marketplace was not always intuitive. For example, participants struggled initially to find their challenges: *"So I am here, what should I do?"* (CA). Completing the first project required significant time to understand the marketplace tools. *"You have to understand how it is done in the marketplace, but then you can reuse your knowledge for another application or challenge"* (CA).

Adaptability. There was a need to adapt a content mask: *"We would like to add 'Proof of Concept' to the question about AI component maturity. Also, the contact information* *should be condensed. Name, Email, and Company should be enough"* (CB). Additionally, some effort is required to work with the marketplace, adding overhead compared to how participants developed their AI systems without the marketplace: *"The YML files require a good understanding, and they have to be set up. This was not necessary before"* (CB).

Compatibility. The marketplace is changing AI development, requiring organisations to adapt their internal processes. *"We have to adapt our internal processes to the way the marketplace is designed [...] to be compatible with its standards and formats"* (CB). Technical incompatibility issues were reported, e.g., missing ONNX support, that affected interoperability: *"if you restrict people to use only one machine learning framework, then you lose a huge part of the community"* (CA). Also, older Linux versions, some platforms, and some hardware lacked support. For example, drowsiness detection in CB could not run because the camera was not supported on the chosen board.

Scope. The marketplace has been criticised for not addressing a major part of AI development: cleaning and preparing data for training. This may hinder its adaption: *"[parties might not] share their data or create a challenge because they have to do 80% of the work before they can even upload a challenge"* (CB).

User Scenarios. The marketplace did not support all AI use cases of the participating organisations. When asked about future use, a participant responded: *"Yes, with partners"* (CA) or *"[...] for deep learning research, so to say, rather not, but now just [for] something old and proven, proof of concept so to say: ok that works, that's what it is good for!"* (CA). The automotive engineer of CB noted that the marketplace is helpful for those unfamiliar with machine learning, but the way the marketplace encoded the AI challenge may be too elaborate: *"A shorter form would be helpful"* (CB).

Hardware Support. The marketplace targeted AI applications for embedded devices based on specific hardware, such as the AMV ALPHA Board. However, the participants of CB faced an issue: the camera they used was not supported on the chosen platform. Also, the operation of the secure premise required multiple machines. These requirements could cause issues if the necessary hardware were unavailable. In one case, a non-professional server failed overnight, preventing access to the secure premise the next day.

Compliance. The marketplace could not manage non-disclosure agreements (NDAs), which would be necessary for projects beyond proof of concepts: *"For large projects, there needs to be an NDA so that you can collaborate"* (CB). CB suggested linking or uploading NDAs to the marketplace. Also, the automotive engineer of CB wanted more control over licences: *"If I can create and provide a restriction or licence myself, I have much greater confidence in it"* (CB).

Long-Term Collaboration Support. Since the marketplace allows the parties to work autonomously, this can also lead to an increased perceived distance between them: *"In a multi-party project, we lose different ways of feedback. We just get the benchmark results, which will be not sufficient"* (CB).

Size of User Community. The marketplace still needed more users. CA compared it to TensorFlow: *"They did it right there, with a lot of tutorials and a lot of example codes. The community was growing... took off"* (CA).

Data Access Constraints. Access to data involved a trade-off when using the secure premise, which does not give visibility to the data and only allows certain operations to be executed on the data: *"If you don't have all the data, the model sucks. If I give you all the data, then I give you all the data [...]. It is crucial now how to perform the training via the secure premise"* (CA).

Cybersecurity. Some security issues were reported, as the marketplace's technical security requirements were not fully implemented. It required full access to participants' GitLab accounts, raising concerns about the visibility of other projects in their accounts. Security, in general, was important for participants. Here is an example quote of a participant questioning the marketplace developer wanting to ensure that challenges are secured: *"You would upload your sample data, everything in there[challenge package]. But in a packed and secured way? So you can only open or access it [the challenge] if you are assigned to it?"* (CA). Additionally, corporate firewalls and corporate infrastructure restrictions limited access, forcing participants to find workarounds or work from home.

Pricing. The cost of assets could hinder their use. Although prices weren't set and participants didn't pay, one noted that future use *"depends on the actual cost"* (CA).

5 Discussion

5.1 Contribution

We empirically studied the perception of a marketplace in terms of value creation and barriers to multi-party collaborative AI development. The specific marketplace advertised AI challenges and applications and supported collaboration with a secure virtual premise of safeguarding machine learning from the threat of data theft.

We found that the ability to exchange assets and use marketplace tools in data processing pipelines contributes to the work efficiency of AI systems development. Reusing assets across organisations and flexibility in working in parallel enabled such efficiency. Self-service exploration of assets promoted independence and freed resources spent on discovering and communicating requirements. Asset protection eased collaboration and contributed to trust.

We identified several barriers to value creation in the marketplace. Beyond issues of maturity, such as incomplete documentation, tutorials, and bugs, factors like learning time, intuitiveness, support, pricing, community size, legal concerns, and internal technical restrictions affected the willingness to adopt the Bonseyes marketplace. Incompatibility with existing AI development processes limited its use cases, and lack of support for key tasks like data labelling, cleaning, and preparation further restricted its application. Privacy, asset protection, and access control concerns must also be addressed.

5.2 Implications for Multi-party Collaboration in AI Systems Development

Our identified benefits of using Bonseyes align well with the literature, showing that collaboration in AI enhances work efficiency [18–21]. The Bonseyes marketplace facilitated asset exchange and tool use in AI pipelines, such as the LPDNN (Low Power Deep Neural Network) for embedded devices. Our results suggest that specialisation for diverse AI pipelines beyond deep neural networks [34, 35] and coverage of the complete pipelines, including data collection, model training, and deployment on constrained platforms, will likely increase visibility and efficiency.

Organisations must invest time in adapting their processes to benefit from a marketplace. If they do so, they may benefit from faster development, especially for developing proof of concepts and finding suitable assets. Digital datasheets [36] can be important in specifying assets to be procured or advertised. Suppliers may benefit from promotion and reduced communication needs due to the self-service model offered by a marketplace. There are also opportunities for suppliers to offer data collection and annotation tools, a need not met at the time of the study.

To collaborate effectively, organisations must be willing to open internal infrastructures or invest in external capacity. Compatibility requires uniform interfaces and packaging of assets [37]. Decentralised architecture for marketplaces may limit the organisation's openness to specifically selected partners [38, 39]. Finally, marketing and support resources and pricing strategies [40] are essential for challenge creators and asset suppliers to grow the community of peers, customers, and suppliers.

5.3 Implications for Marketplace Developers

To ensure success, future AI marketplaces must offer sufficient documentation, tutorials, and personal developer support. The support for AI assets should cover the entire value chain, from data collection to model deployment, and their descriptions should balance detail and ease of input for users. Marketplaces must support iterative work and offer flexibility in where parts of the AI pipeline are executed. They should support commonly used AI development frameworks and, where applicable, technical standards, offer templates for contracts and related legal documents and ensure asset and licence compatibility.

Asset compatibility, protection mechanisms, and legal agreement temples are crucial for adopting an AI marketplace. An AI marketplace should also aim to increase end-user automation, but trade-offs between flexibility and use case coverage must be considered. Automation should consider comprehensive asset lifecycle management, versioning and tracking of deployments, and verifiable benchmarking, essential for trust-building. The automation should be implemented with an intuitive design for end-users and robust IP protection and security features.

When launching the marketplace, efforts should focus on advertising, community growth, and long-term relationship management through forums, events, and reward systems. Finally, helping the marketplace users identify and explore sustainable monetisation models is key, with more research on pricing for different assets still needed.

6 Summary and Conclusions

We studied AI developers' and data scientists' views on the value creation of a marketplace supporting three cases of multi-party collaborative AI systems development: university collaboration, a large company outsourcing data science, and a small company offering AI models as products. The marketplace facilitated advertising AI challenges and AI models and supported multi-party collaboration with secure data and AI model protection. Our work contributed to developing the Bonseyes marketplace, which led to the European BonsAPPs and dAIEDGE projects.

Our results show that the marketplace contributes to value creation in AI systems development through improved efficiency, streamlined communication, trust in collaboration, asset reuse, self-service, and flexibility. Adoption barriers include a lack of documentation, technical issues, low intuitiveness, learning curve, support dependency, compatibility issues, limited scope, legal constraints, small user base, security, and pricing. Collaborative AI development requires adapting assets to specific machine learning pipelines, with organisations needing to invest in expertise and adjust processes.

Acknowledgements. This work has received funding from the European Union's Horizon 2020 research and innovation programme under grant agreement No 732204 (Bonseyes) and from the Swiss State Secretariat for Education, Research and Innovation (SERI) under contract number 16.0159. The opinions expressed and arguments employed herein do not necessarily reflect the official views of these funding bodies.

References

1. Chui, M., Hazan, E.R., et al.: The Economic Potential of Generative AI - The Next Productivity Frontier. McKinsey&Company, New York (2023)
2. Cockburn, I.M., Henderson, R., Stern, S.: The impact of artificial intelligence on innovation (No. 24449). National bureau of economic research (2018)
3. Amershi, S., Begel, A.B., et al.: Software engineering for machine learning: a case study. In: 2019 IEEE/ACM 41st International Conference on Software Engineering: Software Engineering in Practice (ICSE-SEIP), pp. 291–300 (2019)
4. Baylor, D., Breck, E., Cheng, H.-T., et al.: TFX: a tensorflow-based production-scale machine learning platform. In: KDD '17: Proceedings of the 23rd ACM SIGKDD International Conference on Knowledge Discovery and Data Mining, pp. 1387–1395 (2017)
5. Domingos, P.: A few useful things to know about machine learning. Commun. ACM **55**(10), 78–87 (2012)
6. Llewellynn, T., Fernández-Carrobles, M.M.D., et al.: BONSEYES: Platform for Open Development of Systems of Artificial Intelligence: Invited paper. CF'17: Proceedings of the Computing Frontiers Conference, pp. 299–304 (2017)
7. Tan, L.: A Survey of NLP Annotation Platforms (2020). https://github.com/alvations/annotate-questionnaire
8. Shao, Z., Yuan, S., Wang, Y.: Institutional collaboration and competition in artificial intelligence. IEEE Access. **8**, 69734–69741 (2020)
9. Hu, H., Wang, D., Deng, S.: Global collaboration in artificial intelligence: bibliometrics and network analysis from 1985 to 2019. J. Data Inf. Sci. **5**(4), 86–115 (2020)

10. Tarun, G., Husain, S., Hussein Al-Saidi, I., Vats, S., Raad Ali, R., Qusay Jawad, A.: Analysing technical and economic dimensions using AI Techniques. In : 4th International Conference on Advance Computing and Innovative Technologies in Engineering (ICACITE). Greater Noida, India (2024)

11. Panchal, D., Verma, P., Baran, I., Hsiung, T., Musgrove, D., Lu, D.: Reusable MLOps: reusable deployment, reusable infrastructure and hot-swappable AI models and services. In: 10th International Conference on Smart Computing and Communication (ICSCC). Bali, Indonesia (2024)

12. Mehri, V.A., Ilie, D., Tutschku, K.: Designing a secure IoT system architecture from a virtual premise for a collaborative AI lab. In : Proceedings of 2019 Workshop on Decentralized IoT Systems and Security (DISS), San Diego, CA, USA (2019)

13. McMahan, H.B., Moore, E.R., et al.: Communication-efficient learning of deep networks from decentralized data (2017). Preprint arXiv:1602.05629v3 [Cs.LG]

14. Yin, R.K.: Case Study Research and Applications: Design and Methods (6th ed.). Sage Publications, Inc., Thousand Oaks (2018)

15. Hsieh, H.-F., Shannon, S.: Three approaches to qualitative content analysis. Qual. Health Res. **15**(9), 1277–1288 (2005)

16. Hobbs, R.W.: Leadership through collaboration. AIArchitect **3**(11) (1996)

17. Priego-Roche, L.M., Front, A., Rieu, D.: A framework for virtual organization requirements. Requirements Eng. **21**(4), 439–460 (2016)

18. Bogdanova, A., Attoh-Okine, N., Sakurai, T.: Risk and advantages of federated learning for health care data collaboration. ASCE-ASME J. Risk Uncertainty Eng. Syst. Part A: Civ. Eng. **6**(3), 04020031–1–6 (2020)

19. Imakura, A., Sakurai, T.: Data collaboration analysis framework using centralization of individual intermediate representations for distributed data sets. ASCE-ASME J. Risk Uncertainty Eng. Syst. Part A: Civ. Eng. **6**(2), 04020018–1–8 (2020)

20. Konečný, J., McMahan, H.B., Yu, F.X., et al.: Federated Learning: Strategies for Improving Communication Efficiency (2017). Preprint arXiv:1610.05492v2

21. Sheller, M.J., Edwards, B., Reina, G.A., et al.: Federated learning in medicine: facilitating multi-institutional collaborations without sharing patient data. Sci. Rep. **10**(1), 12598 (2020)

22. Jaakkola, H., Henno, J., Thalheim, B., Makela, J.: Collaboration, distribution and culture—challenges for communication. In: 38th International Convention on Information and Communication Technology, Electronics and Microelectronics (MIPRO), pp. 657–664 (2015)

23. Deelman, E., Chervenak, A.: Data management challenges of data-intensive scientific workflows. In: 2008 Eighth IEEE International Symposium on Cluster Computing and the Grid (CCGRID), pp. 687–692 (2008)

24. Maksimov, Y.V., Fricker, S.A., Tutschku, K.: Artifact compatibility for enabling collaboration in the artificial intelligence ecosystem. In: International Conference on Software Business (ICSOB 2018), pp. 56–71 (2018)

25. Freire, J., Silva, C.T., Callahan, S.P., Santos, E., Scheidegger, C.E., Vo, H.T.: Managing rapidly-evolving scientific workflows. In: Moreau, L., Foster, I. (eds.), Provenance and Annotation of Data, vol. 4145, pp. 10–18. Springer, Berlin, Heidelberg (2006)

26. Moreau, L., Ludäscher, B., Altintas, I., Barga, R.S., et al.: Special issue: the first provenance challenge. Concurr. Comput. Pract. Exp. **20**(5), 409–418 (2008)

27. Moreau, L., Clifford, B., Freire, J., et al.: The Open Provenance Model core specification (v1.1). Futur. Gener. Comput. Syst, **27**(6), 743–756 (2011)

28. Kumar, A., Finley, B., Braud, T., Tarkoma, S., Hui, P.: Sketching an AI marketplace: tech, economic, and regulatory aspects. IEEE Access **9**, 13761–13774 (2021)

29. Gordijn, J., Yu, E., van der Raadt, B.: E-service design using i* and e3value modeling. IEEE Softw. **23**(3), 26–33 (2006)

30. Runeson, P., Höst, M.: Guidelines for conducting and reporting case study research in software engineering. Empir. Softw. Eng. **14**(2), 131–164 (2009)
31. Kontio, J., Lehtola, L., Bragge, J.: Using the focus group method in software engineering: obtaining practitioner and user experiences. In: Proceedings of 2004 International Symposium on Empirical Software Engineering, 2004. ISESE '04, pp. 271–280 (2004)
32. Hove, S.E., Anda, B.: Experiences from conducting semi-structured interviews in empirical software engineering research. In: 11th IEEE International Software Metrics Symposium (METRICS'05), p. 23 (2005)
33. Saldaña, J.: The Coding Manual for Qualitative Researchers (3rd ed.). Sage Publications, Ltd., Thousand Oaks (2016)
34. de Prado, M., Denna, M., Benini, L., Pazos, N.: QUENN: QUantization engine for low-power neural networks. In: CF'18: Proceedings of the 15th ACM International Conference on Computing Frontiers, pp, 36–44 (2018)
35. Moor, L., Bitter, L., de Prado, M., Pazos, N., Ouerhani, N.: IoT meets distributed AI - deployment scenarios of Bonseyes AI applications on FIWARE. In: 2019 IEEE 38th International Performance Computing and Communications Conference (IPCCC) (2019)
36. Masiero, S., Qosaj, J., Cutrona, V.: Digital datasheet model: enhancing the value of AI digital platforms. Procedia Comput. Sci. **232**, 149–158 (2024)
37. Riedlinger, M., Bernijazov, R., Hanke, F.: AI Marketplace: serving environment for AI solutions using kubernetes. 13th International Conference on Cloud Computing and Services Science (CLOSER 2023). Prague, Czech Republic (2023)
38. Yazdaninejad, H., Rajarajan, M., Krol, M.: A Blockchain-enabled and transparent evaluation of ml models in the decentralised marketplace. In: IEEE International Conference on Blockchain (Blockchain 2024). Copenhagen, Denmark (2024)
39. Dixit, A., Singh, A., Rahulamathavan, Y., Rajarajan, M.: FAST DATA: a fair, secure, and trusted decentralized IIoT data marketplace enabled by blockchain. IEEE Internet Things J. **10**(4), 2934–2944 (2024)
40. Fricker, S.A., Maksimov, Y.V.: Pricing of data products in data marketplaces. In: Ojala, A., Holmström Olsson, H., Werder, K. (eds.), Software Business, vol. 304, pp. 49–66. Springer, Cham (2017)

Data-Limited Continuous Experimentation (dlCE): A Literature Review

Stanislav Chren[1](✉)[iD], Fabian Fagerholm[1][iD], Elizabeth Bjarnason[2][iD],
Johan Linåker[2][iD], Saima Rafi[3][iD], Bettina Lehtelä[1][iD], Per Runeson[2][iD],
and Marjo Kauppinen[1][iD]

[1] Aalto University, Espoo, Finland
{stanislav.chren,fabian.fagerholm,bettina.lehtela,
marjo.kauppinen}@aalto.fi
[2] Lund University, Lund, Sweden
{elizabeth.bjarnason,johan.linaker,per.runeson}@cs.lth.se
[3] Edinburgh Napier University, Edinburgh, United Kingdom
s.rafi@napier.ac.uk

Abstract. Continuous experimentation (CE) is a software development approach where product decisions are data-driven. Large global internet-facing companies such as Microsoft, Google, and Facebook apply the practice by leveraging their massive user bases to obtain high statistical significance in experimentation results. However, companies with smaller user bases, such as small- and medium-sized enterprises (SMEs) and early-stage software startups, struggle to adopt CE due to limitations in user data. Our goal is to increase understanding of situations in CE where data limitations occur, as observed in the research literature. We investigate data limitations and challenges related to them, including their characteristics, and solutions and practices that may address these. We conducted a rapid review of CE papers from a previous systematic literature review, and analysed these to identify scenarios that exhibit data limitations in CE. We present a framework that illustrates different dimensions of data-limited CE (DLC) and connects scenarios to challenges and their potential future solutions. Most challenges and potential solutions that we found are related to the amount of data. We also note examples of other limitations related to, e.g., evaluation metrics, that provide interesting avenues for further research.

Keywords: Continuous experimentation · Software engineering · User data

1 Introduction

Continuous experimentation (CE) is an established industrial practice where product decisions are based on user behaviour data rather than on company-internal guesswork [14,24]. The practice is commonly applied for consumer products and services provided by large internet-facing companies such as Microsoft,

E. Papatheocharous et al. (Eds.): ICSOB 2024, LNBIP 539, pp. 324–339, 2025.
https://doi.org/10.1007/978-3-031-85849-9_26

Google, Netflix, eCommerce applications but has also been used in other domains such as cyberphysical systems [16,17]. Through field experiments, the development is steered towards problem-solution fit and improved user satisfaction, using quantitative metrics based on very large volumes of user data [24,34]. In contrast, many other product development companies struggle to obtain statistically significant CE results due to data limitations.

While the practice of CE is well-established for large, mature internet-facing companies with ample access to large volumes of quantitative user data, there are challenges when applying CE in other contexts. Examples of such contexts include development of internal tools with (only) hundreds of users [32]; software in business-to-business (B2B) settings [40]; embedded software products with resource-constrained hardware and longer development cycles [16,18]; AI-based applications where AI models need to be matched to user and business level values [29]; and initial product versions in software startups with small user bases and wide variations in competence regarding CE [28]. Many of these challenges boil down to obtaining sufficiently powerful and relevant metrics to support timely decisions, and thus relate to the *volume* and *type* of user data available; an area for which there is very little research.

Some companies may apply CE despite having limited user data. We refer to such situations as data-limited CE (dlCE). The nature of these limitations can vary. In this paper, we use a literature review inspired by the rapid review [5] approach to produce a framework for characterising dlCE scenarios, their contextual factors, challenges, and potential solutions to guide further research on the subject. We contribute an understanding of dlCE contexts, exploring the dimensions of *user data volumes, data types*, i.e. qualitative and quantitative, and *product and business maturity*.

2   Continuous Experimentation in Software Engineering

Continuous Experimentation (CE) has become a well-established practice in the software industry and is well documented in the scientific literature [3,14,18]. By systematically running product feature experiments, companies applying CE aim at fast feedback acquisition. The goal is to reduce the risk of pursuing unprofitable directions in product development and to increase the likelihood of providing products that satisfy the needs and expectations of their end users.

CE is a practice within the area of Continuous Software Engineering [15]. Several models of how to perform CE have been proposed, e.g. HYPEX [31] and RIGHT [14]. The core of these models is to first formulate hypotheses about product features, then deploy variants of the software to users, collect usage data, followed by analysis of the experiment results and making decisions based on the outcome. These decisions can be to fully implement a new feature tested in the experiment, to discontinue a previously implemented feature, or to keep the current product version as it is. The decisions can also include designing further (follow-up) experiments.

Existing literature provides some ideas but no definitive solutions for how to deal with limited data in CE. A potential avenue is to consider improvements in statistical analysis. For instance, metrics with higher sensitivity [4] can make more effective use of available data. Another approach to deal with data limitations is to draw on qualitative strategies for feedback acquisition [39], if the automatically collected (quantitative) data is insufficient.

However, as there are no definite solutions so far, we search for new ways of dealing with data limitations in dlCE. The results are expected to expand the range of companies that can utilise CE, including organisations who are subject to different forms of data limitations.

There have been earlier literature studies investigating aspects of CE. A previous review by Auer et al. [3] focused on main steps in the experimentation process, solutions are used in these steps, and on reported challenges with and benefits from CE. It was based on two previous mapping studies by Auer et al. [2] and Ros et al. [35], in which the authors investigated topics such as by whom, how, with what topical focus, and in which domains CE has been researched. A more recent literature study by Erthal et al. [13] in turn, is more concerned with expressions and definitions, processes and experiment approaches used when describing CE. These previous literature reviews are different from our study, since we focus specifically on data limitations in the context of CE.

3   Method

The focus of this study is to gain a better understanding of situations in which data limitations occur in CE. We initially developed dlCE scenarios in a brainstorming session, followed by a literature review to expand the scenarios into a framework with dlCE dimensions. We address the following research questions:

RQ1: In which scenarios do data limitations occur when applying CE?
RQ2: What contextual and experiment-related factors occur in these scenarios?
RQ3: What challenges and potential solutions related to dlCE exist?

The first research question aims to explore and learn about the state of the practice regarding the problem of dlCE by identifying scenarios which represent contexts where this occurs. The second question aims to identify and describe dlCE scenarios in more detail. Finally, the third question aims to collect information on challenges and corresponding solutions that have been proposed in the literature.

3.1   Scenario Creation

At a brainstorming session, the first three authors identified an initial set of dlCE scenarios based on previous knowledge of CE. We discussed previous studies, conducted by ourselves and by others, where data limitations had come up although they had not necessarily been the focus of the studies. We listed these observations and defined a set of dlCE scenarios to capture them. Later, we also used our analysis of the literature to refine the scenarios.

3.2   Literature Review Approach and Paper Selection

Our literature review is inspired by the rapid review (RR) approach [5], with some adaptations. Rapid reviews are lightweight and focus on supporting practitioners with research evidence in a timely manner, and are recommended to be conducted in collaboration with practitioners in a practical context. They typically limit the search and analysis to focused issues [20]. Since we are currently interested in structuring specific knowledge of dlCE through a wide range of cases, we chose not to engage directly with practitioners in any particular context at this time. Instead, we examined reports from real-life cases, which we believe reveal important practical concerns about dlCE. Thus, we omit the condensed practitioner reporting of RRs but retain the tight focus and descriptive summarisation and categorisation that characterises RR results.

We used the literature review by Auer et al. [3] as a foundation for the paper selection, since this is the most recent and comprehensive summary of the state-of-the-art in the CE domain. We conducted a full-text analysis of the starting set of 160 papers. The inclusion and exclusion of each paper was proposed by two authors. In case of disagreement, a third author analysed the paper, and the final decision was made after discussion. For a paper to be included, it had to contain a description of at least one software product experimentation case. Additionally, it had to be relevant to dlCE by mentioning dlCE scenarios, challenges, or solution methods. In total, 23 papers were included. We provide a list of all papers as supplementary material [6].

3.3   Data Extraction and Analysis

We extracted information about domain, maturity, user base, type of product change, and metrics from each paper. We also extracted information relevant to dlCE. For each paper, one author performed the extraction and another author validated it. Discrepancies were resolved through discussion.

We matched the information in the papers with our dlCE scenarios to see where they occurred. We also analysed the cases reported in the papers to see how product domains (P), types of changes (C), and types of metrics (M) occurred together with different scenarios. Finally, we analysed the challenges reported in the papers and possible proposed solutions. The extracted data is available in the supplementary material [6].

4   Characterising Data-Limited CE (dlCE)

Our framework for dlCE consists of three parts that correspond to our research questions. The first part is a set of dlCE scenarios that illustrate contexts in which data limitations may affect CE practices. The second part is a taxonomy that can be used to describe the context and characteristics of these dlCE scenarios. Finally, the third part is a categorisation of dlCE challenges and potential solutions.

4.1   Scenarios for dlCE (RQ1)

We defined nine initial scenarios (S0-S9) based on our experience of CE companies [34,40,41]. These scenarios were derived from our expert knowledge and also observed in our (rapid) literature review. Additionally, based on the literature review, we identified one extra scenario (S9), resulting in a total of ten scenarios. Each scenario represents a distinct contextual circumstance in which dlCE problems can occur. Moreover, for each scenario, we have identified experimentation cases exposing the scenario. The scenarios and the number of cases found for each are shown in Table 1.

Table 1. Scenarios (S0-S9) for dlCE and the number of papers and cases describing each scenarios.

ID	Scenario name	Papers	Cases
S0	Insufficient amounts of user data for statistically significant results	15	18
S1	Parts of a system with insufficient user traffic	7	8
S2	System and its environment is too big for experimentation	3	22
S3	The cost of experimentation for a very large system is too high	1	1
S4	Long product cycles lead to metric data not being available for timely product design decisions	5	6
S5	Limited resources prohibit running all interesting experiments	3	3
S6	Legislation, policy, or licensing constrains the collection or use of data	1	1
S7	Lack of usable metrics hinders experimentation	4	4
S8	Lack of data on long-term impact	2	4
S9	Incremental introduction of errors into data	1	2

S0: Insufficient Amounts of User Data for Statistically Significant Results. The product may be in an early development stage or the number of users is limited by the nature of the product [16,18,28,32]. This baseline scenario represents the most obvious case of data limitations impacting CE. However, data may also be limited in several other ways, as the other scenarios illustrate.

S1: Parts of a System with Insufficient User Traffic. Even in systems with large amounts of user interaction, some parts may be used less, and thus result in lower amounts of user traffic [10,12]. Such limitations may lead to challenges in collecting enough data to gain statistically sound results within a reasonable time. Ros et al. note that the experimentation speed is thus reduced, affecting CE throughput and, thus, the efficiency of experimentation [34]. They suggest making power calculations for the number of data points required for significant results and optimising the statistical test to the given situation.

S2: System and Its Environment is too Big for Experimentation. Software product experimentation requires precisely defined, testable hypotheses that pertain to well-bounded portions of a system and its environment. When user functionality crosses system or organisational boundaries, e.g., in large systems, it may not be possible to access the data needed for desired experiments and their associated metrics [40]. This also relates to challenges in defining metrics that capture product-market fit for products that offer complex user functionality [34], such as a platform where users can define business KPIs.

S3: The Cost of Experimentation for a Very Large System is too High. A large system typically calls for a larger team of developers requiring more resources for maintaining well-working collaboration. In such situations, experimentation brings in additional effort to maintain and deploy multiple variants of the system and coordinate simultaneous experimentation [24,25]. From the data perspective, the storage and maintenance of experiment data, including the technical, legal and ethical considerations, also result in additional effort and costs, limiting the feasibility of the experimentation.

S4: Long Product Cycles Lead to Metric Data not being Available for Timely Product Design Decisions. Some software products have significantly longer cycles, with new versions being developed even for several years before being released and used by end users. Part of the cycle length may be due to procedures that occur after development, such as certification or complicated upgrade procedures during deployment [18], and that are not worth performing for every small change. Regardless of the reason, when data is not available soon enough, product development decisions cannot rely primarily on experiments. Long cycle times affect the speed of CE and thus influences the throughput and efficiency of CE. Additional complications include the interference of other product changes making CE results invalid, and challenges making experimentation *continuous* when the cycle time is very long [34].

S5: Limited Resources Prohibit Running all Interesting Experiments. After learning the basics of CE, practitioners can relatively easily identify and define a large number of software product experiments. However, few companies have the resources to carry out more than a fraction of these. This is particularly true in smaller companies, including software startups where product development is already challenged by extreme resource constraints [39]. Running experiments in parallel can allow running more of them, but risks interference between experiments and requires more coordination resources. The problem is to obtain a sufficient amount of data for making the most important decisions with a limited number of experiments. This may be achieved through data-driven prioritisation that then increases the efficiency of the experimentation process, a practice applied by some but not all companies [34].

S6: Legislation, Policy, or Licensing Constrains the Collection or Use of Data. Data cannot always be collected or used due to legal constraints. For example, the

GDPR places requirements on data collection within the EU. Similarly, company policy enacted to comply with certain laws, may place restrictions that influence how experimentation may be done [39], as can user license agreements. Finally, some data may be bought from third parties but come with licensing conditions that may limit or completely prohibit the use of data for certain purposes.

S7: Lack of Usable Metrics Hinders Experimentation. Ideas for experimentation should include assumptions about how a new or changed product feature affects some outcome, such as user behaviour. However, it is not always straightforward to operationalise the outcome as a usable metric. As a result, an experiment may never be run because no actionable metric can be found, or the experiment is run but the resulting data is of low quality because the chosen metric does not adequately represent the outcome that was part of the original assumption. Consequently, wrong conclusions may be drawn [8,39].

S8: Lack of Data on Long-term Impact. Experiments may indicate encouraging, but spurious, results. A novelty effect could, for instance, cause adoption numbers to increase in the short term, and the experiment would then indicate a positive outcome. In the long run, the effect may not persist. Monitoring the outcome to determine if the effect is lasting would require rerunning the experiment in some form over time, which might be costly. As a result, there will be a lack of data on the long-term impact of product changes [10].

S9: Incremental Introduction of Errors into Data. Not all experiments rely on A/B testing of product features. Instead, controlled experiments can focus on parameter optimisation, for example, Facebook's ranking system or randomised controlled benchmark to optimise server performance [26]. Optimisation experiments often rely on some form of machine learning (ML) methods. The performance of these methods depends on the quality of input data, which can come from many interconnected retrieval and ranking systems. Outcomes directly affected by ML methods can be significantly skewed, and if they are incrementally used as inputs for other experiments, more measurement errors and uncertainty are introduced in the data [26].

We extracted information relevant to dlCE from the literature and related them to each scenario. We then analysed them to identify what broad aspect of data limitations they represent. The resulting dlCE dimensions (*user data volume, data type,* and *product/business maturity*) and their relation to the scenarios are shown in Figure 1.

4.2   Taxonomy of Factors Characterising dlCE Scenarios (RQ2)

We categorised the experimentation cases from the literature according to (1) the domain of the product experimented on (a contextual factor), (2) the type of product changes that were evaluated by the experiments, and (3) the type of metrics that were collected within the experiment, the latter two factors describing characteristics of the experiment itself. This allows us to explore potential relationships between factors concerning the context and characteristics of an

	User data volume		Data type		Product/business maturity	
	Low	High	Quantitative	Qualitative	Early stages	Mature
S0	•		•	•	•	•
S1	•	•	•		•	•
S2	•	•	•			•
S3		•	•			•
S4	•	•	•		•	•
S5	•		•	•	•	
S6	•	•	•	•	•	•
S7	•	•	•	•	•	
S8	•		•	•	•	
S9	•	•	•			•

Fig. 1. Scenario classification according to dlCE dimensions.

experiment, and the scenarios that appear in each case. The occurrences of these are shown in Table 2.

The most common product **domain** found is *search engines* (D1), which is not surprising given CE forerunners like Google and Microsoft (Bing) with many articles on their experiments. However, it is less obvious that this domain would be connected to dlCE scenarios, given the huge amounts of end users available for experiments in this domain. Still, a quarter (26%) of these cases have *Insufficient amounts of user data* (S0), more than third (35%) report issues related to *System too big for experimentation* (S2), and other mentioned scenarios include *Parts of the system with insufficient traffic* (S1, 16%), *Long product cycles* (S4, 7%) and *Lack of data on long-term impact* (S8, 7%). This evidence indicates that dlCE can occur even in domains with access to very large amounts of user data.

Another observation is that the dlCE scenarios occurring in the literature differ across domains. The two scenarios with most cases reported across all domains are *Insufficient amount of data* (S0) and *System too big for experimentation* (S2), while others appear predominantly in specific domains. For example, *Legislation, policy, licensing* (S6) occurs only in one gaming case (D7), and *Lack of data on long-term impact* (S8) occurs only in business monitoring (D3) and search engines (D1). While the data may be too sparse to state with certainty what scenarios are most common in what domains, the evidence does indicate that the product domain, with the technical and circumstantial aspects that it brings, plays a role in the type of data limitations that occur in real-life cases.

The type of **change** (C1-C6) evaluated through CE varies for different scenarios and the evidence shows that it is important for understanding what data limitations can occur. Changes to product processes (C1) occur in our data when there is *Insufficient amount of user data* (S0, 38%), a *System too big for experimentation* (S2, 21%), and *Long product cycles lead to metrics being unavailable for timely decisions* (S4, 17%). *System is too big for experimentation* (S2) is the most common scenario when experimenting with changes to *algorithms* (C2, 46%) and *user interfaces* (C3, 50%). However, changes related to *source code* (C4), *degradation* (C5), and *infrastructure* (C6) – which are more focused or technical in nature – are less frequently reported with data limitations.

The type of **metrics** (M1-M6, see Table 2) used in the cases also varies for different scenarios. We observe that *usage metrics* (M1) most commonly appear

Table 2. Number of cases for factors (rows) and scenarios (columns). Factors are grouped according to product domain (D), change types (C) and metrics types (M). The percentages show the relative amount of cases for a factor, i.e., a row.

	S0	S1	S2	S3	S4	S5	S6	S7	S8	S9	# Scn.
Domains											
D1 Search engine	11 (26%)	7 (16%)	15 (35%)	1 (2%)	3 (7%)	1 (2%)	–	2 (5%)	3 (7%)	–	8
D2 Media platf.	1 (33%)	1 (33%)	–	–	–	1 (33%)	–	–	–	–	3
D3 Business mon.	2 (29%)	–	1 (14%)	–	2 (29%)	–	–	1 (14%)	1 (14%)	–	5
D4 e-Commerce	1 (33%)	–	2 (67%)	–	–	–	–	–	–	–	2
D5 Automotive	–	–	–	–	–	1 (100%)	–	–	–	–	1
D6 Int. browser	1 (100%)	–	–	–	–	–	–	–	–	–	1
D7 Gaming	1 (33%)	–	–	–	–	–	1 (33%)	1 (33%)	–	–	3
D8 Telecom	1 (33%)	–	1 (33%)	–	1 (33%)	–	–	–	–	–	3
D9 Web app.	–	–	2 (100%)	–	–	–	–	–	–	–	1
D10 Soc. net. site	–	–	1 (33%)	–	–	–	–	–	–	2 (67%)	2
D11 Web portal	–	–	1 (100%)	–	–	–	–	–	–	–	1
# Domains	7	2	7	1	3	3	1	3	2	1	
Change types											
C1 Process	9 (38%)	2 (8%)	5 (21%)	–	4 (17%)	1 (4%)	1 (4%)	2 (8%)	–	–	7
C2 Algorithm	1 (8%)	1 (8%)	6 (46%)	–	1 (8%)	–	–	1 (8%)	1 (8%)	2 (15%)	7
C3 User interface	5 (21%)	3 (13%)	12 (50%)	–	1 (4%)	–	–	–	3 (13%)	–	5
C4 Source code	1 (33%)	–	1 (33%)	–	–	–	–	–	1 (33%)	–	3
C5 Degradation	–	–	4 (100%)	–	–	–	–	–	–	–	1
C6 Infrastructure	–	–	1 (100%)	–	–	–	–	–	–	–	1
# Change types	4	3	6	0	3	1	1	2	3	1	
Metrics types											
M1 Usage	6 (22%)	4 (15%)	13 (48%)	1 (4%)	1 (4%)	–	–	2 (7%)	–	–	6
M2 Operation	–	–	3 (100%)	–	–	–	–	–	–	–	1
M3 Process	2 (18%)	–	8 (73%)	–	1 (9%)	–	–	–	–	–	3
M4 Business	3 (17%)	–	8 (44%)	–	1 (6%)	–	1 (6%)	2 (11%)	3 (17%)	–	6
M5 Quality	1 (33%)	–	–	–	–	–	–	–	–	2 (67%)	2
M6 Satisfaction	2 (50%)	–	1 (25%)	–	–	1 (25%)	–	–	–	–	3
# Metric types	5	1	5	1	3	1	1	1	2	1	

in cases related to Scenarios S0-S5. In contrast, *business metrics* (M4) are among the only ones present in cases related to the more high-level Scenarios S6-S8. The evidence thus indicates that there is a relationship between data limitations and the types of metrics used.

4.3   Challenges and Solutions (RQ3)

Based on a full-text review of the selected papers, we identified four main dICE challenges: *Unavailable user data*, *Low metrics sensitivity*, *Low results validity*, and *Other*. For each main challenge, we identified sub-challenges and potential solutions presented in the selected papers. Unlike scenarios, which describe dICE-relevant circumstances, challenges and sub-challenges represent specific dICE problems that can occur within one or more scenarios. An overview of challenges, sub-challenges, solutions and the mapping to scenarios is shown in Figure 2.

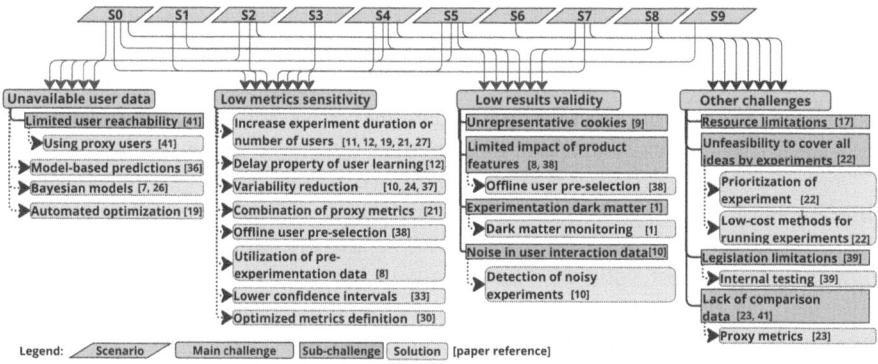

Fig. 2. Overview of dlCE challenges and solutions.

Unavailable user data includes challenges related to *insufficient amounts of user data needed for statistically significant results* (S0). Moreover, Yaman et al. [41] report on challenges with *user reachability* that affect the experiment validation cycle involving direct interaction with customers and analysis of qualitative data. In their experience, problems with reaching users to collect qualitative feedback result in low amounts of data. The use of *proxy users*, such as internal employees, was suggested as a solution. Alternatively, Speicher et al. [36] propose using *model-based predictions*·where user interactions are used for learning models to predict product usability without explicit user feedback. This solution approach focuses purely on usability data, thus limiting its applicability. Deng et al. [7] propose replacing missing data with data from similar experiments using *Bayesian models* (BMs) based on several similarity criteria. However, it was shown that too many criteria can result in insufficient data to train the BMs. The authors suggested hierarchical BMs to reduce the amount of input data needed. Letham et al. [26] also use *Bayesian techniques*, in their case to optimise experimentation parameters. The drawbacks of their method were performance degradation and introduction of measurement errors. Another *automated optimisation* method was introduced by Iitsuka et al. [19] as an alternative to A/B testing for website experimentation with a small user base. The proposed solution showed better results than A/B testing on the same sample size, but its application was limited to web page user interface elements and low scaling of performance.

Low metrics sensitivity represents the inability of a metric to detect the treatment effect of controlled experiments in a cost-effective manner. The most obvious solution for improving metric sensitivity is *increasing the experiment duration and/or the number of users* [27]. However, this is not always possible or desirable [11]. First, the growth of traffic per experiment reduces the number of experiments per time unit [11], and for experiments with longer duration, the results can be affected by seasonal effects, such as holiday sales [19]. Second, increasing the size of the treatment group can be risky due to the treatment potentially having a negative effect on the user base [11]. A preferred way of improving the sensitivity is *variability reduction* of the metric. Dmitriev and Wu [10] proposed a truncation strategy to remove outliers from the data. Kohavi et al. [25] suggested relying on metrics that have inherently lower variability and filtering out users who are included in target metrics but were not exposed to treatment variants. A similar approach was chosen by Wang et al. [37], who utilised covariates that are highly correlated to the response metric while having lower variance. Another solution approach involves *combining several proxy metrics* proposed by Kharitonov et al. [21]. However, their approach might require further validation since only a few of their experiments showed statistical significance. Drutsa et al. [12] proposed a method based on the *delay property of user learning*. Both Xie et al. [38] and Deng et al. [8] proposed methods based on preprocessing of experiment input data. The former used *offline user pre-selection* to reduce the number of test cells, which increased the users' allocation to test groups, resulting in better sensitivity. The latter *utilised pre-experimentation data* to divide sampling region into smaller sub-regions, whose combined estimate was more sensitive. The disadvantage of their method was possible unavailability of the pre-experimentation data, or its usage might be unclear when the analysis unit is not a user [8]. Nikolaev et al. [30] introduced a method for *optimised metrics definition* of more sensitive target metrics based on the evaluation of metric distributions. Finally, Rissanen et al. [33] discussed trade-offs such as using lower sensitivity metrics while accepting *lower confidence intervals* for decision-making or increased reliance on high conversion rates.

Low results validity is a common concern in dlCE since limited amounts of user data often lead to lower statistical significance and generalisability of results. In particular, Dmitriev et al. [9] discuss the challenge of using *unrepresentative internet cookies* to identify users in experiments, which could lead to selection bias [9]. Xie et al. [38] and Deng et al. [8] identify a similar problem related to *limited impact on product features* that affects only a small portion of the user base. When running several experiments at the same time, there might not be enough available users for the evaluation of a particular feature. Xie et al. [38] suggest a solution involving an *off-line preselection* of experiments to reduce the number of test cells. Furthermore, Dmitriev and Wu [10] emphasise the possibility that the *noise in user interaction data* can drown the feature effect, producing statistically insignificant results for key metrics. Their solution focuses on the *detection of noisy experiments*. Appiktala et al. [1] introduce the notion of *experimentation dark matter* as a potential issue in experimentation. Dark matter refers to a discrepancy between planned and actual sizes of representative partitions of the traffic domain. The presence of dark matter poses a challenge as it is invisible for standard A/A or A/B validation, and might result in a negative impact on the representativeness of the population and a loss of statistical power. As a solution, the authors developed a framework for *dark matter monitoring* [1].

Other challenges cover miscellaneous challenges not related to any of the other main challenges. Giaimo et al. [17] describe computational *resource limitations* in experiments in the automotive domain due to the capacity available in cyberphysical systems. Kohavi et al. [22] described that it is often *infeasible to cover all ideas by experiments* due to potentially high implementation costs. As a solution, the authors recommend *prioritisation of experiments* with only the most interesting ideas, and to use *low-cost methods for running experiments*, such as mock-up reviews [22]. Yaman et al. [39] discussed *legislative limitations* related to confidentiality within mobile game development. For example, in some stages of development, experimentation with real users may not be possible due to restrictions in sharing of unpublished games. As a solution, *proxy users* can be used instead, which is, however, likely to introduce biases. Although the main dlCE problems described by S4 are caused by long product development cycles, Kohavi et al. [22] observed that opposite circumstances, i.e. too short development cycles, can be problematic, too. A rapid development might suffer from the unavailability of earlier implementations and, consequently, a *lack of comparison data*. This can prevent teams from forming experimentation hypotheses or defining success criteria [41]. The *lack of comparison data* can also be caused by an inability to collect data from third-party systems [23]. In such a case, Kohavi et al. suggested using *proxy metrics* as a replacement for the unavailable ones.

4.4   Discussion

The answers to our research questions are provided by the framework presented above. We now further discuss and analyse dlCE through the lens of our framework and using the literature chosen for our review.

The dlCE scenarios presented above provide insights into what data limitations may exist in CE (RQ1). We see three main data limiting dimensions at play in the scenarios, namely *user data volume*, *data type*, and *product and business maturity* (see Figure 1). We note that the issues observed in the scenarios are not only due to low *user data volume*, i.e. lack of user data, but can also occur in scenarios where there are exceptionally high volumes of user data. Both situations occur with almost the same frequency in the cases we found, and some cases report on both simultaneously. We can thus conclude that dlCE is not only about user data volume but includes several other aspects.

Regarding the *data type* used for experimentation, the articles analysed in our study all report issues related to quantitative data. However, more than half of the studies also report issues related to qualitative data. The solutions proposed concentrate to a large extent on statistical techniques for dealing with low data volumes, while solutions going beyond quantitative data are scarce (RQ3). This suggests a need for better understanding of how to combine quantitative and qualitative data, as well as addressing data limitations prior to data collection (e.g., in prioritising which assumptions to test and in experiment design).

The cases found are not limited to startups or SMEs, but dlCE challenges are reported also in larger and more mature companies with more established products (RQ2). This suggests that dlCE may be widely applicable and that challenges with becoming a data-driven software organisation exist in many types of organisations, although they may be of different nature for companies of different size, maturity, and domain. Further investigation is needed to provide more detail beyond this preliminary summary.

4.5   Threats to Validity

The internal validity in this study is high due to the selection of studies that are highly representative of the phenomenon under study, as they are based on an existing systematic literature review. The examples we found come from real-life cases with high relevance for CE. We also followed systematic procedures for the literature review, ensuring that the results are based closely on the evidence. External validity is threatened by the small number of cases in the literature we found. This means that we cannot claim our set of scenarios, characteristics, and factors to be comprehensive. Other cases may represent different scenarios, product domains, change types, metric types, and they may detail additional classes of challenges and solutions.

5   Conclusions

We systematically analysed 23 articles reporting data-related challenges in CE. Combined with brainstorming, we created a set of dlCE scenarios to which we then related product domain, change type, and metric type factors to detail the circumstances that may lead to different scenarios occurring. We also extracted dlCE challenges and proposed solutions and created a categorisation of them. Together, these parts provide a dlCE framework that can help practitioners understand their dlCE problem and address it.

Based on the evidence, dlCE scenarios are dependent on both contextual and experimentation factors, many of which can be derived from the product domain. The maturity of CE in an organisation, but also the inherent difficulty of conducting continuous experiments in different domains, may cause different kinds of data-related limitations. We believe that dlCE challenges will occur more often in changes that span multiple parts of the system (process changes), have wide-ranging effects (algorithm changes), or have complicated behavioural effects (changes to the user interface). We observe a relationship between data limitations and the types of metrics used. It is interesting to ask whether guidance on metrics choices is sufficient to address the issues of dlCE. We speculate that improved analysis of the product assumptions to be tested, the experimentation goals, and a better and more informed choice of metrics are examples of solution approaches that should be explored. We also see potential fruitful results from analysing dlCE through the lens of the FACE theory [34]. What challenges are related to problem-solution fit, product-market fit, and what are the incentives involved?

In the next steps of our work, we will continue the analysis of papers from the Included category. We aim to extract information about specific experimentation cases, such as contextual factors, experiment assumptions, inputs, methods, tools, participants, metrics and outputs or decisions. Based on these results, we envision development of new approaches that enable more companies to benefit from applying CE, in particular, in the context of early development stages as well as mature systems with relatively few users.

Acknowledgments. This work was supported by the Wallenberg Artificial Intelligence, Autonomous Systems and Software Program (WASP) funded by Knut and Alice Wallenberg Foundation and the Research Council of Finland (project no. 349574, Naturalistic decision-making in Continuous Experimentation).

References

1. Appiktala, N., Chen, M., Natkovich, M., Walters, J.: Demystifying dark matter for online experimentation. In: IEEE International Conference on Big Data, pp. 1620–1626. IEEE (2017)
2. Auer, F., Felderer, M.: Current state of research on continuous experimentation: a systematic mapping study. In: 2018 44th Euromicro Conference on Software Engineering and Advanced Applications (SEAA), pp. 335–344. IEEE (August 2018)
3. Auer, F., Ros, R., Kaltenbrunner, L., Runeson, P., Felderer, M.: Controlled experimentation in continuous experimentation: knowledge and challenges. Inf. Softw. Techn. **134**, 106551 (2021)
4. Budylin, R., Drutsa, A., Katsev, I., Tsoy, V.: Consistent transformation of ratio metrics for efficient online controlled experiments. In: Proceedings of the 11th ACM International Conference on Web Search and Data Mining, pp. 55–63. WSDM '18, ACM (2018)
5. Cartaxo, B., Pinto, G., Soares, S.: Rapid reviews in software engineering. In: Felderer, M., Travassos, G.H. (eds.) Contemporary Empirical Methods in Software Engineering, pp. 357–384. Springer International Publishing, Cham (2020)
6. Chren, S., et al.: Supplementary material for the paper data-limited continuous experimentation (dlCE): a literature review (November 2024). https://doi.org/10.5281/zenodo.14025937
7. Deng, A.: Objective bayesian two sample hypothesis testing for online controlled experiments. In: Proceedings of the 24th International Conference on WWW, pp. 923–928 (2015)
8. Deng, A., Xu, Y., Kohavi, R., Walker, T.: Improving the sensitivity of online controlled experiments by utilizing pre-experiment data. In: Proceedings of the 6th ACM International Conference on Web Search and Data Mining, pp. 123–132 (2013)
9. Dmitriev, P., Frasca, B., Gupta, S., Kohavi, R., Vaz, G.: Pitfalls of long-term online controlled experiments. In: IEEE International Conference on Big Data, pp. 1367–1376. IEEE (2016)
10. Dmitriev, P., Wu, X.: Measuring metrics. In: Proceedings of the 25th ACM International Conference on Information and Knowledge Management, pp. 429–437 (2016)
11. Drutsa, A., Gusev, G., Serdyukov, P.: Future user engagement prediction and its application to improve the sensitivity of online experiments. In: Proceedings of the 24th International Conference on WWW, pp. 256–266 (2015)

12. Drutsa, A., Gusev, G., Serdyukov, P.: Using the delay in a treatment effect to improve sensitivity and preserve directionality of engagement metrics in A/B experiments. In: Proceedings of the 26th International Conference on WWW, pp. 1301–1310 (2017)

13. Erthal, V.M., de Souza, B.P., dos Santos, P.S.M., Travassos, G.H.: Characterization of continuous experimentation in software engineering: expressions, models, and strategies. Sci. Comput. Program. **229**, 102961 (2023)

14. Fagerholm, F., Guinea, A.S., Mäenpää, H., Münch, J.: The RIGHT model for continuous experimentation. J. Syst. Softw. **123**, 292–305 (2017)

15. Fitzgerald, B., Stol, K.J.: Continuous software engineering: a roadmap and agenda. J. Syst. Softw. **123**, 176–189 (2017)

16. Giaimo, F., Andrade, H., Berger, C.: Continuous experimentation and the cyber-physical systems challenge: an overview of the literature and the industrial perspective. J. Syst. Softw. **170**, 110781 (2020)

17. Giaimo, F., Berger, C., Kirchner, C.: Considerations about continuous experimentation for resource-constrained platforms in self-driving vehicles. In: Proceedings of the 11th European Conference on Software Architecture, pp. 84–91. Springer (2017)

18. Holmström Olsson, H., Bosch, J.: Data driven development: challenges in online, embedded and on-premise software. In: Proceedings of the PROFES, pp. 515–527. Springer (2019)

19. Iitsuka, S., Matsuo, Y.: Website optimization problem and its solutions. In: Proceedings of the 21th ACM SIGKDD International Conference on Know Discovery and Data Mining, pp. 447–456 (2015)

20. Khangura, S., Konnyu, K., Cushman, R., Grimshaw, J., Moher, D.: Evidence summaries: the evolution of a rapid review approach. Syst. Rev. **1**(10) (2012)

21. Kharitonov, E., Drutsa, A., Serdyukov, P.: Learning sensitive combinations of a/b test metrics. In: Proceedings of the 10th ACM International Conference on Web Search and Data Mining, pp. 651–659 (2017)

22. Kohavi, R., Deng, A., Frasca, B., Walker, T., Xu, Y., Pohlmann, N.: Online controlled experiments at large scale. In: Proceedings of the 19th International Conference on Knowledge Discovery and Data Mining, pp. 1168–1176 (2013)

23. Kohavi, R., Deng, A., Longbotham, R., Xu, Y.: Seven rules of thumb for web site experimenters. In: Proceedings of the 20th ACM SIGKDD International Conference on Knowledge Discovery and Data Mining, pp. 1857–1866 (2014)

24. Kohavi, R., Henne, R.M., Sommerfield, D.: Practical guide to controlled experiments on the web: listen to your customers not to the hippo. In: Proceedings of the 13th ACM SIGKDD International Conference on Knowledge Discovery and Data Mining, pp. 959–967 (2007)

25. Kohavi, R., Longbotham, R., Sommerfield, D., Henne, R.M.: Controlled experiments on the web: survey and practical guide. Data Min. Knowl. Disc. **18**, 140–181 (2009)

26. Letham, B., Karrer, B., Ottoni, G., Bakshy, E.: Constrained Bayesian optimization with noisy experiments. Bayesian Anal. **14**(2), 495–519 (2019)

27. Machmouchi, W., Awadallah, A.H., Zitouni, I., Buscher, G.: Beyond success rate: utility as a search quality metric for online experiments. In: Proceedings of the ACM Conference on Information and Knowledge Management, pp. 757–765 (2017)

28. Melegati, J., Chanin, R., Wang, X., Sales, A., Prikladnicki, R.: Enablers and inhibitors of experimentation in early-stage software startups. In: Proceedings of the PROFES, pp. 554–569. Springer (2019)

29. Nguyen-Duc, A., Abrahamsson, P.: Continuous experimentation on artificial intelligence software: a research agenda. In: Proceedings of the 28th ACM Joint Meeting on European Software Engineering Conference and Symposium on the Foundations of Software Engineering, pp. 1513–1516 (2020)

30. Nikolaev, K., Drutsa, A., Gladkikh, E., Ulianov, A., Gusev, G., Serdyukov, P.: Extreme states distribution decomposition method for search engine online evaluation. In: Proceedings of the 21th ACM SIGKDD International Conference on Knowledge Discovery and Data Mining, pp. 845–854 (2015)

31. Olsson, H.H., Bosch, J.: The HYPEX model: from opinions to data-driven software development. In: Bosch, J. (ed.) Continuous Software Engineering, pp. 155–164. Springer, Cham (2014)

32. Paulsson, A., Runeson, P., Ros, R.: A/B testing in the small. In: Proceedings of the PROFES, pp. 449–463. LNCS, vol. 13709, Springer, Jyväskylä, Finland (2022)

33. Rissanen, O., Münch, J.: Continuous experimentation in the B2B domain: a case study. In: 2015 IEEE/ACM 2nd International Workshop on Rapid Continuous Software Engineering, pp. 12–18. IEEE (2015)

34. Ros, R., Bjarnason, E., Runeson, P.: A theory of factors affecting continuous experimentation (FACE). Emp. Softw. Eng. **29**(1), 21 (2024)

35. Ros, R., Runeson, P.: Continuous experimentation and A/B testing: a mapping study. In: IEEE/ACM 4th International Workshop on Rapid Continuous Software Engineering, pp. 35–41. RCoSE '18, ACM (May 2018)

36. Speicher, M., Both, A., Gaedke, M.: Ensuring web interface quality through usability-based split testing. In: Proceedings of the 14th International Conference of Web Engineering, pp. 93–110. Springer (2014)

37. Wang, J., Goldberg, D., Burke, P., Bhoite, D.: Designing and analyzing a/b tests in an online marketplace. In: International Conference on Data Mining Works, pp. 1447–1452 (2018)

38. Xie, H., Aurisset, J.: Improving the sensitivity of online controlled experiments: case studies at netflix. In: Proceedings of the 22nd ACM SIGKDD International Conference on Knowledge Discovery and Data Mining, pp. 645–654 (2016)

39. Yaman, S., Mikkonen, T., Suomela, R.: Continuous experimentation in mobile game development. In: 44th SEAA, pp. 345–352 (2018)

40. Yaman, S.G., et al.: Transitioning towards continuous experimentation in a large software product and service development organisation–a case study. In: Proceedings of the PROFES, pp. 344–359. Springer (2016)

41. Yaman, S.G., et al.: Introducing continuous experimentation in large software-intensive product and service organisations. JSS **133**, 195–211 (2017)

The Concept of a Web App to Find Educational VR Apps

Nadine Bisswang[1,2] ⓘ, Dimitri Petrik[2(✉)] ⓘ, and Sebastian Richter[1] ⓘ

[1] Baden-Wuerttemberg Cooperative State University, Paulinenstr. 50, 70178 Stuttgart, Germany
nadine.bisswang@dhbw-stuttgart.de
[2] University of Stuttgart, Keplerstr. 7, 70174 Stuttgart, Germany
dimitri.petrik@bwi.uni-stuttgart.de

Abstract. The integration of virtual reality (VR) into higher education has great potential, such as enhancing the understanding of complex concepts. However, university lecturers struggle to find suitable VR applications due to inadequate filters in app stores. To address this challenge, we developed a concept of a publicly accessible overview suitable for Information Systems education, based on metadata. We identified nine VR applications through a systematic search of five common app stores. We classified and coded them by deductively applying an existing taxonomy and inductively deriving new metadata categories. The results are presented as a web app so that university lecturers can search for VR applications tailored to their specific educational needs. For researchers, the defined metadata attributes serve as a foundation for developing web-based platforms where educational VR apps can be effectively searched and filtered according to academic requirements. For practitioners, the web app provides a practical tool to find VR applications that align with their teaching objectives.

Keywords: Virtual reality applications · market analysis · metadata

1 Introduction and Theoretical Background

Imagine a university lecturer who wants to integrate virtual reality (VR) into lectures to help students understand complex concepts. Actually, there is a growing interest in the adoption of VR in higher education, driven by technological advancements, decreasing equipment costs, and the increasing accessibility of consumer-grade VR headsets [1]. But to identify appropriate VR applications ('apps') is challenging for lecturers. Although commercial app stores, such as Google Play and Steam, offer many VR apps, they lack a filter for educational purposes. Thus, the search is time-consuming and frustrating – the problem, this article addresses.

Previous systematic literature reviews (SLRs) on educational VR apps highlight VR design elements [1] or application domains [2]. However, these studies do not support the exploration of the identified VR apps. Public platforms such as the Digital Learning Map[1] or the VR Use Case Catalog[2] list prototypical VR apps to inspire educators and

---

[1] https://www.e-teaching.org/community/digital-learning-map.
[2] https://www.uni-giessen.de/de/studium/lehre/projekte/nidit/goals/vrusecases.

E. Papatheocharous et al. (Eds.): ICSOB 2024, LNBIP 539, pp. 340–347, 2025.
https://doi.org/10.1007/978-3-031-85849-9_27

facilitate networking. Yet they do not provide searchable VR apps. Based on these challenges, we formulate two research questions (RQ):

RQ 1: *Which VR apps are currently available for higher education, using the field of information systems as an example?*
RQ 2: *How can the search for relevant VR applications in higher education be narrowed down to meet specific educational needs?*

To answer RQ 1, this study conducts a systematic search to develop an exemplary publicly accessible overview of VR apps for higher education focusing on information systems (IS) because all authors are IS scholars.

To answer RQ 2, we conceptualize a metadata-based search approach. Metadata is structured information that describes objects and makes them easier to identify [3]. For instance, the IEEE Learning Object Metadata (LOM) Standard offers a conceptual schema for describing learning objects to enhance their discovery and use [3]. Searching or filtering by using metadata is a well-established concept that app stores use as well. However, app stores do not provide metadata for the specific goals and needs of higher education institutions.

The remainder of this paper is organized as follows. Following the description of related work and the theoretical background in the introduction, the research method is explained. In the results section, the identified metadata attributes are described. Next, an overview of VR apps and their associated metadata is presented. Finally, we summarize the findings, outline future research directions, and highlight the implications for both research and practice.

2   Research Method

To identify the available VR apps for higher education (RQ 1) in the IS field, a systematic search akin to an SLR was conducted, following the PRISMA guidelines [4]. We adopted these guidelines for the VR app search and analysis to ensure a structured and transparent review.

Data Analysis. We searched five common app stores from April to September 2024: Steam (https://store.steampowered.com/), Google Play (https://play.google.com/), Meta Store (https://www.meta.com/), Apple App Store (https://apps.apple.com/), and Pico Store (https://store-global.picoxr.com/). The Meta Store, Apple App Store, and Pico Store were selected due to their significant market shares in 2024 [5]. Steam and Google Play were chosen because they offer device-independent apps compatible with various Android-based VR systems, such as Meta Quest and Pico VR glasses.

The keywords for the search derived from the core modules of the Bachelor's degree program in IS at the Baden-Wuerttemberg Cooperative State University Stuttgart, excluding the bachelor's thesis and project-related modules due to their annually changing topics. Module names were modified for search terms after a pilot search (e.g., shortening "Introduction to Business Administration" to "Business Administration") to get more results. This process identified 22 apps (cf. Fig. 1).

Data Filtering Approach. We reviewed 22 VR apps for their relevance to higher education by examining descriptions and preview videos, categorizing them as 'relevant,' 'questionable,' or 'not relevant.' Apps not targeting higher education content or audiences were excluded. For example, some 'mathematics' apps focused on secondary school topics like spatial geometry and volume calculations, which do not align with university-level subjects. The research team members independently categorized the apps, resolving disagreements through discussion. The final list comprised nine apps.

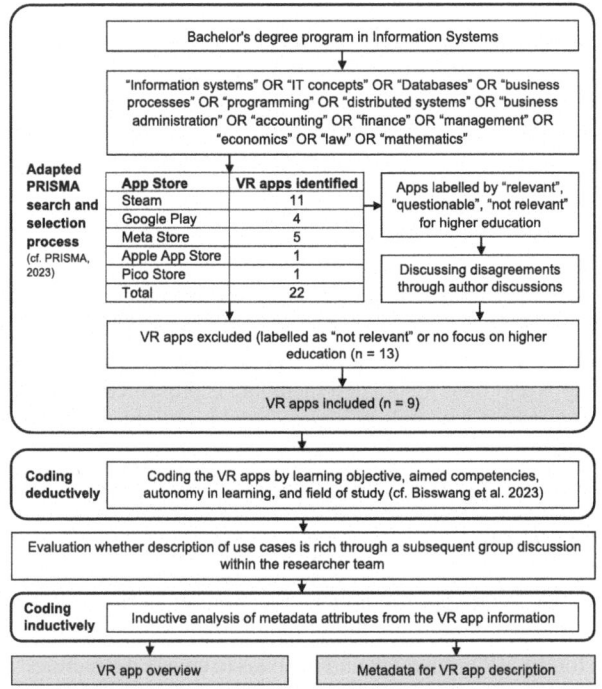

Fig. 1. VR applications search, selection, and coding process.

Coding Process. Initially, metadata attributes were defined using a taxonomy for VR use cases [6]. This taxonomy entails 17 dimensions and 37 characteristics grouped in 'VR', 'use case', 'education', and 'modalities' as meta-concepts. We focus on the meta-concept 'education' as the other three do not contribute to understand educational objectives. Following, additional metadata categories were derived inductively by analyzing the VR apps to identify essential elements not addressed in the literature so far.

3   Result and Prototypical Demonstration

Nine VR apps for IS education were identified and coded using the VR use case taxonomy's dimensions of the meta-concept 'education' [6]. The characteristics of the dimensions serve as controlled vocabulary (cf. Table 1).

Table 1. Metadata derived deductively.

Metadata	Description	Vocabulary
Learning objectives	The specific learning objective targeted, based on Bloom's Taxonomy [6]	Remember, understand, apply, analyze, evaluate, create
Aimed competencies	Competencies such as social-emotional, cognitive, or psychomotor skills [6]	Social-emotional, cognitive, psychomotor
Autonomy in learning	Indicates whether learning is self-directed or guided [6]	Self-determined, externally imposed
Field of study	The academic discipline for which the application is designed [6]	1) humanities, 2) sports, 3) law, economic and social sciences, 4) mathematics and natural sciences, 5) human medicine and health science 6) agricultural, forestry and food sciences, veterinary medicine, 7) engineering sciences, and 8) arts and art sciences

Each metadata category was coded for the identified VR apps ($n = 9$), with information derived from app store pages. If an app had an additional website, its information was also considered. The final metadata attribution was agreed upon through group discussions. Table 2 provides an example of how the metadata was applied.

Table 2. An example of deductive metadata labeling.

Metadata	Information	Used vocabulary
Learning objectives	"In PC Virtual LAB you'll learn the different components of your computer. Different levels (…) put your computer skills into practice." [7] "To complement the theory seen in the classroom with an educational game (…)." [8]	Understand and apply cf. [9]
Aimed competencies		Cognitive and psychomotor cf. [6]
Autonomy in learning	The video shows how to assemble the computer using specific instructions [8]	Externally imposed cf. [6]
Field of study	"Tested in the introduction to Computer Science subjects (…) of the University of Burgos." [8]	Mathematics and natural sciences cf. [6]

Following the deductive coding procedure, the authors discussed whether the app descriptions were detailed enough. Although the deductively applied categories addressed key educational elements, they do not encompass all the details necessary for university lecturers to search and filter VR apps. Consequently, we identified additional metadata categories, as shown in Table 3.

Table 3. Metadata derived inductively.

Metadata	Description	Vocabulary
Name	The official name of the VR application	–
Description	A detailed explanation of the application's purpose and functionality	–
Addressed problem	The educational challenge the application addresses	–
Cost	The price or license model of the application, indicating whether it is free or requires a one-time payment	Free, subscription-based, one-time payment
URL	A direct link to the application's store page	–

For the metadata category "cost," we defined the vocabulary 'free', 'subscription-based' and 'one-time payment'. App stores transparently indicate an app's pricing model. However, for the further categories, no controlled vocabulary was appropriate due to content variations of the apps. Table 4 indicates how the inductively derived metadata attributes were applied.

To ensure accessibility of our results, we developed a web app[3] (cf. Fig. 2) using React (https://react.dev/). Therefore, each VR app is described by a JavaScript Object Notation (JSON) file according to the defined metadata structure (see an excerpt below).

```
{"name": "PC Virtual Lab",
"description": " The PC Virtual Lab app offers an interactive platform to
learn about the components of a computer through practice-orientated learn-
ing.",
...}
```

To facilitate the expansion of the application, researchers and university lecturers can use a submission form to submit further VR apps. The form is structured according to the metadata. We encourage all users of the web app and readers of the paper to contribute to the database and engage with us. Quality control will initially be conducted manually, although an automated solution is aimed for future implementation.

---

[3] Publicly accessible at https://vr4highereducation.de/.

Table 4. An example of inductive metadata labeling.

Metadata	Information	Used vocabulary
Name	"PC Virtual Lab" [8]	PC Virtual Lab
Description	"PC Virtual Lab is a video game to improve learning in basic computer concepts." [8] "In PC Virtual LAB you'll learn the different components of your computer (…). Put your computer skills into practice" [7]	The PC Virtual Lab app offers an interactive platform to learn about the components of a computer through practice-orientated learning
Adressed problem	"To complement the theory seen in the classroom with an educational game that serves to fix these concepts." [8] "An environment where to practice and fail without risk that allows unlimited repetition." [8]	A repeatable environment for comprehending and assembling computer components
Cost	"Free" [8]	Free
URL	https://store.steampowered.com/app/1825460/PC_Virtual_LAB/	https://store.steampowered.com/app/1825460/PC_Virtual_LAB/

Fig. 2. Web application screenshot.

4 Conclusion

This study identifies nine relevant VR apps for higher IS education (RQ1) and defines a set of metadata (RQ2), offering university lecturers a convenient search for VR apps.

A key limitation is the focus on one single discipline – IS, which we used as an example. Future research should expand this approach to other fields, such as human medicine and engineering. For instance, there are VR apps available for understanding heart anatomy[4] for medical education and for practicing robotic programming for engineering education[5].

Furthermore, the prototype web app is in an early development stage and has not yet been evaluated for usability by university lecturers. As a next step, we plan to gather feedback from university lecturers who teach IS courses to assess if the metadata and search functionality meet their educational needs. This feedback will guide us in refining, expanding, and improving both the metadata and the web app.

To keep the web app up-to-date with evolving VR offerings, automating the update process is necessary. We propose a semi-automated solution using web scraping [10] to extend the VR application to other disciplines (e.g., medicine) with a semi-automated search selection and coding process. Since VR app descriptions often lack a direct mapping to the proposed metadata (cf. Table 2), manual verification or a machine learning algorithm would be required to interpret attributes such as learning objectives. Initially, a manual quality control process is proposed to validate data before it is published on the web app.

To foster a collaborative community, partnerships with universities and platform owners, such as the Digital Learning Map[6] and VR Use Case Catalog[7], could be beneficial for further development.

References

1. Radianti, R., Majchrzak, T.A., Fromm, J., Wohlgenannt, I.: A systematic review of immersive virtual reality applications for higher education: design elements, lessons learned, and research agenda. Comput. Educ. **147**, 1–29 (2020)
2. Radianti, J., Majchrzak, T.A., Fromm, J., Stieglitz, S., vom Brocke, J.: Virtual reality applications for higher educations: a market analysis. In: Proceedings of the 54th Hawaii International Conference on System Sciences, 5–8 January, Kauai, Hawaii, USA, pp. 124–133 (2021)
3. IEEE: IEEE Standard for Learning Object Metadata, 1484.12.1TM (2020)
4. PRISMA: The PRISMA 2020 statement: an updated guideline for reporting systematic reviews (2023)
5. IDC: Virtual reality glasses - market share of sales worldwide. https://de.statista.com/statistik/daten/studie/1230812/umfrage/marktanteile-der-hersteller-am-weltweiten-absatz-von-virtual-reality-brillen/. Accessed 24 Sep 2024
6. Bisswang, N., Petrik, D., Heumüller, E., Richter, S.: What is your VR use case for educational like: a state-of-the-art taxonomy. Electron. J. e-Learn. (EJEL) 46–62 (2023)

---

[4] https://www.meta.com/de-de/experiences/xr-heart-anatomy/6754548357996524/.

[5] https://store.steampowered.com/app/683880/VR_Robotics_Simulator/.

[6] https://www.e-teaching.org/community/digital-learning-map.

[7] https://www.uni-giessen.de/de/studium/lehre/projekte/nidit/goals/vrusecases.

7. Universidad de Burgos, PC Virtual Lab – Game for Learning. http://pcvirtuallab.com/. Accessed 24 Sep 2024

8. Valve Corporation, PC Virtual LAB bei Steam. https://store.steampowered.com/app/182 5460/PC_Virtual_LAB/. Accessed 24 Sep 2024

9. Anderson, L.W., Krathwohl, D.R.: A Taxonomy for Learning, Teaching, and Assessing: A Revision of Bloom's Taxonomy of Educational Objectives, 1st edn. Longman, New York (2001)

10. Zhao, B.: Web scraping, in encyclopedia of big data. In: Schintler, L.A., McNeely, C.L. (eds.) Springer, Cham, pp. 1–3 (2017)

Tools in Software Ecosystems

How Do ML Students Explain Their Models and What Can We Learn from This?

Ulrik Franke[1,2]($\boxtimes$) ⓘ

[1] RISE Research Institutes of Sweden, 164 29 Kista, Sweden
`ulrik.franke@ri.se`
[2] KTH Royal Institute of Technology, 100 44 Stockholm, Sweden

Abstract. In recent years, artificial intelligence (AI) has made great progress. However, despite impressive results, modern data-driven AI systems are often very difficult to understand, challenging their use in software business and prompting the emergence of the explainable AI (XAI) field. This paper explores how machine learning (ML) students explain their models and draws implications for practice from this. Data was collected from ML master students, who were given a two-part assignment. First they developed a model predicting insurance claims based on an existing data set, then they received a request for explanation of insurance premiums in accordance with the GDPR right to meaningful information and had to come up with such an explanation. The students also peer-graded each other's explanations. Analyzing this data set and comparing it to responses from actual insurance firms from a previous study illustrates some potential pitfalls—narrow technical focus and offering mere data dumps. There were also some promising directions—feature importance, graphics, and what-if scenarios—where the software business practice could benefit from being inspired by the students. The paper is concluded with a reflection about the importance of multiple kinds of expertise and team efforts for making the most of XAI in practice.

Keywords: explainable AI · experiment · insurance · GDPR

1 Introduction

In recent years, artificial intelligence (AI) and in particular its subset machine learning (ML) has made astounding progress. Tasks which used to be exclusively human—such as reading texts [9], identifying the contents of images [52], or diagnosing disease [40]—are now possible to automate. However, despite encouraging and impressive results, modern AI systems often suffer from being exceedingly difficult to understand and interpret. Their success factor, automatic training on large data sets, is also their Achilles heel in that the large number of parameters makes the result almost impossible to explain. In this sense, such systems are like black boxes [7].

E. Papatheocharous et al. (Eds.): ICSOB 2024, LNBIP 539, pp. 351–365, 2025.
https://doi.org/10.1007/978-3-031-85849-9_28

This poses new challenges for all kinds of enterprises and software business actors wishing to reap the benefits of modern AI. People may be reluctant to trust automated decisions if the systems making them cannot be inspected. This has prompted calls for enhanced transparency—sometimes enshrined in law. For example, the EU General Data Protection Regulation (GDPR) gives people the right to "meaningful information about the logic involved" in "automated decision-making" (Article 15), and the EU AI Act gives a similar right to "clear and meaningful explanations of the role of the AI system in the decision-making procedure and the main elements of the decision taken" for high-risk AI systems (Article 86). More generally, the need for improved AI governance is increasingly acknowledged [27, 29], and enterprises need to respond to remain competitive in the AI playing field.

One set of tools to address such problems comes from explainable AI (XAI)— techniques to open up the black boxes, often by generating simpler and more understandable proxy models such as decision trees from underlying complicated ones such as neural networks (for some reviews of the area, see, e.g., [11, 17, 22, 25]). Being able to explain model behavior in such ways has long been seen as valuable [23], even though other goals may be even more important in some contexts [28].

However, XAI techniques alone are no panacea. Enterprises which focus only on technology rather than its use in the organizational context may neglect important requirements [41], leading to failed projects and lost business opportunities. A broader understanding of the relationship between technology, processes, and people is typically required. Some studies suggest that the discipline of Enterprise Architecture—which aims precisely to systematically document a birds-eye-view of the enterprise—helps AI adoption through mechanisms such as better requirements analysis [41, 45]. A recent literature review on requirements and procurement of explainability argues that there is still a lack of studies acknowledging that explainability can serve many different purposes, and that different kinds of explainability are thus required in different situations [24].

To summarize: As AI has become more capable, pressure from regulators and customers to be able to explain automated decisions has increased. Successful software businesses will need to respond to this pressure, preferably in a way which acknowledges that such explanations may serve many purposes and should be tailored accordingly. It is against this background that this paper explores how ML students explain their models and draws implications from this. To be successful in AI-powered software business, decision-makers need to understand not only the technology, but also the processes and the people involved. Today's students are tomorrow's practitioners, and understanding how they approach XAI is valuable to make sure that XAI—and indeed AI more broadly—reaches its full potential in software business.

More precisely, the following research questions are addressed:

RQ 1 How do ML engineering students explain their models to non-experts?

RQ 2 What kind of model explanations do ML engineering students consider good or bad?

RQ 3 How do explanations from ML engineering students differ from explanations given by companies?

RQ 4 What implications for XAI practice can be inferred from how ML engineering students write and grade model explanations?

RQs 1, 2, and 3 are qualitative and descriptive; their answers lay the foundation for also addressing the more interesting RQ 4. While the paper does not pretend to answer these RQs exhaustively, it does make an initial contribution, hopefully one that can inspire more research into this important area.

The remainder of this paper is structured as follows: The next section describes some related work on XAI with a particular focus on user experiments. Section 3 explains the method before Sect. 4 describes the results. The results and their implications are discussed in Sect. 5, before Sect. 6 concludes the paper.

2 Related Work

The majority of XAI work is conducted within computer science and involves developing and testing technical solutions with little or no user involvement—one review found that only a fifth of XAI papers evaluate their results with users [37]. Clearly, such technically oriented work is necessary for successful development of XAI—this is where XAI techniques come from. But equally clearly, technically oriented work is not sufficient—unless users, or stakeholders more broadly, are involved in the design and evaluation of XAI, it will almost certainly end up not meeting expectations. Therefore, it is increasingly acknowledged that XAI also has to be studied from other complementary non-technical perspectives, such as human-computer interaction (HCI) [1,19,21], organizational governance [35,41,42] as well as requirements and procurement [15,24].

The present paper reports on an XAI user study. Most such studies evaluate particular XAI techniques or styles on end-users in particular settings, e.g., rule-based and example-based explanations in a diabetes self-management scenario [48], post-hoc example-based explanations of classifications of handwritten digits [31], virtual agents explaining speech recognition [51], feature importance, feature contribution, nearest neighbors, and counterfactual explanations in different domains [50], or various explanation types focused on the goals and beliefs of autonomous belief-desire-intention agents in a cooking scenario [5]. A common feature of this line of research is a focus on the techniques or styles themselves, which is more narrow than the focus of the study reported here.

Indeed, it is increasingly recognized that XAI research should look more closely at the needs of different stakeholders [4,18], different stages in the AI lifecycle [14], different legal requirements [2,26], etc. It is in this spirit that the present paper investigates explanations from ML engineering students in the context of a GDPR Article 15 request for meaningful information, in order to infer practically relevant lessons. Thus, the paper makes a contribution to the growing strand of the literature concerned with what to do [47] and what to avoid [6,20] when using explainability in practice.

3   Method

To investigate the research questions identified in Sect. 1, data was collected from the students at the master's degree program in Machine Learning at KTH Royal Institute of Technology.[1] More precisely, as part of a mandatory course designed to integrate the skills and knowledge gained from other courses, and make the students reflect about responsibilities, ethical issues, and the use of ML outside academia,[2] the students were given a two-part assignment to complete individually or in pairs:

Model development In the first part of the assignment, students were asked to imagine themselves working in an insurance company and were tasked to analyze a dataset of car insurance claims.[3] The students were tasked to develop a model for predicting claims based on the nine attributes included in the data; to choose the model that "is going to save us money and make our customers happy", not to spend more than half a day doing the work, and to submit a short (no more than two pages) report describing the model, motivating the choice of model, and summarizing its performance. In line with the intended learning outcomes of the course, the task was deliberately open-ended so as to mimic the experience of being a data scientist or machine learning expert outside academia. To calibrate the difficulty of the task, students were also provided with Python code for training some simple regressors and a neural network.

Request for explanation A few days after the deadline of the first part of the assignment, a second part was released (when doing the first part, students were aware that a second part was coming, but not aware of its contents). In the second part, students were asked to imagine that their model from the first part has been put into production to calculate the premiums of customers. Now, however, two customers have issued GDPR requests for explanations of their premiums as shown in Fig. 1. (This request is identical to the one given to actual insurers in [13], with 'home insurance' changed into 'car insurance'.) In addition to the requests, the students were also given the attributes of the two customers and tasked to draft answers to the customers. As a word of caution, the students were reminded that there is no reason to believe that the customers have any specialist knowledge about machine learning, computer science, or mathematics, but are still entitled to explanations of their premiums. The students were given some ten days to complete this second assignment.

As part of the submission, informed consent was collected. Students were given to option to participate in the scientific study to be published. They were informed that if they agreed, their answers would be part of the analysis,

---

[1] https://www.kth.se/en/studies/master/machine-learning.
[2] https://www.kth.se/student/kurser/kurs/DD2301?l=en.
[3] The French Motor Third-Party Liability Claims dataset (https://www.openml.org/d/41214), slightly cleaned up and partitioned into training, validation and test splits was used. See [38] for more details on this data set.

but no personally identifiable information would be used, that they would remain anonymous, and that their answers would be valuable to the scientific community. It was particularly stressed that participation in the study was voluntary, having no effect on completing the assignment (only P/F) with a passing grade.

```
Hi!

In accordance with article 15, section 1h, of the General Data
Protection Regulation 2016/679 I would like information on how
the premium of my car insurance is determined. This article in
the regulation should be applicable if pricing (i) is automated
and (ii) is based on personal data (both collected from me and
collected by other means).

I would be pleased to receive this information in suitable form
(e.g., mathematical formulæ or descriptive text) that meets the
requirements of the regulation on meaningful information about the
logic involved in automated decision-making. Thanks a lot for your
help!

Best regards
```

Fig. 1. The request for pricing information given to the students.

After the assignment deadline the author gave a lecture on XAI to the students (with key references as cited on the following), introducing problems of bias and discrimination [8, 32, 39], calls for a right to explanation [36], methods for explaining black box models [25], something about what explanations are for [30], and the GDPR article 15, Section 1h. In particular, the results from [13]—where actual insurers answered precisely the kind of requests for explanation that the students themselves answered in the second part of the assignment—were shown and discussed in class. After a Q&A session, at the end of the lecture, students were given a final assignment—to peer review and grade each other's explanations. To facilitate this, assignments from those students who had given their consent had been printed beforehand (in multiple copies, since not everyone had consented) and were distributed throughout the auditorium. The minimum requirement for the task was to set a grade (A–F, following the ECTS grading scale), with the additional option to give a written free text comment motivating the grade given. It was stressed that these peer grades did not have any impact on passing the assignment (only P/F) as such.

Thus, having followed the steps above, the data set used throughout the analysis in the next sections was obtained: (i) a set of explanations of ML systems used for decisions affecting individuals, written by the coders who have designed those systems, trying to communicate with consumers rather than technical experts, most of which were (ii) assessed by their peers.

Turning to analysis, summary statistics of grades and features were first compiled. The main effort, however, consisted in qualitative assessments of explanations, grades, comparison to insurance practice, and—most importantly—the inference of implications in line with RQ 4.

4   Results

32 explanations peer-graded once, twice or three times (with a total of 67 individual grades) were obtained. In addition, 10 explanations were received but were, due to chance in the distribution of explanations for grading, not peer-graded. RQs 1, 3, and 4 could thus be answered based on the union of graded and ungraded sets—42 explanations in total—whereas RQ 2 could only be answered using the 32 graded explanations. (Note that each explanation out of these 32 or 42, respectively, contains one part for each of the two different customers in the scenario, both parts following the general template developed by the student, differing only in the customer details.)

4.1   Overview of Explanations (RQ 1)

As a general characterization, the typical explanation is a technically oriented description.

34 explanations (a large majority of 81%) list some or all of the features used in the model, and 10 of these (24%) also list the values of these features. Some explanations list features (and their values) as variable names (e.g. `VehAge: 0.0`), whereas others (also) spell the features out (e.g. vehicle age), and yet others (also) offer textual explanations in natural language (e.g. the age of the car). This is in line with the results from [43], where input parameters was one of the most frequently selected explanations for all automated decision-making systems in insurance. 6 explanations (14%) list not only features (and their values) but also offer some quantitative measure of how much each feature affects the outcome, corresponding to the 'input influence' explanatory style from [3].

A similarly large majority of 34 explanations (81%) use technical terms to describe the model developed. Some examples of such terms include *neural network, regression tree, accuracy, boosting, Poisson distribution, loss function, ReLu activation functions, random forest, logarithmic transformation,* and *Lorenz curves.*

7 explanations (17%) include graphics, such as diagrams of feature impact or examples of decision trees. One interesting use of graphics is to show how the customer is positioned within the entire feature space, in the spirit of the 'demographic' explanatory style from [3]. Four explanations (10%) also emphasize that the data processing at the insurance company is legal. Four explanations (10%) stress confidentiality issues, i.e., that full explanations cannot be given because some data, such as information on other customers, cannot be shared.

Only 3 explanations (7%) include mathematical formulæ. Furthermore, 2 explanations (5%) highlight the black box-nature of the model developed, i.e., that exact descriptions of model outcomes cannot be had, though approximations and indications are possible.

4.2   Characteristics of Explanations Graded High and Low (RQ 2)

16 explanations (50% of the 32 graded explanations) were peer-graded with high grades, operationalized as an average grade equal to or greater than a B. They are not notably different from the whole population with respect to features mentioned, use of technical terms, graphics, or formulæ. Their common characteristic is rather that they take care to offer pedagogical plain language textual explanations of what they seek to explain, such as features and their relevance (e.g., "Older vehicles have higher rates of malfunctioning due to worn out parts, hence causing a higher risk"), particular models such as decision trees (e.g., "For example, the decision tree may split the data according to whether the Driver's age is above 35"), what-if scenarios (e.g., "All else equal, the risk we estimate for you will likely decrease in a few years because your car will be older, and you will be as well") or the general logic of the model developed (e.g., "For example, if your information (like car condition, driver's age, etc.) shows high similarity with a past customer's information, the expected frequency of the claims you are going to make will be predicted to be a similar result as the real frequency of claims made by that past customer"). This is well in line with the preferred scenario identified for this kind of insurance system (*GLM and classification*) in the Delphi study reported by [43], which was precisely to combine input parameters with the general idea behind the data expressed in natural language.

Only 2 explanations (6% of the 32 graded explanations) were peer-graded with low grades, operationalized as an average grade equal to or less than a D. They have no non-trivial common characteristics; one being very short, just listing features, the other being considerably longer, aiming to explain the general logic of AI without mentioning the features in the particular case.

When an explanation was graded by several peers, the grades were most often close. However, in some cases the grades diverged considerably; a difference of at least three steps (e.g., an A and an E, or a C and an F) were recorded in just four cases (13% of the 32 graded explanations).

4.3   Comparison with Practice (RQ 3)

Comparing the student explanations with the explanations provided by actual insurers in the empirical study [13], some similarities and differences can be identified. With respect to features (i.e. what is listed as pricing information in Table 2 from [13]), the two sets of explanations are quite similar in that a list of features is a core component in both sets and, conversely, in that just a few explanations in either set do *not* list features.

With respect to procedural information (i.e. what is listed in Table 3 from [13]), however, the two sets of explanations are quite different. As mentioned in Sect. 4.1, just a few of the student explanations mention legality or confidentiality, whereas these aspects were mentioned more often by insurers (in Table 3 from [13], 9 out of 26 insurers mention legal concerns and 11 mention business confidentiality). Other aspects frequently explained by insurers, such as the general logic by which insurance works and the process for answering the request are virtually absent from the student answers. Here, it seems that the practice is ahead of the students with respect to moving from (mere) explainable algorithms to (more comprehensive) explainable processes, as called for in [6]. Interestingly, however, the claim that the (automated) insurance process is fair was seen in similar numbers in the two sets, though somewhat more commonly among insurers (3 out of 42 student explanations vs. 3 out of 26 insurers).

Unsurprisingly, the explanations offered by the ML students are generally more technically oriented than the explanations offered by actual insurers, for instance reflected in the prevalence of technical terms, mathematical formulæ, and graphics in the student explanations—elements completely absent from the insurer explanations. For a complete example of a representative actual insurer explanation, see Fig. 2 in [13].

5   Discussion (RQ 4)

Whereas the answers to RQs 1–3 are suitable for concise reporting as in Sect. 4, the answer to RQ 4 rather emerges in the following synthesis and critical discussion.

Experiments with students are sometimes criticized for sacrificing validity for convenience (for some perspectives, see [16,33]). In the study reported here, however, students are not just a convenient proxy for some very different population which is the actual object of interest. On the contrary, the participating students will very soon be practitioners themselves, working with ML in a plethora of companies and other enterprises, such as government agencies and non-profits. They will be called upon to explain their models, internally and externally, and thus make their mark on how XAI is implemented in practice. Understanding how they go about this is of profound interest both (i) in order to understand what can and cannot be expected from XAI efforts and (ii) in order to affect this development for the better. In these respects, the student explanations illustrate both some potential pitfalls and some promising directions.

Starting with some pitfalls to be avoided—informally, explanatory techniques which impede understanding on the part of the receivers—one such is a *technical focus* that leaves the non-expert reader puzzled. Some technical terms used by the students were listed in Sect. 4.1. Something similar holds for the use of mathematical formulæ. Though technical terms and formulæ are excellent for communicating in a precise and concise manner between experts, they are rarely the best vehicles for explanations aimed at the general public. Thus, it has been argued that we should go from explaining AI to explaining decisions produced using AI [6]. (In fairness, it should be noted that the request in Fig. 1 does suggest mathematical formulæ as examples of explanations, and students may have leaped at this opportunity, knowing that their teachers are mathematically literate, even if it stretches the consumer request scenario.) The actual insurers do not make this mistake, because their explanations have probably (this is a speculation, though it seems well-founded) not been compiled by engineers.

Another pitfall is to merely offer *a list of features along with their values* as an explanation (i.e., a 'data dump'). Offering access to the personal data held may of course be valuable, but this is a separate *right to data portability* (GDPR Article 20), not to be confused with the *right to meaningful information* (GDPR Article 15). While none of the student explanations is a mere data dump, two resemble it, listing features and their values as the most prominent part of the explanation, with the explanatory text about how this data is used in the model being comparatively brief (though, in fairness, not at all uninformative). This pitfall is in line with the empirical finding in the literature that companies sometimes do not differentiate between Articles 15 and 20, and respond to Article 15 requests in a way more appropriate for an Article 20 request [44].

Turning to promising directions, one such found among the student explanations is the use of numerical *indications of how important different features are* for the model outcome. For example, Shapley additive explanations (SHAP) [34] can be offered as numerical or graphical explanations, as was the case in 3 (7%) student explanations. On their own, such explanations may be difficult to interpret. Combined with suitable pedagogical textual descriptions, however, they offer the prospect of increased understanding and precision. (A fully interactive SHAP interface is probably even better [10], but may not always be an option.)

This leads to a more general promising direction, namely *graphics*. Though it is well-known that some things are much easier to communicate using suitable graphical depictions ([46] is a classic treatment of dos and don'ts), graphics are wholly absent from the insurer explanations [13]. Here, the disposition of the students to make use of graphics should be seen as an inspiration.

A third promising direction is counterfactual explanations or *what-if scenarios* [49], i.e., explanations of how an automated decision would change under different conditions. For example, one what-if scenario is to say that with a newer vehicle, the insurance premium would decrease; another what-if scenario is to say that the premium will decrease with the collection of more claim-free years. Such explanations are practically useful to the recipients, empowering them as consumers, and deserve more attention. (See also the discussion of actionability in [47].)

5.1 Validity and Reliability

With respect to the instrument used, it is clear that it collects explanations of AI decision-making, i.e., what needs to be measured to answer the RQs, and it has been used before to investigate actual companies [13]. With respect to the student population, it offers reasonable ecological validity—they are not just students used for convenience, but their explanations have independent interest as a gauge of how recently graduated ML experts will behave within actual companies and other enterprises, such as government agencies and non-profits.

One possible threat to validity is that the explanations from the students were not explicitly checked for correctness. However, since the students were at liberty to implement whatever model they wanted and coded these models themselves, it is almost impossible that their descriptive explanations of features used (e.g., vehicle age) or algorithms implemented (e.g., regression tree) are wrong. The risk of errors in more elaborate explanations is slightly higher (e.g., which features were the most important, or SHAP graphs) but still low since standardized XAI software packages were typically employed. Furthermore, it is not clear that implementation errors in these explanations actually threaten the validity of observations made to answer the RQs. For example, if a student has made a calculation error in the SHAP values, this does not change the observations that the student used SHAP values to explain the model (RQ 1), that the student's peers graded the explanation using SHAP values in a certain way (RQ 2), that explanations using SHAP values could be seen in the student population but not among the explanations from actual insurance companies (RQ 3), or that SHAP values may indeed be useful to consider in practical software business applications (RQ 4). Thus, on a balance, not explicitly checking the explanations from the students for correctness seems like a minor threat to validity.

Another threat to validity is the fact that the peer-grading by the students (the data used to answer RQ 2) happened after the lecture on XAI, as this might have affected the grading. In particular, the lecture mentioned three features of bad explanations from [30], viz. circularity, lack of relevance, and lack of coherence. The results reported in Sect. 4.2 should be interpreted with this in mind. However, it should be noted that these three features could be expected to be already known (at least implicitly) by master level university students, so that highlighting them in the lecture would serve as a reminder rather than the introduction of something genuinely novel. Furthermore, recall that only 2 explanations (6% of the 32 graded explanations) were peer-graded with low grades, whereas 16 (50% of the 32 graded explanations) were peer-graded with high grades. This suggests that the practical impact on RQ 2 of mentioning features of *bad* explanations is negligible. The interesting results from RQ 2 rather concern the *good* explanations—and no criteria for goodness were explicitly mentioned in the lecture.

While the students represent an interesting population, there is no claim to having sampled this population (ML students) in a way that warrants statistical generalization. Thus, all figures should be read with this in mind. The claim is not to statistical generalization but to analytic generalization—for example, the claim is not that if ML students at another university were tested, some 80% would list features and some 14% would list measures of how much each feature affects the outcome, but rather (something like) that feature lists are probably much more common than 'input influence' explanations, with the implication that if mere feature lists are not good enough, then some active effort is needed.

In short, the sample population does not allow statistical generalization, but the study provides interesting analytical insights nonetheless.

6   Conclusions

This paper has reported an experiment on how ML students explain their models to non-experts, using a motor insurance example and the scenario of a GDPR Article 15 request for meaningful information. Scrutinizing the findings (Sect. 4), it was observed that the explanations are quite technically oriented compared to explanations offered by actual insurance companies, suggesting both pitfalls to be avoided and promising directions to be further explored (Sect. 5).

One important observation is that in order to avoid the pitfalls and make the most of the promising directions, management attention is needed. It is useful to consider this from a quality assurance perspective. If XAI is left to chance by delegation to individual ML graduates—however talented—some explanations will be great but others will be feeble. Whenever this is not good enough, deliberate effort is required. This is difficult and there is no universal solution—even managers who believe in the benefits of XAI and transparency more broadly sometimes struggle to articulate more precisely how to reap them [12]. But one likely aspect of the solution is more collaboration. The students represent one particular kind of expertise—technical ML experts—which is necessary but far from sufficient to make the most of XAI. Complementary expertise—in other kinds of engineering, law, human-computer interaction, marketing, management, ethics, etc.—is also needed. Meaningful XAI practices are a team effort and XAI work in modern software business should be designed with this in mind.

Acknowledgments. This research was partially funded by the Swedish Competition Authority, grant no 456/2021. The author is grateful to Josephine Sullivan for making the data collection possible, and to Jacob Dexe and Henrik Artman for the discussions that spawned the idea of an experiment in explainability as well as for reading a first draft of the manuscript.

Disclosure of Interests. The author has no competing interests to declare that are relevant to the content of this article.

References

1. Abdul, A., Vermeulen, J., Wang, D., Lim, B.Y., Kankanhalli, M.: Trends and trajectories for explainable, accountable and intelligible systems: an HCI research agenda. In: Proceedings of the 2018 CHI Conference on Human Factors in Computing Systems, pp. 1–18 (2018). https://doi.org/10.1145/3173574.3174156
2. Bibal, A., Lognoul, M., de Streel, A., Frénay, B.: Legal requirements on explainability in machine learning. Artif. Intell. Law **29**(2), 149–169 (2021). https://doi.org/10.1007/s10506-020-09270-4

3. Binns, R., Van Kleek, M., Veale, M., Lyngs, U., Zhao, J., Shadbolt, N.: 'It's reducing a human being to a percentage': perceptions of justice in algorithmic decisions. In: Proceedings of the 2018 CHI Conference on Human Factors in Computing Systems, pp. 1–14. CHI '18, ACM (2018). https://doi.org/10.1145/3173574.3173951
4. Brennen, A.: What do people really want when they say they want "Explainable AI?" We asked 60 stakeholders. In: Extended abstracts of the 2020 CHI Conference on Human Factors in Computing Systems, pp. 1–7 (2020). https://doi.org/10.1145/3334480.3383047
5. Broekens, J., Harbers, M., Hindriks, K., van den Bosch, K., Jonker, C., Meyer, J.-J.: Do you get it? User-evaluated explainable BDI agents. In: Dix, J., Witteveen, C. (eds.) MATES 2010. LNCS (LNAI), vol. 6251, pp. 28–39. Springer, Heidelberg (2010). https://doi.org/10.1007/978-3-642-16178-0_5
6. de Bruijn, H., Warnier, M., Janssen, M.: The perils and pitfalls of explainable AI: strategies for explaining algorithmic decision-making. Gov. Inf. Q. **39**(2), 101666 (2022). https://doi.org/10.1016/j.giq.2021.101666
7. Castelvecchi, D.: Can we open the black box of AI? Nature News **538**(7623), 20 (2016). https://doi.org/10.1038/538020a
8. Cavazos, J.G., Phillips, P.J., Castillo, C.D., O'Toole, A.J.: Accuracy comparison across face recognition algorithms: where are we on measuring race bias? IEEE Transactions on Biometrics, Behavior, and Identity Science (2020). https://doi.org/10.1109/TBIOM.2020.3027269
9. Chowdhary, K.: Natural language processing. Fundam. Artif. Intell. 603–649 (2020). https://doi.org/10.1007/978-81-322-3972-7_19
10. Chromik, M.: Making SHAP rap: bridging local and global insights through interaction and narratives. In: Ardito, C., et al. (eds.) INTERACT 2021. LNCS, vol. 12933, pp. 641–651. Springer, Cham (2021). https://doi.org/10.1007/978-3-030-85616-8_37
11. Chromik, M., Butz, A.: Human-XAI interaction: a review and design principles for explanation user interfaces. In: Ardito, C., et al. (eds.) INTERACT 2021. LNCS, vol. 12933, pp. 619–640. Springer, Cham (2021). https://doi.org/10.1007/978-3-030-85616-8_36
12. Dexe, J., Franke, U., Rad, A.: Transparency and insurance professionals: a study of Swedish insurance practice attitudes and future development. Geneva Pap. Risk Insur. Issues Pract. **46**, 547–572 (2021). https://doi.org/10.1057/s41288-021-00207-9
13. Dexe, J., et al.: Explaining automated decision-making—a multinational study of the GDPR right to meaningful information. Geneva Pap. Risk Insur. Issues Pract. **47**, 669–697 (2022). https://doi.org/10.1057/s41288-022-00271-9
14. Dhanorkar, S., Wolf, C.T., Qian, K., Xu, A., Popa, L., Li, Y.: Who needs to know what, when?: Broadening the Explainable AI (XAI) design space by looking at explanations across the AI lifecycle. In: Proceedings of the 2021 ACM Designing Interactive Systems Conference, pp. 1591–1602 (2021). https://doi.org/10.1145/3461778.3462131
15. Dor, L.M.B., Coglianese, C.: Procurement as AI governance. IEEE Trans. Technol. Soc. **2**(4), 192–199 (2021). https://doi.org/10.1109/TTS.2021.3111764
16. Druckman, J.N., Kam, C.D.: Students as experimental participants: a defense of the "narrow data base". In: Druckman, J.N., Greene, D.P., Kuklinski, J.H., Lupia, A. (eds.) Cambridge Handbook of Experimental Political Science, pp. 41–57. Cambridge University Press (2011). https://doi.org/10.1017/CBO9780511921452.004
17. Du, M., Liu, N., Hu, X.: Techniques for interpretable machine learning. Commun. ACM **63**(1), 68–77 (2019). https://doi.org/10.1145/3359786

18. Ehsan, U., et al.: The who in XAI: how AI background shapes perceptions of AI explanations. In: Proceedings of the CHI Conference on Human Factors in Computing Systems, pp. 1–32 (2024). https://doi.org/10.1145/3613904.3642474

19. Ehsan, U., Riedl, M.O.: Human-centered explainable AI: towards a reflective sociotechnical approach. In: Stephanidis, C., Kurosu, M., Degen, H., Reinerman-Jones, L. (eds.) HCII 2020. LNCS, vol. 12424, pp. 449–466. Springer, Cham (2020). https://doi.org/10.1007/978-3-030-60117-1_33

20. Ehsan, U., Riedl, M.O.: Explainability pitfalls: beyond dark patterns in explainable AI. Patterns **5**(6) (2024). https://doi.org/10.1016/j.patter.2024.100971

21. Ehsan, U., et al.: Human-Centered Explainable AI (HCXAI): beyond opening the black-box of AI. In: CHI Conference on Human Factors in Computing Systems Extended Abstracts, pp. 1–7 (2022). https://doi.org/10.1145/3491101.3503727

22. Ferreira, J.J., Monteiro, M.S.: What are people doing about XAI user experience? A survey on AI explainability research and practice. In: Marcus, A., Rosenzweig, E. (eds.) HCII 2020. LNCS, vol. 12201, pp. 56–73. Springer, Cham (2020). https://doi.org/10.1007/978-3-030-49760-6_4

23. Fleischmann, K.R., Wallace, W.A.: A covenant with transparency: opening the black box of models. Commun. ACM **48**(5), 93–97 (2005). https://doi.org/10.1145/1060710.1060715

24. Franke, U., Helgesson Hallström, C., Artman, H., Dexe, J.: Requirements on and procurement of explainable algorithms—a systematic review of the literature. In: de la Iglesia, D.H., de Paz Santana, J.F., López Rivero, A.J. (eds.) New Trends in Disruptive Technologies, Tech Ethics, and Artificial Intelligence. DiTTEt 2024. AISC, vol. 1459. Springer, Cham (2024). https://doi.org/10.1007/978-3-031-66635-3_4

25. Guidotti, R., Monreale, A., Ruggieri, S., Turini, F., Giannotti, F., Pedreschi, D.: A survey of methods for explaining black box models. ACM Comput. Surv. (CSUR) **51**(5), 1–42 (2018). https://doi.org/10.1145/3236009

26. Hacker, P., Passoth, J.H.: Varieties of AI explanations under the law. From the GDPR to the AIA, and beyond. In: Holzinger, A., Goebel, R., Fong, R., Moon, T., Müller, KR., Samek, W. (eds.) xxAI - Beyond Explainable AI. xxAI 2020. LNCS, vol. 13200, pp. 343–373. Springer, Cham (2020). https://doi.org/10.1007/978-3-031-04083-2_17

27. Hechler, E., Oberhofer, M., Schaeck, T.: Deploying AI in the Enterprise. Springer, Cham (2020). https://doi.org/10.1007/978-1-4842-6206-1, see especially the chapter *AI and Governance*, pp. 165–211

28. Holm, E.A.: In defense of the black box. Science **364**(6435), 26–27 (2019). https://doi.org/10.1126/science.aax0162

29. Jonk, E., Iren, D.: Governance and communication of algorithmic decision making: a case study on public sector. In: 2021 IEEE 23rd Conference on Business Informatics (CBI), vol. 1, pp. 151–160. IEEE (2021). https://doi.org/10.1109/CBI52690.2021.00026

30. Keil, F.C.: Explanation and understanding. Annu. Rev. Psychol. **57**, 227–254 (2006). https://doi.org/10.1146/annurev.psych.57.102904.190100

31. Kenny, E.M., Ford, C., Quinn, M., Keane, M.T.: Explaining black-box classifiers using post-hoc explanations-by-example: the effect of explanations and error-rates in XAI user studies. Artif. Intell. **294**, 103459 (2021). https://doi.org/10.1016/j.artint.2021.103459

32. Köchling, A., Wehner, M.C.: Discriminated by an algorithm: a systematic review of discrimination and fairness by algorithmic decision-making in the context of HR recruitment and HR development. Bus. Res. **13**(3), 795–848 (2020). https://doi.org/10.1007/s40685-020-00134-w

33. Liyanarachchi, G.A.: Feasibility of using student subjects in accounting experiments: a review. Pac. Account. Rev. **19**(1), 47–67 (2007). https://doi.org/10.1108/01140580710754647

34. Lundberg, S.M., Lee, S.I.: A unified approach to interpreting model predictions. In: Guyon, I., Luxburg, U.V., Bengio, S., Wallach, H., Fergus, R., Vishwanathan, S., Garnett, R. (eds.) Advances in Neural Information Processing Systems, vol. 30. Curran Associates, Inc. (2017). https://proceedings.neurips.cc/paper/2017/hash/8a20a8621978632d76c43dfd28b67767-Abstract.html

35. Mäntymäki, M., Minkkinen, M., Birkstedt, T., Viljanen, M.: Defining organizational AI governance. AI Ethics **2**(4), 603–609 (2022). https://doi.org/10.1007/s43681-022-00143-x

36. More accountability for big-data algorithms: Nature **537**(7621), 449 (2016). https://doi.org/10.1038/537449a

37. Nauta, M., et al.: From anecdotal evidence to quantitative evaluation methods: a systematic review on evaluating explainable AI. ACM Comput. Surv. **55**(13s), 1–42 (2023). https://doi.org/10.1145/3583558

38. Noll, A., Salzmann, R., Wuthrich, M.V.: Case study: French motor third-party liability claims (2020). https://doi.org/10.2139/ssrn.3164764

39. Obermeyer, Z., Powers, B., Vogeli, C., Mullainathan, S.: Dissecting racial bias in an algorithm used to manage the health of populations. Science **366**(6464), 447–453 (2019). https://doi.org/10.1126/science.aax2342

40. Richens, J.G., Lee, C.M., Johri, S.: Improving the accuracy of medical diagnosis with causal machine learning. Nat. Commun. **11**(1), 3923 (2020). https://doi.org/10.1038/s41467-020-17419-7

41. Sandkuhl, K.: Putting AI into context – method support for the introduction of artificial intelligence into organizations. In: 2019 IEEE 21st Conference on Business Informatics (CBI), vol. 1, pp. 157–164. IEEE (2019). https://doi.org/10.1109/CBI.2019.00025

42. Schneider, J., Abraham, R., Meske, C., vom Brocke, J.: Artificial intelligence governance for businesses. Inf. Syst. Manag. **40**(3), 229–249 (2023). https://doi.org/10.1080/10580530.2022.2085825

43. Schotman, E., Iren, D.: Algorithmic decision making and model explainability preferences in the insurance industry: A Delphi study. In: 2022 IEEE 24th Conference on Business Informatics (CBI), vol. 1, pp. 235–242. IEEE (2022). https://doi.org/10.1109/CBI52690.2021.10055

44. Sørum, H., Presthus, W.: Dude, where's my data? The GDPR in practice, from a consumer's point of view. Inf. Technol. People **34**(3), 912–929 (2020). https://doi.org/10.1108/ITP-08-2019-0433

45. Stecher, P., Pohl, M., Turowski, K.: Enterprise architecture's effects on organizations' ability to adopt artificial intelligence–a resource-based perspective. In: Proceedings of the 28th European Conference on Information Systems (ECIS). Association for Information Systems (2020). https://aisel.aisnet.org/ecis2020_rp/173

46. Tufte, E.R.: The Visual Display of Quantitative Information, 2nd edn. Graphics Press, Cheshire, CT (2001)

47. Vermeire, T., Laugel, T., Renard, X., Martens, D., Detyniecki, M.: How to choose an explainability method? Towards a methodical implementation of XAI in practice. In: Kamp, M., et al. (eds.) Machine Learning and Principles and Practice of Knowledge Discovery in Databases. ECML PKDD 2021. CCIS, vol. 1524, pp. 521–533. Springer, Cham (2021). https://doi.org/10.1007/978-3-030-93736-2_39

48. van der Waa, J., Nieuwburg, E., Cremers, A., Neerincx, M.: Evaluating XAI: a comparison of rule-based and example-based explanations. Artif. Intell. **291**, 103404 (2021). https://doi.org/10.1016/j.artint.2020.103404
49. Wachter, S., Mittelstadt, B., Russell, C.: Counterfactual explanations without opening the black box: automated decisions and the GDPR. Harv. J. Law Technol. **31**, 841–887 (2017)
50. Wang, X., Yin, M.: Are explanations helpful? A comparative study of the effects of explanations in AI-assisted decision-making. In: 26th International Conference on Intelligent User Interfaces, pp. 318–328 (2021). https://doi.org/10.1145/3397481.3450650
51. Weitz, K., Schiller, D., Schlagowski, R., Huber, T., André, E.: "Do you trust me?" Increasing user-trust by integrating virtual agents in explainable AI interaction design. In: Proceedings of the 19th ACM International Conference on Intelligent Virtual Agents, pp. 7–9 (2019). https://doi.org/10.1145/3308532.3329441
52. Zhao, Z.Q., Zheng, P., Xu, S.T., Wu, X.: Object detection with deep learning: a review. IEEE Trans. Neural Netw. Learn. Syst. **30**(11), 3212–3232 (2019). https://doi.org/10.1109/TNNLS.2018.2876865

npmSECO: A Tool for Integrating Trust into the Software Ecosystem

Fang Hou$^{(\boxtimes)}$ ⓘ, Angel Temelko, and Martijn Voordouw

Utrecht University, Utrecht, The Netherlands
{f.hou,m.n.voordouw}@uu.nl, a.temelko@students.uu.nl

Abstract. Selecting software packages is challenging due to the multitude of trust factors involved, such as functionality, compatibility, security, or maintenance, which often requires comprehensive analysis and cross-referencing. Additionally, the tons of software packages and their dependencies can overwhelm decision-makers, leading to potential oversights and inefficiencies in the selection process for critical vulnerabilities. This paper introduces npmSECO, an open-source initiative designed to evaluate the trust and security of software packages before and after installation. We infuse trust data, including trust factors and scores, into a package ecosystem - npm, which is well known for its vulnerabilities and extensive dependency tree to create a more secure environment for software engineers to produce software in. Trust scores and factors are displayed in the command line interface, helping software engineers access rich information for software evaluation in one place before the package installation. We conducted 20 interviews with software engineers to assess this tool. Preliminary feedback indicates that npmSECO offers a high level of usability.

Keywords: Software Ecosystem · Software Package · Package Evaluation · Software trust

1 Introduction

A software ecosystem (SECO), for instance, the iOS ecosystem or Node package manager (npm) ecosystem, comprises actors working collaboratively on a shared platform to produce software products or services [9]. Within these ecosystems, the software supply chain comprises interdependent dependencies, modules, libraries, packages, or imports, facilitating this collaborative process [13]. This study uses the term "package" to refer to these components. These packages are expected to perform their intended functions while managing associated risks, which forms the basic concept of software trust. Software trust refers to *the willingness of SECO actors to accept risks based on subjective beliefs. It is essentially an upstream trust in that actors expect assurance that other actors on top of a common technology platform can exhibit reliable behavior and provide valuable software products* [7]. This concept is the basis of this research. It is not just

© The Author(s), under exclusive license to Springer Nature Switzerland AG 2025
E. Papatheocharous et al. (Eds.): ICSOB 2024, LNBIP 539, pp. 366–381, 2025.
https://doi.org/10.1007/978-3-031-85849-9_29

an abstract concept, but an important determinant of packages' adoption and projects' success. It requires continuous assessment and improvement to ensure that all hubs and actors within the SECO can collaborate while managing the risks.

Untrustworthy packages may pose risks to downstream hubs and actors, causing incorrect outputs, system failures, crashes, and other serious consequences. Especially, software vulnerabilities may be intentionally introduced or accidentally embedded within software packages by attackers, disrupting the entire software supply chain.

Software engineers, particularly those involved in open-source software (OSS) development, often lack formal processes for evaluating or selecting software packages [8]. Common practices may only include reviewing a package's documentation or assessing its compatibility, installation feasibility, and the reputation of its providers through online sources. It is important to note that while software-producing organizations bear significant responsibility for securing SECOs, software-consuming organizations have a smaller role in managing the overall software supply chain's security.

We introduce the npmSECO tool, which integrates trust knowledge into a software engineer's workflow, including before and after package installation. Trust knowledge encompasses factors that can be transformed into actionable information, such as download counts, open issues, licenses, detected vulnerabilities, and the trust of direct and transitive dependencies [6,7]. For the evaluation, We collected feedback from 20 software engineers through interviews to evaluate npmSECO based on its features, performance, and usability. Please note that this paper focuses on how software engineers interact with this data through npmSECO, rather than on the calculation of trust scores, which is addressed in previous works.

The rest of this paper is structured as follows. Section 2 introduces the preliminary project design and existing knowledge. Section 3 presents the npmSECO tool. Section 4 shows the results of the npmSECO evaluation based on a set of interviews. In Sect. 5, we discuss the tool, compare it with the existing approaches from the literature, and highlight its limitations. Finally, Sect. 6 concludes this study with an outline of future work.

2   Foundations and Preliminary Design

2.1   Identifying the Gap in Existing Tools

We conducted a Systematic Literature Review (SLR) to explore the state-of-the-art trust reinforcement mechanisms in the software package ecosystem [15]. The results show that most of the tools: (1) focus primarily on post-installation detection rather than proactive warnings about software trust before the package is installed. Typically, these tools are designed for vulnerability detection and employ a variety of techniques, including dynamic and static analysis, build automation, sandboxing, and machine learning. This reactive approach is effective in identifying existing vulnerabilities after installation, but it does not address the critical need for assessing the packages before installation. (2) It is worth noting that software engineers focus on a wide range of trust factors when selecting third-party packages, not just security or vulnerability [6,7]. Whereas current package manager tools focus primarily on security. (3) Some of the tools have limitations, such as high rates of false positives and negatives, inconsistent performance metrics, and lack of validity. As a result, we need a tool that will not only assess security but also provide richer metrics about software trust that may be accessed and acted on during the selection process of packages.

2.2   A Comprehensive Framework for Software Ecosystem Trust

To bridge this gap, we propose npmSECO, a tool designed to provide software engineers with trust scores and trust knowledge for npm packages before installation. This tool is based on the TrustSECO framework, which we previously developed to enhance trust in SECOs by aggregating trust data, such as the number of downloads, open issues, license information, and known vulnerabilities, from multiple sources such as GitHub, Libraries.io, and CVE databases [5]. The data is used to generate a trust score, which provides a straightforward, numerical assessment of a package's trustworthiness. We integrate TrustSECO to npm, a well-known software package manager. It is able to assist software engineers in making informed decisions about package adoption when using npm, by offering both pre-installation and post-installation assessments. Figure 1 illustrates the framework. Please note that while we provide an introduction to trust data and scores here, these details are not the primary focus of this study.

Trust knowledge was derived from interviews with 24 software engineers to explore package selection protocols and trust knowledge affecting selection [6]. The interview results also reveal that software engineers preferred simple scoring methods to complex ones. They believe numerical forms of trust assessment to be particularly effective. Based on this insight, we developed a trust score calculation mechanism that assigns weights to each factor according to their perceived importance reported in the interviews. This means that the more participants perceive the factor as important, the higher the weight of the factor. The trust assessment is presented as a numerical score ranging from 0 to 100. Higher trust scores indicate greater trust. This approach ensures that the trust score reflects the real-world priorities and practices of software engineers, providing a direct and simple assessment of software trust.

2.3   Objectives to Address the Research Gap

npmSECO addresses a critical gap in current software package evaluation tools, which often focus solely on identifying security vulnerabilities while neglecting other essential trust factors such as maintainability and community support. Existing solutions lack a comprehensive, proactive approach to evaluating the overall trustworthiness of packages before installation. npmSECO fills this gap by automating and streamlining the trust evaluation process, providing engineers with real-time insights into security risks, maintenance activity, and community

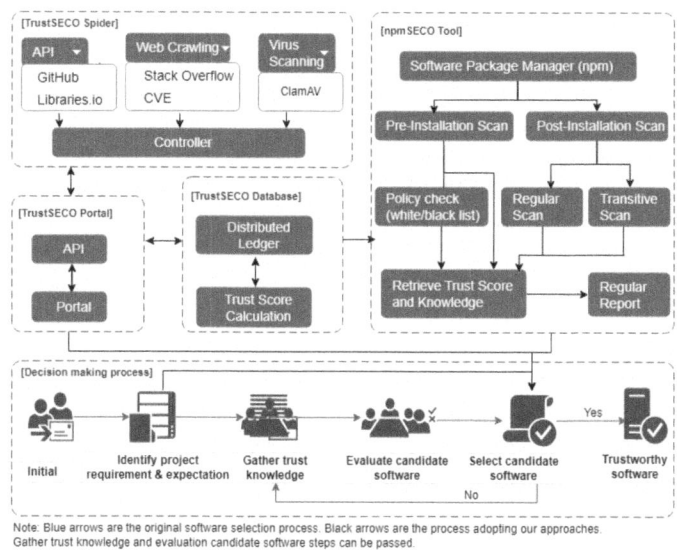

Fig. 1. Overview of npmSECO. In order to clarify the background of the entire project, the framework and relationship of TrustSECO are also shown.

engagement. In particular, it enables engineers to understand the trust of packages before they are installed, thus avoiding the need to manually cross-check multiple sources, reducing the risk of introducing insecure or poorly maintained packages, and preventing costly security issues or disruptions later in the development process.

Here are two sample use scenarios. For instance, a software engineer is tasked with selecting a package for a critical web application. Using npmSECO, they check the trust scores of potential npm packages and discover that one package has a low trust score due to security vulnerabilities, prompting them to choose a more trustworthy alternative to ensure the application's security. Another scenario is when they are reviewing third-party packages used in their organization's software, they can identify a package with outdated dependencies and a low trust score, enabling them to block its use to comply with the institution's strict security policies.

3   Trust Knowledge Integration to npm

We demonstrate npmSECO in Fig. 1. The artifacts, including TrustSECO and npmSECO, are ready to use, and available in an online repository. npmSECO builds on the work of TrustSECO to seamlessly assist software engineers in assessing the trust of packages before and after installation, helping them avoid installing untrustworthy packages via the npm command line interface (CLI). Its main features include the evaluation in both pre-installation and post-installation.

Pre-Installation: The *install* command allows software engineers to check trust scores and knowledge for certain packages by providing the name and version before installation. If the trust score falls below a predefined threshold, e.g., 80, a prominent yellow warning is displayed.

This command includes policy enforcement designed to enforce custom installation policies by using a JSON file located in the project's root directory. This file allows users to define lists of allowed and/or disallowed packages. If the JSON file is absent or empty, npmSECO defaults to the standard npm behavior, displaying only trust information and indicating whether a package's trust score meets the required standard, as illustrated in Fig. 2. When any packages are set in the approved and/or blocked list in the file, the policy checker activates and verifies the packages intended for installation against these lists to ensure compliance. The approved list functions as a whitelist, containing only the packages that are approved for installation. Packages not listed are automatically prohibited with a warning message. The blocked list functions as a blacklist. It catalogs all packages that are banned. Detailed examples of these lists are provided in Fig. 3. This feature is particularly valuable for large-scale organizations or sectors with high-security needs, such as banking and military, which often restrict software installations to components on an approved list [6]. By incorporating known malicious packages into a blocked list, software engineers can prevent their inadvertent installation, thereby enhancing security and adhering to stringent organizational requirements.

After verifying compliance with the policies (if they are set up), npmSECO retrieves the trust score and relevant data from the TrustSECO database. This information is presented in a user-friendly ASCII table format, improving the tool's overall usability. To enhance clarity and usability, npmSECO organizes data into distinct tables, which helps software engineers quickly interpret and act on the trust information.

Given that software engineers might want to review package details and trust scores before proceeding with installation, npmSECO offers the *info* command. This command presents the package summary, information on vulnerabilities, and a set of trust knowledge. The output is akin to what the *install* command generates, as illustrated in Fig. 2, just without the warning messages.

npmSECO provides the *view tree* command to inspect transitive dependencies without downloading the software package or navigating to the portal. By employing this command, software engineers can visualize the transitive dependencies and trust scores. The view is similar to the demonstration in Fig. 4.

Post-Installation: While npmSECO is primarily designed to enforce pre-installation verification to prevent the inclusion of malicious packages, it also offers basic post-installation capabilities. This feature is particularly beneficial for scanning packages already installed in projects. npmSECO enables regular and transitive dependency scans through the use of flags that extend existing commands, rather than requiring additional arguments or separate commands.

When the flag of *report* is executed, npmSECO performs a regular scan by iterating through the *packages.json* file of installed packages, listing all pack-

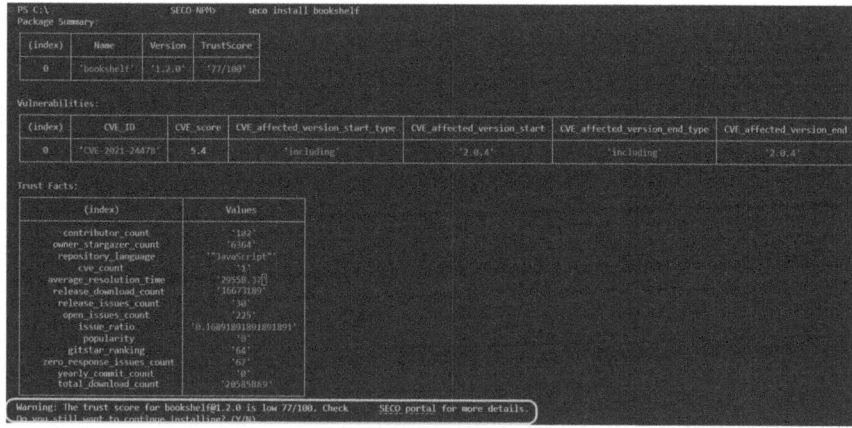

Fig. 2. Screenshot of package installation with warning message

```
PS C:\,              :\Code\SecureSECO-NPM> trustseco install bookshelf
Warning: The package bookshelf is blocked by your organization's policy.
Do you still want to continue installing? (Y/N) 

PS C:\,              :\Code\SecureSECO-NPM> trustseco install bookshelf
Warning: The package bookshelf is not on the allowed list.
Do you still want to continue installing? (Y/N) 
```

Fig. 3. Policy Verification screens for a package installation message when it is listed in the disapproval list and not in the approval list. The top one is for the disapproval list function. The bottom one is for the approve list function.

```
 PS C:\                          SECO-NPM>          seco scan -d
npm-trust-score-script@1.0.0 TrustScore:82
     ├── commander@11.0.0 TrustScore:54
     ├── node-fetch@2.7.0 TrustScore:63
     │   ├── encoding@undefined TrustScore:47
     │   └── whatwg-url@5.0.0 TrustScore:17
     │       ├── tr46@0.0.3 TrustScore:22
     │       └── webidl-conversions@3.0.1 TrustScore:62
     ├── oo-ascii-tree@1.88.0 TrustScore:68
     ├── ora@5.4.1 TrustScore:2
     ├── bl@4.1.0 TrustScore:92
     ├── buffer@5.7.1 TrustScore:89
     │   ├── base64-js@1.5.1 TrustScore:34
     │   └── ieee754@1.2.1 TrustScore:77
```

Fig. 4. Screenshot of Transitive Dependency Scan

```
 PS C:\        \Code\S:   :SECO-NPM>        scan -r
The following libraries have trust scores below the acceptable threshold:
bookshelf@^1.2.0 - TrustScore: 42
node-fetch@^2.6.6 - TrustScore: 55                              I
oo-ascii-tree@^1.88.0 - TrustScore: 46
ora@^5.4.1 - TrustScore: 35
semver@^6.3.1 - TrustScore: 63
typescript@^5.2.2 - TrustScore: 20
For more information, visit    SECO-portal.

A report has been created in the root folder of this project named trust_scores_report.csv
```

Fig. 5. Screenshot of Regular Scan

ages that fall below the trust score threshold. Details are shown in Fig. 5. This feature improves reporting capabilities for engineers and assists in the ongoing enhancement of their untrusted dependencies.

The flag of *dependencies* activates the *npm ls* command provided by npm to gather all transitive dependencies and their trust scores in a tree visualization, which gathers all transitive dependencies and visualizes them in a tree structure, as shown in Fig. 4. Although *npm ls* command delivers a comprehensive view of the dependency tree, npmSECO independently calculates the trust score for each package. Dependencies with trust scores below the specified threshold are highlighted in yellow to ensure they receive engineers' attention. Given the potentially large number of packages, this process requires significant recursion. To optimize this process, npmSECO utilizes caching mechanisms. If a trust score for a package has previously been calculated and there have been no updates in the TrustSECO database, it is retrieved from the cached data. Dependencies with trust scores below a specific threshold are highlighted in yellow to draw engineers' attention. Both regular scan and transitive scan results can be added to generate a file at the project's main root.

4   Evaluation

We conducted semi-structured interviews based on the guide developed by Kallio et al. [10] to gather feedback from experienced software engineers on their typical software evaluation practices and their assessment of the npmSECO tool. The purpose was to evaluate the tool's features, performance, comparative advantages, and areas for improvement. The interviews, which lasted approximately 30–40 minutes each, were conducted either online or in person and were recorded. Participants were recommended to be fully familiar with the tool. Before the interviews, if participants were unable to install the tool, they were provided with a video demonstration to help them familiarize the features for a more effective discussion. During the interview, participants had the opportunity to request live demonstrations of the features to gain a deeper understanding of the tool. After the interviews, transcripts were sent back to participants for verification and any necessary corrections.

A total of 20 software engineers participated in the study, distinct from those who contributed to the initial collection of trust knowledge. Participants were selected based on their professional experience, with each having at least two years in the field. They were recruited primarily through the co-authors' professional networks and met the following criteria: (1) proficient in English; (2) holding at least a bachelor's degree in computer science or related fields; (3) domain experts from software companies involved in the search for software packages (15 participants indicated a frequency score of 4 or higher, on a scale of the frequency of searching for software packages, 1–5 indicating from "never" to "very often"; mean = 3.85, median = 4, which underscores they are well experienced and expectant about the software package selection); (4) the majority, comprising 14 participants, are full-stack engineers, meaning they have experience with both the UI and server sides of systems, which gives them a comprehensive perspective when discussing npm packages. Notably, three participants are cloud architects, adding further diversity and expertise to our study; (5) between two to 29 years of industry experience (mean = 10, median = 7); and (6) employment across various industries and company sizes. Then we adopted convenience sampling (contacted the practitioners who meet such requirements) and snowball sampling (consulted eligible practitioners referred by participants). The demographic characteristics of the interview participants are presented in Table 1. Interview protocol and participant feedback are saved as online materials[1].

Table 1. Demographic Information of Software Engineers

ID	Years	Role	Size	Utilization
I1	3	Full-Stack	17	3
I2	23	Full-Stack	30,000	5
I3	20	Full-Stack	300	5
I4	15	Full-Stack	40,000	4
I5	29	Cloud Architect/Full-Stack	350	5
I6	10	Cloud Architect/Full-Stack	20	4
I7	15	Full-Stack	300	4
I8	3	Front-End	20	4
I9	3	Full-Stack	80	2
I10	10	Full-Stack	250	4
I11	6	Full-Stack	10	2
I12	3	Full-Stack	20	4
I13	3	Front-End	200	3
I14	3	Front-End	200	4
I15	11	Full-Stack	400	4
I16	8	Full-Stack	90,000	3
I17	2	Full-Stack	10	4
I18	25	Full-Stack	20,000	4
I19	6	Full-Stack	400	4
I20	2	Full-Stack	130	5

Year - Years of experience of the participants;

Size - Size of the company;

Utilization - How frequently search software packages

---

[1] https://figshare.com/s/4db3d34847d97fd65953.

4.1   Software Selection Process

We interviewed participants regarding their typical software selection process. While it is not directly related to assessing this tool, the discussion provides valuable insights into the participants' protocol and the trust knowledge in software package evaluation or selection. This understanding is crucial to ascertain whether our tool could address the challenges faced by software practitioners in evaluating or selecting software, thereby enhancing or streamlining the process. The results align with interview findings [6] and relevant literature [12].

Nineteen participants point out that they do not adopt any tools for software evaluation but rely on manual checks from open-source communities or feedback from the npm install process. Only I20 utilizes a prebuilt CI tool in their work. Interestingly, engineers from smaller companies often report a lack of formal policies regarding third-party component usage [6]; these companies tend to trust their engineers' judgment in selecting appropriate libraries. In contrast, those employed by enterprise-level organizations or within specific sectors indicate stringent regulations and policies. I7 believes that *"It was a more structured and strict enforcement of third-party library use policies. The financial institution has a list of approved packages. If someone wants to use a different package, they can't just decide independently. They need to discuss it with the team. If the team agrees, they still need permission from higher-ups."*.

Participants believe preventing application bloat and maintaining optimal performance is more important than security. Twelve participants consider popularity such as the number of downloads and GitHub Stars as a major factor; maintenance activity such as the number of releases, and the number of open or closed issues are significant for 11 participants; known vulnerabilities and community support are crucial for five and four participants; licensing, trust knowledge source, and package size, each influenced less than three participants. However, two participants prioritize dependency issues over these factors, focusing more on package installation impacts.

4.2   Features

Trust Knowledge: Overwhelmingly positive feedback emerges from the surveyed engineers. Specifically, 19 participants believe this feature improved their understanding of the packages they considered, promoting more careful decision-making. I8, I10, and I13 confirm that they often overlook the details included in the trust knowledge. I5 highlights that *"Trust scores provide the information that decides not to install a package. The trust score should make me pause and consider for a few seconds longer before installing, especially from a security standpoint"*. According to I9 and I14, they rarely check trust knowledge but only care about whether or not the packages can be successfully installed through npm. This tool enables them to consider the trust before the installation. By utilizing this tool, they may be aware that it is imperative to exercise caution before utilizing external libraries, particularly in large projects that may consist of a variety of libraries. I2 and I20 contend that sometimes software engineers overlook details about a package. Trust scores serve as a guide or alert to help prevent such errors from occurring.

Trust Score: Some participants point out that trust scores do not fully reflect the trust of a software package. For instance, I6 highlights that the trust score may introduce an unfair bias towards new packages due to insufficient trust knowledge. For instance, total downloads, number of software engineers, or frequency of releases, may have low values for new packages, leading to lower trust scores unfairly impacting their evaluation. I10 notes that the trust of a package may not depend on frequent updates. It could be a well-functioning tool that does not require constant changes. Similarly, trust knowledge, such as the number of GitHub stars may not always reflect the true value of a library, and a perfectly functioning package does not need to commit anything, so the number of commits per year drops to close to zero. Another one is the contributor count. I20 points out that most software engineers could see no reason why the number of people working would affect software trust. Four participants highlight certain trust knowledge, such as GitHub Star, first release date, and contributor count, is redundant or not particularly useful. While understanding the feature's broader appeal, I3, I6, and I20 personally prefer accessing information directly from GitHub or sticking to their existing processes. In addition, some participants propose enhancements to the trust score calculation process. For example, I3 and I20 emphasize the importance of the dependencies. They point out that a package's trust score should not exceed that of its lowest scoring dependency.

Pre-Installation Scan: All participants appreciate the pre-installation scan feature, recognizing it can help them get more clear, comprehensive, and transparent insights into the package's trust before the installation. As a result, it can save them time in collecting information from various sources, especially for large organizations where strict guidelines govern the use of packages. According to I3, I15, I18, I19, and I20, most security or quality evaluation tools are post-installation verifications. To the best of their knowledge, this tool is almost the first CLI tool being developed specifically for npm to enhance trust in packages for pre-installation. The policy enforcement feature can block packages that are not allowed for specific companies or fields. I6 and I20 suggest that this tool can be included in the DevOps pipeline and automated pipeline. Especially when one of the dependencies becomes vulnerable, it automatically gets warned. However, most participants do not have an interest in post-installation, so it is possible to determine the trust of the packages they use in more ways.

Transitive Scan: Most participants consider it an impressive feature as it offers extensive information about where each element fits within the overall stack of dependencies. Specifically, 19 participants recognize its benefits, with 15 even considering it the most beneficial feature of the tool. I6 and I16 state that software engineers usually ignore the packages depending on the others, and this feature can help them pre-check the quality of the libraries deeply. I20 states that *"I think checking transitive dependencies should not even be a question. Check everything I am installing every time, please"*.

CSV Report: The participants offer varied feedback for the report of post-installation verification. Twelve of them regarded it as a highly useful tool for reporting purposes. I2, I6, and I15 express interest in using the feature but suggest enhancements, such as customizable headers, tables, and the option to export to HTML.

CLI: Participants believe it is significant assistance during their package library research and appreciated the convenience of quick lookups. However, whilst they recognize its usefulness, consistent feedback highlights concerns about how trust knowledge is presented. Participants suggest that the naming of the trust knowledge could be clearer and more intuitive for the values presented.

4.3 Performance and Usability

Performance: Regarding performance, most participants confirm that they did not notice any significant performance issues. I14 and I17 indicate that performance is not their primary concern when using the tool. The benefits of ensuring trust outweighed any potential performance flaws. Comparing speed to the trust knowledge provided, they are willing to sacrifice speed in expectation of more knowledge. This is because they usually spend a long time gathering trust knowledge. The tool's responsiveness is viewed differently. Sixteen respondents agree that a scan time of 137 seconds for 12 packages is reasonable. According to I1 and I13, gathering all of the transitive dependencies manually could take several hours. I3 and I10 appreciate it as a confirmation that the tool is functioning and has not stalled. However, I19 and I20 express dissatisfaction with the slow response of npmSECO. I19 states that *"Depending on the project's size and number of dependencies, the tool might take longer to produce results. Optimization might be needed since users might not have the patience for long waits"*. According to I20, *"I don't care about the package installation process that much. Even if it was significantly slower, I just waited for it one time and never again. I think performance matters for the scan feature, that is, the one that would be running over and over on a CI agent"*.

Usability: Most participants believe the tool is user-friendly, with its installation and setup as straightforward as adding a standard npm package. Additionally, they confirmed that npmSECO automates the evaluation process by retrieving trust data for packages, simplifying the process of acquiring trust knowledge and scores. Especially, it seamlessly integrates with existing workflows, enabling them to utilize the tool without interruption. Furthermore, participants stated that the tool could be used to reduce the time spent manually evaluating packages. However, I2 and I20 highlight that the trust knowledge provided by npmSECO is insufficient. They are looking for additional details, such as license or code size, to more comprehensively evaluate the trust of a package.

Time-Saving: Thirteen participants find the information from npmSECO sufficient for their initial assessment, potentially saving them between one to five hours. I1 and I2 note the tool could save them additional time since they typically inspect the issues within package dependencies. For I9 and I14, previously unfamiliar with the trust knowledge in package evaluation, npmSECO introduces new perspectives to their assessment process, making it challenging to quantify the time savings. Meanwhile, two other participants, I2 and I10, estimate a time saving of one to two hours by using the tool to check a package's popularity, maintenance, and support, though they still need to review other trust knowledge, such as the documentation, code, and license.

5 Discussion

Software engineers currently rely on manual checks when selecting packages, for example, considering the popularity of the package, the number of downloads, and basic information about the npm installation process. Very few automated tools are used for package evaluation. npmSECO fills this critical gap by automating key parts of the selection process, providing trust knowledge and actionable insights to help engineers make safer decisions. The automation provided by npmSECO is a major contribution. Instead of manually cross-referencing various sources for information, npmSECO automates the gathering of trust knowledge and the evaluation of packages, making the software selection process far more efficient. The automated trust evaluation process combined with its policy enforcement capabilities is useful for teams working on large projects or in highly regulated industries. For these users, npmSECO not only streamlined the selection process but also ensured that organizational security policies were upheld throughout the development lifecycle.

Comparison with Existing Tools: According to SLR for the trust reinforcement mechanisms in npm ecosystem [15], various tools adopt different methodologies focusing on vulnerability detection, such as dynamic and static analysis, sandboxing [16], and machine learning techniques [4]. These tools are often integrated into CI/CD pipelines and address a range of threats, including transitive vulnerabilities, code injections, zero-day vulnerabilities, clone packages, malicious code, and permission systems. Despite these advancements, a significant gap persists in pre-installation safeguards [1,17]. While many tools excel in detecting vulnerabilities, they frequently fall short in providing a comprehensive evaluation of package trust. There is a clear need for tools that offer a richer set of information about packages, extending beyond mere vulnerability detection, to enable a more thorough assessment of their overall trust prior to installation. npmSECO integrates seamlessly with the npm CLI, providing software engineers with direct access to trust knowledge within their development workflow. This integration streamlines data collection and improves efficiency by embedding trust evaluation into the installation process. The tool adopts an evidence-based approach combined with pre-installation verification. It offers comprehensive trust scores and detailed knowledge of packages and their dependencies, including knowledge such as quality, maintenance, support status, vulnerabilities, and virus information. By presenting this information, npmSECO enables software engineers to assess the overall trust of a package before installation, thus helping to prevent the inclusion of malicious software in their projects.

Comparison with npms and Snyk Score: npm score[2] and Snyk score[3] are web-based platforms offer distinct approaches to evaluating package trust. *npms* focuses on package quality, popularity, and maintenance by analyzing trust knowledge such as license, vulnerable dependencies, downloads, stars, releases, and issues, with a weighted scoring system whose method is not fully disclosed. It provides separate scores for quality, popularity, and maintenance, updated bi-weekly. *Snyk* similarly assesses security, popularity, maintenance, and community, presenting data through text and charts. npmSECO, in contrast, provides comprehensive trust knowledge before the package installation. Particularly, it emphasizes vulnerability status on the top of the npm CLI to draw attention to the existing disclosed issues. However, npmSECO's presentation of trust knowledge could be improved. Some aspects, such as the unit for resolution time, are unclear, and the calculation methods for trust scores are not transparent to users who are not logged into the TrustSECO portal. This lack of clarity can hinder users' understanding of the trust knowledge provided by npmSECO.

To analyze the factors affecting npmSECO, we discuss the threats to validity as outlined below.

Internal Validity: The evaluation of npmSECO is based on the experiences and observations of the participants with diverse backgrounds, including varying work experiences, educational levels, cultural contexts, roles, and industry contexts. Therefore, the results may not fully represent the perspectives of all software engineers [3]. For example, for software engineers who are only focused on the successful installation of a software package, npmSECO can provide them with enhanced trust knowledge to assist them in avoiding issues during package installation, such as software compatibility, quality, or vulnerability issues. Conversely, those who fully realize the role of trust may have different requirements for npmSECO. For example, some software engineers need npmSECO to be customized or to provide compliance or specific formats for reporting. Or closed software engineers may pay attention to security and licenses (one of the structure assurance trust factors), while OSS engineers tend to ignore them. We recognize that there is no one-size-fits-all tool, npmSECO is designed to incorporate a variety of trust knowledge, related information, and features to provide software engineers with a more comprehensive view of a package's trust. While certain relevant information, such as deprecated project flags [11], may not contribute directly to the trust score calculation, it serves to alert engineers about abandoned packages or dependencies. This approach helps engineers save time and gain a deeper understanding of packages.

---

[2] https://npms.io/about.
[3] https://snyk.io/advisor/python.

External Validity: Feedback from our interviews indicated potential biases in trust knowledge such as download counts, GitHub Stars, or update frequency, which might unfairly lower the trust scores for newer or less frequently updated packages. We acknowledge that packages with low trust scores are not necessarily untrustworthy and are exploring ways to help engineers identify such packages more accurately. This bias, however, is one for which we have not found an effective solution in the relevant literature. In contrast to npm and Snyk scores, npmSECO does not assign more than 30% weight to package maintenance and popularity. The deviations do not pose a significant problem for npmSECO.

6   Conclusion and Future Work

In the face of the growing complexity and risks associated with software supply chains [2], existing methods have proven inadequate in fully evaluating and selecting software packages [14]. To address this critical real-world problem faced by software engineers and organizations, we introduce npmSECO, a tool designed to enhance the trust of SECOs by significantly improving the package evaluation process. npmSECO provides a pre-installation evaluation mechanism that assesses the trust of software packages before they are integrated into a project. It incorporates a policy enforcement feature that functions similarly to whitelists and blacklists, enabling the installation of only approved packages or blocking disapproved ones. This feature bolsters security protocols and improves the management of software assets in organizations. Additionally, npmSECO offers a post-installation assessment that continuously monitors and evaluates the security of installed packages and their dependencies, thereby increasing the overall software trust.

The evaluation of npmSECO emphasizes how software engineers engage with and interpret the provided trust data through the tool's interface. This interaction, rather than the mathematical intricacies of calculating trust scores, forms the core of this study. Our focus lies in how npmSECO facilitates informed decision-making and trust assessment during the software package selection process, particularly through its user-centered design and the real-time display of trust factors.

The key innovation of npmSECO lies in its seamless integration with npm, enabling real-time, pre-installation trust evaluations that extend beyond traditional post-installation vulnerability checks. With features such as customizable allow and block lists, npmSECO not only ensures compliance with security policies but also enhances package governance for organizations, particularly large-scale or specialized ones, by improving oversight and decision-making. Insights from practitioners highlight the utility of trust scores as an effective decision-making tool, offering critical feedback on package reliability and security. These insights reinforce the need for comprehensive trust assessments in software package management, demonstrating the practical impact of npmSECO in real-world scenarios.

The future work includes (1) an improved presentation of trust knowledge, with detailed displays of trust scores across various dimensions, and making it more presentable for organizations; (2) providing additional markings and descriptions for newly created packages; (3) refining the formatting of reports to enhance usability; (4) integrating trust knowledge into other platforms and extend it across various ecosystems and tool portfolios; and (5) including the business perspective by integrating other standards, for instance, ISO/IEC 20243-1:2023, ISO 22385:2023 and, ISO/IEC 18974:2023. Additionally, we intend to collaborate with other organizations to incorporate a broader range of their software packages and infrastructure.

References

1. Arteca, E., Turcotte, A.: Npm-filter: automating the mining of dynamic information from npm packages. In: Proceedings of the 19th International Conference on Mining Software Repositories, pp. 304–308. MSR '22, Association for Computing Machinery, New York, NY, USA (2022)
2. Duan, R., Alrawi, O., Kasturi, R.P., Elder, R.S., Saltaformaggio, B., Lee, W.: Towards measuring supply chain attacks on package managers for interpreted languages. Network and Distributed Systems Security (NDSS) Symposium 2021 (2021)
3. Ewers, R.M., Didham, R.K.: Confounding factors in the detection of species responses to habitat fragmentation. Biol. Rev. **81**(1), 117–142 (2006)
4. Garrett, K., Ferreira, G., Jia, L., Sunshine, J., Kästner, C.: Detecting suspicious package updates. In: 2019 IEEE/ACM 41st International Conference on Software Engineering: New Ideas and Emerging Results (ICSE-NIER), pp. 13–16 (2019)
5. Hou, F., Farshidi, S., Jansen, S.: Trustseco: a distributed infrastructure for providing trust in the software ecosystem. In: International Conference on Advanced Information Systems Engineering, pp. 121–133. Springer (2021)
6. Hou, F., Jansen, F., De Vries, A., Jansen, S.: The role of software trust in selection of open-source and closed software. In: 2023 IEEE/ACM 11th International Workshop on Software Engineering for Systems-of-Systems and Software Ecosystems (SESoS), pp. 30–37. IEEE (2023)
7. Hou, F., Jansen, S.: A systematic literature review on trust in the software ecosystem. Empir. Softw. Eng. **28**(1), 8 (2023)
8. Jansen, F., Jansen, S., Hou, F.: TrustSECO: an interview survey into software trust. arXiv preprint arXiv:2101.06138 (2021)
9. Jansen, S., Cusumano, M.A., Brinkkemper, S.: Software Ecosystems: Analyzing and Managing Business Networks in the Software Industry. Edward Elgar (2013)
10. Kallio, H., Pietilä, A.M., Johnson, M., Kangasniemi, M.: Systematic methodological review: developing a framework for a qualitative semi-structured interview guide. J. Adv. Nurs. **72**(12), 2954–2965 (2016)
11. Miller, C., Kästner, C., Vasilescu, B.: We feel like we're winging it: a study on navigating open-source dependency abandonment. In: Proceedings of the 31st ACM Joint European Software Engineering Conference and Symposium on the Foundations of Software Engineering, pp. 1281–1293 (2023)
12. Mujahid, S., Abdalkareem, R., Shihab, E.: What are the characteristics of highly-selected packages? A case study on the npm ecosystem. J. Syst. Softw. **198**, 111588 (2023)

13. Ohm, M., Stuke, C.: SOK: practical detection of software supply chain attacks. In: Proceedings of the 18th International Conference on Availability, Reliability and Security, pp. 1–11 (2023)

14. Samoaa, H.P., Longa, A., Mohamad, M., Chehreghani, M.H., Leitner, P.: TEP-GNN: accurate execution time prediction of functional tests using graph neural networks. In: International Conference on Product-Focused Software Process Improvement, pp. 464–479. Springer (2022)

15. Temelko, A., Hou, F., Farshidi, S., Jansen, S.: Systematic literature review of the trust reinforcement mechanisms exist in package ecosystems. arXiv preprint arXiv:2407.02522 (2024)

16. Vu, D.L., Pashchenko, I., Massacci, F., Plate, H., Sabetta, A.: Towards using source code repositories to identify software supply chain attacks. In: Proceedings of the 2020 ACM SIGSAC Conference on Computer and Communications Security, pp. 2093–2095. CCS '20, Association for Computing Machinery, New York, NY, USA (2020)

17. Zahan, N., Kanakiya, P., Hambleton, B., Shohan, S., Williams, L.: Preprint: can the openssf scorecard be used to measure the security posture of npm and pypi? arXiv preprint arXiv:2208.03412 (2022)

Governance Practices for Open Source Foundations in the Healthcare Sector

Elçin Yenişen Yavuz[1]([✉]), Akshat Shrivastava[1], Dirk Riehle[1], and Florian Putz[2]

[1] Friedrich-Alexander-University Erlangen-Nürnberg, Erlangen, Germany
{elcin.yenisen,akshat.shrivastava}@fau.de, dirk@riehle.org
[2] Universitätsklinik Erlangen-Nürnberg, Erlangen, Germany
florian.putz@uk-erlangen.de

Abstract. Open source (OS) foundations are non-profit organizations that support open-source software development projects. OS foundations can be categorized based on their membership and governance structures. This study focuses on vendor-led and user-led OS foundations operating in the healthcare sector. The study has two objectives. The first objective is to explore the similarities and differences of vendor-led and user-led OS foundations. The second objective is to explore and define governance practices applied in these foundations to achieve success. To address these objectives, we performed multiple-case study research, with the openEHR Foundation and the RACOON consortium as our cases. We performed interviews with key stakeholders and applied thematic analysis to derive the results. We present differences and similarities of these foundations with respect to membership and organizational structure. We also present members' motivation to engage with these foundations. Furthermore, we identify and explain 32 governance practices applied in nine contexts related to OS foundations in the healthcare sector.

Keywords: open source foundation · governance practices · best practices · openEHR · RACOON

1 Introduction

The development of open-source software (OSS) is a process in which participants cooperate to produce better software with openness as a key element. OSS projects started with developer communities followed by the participation of companies and the establishment of open source (OS) foundations. OS foundations are non-profit organizations that offer neutral organizational platforms for OSS projects. They are legal entities that play a role in collecting and allocating funds to sustain these projects and protecting the rights of project contributors. They may provide assistance in governance mechanisms and technical infrastructure for the projects they host [1,2].

To provide an understanding of OS foundations, [3] introduced a classification which distinguish three types of OS foundations regarding the legal entity and

E. Papatheocharous et al. (Eds.): ICSOB 2024, LNBIP 539, pp. 382–397, 2025.
https://doi.org/10.1007/978-3-031-85849-9_30

motives of their leading members: community-led OS foundations, vendor-led OS foundations, and user-led OS foundations.

In community-led OS foundations, projects are steered by individuals, who may be both developers and users of the software they contribute to. Contributors to these community-led OS projects can be either volunteers or paid employees of companies [3]. An example of this type of foundations is the Apache Software Foundation.

In vendor-led OS foundations, the leading members are information technology (IT) companies collaborating to develop OSS components [1,4]. Vendors' involvement in OSS projects evolved from sponsoring OSS communities to creating OSS consortia with their competitors and leading the development process collaboratively. Two examples of vendor-led OS consortia are the Linux Foundation (LF) Edge consortium, and the Open Infrastructure Foundation.

In user-led OS foundations, the leading members are end-user organizations, mostly from non-software industries. These organizations collaborate with the focus of developing software applications to use in their internal processes [3]. In these foundations, key members are organizations, not individual software developers. User-led OS foundations emerged in higher education in the early 2000s, driven by the need for tailored software and vendor independence, with the universities in the United States (US) at the forefront. Notable early projects include the Kuali Financial Systems and the Sakai Learning Management System. Some other examples are openKonsequenz from the energy industry [5], and openMDM from the automotive industry [3]. However, we did not encounter any research papers about user-led OS foundations in the healthcare sector.

In the late 1990s, healthcare providers began integrating IT systems to develop comprehensive care delivery systems. Faced with challenges in conventional software, they turned to OSS alternatives [6]. OSS has since grown in importance in healthcare, contributing to improved care quality while reducing costs-an advantage particularly valuable in low-resource settings [7].

This study focuses on the OS foundations operating in the healthcare sector steered by organizational members (corporate entities). Our goal is to investigate the similarities and differences of vendor-led and user-led OS foundations and to define the governance practices which help to achieve the success of OS foundations. Our research questions are:

- RQ1: What are the differences and similarities between vendor-led and user-led open source foundations in the healthcare sector concerning governance structures and member engagement motivations?
- RQ2: What governance practices enable foundations in the healthcare sector to achieve success?

To address these problems, we performed case study research with two cases. We selected openEHR as an example of a vendor-led OS foundation and RACOON (Radiological Cooperative Network) as an example of a user-led OS foundation. openEHR is a non-profit organization that provides technical specifications for Electronic Health Record (EHR) platforms, as well as domain-specific clinical models for defining content. RACOON is a consortium focusing on collaborative work among university clinics in Germany to provide better medical care against COVID-19 and cardiac diseases. Consortium here means a formally organized community of organizations with a defined governance structure and processes. The specific legal form of incorporation does not matter. We therefore use the terms foundation and consortium synonymously.

The structure of this paper is as follows: In Sect. 2, we present the related work on OS foundations in healthcare and governance practices of organization-led open source foundations. In Sect. 3, we describe the methodology we employed. We present the results in Sect. 4, and discussion in Sect. 5. In Sect. 6, we discuss the limitations, and in Sect. 7 we present the conclusion.

2   Related Work

2.1   Open Source Foundations in Healthcare Sector

OS foundations in healthcare play a role in shaping a procurement strategy that maximizes resource utilization, prioritizes patient safety, increases standardization and improves healthcare services quality [8].

[9] identified the five most popular open-source Electronic Health Records (EHR) systems and compared them by focusing on their features, functionalities and performances. These systems were: OSEHRA VistA, GNU Health, Open Medical Record System (OpenMRS), Open Electronic Medical Record (OpenEMR), and OpenEHR. **VistA**(Veterans Health Information Systems and Technology Architecture) was one of the early examples of OSS projects in the healthcare sector. VistA was initiated by the US Veterans Health Administration in 1982. As a federal project, its source code was public domain. Although it was open to use by other organizations, it was not officially OSS until 2003. Applying OSS principles and building a community around the system was essential to attract talented developers to contribute to VistA [10]. [10] identified the challenges VistA faced during this transformation process. These challenges include creating a technical infrastructure for collaboration, establishing governance mechanisms to balance stakeholders' demands, acquiring domain experts beyond computer science, and deciding on intellectual property licensing. **OpenMRS** was initiated by the Regenstrief Institute and the Medical Research Council of South Africa for use by low income and developing countries [11,12]. [11] investigated the impact, opportunities, and challenges of openMRS implementation in hospitals. **LibreHealth:RIS** is an open-source radiology information system (RIS) that began as a small module of openMRS. As of 2017, it has continued as an independent RIS project under LibreHealth [12]. [12] described the specifications and development process of LibreHealth:RIS. **OpenEMR** is an open-source EHR and medical practice management solution. Although it started as a commercial product in 2001, in 2004 it was released as an OSS project. It is supported by the community-led openEMR Foundation and available for the use of medical practitioners [13]. [13] investigated the project's success in terms of the roles of the developers and the influence of the OSS development approach. The **openEHR** project was initiated in England and extended to other countries.

[14] explained the technical specifications about openEHR and establishment process of openEHR Foundation. **GNU Health** is a community-led OS health and hospital information systems project. It is supported by the GNU Solidario Foundation [15]. As of this writing, we did not encounter any research papers in English on the governance aspect of GNU Health.

Related work results show that there is a lack of literature about OS foundations in the healthcare sector focusing on the governance aspect.

2.2 Governance Practices of Organization-Led Open Source Foundations

[16] look into the **governance mechanisms** of software ecosystems in both proprietary and open-source contexts. They categorize these mechanisms into *value creation, coordination of players,* and *organizational openness and control.* Their findings highlight the most frequently cited governance mechanisms are *attracting and maintaining partners, sharing knowledge, promoting innovation, and managing licenses.* [17] explore the management of **commercial conflicts** in OS Foundations. To prevent conflicts, they emphasize establishing a screening process before accepting new members, defining governance rules, applying distributed decision making mechanisms and prevention strategies to protect culture, values and common interests. The governance rules include *separation of powers, tiered membership, limited representation from the same company,* and *having independent management entities that are not in relation with any of the member companies.* Prevention strategies include, allowing community participation, enforcing public communication, and ensuring openness and transparency. [3] analyze **the success factors within a user-led OS consortium**, emphasizing governance practices critical for its sustained effectiveness. They identify specific governance practices that bolster success, including *clearly defined rules and boundaries, collective prioritization, openness and transparency, shared resources and equality, commitment of members, inheriting established governance rules and legal structures, periodic communication, organizing events,* and *promoting hosted projects.*

3 Methodology

We conducted multiple-case case study research by following the guidelines of [18]. We chose a case study approach primarily to observe real-case dynamics in a natural setting [19].

3.1 Case Selection

We used polar sampling to select two cases [18]. Our first consideration was the type of foundation, choosing one vendor-led and one user-led OS foundation in healthcare. Additional selection criteria included the foundation's size, scope, geographical activity area, focus, and maturity level. We compiled a list of OS foundations in the healthcare sector, including the Cerner Open Source

Platform, LibreHealth, openEMR, and openMRS. After investigating the governance and membership structures of these foundations, we selected openEHR and RACOON. Detailed sampling information and background on both consortia are provided in External Appendix [23].

The **openEHR** Foundation, established in 2003, has a Governing Board consists of representatives from different membership types, including organizational members, industrial partners, individuals and professionals. openEHR is a vendor-led OS foundation, because the majority of the governing board members are representatives of vendor companies. Although founded in England, it is internationally recognized and operates in various countries, including Australia, and Canada. Its mission is to standardize Electronic Health Record (EHR) data, promoting interoperability and efficient healthcare data exchange and management.

RACOON, established in 2020, is currently active in one country (Germany). RACOON is a user-led OS consortium, because its governing board consists of representatives of user organizations (University Clinics). RACOON aims to build a national system for multicentric analysis of radiological data.

3.2 Data Collection and Data Analysis

We collected data from case websites, focusing on foundations' history, membership, and vision. Then, we conducted semi-structured interviews with key informants, using open-ended questions to allow flexibility during the discussions [20]. Before conducting interviews, we prepared an interview protocol including questions aligned with our research objectives. We performed seven online interviews in English from July to September 2023, each lasting one to two hours. Four interviews involved openEHR members, and three involved RACOON members. Following each interview, we shared transcriptions with the respective interviewees for confirmation. We assigned each interviewee and data source a unique identification number (ID) and employed these IDs in the results section to clearly attribute the sources of our findings. We share our interview questions in External Appendix [23]. Table 1 presents an overview of the interview sessions and Table 2 presents the online data sources.

Table 1. Interviewees and Identifiers

ID	Foundation	Responsibility in the Foundation	Interview Date
I1	openEHR	Former Chair of the Management Board	21.07.2023
I2	openEHR	Board Member of the CIC	25.07.2023
I3	openEHR	Chief Executive Officer of the CIC	28.07.2023
I4	openEHR	Board Member of the CIC	26.09.2023
J1	RACOON	User-Member	07.09.2023
J2	RACOON	User-Member	08.09.2023
J3	RACOON	User-Member	22.09.2023

We analyzed the interviews using thematic analysis. We followed the guidelines of [21]. First, we reviewed interview scripts to gain an overall understanding. Starting from the second step, we used a qualitative data analysis tool, QDAcity[1], and generated codes. In the third step, we refined the coding scheme by clustering initial codes into themes. Following this step, we reviewed our codes and their associations with the emerging themes. We continually revised and updated the codes and themes as necessary. After providing names and explanations for the themes, we organized themes in a logical manner and grouped different subsets within the same set to form a larger category. As the final step, we present our data analysis results in the results section of this paper.

Table 2. Online Data Sources and Identifiers

ID	Official Website and Content	Link
W1	openEHR/About openEHR	https://openehr.org/about_us
W2	openEHR/What is openEHR?	https://openehr.org/about/what_is_openehr
W3	openEHR/History 2002-2018	https://openehr.org/about/history_2002_2018
W4	openEHR/Membership	https://openehr.org/community/membership/
V1	RACOON/Project Team	https://racoon.network/?page_id=7844
V2	Charité Berlin/RACOON	https://num.charite.de/teilprojekte/laufende_projekte/racoon/
V3	Network of University Medicine /About us	https://www.netzwerk-universitaetsmedizin.de/ueber-uns/
V4	RACOON/RACOON Base	https://racoon.network/?page_id=1638

4 Results

4.1 The Differences and Similarities Between Vendor-Led and User-Led OS Foundations in the Healthcare Domain

We present results in this section and a summary in External Appendix [23].

Organizational and Membership Structure. *openEHR* consists of two organizational entities: the openEHR Foundation and the openEHR International Community Interest Company (CIC). The Foundation owns and safeguards openEHR's intellectual property. The openEHR International is responsible for handling day-to-day businesses within the openEHR community (I1, W1). *openEHR* comprises four membership types; organizational partners, industry partners, professional members, and individual members (I1, W4). Organizational partners represent healthcare institutions and provide input about user expectations (I1, I3, W4). An example is the Catalan Health Service (W4). Industry partners are software vendors which build products or services on top of openEHR specifications (I3). They provide financial and human resources (I1,

[1] https://qdacity.com/.

W4). An example is EY-Health (W4). Professional members are individuals who offer consultancy and training services. Individual members are individuals who contribute to and influence the community (I1, I3).

RACOON was created as part of the German Network University Medicine, which was founded by the German Government (V3). Project coordination is performed by the University Hospital Frankfurt and the Charité Universitätsmedizin Berlin (V2). *RACOON* accepts only organizations as members (J1). There are two types of members: user members which are the university clinics, and technical partners which perform development work in coordination with user members. All University Clinics in Germany are members of the consortium. Two examples of technical partners are Mint Medical and Fraunhofer Mevis (J1, V1).

Governance Structure. *openEHR* has a two-layer governance structure. The first layer is the steering board. It is the main decision organ, and consists of members from different membership categories (I4). Members vote on the allocation of resources and priorities (I1, I3). The second layer is the program boards with their independent governance mechanisms. As of 2023, there are four programs with governing boards: Specifications, Clinical Modeling, Software, and Education (I4, W1). Each program board represents different areas of expertise. For instance, the Specifications Program Board is governed by the technical experts, while the Education Program Board consists of experts in training and academia (I4, W1). Program board members collaboratively set priorities and define requirements (I2). Disagreement within the community are handled through the program boards. In the situation of unresolved disagreements, the issue is escalated to the steering board and decided by vote if necessary (I3, I4). Governing mechanisms of *RACOON* include the General Assembly, a steering committee, and coordination teams (J1). The General Assembly consists of members from all partner hospitals (J1). The steering committee consists of healthcare professionals representing different University Clinics (V1). The steering committee is the main source of decisions, including setting priorities and accepting new members (J1, J3). Conflicts and disagreements are addressed in the steering committee (J1). Coordination teams provide information flow between working groups and the steering committee (J3).

Financement. Financement of *openEHR* depends on annual membership fees. Membership fees vary by category, ranging from €150 for individuals to €17,010 for organizations (W4). The *RACOON* is funded by The Federal Ministry of Education and Research Germany for three years and as of 2023 does not collect any membership fees (J1).

Development and Output. The focus of *openEHR* is to develop data models and specifications (I1). For the development of data models, both volunteer developers and employees of partner institutions collaborate (I3). openEHR works on the data application layer, while industrial partners work on the application layer to offer projects compatible with openEHR specifications (I1, I3). Industry partners are not required to open source application-layer projects;

they may choose to release them as OSS or proprietary software (I1). On the other hand, openEHR has also an OSS development project, which, however, is not suitable for large deployments (I3). In *RACOON*, user members define the requirements and steer the development direction (J1, J2). Being in charge of the steering process allows users to be more creative in solving problems and fulfilling their functional expectations (J2). Each of the user members have an IT-specialist employed specifically for this project (J2). Technical partners perform the development work and are paid for it (J1, J2, J3). In this initial phase, the consortium only accepts contributions from its members and not from outside organizations or volunteers (J1).

Members' Engagement Reasons. A key challenge in healthcare is the variation in medical data structures, leading to unstandardized models and inconsistent data logging, which can impact patient care. The ***need for standardized data models*** has driven organizations to establish the *openEHR* community (I3). With rapid advancements in healthcare technology, traditional data models can become obsolete, highlighting the need for adaptable frameworks (I1, I2). Semantic interoperability enables information exchange across healthcare systems without altering data meaning, reducing uncertainties, improving patient care, and fostering progress. ***Addressing interoperability challenges*** is another key motivator for organizational involvement (I1, I2, I4). Since openEHR specifications are open source, organizations can continue development even if openEHR is discontinued, ensuring ***investment security*** (I2, I4). Ethically, especially for organizations using public funds, investing in open source that ***benefits the community*** is an additional incentive (I4). Industry partners can develop application layers using open specifications, ensuring ***vendor neutrality*** and reducing lock-in, which allows organizations to choose vendors based on their specific needs (I1, I2). Industry partners offer commercial services around openEHR specifications, helping them ***save costs*** by utilizing existing data models (I1). To sustain a healthy community, member companies are encouraged to support the foundation through membership fees (I2).

RACOON was initiated during the COVID-19 pandemic, while the knowledge on the disease was limited. Healthcare practitioners needed data to gain deeper understanding about the disease. The RACOON consortium aimed to create a platform that enables data sharing and analysis among radiological departments from university hospitals, to ***enhance understanding about the disease and provide better medical care*** to patients (J1, J2). ***Expanding research opportunities*** is another motive for organizations to join in RACOON consortium. Beyond COVID-19, data sharing extended to medical imaging data on cancer and cardiac conditions. One use case of the collected data is training artificial intelligence and machine learning to improve the pattern recognition in Computed Tomography (CT) scan (J2, V4). Researchers can propose research topics, and once approved, work on the platform. Students gain access to a ***larger pool of data*** compared to what their university alone provides (J2). The platform facilitates communication and ***strengthens networking*** among university hospitals. Its transparency policy allows any interested party to join proposed research projects (J1). The platform **enhances collaboration opportunities** among university clinics (J1, J2, J3).

4.2 Governance Practices for Open Source Foundations in the Healthcare Sector

We identified 32 governance practices in nine contexts which are associated with the OS foundations in the healthcare sector. In this section, we detail each context (C), with explanation (E) and practices (Pr). We present the list of these practices in External Appendix [23].

C-1. Mitigating the Domination of Any Single Member

C-1.E. The openEHR Foundation was founded as a partnership between University College London (UCL), a non-profit organization, and Ocean Informatics, a commercial entity. Some community members perceived the foundation as a front for Ocean Informatics' commercial operations, which negatively affected the community dynamics (I1).

C-1.Pr. openEHR addressed this challenge by restructuring its membership structure and selecting **representatives from all membership categories for the governing board**. This approach ensures that diverse viewpoints are represented within the foundation (I1, I3, I4). The revised structure emphasizes transparency and embraces a democratic approach (I1). The governing board makes decisions about **resource allocations based on votes** among its members (I3, I4). **Including representatives from competing companies on the board** helps avoid dominance by any single organization (I1). Another practice is **rotating members on the governing board**, which prevents prolonged influence by the same individuals and encourages diverse viewpoints (I4).

I1 shared the following words: *"Our structure aims to ensure that different member categories feel represented on the board without giving too much influence to national or commercial organizations."*

C-2. Focusing In-Depth on Specific Issues

C-2.E. Collaborative work may involve diverse needs and expertise requirements, requiring insights from both clinical and technical perspectives (I3).

C-2.Pr. openEHR has four **sub-groups that focus on different areas of expertise**, addressing the needs of various stakeholders (I2). Prioritization, decision making, and disagreement resolution are expected to be managed within these groups (I2). In the case of unsolved issues, the matter is escalated to the governing board (I3). These groups are open and inclusive, welcoming organizations and individual members with diverse skills and experiences (I2, I3, I4).

RACOON follows a similar approach, organizing **working groups** to focus on specific issues, such as quality assurance (J1, J3). Each working group has its own leader, chosen by the group members (J3). These groups are open to all interested members and encourage collaborative work (J1, J3). Working groups hold weekly meetings to share updates (J3). Furthermore, each user institution in the RACOON consortium has a **dedicated IT-specialist.** These specialists communicate and collaborate with each other and with technical partners, positively impacting the project (J1, J2).

C-3. Facilitating Mediation Among Diverse Expert Opinions

C-3.E. A common challenge in collaborative projects is that, when multiple experts with unique visions, perspectives, and experiences, come together, decision-making can become difficult. They may have different functional expectations, technical preferences, and approaches, making it challenging to reach common ground (J1, I1).

C-3.Pr. It is essential to **acknowledge and value the expertise and abilities of all individuals involved** when addressing issues (J2). The subsequent stage involves **fostering a dialogue where each person has the opportunity to express their perspectives** (J1, J2, J3). **Showing mutual respect and understanding** is crucial for finding common ground among diverse interests and viewpoints, creating a harmonious environment and an inclusive spirit aligned with the organization's goals (J1, J2, J3, I1, I3).

C-4. Safeguarding Data Privacy and Security

C-4.E. Meeting data privacy and security regulations is a time-consuming and complex process due to varying requirements and complicated nature of the task (J1, J3). The primary challenge is to protect stored patient data against unauthorized access, while enabling multicentric scientific research using data from all member institutions (J1).

C-4.Pr. To safeguard data privacy and security, RACOON **anonymizes data stored on its cloud server and restricts access to authorized individuals** (J2). Measures such as data encryption and access controls help prevent misuse or leaks (J2). The openEHR Foundation does not store patient data (I1, I3). While cloud servers may store databases related to tools and design models, no sensitive information is kept there (I1). In both openEHR and RACOON, **the responsibility for securing patient data belongs to the data-owning organizations**, not to the foundation (I1, I3, J1, J3).

openEHR ensures that its platform and published data models comply with General Data Protection Regulation in Europe and Health Information Privacy Standards in the US (I3). Similarly, RACOON **stays in alignment with the data security and privacy regulations** (J1, J3).

C-5. Building Trust and Relationship Among Members

C-5.E. Networking and maintaining strong relationships, even with competitors, is essential for sustaining continuity of the collaboration (I1).

C-5.Pr. Face-to-face communication positively impacts trust-building and relationships among members (I1, J3). In-person gatherings also increase energy and commitment (I1). For example, RACOON organizes sessions at conventions and conferences, which foster communication and help members build personal connections (J3). Similarly, openEHR members benefit from face-to-face meetings, which aid in resolving disagreements (I1). **Regular meetings** increase information flow and facilitate direct communication between members (J3). Additionally, an **online platform** enables ongoing member interaction (J3). **Ensuring transparency** further contributes to building trust (I1, I4).

C-6. Attracting New Members

C-6.E. Attracting new members who align with project objectives is essential for ensuring the continuity and financial sustainability of OSS projects (I1, I4).

I1 shared these words: *"You need to have mechanisms for generating new money. It's challenging to keep the project going, and you can't always rely on old members. New ones must come in, and they have to be convinced to put money into the project."*

C-6.Pr. In both the openEHR and RACOON communities, the primary goal is to provide better medical care and improve patient health outcomes (I4, J3). Although companies may have economic interests, it is important that they do not act with avarice (I4). For an OS foundation to succeed, it must **strike a balance** that honors OS principles—including transparency and openness—while also considering financial sustainability (I1, I4). The inclusion of commercial entities in the consortium positively impacts resource generation and enhances service provision for user organizations (I1).

Outreach and marketing efforts are essential to reach and onboard likeminded individuals by **communicating the foundation's activities** (I4). Organizations familiar with existing projects are more likely to get involved. **Encouraging interested organizations** to use the technology and engage with the community also helps attract new members (I2).

I2 shared these words: *"The process of selecting and onboarding new members into the openEHR community is often driven by the existing projects and usage of the technology. When companies start using openEHR and experience its benefits, they naturally become interested in becoming part of the community."*

C-7. Providing an Inclusive and Open Environment

C-7.E. Besides attracting new members, it is also essential to motivate them to engage in community (I2).

C-7.Pr. This issue can be addressed by providing new members with **comprehensive information** on the governance structure and regulations through resources like onboarding protocols, the website, and consortium wiki pages (J1). **A structured onboarding protocol** that clearly defines regulations can simplify complexities for the newcomers (J1). **Transparency about projects and processes**, along with open information-sharing with new members, is essential for building trust, fostering confidence, and encouraging active participation in projects (J1). **Recognizing success, appreciating contributors**, and offering them with opportunities to speak at conferences are additional practices that motivate members to engage in projects. Additionally, **explaining the impact of projects and sharing experiences within the community** are effective ways to attract new contributors (I3). In an open environment, even competitive vendors can share experiences and knowledge as long as the shared objective of **open standards** is maintained (I2).

I3 shared the following words: *"it's about celebrating collaboration, reflecting on what works well, and explaining why we're doing what we're doing. For example, if we're talking about care planning, we don't just discuss the data items needed for care planning. We also talk about what care planning is, how it makes a difference to humans, why we need to tackle it. It's about being explicit with clinicians and operational people, bringing the impact to life."*

C-8. Ensuring Transparency

C-8.E. Transparency helps in building trust among community members. Contributions to the foundation and its projects happen in different forms, including technical, financial, and intellectual support (I4). In collaborative efforts toward a common goal, it is essential to provide openness and transparency among members (J3). Transparency ensures that decisions are not made in isolation, information is communicated effectively and every member has the information they need for contribution (I4, J2).

C-8.Pr. To ensure transparency, openEHR **documents the foundation's decisions** and **keeps the community informed** about the roadmap and resource allocation (I3, I4). For instance, openEHR organizes annual meetings to share information about foundation's progress and status (I2). **Publishing meeting minutes and sharing related information** about specific topics-such as member responsibilities, contact details, and clinical content documentation-further supports information flow (I4, J3). Additional practices include **providing an open environment** where community members can engage in dialogue with board members (I3) and allowing interested members to attend subprogram board meetings (I3, J3).

C-9. Aligning with Market Needs and Diverse Data Regulations

C-9.E. Alignment with market needs is essential for an impact and success on the market (I3). In the healthcare sector, foundations must stay informed about market trends and regulations (I1). Each country has distinct regulations, making it challenging to ensure data model compliance across borders (I1, I3). Deploying openEHR in different countries requires mapping between openEHR standards and the specific standards employed in clinics (I1).

I1 highlighted this problem: *"Addressing varying regulations and requirements in different international markets is a significant challenge. There's no one-size-fits-all solution in healthcare makes it even more complex. Healthcare systems, funding models, and regulatory frameworks differ greatly between countries. [...] These differences significantly impact the mindset of vendors and clinicians."*

C-9.Pr. Policymakers' involvement in the community is beneficial, as it allows the community to stay informed about data regulations and address specific requirements (I3). Another approach is to develop open-source mapping tools to **establish mapping guidelines**. Although these tools cannot accommodate all variations due to the diversity of needs, they can serve as a foundational basis. Industry partners can customize these solutions to meet the specific institutional requirements. The main focus in addressing this challenge is to **establish interoperability** and **create uniform standards** (I1).

5   Discussion

In openEHR, the membership structure includes both individuals and organizations; however, governance is driven by organizational members. Vendors provide financial support for the community and hold the majority on the governance board. The continuity of the foundation is important for them, as they offer commercial services based on the specifications provided by the foundation. User members in openEHR provide input for the specifications. On the other hand, RACOON only accepts organizations as member. Governance is led by user organizations, meaning that development direction and priorities are steered by the user organizations. Vendors work on platform development for a fee. openEHR needs to balance commercial interests with open-source values. In contrast, RACOON does not face this challenge, as its ultimate goal is to enhance research collaboration and gain deeper insights into diseases. RACOON is funded by the German Government, so there were no financial concerns as of 2023. openEHR, however, requires resources from its members to ensure sustainability and must balance the expectations of both user organizations and vendor companies.

Organizations engage in OS foundations for various reasons. In the case of openEHR, the primary motivation is the need for standardized data models. Another motivation is vendor neutrality, a motive observed in both vendor-led and user-led OS foundations. For instance in the openKonsequenz case, one reason for users involvement was to eliminate vendor lock-in [5]. Vendors are motivated to offer commercial services around the OS data specifications. From the vendors' perspective, having standardized data models enables cost savings. In RACOON, the primary motivation is to create a platform that facilitates collaboration and data sharing. User members participate in this project to utilize the system in their clinics.

To address this study's second objective, we identified 32 governance practices across nine contexts. Seven of these contexts were utilized by both openEHR and RACOON in developing their practices, while two contexts were specific to openEHR. The first difference is the challenge of preventing any single company from dominating the foundation's governance. openEHR was initiated by a university and a commercial organization, and the community perceived the founders' dominance in the governance process. To ensure the foundation's health and sustainability, the governance structure was revised to become more inclusive and democratic by incorporating stakeholders from different membership categories. Tiered membership structure is also a reported practice in [17] to avoid domination of one single company in OS foundations. In the RACOON consortium, governance is collaboratively led by user institutions. None of the interview partners reported concerns about any member institution dominating the governance process. The second difference relates to adapting to market conditions and data regulations. This differentiation may stem from the scope of each foundation's activities: openEHR operates internationally and must adapt to varying regulations across countries, while RACOON is active only in Germany.

Common contexts include focusing on issues in-depth, facilitating mediation among diverse expert opinions, safeguarding data privacy and data security. Additionally, building trust and relationships among members, attracting new members, providing an inclusive and open environment, and ensuring transparency are contexts investigated in the literature [3, 16].

6   Limitations

We have employed [22]'s trustworthiness metrics to evaluate our research. **Credibility** relates to the accuracy of research findings. We applied prolonged engagement over eight-months. The first and second authors held weekly meetings to discuss progress, including interviews, qualitative analysis, and reporting. Both authors independently analyzed all interview transcripts. **Transferability** refers to generalizability of findings. To enhance transferability, we used polar sampling, considering various dimensions. We investigated similarities and differences between these two cases. Seven out of nine governance contexts were similar for both of these cases, indicating potential for broader application. However, it remains for future work to determine whether these findings apply to other industries. **Dependability** determined by the traceability and reliability of the findings. To ensure this, we transparently report our research steps in the methodology section. Due to data privacy concerns, we did not share transcripts, however, we included interview quotations to support our findings. Furthermore, we referenced results using IDs for traceability. **Confirmability** refers neutrality and involves conducting unbiased data analysis. To avoid researcher bias, we used interview protocol. Two authors analyzed the interview transcripts by following thematic analysis guidelines and reached similar results.

7   Conclusion

This study had two objectives. First one was to explore the similarities and differences between user-led and vendor-led OS foundations in the healthcare sector. The second objective was to explore and define the governance practices applied in these foundations to achieve success. To address these objectives, we focused on two cases: openEHR and RACOON. We compared these cases by focusing on their membership structure, governance structure, and members' motivation to engage. To address our second objective, we identified 32 governance practices across nine contexts. These contexts include mitigating the domination of any single member, focusing in-depth on specific issues, facilitating mediation among diverse expert opinions, safeguarding data privacy and data security, building trust and relationships among members, attracting new members, providing an inclusive and open environment, ensuring transparency, and aligning with market needs and diverse data regulations. We explained each of the contexts, and applied practices in detail.

References

1. Riehle, D., Berschneider, S.: A model of open source developer foundations. In: IFIP International Conference on Open Source Systems, pp. 15–28. Springer, 2012
2. Eckert, R., Stuermer, M., Myrach, T.: Alone or together? Inter-organizational affiliations of open source communities. J. Syst. Softw. **149**, 250–262 (2019)
3. Yenişen Yavuz, E., Barcomb, A., Riehle, D.: Problems, solutions, and success factors in the openMDM user-led open source consortium. Commun. Assoc. Inf. Syst. **51**(1), 13 (2022)
4. Schaarschmidt, M., Bertram, M., von Kortzfleisch, H.: In Governance and Sustainability in Information Systems. Managing the Transfer and Diffusion of IT: IFIP WG 8.6 Int. Working Conference, Hamburg, Germany, pp. 16–28. Springer, Cham (2011)
5. Schwab, B., Riehle, D., Barcomb, A., Harutyunyan, N.: The ecosystem of openKonsequenz, a user-led open source foundation. In: Open Source Systems: 16th IFIP WG 2.13 International Conference, OSS 2020, pp. 1–13. Springer, Cham (2020)
6. Goulde, M., Brown, E.: Open source software: a primer for health care leaders (2006)
7. Bagayoko, C.O., Dufour, J.C., Chaacho, S., Bouhaddou, O., Fieschi, M.: Open source challenges for hospital information system in developing countries: a pilot project in Mali. BMC Med. Inform. Decis. Mak. **10**, 1–13 (2010)
8. Reynolds, C.J., Wyatt, J.C.: Open source, open standards, and health care information systems. J. Med. Internet Res. **13**(1), e1521 (2011)
9. Purkayastha, S., Allam, R., Maity, P., Gichoya, J.W.: Comparison of open-source electronic health record systems based on functional and user performance criteria. Healthc. Inform. Res. **25**(2), 89–98 (2019)
10. West, J., O'Mahony, S.: Contrasting community building in sponsored and community founded open source projects. In: 38th HICSS, p. 196c. IEEE, 2005
11. Verma, N., Mamlin, B., Flowers, J., Acharya, S., Labrique, A., Cullen, T.: OpenMRS as a global good: impact, opportunities, challenges, and lessons learned from 15 years of implementation. Int. J. Med. Inform. **149** (2021)
12. Gichoya, J.W., Kohli, M., Ivange, L., Schmidt, T.S., Purkayastha, S.: A platform for innovation and standards evaluation: a case study from the OpenMRS open-source radiology information system. J. Digit. Imaging **31**, 361–370 (2018)
13. Noll, J., Beecham, S., Seichter, D.: A qualitative study of open source software development: the openEMR project. In: 2011 International Symposium on Empirical Software Engineering and Measurement, pp. 30–39. IEEE
14. Kalra, D., Beale, T., Heard, S.: The openEHR foundation. Stud. Health Technol. Inform. **115**, 153–173 (2005)
15. GNU Health: Welcome to GNUHealth (2020). https://gnuhealth.org/about-us.html

16. Alves, C., de Oliveira, J.A.P., Jansen, S.: Software ecosystems governance-a systematic literature review and research agenda. ICEIS **3**, 215–226 (2017)
17. Weikert, F., Riehle, D., Barcomb, A.: Managing commercial conflicts of interest in open source foundations. In: ICSOB 2019, pp. 130–144. Springer, Cham (2019)
18. Eisenhardt, K.M.: Building theories from case study research. Acad. Manag. Rev. **14**(4), 532–550 (1989)
19. Yin, R.K: Case Study Research and Applications. Sage, Thousand Oaks, CA (2018)
20. Bryman, A.: Social Research Methods. Oxford university press, Oxford (2016)
21. Braun, V., Clarke, V.: Using thematic analysis in psychology. Qual. Res. Psychol. **3**(2), 77–101 (2006)
22. Guba, E.G.: Criteria for assessing the trustworthiness of naturalistic inquiries. Ectj **29**(2), 75–91 (1981)
23. Yenisen Yavuz, E., Shrivastava, A., Riehle, D., Putz, F.: External Appendix of Governance Practices for Open Source Foundations in the Healthcare Sector. https://faubox.rrze.uni-erlangen.de/getlink/fiHtE95Cg18T96CQtdqn5w/

Adoption of Cloud Platforms Among Independent Software Vendors

Lucas Constantin Mangold, Monty Lukas Meier, and Maximilian Schreieck$^{(\boxtimes)}$

University of Innsbruck, Innrain 52, 6020 Innsbruck, Austria
{lucas.mangold,monty.meier}@student.uibk.ac.at,
maximilian.schreieck@uibk.ac.at

Abstract. The transition from on-premises to cloud-based enterprise software influences independent software vendors (ISVs) to build their solutions upon the software offered by well-established vendors. This paper evaluates different strategies in this transition. The study is based on a data set of 1,652 ISVs that match appropriate characteristics, which forms the basis for this study. We obtained unexpected results regarding growth opportunities for ISVs joining a cloud platform. We did not find a significant effect of cloud adoption on ISV's growth opportunities, and we still see growth opportunities for ISVs who run their software on-premises. In addition, we found that ISVs showed higher growth opportunities when single-homing compared to multi-homing. These findings contribute to understanding ISV's challenges in transitioning from on-premises to the cloud. In the near term, there still seem to be business opportunities for maintaining customers' on-premises landscapes. Furthermore, it is costly to develop the capabilities for a cloud platform ecosystem; thus, focusing on one of the large vendors' ecosystems could be a promising strategy for ISVs.

Keywords: independent software vendors · on-premise software · cloud software · single-homing · multi-homing

1 Introduction

Cloud computing is taking over on-premises technology in the enterprise software industry. Platform owners co-create value with independent software providers (ISVs) in their platform ecosystems by promoting complementary ISV innovation and leveraging indirect network effects. Conversely, ISVs join a platform ecosystem to benefit from the infrastructure and installed base of the platform owner [1]. Running a complement on multiple platforms is knowns as multi-homing. It is also gaining popularity in many platform markets because it helps providers to increase their market reach [2].

This short paper aims to identify and evaluate relevant strategies for ISVs to join a cloud platform in terms of growth opportunities. Thus, we answer the following research questions: *(1) What impact on the growth opportunities does the adoption of cloud platforms have among ISVs compared to on-premise solutions? (2) Does the impact on the growth opportunities of choosing a single or multi-homing cloud platform strategy among ISVs differ?*

E. Papatheocharous et al. (Eds.): ICSOB 2024, LNBIP 539, pp. 398–403, 2025.
https://doi.org/10.1007/978-3-031-85849-9_31

2 Background

The Platform Ecosystem Model. According to the information systems literature, platform ecosystems are networks of businesses that produce value on a digital platform. A digital platform ecosystem comprises a platform owner who implements governance mechanisms to enable value-creating procedures on a digital platform between the platform owner and an ecosystem of complementors and users. Applications from complementors (in the enterprise software industry, often referred to as ISVs) increase the platform's functionality and benefit users in other industries [1]. Companies from various industries are moving towards a platform ecosystem strategy. They seek an advantage by collaborating with complementors using cloud computing technology [3].

Cloud Computing. The trend known as cloud computing separates integrated components of company infrastructure and applications into services that can be provided by internal or external service providers. Providing services via cloud computing enables access at any time and location, as well as data sharing and collaboration. Service providers benefit from substantially more straightforward software setup, ongoing support, and centralized versioning control. With cloud computing, more application vendors have the option to offer their applications as Software as a Service (SaaS) without setting up a data center first. An important decision for vendors such as ISVs is whether to single- or multi-home on cloud computing platforms. Multi-homing, known as multi-cloud, is a potential way to improve the availability of one's own service by relying on the cloud computing platforms of multiple providers [4]. To avoid vendor lock-in, interoperability and portability among cloud providers is crucial. An increasing number of companies realize that a multi-cloud setup which uses multiple public cloud services for distinct purposes provides the best of each. Moreover, organizations can use resources from several cloud providers to access the best services offered by each cloud vendor instead of relying just on a single cloud's services [5].

3 Hypotheses Development

Cloud. vs. On-Premises. Cloud-based enterprise software offers benefits to both service providers and end users. Since technical operations are integrated into the cloud offering, pay-per-use cloud solutions do not require maintenance contracts for technical support, unlike on-premise solutions [6]. Furthermore, major providers of ERP systems, including SAP, Microsoft, and Oracle, are now providing their ERP in a cloud-based setting [7]. This suggests a shift in how customers use computing resources and a positive change in how vendors and their partners' business models create value [6]. Entering a cloud-based platform ecosystem allows the ISV to penetrate the platform's installed base more quickly and effectively. As well-known platform owners have a substantial installed base, partnering opens up a larger potential market for an ISV. Additionally, an ISV may need to undergo a certification procedure to be considered as an authorized provider for a platform. This certification by a prominent platform owner could signal quality to new clients and increase sales [8]. As a result, the financial markets should view these partnerships positively, and investors will be more confident in the company's ability to generate profit in the future. Therefore, we develop the following hypothesis:

H1: The long-term growth opportunities are higher for ISVs that are part of a cloud-based ecosystem than for those part of an on-premises ecosystem.

Single-Homing vs. Multi-Homing. On the one hand, enterprise software providers can experience difficulties in multi-homing as they must master the technical challenges of integrating with the platform and the business processes and industry environment of the platform's users [9]. On the other hand, there are several reasons for complementors to collaborate with multiple platforms. Complementors may find it easier to reduce uncertainty about potential technical and organizational difficulties when using multi-homing. Also, they frequently benefit from cross-platform scale economies, encouraging them to multi-home. The benefits of reaching a broader market could outweigh the costs associated with adapting products to multiple platforms. Complementors can further reduce the risk of lock-in by using multi-homing [10]. By modifying existing products for new platform ecosystems, complementors create expansion strategies to take advantage of the network benefits of a broader installed base. To maintain bargaining power, many complementors partner with multiple platform owners [11]. From this, we develop the second hypothesis:

H2: The long-term growth opportunities are higher for ISVs that multi-home compared to those that single-home.

4   Study Design and Data Sample

To analyze the growth opportunities of cloud adoption strategies among ISVs, we conducted a quantitative study based on a dataset from ISVWorld. It is considered the ISV data reference platform for 80% of the Fortune 500 tech-active companies. Among other things, ISVWorld lists companies with revenue, headquarters country, and long-term growth forecasts and classifies them into industries, horizontal applications, and ecosystems [12]. For this study, we focused on ISVs in the SAP ecosystem because SAP is the world's leading ERP vendor. We filtered the "application" category to "ERP & Process Management" since these applications reflect the core ERP applications. As we are interested in small and medium-sized ISVs within Europe, we also focused on ISVs with revenue lower than 5 million USD and headquartered in Europe. This step led to a set of 1,729 software vendors. Finally, we removed ISVs that did not have a measurement for long-term growth in the ISVWorld data. This approach led to 1,652 valid cases of ISVs for further analysis.

As our study's dependent variable, we used the ISVs' long-term growth forecast by ISVWorld, which describes the expected growth of ISVs over the next 12 months. This long-term growth thus reflects the **growth opportunities** of the ISVs. As independent variables, we differentiate whether ISVs are part of a cloud-based ecosystem (any cloud vs. non-cloud ecosystem) and whether they are active in a single (SAP) or also in multiple ecosystems (Microsoft or Oracle), i.e., whether they single-home or multi-home. To test the hypotheses and identify differences between the different ecosystems, we formed groups of ISVs with a non-cloud or cloud strategy and, in the case of a cloud strategy, a single-homing or multi-homing strategy.

5 Findings

Table 1 presents a descriptive analysis of long-term growth rates across the different groups comprising different combinations of ecosystems. The data gives a first impression that the mean value of long-term growth is higher for ISVs in non-cloud ecosystems and for those who single-home.

Table 1. Descriptive statistics of dependent variable Long-Term growth in groups.

Long-term growth per group	Mean value	Standard deviation
Non-cloud ecosystem ($n = 114$)	75.44	15.677
Any cloud ecosystem ($n = 1,538$)	72.54	15.434
Single-homing ($n = 201$)	75.02	16.774
Multi-homing ($n = 1,337$)	72.17	15.194

To statistically evaluate these findings, we first analyzed whether the data for the groups followed a normal distribution using the Kolmogorov-Smirnov test [13]. All four groups showed statistically significant deviations from the expected normal distribution, indicating non-normality in the long-term growth distribution ('non-cloud': 0.179, 'any-cloud': 0.196, 'single-homing': 0.188, 'multi-homing': 0.197). Therefore, we conducted a Mann-Whitney U Test to make statistically valid comparisons between the groups of ISVs in our sample. The Mann-Whitney U test is a statistical tool used to compare two groups based on a single ordinal variable without any particular distribution. Table 2 presents the tests' results to evaluate hypotheses 1 and 2.

Table 2. Results of Mann-Whitney U test and validation of the hypotheses.

Hypothesis	Groups tested	Comparison of means	p-value	Confirmed
H1	Non-cloud ecosystem vs. Any cloud ecosystem	75.44 vs. 72.54	0.06	No
H2	Single-homing vs. Multi-homing	75.02 vs. 72.17	0.04	No
Posthoc	Single-homing vs. Multi-homing (SAP and Microsoft)	75.02 vs. 71.93	0.02	-
	Single-homing vs. Multi-homing (SAP and Oracle)	75.02 vs. 76.5	0.64	-

The purpose of **Hypothesis 1** was to determine if the group of ISVs that had joined a cloud-based ecosystem (group 'any cloud ecosystem') had significantly higher growth opportunities than the group of ISVs that still focused on on-premises software (group 'non-cloud ecosystem'). Interestingly, the mean of the long-term growth is higher for the group 'non-cloud ecosystem,' and the difference between the groups is statistically significant at the 10% level (p-value of 0.06). Therefore, we could not support Hypothesis 1. **Hypothesis 2** aimed to examine differences in long-term growth between the group' single-homing' and the group' multi-homing', hypothesizing that growth opportunities would be higher for ISVs that multi-home. However, we found a statistically significant difference at the 5% level (p-value of 0.04) when comparing the two groups in terms of long-term growth, indicating that the group' single-homing' with a mean of 75.02 has higher long-term growth than the group' multi-homing' with a mean of 72.17. Therefore, we could not support Hypothesis 2.

In a **posthoc** test, we differentiated multi-homing on SAP and Microsoft platforms and multi-homing on SAP and Oracle platforms. Only when comparing single-homing (with SAP) and multi-homing with SAP and Microsoft did we find a significant difference in the growth opportunities with higher growth opportunities for the ISV that single-homed. For the comparison of single-homing and multi-homing with SAP and Oracle, the multi-homing ISVs saw higher growth opportunities; however, the difference was insignificant. Overall, the negative effect of multi-homing compared to single-homing seems to stem from combining the SAP and the Microsoft ecosystems.

6   Discussion and Conclusion

The indications that growth opportunities are significantly higher for ISVs in non-cloud ecosystems than in cloud ecosystems are surprising, given the general technological advantages of cloud platforms and cloud computing. There are two possible explanations for our findings. First, the competition among ISVs on the large cloud platforms is intense. Many new startups join the cloud platforms and compete with established ISVs transitioning from on-premises to the cloud. Second, the customers' transitions from on-premises will continue for the coming years, leaving a window for ISVs to focus on on-premises offerings. For example, SAP offers extended maintenance of its long-standing ERP suite, SAP R/3, until 2030. Maintaining the extensions of these on-premises landscapes will still be a lucrative business for some ISVs.

Regarding the comparison of single-homing and multi-homing, we found significantly higher growth opportunities for ISVs that single-home (on SAP's cloud platform). This trend is surprising because we expected that multi-homing would lead to higher growth opportunities. One explanation relates to the investments needed to bring specialized business applications to multiple cloud platforms, as complements must often be customized to each platform. Interestingly, our findings indicate that multi-homing with SAP and Microsoft seems less promising compared to multi-homing with SAP and Oracle. These results deserve further investigation, as enterprise users widely trust Microsoft Azure [14]. Overall, we contribute to the information systems research on digital platforms, particularly in the enterprise software industry [1, 3]. Highlighting the transition challenge, we show that the transition to cloud platforms is not necessarily smooth for ISVs and might even hamper their growth opportunities [15].

Acknowledgments. We thank the University of Innsbruck's Network Banking, Accounting, Auditing, Finance & IT (BAFIT) for their financial support to access the ISVWorld data. This work was partly funded by the Austrian Science Fund (FWF) [project no. https://doi.org/10.55776/I6567].

References

1. Ceccagnoli, M., Forman, C., Huang, P., Wu, D.J.: Cocreation of value in a platform ecosystem: the case of enterprise software. MIS Q. **36**, 263–290 (2012)
2. Cennamo, C.: Building the value of next-generation platforms: the paradox of diminishing returns. J. Manag. **44**, 3038–3069 (2018)
3. Schreieck, M., Wiesche, M., Krcmar, H.: Capabilities for value co-creation and value capture in emergent platform ecosystems: a longitudinal case study of SAP's cloud platform. J. Inf. Technol. **36**, 365–390 (2021)
4. Naldi, M.: Balancing leasing and insurance costs to achieve total risk coverage in cloud storage multi-homing. In: Altmann, J., Vanmechelen, K., Rana, O.F. (eds.), pp. 146–158. Springer International Publishing (2014)
5. Fadziso, T., Adusumalli, H.P., Pasupuleti, M.B.: Cloud of things and interworking IoT platform: strategy and execution overviews. Asian J. Appl. Sci. Eng. **7**, 85–92 (2018)
6. Boillat, T., Legner, C.: From On-premise software to cloud services: the impact of cloud computing on enterprise software vendors' business models. J. Theor. Appl. Electron. Commer. Res. **8**, 39–58 (2013)
7. Chen, C.-S., Liang, W.-Y., Hsu, H.-Y.: A cloud computing platform for ERP applications. Appl. Soft Comput. **27**, 127–136 (2015)
8. Arora, A., Asundi, J.: Quality certification and the economics of contract software development a study of the Indian software industry. Nat. Bur. Econ. Res. (1999)
9. Chatterjee, J.: Strategy, human capital investments, business-domain capabilities, and performance: a study in the global software services industry. Strateg. Manag. J. **38**, 588–608 (2017)
10. Huang, P., Ceccagnoli, M., Forman, C., Wu, D.J.: Appropriability mechanisms and the platform partnership decision: evidence from enterprise software. Manage. Sci. **59**, 102–121 (2013)
11. Wang, R.D., Miller, C.D.: Complementors' engagement in an ecosystem: a study of publishers' e-book offerings on Amazon Kindle. Strateg. Manag. J. **41**, 3–26 (2020)
12. https://www.isvworld.com/
13. Wilcox, R.R.: Some practical reasons for reconsidering the Kolmogorov-Smirnov test. Br. J. Math. Stat. Psychol. **50**, 9–20 (1997)
14. Gupta, B., Mittal, P., Mufti, T.: A review on amazon web service (AWS), Microsoft Azure & Google cloud platform (GCP) services. In: 2nd International Conference on ICT for Digital, Smart, and Sustainable Development (ICIDSSD), Jamia Hamdard, New Delhi, India (2020)
15. Schreieck, M., Wiesche, M., Kude, T., Krcmar, H.: Shifting to the cloud–how SAP's partners cope with the change. In: Hawaii International Conference on System Sciences, Maui, Hawaii, USA (2019)

Software Startups and Digital Transformation

Technology Change Adoption in Organizations: Drivers, Challenges, and Success Enablers

Maryam Gulzar[✉] [iD], Bilal Naqvi [iD], and Kari Smolander [iD]

LENS Software Engineering Department, LUT University, Lappeenranta, Finland
{Maryam.Gulzar,Syed.Naqvi,Kari.Smolander}@lut.fi

Abstract. Change adoption and management are paramount to organizations' operations and continuous service delivery. Analysis of the extant literature reveals challenges organizations face while adopting new technologies within their information technology (IT) infrastructures. The paper presents an empirical study featuring semi-structured interviews with IT practitioners (from 13 IT organizations operating in Finland) while considering, (i) *why* organizations adopt the latest technologies, (ii) *what* challenges arise by adopting the latest technology, and (iii) *how* the organization makes the adoption process successful. In line with these questions, 14 motivational drivers, 24 challenges, and 12 success enablers were identified. In addition, the paper also presents a conceptual framework of identified drivers, challenges, and success enablers, that govern the successful adoption of the latest technologies. The framework also helps practitioners to understand the technology adoption process by analyzing the motives, identifying the challenges, and overcoming challenges through success enablers.

Keywords: Adoption Model · IT Infrastructure · Technology Change

1 Introduction

The rapid evolution of digital technology has transformed the IT infrastructure (ITI) across all sectors including education [1], health [2], the IT industry [3], the construction industry [4], and the manufacturing industry [5] among others. These organizations continually adapt and integrate the latest advancements into their operations and update their ITI. ITI is using IT components upon which systems and services are built and run, to manage and process information [6] within organizations. Adopting new relevant technologies such as cloud computing, artificial intelligence, the Internet of Things, and blockchain, among others across these sectors, has become necessary in today's competitive environment [7]. The technology adoption arises from several factors including the need to remain competitive, enhance operational efficiency, drive innovation, ensure security, and meet evolving customer expectations [3].

However, the adoption of digital technologies does not always succeed [8]. A few studies discuss the failure of digital transformation to deliver the expected business value within industrial fields [9, 10]. The disconnection between the strategy formulation and implementation often causes failure [8]. Inappropriate adoption of digital

E. Papatheocharous et al. (Eds.): ICSOB 2024, LNBIP 539, pp. 407–422, 2025.
https://doi.org/10.1007/978-3-031-85849-9_32

technologies may result in disruptive change, leading to high risk and uncertainty during the transformation [3, 11].

The adoption of digital technology is significantly affected by technological, organizational, environmental, and managerial factors [3, 12, 13]. Therefore, before adopting new technologies, organizations must understand the purpose of the adopted technology and the determinants of IT adoption [14]. In addition, the organizations need to analyze what might happen in the technology adoption process, and how they make the technology adoption process successful. In other words, organizations need to start by analyzing "why" (representing the drivers, purposes, and motives), followed by "what" (representing the challenges, outcomes, or results) and "how" (representing the success enablers, achievers, or required attributes). Despite the growing research interests in the area, the current understanding of these three aspects (i.e., why, what, and how) concerning the adoption of digital technologies within the ITI of organizations is limited [10, 15, 16].

In this context, we conducted interviews to grasp perspectives from organizations by utilizing an exploratory approach that investigates the motives, challenges, and success enablers to overcome challenges during the technology adoption process. The purpose of this study is to explore three main factors, (i) motivational drivers that push industries to adopt new technologies, (ii) challenges that offer a comprehensive understanding of the complexities in this process, and (iii) identified success enablers that help organizations towards successful adoption of new technologies. For exploration purposes, a semi-structured interview protocol was followed and 21 field experts from 13 organizations were interviewed to explore the technology change adoption process.

2 Related Work

Existing research highlights that organizational and IT readiness are key factors in IT adoption [17]. These studies often consider internal technological factors like top management support, organizational structure, and culture based on the technical, organizational, and environmental (TOE) framework [18]. The diffusion of innovation (DOI) theory [19] is also used to explore technological readiness and expertise in IT innovation. Asiaei et al. [20] focused on non-technical aspects of the TOE framework, using a structural model to explore cloud computing adoption. This study identified critical factors like data security, top management support, and technology readiness, but the technological aspects of the TOE framework were overlooked.

Ghani et al. [21] studied AI adoption in manufacturing using the TOE framework, with an emphasis on IT capability, top management, and government support. Salih et al. [22] explored the post-implementation phase of ERP systems, highlighting the role of top management in user training, internal IT competency, and communication but observed it less significant for ongoing vendor support.

However, these [17, 20–22] studies rely on quantitative data and a narrow set of factors from established frameworks. Our research adopts a qualitative approach, exploring motivational drivers, challenges, and success enablers not only based on existing frameworks but also on industry practices. While some qualitative studies, such as Malik et al. [23], used interviews to explore blockchain adoption, they lacked comprehensive coverage of influencing factors and had limited generalizability. Khin and Kee [24] examined

Industry 4.0 adoption but failed to identify social, economic, and technological drivers, as well as the internal relationships between influencing factors.

A key research gap arises in the lack of focus on the dynamic nature of technological development and how organizations adjust to these changes over time. Existing studies fail to explore the organizational perspective on why technology change is needed, the challenges that arise, and how successful adoption can be achieved. To address this, the research community needs to develop new frameworks that consider the complexity of modern technology adoption, providing a better understanding. Our research extends the TOE framework by including social and managerial factors, identifying 14 motivational drivers, 24 challenges, and 12 success enablers that have not been covered in previous studies.

3   Research Methodology

An exploratory approach was adopted for the study and semi-structured interviews in line with the factors presented earlier were conducted. The data from the interviews was analyzed qualitatively using Nvivo and a thematic analysis was performed to identify broad category themes related to motivations, challenges, and success enablers concerning the aims and objectives of the study. The questions were mostly related to mainly technology adoption process within ITI, motivations, and pre- and post-adoption effects. Through semi-structured interviews, the interviewer ensures that all key questions are covered while allowing the interviewee to reflect and share relevant experiences.

3.1   Data Collection

Participants were contacted via email through the industry-academia network at the author's university. In total, 105 emails were sent (between Sep 2023 and Feb 2024), and 21 practitioners from 13 organizations were interviewed after pre-screening for relevant expertise. We reached the data saturation point after 15 interviews, but six more interviews were conducted to reduce the risk of data bias and increase the reliability of the findings. The interviews, averaging 50 min, involved various roles like CEOs, CIOs, IT managers, etc. Ethical concerns in this regard were followed including informed consent and non-disclosure of participant details at any stage of the study. Table 1 presents the info about the organizations and roles of the interviewee.

3.2   Data Analyses

We applied an open coding technique to examine our data [25]. Our analysis involved transcribing the interviews into text format and then importing them into Nvivo software, which is designed for qualitative analysis purposes. Using the open coding technique, we labeled the paragraphs and sentences based on their contexts. For instance, "motivational drivers", "challenges", and "success enablers" are examples of the first level of coding that we conducted. In this stage, more than 300 codes that indicated the general ideas of paragraphs or sentences were generated.

In the next step, the focus was only on the parts labeled as motivational drivers, challenges, and success enablers. The more precise and meaningful phrases for each of above mentioned three aspects were assigned. The second level of coding with more than 100 codes that indicated different and mostly similar motivations drivers, challenges, and success enablers of technology adoption were obtained. For example, in terms of motivational drivers, "emphasis on scalability", "cloud migration for flexibility", and "modular IT infrastructure" were all grouped into the main category named "strive for scalability & flexibility". After grouping similar drivers 14 different motivational drivers that are presented in Fig. 2 were established.

The same coding process was followed in challenges, "need stakeholder alignment", "cross-functional collaboration issues", "dependence on external vendors", and "Inefficiency of vendors" which were all grouped into one category named "collaboration issues". After grouping similar issues, 24 challenges were established (see Table 2).

Like success enablers, "protection of sensitive data", "customer trust and loyalty" and "protection against cyber threats" are categorized into one named "enhanced security protocols". After grouping similar attributes 12 different success enablers that are presented in Fig. 3 were established.

To enhance the clarity of the identified motivational drivers, challenges, and success enablers within their respective contexts, 4 themes were selected e.g., environmental, technical, organizational, and managerial. In the case of motivational drivers, managerial factors were replaced with social factors due to the nature of the data.

4   Results

Based on interview outcomes and qualitative inductive analysis, a conceptual framework (Fig. 1) was developed. It comprises motivational drivers, challenges, and success enablers in adopting new technologies, and a detailed taxonomy is provided in the subsequent sub-sections.

4.1 Motivational Drivers

These drivers push organizations or individuals to adopt new technological advancements [26] and are classified into two main types of motives: rationalistic and intuitive.

Figure 2 shows the proposed taxonomy of the motivational drivers.

Rationalistic Motivation. These motives come from logical reasoning, practical considerations, and objective assessments of potential benefits. The drivers are categorized into three main themes:

Technical Drivers. Organizations aim to implement scalable and flexible technology to accommodate growth and evolving needs. They are striving for scalability and flexibility by migrating to the cloud. The senior service operations manager from Case E stated: *"By adopting cloud solutions, there is a need to create a setup that is not only more adaptable, flexible, and scalable but also more efficient in terms of cost management and resource utilization"*. Improving security serves as a key driver for adopting new technologies such as cyber security. The CIO of Case F highlighted secure and efficient

Table 1. Information about conducted interviews and the organizations

Cases	Industry	Company size	No. of interviews	Interviewee's roles
A	IT services and consulting company	220,000	4	Cloud Infra Services Specialist, Technical Expert, Sr. Specialist, Infra Leader
B	IT services and consulting company	15,000	1	IT Manager
C	A telecom and ICT services industry	10000	2	Software Services Advocate
				Service Manager
D	IT services and consulting company	5000	1	Head of Professional Services
E	IT services and consulting company	5000	2	Sr. Service Operations Manager
				VP of Customer Service
F	IT services and consulting company	5000	1	CIO
G	IT services and tactical communication industry	1000	1	Director of IT and Digital Services
H	IT services and consulting company	500	1	Team leader
I	IT services and consulting municipal operators	500	2	Head of User Services
				Service Manager
J	IT services and consulting company	200	1	CEO
K	IT services and consulting company	50	1	Operational Officer
L	IT services and consulting company	10	3	Service Manager
				IT Manager
				CTO
M	IT services and consulting company	10	1	CEO

software provisioning, stating, *"The adoption offers innovative solutions and advanced capabilities that are specifically designed to address modern cybersecurity challenges"*. The rapid pace of technological innovation necessitates proactive measures to stay ahead of emerging threats and vulnerabilities.

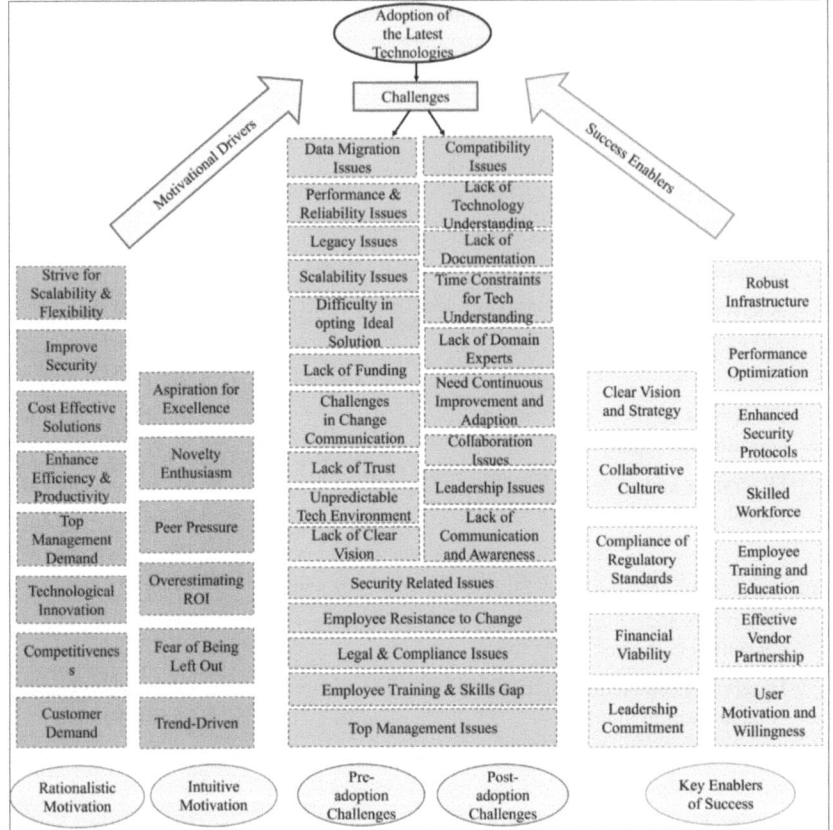

Fig. 1. Technology change adoption framework

Organizational Drivers. New technologies offer innovations that reduce costs compared to older ones. Experts from Cases A, E, F, L, and I emphasized cost-effective solutions by providing scalable setups. The IT manager from Case L stated, *"Advancements in cloud computing and virtualization have significantly reduced hardware and maintenance costs for businesses, making it more cost-effective and will go forward to adopt these technologies compared to maintaining on-premises infrastructure"*. Operational efficiency and productivity are vital for service businesses. The senior service operators from Case E stated, *"We are constantly looking to optimize our ways of working by investing less time, reducing cost, and getting more productivity in terms of giving better services and solutions"*. In Case J, the CEO highlighted that the top management demands drive innovation and efficiency, by adopting technology successfully.

Environmental Drivers. Most practitioners emphasize technological innovation driving industries toward adoption. The infra leader of Case A said, *"Organizations are keen on using AI solutions, but to do that, they often need to shift their data to the cloud. This requires good infrastructure set up to handle data migration effectively"*. A competitive business aims to stand out by delivering superior products or services.

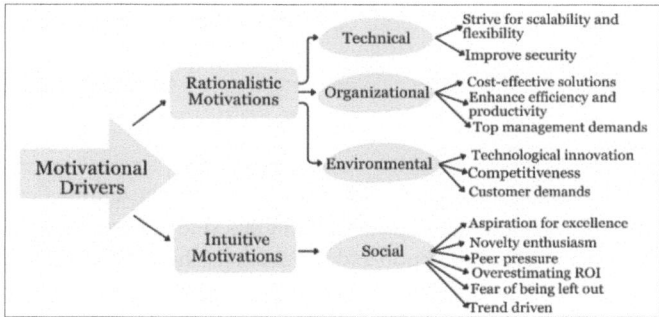

Fig. 2. Taxonomy of Identified Motivational Drivers

The head of user services from Case I stated, *"If we as an organization don't change or look at new technologies, the competitor will come, and they will use the new technology and deliver more efficient services"*. In general, the world and technology are constantly advancing. Experts from Cases A, C, D, E, and H highlighted that offering the latest solutions is a key customer demand. Senior infra experts from Case A added *"Everything revolves around meeting customer needs and aligning with their actions. We strive to stay one step ahead, continuously providing and assisting with the latest solutions to best serve our customers"*.

Intuitive Motivation. Intuitive motives are driven by subjective perceptions, emotions, and instincts rather than rational analysis influenced by psychological, cultural, or social factors as shown in Fig. 2.

Social Drivers. The aspiration for excellence drives individuals to strive for higher performance. The IT manager from Case B stated, "The desire to adopt new technology quickly is strong, but it's important to understand that this process takes time, particularly with security verifications, ensuring safe and effective adoption". Novelty enthusiasm adds excitement for innovation. In Case K, the operational officer said "Our involvement in developing the new technology drives the need for speed. We should react fast to the latest adoption without spending extra time thinking". Peer pressure shapes motivations for tech adoption. The Director of IT and digital services of Case G stated "In rapidly evolving industries, there is often a "race" among competitors to innovate and introduce modern technologies. Organizations may feel pressure to adopt these innovations to keep pace with competitors". Organizations often overestimate ROI from investments. The director of IT from Case G mentioned "The organization's ultimate goal is to generate revenue and profitability, but there is always the risk of overestimating ROI that needs to be assessed carefully considering costs and market dynamics". Organizations perceive fear of being left out with the pace of change that drives technological advancement. The IT manager of Case B said, "When technology advances rapidly, it's crucial to keep pace consistently. If companies don't adopt these new technologies, they could fall behind". Moreover, the trend-driven decisions influence its adoption. The CTO from Case L communicated about trend-driven decision-making to adopt modern technology, he said: "Organizations need to make decisions by adopting trendy technologies to enhance their image or reputation by adding more value to their business because reputable firms are doing the same".

4.2 Challenges

These refer to the obstacles, difficulties, or barriers that organizations face when integrating new technologies into their current ITI. In this study, these challenges are categorized into two stages (i) pre-adoption and (ii) post-adoption challenges. Furthermore, all these challenges are categorized into major themes, which are discussed below in detail sections and presented in Table 2.

Pre-adoption Challenges. These refer to the issues organizations were facing in their current ITI before adopting new technologies.

Technical Challenges. Data migration is a critical process in IT and business operations, often undertaken when adopting new technologies, upgrading systems, or merging data from multiple sources. The team leader of Case H mentioned *"Transitioning from on-premises to the cloud involves various technology transition issues and the main reason is lack of planning and beforehand migration analysis"*. The early adoption of the latest technology is necessary to achieve operational excellence in the organization. The infra specialist from Case A discussed performance and reliability concerns by saying *"Delayed adoption of cloud technologies can hinder organizational productivity and effectiveness. Without access to cloud-based AI solutions and optimization tools, organizations may struggle to streamline operations and deliver efficient services to citizens"*. The difficulties arise due to existing systems/technologies within an organization because they are outdated for current needs. Infra services specialist from Case A discussed legacy issues, he stated: *"Some customers want to use solutions in their data centers where cloud-based options aren't feasible and posing a challenge for both the customers and us when we try to introduce these new technologies but encounter resistance to cloud-based solutions"*. Organizations facing scalability issues as delaying upgrades can lead to unsupported environments and skill shortages. The CEO of Case M specified issues about the novelty-driven system and their training by saying *"Our primary challenge from a business and scalability standpoint is creating something entirely new that requires time, awareness, and some education before we can establish a truly scalable business model and technology infrastructure"*. Experts from different cases raised concerns about security issues. They emphasized the importance of thorough data protection assessments for new technologies to comply with regulations. They also mentioned the need for effective communication between software for better security integration. However, costly advanced security services may not fit many organizations' budgets. Additionally, the team Leader from Case H highlighted the need for training concerning security usage and stated, *"People need to understand how to use security measures effectively to safeguard sensitive data"*.

Organizational Challenges. Experts face challenges by opting for an ideal solution. According to experts from Case K and L, the main challenge is to select the best-fit solution available in the market. This process demands significant time to evaluate options that align with future demands. Organizations are facing a lack of funding challenges because they underestimate the financial costs of adopting new technology, which is influenced by biases. Upgrading technology often requires additional investments in computing power or storage to maintain service quality. There are resource allocation issues discussed that need to implement regular audits of software usage that can help ensure that licenses are allocated efficiently and not wasted on unused subscriptions. There are challenges in change communication as the reason for the change is always hard to communicate the team leader from Case H stated, *"Communicating the rationale behind the change, its benefits, and the expected outcomes clearly and effectively is a challenge before adopting the latest technology"*. A few organizations may have hesitancy or lack of trust in relying on cloud-based services due to security concerns. The experts from Case A and C mentioned, *"Challenges in adopting cloud solutions include fears of public cloud security and reluctance from few customers to store data outside of Finland due to national boundaries concerns"*. Employees resist change especially when they have been using a particular tool for many years. They argue about change because they don't fully understand the rationale behind the proposed change. Technical infra expert from Case A stated, *"Employees are resistant due to a fear of new technology, often stopping their ability to adapt, concerns about job security, or anxiety to learn new skills"*.

Environmental Challenges. The infra services specialist mentioned that legal & compliance issues can hinder the adoption of new technologies by citing *"Organizations may be restricted from using certain technologies or be required to conduct extensive assessments to ensure compliance with data security and protection regulations"*. Employees may encounter challenges in utilizing AI assistant development tools due to legal considerations and the need for compliance. One of the major challenges is the unpredictable technological environment. The CEO from Case M stated, *"Technology is evolving rapidly, with concepts such as the metaverse and AI, gaining fame at different times"*. This dynamic nature of the technological landscape poses a challenge for organizations, requiring them to adapt quickly to stay relevant.

Managerial Challenges. Experts from Cases F and G discussed the lack of clear vision, noting that without understanding organizational goals, *"Hasty adoption of AI driven by social media hype without having a concrete understanding of why, what, and how can lead to unsatisfactory outcomes when objectives and strategies are unclear"*. They emphasized the need for more precise requirements and business maturity for successful adoption. Challenges in employee training and skills gaps also arise. In Cases M and D, experts stated, "There is a need to ensure that users understand how to utilize the technology effectively, meet expectations, use it responsibly, and undergo the necessary training". The experts from Cases C and L highlighted the top management issues by stating, "It is challenging to convince higher-ups about the value and investment in adopting new technologies, even when the talented workforce recognizes their potential". This resistance may arise from a gap in management's tech knowledge affecting decision-making and technology understanding.

Post-adoption Challenges. These refer to the issues organizations were facing after adopting new technologies.

Table 2. Taxonomy of Identified Challenges

Challenges	Pre-adoption Challenges	Post-adoption Challenges
Technical [Issues related to legacy systems, performance, and security vulnerabilities]	Data migration issues	Compatibility issues
	Performance and reliability	Lack of technology understanding
	Legacy issues	
	Scalability issues	
	Security issues	
Organizational [Issues related to resources, personnel communication, and change resistance]	Difficult to opt ideal solution	Lack of documentation
	Lack of funding	Time constraints for tech understanding
	Challenges in change communication	Lack of domain expert
	Lack of trust	Need improvement and adaption
	Employee resistance to change	
Environmental [Issues related to the inter- and intra-org. Environment]	Unpredictable technological environment	Collaboration issues
	Legal & compliance issues	
Managerial [Issues related to management, leadership, and personnel skills]	Lack of clear vision	Leadership issues
		Lack of communication and awareness
	Employee training and skills gap	
	Top management issues	

Ensuring compatibility and smooth integration with existing infrastructure is crucial. The CTO from Case L indicated potential reliability and compatibility issues by stating, *"When the container stops unexpectedly, without logging information, it makes it difficult to understand what went wrong inside the container".* Challenges include integration issues with legacy systems, lack of technology understanding, and overcoming language barriers that hinder tech understanding as highlighted by the head of professional services from Case D *"In Finland, most of the companies, give priority to finish language so they make communication easier within their environment".* Security issues, such as data protection and compliance with international standards, are significant, with the Service Manager from Case C stating, *"The protection of sensitive information is a challenging thing to prevent unauthorized access, breaches, theft, or misuse of data while ensuring compliance with international regulations and standards globally".* Cloud security vulnerabilities also pose a risk. Hindering the organization from utilizing public cloud services.

Organizational Challenges. New technologies often come with refinement needs and a lack of documentation. The IT manager from Case L highlighted, *"Finding real-world experiences with novel technologies can be challenging"* emphasizing the need for comprehensive documentation. Within a complex organizational environment, there are always time constraints for tech understanding. The primary challenges revolve around the lack of domain experts and resources for implementing new technology. The head of professional services from case D discussed the shortage of skilled leaders: *"It's difficult to find experienced leaders with broad expertise and strong interpersonal skills, which is daunting given the competitive nature of the technology sector".* With continuous change, organizations need continuous improvement and adaptation effectively where needed. Lack of user involvement in the adaptation process can result in technologies being imposed on users without their understanding leading to employee resistance to change. The cloud infra leader from Case A highlighted job displacement by stating, *"The transition from on-premises infrastructure to cloud-based data centers can result in job displacement".* This sudden change can cause stress as employees adjust to new roles or seek alternative employment opportunities.

Environmental Challenges. Legal & compliance issues, such as those affecting AI tools, need to be addressed. The operational officer from Case K discussed productivity impact, *"Employees may face productivity hurdles when seeking to use specific tools due to unresolved legal concerns like intellectual property rights or copyright issues, causing delays in their access and utilization".* Collaboration and stakeholder alignment is crucial, as highlighted by the CIO from case F: *"The organization's dependence on external vendors introduces challenges, particularly when the vendors may take time to build the capacity and competence required for the adoption of new technologies".*

Managerial Challenges. Identifying and empowering proactive influencers is difficult. The CEO from Case J mentioned, "It's difficult to identify who is responsible for processes, applications, and data, especially in organizations with poorly defined process models". Experts from A, D, F, and L mentioned the lack of effective people management and lack of interactive support which happens due to inadequate leadership skills and poor teamwork. These leadership issues and lack of communication can hinder engagement and productivity. The director of IT from Case G stated: "Challenges arise when there is a mismatch between the communicated purpose of the technology and the actual problems it is intended to solve. Lack of clarity in communication can lead to a wrong fit". Continuous employee training and skills sessions are required so that they can meet the demands of evolving technologies. Talent acquisition and training are challenges as the CIO from Case G discussed the difficulty of providing relevant training. The experts from Case A, C and I mentioned "We need to reallocate the work or provide training to those who may have lost their jobs and it's more challenging to find the right individuals to support the technology and provide education, especially for complex technologies like AI". The CEO from Case M stated top management issues within the organization by citing "Around 70% of employees in many organizations consider changing jobs due to poor management practices". Lack of ownership in change management poses a challenge, particularly in IT projects. It's essential to determine who should take ownership and make decisions.

4.3 Success Enablers

Success enablers are factors that help in overcoming obstacles, mitigating risks, and achieving technology adoption goals. This study categorizes these enablers into major themes, discussed in detail and shown in Fig. 3.

Technical Factors. A <u>robust infrastructure</u> is needed to ensure all components like networking, security, access management, and cloud services, are in place and scalable as needed. A cloud infra services specialist said that the shift to cloud solutions was growing due to scalability and added, *"The ability to scale resources up or down easily is a key benefit that cloud solutions have brought about, marking a significant change in how ITI is managed and utilized"*. Continuous improvement is crucial for <u>performance optimization</u> requiring ongoing dialogue with the business to align technology adoption with evolving needs. The CIO of case F stated that. "The experimental approach *allows the organization to test and validate the feasibility of new technologies in real-world scenarios before committing to larger-scale implementations"*. <u>Enhanced security protocols</u> are vital to protect data, systems, and networks. Experts from Cases A, C, and I emphasized *"It is important to maintain the privacy and security of individuals and organizations and prevent potential negative consequences like identity theft, financial loss, or reputational damage"*. As new technologies introduce vulnerabilities and robust cyber criminals' measures are essential to protect against threats.

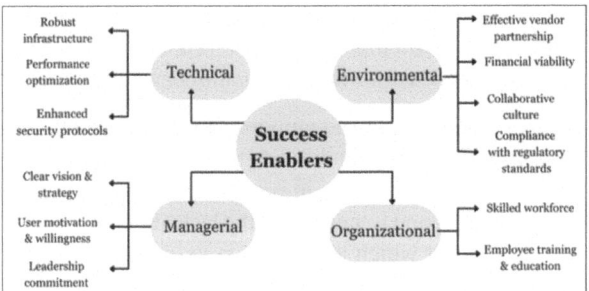

Fig. 3. Taxonomy of Identified Success Enablers

Organizational Factors. A <u>skilled workforce</u> is essential for innovation, productivity, and competitiveness. The software services advocate from Case C emphasized the need for in-house expertise to develop new technologies. Successful technology adoption requires effective employee engagement. Experts from Cases A, D, and K highlighted recruiting the right candidate by stating *"It's important to prioritize candidates with the required competencies, skills, and a mindset focused on continuous self-development and adaptability to new technologies during the hiring process"*. The IT manager from Case B stated the importance of tech-savvy decision-makers. <u>Employee training and education</u> are essential to boost retention and productivity. Experts from Case A stated, *"Enhancing employee skills and educating them on technology use through training and development is essential"*. The director of IT from case G added *"Conduct interactive learning sessions to facilitate hands-on learning and skill development among employees regarding the use of technology".*

Environmental Factors. Experts discussed the importance of effective vendor partnerships for adopting new technologies. Organizations must proactively find suitable vendors for infrastructure readiness. The Infra leader from Case A emphasized close relationships with vendors, stating, *"This collaboration ensures that the organization receives the necessary support and guidance from experts in the technology field".* In service business, strategic vendor management is key, with dedicated teams for managing IT vendors as many IT tasks are outsourced. Cost Management ensures financial viability. The service operation manager from Case E stated, *"Identifying risk and opportunities are important for maximizing returns and minimizing losses".* Investments must align with strategic goals for long-term financial success. The IT director of Case G added, *"Focuses on whether the new technology contributes to revenue generation and provides other benefits that make it a viable addition to the organization".* A collaborative culture, among teams and partners, is essential for alignment with organizational goals. Experts from Case A, C, and G stated, *"Effective and constant collaboration is important by involving stakeholders in discussions, understanding their needs, and addressing concerns which contribute to successful technology adoption".* The Technical expert from Case A highlighted regulatory standards compliance as a success enabler, stating, *"The adherence of an organization to the laws, regulations, rules, and guidelines that govern its operations, products, services, and interactions with various stakeholders".*

Managerial Factors. Establishing a clear vision and strategy provides the organization direction. Experts from Cases A and G stated that alignment with process improvement ensures, *"Organizational processes, workflows, and practices are designed and optimized to support the achievement of strategic objectives".* Effective decision-making is compulsory for organizations to make timely and informed decisions. The CEO from Case J emphasized the business demand-driven way by stating *"Aligning technology adoption with business demand ensures that the adoption efforts are focused on addressing actual business needs, making the technology more relevant and valuable".* Motivated and willing users are essential for successful adoption. Technology. The head of the professional services from Case D said, *"Users should be well-informed about the purpose of the technology and how it aligns with their work".* Building internal competencies equips the workforce with the skills and knowledge needed for new technologies. Leadership commitment drives strategic planning and improvement. The infra leader from Case A highlighted, *"Adopting new technologies isn't solely about the technology itself. It involves redesigning processes, scaling employees, and reorganizing structures within a firm".*

5   Discussion

This work identified 14 motivational drivers, 24 challenges, and 12 success enablers with implications for both research and practice. While existing works [9, 12, 13] focused on challenges during the adoption process, our study covers both pre- and post-adoption challenges and identifies motivation factors and success enablers. Existing studies [11,

26] discuss drivers like competitive trends, customer-driven trends, technology trends, and cost-effectiveness, but our study introduces new rationalistic and intuitive motivations categorized into technical, organizational, environmental, and social drivers. Rationalistic motivations include motivations striving for scalability & flexibility, improving security, enhancing efficiency & productivity, and top management demands. Intuitive motivations (e.g., aspiration for excellence, novelty enthusiasm, peer pressure, fear of being left out, and trend-driven decisions) are often overlooked but can lead to failure if not aligned with long-term goals.

Previous research emphasized technical challenges like integration and security [7, 16]. Our findings also highlight organizational, environmental, and managerial challenges, such as lack of vision, communication difficulties, and trust issues in pre-adoption, and technology understanding and continuous improvement in post-adoption. Some challenges, like security, employee resistance, and legal issues, are included in both stages (pre- and post-adoption).

Additionally, we identify technical, organizational, environmental, and managerial factors success enablers such as robust infrastructure, performance optimization, security protocols, vendor partnerships, and compliance, which were previously overlooked. Existing research found that encouraging a learning culture, employee empowerment, and engaging external stakeholders helps to build innovation capabilities as success enablers of technology adoption [3, 27]. These enablers, like enhanced security, can address cybersecurity concerns and boost organizational performance. For example, enhancing security protocols can address cyber and cloud security concerns by protecting sensitive data from threats and maintaining customer trust and loyalty concerning digital services.

The findings of the paper contribute to the academic discourse on technology adoption by advancing theoretical understanding and providing empirical evidence on the diverse factors influencing technology adoption processes in organizational contexts. It empowers organizations to navigate the complexities of technology implementation and capitalize on the transformative potential of new technologies. The study's findings act as a checklist for practitioners to prepare their organizational setup for the adoption and implementation of new technology. The findings from empirical investigation serve as valuable insights to enhance the effectiveness of the technology initiatives within organizations.

6 Conclusion

The current study addresses three research questions related to the adoption of new technologies in organizations. These questions have been answered by conducting interviews with professionals to understand the technology adoption process within ITI in the context of Finnish digital services providers. This study proposed a technology change adoption framework and provided relevant factors that enhance the understanding of the motivation behind technology adoption, challenges they face before and after technology adoption, and enablers to make the technology adoption process successful. Industrial professionals and researchers should consider these factors when examining or adopting any new technologies within the organizational environment.

One of the limitations of the work is that the quality of data could have been influenced by the type of organizations who participated in the interviews affecting global generalizability and focuses only on management roles. Future work aims to (i) expand the study to other stakeholders (e.g., consultants, users) and other organizations across the EU, (ii) explore relationships (e.g., cause and effect) between drivers, challenges, and enablers, and (iii) conduct a survey to improve the generalizability of the findings.

References

1. Alenezi, M.: Digital learning and digital institutions in higher education. Educ. Sci. **13**(1), 88 (2023)
2. Junaid, S.B., et al.: Recent advancements in emerging technologies for healthcare management systems: a survey. In: Healthcare, vol. 10, no. 10, p. 1940. MDPI (2022)
3. Müller, J.M., et al.: Barriers and enablers for Industry 4.0 in SMEs: a combined integration framework. IEEE Trans. Eng. Manage. (2024)
4. Sharma, S., Malik, A., Sharma, C., Batra, I., Kaswan, M.S., Garza-Reyes, J.A.: Adoption of Industry 4.0 in different sectors: a structural review using natural language processing. Int. J. Interact. Des. Manuf. (IJIDeM), 1–23 (2023)
5. Yang, L., Zou, H., Shang, C., Ye, X., Rani, P.: Adoption of information and digital technologies for sustainable smart manufacturing systems for industry 4.0 in small, medium, and micro enterprises (SMMEs). Technol. Forecast. Soc. Change **188**, 122308 (2023)
6. Sirkemaa, S.: IT infrastructure management and standards. In: Proceedings International Conference on Information Technology: Coding and Computing, pp. 201–206. IEEE (2002)
7. Coeurderoy, R., Guilmot, N., Vas, A.: Explaining factors affecting technological change adoption: a survival analysis of an information system implementation. Manage. Decis. **52**(6), 1082–1100 (2014)
8. Correani, A., De Massis, A., Frattini, F., Petruzzelli, A.M., Natalicchio, A.: Implementing a digital strategy: learning from the experience of three digital transformation projects. Calif. Manage. Rev. **62**(4), 37–56 (2020)
9. Brunetti, F., Matt, D.T., Bonfanti, A., De Longhi, A., Pedrini, G., Orzes, G.: Digital transformation challenges: strategies emerging from a multi-stakeholder approach. TQM J. **32**(4), 697–724 (2020)
10. Prause, M.: Challenges of industry 4.0 technology adoption for SMEs: the case of Japan. Sustainability **11**(20), 5807 (2019)
11. Van de Vrande, V., De Jong, J.P., Vanhaverbeke, W., De Rochemont, M.: Open innovation in SMEs: trends, motives and management challenges. Technovation **29**(6–7), 423–437 (2009)
12. Gutierrez, A., Boukrami, E., Lumsden, R.: Technological, organizational, and environmental factors influencing managers' decision to adopt cloud computing in the UK. J. Enterp. Inf. Manag. **28**(6), 788–807 (2015)
13. Yadegaridehkordi, E., Hourmand, M., Nilashi, M., Shuib, L., Ahani, A., Ibrahim, O.: Influence of big data adoption on manufacturing companies' performance: an integrated DEMATEL-ANFIS approach. Technol. Forecast. Soc. Change **137**, 199–210 (2018)
14. Straub, E.T.: Understanding technology adoption: theory and future directions for informal learning. Rev. Educ. Res. **79**(2), 625–649 (2009)
15. Ntorukiri, T.B., Kirugua, J.M., Kirimi, F.: Policy and infrastructure challenges influencing ICT implementation in universities: a literature review. Discov. Educ. **1**(1), 19 (2022)
16. Kumar, P., Bhamu, J., Sangwan, K.S.: Analysis of barriers to Industry 4.0 adoption in manufacturing organizations: an ISM approach. Procedia Cirp **98**, 85–90 (2021)

17. Ali, O., Murray, P.A., Muhammed, S., Dwivedi, Y.K., Rashiti, S.: Evaluating organizational level IT innovation adoption factors among global firms. J. Innov. Knowl. **7**(3), 100213 (2022)
18. Tornatzky, L.G., Fleischer, M.: The Process of Technological Innovation. Lexington Books, United Kingdom (1990)
19. Rogers, E.M.: Diffusion of Innovations, vol. 32, pp. 891–937. Glencoe Free Press (2003)
20. Asiaei, A., Ab. Rahim, N.Z.: A multifaceted framework for adoption of cloud computing in Malaysian SMEs. J. Sci. Technol. Policy Manage. **10**(3), 708-750 (2019)
21. Ghani, E.K., Ariffin, N., Sukmadilaga, C.: Factors influencing artificial intelligence adoption in publicly listed manufacturing companies: a technology, organisation, and environment approach. Int. J. Appl. Econ. Financ. Acc. **14**(2), 108–117 (2022)
22. Salih, S.H., et al.: Critical success factors for ERP systems' post-implementations of SMEs in Saudi Arabia: a top management and vendors' perspective. IEEE Access **10**, 108004–108020 (2022)
23. Malik, S., Chadhar, M., Chetty, M., Vatanasakdakul, S.: Adoption of blockchain technology: exploring the factors affecting organizational decision. Hum. Behav. Emerg. Technol. **2022**(1), 7320526 (2022)
24. Khin, S., Kee, D.M.H.: Factors influencing Industry 4.0 adoption. J. Manuf. Technol. Manage. **33**(3), 448–467 (2022)
25. Corbin, J.M., Strauss, A.: Grounded theory research: procedures, canons, and evaluative criteria. Qual. Sociol. **13**(1), 3–21 (1990)
26. Hrustek, L., Furjan, M.T., Pihir, I.: Influence of digital transformation drivers on business model creation. In: 42nd International Convention on Information and Communication Technology, Electronics and Microelectronics (MIPRO), pp. 1304–1308. IEEE (2019)
27. Ediriweera, A., Wiewiora, A.: Barriers and enablers of technology adoption in the mining industry. Resour. Policy. Policy **73**, 102188 (2021)

Too Tight or Too Loose? Toward Effective Governance for Corporate Startup Autonomy

Konstantin Garidis[1]([⊠]) [iD], Alexander Rossmann[2] [iD], Alan Murray[1],
and Dominik Augenstein[3]

[1] University of the West of Scotland, Paisley, Scotland, UK
konstantin.garidis@reutlingen-university.de,
alan.murray@uws.ac.uk
[2] Reutlingen University, Reutlingen, Germany
alexander.rossmann@reutlingen-university.de
[3] Hochschule Karlsruhe, Karlsruhe, Germany
dominik.augenstein@hs-karlsruhe.de

Abstract. Engaging with start-ups has become crucial for large, established firms to drive digital innovation and foster an entrepreneurial culture. Start-ups are valued for their autonomy and freedom of choice. However, giving corporate start-ups (CSs) the right level of autonomy is challenging for firms. Effective CS governance requires balancing integration and independence. While previous research has explored corporate venturing, there is a lack of empirical evidence on the governance mechanisms that foster successful CSs. We conducted 40 semi-structured interviews with CEOs and managers in the German-speaking DACH region to address this, providing unique insights and empirical evidence on CSs. We develop a framework consisting of three dimensions and fourteen underlying mechanisms for managing CS governance and autonomy that can be applied to different situations and objectives. This framework is a valuable resource for researchers and practitioners in corporate entrepreneurship and digital innovation.

Keywords: Corporate entrepreneurship · Corporate startups · Governance · Autonomy

1 Introduction

Engaging with startups is not just a trend but a crucial strategy for digital innovation and culture-building for large, established firms. Every established industry faces the threat of disruption from some form of digital business model innovation. However, driving digital innovation is complex, especially for non-tech firms [16]. These firms often lack IT knowledge and digital culture, which hinders their ability to adapt to the rapidly changing digital landscape. In the past, this led to many established industry leaders being displaced by a new disruptive and innovative market entry [15]. However, established firms are designed to exploit their traditional business model, which leads to a structural model that executes the existing business model most efficiently—leaving no room for exploring digital business models apart from the core business. While traditional R&D departments drive innovation in core businesses and technologies, firms try to facilitate digital innovation with various models that are in part structurally separated from the core business, such as innovation labs or incubators. Over the years, firms have introduced and tested many models. These initiatives are ever-changing because of strategy changes or failure to achieve objectives. However, the basic idea of setting up these initiatives is the same: to provide an environment for innovation teams separate from the core business and the firm's legacy that mimics the design of tech startups to drive entrepreneurial culture in the company. This concept of corporate startups (CSs) is being pursued through various approaches [19]. However, researchers and practitioners are still determining how the tension between managing CSs on the one hand and maintaining extensive autonomy for startups on the other hand can be reduced. Autonomy is an essential feature for the success of startups and is required for build–measure–learn cycles during innovation testing [1].

Organizations often face difficulties in providing the desired level of autonomy to their CSs [2]. Research indicates that there is no one-size-fits-all approach to setting up a CS [12]. Firms may choose to offer no autonomy and keep the CS closely integrated with the core business or offer maximum autonomy by completely separating it from their own structure. CS autonomy (CSA) and its influences have been discussed in research from different perspectives. Some studies address firms' structural separation by, for example, setting up a different legal entity [13], whereas others view autonomy from a strategic perspective and describe it as the ability of the CS to set up its plans and decisions independently [9]. While some scholars might argue that a high level of CSA is the desired model, research shows that, in some cases, a more integrated model can be beneficial for innovation goals [2].

Despite the possibility that governance, the way to set up processes and structures, and the explorative nature of a startup might contradict each other, some form of CS governance will always exist in a corporate setting, whether implicitly grown or explicitly managed. Therefore, analyzing how governance mechanisms influence CSA is essential to actively enable the proper CSA setup for the desired goal. Unfortunately, empirical evidence on actual CS initiatives is lacking in this context.

The ongoing debate in research and the struggle in practice show the complexity of the CSA phenomenon. As more CS models pursue different goals and various degrees of CSA exist, steering CSA becomes increasingly complex [3, 10].

While there is no one way to approach the complex problem of steering CSA, there are multiple ways to analyze it. What is missing, however, is a reference for research and practice to orient to and find solutions that fit their situations [5]. This research addresses these issues by building a reference model from a governance perspective. This perspective is broad enough to be applied and adapted to different circumstances and goals. In the pursuit of developing a CS governance model, we follow a qualitative research approach, conducting 40 semi-structured interviews with experts who are implementing and managing these models, as well as CS founders and managers in the DACH region. Following this approach, we focus on the following research questions:

RQ1: Which governance mechanisms are implemented in managing CSs?

RQ2: How do these mechanisms effectively influence CSA?

RQ3: How can a comprehensive governance model for CSA be structured?

The paper is structured as follows: Sect. 2 briefly explains the theoretical foundation of CSs, governance, and autonomy. Our qualitative research is deductively based on the concepts defined in that section. Section 3 describes the methodology and our research process. Section 4 provides a descriptive overview of our sample. In the analysis, we reference the interviews provided in Table 1 in this section. We provide our main study and the description of the developed framework on governance and autonomy in Sect. 5, in which we describe the applied governance mechanisms and their influence on CSA. Section 6 discusses how the experts view their level of autonomy and how it is characterized. Finally, in Sect. 7, we conclude the results and offer directions for future research.

2   Theoretical Foundation

We adapt the definition of CS by Weiblen and Chesbrough [19] which we describe in Sect. 2.1, as their definition encompasses various types of CSs. It focuses on the innovation flow but does not include governance mechanisms used to design CSs. To conduct our research deductively, we base our model on the CS governance dimensions and mechanisms identified from empirical research by Garidis et al. [18]. As our study focuses on qualitatively understanding how these mechanisms are implemented today and how they influence CSA, we only briefly describe the theory herein. In their literature review, Garidis et al. [6] describe the framework extensively.

2.1   CSs Defined

Incumbent companies adopt different CS models to pursue their innovation goals. Over time, several such models have become established in practice. A wealth of research has described these models and their attributes. While these concepts are valuable for analyzing the respective corporate strategy model, a typology encompassing all models is required to investigate the applied governance mechanisms. Weiblen and Chesbrough's [19] approach explains different models by classifying corporate strategy models following innovation flow and equity involvement:

Inside-out Models: Corporate incubation is often nested in a structured program in which internal innovation processes are streamlined into a more agile entity. Firms usually apply these models to innovations that differ significantly from their core business, indicating a need for structural autonomy. Start-ups emerging from this type are often called spinoffs. The term incubation is also used for outside-in entities cooperating with startups by providing facilities, mentoring, and other services.

Outside-in Models: Corporate venturing describes a well-established model of investing in existing startups depending on the strategic goal set by the corporate entity. The process involves individual steps such as scouting for fitting startups or undertaking due diligence. A startup program is a model used to make promising innovations and products by startups available for the offering entity. The format allows the incumbent to engage with several startups and explore possibilities. In exchange, the startups receive benefits such as consulting or access to the corporate ecosystem. In this paper, the term

CS encompasses models that fit into these descriptions of inside-out and outside-in models, as both aim for an environment that enables innovation.

2.2 Governance and Autonomy

CS research has long debated the notion of CSA [4]. Many studies suggest that a CS needs a certain level of CSA to enhance its learning and fully develop innovation capability [14]. This idea is substantiated by structural ambidexterity, which suggests separating organizational structures into entities according to the two objectives of exploiting existing markets and exploring new ones [17]. The premise of CSA is to create an environment for the CS that promotes creativity and flexibility to enable exploration. Other research shows that high CSA can adversely affect CS performance as it impedes knowledge exchange between the CS and the parent firm [7].

Thus, there is a "tug of war" between granting CSA to develop a creative environment that promotes exploration and establishing structures and processes that integrate the CS into the parent firm to secure alignment between the two. Researchers have addressed this issue by distinguishing different types of CSA [5]. Structural autonomy refers to the extent to which a CS is separated from its parent. Operational autonomy describes how CS operations, such as human resources, are shared with the parent firm. Planning autonomy represents the strategic aspects of CSA and describes the CS's ability to set its goals and strategic directions autonomously [9].

Governance research has established similar dimensions that address comparable design aspects of a firm, namely *structures*, *processes & operations*, and *relational mechanisms* [18]. Garidis et al. [5] conducted a systematic literature review and mapped mechanisms found in empirical research on CSs onto an established governance model comprising these three governance dimensions. We use their framework as a foundation to develop and expand the model with empirical evidence by researching how these identified dimensions and their respective mechanisms are implemented in practice today to steer CSA.

3 Methodology

We follow a qualitative research approach using semi-structured interviews [11]. The process consists of four phases: (1) questionnaire design, (2) pretest, (3) main study, and (4) qualitative analysis with MaxQDA. In the first phase, we developed a semi-structured questionnaire. In the second phase, we conducted a pretest to ensure that the questions were adequately designed and could be easily understood by the interviewees. We also used this pretest to check whether the responses to the initial questions were relevant to the research objectives or if they needed to be modified. Using the insights from the previous phases, we were able to design the final questionnaire and conduct the main study.

(1) **Developing the questionnaire:** To deductively analyze the applied mechanisms, we derived the questions from the CS governance model described in the theory section and structured the questionnaire in five main areas: descriptive questions about the interviewee, the firm, and the CS model they apply (Sect. 4); questions

on the *structural* mechanisms applied in their model (Sect. 5.1); questions on the *processes & operational* mechanisms (Sect. 5.2); questions on the *relational mechanisms* (Sect. 5.3); and the mode of CSA and its implications (Sect. 6). For every dimension, we openly asked which mechanisms they apply, e.g., "How is the cooperation between the parent firm and the start-ups structurally organized?" Based on the mechanisms listed at that time, we asked how the mechanisms in place relate to CSA. In this way, all implemented governance mechanisms were listed, and their relationship to CSA was discussed after all mechanisms were listed. This procedure ensured that mechanisms intended to manage CSA, as well as those that unintentionally influence CSA, were captured.

(2) **Interview pretest:** We conducted a pretest with five experts to ensure the questionnaire was adequately designed to answer the research objectives. The goal was to test whether the interviewees understood the questions and whether the answers provided the information needed to answer them. The pretest also confirmed that the interviews could be completed within 45–60 min.

(3) **Main study:** In the pretest, we discovered that asking interviewees to describe the applied mechanisms for each dimension alone might not fully capture the nuance of the phenomenon. As a result, we added a question about the challenges and successes associated with setting up these mechanisms. All interviews were recorded over online video calls and fully transcribed. We conducted five consecutive interviews and then assessed whether new insights emerged. We repeated this process until no new insights were found. At 40 interviews, we interviewed a balanced number of experts from various CS models and the corporate and CS sides. The last five interviews provided no new implementations of the researched mechanisms reaching saturation.

(4) **Analysis:** In this phase, we used qualitative content analysis following Kuckatz and Rädiker [11] to extract and analyze the transcripts using the software MaxQDA. We adopted a deductive approach by structuring the codes on a top level according to Garidis et al. [5]. The code system was applied to the transcripts by coding each passage a mechanism is mentioned. We also extended the model's described mechanisms by incorporating new insights from the interviews inductively. This combination of deductive and inductive analysis allowed us to add to existing research, update known mechanisms, and introduce new ones to the model.

4 Description of the Sample

We interviewed 40 experts from the industry, mainly in the German-speaking DACH region. All experts have several years of experience in several different CS settings. We ensured we interviewed experts working in outside-in and inside-out models, with some working in both. All interviewees are in leading roles such as CS CEOs, department or area heads, or managers. These positions typically set up the mechanisms we are analyzing herein. This gives us a unique view of the mechanisms applied from the corporate and CS sides, diversifying the collected data. Table 1 lists the experts, their roles, and the respective models they implemented. We ensured we interviewed experts from a diverse industry background such as: tech, home appliances, chemical and pharmaceutical, energy, insurance, manufacturing, automotive, and consumer goods. Although not all initiatives focus solely on digital innovation, for all of them, digital (business model) innovation is an integral part of their innovation output.

Table 1. List of Interviews

No	Position	C/S	Model	No	Position	C/S	Model
INT1	Business development	C	Oi	INT21	Partner Manager	S	Oi
INT2	CEO	S	Io	INT22	CEO	S	Io
INT3	Head of	C	Oi	INT23	Innovation Manager	C	Both
INT4	Head of	C	Oi	INT24	Partner Manager	C	Oi
INT5	CEO	S	Oi	INT25	Head of	C	Both
INT6	Innovation Manager	C	Oi	INT26	Innovation Manager	C	Io
INT7	Innovation Manager	C	Oi	INT27	Innovation Manager	C	Oi
INT8	Innovation Manager	C	Io	INT28	Head of	C	Both
INT9	Innovation Manager	C	Io	INT29	Innovation Manager	C	Io
INT10	Innovation Manager	S	Io	INT30	Innovation Manager	S	Io
INT11	Innovation Manager	C	Both	INT31	CEO	S	Io
INT12	Innovation Manager	C	Both	INT32	CEO	S	Io
INT13	Innovation Manager	C	Io	INT33	Innovation Manager	C	Oi
INT14	Innovation Manager	C	Io	INT34	Head of	C	Both
INT15	CEO	S	Oi	INT35	Head of	C	Io
INT16	Innovation Manager	C	Io	INT36	Head of	C	Io
INT17	Innovation Manager	C	Io	INT37	Head of	C	Oi
INT18	Innovation Manager	C	Io	INT38	Innovation Manager	C	Both
INT19	Innovation Manager	C	Oi	INT39	Innovation Manager	C	Both
INT20	Innovation Manager	C	Both	INT40	Innovation Manager	C	Oi

C/S: C = corporate representative; S = start-up representative Model: Oi = outside-in; Io = inside-out.

5 CS Governance Model

Using the model described in Sect. 2 as a framework, we describe how the experts implement the mechanisms of the three governance dimensions (i.e., *structures, processes & operations,* and *relational mechanisms*), as well as their influence on *autonomy* as a CS-specific dimension. Therefore, we synthesize the implementations and provide a few examples for each mechanism we observed. This ensures that all dimensions, their underlying mechanisms, and their respective influence on CSA are described in our model. Figure 1 depicts the final model. It's mechanisms are based on a combination of deductive and inductive coding as described in Sect. 3.

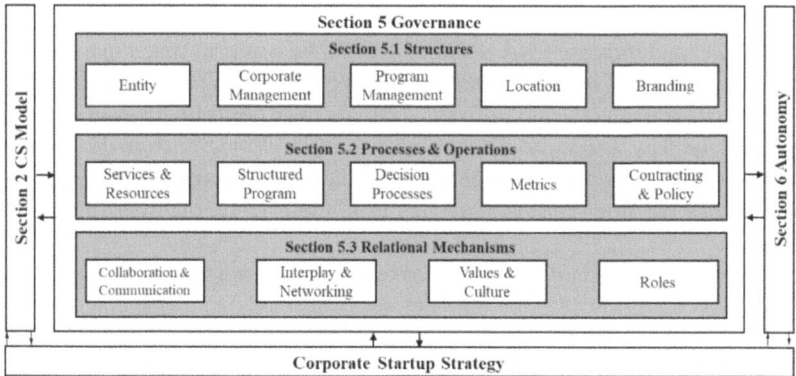

Fig. 1. CS Governance Dimensions and their Mechanisms

5.1 Structures

Structures provide the environment in which the CS operates and encompass five mechanisms. *Entity* defines how the unit is legally embedded in the corporate structure. *Corporate management* describes management's involvement in the CS and its implications. *Program management* describes the team or unit that manages and designs the CS initiatives. *Location* describes where the CSs are located in relation to the headquarters and how this influences CSA. Finally, *branding* discusses whether the CS uses corporate branding and how this restricts CSA.

Entity: Inside-out setups range from a classic department to an separate legal entity, sometimes even with third-party investments or as a joint venture. Some programs are designed to develop CSs founded as separate legal entities (INT9, INT14). In contrast, others identify as venture-building programs but aim to build new business units without legal separation (INT10).

Others leave both options open and decide individually depending on the CSA needs of a CS (INT25). The way the experts interpret the effect of the dimension on CSA varies. INT2, INT22, INT31, and INT32 are CEOs of CSs that are not separate legal entities and thus still have a high level of autonomy. INT16 stated that the legal separation was a critical success factor for one of his CSs, as the corporate structures and *decision processes* would not have allowed the development of a business model.

We observe a clear connection between the desired level of CSA and the design of the *entity* mechanism, as the question of how to facilitate the *entity* was described by all interviewees as a matter of the desired CSA. However, how the manifestation of the dimension affects CSA depends on subsequent mechanisms. As INT2 stated, although the CS is not a legal *entity*, it has the freedom to decide which corporate resources to use. INT30 stated that *decision processes* and internal politics slowed the CS considerably and that moving the CS into a separate legal *entity* would have saved it from these barriers.

In outside-in cases, the *entity* dimension primarily describes whether the corporation holds equity. We find that corporations mostly separate investments and (strategic) cooperation initiatives. However, in some cases cooperation and investment are combined but there are plans to separate these initiatives in the future to maintain an objective view of the cooperation and increase CSA (INT23). INT24, by contrast, stated that they plan to make small investments in their startup program possible. The program is set up so that the firm can integrate the startup's offerings into its sales portfolio. Investing in startups that are in demand by their customers generates additional income from the cooperation by leveraging the cooperation through *equity*. In this case, decreasing the level of CSA is done because the firm considers insights from the customer demand a competitive advantage.

Corporate Management: Research has repeatedly shown that management support is a critical success factor [8]. Ten interviewees confirmed that management support is important for their initiative. INT10 noted that management supports their initiative and opens doors into corporate units if requested. This is especially important for inside-out models and models that are more integrated into the corporate structure. For example, INT10 and INT34 indicated that their CS initiatives report directly to higher corporate management, providing them a unique position and backing in the corporation. Downsides also exist though; INT14 noted that a high level of management attention also comes with a high demand for reporting, which diverts resources from developing innovation to building high-quality slides for corporate reporting. INT29 compared two CS experiences he was part of, with one located on a different continent and the other close to the headquarters. INT29 noted that the one on the different continent could act more autonomously than the one near headquarters as it was not directly observed by management and therefore did not need to adhere to the corporate policy as much. This may reflect a form of shadow innovation similar to shadow IT, in which CS innovation thrives because it can explore not by design but because of the lower degree of corporate management attention.

Program Management: Some CSs emerged from a strategic impulse or an innovation opportunity without specific *program management* and with no plans to implement it (INT2). This was the case for INT30, but the corporation took this opportunity and is now in the process of setting up a program learning from the insights of its project. Conversely, others started by setting up a *program management* unit that oversees innovation efforts (INT14, INT20, INT23). Some initiatives are set up as departments to develop innovation in a startup-like manner (INT13, INT17, INT18). Most *program management* units are departments in the traditional sense, they employ different measures such as an own *branding* to increase CSA. In a few cases (INT14, INT20), the *program management* itself is set up as a separate legal *entity*. This is done to establish special *services & resources* for their innovation process. For example, INT14 runs an excubation program, and the separate *entity* enables it to set up *processes & operations* according to its needs, decoupled from the corporation, and therefore increasing CSA. The *program management* usually is the team that establishes *processes & operations*, manages the portfolio, and draws up *contracts & policies*. Some interviewees described their role as a security layer between the corporate processes & policies and the innovation teams (INT7, INT24). In other cases, *program management* also develops the innovation (INT13, INT17, INT18). According to INT23, handover of innovation can be challenging if the people in the business unit are not involved in the development. In summary, while *program management* can be the central setup in the form of a legal *entity* to ensure CSA, it can also function as a mediator that, though the CS initiatives are happening inside corporate structures, helps CS teams decouple from the challenges of steering corporate processes and provide *services & resources.*

Location: The *location* aids in creating CSA. Only two cases that mentioned location during the interview located the CS or *program management* in the offices like any other department. Ten cases explicitly opened or rented offices outside the headquarters to create distance from the everyday work at the business units. INT34 located the initiative in Berlin, where many tech firms and startups are located, to be closer to talent. INT10 stated that being distant from the headquarters also comes with challenges, as the physical distance hinders close cooperation with the business units.

Branding: As an inside-out case, INT14 tests *branding* to determine which brand, the corporate brand or a new one, resonates best with the target audience. Strong corporate brands can be leveraged to gain trust and open doors in the market, but they also come with requirements in quality and reliability for the CSs products, limiting CSA. *Branding* is also crucial for attracting digital-savvy talent who might not be attracted to the legacy corporate brand. The corporate brand is valuable, especially for business-to-business (INT19). Co-branding may occur in outside-in partnerships as a potential benefit for external startups. In some cases, *program management* builds its brand for internal and external visibility (INT3, INT14, INT17).

In summary, there is a clear connection between structural governance and CSA. Firms leverage these mechanisms to steer CSA toward their desired outcome. Although there is still much movement in how firms design *structures*, they are ever-learning what their optimal setup could look like. We also observe a clear interrelation not just between the *structural* mechanisms but also between other dimensions such as *processes & operations.*

5.2 Processes and Operations

This dimension describes the CSs' operations and those the parent firm provides. This includes five mechanisms. *Services & resources* are mechanisms designed to provide the CS with basic resources, administrative services, and specialized resources such as manufacturing. A *structured program* refers to an innovation process or other types of programs designed to enable and streamline CSs. *Decision processes* describe where and how decisions are made and how these influence CSA. *Metrics* describes how target figures such as key performance indicators are used to steer CSs. Finally, *contracting & policy* describe legal boundaries set up by general corporate policy or by individual contracting between the parties.

Services and Resources: The interviewees mentioned a plethora of services offered, ranging from administrative tasks such as HR, legal, or financial administration; to operative tasks such as marketing and facilities; to specialized services such as training, professional equipment, and infrastructure; to resources such as financial support, materials, and manufacturing. To understand how these services affect CSA, discussing how they are provided is essential. This is closely related to the mechanisms *entity, program management*, and *structured programs* as these, in part, already dictate how services are provisioned. For example, INT2, as a CS uses the same administrative functions, such as HR, as any other department, though it is free to build its own processes and resources if needed. It did this in the case of marketing and sales as it only used digital channels, which the corporation did not provide. Other CSs built similarly do not have this freedom and are constrained by corporate processes and policies (INT30). If the *program management* facilitates a *structured program*, this usually comes with services customized for the program. For example, INT4 and INT13 often need manufacturing components, so they have manufacturing possibilities within their program, such as equipment and access to corporate manufacturing resources. In some programs, these resources are structured with a fixed budget, such as a set number of days to use a legal service. Other programs allow the CSs to access resources from the corporation, but these are based on the willingness to cooperate by other units. In some cases, this works well because the corporate *culture* is very supportive, and all units are willing to support (INT10). Other cases (INT8, INT20) reveal that despite people's willingness to support, they are overburdened and have no resources allocated to participate in innovation. The setup with the highest CSA we observed is when the CS is provided a budget and can spend it freely. In some cases, the budget is fixed for the first validation phase (INT5); in other cases, the budget is negotiated, depending on the CS's needs (INT9). Although these budget setups do not provide full CSA, as the corporation expects reporting on the spending.

Structured Program: There are various *structured programs*, but all are managed by some form of *program management*. In most cases, we observed that the *structured program* is facilitated by an innovation process that streamlines the development of CSs, depending on the innovational goal of the program. For example, in an inside-out setting, this could be a ruleset that regulates how employees are exempt from their everyday jobs during the different phases. E.g. INT14 noted that employees only get to work on a project one day a week in the early phases. If the project matures, they can be completely exempt from their job for a specific period. Most interviewees stated that some form of innovation process as a guideline is important, especially for providing services and the discussed allocation of resources and other formalities. Most try to keep this as lightweight as possible to preserve CSA and enable the CSs to individually develop their ideas in a way that fits their needs. INT5 stated that he attended an accelerator at a corporation and was restricted to many events, training, and other resources set up by the program that did not benefit the specific project. According to our interviews, to enable CSA, firms set up programs in a way that offers services, establishes rules for allocating working hours, offers access to internal or external experts, dictates how resources are provided, and so on. While this lightweight approach helps achieve CSA, having no program at all does not increase CSA. The program also functions as a way to decouple the CSs from the corporate processes by clarifying many formalities beforehand.

Decision Processes: The *structured program* often dictates *decision processes*. A program created to validate ideas and guide them through an innovation process until some become actual products typically has clear rules in place. These rules may include goals set by the CSs themselves or potential revenue targets to determine which projects advance to the next phase. We did not observe any CSs whose corporate management takes top-down decisions. In some cases, there are steering committees, but these mostly decide on continuing funding or have a role similar to a supervisory board. None of the interviewees stated that decisions on product issues were made by corporate management. The limiting factors here are usually corporate processes and decisions happening in those processes. INT30 noted that while setting up different parts of their product (e.g., infrastructure, branding), so many people were involved in deciding whether they could do it or not that this was the most limiting factor for their CS. Many interviewees also noted that purchasing and procurement decisions are a central limiting factor for development. INT11 even stated that in their experience, purchasing/procurement and IT are the two things that have to be set up first autonomously, as those have the most regulatory limitations. This is why different measures are implemented to circumvent these limitations. Some of these measures were discussed in the previous section on the *entity* mechanism, as building a separate legal entity usually frees the CS from purchasing guidelines. In some cases, essential equipment or software (e.g., prototyping) is provided already to limit the need for purchasing during initial development. INT2 stated that the CS has the freedom to procure anything it needs. In some cases, the *program management* manages the CSs' processes so that they can focus on their project.

Metrics: *Metrics* can be used to steer CSs' goals in the context of CSA. Metrics entirely set by corporate management often lead to low CSA. Our sample did not observe any cases in which the metrics caused an issue. In most cases using metrics, the metrics were set up by *program management* in cooperation with the corporation.

Contracting and Policy: While setting rules for the relationship via contracts is the norm in business, the uneven relationship between the corporation and the CS, inside-out or outside-in, might lead to a one-sided ruling, influencing CSA negatively. This refers to cooperate contracts handling the relationship specifically and corporate policies that actors in the corporate space must obey. For outside-in cooperations, we observed that program management often implements lightweight contracts that handle, for example, intellectual property. For INT33, there is a clear separation between what is owned by the corporation and what is owned by the CSs. INT3 stated that the firm structures its initial projects so that there will be no new intellectual property to handle. Regarding onboarding startups as solutions suppliers, corporations usually have strict entry boundaries and policies for suppliers. INT7 described that the firm could not implement a process specifically designed for startups, though it was able to structure the process in a way that aligns better with the nature of startup cooperations. Examples of such structures include the idea that comparison offers are unnecessary because of the experimental nature of these collaborations, and payment terms are much shorter because startups typically require liquidity. INT19 described that every CS must meet high regulatory standards as the corporation is in a highly regulated industry. The solution is to collaborate only with established startups in the industry that already meet those standards. In the case of inside-out, we already discussed some policy and legal aspects in the sections on entity, branding, and *program management.* Securing the startup from corporate policy restrictions was often accomplished by founding a separate entity, separating *branding*, or having the *program management* handle all the regulations and protect the CSs from those barriers.

In summary, while many firms try to build services and resources for the CS to use freely, this often comes with challenges from corporate policies. While there is some movement to decouple these resources and provide CSA, the link is not as clear as in the *structures*. While *structures* do offer a certain level of CSA, firms can also provide a certain level of CSA by designing *processes & operations* in a desired way without providing full autonomy through their *structures*. Furthermore, we observe that the capacity to build these processes often rests on an open and supportive corporate culture and on enabling collaboration through *relational mechanisms*.

5.3 Relational Mechanisms

Relational mechanisms describe mechanisms designed to enable interpersonal relationships and encompass four factors: *Collaboration & communication* describe the relationships between the CS and the parent firm. *Interplay & networking* define mechanisms to enable an interplay between different initiatives and internal and external networks. *Values & culture* highlight how culture enables innovation. Finally, *roles* describe the established roles and their jobs.

Collaboration and Communication: We observe that most collaborations follow an informal style to ensure the freedom of both cooperation partners. In our sample, the initiatives designed to enable outside-in cooperations focus on cooperating with startups that already work with corporations and therefore have some experience in handling corporate processes. Most reported that they also looked at early-stage startups initially but changed their focus because some collaborations failed. This would lead to business units losing trust in startups in general (INT7, INT19). INT3 noted that the firm looks for strong cooperation partners in startups to ensure the relationship is on equal footing. In general, corporations try to provide external startups with CSA in terms of *collaboration & communication* on an informal basis without any rigid structures or rules. They tend to focus on building trust on both sides, the business units on the corporate side and those on the startup side. A view of both sides in research on interpersonal relationships is necessary to reliably analyze whether this relationship structure affects CSA. When asked if there was an uneven relationship between the two players, corporate experts explained that they ensure they stay on an equal footing (INT3, INT19). On the startup side, a CEO stated that the CS is highly reliant on corporate management and that it has a "big influence" (INT15).

Interplay and Networking: This mechanism can be viewed from two angles: access to corporate customers and the internal network within the corporation. For inside-out models, access to corporate customers differs for cases that use corporate branding and cases in which branding is separate. So, when there is a lower degree of CSA with combined branding, the hurdle of providing customer access is much lower. In the case of INT16, one of the CSs was intentionally designed with different branding; therefore, no customer access was granted. In the cases of INT11 and INT13, the CSs openly acted under corporate branding to work with corporate customers intentionally. As discussed under the *branding* mechanism, acting under corporate branding decreases CSA, as it comes with policy restrictions while enabling customer access, which provides a considerable advantage. In the case of outside-in models, INT6 described customer access as one of the critical motivations for startup cooperation partners, and the firm is trying to enable this by implementing networking events. INT24 described customer access as a critical component of the startup program. This acts as quality control of the startups, and startups that fit into the program get customer access by integrating their solutions into the corporate sales portfolio. In contrast, INT33's program is designed so that startups can develop new solutions using the corporate solution portfolio. Still, sales integration is not a part of the strategy to ensure CSA. Overall, customer access is treated highly individually but is dependent on CSA. Views of the internal network are just as individual. INT10 and INT13 agreed that the internal network is based on the network of the CS's employees, as they are long-term corporate employees who transferred to the CS. INT20 described their role in building an internal network for the CS actors over time.

Values and Culture: Informal collaborations work exceptionally well when the corporation already has an open and supportive culture. Many interviewed experts described the corporation's open and supportive culture as a critical success factor (INT10, INT18, INT19, INT30). INT30 even stated that the open and supportive culture enabled the firm to push back on the hurdles the corporate structures created.

Roles: *Program management* mediates between the corporation and the CSs. As described in Sect. 5.1, it takes this role as a mediator in charge of tasks. It is a translator between corporate management and the startups and ensures a respectful, professional, and trustful relationship. It also acts as a firewall between the two so that the CSs are protected by corporate processes and policies, increasing CSA (INT7). One particular case was the role of the internal investor described by INT9. He describes it as an internal business angel for CSs. The idea is to provide the same financing structures a startup would have on the free market, provide the same incentive structures, and ensure that the CSs are not dependent on traditional budgeting like other projects.

In summary, while we only observed minor cultural challenges, a prevalent open and supportive culture is the base for enabling the effectiveness of the other dimensions. Especially in the context of CSA, culture is the "binding agent" that keeps the initiatives and mechanisms together and enables innovation without strict processes.

6   Discussing Autonomy

We identified how governance mechanisms can be implemented to steer CSA and the interrelations between them. When asked how much CSs can act autonomously, most interviewees agreed that they can act highly autonomously. However, this contradicts some of their previous statements, in which they noted that CSs must follow corporate guidelines or cannot circumvent the purchasing and procurement processes. For most experts, a central goal is to ensure CSA. For many experts in our sample, CSA is understood as the ability to make decisions and test ideas independently. Prior research has referred to this as planning autonomy [9]. Many experts, however, neglect the structural dependencies CSs have and their impact on innovation development. While these dependencies may come with a competitive advantage, they are by design, or the goal for these solutions is to be integrated into the corporate portfolio, in which they need to follow corporate policies anyway. To manage CSA effectively, research needs to understand how these mechanisms influence CSA. Our model, depicted in Fig. 1, provides a framework to guide practitioners and researchers in the pursuit of steering CSA through effective governance mechanisms.

Some CSs intentionally limit CSA, primarily entities that innovate close to the core business. For example, one innovation lab (INT13) is designed to develop new ideas as add-ons to the core business and must cooperate closely. However, it is granted operational autonomy by having a budget it can use freely and not being restricted to purchasing and procurement processes. It is also provided with a credit card and can buy anything needed. Corporate policies should be kept in mind as innovation will be integrated into core business in the future.

Many of the challenges and future improvements the experts stated are related to managing CSA. A few said they would like a separate legal *entity* to decouple the CS initiative (INT16, INT24). In addition, ten interviewees said that extensive or even unknown corporate processes slow them down. Some also stated that the dependencies on corporate business units slow them down as the business units do not have enough resources allocated to innovation, if any (INT8, INT9, INT17, INT18). Others stated that internal marketing, reporting efforts, and building the internal network take significant resources away from developing innovation (INT11, INT14, INT22, INT25).

In summary, the experts are actively steering CSA, and none stated that complete autonomy is the golden way. However, finding the proper balance for their innovation goals is still a considerable challenge, and they are still on their way to testing different mechanisms and developing a suitable setup.

7   Conclusion, Limitations and Future Research

The challenges of designing CS models to drive digital innovation are just as diverse as those of digital innovation itself. The presented empirical research clarifies that a lot of different governance mechanisms are used for CS initiatives at different levels. Generally, the mechanisms identified on the basis of qualitative interviews can be categorized in existing governance models [5]. However, for the first time, this research offers a detailed and empirically sound insight into individual mechanisms and their impact on CSA.

While general concepts are clear, knowing which mechanisms to implement to achieve the desired CSA is still challenging, and models are ever-changing. Firms aim for different innovation goals and, therefore, follow different strategies. To assist firms in this endeavor, we based our model on existing research and were able to build a sophisticated CS governance model for CSA based on empirical evidence acquired through 40 expert interviews. Our model defines the main mechanisms applied to manage CSA. Most CS experts agreed that managing CSA is an integral part of their business and noted that they built their structures with CSA in mind. Most still need assistance setting up a suitable model for their CSA needs. The degree of CSA desired depends on the strategic goal of the CS initiative. Our findings suggest that the closer the desired innovation is to the core business, the less the CS benefits from specific CSA mechanisms. Although this is just a rule of thumb and in an effort to balance between CSA and corporate relationship, CS experts are struggling with implementing a CS model that benefits their strategic goals.

Like every research, this study has some limitations. While we ensured a diverse sample, multiple interview perspectives, and interviews from the corporate and startup sides, we only analyzed data from respondents in the German-speaking DACH region. Although we investigated globally acting corporations, the analyzed phenomenon could have cultural influences that only apply to German corporations. Further research with an international sample is required to apply the model in a global context and to assess its validity with a more extensive data set.

Various directions can be derived for further research. First, further empirical data is needed to investigate the relationship between different forms of CSs, strategic objectives, specific governance mechanisms and the desired level of CSA. This research provides an initial basis. Initial patterns can be derived from the available data presented in this paper. However, this must be explored in greater depth in further research. The model developed in this study can be applied as a framework in this pursuit. Mapping the implemented mechanisms onto strategic pathways will give corporations a clearer picture on which mechanisms benefit their strategic goals. Our model provides a foundational framework based on the three established governance dimensions: *structures, processes & operations*, and *relational mechanisms*. Practitioners can apply this framework to analyze their CSA setup and identify possible opportunities for improvement.

References

1. What's A Startup? First Principles. https://steveblank.com/2010/01/25/whats-a-startup-first-principles/. Accessed 18 May 2022
2. Covin, J., et al.: Short leash or long leash? Parenting style, initial strategic clarity, and the development of venture learning proficiency. J. Bus. Ventur. **35**, 4 (2020)
3. Feldman, E.R.: Dual directors and the governance of corporate spinoffs. Acad. Manag. J. **59**(5), 1754–1776 (2016)
4. Gard, J., et al.: An integrating model of autonomy in corporate entrepreneurship. In: International Conference on Engineering, Technology and Innovation (2015)
5. Garidis, K., et al.: Corporate startups: a systematic literature review on governance and autonomy. In: ICSOB (2024)
6. Garidis, K., Rossmann, A.: A framework for cooperation behavior of start-ups. J. Small Bus. Enterp. Dev. **26**(6/7), 877–890 (2019)
7. Garrett, R.P., Covin, J.G.: Internal corporate venture operations independence and performance: a knowledge-based perspective. Entrep. Theory Pract. **39**(4), 763–790 (2015)
8. Garrett, R.P., Neubaum, D.O.: Top Management support and initial strategic assets: a dependency model for internal corporate venture performance. J. Prod. Innov. Manag. **30**(5), 896–915 (2013)
9. Johnson, K.L.: The role of structural and planning autonomy in the performance of internal corporate ventures. J. Small Bus. Manage. **50**(3), 469–497 (2012)
10. Kötting, M., Kuckertz, A.: Three configurations of corporate innovation programs and their interplay. Eur. J. Innov. Manag. **23**(1), 90–113 (2020)
11. Kuckatz, U., Rädiker, S.: Qualitative Inhaltsanalyse. Methoden, Praxis, Computerunterstützung (2022)
12. Lee, S.U., et al.: The double-edged effects of the corporate venture capital unit's structural autonomy on corporate investors' explorative and exploitative innovation. J. Bus. Res. **88**, 141–149 (2018)
13. Li, H., et al.: Corporate governance in entrepreneurial firms: a systematic review and research agenda (2020)
14. Schuh, G., et al.: Deriving requirements for the organizational structure of corporate incubators. In: PICMET 2018, pp. 1–8 IEEE (2018)
15. Skog, D.A., et al.: Digital disruption. Bus. Inf. Syst. Eng. **60**(5), 431–437 (2018)
16. Svahn, F., et al.: How volvo cars managed competing concerns. MIS Q. **41**(1), 239–254 (2017)

17. Tushman, M.L., O'Reilly, C.A.: Ambidextrous organizations: managing evolutionary and revolutionary change. Calif. Manage. Rev. **4**, 8–30 (1996)
18. Vejseli, S., et al.: The concept of agility in IT governance and its impact on firm performance. In: ECIS 2022 Research Papers, p. 98 (2022)
19. Weiblen, T., Chesbrough, H.W.: Engaging with startups to enhance corporate innovation. Calif. Manage. Rev. **57**(2), 66–90 (2015)

The Use of Generative AI Tools in the Inception Stage of Software Startups

Triando[1]([✉]) [iD], Mario Simaremare[2] [iD], Xiaofeng Wang[1] [iD],
and Akshy Sripad Raghavendra Prasad[1] [iD]

[1] Free University of Bozen-Bolzano, Bolzano, Italy
{Dtriando,Xiaofeng.Wang,Akshysripad.Raghavendraprasad}@unibz.it
[2] Department of Software Engineering, Blekinge Institute of Technology,
Karlskrona, Sweden
mario.simaremare@bth.se

Abstract. Generative Artificial Intelligence (GenAI) is disrupting numerous fields of human endeavors, including software startups. While GenAI tools hold the promise of accelerating innovation, improving product quality, and enhancing decision-making, software startups during their inception stage, a phase characterized by high uncertainty and limited resources, may face significant challenges in using these technologies. However, understanding the opportunities and challenges that GenAI brings to software startups is scarce due to the nascent nature of GenAI tools. Our study aims to provide an initial understanding of the intriguing research phenomenon of GenAI application in early-stage software startups. An action case study approach is employed in our study. We examined two software startups within a university setting, focusing on how these teams utilized GenAI tools in the inception stage. The findings revealed 11 opportunities and 10 challenges of using GenAI tools in the inception stage. Novel findings in the startup context include opportunities like brand identity development, generating landing pages, simulating customer feedback, and validating MVP. In contrast, challenges include a function-oriented rather than problem-oriented and a tendency to please rather than provide critical feedback. The findings suggest that while GenAI tools offer valuable benefits for startups, successful adoption requires careful consideration of technical and non-technical factors. This research opens avenues for future studies on integrating GenAI in early-stage software startups.

Keywords: Software Startup · Inception Stage · Generative AI · Action Case Study

1 Introduction

"Change the world for a better place" is a well-known motto that millions of startup companies worldwide embrace. Startups do not just adapt to the future - they create it. However, it is challenging to build a startup due to the inherent

E. Papatheocharous et al. (Eds.): ICSOB 2024, LNBIP 539, pp. 439–453, 2025.
https://doi.org/10.1007/978-3-031-85849-9_34

uncertainty associated with the process of "from 0 to 1" [16]. The failure rate is notoriously high [22]. Many startups fail to survive even the earliest inception stage, from the initial conception of a business idea to the point where the startup delivers its first product to a customer [15]. This stage is crucial as the startup works toward achieving problem-solution fit, a milestone indicating that its solution adequately meets the needs of targeted customers [11].

The landscape of startups, including how they can be supported, is disrupted by the recent surge of Generative Artificial Intelligence (GenAI). According to a recent CBInsight report "Generative AI Bible: The ultimate guide to GenAI disruption"[1], an increasing number of startups pile into the GenAI arena, and funding soars as investors flock to catch the trend. In contrast, how GenAI is and will disrupt startups, especially in their early stages, receives much less attention, as the old saying depicts, "the darkest place is under the candlestick."

Like many other fields, GenAI technologies can enable startups to identify opportunities, accelerate innovation, and improve services and product quality, meeting the dynamic and challenging demands of the environments [19,20]. In the meantime, it is essential to address various issues and concerns associated with GenAI, such as bias in models and hallucinations [1], which could affect its applications in critical decision-making contexts. What opportunities and challenges GenAI technologies bring to startups and how startups can reap the benefits and handle the challenges are yet to be understood. These questions are particularly demanding for early-stage startups with limited resources and knowledge to experiment with GenAI, which prevents them from leveraging its potential to support their activities.

Our study aims to provide a good understanding of the potential of GenAI technologies in supporting startups. We focus on the inception stage of software startups. The inception-stage startups resemble infants in their vulnerability and need for support to thrive. They rely heavily on various resources such as incubation programs, mentoring services, and networking opportunities [6]. However, these resources are often limited and not universally accessible, leaving many inception-stage startups without the tailored support they require to address their unique challenges and increase their survival rates [18]. The rationale behind the focus on software startups is that they typically adopt cutting-edge technologies early and are highly influenced by them [10].

In this study, we ask the following research question:

RQ: How is the usage of GenAI technologies perceived by software startups in the inception stage?

To answer the research question, we applied the action case approach [4] and studied two software startups in the university settings in depth. The findings from our study include eleven opportunities and ten challenges associated with the key steps in the inception stage of software startups. The two cases provided a contextual understanding of these opportunities and challenges.

The rest of the paper is organized as follows. Section 2 reviews background literature and existing research relevant to our study. The use of action case as

---

[1] https://www.cbinsights.com/research/report/generative-ai-bible.

the research methodology is explained in Sect. 3, and the data collection and analysis processes are detailed in the same section. The findings are reported in Sect. 4 and discussed in Sect. 5. Section 6 concludes the paper with future work.

2 Literature Review

2.1 Inception Stage of Software Startups

Software startups are the startups in which software plays a central role in the innovations they are working on [17]. Limited resources, limited experiences, and the strong influence of cutting-edge technologies are some of the key characteristics of software startups [24].

A recent study by Klotins et al. [15] models the software startup lifecycle into four stages: inception, stabilization, growth, and maturity. In the inception stage, software startups focus on discovering gaps and developing innovative ideas into viable solutions [15]. Bosch et al. [3] model early-stage software startup development into three phases: idea generation, ideas backlog prioritization, and funneling through problem validation, solution validation, and minimum viable product (MVP) validation on small and large scales.

Studies show that developing viable solutions during the early stages of a software startup is a challenging process [10,25]. For example, Giardino et al. [10] explore the most common challenges early-stage software startups face during the initial period. These challenges include technological issues, customer acquisition, funding, team development, defining MVP, and product-market fit.

2.2 GenAI for Innovation

GenAI refers to AI technologies capable of creating new content [8], such as text, images, audio, video, 3D, and code. These technologies use advanced machine learning techniques and neural networks to analyze vast information and generate original outputs that mimic human-generated content [8]. In the software industry, GenAI has been used to streamline software development processes through task automation, such as image generation, code generation, testing, debugging, deployment, expert replacement, and documentation [12,13,23]. Conversely, this technology has various challenges, including bias, hallucination, and inaccurate responses [12,13,23].

Studies point out the potential use of GenAI to foster and accelerate innovations [2,9]. GenAI can help companies in the initial stage of their innovation initiatives, from ideation to the solution validation phase [9]. In the ideation phase, GenAI can assist idea generation from nothing or from an analysis of existing data, e.g., customer reviews and behavior, to capture patterns and uncover problems from which new ideas emerge. Later, GenAI can also assist innovation teams in evaluating these new ideas and creating assumptions, i.e., hypotheses. Following that, GenAI can help with product validation purposes, which benefits teams without tech-savvy personnel [9]. Moreover, GenAI also has the potential to assist in organizational, managerial, and customer-related activities such as customer support and analytics for recommendation systems [9].

Apart from these few studies that explore the potential of GenAI in the software industry and to support innovation in companies, to the best of our knowledge, there is no study on the opportunities and challenges brought by GenAI to software startups. Our study intends to bridge this knowledge gap to advance research and practice in the context of software startups.

3   Research Approach

To answer the research question, we applied the action case research method, a hybrid of interpretation and intervention, understanding and change [4]. Action case lies between case study and action research. It introduces small-scale intervention with a deep contextual understanding of a case. We deem action case as an appropriate research method for this study because, when studying a nascent research phenomenon such as GenAI, which is not widespread yet, a researcher needs to take a more active role and be involved in creating change in practice rather than being an observer only.

This study involved two software startups in a university setting. Both teams worked on the startup projects for four months during the data collection in June 2024. The two software startups were in the inception stage since neither has reached a problem-solution fit yet.

One of the authors intervened with the two startup teams by encouraging the teams to utilize GenAI technology to support their startup development. Several tools were recommended, including ChatGPT, the GPT builder (to create digital personas representing early adopters), and mixo.io (automated landing page generation from a stated idea). The teams were not obliged to use the recommended tools and had the liberty to use any GenAI tools they considered appropriate. Additionally, the teams were mentored by university lecturers and local entrepreneurs.

3.1   Data Collection

The primary data collection method was semi-structured interviews with open-ended questions. Since one of the authors was familiar with the two software startup teams already, we kept the part related to the demographic and background of the interviewees minimal. The main part of the interview was guided by the steps that represent the typical steps a startup follows in the inception stage, according to the Lean Startup methodology [21] and the literature reviewed in Sect. 2.1. The first step, **ideation and problem identification**, combines idea generation with ideas backlog prioritization, emphasizing problem identification. The second step is **problem validation**, intending to understand whether the hypothesized customer problems do exist. The third step, **problem-solution fit**, focuses on validating the proposed solution.

For each of the steps, we asked the following open-ended questions in the interviews:

- (Q1) Which GenAI tools did your team use?
- (Q2) How did your team use them?
- (Q3) What are your opinions about the tools used?

Additional questions emerged during the interviews and were followed up wherever possible. The interview protocol used can be accessed online[2]

All team members were interviewed, and their profiles are summarized in Table 1. The table provides background information on each interviewee. Members from the Rapido team are indicated with the prefix **R**, while those from the Blue Dot team are marked with **B**. Each interviewee within their respective teams is assigned a unique identifier in the format **In** (where n represents the interviewee's sequence number).

Three of the four authors were present in all the interviews conducted. The author who intervened with the two teams by introducing GenAI tools to them was the main interviewer. The other two authors acted as observers and asked additional questions when appropriate. All interviews were conducted online using Microsoft Teams[3] The duration of the interviews varies between 30 min to 45 min per interviewee. All interviews were transcribed using OpenAI's Whisper[4] The transcriptions were reviewed, and missed transcribed texts were manually fixed based on the recordings.

In addition to the interviews and observations during them, documents produced by the two teams were collected, including pitch decks, promotion videos, recorded pitches, landing pages, filled lean canvas, learning diaries, and custom GPTs. These documents and observations were used to triangulate the data collected through the interviews.

3.2 Data Analysis

We conducted a thematic analysis of the interview data following the approach outlined by Braun and Clarke [5]. We also followed the guidelines provided by Cruzes et al. [7] to synthesize our findings. Our analysis was both deductive and inductive. Initially, we developed a set of high-level codes aligned with the research question. The first and second authors took primary responsibility for analyzing the interview transcripts. Both authors then independently read the transcripts to understand the content and context. The two authors reconciled their coding, and all authors reviewed the final results for rigor and consistency. The documents, unlike interview data, were analyzed to gain insights into GenAI tool usages.

4 Findings

This section describes how the two startup teams used various GenAI tools and how they perceived the opportunities and challenges associated with the usage of GenAI. Table 2 presents the GenAI tools utilized by the two startups.

---

[2] Interview protocol: https://doi.org/10.5281/zenodo.14036029.

[3] Microsoft Teams: https://www.microsoft.com/en-us/microsoft-teams.

[4] OpenAI's Whisper: https://openai.com/index/whisper.

444   Triando et al.

Table 1. The Profiles of Interviewees

Team	Interviewee	Background Information
Rapido	R-I1	R-I1 is an experienced engineer in front-end, back-end, and full-stack roles. R-I1 has interned in a company based in Italy, working with TypeScript, and holds a bachelor's degree in computer science. R-I1 has experience developing mobile applications and has used Figma for mock-ups
	R-I2	R-I2 is a software developer with experience in both front-end and back-end development from university projects. R-I2 specializes in back-end development and works with C#. Moreover, R-I2 has also developed mobile applications. R-I2 holds a bachelor degree in computer science
	R-I3	R-I3 have experience working as an engineer for websites and mobile applications, with occasional front-end tasks. R-I3 has intervened in a company with a role related to compliance assessment
Blue Dot	B-I1	B-I1 is a full-stack developer, proficient in both back-end and front-end development. B-I1 uses Scala for back-end tasks and PureScript for front-end development
	B-I2	B-I2 has experience with Java, HTML, Python, Node.js, and jQuery for website development and JavaScript for app development. B-I2 has also learned PHP through an internship and has experience writing smart contracts using Solidity, which is based on C++

Table 2. Reported GenAI tools used by the two startups

Name	Type	Usage in the Cases
Gamma.app	Text-to-Image	Create presentations for pitch decks
logomaster.ai	Text-to-Image	Design logos for products or brands
UIZard.io	Text-to-Image	Develop app mockups for user testing and feedback
ChatGPT.com	Text-to-Text	Validate ideas, generate brand names, custom GPTs, and content
Wix.com	Text-to-Text	Build and customize websites for companies
FlexClip.com	Text-to-Video	Create video presentations for pitching ideas
InVideo.io	Text-to-Video	Create video presentations for pitching ideas

The findings are structured using the three steps described in Sect. 3.2. Table 3 overviews the opportunities and challenges identified in the two cases.

Table 3. Opportunities and Challenges of using GenAI Tools

		Case 1. Rapido			Case 2. Blue Dot		
		I&PI	PV	P-S Fit	I&PI	PV	P-S Fit
Opportunities	Op01. Brand identity development	✓					
	Op02. Create mockups and websites		✓				✓
	Op03. Create presentation		✓				
	Op04. Develop interview questions	✓					
	Op05. Domain expert replacement		✓				✓
	Op06. Generate image, audio, and video		✓				
	Op07. Generate landing page		✓				
	Op08. Idea generation and refinement				✓		
	Op09. Language translation	✓					
	Op10. Simulate customer feedback		✓				
	Op11. Validate MVP		✓				✓
Challenges	Ch01. Biased responses		✓				
	Ch02. Cannot represent the actual users		✓		✓		
	Ch03. Felt unnatural		✓				✓
	Ch04. Pricy		✓			✓	
	Ch05. Hard to construct meaningful prompts		✓				
	Ch06. Inaccurate responses		✓				
	Ch07. Function-oriented instead of problem-oriented		✓				
	Ch08. Tend to please instead of being critical					✓	
	Ch09. Lacks of transparency						✓
	Ch10. Unreliable responses		✓				

Note: I&PI: Ideation and Problem Identification; PV: Problem Validation; P-S Fit: Problem-Solution Fit
The highlighted cells indicate that the corresponding challenges are not specific to any steps.

4.1 Opportunities and Challenges Perceived by Rapido

The Rapido team (Table 1: R-I1, R-I2, and R-I3) proposed a digital platform to revolutionize the booking process for sports facilities such as tennis courts and football pitches. This innovative solution replaces traditional manual, paper-based methods with a streamlined and efficient workflow. By integrating online booking capabilities, the platform offers users a convenient and user-friendly experience, allowing them to reserve sports fields effortlessly.

Ideation and Problem Identification. In this step, the team brainstormed and developed **brand identity (Op01)** by using ChatGPT, R-I1 shared, *"We were trying to come up with a few names based on the idea's description. We went through some options, but in the end, we picked the one we liked best"* and created some logos as R-I1 shared, *"It's an AI tool for creating free logos, and* *there are a lot of websites offering something similar"* from which the team then chose one of the given alternatives as their product logo.

Problem Validation. In this step, the team used GenAI to **develop customer interview questions (Op04)**. In this use case scenario, they asked ChatGPT to suggest relevant questions mentioning *"essentially, we wanted to figure out which questions would give us the most useful information. Since the goal of these interviews was validation, we needed to focus on questions that would provide insights we found valuable"* as R-I1 stated. Then using these questions, they interviewed several sports field owners and customers about their experiences and challenges while managing and making reservations.

Some customer interviews were conducted with potential users who speak Spanish due to the connection one team member had back in his home country Peru. Since not all team members are Spanish speakers, they used AI to translate these interview transcriptions into English. In this early step, GenAI's **language translation (Op09)** capability proved useful for the team.

Despite the opportunities, the custom GPTs also brought challenges. Firstly, they potentially generate **biased responses (Ch01)** *"because they were shaped for our needs,"* R-I3 stated. Secondly, the team felt that the custom GPTs **cannot fully represent the actual users (Ch02)**, making validation necessary as R-I3 suggested to *"go into the real world, and it may be different because every person has a different opinion."*

Problem/Solution Fit. In this step, the team used GenAI to help them develop their solution, starting from **creating presentations (Op03), images, audio, video (Op06), mockups (Op02), and landing page (Op07)** using AI-generated prompts. The power of GenAI helped the team fill the need for **expertise in particular fields (Op05)**, in this case, while developing the landing page.

The team utilized two custom GPTs to gather more detailed human-like opinions about their MVPs, allowing them to seek immediate **customer feedback through simulation (Op10)** before collecting input from actual users. This approach was particularly useful as finding actual was challenging, and they *"did not intend to go to ask actual people"* as R-I3 mentioned for a halfway solution, making the simulated interaction a practical alternative. In this case, the team used the custom GPTs to **validate their MVP (Op11)**, such as their landing page and video. The custom GPTs developed by this group can be found in Appendix A.

Despite the opportunities, GenAI's outputs were sometimes **felt unnatural (Ch03)**, R-I3 shared an example of this challenge, *"the generated images sometimes were kind of unnatural, and we can see that they are AI-generated."*

Challenges Across All Steps in the Inception Stage. The first challenge was **high price (Ch04)**, R-I3 stated *"these [features] are more advanced and* *you have to pay for them. Since we do not have much money. It's difficult"* for the team to enjoy the full potential of GenAI tools and had to be satisfied with limited customizations and watermarks. Unfortunately, it was **hard to construct meaningful prompts (Ch05)**, R-I3 stated, *"prompting the right term to the right input is crucial ... We need to know very well what to be written is exactly what is in our mind."* Otherwise, **inaccurate responses (Ch06)**, R-I3 continued, *"you can get some results that are not so aligned with your mind, your idea."* Another reported challenge was the available GenAI tools were more **function-oriented instead of problem-oriented (Ch07)**. R-I1 argued that instead of having separate tools for image, logo, and text generation to develop a webpage, *"it would be great if we could find a tool that takes all of them in one place."* The team also experienced GenAI produced **unreliable responses (Ch10)**, *"sometimes the response is good, sometimes it needs small adjustments, and sometimes it is unacceptable,"* R-I3 shared.

4.2 Opportunities and Challenges Perceived by Blue Dot

The Blue Dot team (Table 1: B-I1, and B-I2) was building a community-based travel platform to facilitate ride-sharing for short distances within urban areas. This solution addresses several common urban transportation challenges, including difficulties in finding public transport in certain areas and the scarcity of parking spots for private vehicles. By enabling people to share rides, the platform aims to enhance urban mobility, reduce traffic congestion, and promote a more sustainable mode of transportation.

Ideation and Problem Identification. In this step, the team used GenAI tools for **idea generation and refinement (Op08)**. They found ChatGPT particularly effective at generating ideas and refining concepts, noting that it was *"very good at generating stuff and coming up with ideas,"* as B-I1 mentioned. This approach was especially valuable in the inception stage of a startup, providing crucial guidance that helped them shape their initial ideas.

Problem Validation. In the problem validation step, the team developed a custom GPT and considered the possibility of validating the hypothesized customer problems using the custom GPT. However, the team pointed out that they were worried that the custom GPT **cannot represent the actual users (Ch02)**, emphasizing the need to *"go and talk to [real] people to understand the problem,"* B-I1 shared, highlighting the limitation of GenAI in replacing direct user interaction for problem validation purpose. The custom GPTs developed by this group can be found in Appendix A.

Problem/Solution Fit. In this step, the team used GenAI tools like UIZard[5] to **create mockups (Op02)** as B-I1 mentioned *"We briefly used AI to create*

---

[5] UIZard: https://uizard.io.

the app mockup because the software we were using only accepts prompts. For example, we enter something like build a ride-hailing app," they generated basic screens that helped visualize the application.

The team also identified an opportunity for **domain expert replacement (Op05)**, where B-I1 mentioned *"If you are developing a software solution, GenAI can be a big help in creating an initial prototype. If you do not know how HTML, CSS, or JavaScript work, especially for those without a technical background,"* also offering assistance to **validate MVP (Op11)** by refining the content for their product as mentioned by B-I1 *"On Netlify, I believe we selected a template. In the beginning, we may have used the persona to help validate some of the text being added to our MVP website".*

Despite this, the team experienced challenges when creating MVPs, such as promotional videos and landing pages. The responses generated by GenAI **felt unnatural (Ch03)**, with videos appearing *"strange and a bit unsteady"* as mentioned by B-I2. Furthermore, there were **lacks of transparency (Ch09)** in GenAI tools, where the team perceived it as a *"black box magic machine that brings out code"* as mentioned by B-I1.

Challenges Across All Steps in the Inception Stage. One of these challenges was GenAI is **pricy (Ch04)** as premium subscriptions were required for premium features. This was not affordable for the team, and they had to create multiple trial accounts to enjoy premium features. B-I1 shared an example of this challenge, *"I think I had to create four different accounts because we changed ideas. As a student trying to save money."* Additionally, GenAI tools tended to **please the users instead of being critical (Ch08)**, B-I1 shared, *"I think AI tends to please and agree with you."*

4.3   Cross-Case Comparison

The use of GenAI tools provided various opportunities to the two studied software startups, particularly in areas such as creating mockups and validating MVPs. The ability to quickly generate mockups (Op02) was perceived as beneficial by both teams, enabling them to rapidly visualize their ideas without needing extensive design expertise or resources. This efficiency saved time and allowed the teams to iterate on their designs more effectively. Similarly, using GenAI to validate MVPs (Op11) offered a streamlined approach to gathering feedback and making necessary adjustments before presenting the product to actual users. This capability was particularly valuable for early-stage startups, where resources are limited, and the need for quick, cost-effective validation processes is critical.

However, these opportunities were also accompanied by several common challenges. Both teams encountered issues with the limitations of GenAI, such as the inability to fully represent actual users (Ch02), leading to concerns about the accuracy and relevance of the feedback generated by GenAI tools. Additionally, the output generated by GenAI sometimes felt unnatural (Ch03), which affected the overall quality of the prototypes and MVPs. The high cost of premium GenAI tools (Ch04) was another shared challenge, particularly for startups operating on tight budgets. These challenges underscore the need for careful consideration when integrating GenAI into the early stages of product development, balancing the benefits of efficiency and innovation with the potential drawbacks of cost and accuracy.

There was a noticeable difference in the confidence levels regarding using GenAI tools. **Rapido** team demonstrated a strong confidence in the potential of GenAI tools, integrating these tools extensively into their workflow, trusting the technology to enhance their startup development. Their confidence in GenAI led them to explore and leverage GenAI tools capabilities. In contrast, **Blue Dot** team was more hesitant and relied heavily on their own experience, expressing significant doubts about the effectiveness of GenAI tools. Their skepticism made them cautious in adopting GenAI, and they were more comfortable relying on their expertise. This team is concerned about the risks and limitations GenAI tools might pose, which affected their willingness to integrate them into their startup development.

5 Discussion

The inception stage of software startups is marked by high uncertainty and limited resources, making it a critical period for innovation and strategic decision-making. To address the research question, **How is the usage of GenAI technologies perceived by software startups in the inception stage?**, findings from the action case study of two inception-stage software startups reveal that GenAI tools can offer substantial **opportunities** in this phase by providing functionalities that streamline processes, enhance creativity, and accelerate product development, while also introduces significant **challenges** that must be carefully managed.

The eleven opportunities and ten challenges identified in this study can be viewed from both business and technical perspectives. From the business perspective, opportunities involve evaluating how GenAI can address the startup's core business problems, while the technical perspective focuses on the functionalities that GenAI offers. For example, Team **Rapido** used GenAI to create a landing page (Op07), a prototype of their solution (i.e., business aspect), without having to write codes manually (i.e., technical aspect).

These perspectives are natural, given that the primary goal of a software startup is to develop viable business ideas while managing the technical aspects of implementation. Consequently, the identified opportunities can be categorized into business opportunities (Op01, Op02, Op03, Op04, Op05, Op07, Op08, Op10, Op11) and technical opportunities (Op06, Op09). Likewise, the challenges fall into business challenges (Ch02, Ch04, Ch07, Ch08) and technical challenges (Ch01, Ch03, Ch05, Ch06, Ch09, Ch10). These opportunities and challenges are highly relevant to the startup context, aligning with the critical role of GenAI in driving business model innovation, which is particularly crucial for startups striving to maintain competitiveness [14].

From our analysis, we found that several opportunities (Op02, Op03, Op04, Op05, Op06, Op08, Op09) and challenges (Ch01, Ch03, Ch04, Ch05, Ch06, Ch09, Ch10) have also been reported in prior studies [12,13,23], thereby consolidating the existing knowledge related to GenAI. However, we also identified novel opportunities such as brand identity development (Op01), generating landing pages (Op07), simulating customer feedback (Op10), and validating MVP (Op11). Additionally, we discovered novel challenges where existing GenAI tools are more function-oriented than problem-oriented (Ch07) and tend to please rather than provide critical feedback (Ch08). These novel findings are particularly pertinent to the startup context, offering new insights into how GenAI can be both a powerful tool and a potential pitfall in the early stages of software startup development.

Limitation. A potential threat to the internal validity of our findings is the intervening nature of the action case study. One of the authors introduced and encouraged the teams to use GenAI tools in their startup development. This may have influenced the teams to be more positive towards the use of GenAI tools to support their startup activities. To mitigate this potential threat, we avoided any leading questions and tried our best to keep a neutral tone during the interviews. We also triangulated interviewees' opinions using the documents and observations we gathered as part of the action case study.

As with any case study, a limitation of this research is the generalizability of the findings. A small number of cases were studied. The opportunities and challenges identified from the two studied cases may be incomplete and not representative for the general population of software startups. The study's exploratory nature and the multiple-case design mitigated this validity threat to a certain extent.

Another limitation of the study is that it focused on inception-stage software startups within a specific university setting, which may not reflect the experiences and challenges of software startups in industries, even though it is not uncommon for startup teams to initiate their startup development journey while they are university students. Further investigation is necessary to explore the use of GenAI tools across a broader range of startup ecosystems. This would help understand the full potential and limitations of GenAI tools in various contexts, providing a more comprehensive view.

6   Conclusion

GenAI became a disruptive force to all walks of life only less than two years ago. We are yet to fully grasp its potential to support startup endeavors. Our study is one of the first attempts that aspires to bring insights on how to utilize GenAI effectively in the startup context. It highlighted the use of GenAI tools in the inception stage of software startups, presenting significant opportunities and challenges. While GenAI can accelerate innovation, streamline product development, and offer cost-effective solutions, its application has risks, such as generating biased outputs, high costs for premium features, and difficulties in fully representing actual user needs. The findings underscore the need for early-stage startups to strategically integrate GenAI, balancing its potential benefits with carefully considering its limitations.

Following this initial step, we will study more early-stage software startups to consolidate and extend the findings reported in this study and map specific GenAI tools to relevant opportunities and challenges through multiple case studies and survey studies. We also plan to cover other stages of software startups, including stabilization, growth, and mature stages, in our future research.

Acknowledgements. This work has been partially supported by ELLIIT, the Swedish Strategic Research Area in IT and Mobile Communications, and supported by European Union with Piano Nazionale di Ripresa e Resilienza (PNRR) funds.

Appendix

A   Custom GPTs

The Rapido team created two custom GPTs backed with the two identified personas and used these custom GPTs to validate the problem further. The team derived two personas based on the customer interviews. One is called Laura Fajitas, representing the sports field owners. Laura *"is 33 years old, Peruvian-Italian, manages football field reservations in Pescara, Italy"*. The other is called Alex Sportivo, representing a sports facility user. Alex is *"a 27-year-old young man in Italy who supports Modena FC and Real Madrid, and whose favorite tennis player is Rafael Nadal. Alex plays as a left-footed defender in soccer and enjoys tennis to unwind"*.

Similarly, the Blue Dot team created a persona called Luca to represent potential platform users and built a custom GPT to represent Luca digitally. Luca is *"a student and part-time worker living in Ravenna. He juggles his university classes in the morning and work in the afternoon, all while trying to balance life with his girlfriend. He commutes around the city a lot and tries to avoid using his car whenever he can because finding parking is a pain, and fuel is expensive. When he's not working or studying, he either hangs out with friends or runs errands like grocery shopping and cooking dinner at home"*.

References

1. Banh, L., Strobel, G.: Generative artificial intelligence. Electr. Markets **33**(1) (2023)
2. Bilgram, V., Laarmann, F.: Accelerating innovation with generative AI: AI-augmented digital prototyping and innovation methods. IEEE Eng. Manage. Rev. **51**(2), 18–25 (2023)

3. Bosch, J., Holmström Olsson, H., Björk, J., Ljungblad, J.: The early stage software startup development model: a framework for operationalizing lean principles in software startups. In: Fitzgerald, B., Conboy, K., Power, K., Valerdi, R., Morgan, L., Stol, K.J. (eds.) Lean Enterprise Software and Systems, pp. 1–15. Springer, Berlin Heidelberg (2013)
4. Braa, K., Vidgen, R.: Interpretation, intervention, and reduction in the organizational laboratory: a framework for in-context information system research. Account. Manag. Inf. Technol. **9**(1), 25–47 (1999)
5. Braun, V., Clarke, V.: Using thematic analysis in psychology. Qual. Res. Psychol. **3**(2), 77–101 (2006)
6. de Carvalho, J.V., Teixeira, S.F.: Developing a digital business incubator model to foster entrepreneurship, business growth, and academia-industry connections. Sustainability **15**(9), 7209 (2023)
7. Cruzes, D.S., Dyba, T.: Recommended steps for thematic synthesis in software engineering (2011)
8. Ebert, C., Louridas, P.: Generative AI for software practitioners. IEEE Softw. **40**(4), 30–38 (2023)
9. Füller, J., Hutter, K., Wahl, J., Bilgram, V., Tekic, Z.: How AI revolutionizes innovation management - perceptions and implementation preferences of AI-based innovators. Technol. Forecast. Soc. Change **178**, 121598 (2022)
10. Giardino, C., Bajwa, S.S., Wang, X., Abrahamsson, P.: Key challenges in early-stage software startups. In: Lassenius, C., Dingsøyr, T., Paasivaara, M. (eds.) Agile Processes in Software Engineering and Extreme Programming, pp. 52–63. Springer (2015)
11. Giardino, C., Wang, X., Abrahamsson, P.: Why early-stage software startups fail: a behavioral framework. In: The 5th International Conference on Software Business, pp. 27–41. Springer (2014)
12. Haji, S., Sheehy, W.: Exploring the impact of AI tools on Swedish startups - a qualitative analysis of operations optimization and alignment with the lean startup development. Ph.D. thesis, Uppsala University (2023)
13. Hou, X., et al.: Large language models for software engineering: a systematic literature review (2024). https://doi.org/10.48550/arXiv.2308.10620
14. Kanbach, D.K., Heiduk, L., Blueher, G., Schreiter, M., Lahmann, A.: The GenAI is out of the bottle: generative artificial intelligence from a business model innovation perspective. RMS **18**(4), 1189–1220 (2024)
15. Klotins, E., et al.: A progression model of software engineering goals, challenges, and practices in start-ups. IEEE Trans. Software Eng. **47**(3), 498–521 (2021)
16. Masters, B., Thiel, P.: Zero To One: Notes on Start Ups, Or How to Build the Future. Random House (2014)
17. Melegati, J., Edison, H., Wang, X.: XPro: a model to explain the limited adoption and implementation of experimentation in software startups. IEEE Trans. Software Eng. **48**(6), 1929–1946 (2022)
18. Nijssen, E., et al.: Business incubator and economic development. IntechOpen (2023). https://www.intechopen.com/chapters/76123
19. Ozkaya, I.: The next frontier in software development: AI-augmented software development processes. IEEE Softw. **40**(4), 4–9 (2023)
20. Patel, L.: Lean AI: How Innovative Startups Use Artificial Intelligence To Grow. O'Reilly Media (2020)
21. Ries, E.: The Lean Startup: How Today's Entrepreneurs Use Continuous Innovation to Create Radically Successful Businesses. Crown Currency (2011)

22. Santisteban, J., Morales, V., Bayona, S., Morales, J.: Failure of tech startups: a systematic literature review. In: International Conference on Computer Science, Electronics and Industrial Engineering, pp. 111–126. Springer (2022)
23. Simaremare, M., Edison, H.: The state of generative AI adoption from software practitioners' perspective: an empirical study. In: The 2024 50th Euromicro Conference on SEAA, pp. 106–113. IEEE (2024)
24. Sutton, S.M.: The role of process in software start-up. IEEE Softw. **17**(4), 33–39 (2000)
25. Wang, X., Edison, H., Bajwa, S.S., Giardino, C., Abrahamsson, P.: Key challenges in software startups across life cycle stages. In: Sharp, H., Hall, T. (eds.) Agile Processes, in Software Engineering, and Extreme Programming, pp. 169–182. Springer (2016)

Smart Scaling for Software Startups Through Financial Requirements Prioritization Criteria

Frédéric Pattyn[1] and Usman Rafiq[2]

[1] Department of Business Informatics and Operations Management,
Ghent University, Ghent, Belgium
Frederic.Pattyn@ugent.be
[2] Faculty of Engineering, Free University of Bozen-Bolzano, Bolzano, Italy
usman.rafiq@unibz.it

Abstract. Software startups play a critical role in driving innovation and boosting the economy. However, building these distinguished companies is extremely challenging and often comes with an alarmingly high failure rate. The failure reasons include but are not limited to, product development issues, premature scaling, cash flow mismanagement, and difficulties in securing investment. The current study aims to explore the role of prioritization of financially related requirements in the success of startups. We performed a multiple-case study with 16 software startups. We primarily collected data through 29 semi-structured interviews with these companies and analyzed data using thematic analysis. Our findings reveal a strong correlation between using financially focused requirements prioritization criteria such as estimated revenue, return on investment, time to value, cost of development, and the probability of startup success. We also demonstrate that successful startups prioritize product features with a solid business case, optimizing for time to value. In contrast, startups that neglect the cost of feature development increase the likelihood of failure. We conclude our study by highlighting the relationship between feature requirements prioritization activities and their impact on the financial metrics of startups, such as burn rate and runway.

Keywords: Startups · Requirements Prioritization · Prioritization Criteria · Requirements Engineering · Cash Flow

1 Introduction

Software startups are companies that aim to develop innovative and software-intensive products or services under extreme conditions of uncertainty [18]. These companies are known for their rapid pace, dealing with uncertainty, and operating under resource scarcity. Such distinguished characteristics pose unique challenges for them. The existing literature highlights various prominent challenges, such as product development issues [6], premature scaling [12] cash flow mismanagement [14], difficulties in securing investment [13] and simply running out of funds, which impacts between 21% and 44% of startups [14]. With the failure rate of more than 90% [16], it becomes evident that addressing these unique challenges is critical for their survival. A majority of these failed companies struggled to conduct sufficient market research or business case analysis [13], which led to inefficient requirements selection process [17], poor allocation of critical resources [5], and an over-commitment to solutions that do not meet market needs [10]. As a result, startups often face the risk of not achieving product-market fit [5] [6], and struggle with acquiring their first paying customers [6]. These factors put the runway (the number of months a startup company has left until cash runs out) at risk and therefore restrict their likelihood of success.

In this challenging environment, effective cash flow management, strategic planning, and efficient resource allocation become significant for the survival of startups [15]. While the research on startups is growing [18], one key research area that is overlooked in the startup literature is financial requirements prioritization criteria. It is an approach that can be linked back to budget or cost and considers financial considerations in the decision-making process [3]. This means that the strategic criteria is tied to the budget or cost [3]. A few other studies even extend it beyond budget concerns and include variables, such as expected profitability [8], return on investment (ROI) [1], net present value [9], break-even point [7], internal rate of return [4] and estimated market share [2]. Therefore, to address the highlighted research gaps and to explore the practice of these variables, we set the current study to address the following research question (RQ):

RQ: How do startups use financially oriented requirements prioritization criteria?

To answer the RQ, we conducted 29 semi-structured interviews with 16 software startups. The interviews elicited the startup journey, from concept to reality, including their early failures and successes. The study results enable us to contribute in terms of providing initial observations regarding the decision-making processes of these companies, distinguishing between those that thrive and those that do not. These collective insights can inform startup founders in their quest to enhance their startup's success probability.

2   Research Approach

Considering the nature of the RQ, we decided to conduct case studies with startups. Therefore, based on purposive sampling, we conducted case studies with 16 startups. All our studied startups were part of an accelerator based in Belgium. In particular, startups were part of the quarterly cohort. We studied between Q4 of 2022 and Q2 of 2024.

We mainly used semi-structured interviews to collect the data. Overall, we conducted 29 semi-structured interviews with startup co-founders, with an average duration of 63 min. We prepared the interview guide before conducting each interview. The complete guide is accessible at https://tinyurl.com/34wc6muy and the details of our cases are presented in Table 1. In addition to interviews, we also collected additional information about the startups from various online sources.

Table 1. Startups profiles

ID	Description	Interviews	Years active
S1	Football data analytics	1 (1h15)	3
S2	Security platform	2 (2h07)	2
S4	Web3 SocialFi	3 (2h45)	3
S5	PLG platform	2 (1h13)	4
S7	HR tech	1 (0h45)	2
S8	Logistical solution	1 (1h25)	3
S9	Form builder	3 (3h24)	3
S10	Web2 credit market	2 (1h45)	3
S11	HR tech	3 (2h53)	3
S12	Healthcare platform	2 (1h48)	2
S13	HR tech	2 (1h15)	3
S14	HR tech	1 (2h11)	3
S15	Data document management	3 (2h41)	3
S16	Fashion tech	1 (0h58)	2
S17	AI for trends analysis	1 (1h23)	4
S18	HR tech	1 (0h51)	4

We used thematic analysis [11] to analyze the interview data. On the other hand, the additional information we collected from online sources helped us to build the context regarding our cases and facilitated us to understand requirements prioritization criteria.

To study which requirements prioritization criteria or processes could be considered predictive or at least to get a shared correlative indication among the best-performing startups, we also ranked the criteria. Based on the interviews and online information about our cases, we analyzed data on (1) the number of funding rounds, (2) total funding raised, (3) revenue generated in the most recent year, (4) profits generated in the most recent year, (5) remaining runway in months and (6) if they are still in business or not. We then compared startups with each other and ranked accordingly for each dimension. When having the same results, the same ranking value was considered. We left the information empty if it was not available. The final ranking was calculated as the average of their respective rankings. This means those with the lowest ranking are considered the best-performing startups on average (see Table 2). This ranking provides us with four tiers of comparable startups; tier 1 (green, including S2, S10, and S11): top of their class with a ranking score below average, tier 2 (yellow, including S18, S15, S12, S17, and S4): scores that are between average and average plus a standard deviation, tier 3 (light orange, including S9, S1, S8, S13, and S16): scores that are less than average plus 2 standard deviations, and finally tier 4 (pink, including S14, S5, and S7), those that are no longer in business.

Table 2. Startups and Interviews

ID	(1)	(2)	(3)	(4)	(5)	(6)	Final Ranking
S2	1	2	3	4		Y	2.5
S10	1	1	1	11	2	Y	3.2
S11	3	5	2	3	5	Y	3.6
S18	3	13	4	1	1	Y	4.4
S15	2	4	5	9	4	Y	4.8
S12	3	9	7	1	5	Y	
S17	3	3	9	10	3	Y	5.6
S4	2	6	10	5		Y	5.7
S14	3	7	6	6	11	N	6.6
S5	3	8	10	8	6	N	7.0
S9	3	11	9	5	7	Y	7.0
S1	3	10	10	7	8	Y	7.6
S8	4	14	9	2	10	Y	7.8
S13	4	14	8	4	11	Y	8.2
S16	3	12	10	9		Y	8.5
S7	4	14	10		12	N	10

3   Results and Discussion

Our study results are demonstrated in Fig. 1. The results show the relationship between the use of financially related requirements prioritization criteria and the performance of the startups. As one might observe a pattern in the figure, indicates that startups employing this criteria tend to achieve higher rank. We provide further insights from our interviewee participants by referring to the original interview excerpts:

Early-stage startups are struggling with prioritization. They are doing it based on gut feeling, as illustrated by the co-founder of S1: *"based on our gut feeling, we give a score between 1 and 10"*. The co-founders of startup S7 and S14 reported the same. Additionally, some startups failed to grasp the importance of considering the cost of building a feature. The CEO of S5 who filed for bankruptcy due to cash flow challenges confirmed this: *"we don't consider the cost of building a feature; we have the 'it's done when it's done' philosophy. We release when it is perfect."* In contrast, most startups do consider the cost of implementing a feature, as shared by the founder of S6: *"ideas get valued against their cost and PR-value."* More successful startups pair this in their business case, ensuring not only customers are interested but also willing to pay for the feature sooner rather than later. It is evident in the excerpt shared by the co-founder of S2: *"[we] use a quadrant-based approach to prioritize ideas based on value and effort"*, while the founder of S8 mentioned: *" we have a wall with*

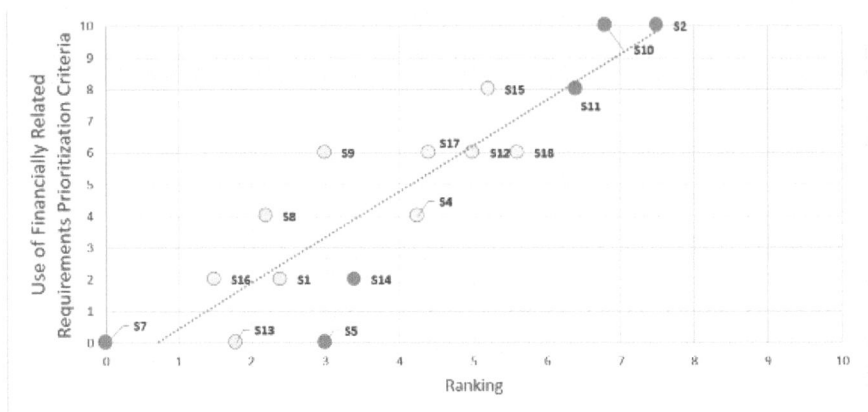

Fig. 1. Use of Financially Related Requirements Prioritization Criteria Versus anking

X and Y axis on it, X as the features according to their estimated effort and complexity, the Y axis the number of customers that want it. We only pick them up when there's at least a single customer willing to pay for it." This focus on revenue generation is also emphasized by the founders of startups S9, S11, S15, and S17.

Some startups considered the business case but eventually abandoned the effort, as shared by the founder of S4: *"we don't consider the business case anymore."* Conversely, other startups recognized the value of financially focused prioritization criteria over time. The S9 co-founder stated that if he could start over, he would: *"start selling the idea faster, talk to more potential customers, and secure paid commitments at hand."* Therefore, depending on the startup and its financial situation in terms of burn rate and remaining runway, it is highly advised to understand the estimated probability and business case of features being released. If there is no direct financial upside or if it is highly underestimated due to an incorrect confidence level, any startup will face cash flow challenges and potentially go bankrupt. This is especially true for startups with short runways and who are in desperate need of cash from investors or paying customers. It is never too late to start considering financially related prioritization criteria. However, we noted that startups enjoying a successful journey utilize this from the beginning, which provides them with an average runway of two years. On the contrary, startups that do not consider the costs at all might be getting only three months of cash left to survive.

4   Conclusions and Future Work

We conclude our study by highlighting that the ability to integrate financially oriented criteria into the requirements prioritization process is not just beneficial, but essential. Our results demonstrate that startups that systematically evaluate feature business cases by considering financial aspects, by balancing revenue potential, cost, and ROI, are better positioned to make informed decisions, maximize value, and ensure sustainability. However, with a limited number of startups from Belgium, our findings lack diversity in terms of prioritization criteria. Therefore, to fully understand the complexities of these dynamics, future studies should aim for larger, more diverse samples and employ quantitative methods to validate these findings across different startup ecosystems.

References

1. Boehm, B.: Value-based software engineering: reinventing. ACM SIGSOFT Softw. Eng. Notes **28**(2), 3 (2003)
2. Boehm, B.: Some future trends and implications for systems and software engineering processes. Syst. Eng. **9**(1), 1–19 (2006)
3. Cleland-Huang, J., Denne, M.: Financially informed requirements prioritization. In: Proceedings of the 27th International Conference on Software Engineering, pp. 710–711 (2005)
4. Cosse, T.J., Swan, J.E.: Strategic marketing planning by product managers-room for improvement? J. Mark. **47**(3), 92–102 (1983)
5. Eisenmann, T.R.: Determinants of early-stage startup performance: survey results. Harvard Business School Entrepreneurial Management Working Paper (21-057) (2020)
6. Giardino, C., Bajwa, S.S., Wang, X., Abrahamsson, P.: Key challenges in early-stage software startups. In: Agile Processes in Software Engineering and Extreme Programming: 16th International Conference, XP 2015, Helsinki, Finland, 25-29 May 2015, Proceedings 16, pp. 52–63. Springer (2015)
7. Gorchels, L.: Transitioning from engineering to product management. Eng. Manag. J. **15**(4), 40–47 (2003)
8. Gordijn, J., Akkermans, J.: Value-based requirements engineering: exploring innovative e-commerce ideas. Requirements Eng. **8**, 114–134 (2003)
9. Guyon, I., Elisseeff, A.: An introduction to variable and feature selection. J. Mach. Learn. Res. **3**(Mar), 1157–1182 (2003)
10. Insights, C.: The top 12 reasons startups fail. https://www.cbinsights.com/research/report/startup-failure-reasons-top/ (2021). Accessed 21 Oct 2024
11. Kiger, M.E., Varpio, L.: Thematic analysis of qualitative data: AMEE Guide No. 131. Med. Teach. **42**(8), 846–854 (2020)
12. Marmer, M., Herrmann, B.L., Dogrultan, E., Berman, R., Eesley, C., Blank, S.: Startup genome report extra: premature scaling. Startup Genome **10**, 1–56 (2011)
13. Michael, F.: Small business cash flow management: strategies for success (2020). https://preferredcfo.com/cash-flow-reason-small-businesses-fail/. Accessed 21 Oct 2024
14. Pattyn, F.: The hidden costs of ignoring cash flow: a call for strategic requirements prioritization at startups during an era of rising interest rates. In: IEEE 31st International Requirements Engineering Conference Workshops (REW). IEEE (2023)
15. PitchBook: European venture report (q2/2024). Technical report (2024)
16. Rafiq, U., Pattyn, F., Wang, X.: Practitioner views on analytics for software startups: A preliminary guide based on gray literature. In: International Conference on Software Business, pp. 315–323. Springer (2023)

17. Svahnberg, M., Gorschek, T., Feldt, R., Torkar, R., Saleem, S.B., Shafique, M.U.: A systematic review on strategic release planning models. Inf. Softw. Technol. **52**(3), 237–248 (2010)
18. Unterkalmsteiner, M., Abrahamsson, P., Wang, X., Nguyen-Duc, A., Shah, S., Bajwa, S.S., et al.: Software startups – a research Agenda. e-Informatica Softw. Eng. J. **10**(1), 89–124 (2016)

Accelerating New Product Development: A Vision on Active Personas

Mario Simaremare$^{(\boxtimes)}$ and Henry Edison

Blekinge Institute of Technology, Karlskrona, Sweden
{mario.simaremare,henry.edison}@bth.se

Abstract. User participation and user feedback are essential to the success of new product development (NPD). Development teams use user feedback to derive requirement engineering artifacts, such as user scenarios, user stories, concept mindmaps, and user personas, to guide them in identifying and addressing a particular user problem. However, finding enough user participation to collect meaningful feedback is challenging, and less attention has been given to addressing this. In this paper, we propose Active Personas (APs), fictional users capable of generating contextual feedback through an interactive multi-modal interaction, such as text, voice, image, and video. APs enable development teams to gather feedback on their solutions through iterative internal experimentation. APs use generative artificial intelligence to enable dynamic multi-modal interaction and utilize user personas to generate contextual feedback. We aim to conduct a series of studies to further validate APs by applying the design science approach as guidance. We plan to develop an initial prototype of APs and conduct studies in a more controlled setting using open-source or completed projects to validate APs. Later, we will transition to ongoing projects in various types and domains.

Keywords: active personas · user personas · generative ai · user participation · user feedback · new product development

1 Introduction

User participation is critical and often endorsed as an intervention in new product development (NPD) [11]. The main argument for this is that users are experts in their own lives. Thus, involving them will help development teams emphasize and gain more detailed knowledge about their specific situations: their needs, wishes, and requirements. In software engineering (SE), user participation has traditionally referred to the roles, responsibilities, and activities that users or their representatives have performed in various phases in the NPD process [7]. This includes idea validation, requirement engineering, design, testing, and support activities [5,20]. User participation enables a development team to identify and understand their users and collect valuable feedback to inform strategic decisions [7,17,20]. For example, teams can synthesize requirement engineering

E. Papatheocharous et al. (Eds.): ICSOB 2024, LNBIP 539, pp. 461–466, 2025.
https://doi.org/10.1007/978-3-031-85849-9_36

(RE) artifacts, such as user scenarios, user stories, concept mindmaps, and user personas [15]. Among these artifacts, user personas help teams portray the characteristics of actual users, develop empathy towards them, reduce assumptions about them, and focus on design decisions [9,18]. User personas have been used as references in clarifying requirements, designing user interfaces and user experiences, and selecting participants for usability testing [10,16].

However, getting enough user participation and meaningful feedback throughout the NPD stages are still unresolved challenges for many reasons [10,14,21], not to mention managing and analyzing the gathered feedback [13]. Users are not always available and willing to participate [10], especially in projects that require long user commitment [22]. Access to a subset of users provides a limited sample of end users' viewpoints. A study suggests that failing to get enough user participation and meaningful feedback contributes to NPD failure [12]. This is exacerbated in the software startup context where a lack of user feedback wastes their limited resources and increases time to market, ultimately putting the company's survival at high risk [14].

To address the challenge, we propose Active Personas (APs), fictional users capable of generating contextual feedback through an interactive multi-modal interaction, such as text, voice, image, and video. Development team members can interact with AP objects to gather feedback on the product under development and make improvements before reaching out to the targeted end users. APs will be particularly useful in the early stage of NPD when users might be difficult to find. The remainder of this paper is organized as follows: the next section discusses existing works relevant to this study. Section 3 elaborates on the proposed solution and a case to illustrate its potential application, and Sect. 4 paves the next step of the study.

2   Related Work

This chapter discusses the importance of user participation, user feedback, and the common usage of user personas in NPD.

2.1   User Participation and User Feedback

User participation and involvement are two indivisible concepts [7]. The earlier focuses on the roles and responsibilities of a person in an NPD, while the latter is about psychological attitudes toward the NPD [7]. Through user participation, development teams can extract feedback and use it to improve their ideas, collect and prioritize requirements, test initial prototypes, and learn from existing solutions offered by competitors [20]. Continuously gathering and incorporating user feedback is essential to ensure the alignment of software product value with user needs [5,13]. A study indicates a strong association between user feedback and product quality, project success, and ultimately, end users' satisfaction [11]. However, finding a representative group of users to work with the team throughout the development and ensuring interaction with various end users can be challenging [10]. Moreover, having access to a subset group of users will only provide a limited sample of end users' viewpoints.

2.2   User Personas

User personas are *"hypothetical archetypes of actual users"* developed iteratively through user research [2,9]. It provides a descriptive model of real users to complement human participation in NPD [2]. This concept is often used in RE activities, solution design, and usability testing [10,16]. For example, capturing user needs and designing user interfaces. A user persona commonly consists of user goals, motivations, pain points, personal characteristics, skills, experiences, environmental, and group characteristics that reflect the actual users [8]. A development team can also use their assumption about the target users [23] as a basis to create initial personas, i.e., proto-personas [9]. Studies show that personas help the development team build empathy towards their users and understand the problems from the users' perspective [9].

User personas are often presented statically on paper as textual descriptions or visual representations to highlight certain human aspects [18]. The personas are referred to when needed during the development [16]. For example, when designing user interfaces, designers refer to the personas of users who will use the interfaces. However, as teams use user personas subjectively, inherent bias can be introduced. When integrating personas into development tasks, the teams' opinions or stances may influence their understanding, leading to misinterpretations and omitting key requirements [9].

3   A Vision on Active Personas (APs)

Active Personas (APs) are dynamic manifestations of user personas that provide contextual and relevant feedback through a dynamic interaction with a development team. This concept is inspired by the Active Record (AR) pattern [6], an architectural pattern where a database tuple or record is encapsulated as an object that behaves according to its state and can interact with other components in the system. For example, in an application, a software component may request an AR object to display its state, i.e., current attribute values. The AR object will inspect and process the request and return a response according to its current attribute values.

An AP encapsulates a user persona or proto-persona, together with other RE artifacts, as an object that shares the characteristics of a group of targeted users. A user persona and the other RE artifacts provide a solid foundation for the AP object to generate contextual and relevant feedback. It is a one-to-one relationship between an AP and its underlying user persona.

To realize APs' dynamic multi-modality interaction, we propose to use Generative artificial intelligence (GenAI) technology [4]. As a subset of AI technology, GenAI can create novel human-like generated content in various modalities [4],

including texts, images, audio, videos, and simulations. This technology leverages advanced machine learning models to recognize patterns and relationships
within a large dataset to generate responses to given inputs. Approaches, such as
retrieval-augmented generation (RAG) and fine-tuning [19], can feed user personas and other RE artifacts into GenAI. To illustrate our proposed solution, a
case application of APs in the context of software startups is described below.

Software startups are emerging market-driven companies that develop innovative software products [15]. Software startups often operate under heavily limited resources and high uncertainty [15]. To minimize the uncertainty, software
startups decompose their vision into testable hypotheses and empirically test
them through the iterative build-measure-learn (BML) cycle [17]. This approach
helps software startups clarify their ideas and avoid spending resources unnecessarily. Experimentation serves two purposes: to discover potential customers,
i.e., problem-solution fit, or to validate the customers, i.e., product-market fit
[3]. The success of an experiment relies on user participation and feedback.

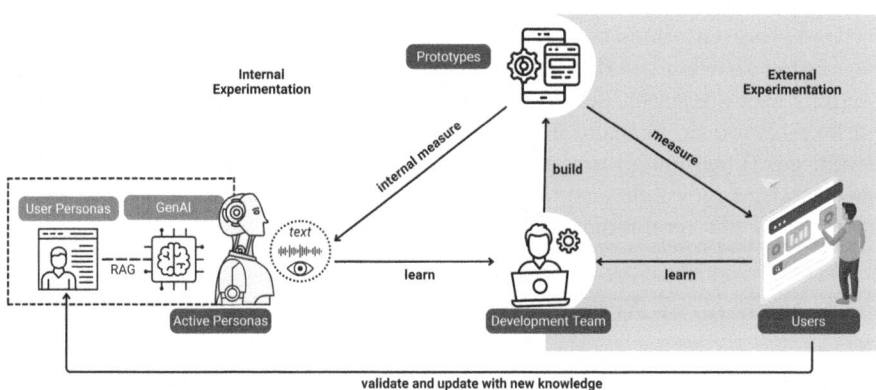

Fig. 1. Active Personas in the search of problem-solution fit

Figure 1 illustrates the role of the APs application in addressing problem-
solution fit. In this illustration, a development team discovers a potential problem
from an initial user reach out. The team then builds a prototype of a hypothetical solution in the form of, for example, a mockup and defines the user personas.
Instead of testing the solution directly to the end users, the team can do iterative internal experimentation with AP instances to get immediate feedback
on the prototype and make improvements (see the left side of the figure). The
interaction can be in various modalities. When the team has confidence in the
prototype, they can reach out to the user for external experimentation (see the
right side of the figure). However, teams should be aware that they should not
overly rely on AP's feedback due to GenAI's potential bias and hallucinations. To
mitigate this issue, teams should conduct external experimentation with actual
users. The feedback from external experimentation is valuable: (1) to validate

the hypothetical solution, (2) to collect new requirements, (3) to measure the alignment of AP's generated feedback, and (4) to update the underlying user personas and RE artifacts.

As discussed, we argue that APs potentially help development teams to address several known inhibitors to conduct valid experiments [14]. For instance, startup founders will have the resources to perform experimentation internally. Moreover, they will have a safe environment for experimentation with not-ready versions that do not threaten their business. Such experimentation does not put any risk on how their customers perceive their product. APs may provide contextual and relevant feedback and insights into the proposed solution, thus reducing the teams' overconfidence before directly validating it to end users.

4   Next Step

We plan to conduct a series of studies to validate APs. Since APs aim to address a practical challenge, we plan to conduct these studies by applying the design science [1] approach. These studies are grouped into the following three phases. In the first phase, we aim to develop a prototype of APs, starting from the simplest modality, text. From there, we will add the other modalities as the studies progress. There are many options for implementation, one of which is ChatGPT[1], capable of handling multiple modalities. The second phase aims to validate APs in a more controlled environment. In this phase, we plan to apply APs to an open-source project from which user personas and other RE artifacts can be derived. Following that, we plan to pilot APs with completed projects from companies to validate it further. In the last phase, we aim to apply APs to ongoing projects in various types and domains with known and unknown markets. In all of these studies, we will identify and work with small hypotheses. Moreover, will also look for representative users matching the underlying user personas to gather feedback to mitigate deviation and validate APs.

Acknowledgements. This work has been supported by ELLIIT, the Swedish Strategic Research Area in IT and Mobile Communications.

References

1. Aken, J.E.V.: Management research based on the paradigm of the design sciences: the quest for field-tested and grounded technological rules. J. Manage. Stud. **41**(2), 219–246 (2004)
2. Cooper, A., Saffo, P.: The Inmates Are Running the Asylum. Macmillan (1999)
3. Cooper, B., Vlaskovits, P.: The Entrepreneur's Guide to Customer Development: A Cheat Sheet to The Four Steps to the Epiphany. Cooper-Vlaskovits (2010)
4. Ebert, C., Louridas, P.: Generative AI for software practitioners. IEEE Softw. **40**(4), 30–38 (2023)

---

[1] OpenAI ChatGPT: https://openai.com/index/chatgpt/.

5. Fabijan, A., Olsson, H.H., Bosch, J.: Customer feedback and data collection techniques in software R&D: a literature review. In: International Conference of Software Business, pp. 139–153 (2015)
6. Fowler, M.: Patterns of Enterprise Application Architecture. Addison-Wesley (2002)
7. Hartwick, J., Barki, H.: Explaining the role of user participation in information system use. Manage. Sci. **40**(4), 440–465 (1994)
8. Karolita., D., Grundy., J., Kanij., T., Obie., H., McIntosh., J.: What's in a persona? A preliminary taxonomy from persona use in requirements engineering. In: The 18th International Conference on ENASE, pp. 39–51 (2023)
9. Karolita, D., Grundy, J.C., Kanij, T., McIntosh, J., Obie, H.O.: Lessons learned from persona usage in requirements engineering practice. In: The 2024 IEEE 32nd International Requirements Engineering Conference, pp. 116–128 (2024)
10. Karolita, D., McIntosh, J., Kanij, T., Grundy, J., Obie, H.O.: Use of personas in requirements engineering: a systematic mapping study. Inf. Softw. Technol. **162**, 107264 (2023)
11. Kujala, S., Kauppinen, M., Lehtola, L., Kojo, T.: The role of user involvement in requirements quality and project success. In: The 13th IEEE International Conference on Requirements Engineering, pp. 75–84 (2005)
12. Lehtinen, T.O.A., Mäntylä, M.V., Vanhanen, J., Itkonen, J., Lassenius, C.: Perceived causes of software project failures - an analysis of their relationships. Inf. Softw. Technol. **56**(6), 623–643 (2014)
13. Li, Z.S., Arony, N.N., Devathasan, K., Sihag, M., Ernst, N., Damian, D.: Unveiling the life cycle of user feedback: best practices from software practitioners. In: The IEEE/ACM 46th ICSE (2024)
14. Melegati, J., Edison, H., Wang, X.: XPro: a model to explain the limited adoption and implementation of experimentation in software startups. IEEE Trans. Software Eng. **48**(6), 1929–1946 (2022)
15. Paternoster, N., Giardino, C., Unterkalmsteiner, M., Gorschek, T., Abrahamsson, P.: Software development in startup companies: a systematic mapping study. Inf. Softw. Technol. **56**(10), 1200–1218 (2014)
16. Pruitt, J., Grudin, J.: Personas: practice and theory. In: Proceedings of the Conference on Designing for User Experiences, pp. 1–15 (2003)
17. Ries, E.: Lean Startup: How Today's Entrepreneurs Use Continous Innovation to Create Radically Successful Businesses. Crown Business (2011)
18. Salminen, J., Jansen, B.J., An, J., Kwak, H., Jung, S.G.: Are personas done? Evaluating their usefulness in the age of digital analytics. Persona Stud. **4**(2), 47–65 (2018)
19. dos Santos Junior, J.C., Hu, R., Song, R., Bai, Y.: Domain-driven LLM development: insights into rag and fine-tuning practices. In: The 30th ACM SIGKDD Conference on Knowledge Discovery and Data Mining, pp. 6416–6417 (2024)
20. Sauvola, T., Lwakatare, L.E., Karvonen, T., Kuvaja, P., Olsson, H.H., Bosch, J., Oivo, M.: Towards customer-centric software development: a multiple-case study. In: The 41st Euromicro Conference on SEAA, pp. 9–17 (2015)
21. Seppänen, P., Tripathi, N., Oivo, M., Liukkunen, K.: How are product ideas validated? In: Software Business, pp. 3–17 (2017)
22. Subramanyam, R., Weisstein, F.L., Krishnan, M.S.: User participation in software development projects. Commun. ACM **53**(3), 137–141 (2010)
23. Zowghi, D., Coulin, C.: Requirements elicitation: a survey of techniques, approaches, and tools, pp. 19–46. Springer (2005)

Author Index

E. Papatheocharous et al. (Eds.): ICSOB 2024, LNBIP 539, pp. 467–468, 2025.
https://doi.org/10.1007/978-3-031-85849-9

The manufacturer's authorised representative in the EU is Springer
Nature Customer Service Centre GmbH, Europaplatz 3, 69115 Heidelberg,
Germany. If you have any concerns regarding our products, please
contact ProductSafety@springernature.com

Printed and bound by CPI Group (UK) Ltd, Croydon, CR0 4YY
29/04/2026
02099541-0009